HERETICS AND COLONIZERS

HERETICS AND COLONIZERS

FORGING RUSSIA'S EMPIRE IN THE SOUTH CAUCASUS

NICHOLAS B. BREYFOGLE

CORNELL UNIVERSITY PRESS
Ithaca and London

First published 2005 by Cornell University Press

Printed in the United States of America

Library of Congress Cataloging-in-Publication Data

Breyfogle, Nicholas B., 1968–
  Heretics and colonizers : forging Russia's empire in the south Caucasus / Nicholas B. Breyfogle.
      p.   cm.
  Includes bibliographical references and index.
  ISBN 0-8014-4242-7 (cloth : alk. paper)
    1. Transcaucasia—History—19th century.   2. Land settlement—Transcaucasia.   3. Transcaucasia—Ethnic relations.   4. Dissenters, Religious—Transcaucasia.   I. Title.
  DK509.B6866   2005
  947.507—dc22

                                                    2004019431

Cornell University Press strives to use environmentally responsible suppliers and materials to the fullest extent possible in the publishing of its books. Such materials include vegetable-based, low-VOC inks and acid-free papers that are recycled, totally chlorine-free, or partly composed of nonwood fibers. For further information, visit our website at www.cornellpress.cornell.edu.

Cloth printing
10 9 8 7 6 5 4 3 2 1

For Jillian and Charlie

"Find a road and we will travel"

CONTENTS

PART III. THE DUKHOBOR MOVEMENT

ACKNOWLEDGMENTS

It is with great pleasure that I express my deep thanks to the many people and organizations that have provided help and support during the long germination of this book. The list is long, and I only wish there were more space to honor publicly their immense assistance and encouragement—but that would require another book altogether. The project began at the University of Pennsylvania, where I had the extremely good fortune to work with Alfred Rieber, an exemplary scholar and teacher. He set me on the path of this study, and his insight, intellectual breadth, and unfailing humanity continue to inspire me. At Penn, my thanks also go to Moshe Lewin, Ann Matter, Jack Reece, and everyone at the Department of History for their many contributions in the early stages. At Brown University, my undergraduate advisors Abbott Gleason and Patricia Herlihy nourished my nascent interest in Russian history with fascinating courses, generous time, and stimulating conversations.

A number of colleagues read the manuscript in its entirety at different stages, and I am extremely grateful to them for their indispensable suggestions, critiques, and encouragement—their collective efforts made this book far better. They include Andy Conovaloff, Laura Engelstein, Daniel Field, David Hoffmann, Eve Levin, Carla Pestana, Roy Robson, Ron Suny, and the two anonymous readers from Cornell University Press. Particular thanks go to Josh Sanborn and Paul Werth, who critiqued the complete manuscript in the crucial final stages, which helped me refine my arguments and prose. Others read parts of the project and provided helpful and heartening feedback: Leslie Alexander, Mansel Blackford, John Brooke, Elizabeth Clement, Michael David-Fox, Sheila Fitzpatrick, Peter Holquist, Austin Jersild, Robin Judd, David Moon, Lucy Murphy, Alison Pion, Gabriella Safran, Abby Schrader, and Judy Wu. I also greatly appreciate the sage contributions of John Ackerman, Karen Laun, Martin Schneider, and the wonderful staff at Cornell University Press.

The book has also profited tremendously from numerous conversations and cups of coffee with friends and colleagues whose ideas, suggestions, and energy have found their way onto these pages. They include Jörg Baberowski, Steve Bittner, Angela Brintlinger, John Bushnell, Ken Church, Heather Coleman, Steve Conn, Saul Cornell, Katja David-Fox,

Russell Field, Eric Jennings, Val Kivelson, Terry Martin, Margaret Newell, Liam Riordan, Nate Rosenstein, Birgitte Søland, John Staples, John Strickland, Willard Sunderland, and Lynne Viola. Aspects of this book were presented at many conferences and lectures, where I invariably benefited from probing questions and comments. I owe particular thanks to the Russian history community at the University of Chicago. Two years attending their Wilder House workshops did much to develop my understanding of the Russian past and sharpen my thinking on this project. The same must also be said of the collegial and productive meetings of the Midwest Russian History Workshop, in which a number of early drafts of certain chapters were discussed. My understanding of Russian colonialism was significantly enhanced by the vibrant discussions at the conference "Peopling the 'Periphery': Slavic Settlers in Eurasia from Muscovy to Recent Times" held at Ohio State University in 2001.

Many people helped to make my time researching in Russia and Georgia a delightful and productive experience. My deepest thanks go to the archivists and scholars who took time from their busy and difficult schedules to help me in my research and discuss history over tea (or the like). In Russia, my appreciation goes especially to B. V. Anan'ich, L. G. Zakharova, I. V. Tarasova, S. A. Inikova, A. Iu. Polunov, I. V. Poltavskaia, S. I. Varekhova, S. A. Kozlov, E. Vorobeva, and all the staff at RGIA, GMIR, GARF, ORRGB, and the Publichka for their many daily kindnesses and professionalism. In Tbilisi, I am particularly grateful to Rezo Khutsishvili, Kristine, the Chikvinidze family, and all the staff at the Central Historical Archive and the National Library. My fond thanks also go to my friends in St. Petersburg, Moscow, and Tbilisi; they made my stays a pleasure and always shared with me all that is most magical about their cities and countries.

This book was improved no end by the stories and wisdom that many Dukhobors, Molokans, and Subbotniks have shared with me about their past. Their commitment to peace and justice remains an example for us all. I am deeply thankful for the hard work and contributions of Victoria Clement, Kristin Collins, and Aaron Retish, who worked as research assistants for the book, and of Ron McLean, who braved the complexities of Caucasian geography in his meticulous preparation of the maps. My appreciation also goes to the staff at the many libraries and archives in North America where I undertook research, particularly Jack McIntosh at the University of British Columbia, Larry Black at CRCR, and Harvey Dyck and Ingrid Epp at PJBRMA.

The research and writing of this book were supported by numerous grants and fellowships, and I am extremely grateful to these organizations for their generous support, including the Fulbright-Hays Doctoral Dissertation Research Abroad Program, the National Endowment for the

Humanities, an independent federal agency, the National Council for Eurasian and East European Research (NCEEER) under authority of a Title VIII grant from the U.S. Department of State, the International Research and Exchanges Board, with funds provided by the U.S. Department of State (Title VIII program), the Kennan Institute for Advanced Russian Studies, the Mershon Center, the College of Humanities and the Department of History at The Ohio State University, and the University of Pennsylvania.

Portions of this book have appeared in print elsewhere, and I am thankful for permission to publish this material here in revised form. An earlier version of chapter five appeared in Russian translation as "Kontakt kak sozidanie. Russkie sektanty i zhiteli Zakavkaz'ia v XIX v." in *Diaspory: nezavisimyi nauchnyi zhurnal* 4, no. 4 (2002). Small passages scattered through the book appeared in *Kritika: Explorations in Russian and Eurasian History* (Fall 2001), 713–50; in Marsha Siefert, ed., *Extending the Borders of Russian History: Essays in Honor of Alfred J. Rieber* (Budapest, 2003), 143–66; in Marshall Poe and Eric Lohr, eds., *The Military and Society in Russian History* (Leiden, 2002), 441–67; and in Andrew Donskov et al., eds, *The Doukhobor Centenary in Canada: A Multi-Disciplinary Perspective on their Unity and Diversity* (Ottawa, 2000), 55–82.

It gives me enormous pleasure to thank my parents, Jo and Peter Breyfogle, for all the love and support they have provided along the way. They gave me my love for learning and have always encouraged me to reach for the best and make all that I can out of this life. To be sure, this book is small return for everything they have done for me. I also want to express my gratitude to my in-laws Jeff Gustin, the late Charlotte Gustin, and Susan Smith, who unwaveringly supported me through the writing process, even if I failed Jeff by not incorporating more "sex and action" to propel the book onto the bestseller lists.

The book is dedicated to two people who not only made it possible in so many ways through their love and support, but made the life around it so worth living. To say that I could not have done this without my wife, Jillian Gustin, is to understate perilously everything that she has given to me and to the project. With clear insight, intelligence, and extraordinary patience, she navigated me through the ups and downs of writing at every stage. Her love, humor, and understanding remain a constant inspiration and my greatest happiness. Lastly, this book is for Charlie, our new addition. He has brought more joy and laughter into our lives than I would ever have thought possible, and his bright-eyed wonder at the marvels and menaces of this world reminds me daily why I became an historian in the first place.

NOTE ON TRANSLATION AND TRANSLITERATION

I have followed the Library of Congress transliteration system, with two exceptions. In the case of famous people, I use the customary English spelling; thus Leo Tolstoy rather than Lev Tolstoi. However, I do use Dukhobor instead of Doukhobor, the more common international spelling. Also, I have dropped the soft sign symbol at the end of words in the text itself, but not in the notes when part of a title. Words from South Caucasian languages are transliterated according to the Cyrillic Russian spelling.

For consistency and accuracy to the given historical moment, I use the version of place names employed in Russia during the nineteenth century. For example, I use Tiflis rather than the current Tbilisi, Kura for the Mktvari River, Elisavetpol for Ganja, and Lake Gokcha for Lake Sevan. I translate the Russian designation *Zakavkaz'e* as both Transcaucasia and the South Caucasus. Administrative divisions in the South Caucasus changed frequently during the nineteenth century. As a general rule, when noting geographical location, I employ the name of the province or region in use at the time I am discussing.[1]

Translations from the Bible are rendered here from the Revised Standard Version.

Tsarist officials used the word "Tatar" as a residual category and catch-all designation to label Muslims in Transcaucasia, although its usage was rarely consistent. In many cases, "Tatars" was used very specifically to refer to the Turkic Azerbaijani people. In other cases, its meaning expanded to include a wide diversity of Muslim peoples in Transcaucasia. It is often difficult to discern which meaning of "Tatar" is intended in a given document. Since "Tatar" is an inappropriate description for these people and causes confusion with the Tatars of Crimea or of the Volga, I use the (also problematic) term "Muslim," for lack of a better word, where nineteenth-century Russians used "Tatar" in its broadest meaning. Whenever possible, I use the more specific name for each ethnicity (particularly Azerbaijani) included under this umbrella term. I occasionally

1. A discussion of these changes with good maps can be found in George A. Bournoutian, *Russia and the Armenians of Transcaucasia, 1797–1889: A Documentary Record* (Costa Mesa, 1998), 473–76, 487–94.

leave "Tatar" in the original in quotations when the Russian choice of words seems to me to be relevant.[2]

I have kept certain words in their original Russian when a suitable translation is not easily available or in the case of certain measurements, although I substitute kilometer for *versta* in translations, even if they are not exactly equivalent (1 versta = 1.06 km).

arshin	measurement equal to 71 cm or 28 inches
ataman	Cossack chieftain
desiatina, desiatiny (pl.)	measurement equal to 1.09 hectares (2.7 acres)
meshchanin, meshchane (pl.)	urban dweller of lower social status, petty bourgeois townsman
odnodvortsy	state peasants originating from petty servitors
soslovie	social estate
stanitsa, stanitsy (pl.)	Cossack village
starshina, starshiny (pl.)	elder, headman of small rural district (*volost'*)

---

2. For a discussion of these issues, with a slightly different resolution to my own, see Audrey Altstadt, *The Azerbaijani Turks: Power and Identity under Russian Rule* (Stanford, 1992), xix–xx.

ABBREVIATIONS

ARCHIVES:

BCA	British Columbia Archives, Victoria
CRCR	Centre for Research on Canadian-Russian Relations, Ottawa
GARF	Gosudarstvennyi arkhiv Rossiiskoi Federatsii, Moscow
GKP	George Kennan Papers, Library of Congress, Washington
GMIR	Gosudarstvennyi muzei istorii religii, St. Petersburg
ORRGB	Otdel rukopisei, Rossiiskaia gosudarstvennaia biblioteka, Moscow
PJBRMA	Peter J. Braun Russian Mennonite Archive, Toronto
RGIA	Rossiiskii gosudarstvennyi istoricheskii arkhiv, St. Petersburg
SSC'SA	Sak'art'velos saistorio c'entraluri saxelmcip'o ark'ivi, Tbilisi

PUBLISHED SOURCES:

AHR	*American Historical Review*
AKAK	*Akty sobrannye Kavkazskoiu Arkheograficheskoiu Kommissieiu*
CAS	*Central Asian Survey*
CSP	*Canadian Slavonic Papers*
DKh	*Dukhovnyi khristianin*
EO	*Etnograficheskoe obozrenie*
ES	*Entsiklopedicheskii slovar'*
EZh	*Ezhemesiachnyi zhurnal literatury, nauki, i obshchestvennoi zhizni*
IJPCS	*International Journal of Politics, Culture and Society*
IKOIRGO	*Izvestiia Kavkazskogo otdela Imperatorskogo Russkogo geograficheskogo obshchestva*
IV	*Istoricheskii vestnik*

HJ	*The Historical Journal*
JGO	*Jahrbücher für Geschichte Osteuropas*
JMH	*Journal of Modern History*
JSH	*Journal of Social History*
KES	*Kavkazskii etnograficheskii sbornik*
KhCh	*Khristianskoe chtenie*
KK	*Kavkazskii kalendar'*
KSKh	*Kavkazskoe sel'skoe khoziaistvo*
MIEB	*Materialy dlia izucheniia ekonomicheskogo byta gosudarstvennykh krest'ian Zakavkazskogo kraia*
MIIRS	*Materialy k istorii i izucheniiu russkogo sektantstva*
MIIRSR	*Materialy k istorii i izucheniiu russkogo sektantstva i raskola*
MO	*Missionerskoe obozrenie*
NP	*Nationalities Papers*
OZ	*Otechestvennye zapiski*
PKEG	*Pamiatnaia knizhka Erivanskoi gubernii*
PS	*Pravoslavnyi sobesednik*
PSPRVP	*Polnoe sobranie postanovlenii i rasporiazhenii po vedomstvu Pravoslavnogo ispovedaniia Rossiiskoi Imperii*
PSZ (1–3)	*Polnoe sobranie zakonov* (in three series)
RA	*Russkii arkhiv*
RH	*Russian History/Histoire Russe*
RHMC	*Revue d'histoire moderne et contemporaine*
RI	*Russkii invalid*
RM	*Russkaia mysl'*
RR	*Russian Review*
RS	*Russkaia starina*
RTKE	*Raion Tiflissko-karssko-erivanskoi zheleznoi dorogi v ekonomicheskom i kommercheskom otnosheniiakh*
RV	*Russkii vestnik*
SEER	*Slavonic and East European Review*
SG	*Soviet Geography*
SMOMPK	*Sbornik materialov dlia opisaniia mestnostei i plemen Kavkaza*
SPChR (1860)	*Sobranie postanovlenii po chasti raskola, sostoiavshikhsia po vedomstvu Sv. Sinoda*
SPChR (1875)	*Sobranie postanovlenii po chasti raskola*
SR	*Slavic Review*
TV	*Tserkovnyi vestnik*
VE	*Vestnik Evropy*
VMU	*Vestnik Moskovskogo Universiteta*
ZKOIRGO	*Zapiski Kavkazskogo otdela Imperatorskogo Russkogo geograficheskogo obshchestva*

ZKOSKh	*Zapiski Kavkazskogo obshchestva sel'skogo khoziaistva*
ZV	*Zakavkazskii vestnik*

ARCHIVAL AND PUBLISHED CITATIONS:

ch.	chast'
d. (dd.)	delo (dela)
doc(s).	document number
d-vo	deloproizvodstvo
f.	fond
k.	kartonka
l. (ll.)	list (listy)
ob.	oborot
op.	opis'
otd.	otdelenie
p. (pp.)	page number
st.	stol
t.	tom

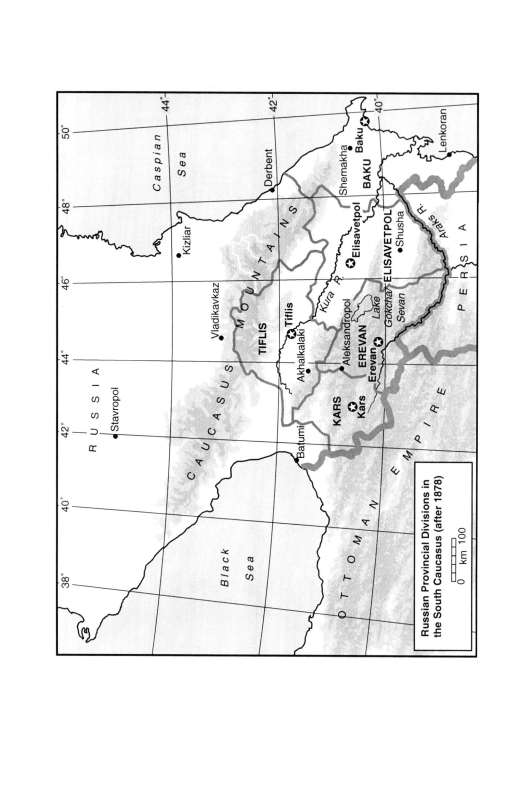

Russian Provincial Divisions in
the South Caucasus (after 1878)

0   km   100

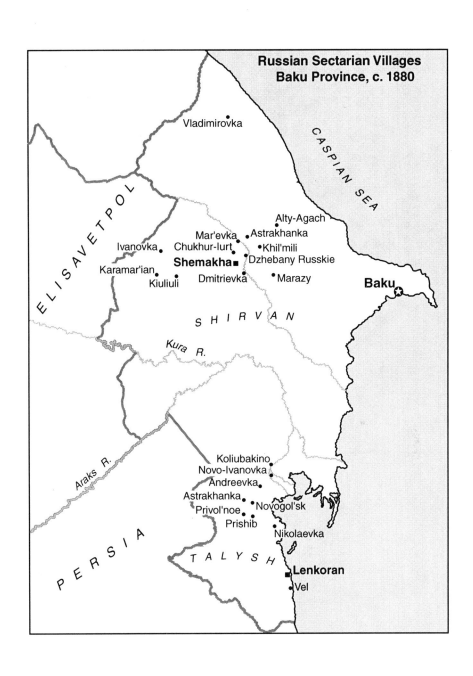

Russian Sectarian Villages
Baku Province, c. 1880

Vladimirovka

CASPIAN SEA

ELISAVETPOL

Alty-Agach

Mar'evka   Astrakhanka
Ivanovka   Chukhur-Iurt
                        Khil'mili
Karamar'ian   Shemakha   Dzhebany Russkie
        Kiuliuli   Dmitrievka   Marazy

Baku

SHIRVAN

Kura R.

Araks R.

Koliubakino
Novo-Ivanovka
Andreevka
Astrakhanka
Privol'noe   Novogol'sk
    Prishib
        Nikolaevka

PERSIA

TALYSH

Lenkoran
Vel

Russian Sectarian Villages
Elisavetpol Province, c. 1880

TIFLIS

Kura R.

Delizhan Novyi
•Golovino Slavianka   Novo-Troitskoe
 •Novo-Saratovka • •Novo-Goreloe   ☆ **Elisavetpol**
Mikhailovka   •Novo-Spasskoe
       •Novo-Ivanovka   • Mikhailovka
                              •Borisy Russkie

E R E V A N

B A K U

■ **Shusha**

•Bazar-Chai   Karabulagh
                         •

K A R A B A G H

Araks R.

P E R S I A

Russian Sectarian Villages
Erevan Province, c. 1880

TIFLIS

ELISAVETPOL

KARS

Voskresenovka

Aleksandropol Nikitino

Semenovka

Elenovka

Konstantinovka

Aleksandrovka

Nadezhdino

Nizhnie Akhty

Novo-Baiazet

Sukhoi
Fontan

Lake
Gokcha/
Sevan

Novonikolaevka

Erevan

Araks R.

Karmalinovka

OTTOMAN
EMPIRE

Araks R.

PERSIA

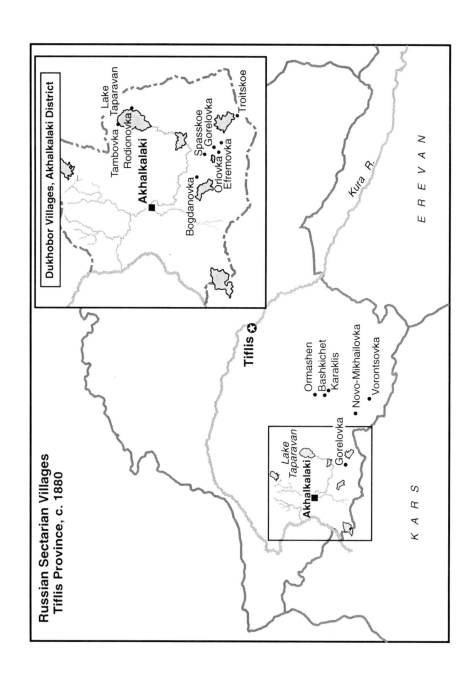

Russian Sectarian Villages
Tiflis Province, c. 1880

Dukhobor Villages, Akhalkalaki District

Lake Taparavan
Tambovka
Rodionovka
Akhalkalaki
Bogdanovka
Spasskoe
Gorelovka
Orlovka
Efremovka
Troitskoe

Tiflis

Ormashen
Bashkichet
Karaklis
Novo-Mikhailovka
Vorontsovka

Lake Taparavan
Gorelovka
Akhalkalaki

Kura R.

EREVAN

KARS

HERETICS AND COLONIZERS

INTRODUCTION

"Migration and colonization of the country constituted the fundamental features of our history, to which all other features were
more or less directly connected."

—V. O. Kliuchevskii

"History shows us no people which from its first appearance has
manifested as persistent and indestructible a drive to colonize as
the Russians."

—August von Haxthausen

"What has been missing, and what is essential to an understanding
of how the borderlands fit into the Russian Empire, is a history of
those who moved there and lived at the edge of empire, how diverse people interacted there, their cultural exchanges, and the
new landscapes, economies, and societies that they created."

—Thomas Barrett

On October 20, 1830, Tsar Nicholas I issued a decree that fundamentally
altered two previously unconnected aspects of Russian history.[1] It redirected the trajectory of Russian colonization in the Empire's southernmost region—the newly incorporated provinces of the South Caucasus—
while simultaneously recasting the fate of Christian religious dissenters

---

1. *PSZ* (2), vol. 5:2 (1830), no. 4010, pp. 169–70. The decree can also be found in RGIA f. 379,
op. 1, d. 1043, 1830–37, ll. 1–10b and *SPChR* (1875), 104–6. Quotations in the epigraph are
from V. O. Kliuchevskii, *Sochineniia v deviati tomakh* (Moscow, 1987), 1:50–51; August von Haxthausen, *Studies on the Interior of Russia*, ed. S. Frederick Starr, trans. Eleanore L. M. Schmidt
(Chicago, 1972), 176; and Thomas Barrett, "Crossing Boundaries: The Trading Frontiers of the
Terek Cossacks," in *Russia's Orient: Imperial Borderlands and Peoples, 1700–1917*, ed. Daniel R.
Brower and Edward J. Lazzerini (Bloomington, 1997), 229.

throughout the Empire.[2] The 1830 edict ordered that all religious sectarians (*sektanty*) who were classified as "especially pernicious" (including
Dukhobors, Molokans, and Subbotniks, but not Old Believers) were to
be relocated to Transcaucasia by either forcible exile or voluntary resettlement. The legislation was a conscious state effort to utilize the Empire's periphery as a means to segregate sectarian Russians from
Orthodox ones—to use communal isolation to resolve the perceived
dilemmas of religious difference. From 1830 through the 1880s, tsarist
policy promoted the relocation of dissenters almost to the exclusion of
other Russians in an effort to eliminate what state and spiritual leaders
saw as their heretical "infection" of Orthodox subjects. Although small
numbers of Russians had moved to Transcaucasia before 1830, the decree turned the trickle into a torrent, as tens of thousands of dissenters
left for the southern frontier. As late as the 1890s, these nonconformists
comprised the overwhelming majority of ethnic Russians in Transcaucasia.[3] The sectarian dominance of colonist communities inextricably
linked popular spirituality with Russian colonialism, indelibly defining
the character of Russia's imperial presence in the region. Their segregation to the southern borderlands simultaneously altered the religious
landscape of the tsarist empire in enduring ways.

If the decree of 1830 opened a new chapter in the long history of Russian settlement in Eurasia, a pacifist insurgency among Dukhobor
colonists brought the era of "sectarian colonialism" to an end late in the
nineteenth century. Acting on their religious beliefs and out of frustration with the demands of an encroaching, "colonizing" state, Dukhobors
refused military service, denounced secular authority, ceased fulfilling
state obligations, and destroyed all of their weapons. Tsarist officials responded with beatings and torture, rape, imprisonment, court trials,
forcible enlistment in disciplinary battalions, and exile. As the first large-
scale antimilitary, antistate demonstration since the military reforms of
1874, their opposition movement altered the relationship between Russian state authority and the sectarian settlers in Transcaucasia. By 1900,
thousands of Dukhobors and Molokans had either emigrated to North
America or were planning to do so, and the tsarist government had begun a substantial campaign to replace the nonconformists with Orthodox migrants.

---

2. The nineteenth-century South Caucasus (also known as Transcaucasia from the Russian *Za-kavkaz'e*) approximates geographically the Republics of Azerbaijan, Armenia, and Georgia, and, after 1878, also included Kars territory that is now in eastern Turkey.

3. Polkovnik Andrievskii, *Voenno-geograficheskoe i statisticheskoe opisanie Kavkazskogo voennogo okruga* (Tiflis, 1908), 71. See also *Svod statisticheskikh dannykh o naselenii Zakavkazskogo kraia, izvlechennykh iz posemeinykh spiskov 1886 g.* (Tiflis, 1893). On Orthodox settlement in the South Caucasus, see D. I. Ismail-Zade, *Russkoe krest'ianstvo v Zakavkaz'e: 30–e gody XIX-nachalo XX v.* (Moscow, 1982), esp. 94–283; and Firouzeh Mostashari, "Tsarist Colonial Policy, Economic Change, and the Making of the Azerbaijani Nation: 1828–1905" (Ph.D. diss., University of Pennsylvania, 1995), 225–50.

The multiple dimensions of Russian colonial settlement in the South Caucasus from the decree of 1830 through the years immediately after the Dukhobor uprising of 1895 are the central focus of this book. In particular, I explore both the role of sectarian colonization in the broader patterns of tsarist empire-building and the peasant migrants' social and cultural experiences in a transformative borderland setting. Colored as they were by their religious dissent, these sectarian colonists were not "average" Russian peasants, and the South Caucasus was a region distinctive in important respects from other tsarist holdings. That said, sectarian migration to Transcaucasia provides a window onto the growth and internal functioning of the tsarist empire, the role of frontier regions in Eurasian historical development, the characteristics of nineteenth-century popular religiosity and peasant life, and the changing parameters of identity.

Discussions of Russian imperialism stressing the bilateral confrontation between Russian state agents and non-Russian peoples have tended to underemphasize the vital role of Russian colonists in forging the Empire.[4] Whether they supported or opposed tsarist power, the sectarian settlers influenced the course of Russia's imperial enterprise through their interactions with colonial authorities, with local inhabitants, and with Transcaucasia's natural environment. At crucial moments, the settlers performed a range of military, economic, and administrative functions essential to Russian empire-building—sometimes unwittingly. At other times, they challenged the legitimacy of tsarist authority and imperial ideology. In either case, peasant borderland settlement was not simply a corollary of territorial expansion, nor was it solely the product of domestic agrarian concerns.[5] The sectarians who migrated to the South Caucasus also played a decisive role in constructing and constituting Imperial Russia as a multi-ethnic, multiconfessional entity. For the peoples

4. In this regard, this book builds on the inventive work of Thomas Barrett and Willard Sunderland. See Thomas Barrett, *At the Edge of Empire: The Terek Cossacks and the North Caucasus Frontier, 1700–1860* (Boulder, 1999); idem, "Crossing Boundaries," 227–48; idem, "Lines of Uncertainty: The Frontiers of the North Caucasus," *SR* 54, no. 3 (1995): 578–601; Willard Sunderland, "An Empire of Peasants: Empire-Building, Interethnic Interaction, and Ethnic Stereotyping in the Rural World of the Russian Empire, 1800–1850s," in *Imperial Russia: New Histories for the Empire*, ed. Jane Burbank and David L. Ransel (Bloomington, 1998), 174–98; idem, "Peasants on the Move: State Peasant Resettlement in Imperial Russia, 1805–1830s," *RR* 52, no. 4 (1993): 472–85; idem, "Russians into Iakuts? 'Going Native' and Problems of Russian National Identity in the Siberian North, 1870s–1914," *SR* 55, no. 4 (1996): 806–25; idem, "The 'Colonization Question': Visions of Colonization in Late Imperial Russia," *JGO* 48, no. 2 (2000): 210–32; and idem, "Peasant Pioneering: Russian Peasant Settlers Describe Colonization and the Eastern Frontier, 1880s–1910s," *JSH* 34, no. 4 (2001): 895–922. See also Daniel Brower, *Turkestan and the Fate of the Russian Empire* (London, 2003), esp. 126–51; and the essays in Nicholas B. Breyfogle, Abby Schrader, and Willard Sunderland, eds., *Peopling the Periphery: Russian Settlement in Eurasia from Muscovite to Soviet Times* (forthcoming).

5. A. A. Kaufman, in his seminal *Pereselenie i Kolonizatsiia* (St. Petersburg, 1905), saw Russia's peripheral regions as "a continuation of Russia" and peasant settlers as internal migrants rather than external colonists. See also Donald Treadgold, *The Great Siberian Migration: Government and Peasant in Resettlement from Emancipation to the First World War* (Princeton, 1957).

of Transcaucasia, the Russian imperial presence was defined in great part by their encounters with the sectarian settlers. The grassroots reality of empire was forged in these "worlds of interaction."[6]

Migration to Russia's borderland regions also produced arenas in which Russians (in this case sectarians) were able to forge alternative existences beyond what was possible in the central provinces. The religious dissenters made their way into an unfamiliar part of the world, one with a human and environmental diversity that challenged their imaginations. Georgians, Armenians, Azerbaijanis, Kurds, Persians, Turks, and Lezgins were only some of the ethno-confessional communities that they encountered as they built new lives in the dramatically varied South Caucasian environment.[7] In the less-regulated spaces of the Transcaucasian frontier and in dynamic interaction with this wide array of Caucasian peoples and physical landscapes, the sectarian colonists elaborated new religious beliefs, social structures, economic practices, and identities. Indeed, the southern periphery proved a fertile space for the nonconformists to contest labels, manipulate categories, and refashion notions of self and community. The use of religious dissenters as colonists altered what "Russian" and "sectarian" identity meant for both tsarist officials and the dissenters themselves, and it destabilized the traditional connection among Orthodox Christianity, Russian ethnicity, and perceived political loyalty. Like the Communards banished from Paris as politically uncivilized yet sent to New Caledonia as the bearers of civilization to the "savage" natives, the religious dissenters cast out to the South Caucasus saw their political and social identities altered in fundamental ways.[8]

Examining the tsarist empire through the lens of the Russian colonists helps us better understand Russia's place in the larger picture of Europe's interactions with the extra-European world in the nineteenth century. Russian empire-building has often been seen as distinct from Western European imperialism because Russia's was an overland rather than an overseas empire. As such, distinctions between "metropole" and "colony" blurred, and "colonies of exploitation" and "colonies of settlement" commingled in the same geographical space.[9] Certainly, the tsarist

6. I take "worlds of interaction" from Sunderland, "Empire of Peasants," 175, 181.

7. On ethno-confessional diversity, see George Bournoutian, "The Ethnic Composition and the Socio-Economic Condition of Eastern Armenia in the First Half of the Nineteenth Century," in *Transcaucasia: Nationalism and Social Change*, ed. Ronald Grigor Suny (Ann Arbor, 1983), 69–86; and N. G. Volkova, "Etnicheskie protsessy v Zakavkaz'e v XIX–XX vv." in *KES*, ed. V. K. Gardanov (Moscow, 1969), 4:3–54. On environment, see N. A. Gvozdetskii, *Kavkaz: Ocherk prirody* (Moscow, 1963).

8. Alice Bullard, *Exile to Paradise: Savagery and Civilization in Paris and the South Pacific, 1790–1900* (Stanford, 2000).

9. Ann Laura Stoler and Frederick Cooper, "Between Metropole and Colony: Rethinking a Research Agenda," in *Tensions of Empire: Colonial Cultures in a Bourgeois World*, ed. Stoler and Cooper (Berkeley, 1997), 23; Geoffrey Hosking, *Russia: People and Empire, 1552–1917* (Cambridge, MA,

state's territorial contiguity produced undeniable peculiarities, but Russia shared many characteristics with Western European imperialism (itself a heterogeneous phenomenon), particularly in terms of the ambiguities, contestations, and hybridity of empire upon which recent scholarship has focused.[10] In particular, scholars of Western European imperialism have embraced the notion that colony and metropole "co-produce each other" in the imperial encounter, and that these concepts need to be examined "in a single analytic field."[11] The story of sectarian colonization in the South Caucasus demonstrates that state-building and social developments "internal" to Russia were often inseparable from empire-building and colonial developments on the periphery, each constituting the other. Conceptions of Russianness, of "nation" and "empire," of faith and religious affiliation, and of "core" and "borderland" were defined and redefined in the colonial encounter.

Russia's sectarian colonists also form part of a centuries-old process of European migration to colonies of settlement, sharing important characteristics with other "white settler colonies." Dissenter colonization in the South Caucasus had much in common with the experience of the British in Rhodesia and Kenya, the French in Algeria, and the Dutch and British in South Africa—all cases in which a numerically predominant indigenous population remained after European conquest and settlement.[12] Colonists often began with assumptions and goals that led them along paths that diverged from those intended by the ruling elites.[13] Settler interactions with indigenous peoples and local ecologies transformed the participants in often unexpected and enduring ways. That said, there were also significant differences between the experiences of

1997), 39–41; and Alfred J. Rieber, "Struggle over the Borderlands," in *The Legacy of History in Russia and the New States of Eurasia*, ed. S. Frederick Starr (Armonk, NY, 1994), 67–68.

10. Stoler and Cooper, *Tensions of Empire*.

11. Quotations are from, respectively, Patrick Wolfe, "History and Imperialism: A Century of Theory, from Marx to Postcolonialism," *AHR* 102, no. 2 (1997): 389; and Stoler and Cooper, "Between Metropole and Colony," 4, passim. See also Catherine Hall, *Civilising Subjects: Colony and Metropole in the English Imagination, 1830–1867* (Chicago, 2002).

12. On white settler colonies, see for example, Dane Kennedy, *Islands of White: Settler Society and Culture in Kenya and Southern Rhodesia, 1890–1939* (Durham, 1987); Alan Lester, *Imperial Networks: Creating Identities in Nineteenth-Century South Africa and Britain* (London, 2001); Daniel Leconte, *Les Pieds-Noirs: Histoire et portrait d'une Communauté* (Paris, 1980); Michael J. Heffernan and Keith Sutton, "The Landscape of Colonialism: The Impact of French Colonial Rule on the Algerian Rural Settlement Pattern, 1830–1987," in *Colonialism and Development in the Contemporary World*, ed. Chris Dixon and Michael J. Heffernan (London, 1991), 121–52; and Daiva Stasiulis and Nira Yuval-Davis, eds., *Unsettling Settler Societies: Articulations of Gender, Race, Ethnicity and Class* (London, 1995). Compare P. J. Marshall, "British Immigration into India in the Nineteenth Century," in *European Expansion and Migration: Essays on the Intercontinental Migration from Africa, Asia, and Europe*, ed. P. C. Emmer and M. Morner (New York, 1992), 179–96.

13. See, for example, the discussion of three models of colonialism among Europeans in South Africa: state colonialism, settler colonialism, and civilizing colonialism, in John Comaroff, "Images of Empire, Contests of Conscience: Models of Colonial Domination in South Africa," in *Tensions of Empire*, 178–91.

the sectarians and most Western European colonists. As "heretics" and peasants, the sectarians, at least initially, were not driven by a colonial mission. Perhaps more important, the nonconformist settlers in the South Caucasus neither erected racial boundaries nor developed systematic, capitalist exploitation of native labor, as was common in other white settler colonies.[14]

Sectarian colonization in some respects also bears a resemblance to overland expansion in North America and Australia, where the native population was either pushed out or was relatively sparse to begin with and where religious nonconformists frequently represented the advance guard of settlement. Invoking the theories of Frederick Jackson Turner, historians have likened Russia's expansion across Eurasia to the Western push that occurred in the United States.[15] However, recent studies in the history of the American West have revised our understanding of the form and function of frontier regions and of the experiences of settlers in creating and transforming them.[16] Scholars have argued that the American frontier was characterized not simply by isolation, as Turner's line of thinking asserted, but also by "connectedness." They also claim that the transformation of "frontiers" into "regions" is best understood as a process which involved such diverse developments as "species shifting," "market making," "land taking," "boundary setting," "state forming" and "self-shaping"—developments that characterize the history of Russia's sectarian colonialism in equal measure. Moreover, these new studies have shifted focus to examine the everyday experiences of frontier settlers. "By keeping close to the land, frontier and regional history can move back and forth between the nitty-gritty details of ordinary life—activities like

14. Compare Kennedy, *Islands of White;* Lester, *Imperial Networks;* Patrick Wolfe, *Settler Colonialism and the Transformation of Anthropology: the Politics and Poetics of an Ethnographic Event* (London, 1999); Donald Denoon, *Settler Capitalism: the Dynamics of Dependent Development in the Southern Hemisphere* (New York, 1983); and Hall, *Civilising Subjects.*
15. Examples of efforts to use Turner's thesis in the Russian case include: Judith Pallot and Denis J. B. Shaw, *Landscape and Settlement in Romanov Russia, 1613–1917* (Oxford, 1990), esp. 13–32; Donald W. Treadgold, "Russian Expansion in the Light of Turner's Study of the American Frontier," *Agricultural History* 26, no. 4 (1952): 147–52; and Joseph L. Wieczynski, "Toward a Frontier Theory of Early Russian History," *RR* 33, no. 3 (1974): 284–95. See also the perceptive discussion in Mark Bassin, "Turner, Solov'ev, and the 'Frontier Hypothesis': The Nationalist Significance of Open Spaces," *JMH* 65, no. 3 (1993): 473–511.
16. The insights and parallels of the following revisionist studies have been influential on this book. William Cronon, George Miles and Jay Gitlin, eds., *Under an Open Sky: Rethinking American's Western Past* (New York, 1992); Patricia Nelson Limerick, Clyde A. Milner II and Charles E. Rankin, eds., *Trails: Towards a New Western History* (Lawrence, 1991); Daniel H. Usner, Jr., *Indians, Settlers and Slaves in a Frontier Exchange Economy: The Lower Mississippi Valley Before 1783* (Chapel Hill, 1992); Richard White, *The Middle Ground: Indians, Empires, and Republics in the Great Lakes Region, 1650–1815* (New York, 1991); William Cronon, *Changes in the Land: Indians, Colonists, and the Ecology of New England* (New York, 1983); and Jeremy Adelman and Stephen Aron, "From Borderlands to Borders: Empires, Nation-States, and the Peoples in Between in North American History," *AHR* 104, no. 3 (1999): 814–41.

growing crops, raising children, building homes—and the larger meanings people have attached to such activities. It can embed people and
their communities in the most abstract of historical processes without losing sight of what it was like to live through those processes."[17]

In addition to its focus on colonization, empire-building, and the lived
experience of migration, this book is a story about popular religiosity and
the role of religion in Russian society and polity. It explores state and
Church policies of intolerance toward non-Orthodox Christians, the
meanings of religious pluralism in tsarist Russia, and the ways in which issues of faith and confessional affiliation helped to define tsarist empire-
building policy.[18] Simultaneously, in examining the development of
long-ignored spiritual movements, the book unveils the rich tapestry of
religious life in nineteenth-century Russia and the porous boundaries
among religious groups. A plurality of Russia's sectarians came to find
their home in the Transcaucasus, thereby providing a thriving territorial
core for the nonconformist population that until then had often been
thinly spread around the central provinces. On the frontier, these communities experienced a spiritual ferment that breathed new life into religious movements that, in the Russian heartland, had been increasingly
constricted.

Since the large majority of sectarians who settled in Transcaucasia
were peasants, their story is also a chapter in the history of the Russian
peasantry. The dissenters' experiences underscore the fact that movement was an intrinsic characteristic of the Russian people throughout the
nineteenth century. Whether to the borderlands, to the cities, abroad, or
to and from seasonal work and pilgrimage sites, migration had ramifications both for the point of departure and the place of destination. The
new worlds forged in the crucible of the South Caucasus were the work
of dynamic peasant communities, whose energetic adjustments to new
conditions belie the Russian peasantry's reputation for resistance to
change.[19] The sectarians' general opposition to state power, expressed

17. William Cronon, George Miles, and Jay Gitlin, "Becoming West: Toward a New Meaning for
Western History," in *Under an Open Sky*, 3–27, quotation on 8.
18. Recent scholarship has explored the importance of religious questions to Russian empire, particularly regarding non-Christian faiths (and especially Islam), missionary efforts, possibilities of
assimilation, ethnic and confessional stereotyping, and the demands for rights to their faiths by
Russia's colonized peoples. Paul Werth, *At the Margins of Orthodoxy: Mission, Governance, and Confessional Politics in Russia's Volga-Kama Region, 1827–1905* (Ithaca, 2002); Robert Paul Geraci, *Window on the East: National and Imperial Identities in Late Imperial Russia* (Ithaca, 2001); Robert Geraci
and Michael Khodarkovsky, eds., *Of Religion and Empire: Missions, Conversion, and Tolerance in Tsarist
Russia* (Ithaca, 2001); and Michael Khodarkovsky, *Russia's Steppe Frontier: The Making of a Colonial
Empire, 1500–1800* (Bloomington, 2002).
19. For an overview of "slow history" and questions of "cohesion, strategy, and equilibrium"
among the central Russian peasantry, see Ben Eklof, "Ways of Seeing: Recent Anglo-American
Studies of the Russian Peasant (1861–1914)," *JGO* 36 (1988): 61–64. See also David Moon, *The
Russian Peasantry, 1600–1930: The World the Peasants Made* (New York, 1999).

most dramatically in the Dukhobor arms burning, highlights the potentially pivotal role of religious belief in originating and channeling peasant resistance movements. Finally, this examination of nonconformist peasants in a multi-ethnic borderland offers a different context in which to explore the much-debated question of peasant identification as Russians and as tsarist political subjects.[20]

WHO WERE THE RELIGIOUS SECTARIANS?

This book focuses on three communities of religious sectarians who may be called Russia's "indigenous" Christian sects: Dukhobors, Molokans (and their different subsects: Pryguny, Obshchie, Postoiannye, Dukhovnye, among others), and Subbotniks (also called Iudeistvuiushchie and Zhidovstvuiushchie).[21] These religious communities broke away from the Orthodox Church to embrace different forms of theology and practice. They are distinguished by their Russian origin from "imported" Western Protestant sects such as Baptists, Shtundists, Mennonites, and Pentecostals, and also from Old Believers (staroobriadtsy, also Old Ritualists), who considered themselves the true practitioners of Orthodoxy. Neither the Protestant sects, nor the Old Ritualists, nor other Russian sects (for instance, the Khlysty and Skoptsy) migrated to Transcaucasia, or else did so in such small numbers as to be tangential to our story. While making these distinctions, it bears noting that throughout much of the nineteenth century Russian authorities used the more inclusive word raskol'niki (schismatics) to refer to both "sectarians" as well as Old Believers. Only in the second half of the century did tsarist discourse apply the term raskol'nik almost exclusively to Old Believers and consistently distinguish sektanty from staroobriadtsy. Additionally, so-called sectarians did not accept the label placed upon them by religious and secular authorities, believing that they practiced and upheld true Christianity in the face of the debauched Orthodox Church and the misguided faith and rituals of other sectarians. Still, the term "sectarian" is used in this study because of its widespread historical usage; such English equivalents as dissenter and nonconformist are included in order to avoid repetition.

Rather than groups with sharply distinct beliefs and practices, Dukho-

20. David Moon, "Peasants into Russian Citizens? A Comparative Perspective," Revolutionary Russia 9, no. 1 (1996): 43–81; James R. Lehning, Peasant and French: Cultural Contact in Rural France During the Nineteenth Century (New York, 1995); Eugen Weber, Peasants into Frenchmen: The Modernization of Rural France, 1870–1914 (Stanford, 1976); and Keely Stauter-Halsted, The Nation in the Village: The Genesis of Peasant National Identity in Austrian Poland, 1848–1914 (Ithaca, 2001).
21. Dukhobors are usually translated as "Spirit-Wrestlers," Molokans as "Milk-Drinkers," and Subbotniks as "Sabbatarians."

bors, Molokans, and Subbotniks should be understood as occupying a certain part of a spectrum of religiosity, with the hues and shades of faith and ritual often blending with one another. These various religious movements shared much in common with other sectarian groups, Old Believers, and even Orthodox Christians. Each of these varieties of Christianity came from similar spiritual roots in the Eastern Christian tradition, and "sectarians" and their "Orthodox" neighbors were not always easily discernible in their day-to-day religiosity.[22] Those who did switch from Orthodoxy to a sectarian faith might continue to attend Orthodox services and fulfill Orthodox religious practices, in part to keep with tradition and in part to avoid persecution for their change of faith.

Moreover, while Dukhobor, Molokan, and Subbotnik religious beliefs and practices were distinct in many vital respects, they shared certain commonalties: they all opposed the institutional Orthodox Church, refuted the need for priests and hierarchies (or any other mediators in a relationship with God),[23] and abjured Orthodox sacraments (most notably water baptism), icons, saints, relics, candles, and churches. Dukhobors and Molokans also shared certain social and political viewpoints that grew out of these common religious beliefs. In the eighteenth and early nineteenth centuries, they rejected secular authorities such as the tsar and state officials and opposed the power of landowners and other social elites, arguing that all humans were equal.

The process by which groups and individual believers were labeled sectarians was also problematic and fraught with incongruities. Dukhobor, Molokan, and Subbotnik were all names that tsarist religious officials gave to these people and, to varying degrees, were later taken up by the sects themselves. Reflecting the concurrent fluidity and stasis of identity categories in Imperial Russia, struggles unsurprisingly erupted between state authorities and sectarians over official labels and self-generated names and notions of self.[24] For example, Molokans called themselves

22. John Eugene Clay, "Russian Peasant Religion and its Repression: The Christ-Faith [Khristovshchina] and the Origins of the 'Flagellant' Myth, 1666–1837" (Ph.D. diss., University of Chicago, 1989); Gregory Freeze, "The Rechristianization of Russia: The Church and Popular Religion, 1750–1850," Studia Slavica Finlandensia 7 (1990): 101–36; Laura Engelstein, Castration and the Heavenly Kingdom: A Russian Folktale (Ithaca, 1999); Nadieszda Kizenko, A Prodigal Saint: Father John of Kronstadt and the Russian People (University Park, PA, 2000) and Pierre Pascal, The Religion of the Russian People (London, 1976).

23. In an exception, certain Subbotnik communities did attempt to integrate Jewish rabbis into their communities and religious services.

24. Alfred Rieber, "The Sedimentary Society," in Between Tsar and People: Educated Society and the Quest for Public Identity in Late Imperial Russia, ed. Edith W. Clowes, Samuel D. Kassow, and James L. West (Princeton, 1991), 343–71; Gregory L. Freeze, "The Soslovie (Estate) Paradigm and Russian Social History," AHR 91 (1986): 11–36; Elise Kimmerling Wirtschafter, Social Identity in Imperial Russia (DeKalb, 1997); Barbara Alpern Engel, "Engendering Russia's History: Women in Post-Emancipation Russia and the Soviet Union," SR 51, no. 2 (1992): 309–21.

"Spiritual Christians," whereas official sources used the same term as an umbrella expression to encompass Dukhobors and Khlysty as well. In addition, tsarist authorities and religious officials were not always aware of the finer theological distinctions involved. They applied labels to people practicing non-Orthodox aspects of faith without considering whether their beliefs and practices actually corresponded to those covered by the categories "Dukhobor," "Molokan," and "Subbotnik." Cases abound of petitions from sectarians expressing their consternation at having been categorized as, say, Dukhobor when they considered themselves Molokan.[25] Furthermore, the labeling of religious beliefs varied according to region. Individuals categorized as belonging to one denomination by administrators in a given locale often found that they had little in common with their ostensible coreligionists in the neighboring province.[26] Such blurred boundaries were exacerbated by the fact that these religious movements were not necessarily self-aware from the outset, nor were their theological beliefs and practices rigidly defined but instead underwent substantive changes over time.

There were, nevertheless, real differences in the faiths of the Dukhobors, Molokans, and Subbotniks, and they quite consciously saw themselves as distinct from one another. At the heart of the Dukhobor faith lay the belief that the spirit of God resides in all human beings, and the essentials of the Dukhobor faith included "the knowledge and recognition of God by internal feeling and experience."[27] As observers of Dukhobor life have written, "the central, constant element in Dukhobor Christianity . . . is the belief in the immanence of God, in the presence within each man of the Christ spirit, which not merely renders priesthood unnecessary, since each man is his own priest in direct contact with the divine, but also makes the Bible obsolete, since every man can be guided, if only he will listen to it, by the voice within."[28] In place of the Bible, Dukhobors maintained a strong oral tradition of psalms and hymns known as the "Living Book," through which they transmitted their beliefs and practices from generation to generation.[29] Since all humans are deified, Dukhobors recognized no social distinctions and refused to take part in violence toward others because such actions represented literal vi-

25. See, for instance, GMIR f. 2, op. 7, d. 596, n.d., ll. 124–27.
26. See, for example, GMIR f. K1, op. 8, d. 516, n.d., ll. 1–5.
27. Orest Novitskii, *O Dukhobortsakh* (Kiev, 1832), 48.
28. George Woodcock and Ivan Avakumovic, *The Doukhobors* (Toronto, 1968), 19. See also S. A. Inikova, "Russkie sekty," in *Russkie*, ed. V. A. Aleksandrov, I. V. Vlasova, and N. S. Polishchuk (Moscow, 1999), 729–32, 736–40; and Nicholas B. Breyfogle "Building Doukhoboriia: Religious Culture, Social Identity and Russian Colonization in Transcaucasia, 1845–1895," *CES* 27, no. 3 (1995): esp. 27–34.
29. The Living Book was published just after the turn of the century. V. D. Bonch-Bruevich, ed., *Zhivotnaia Kniga Dukhobortsev* (St. Petersburg, 1909).

olence against God. The Dukhobors were ruled by a single Christ-leader. In each generation, they believed, a personification of Christ would appear who would manifest the strength and characteristics of the Son of God and who would lead the Dukhobor community. In practice, the Christ-spirit, and with it the leadership, tended to be passed from generation to generation within a single bloodline.

Like Dukhobors, Molokans denied the legitimacy of the Orthodox Church and its sacraments, rites, saints, icons and relics and also forsook all specially designed church buildings.[30] Unlike Dukhobors, however, they believed that the Old and New Testaments of the Bible constituted the only source of religious authority and spiritual teaching. However, while Molokans found no religious legitimacy outside the holy scriptures, they consciously interpreted the Bible and sacraments in allegorical or spiritual terms. They derived their justification for doing so from such verses in the Bible as: "the written code kills, but the Spirit gives life" (2 Corinthians 3:6) and "God is spirit, and those who worship him must worship in spirit and truth" (John 4:24). Thus, they did not practice water baptism because they understood the word water in the nonliteral sense of "living water" (John 7:38) and believed that baptism was concluded by hearing the word of God and living in a godly way. Molokans were also characterized by their fascination with the coming of the apocalypse and their tendency to fracture into "subsects" based on theological differences and the power of certain charismatic leaders. During the nineteenth century, a variety of Molokan groups appeared, including *Molokane Donskogo tolka, vodnye, pryguny, postoiannye, obshchie, dukhovnye, voskresniki,* and *presniki,* to name but a few.

The Molokans' teachings also had important social and political components. They believed that Christ was the only true ruler, that all humans were "brothers" and hence equal, and that disparities of wealth were an affront to God's tenets. Molokan communities did have presbyters and elders, but these leaders were not thought to have received any special powers from God. Despite their extra responsibilities in the community, they were to be approached as spiritual equals. In the early nineteenth century, Molokans did not recognize the tsar as the earthly arbiter of heavenly power, although they did respect him as a secular authority. However, Molokans refused to obey laws that they believed to contradict divine law, often refusing to fulfill military service and swear oaths.[31]

---

30. On the changes in Molokan opposition to designated sacred spaces in the late nineteenth century, see Nicholas B. Breyfogle, "Prayer and the Politics of Place: Molokan Church Building, Tsarist Law, and the Quest for a Public Sphere in Late Imperial Russia," in *Sacred Stories: Religion and Spirituality in Modern Russian Culture,* ed. Heather Coleman and Mark Steinberg (Bloomington, forthcoming).

31. N. B-v, "Molokane," in *ES,* vol.19: 2 (St. Petersburg, 1896): 644–46; A. I. Masalkin, "K istorii

In contrast to Molokans and Dukhobors, Subbotniks adhered to some, if not all, of the tenets and laws of Judaism (as they interpreted them). Scholars and tsarist officials have posited three different origins for the Subbotniks, without reaching any definitive conclusion. Tsarist officials frequently saw the Subbotniks as an outcome of the interaction of Jews and Orthodox Russians. Other commentators argued that the Subbotniks represented a reappearance among Russians of the "Judaizer heresy" which dates back (although not continuously) to the fifteenth century. Finally, scholars have noted that the Subbotniks arose from a divergent wing of the Molokans. Whatever their origins, Subbotniks debated throughout the nineteenth century to what degree a true believer should follow the dictates of Mosaic Law, and how close to Judaism a Christian should gravitate in order to worship God properly. As a result, the beliefs and practices of those who considered themselves Subbotniks (or those who the state labeled as Subbotniks) varied widely. On one end of the spectrum were those who kept the Sabbath on Saturday, believed the Old Testament to be more important than the New, but still considered themselves Christians. At the other end were those who identified themselves as Jewish, followed Jewish law only, hired rabbis to conduct their services in Hebrew, and embraced the Talmud in place of the Bible. In between these poles, Subbotniks followed any combination of the above-mentioned practices as well as circumcision, Jewish dietary restrictions, Jewish holidays (especially Passover), and Jewish services conducted in Russian.[32]

ARCHAEOLOGY OF THE SETTLER EXPERIENCE

The Transcaucasian sectarians represent an exception to the general silence of peasants in nineteenth-century Russia, particularly concerning their personal experiences in resettlement across Eurasia.[33] They left be-

zakavkazskikh sektantov: I. Molokane," *Kavkaz*, no. 306 (November 18, 1893): 2–3; "Istoricheskiia svedeniia o molokanskoi sekte," *PS* (September 1858): 42–80 and (November 1858): 291–327; N. Kostomarov, "Vospominaniia o molokanakh," *OZ*, no. 3 (1869): 57–78; Inikova, "Russkie sekty," 733–40; and Fedor Vasil'evich Livanov, *Raskol'niki i ostorozhniki: ocherki i rasskazy*, 4 vols. (St. Petersburg, 1872–73).

32. A. I. Masalkin, "K istorii zakavkazskikh sektantov: II. Subbotniki," *Kavkaz*, no. 307 (November 19, 1893): 2; Il'ia Zhabin, "Selenie Privol'oe, Bakinskoi gub., Lenkoranskogo uezda," in *SMOMPK*, vol. 27 (Tiflis, 1900), otdel II, 42–94; "Subbotniki," in *ES*, vol. 31 (1901): 874–75; "Iudeistvuiushchie," in *ES*, vol. 13: 2 (St. Petersburg, 1894); "Zhidovstvuiushchie," in *ES*, vol. 11: 2 (St. Petersburg, 1894); and "'Subbotniki' v Erivanskoi gubernii," in *PKEG na 1912 g.* (Erevan, 1912), Lit. otdel, chap. III, 1–11.

33. On the silence of peasant colonial migrants and an exception that proves the rule, see Treadgold, *Siberian*, 82, and Sunderland, "Peasant Pioneering," respectively. On the general quiet of peasant Russia, see Esther Kingston-Mann, "Breaking the Silence: An Introduction" in *Peasant Economy, Culture, and Politics of European Russia, 1800–1921*, ed. Kingston-Mann and Timothy Mix-

hind a rich collection of letters, memoirs, group histories, liturgical texts, and artwork, much of it unpublished. In these sources, the sectarians tell their own story, bringing to life aspects of colonization and popular religiosity that are absent in studies of these topics that rely on state-produced documentation alone. This book combines these sources of settler provenance with those generated by state chancelleries responsible for the administration of empire and the regulation of religious dissenters, and with published materials such as newspapers and journals, ethnographic studies, reports of the local statistical committees, and the religious press.

The sectarians' articulation of their histories came about as a result of three factors. First, literacy spread to the sectarian communities in the second half of the nineteenth century. The dissenters, especially Molokans, began to record their histories and theology and to publish those documents already in their possession.[34] Second, in the wake of the Dukhobor movement of 1895 through 1899 and the emigration of large numbers of Dukhobors and Molokans to North America, V. D. Bonch-Bruevich, an ethnographer and future Bolshevik leader, began a systematic study of Russia's sectarians. Writing to their communities in both Russia and North America, he asked them to record their life stories and to send anything written down that they might have with them. To this request they responded with gusto. Bonch-Bruevich published many of these source materials in a series of volumes before the 1917 revolution.[35] However, the majority of this material remains unpublished and is housed today in St. Petersburg's Museum of the History of Religion (GMIR) and the Manuscript Division of the Russian State Library (ORRGB) in Moscow.[36] Tolstoyans such as V. G. Chertkov, P. I. Biriukov, and I. M. Tregubov carried out a similar gathering and publication of materials, further in-

ter (Princeton, 1991), 3–19; Eklof, "Ways of Seeing"; and David Ransel, "Rural Russia Redux," *Peasant Studies* 18, no. 2 (1991): 117–29.

34. Examples of the publications from this period include: S. K. Zhabin, *K dukhovnomu svetu. Kratkii kurs Zakona Bozhiia dlia dukhovnykh khristian (postoiannykh molokan)* (Tiflis, 1912); *Kratkoe izlozhenie dogmatichesko-religioznogo ucheniia dukhovnykh khristian* (Tiflis, 1909); N. F. Kudinov, *Dukhovnye khristiane. Molokane. Kratkii istoricheskii ocherk* (Vladikavkaz, 1913); I. F. Kolesnikov, *Dogmaty i ustav dukhovnykh khristian molokanskogo veroispovedaniia* (Baku, 1910); P. A. Suvorov, *Uchebnik dukhovnykh khristian*, Izd. 1–oe (Baku, 1915); *Otchet o Vserossiiskom s'ezde dukhovnykh khristian (Molokan), sostoiavshemsia 22 iiulia 1905 goda* (Tiflis, 1907); and the journals *Molokanin, Molokanskii vestnik*, and *Dukhovnyi khristianin*.

35. See V. D. Bonch-Bruevich, *Programma dlia sobranii svedenii po issledovaniiu i izucheniiu russkogo sektantstva i raskola* (St. Petersburg, 1908) and the same author's multivolume series *Materialy k istorii i izucheniiu russkogo sektantstva*, 4 vols. (Christchurch, UK, 1901–02) and *Materialy k istorii i izucheniiu russkogo sektantstva i raskola*, 6 vols., numbered 1–5, 7 (St. Petersburg, 1908–16); and Engelstein, *Castration*, 1–10.

36. On GMIR, see V. I. Rutenburg, "Kratkii putevoditel' po fondam lichnogo proiskhozhdeniia rukopisnogo otdela Muzeia istorii religii i ateizma," in *Ateizm, religiia, sovremennost'* (Leningrad, 1973). On ORRGB, see S. V. Zhitomirskaia, ed., *Vospominaniia i dnevniki XVIII–XX vv.: Ukazatel' rukopisei* (Moscow, 1976); and S. V. Zhitomirskaia, L. V. Gapochko, and B. A. Shlikhter, "Arkhiv V. D. Bonch-Bruevicha," *Zapiski otdela rukopisei*, no. 25 (Moscow, 1962).

creasing the pool of sources available for the historian. Third, in emigration, both Molokan and Dukhobor communities began to write down their histories and theological principles in order to retain their faith and cultural distinctiveness in their new homes and pass them on to their children.[37]

These sources come with their own biases and must be approached with critical caution. Although there are materials and stories dating back to the eighteenth century, the majority was written down only at the end of the nineteenth century, sometimes abroad. As a result, they often reflect a certain refashioning of memory and the concerns of distant generations in different contexts. This is especially true because many were published after the Dukhobor uprising, which altered the sectarians' notions of themselves and their past. Nonetheless, these sources offer an exceptional window onto popular religiosity and Russian settler colonialism, and they help revive the voice of the peasantry under the rule of the tsars.

37. Examples of these publications include: Peter Malov, *Dukhobortsy: ikh istoriia, zhizn' i bor'ba*, vol. 1 (Thrums, BC, 1948); V. A. Sukhorev, *Istoriia dukhobortsev* (Winnipeg, 1944); Koozma Tarasoff, *Plakun Trava: The Doukhobors* (Grand Forks, BC, 1982); S. F. Reibin, *Trud i mirnaia zhizn'. Istoriia dukhobortsev bez maski* (San Francisco, 1952); I. G. Samarin, ed., *Dukh i zhizn'—Kniga Solntse* (Los Angeles, 1928); Morris Mose Pivovaroff, *Moisey: A Russian Christian Molokan* (n.p., 1989); John K. Berokoff, *Molokans in America* (Whittier, CA, 1969); and Maksim Gavrilovich Rudometkin, *Utrenniaia zvezda* (Los Angeles, 1915). My deepest thanks to Morris Pivovaroff for kindly lending me a copy of his self-published book.

PART I

THE ROAD TO TRANSCAUCASIA

TOLERATION THROUGH ISOLATION

The Edict of 1830 and the Origins
of Russian Colonization in Transcaucasia

The statute of 1830 laid the foundation for the systematic settlement of ethnic Russians in the South Caucasus. With a single stroke of the legislative pen, the act opened a striking new chapter in Russia's long history of borderland settlement, transformed the process of Russian imperialism in Transcaucasia, and altered the fate of religious sectarians throughout the Empire. The legislators attempted to combine three goals in the decree. First, and by far the most important, was the desire to weaken religious dissent in the heartland by isolating sectarians on the Empire's Transcaucasian periphery. Such segregation took two forms. Those sectarians found guilty of spreading their heresy, of "tempting" or converting others, or of insolence toward the Orthodox Church and its priesthood, were impressed into Caucasian military service or exiled to the Transcaucasus. Other religious dissidents were encouraged to undertake voluntary resettlement in the South Caucasus in order to purge the interior provinces.[1]

The edict's second objective was to ensure that these religious nonconformists, despite their status as "especially pernicious," would nevertheless fulfill duties beneficial to the Empire, especially to strengthen frontier defense in the volatile Caucasian region through military service. Finally, the law of 1830 was also designed to initiate the process of Russian colonization of Transcaucasia—although this was by far the least important aspect of the decree as far as the legislators themselves were concerned. A broad spectrum of sectarians, especially women, children, those unable to complete military service, and all voluntary settlers were

---

1. *PSZ* (2), vol. 5:2 (1830), no. 4010, p. 169, art. 1, 2, 4–6, 8; RGIA f. 1284, op. 196–1833, d. 33, ll. 90b–10; f. 381, op. 1, d. 23322, 1846, l. 8; f. 1268, op. 8, d. 275, 1856, l. 2; and K. S-A., "Russkie raskol'niki, poselenye v Bakinskoi gubernii," *Kavkaz* no. 9 (January 21, 1868): 2.

to be sent to Transcaucasia in order to begin colonizing the region with Russians. Officials in Transcaucasia were charged with mapping out places for settlement appropriate "as much in respect to populating the region as in respect to terminating the means to spread the sectarian faith."[2]

The administration's decision to send "especially pernicious" sectarians to the South Caucasus appears, at first glance, quite paradoxical. Having only recently been brought within Russia's borders, the region was only nominally under Russian control.[3] Tsarist authorities considered the dissenters to be significant threats to state power and the social order, disrespectful to tsar and Church and antagonistic to the institution of serfdom. Why, then, send disloyal heretics en masse into a region that would seem to require settlement by Russia's most reliable subjects in order to successfully incorporate it into the Empire? The answer lies in the fact that the 1830 statute was driven primarily by the need to resolve the internal tensions caused by religious heterogeneity, not by concerns of empire-building or colonialism. The edict attempted to address an essential dilemma of tsarist religious policy: how to regulate a multiconfessional empire in which one faith—Orthodoxy—was not only privileged, but a state-sponsored national church.[4]

During the first quarter of the nineteenth century, Tsar Alexander I developed the practice of toleration through isolation in response to the complications of religious pluralism. That is, non-Orthodox Russians could be tolerated in the Russian Empire only if they were completely separated from the Orthodox population. This policy was taken up and revised by his successor, Nicholas I—in 1830, Russian officials strove to resolve the tensions of religious diversity by exploiting the Empire's vast size to isolate sectarians on the periphery. Although the edict included a stipulation to ensure their proper settlement in the region, its primary

2. *PSZ* (2), vol. 5:2 (1830), no. 4010, p. 169, art. 2, 3; and "Istoricheskiia svedeniia o molokanskoi sekte," *PS* (November 1858):293.

3. Muriel Atkin, *Russia and Iran, 1780–1828* (Minneapolis, 1980); Ronald Grigor Suny, *The Making of the Georgian Nation*, 2nd ed. (Bloomington, 1994), 42–95; Stephen F. Jones, "Russian Imperial Administration and the Georgian Nobility: The Georgian Conspiracy of 1832," *SEER* 65, no. 1 (1987): 53–76; Firouzeh Mostashari, "Tsarist Colonial Policy, Economic Change, and the Making of the Azerbaijani Nation: 1828–1905" (Ph.D. diss., University of Pennsylvania, 1995); and Moshe Gammer, *Muslim Resistance to the Tsar: Shamil and the Conquest of Chechnia and Daghestan* (London, 1994).

4. This was a question that plagued tsarist Russia until its demise. See Peter Waldron, "Religious Toleration in Late Imperial Russia," in *Civil Rights in Imperial Russia*, ed. Olga Crisp and Linda Edmondson (Oxford, 1989), 103–19; M. A. Reisner, *Gosudarstvo i veruiushchaia lichnost'* (St. Petersburg, 1905); A. M. Bobrishchev-Pushkin, *Sud i raskol'niki-sektanty* (St. Petersburg, 1902); N. L. Solov'ev, *Pol'nyi krug dukhovnykh zakonov* (Moscow, 1907); V. I. Iasevich-Borodaevskaia, *Bor'ba za veru: istoriko-bytovye ocherki i obzor zakonodatel'stva po staroobriadchestvu i sektantstvu v ego posledovatel'nom razvitii* (St. Petersburg, 1912); and K. K. Arsen'ev, *Svoboda sovesti i veroterpimost'* (St. Petersburg, 1905).

goal was to rid the imperial core of religious nonconformists—"to cleanse the internal provinces," as one official described it.[5] The authorities envisioned different possible outcomes in implementing the decree. At the very least, they hoped to control the spread of sectarians by physically removing adherents from Orthodox Russians. Others saw it as a means to eliminate the sectarians altogether, either by exterminating them or converting them to Orthodoxy. Exile to a remote and dangerous area of the Empire was a potentially life-threatening prospect. The threat of banishment to the borderlands, combined with offers of tangible rewards for converts, might convince some to "return" to Orthodoxy.[6]

Only in the final stages of policy formation did tsarist officials give any thought to what would happen to the settlers—or indeed to Transcaucasia—once they arrived. This unintentional colonialism stands in stark contrast to the simultaneous, elaborate plans of tsarist imperialists to exploit the South Caucasus as a colony for economic, political, and military ends. Indeed, in keeping with the multidimensional and uncoordinated nature of tsarist empire-building, Russian elites had at one time discussed plans to colonize the region with Russians in order to enhance economic and military development. Yet, these earlier deliberations about the benefits of colonial settlement played no direct role in the edict, which was formulated strictly as a matter of religious policy. Similarly, other policies concerning the immigration of Armenians and Germans to the South Caucasus, and the emigration of Muslims had no bearing on debates regarding sectarian relocation.[7]

RELIGIOUS DIVERSITY, CONFESSIONAL UNITY, AND THE SECTARIAN DILEMMA

For Russian officials, the problems of managing religious diversity became increasingly pressing during the seventeenth and eighteenth centuries. The combination of imperial expansion, which incorporated large numbers of Muslims, Jews, Catholics, Protestants, Buddhists, and "pagans" into Russia, and the proliferation of schismatic and sectarian reli-

5. RGIA f. 381, op. 1, d. 23297, 1844–45, l. 220b.
6. *PSZ* (2), vol. 5:2 (1830), no. 4010, p. 169; RGIA f. 383, op. 4, d. 3212, 1841–43, l. 1; f. 379, op. 1, d. 1043, 1830–37, ll. 19–190b; *AKAK* vol. 7, doc. 415, p. 466; and GMIR f. 2, op. 7, d. 596, n.d., ll. 47–78, 113–31.
7. G. V. Khachapuridze, *K istorii Gruzii pervoi poloviny XIX veka* (Tbilisi, 1950), passim and 136–41 on colonization; Laurens Hamilton Rhinelander, "The Incorporation of the Caucasus into the Russian Empire: The Case of Georgia, 1801–1854" (Ph.D. diss., Columbia University, 1972); 48–170; Suny, *Georgian Nation*, 63–95; K. A. Borozdin, "Pereselentsy v Zakavkaz'e." *RV*, no. 215 (July 1891): 117–61; and Sergei Glinka, *Opisanie pereseleniia Armian Adderbidzhanskikh v predely Rossii* (1831; repr. Baku, 1990).

gious movements brought the tsarist government face to face with the kaleidoscopic demands of rapidly expanding confessional heterogeneity.[8] Beginning with Peter III, and especially during the reigns of Catherine II and Alexander I, the autocracy introduced varying degrees and forms of religious toleration as it struggled to find an acceptable middle ground between total acceptance and outright criminalization of non-Orthodox Russians. To be sure, their tolerance had its limits. Russian monarchs proved unwilling to accept any challenge to the preeminence of the Orthodox Church and were especially perturbed by the growth of Russian Christian sectarians at the expense of Orthodoxy. As Russians who were not Orthodox, and whose theology challenged state and society, the sectarians posed a particularly vexing dilemma for religious policymakers. Thus, while Catherine the Great implemented broad practices of Enlightenment-derived, utilitarian religious toleration, she could not find it in herself to extend such acceptance to sectarians.[9]

Secular and spiritual authorities in the eighteenth and early nineteenth centuries perceived the sectarians as dangerous opponents of Orthodoxy, autocracy, and serfdom. From a religious perspective, they were heretical lost souls, apostates from the flock of the Orthodox Church. Given the strong bonds between civil and religious authority in Imperial Russia, breaking from Orthodoxy was necessarily a political act as well. As Anatole Leroy-Beaulieu, French observer of Russia during the late nineteenth century, accurately noted, "In the eyes of the government as well as of the people, the quality of Orthodox Christian is (even now) the surest pledge of patriotism and loyalty."[10] In addition, the sectarians challenged the political and social foundations of the tsarist system to their very core. For Russian elites, they were "democratic" and anti-tsar, and imbued with a threatening ideology of Christian equality, freedom, and communalism. Contemporary publications described them as fanatics, easily deluded, given to absurd views, and likely to fall under the sway of charismatic charlatans.[11]

8. On the proliferation of new sectarian movements, see F. V. Livanov, *Raskol'nikii ostorozhniki: ocherki i rasskazy*, 4 vols. (St. Petersburg, 1872–73); Orest Novitskii, *O Dukhobortsakh* (Kiev, 1832), 3–24; John Eugene Clay, "Russian Peasant Religion and its Repression: The Christ-Faith [*Khristovshchina*] and the Origins of the 'Flagellant' Myth, 1666–1837" (Ph.D. diss., University of Chicago, 1989); Laura Engelstein, "Rebels of the Soul: Peasant Self-Fashioning in a Religious Key," *RH* 23, no. 1–4 (1996): 197–213; S. A. Inikova, "Tambovskie Dukhobortsy v 60–e gody XVIII veka," *Vestnik Tambovskogo universiteta. Ser. Gumanitarnye nauki* 1 (1997): 39–53.

9. Gregory L. Bruess, "Religious Toleration in the Reign of Catherine the Great," in *International Perspectives on Church and State*, ed., Menachem Mor (Omaha, 1993), 299–315; George Woodcock and Ivan Avakumovic, *The Doukhobors* (Toronto, 1968), 30–31; and *Obzor meropriiatii ministerstva vnutrennikh del po raskolu s 1802 po 1881 god* (St. Petersburg, 1903), 21–27.

10. Anatole Leroy-Beaulieu, *The Empire of the Tsars and the Russians*, vol. 3, *Religion* (New York, 1896), 510; "Istoricheskiia svedeniia," 291–92; and V. M. Skvortsov, *Zapiska o dukhobortsakh na Kavkaze* (n.p., 1896), 1–7.

11. A. I. Masalkin, "K istorii zakavkazskikh sektantov: I. Molokane," *Kavkaz*, no. 306 (November

The proclamations and actions of Molokans and Dukhobors entrenched officials in their antisectarian views. Molokans asserted that they would obey only God's commandments, and, as self-defined "true Christians," that they stood outside the arbitrary and temporary laws promulgated by human rulers. Earthly authority applied only to "sons of the earth"—since Molokans were of God's world rather than this one, worldly powers were of no consequence to them, citing John 17:14: "They are not of the world, even as I am not of the world."[12] Dukhobors manifested a similar self-understanding, asserting: "There is no Fatherland on earth for us; we are wanderers on the earth."[13] Asked in one psalm "Why do you not obey the government?"—Dukhobors responded "I am a Christian, have known truth and profess the law of my Lord, Jesus Christ, and I cannot [obey the government], . . . because He who sent me into this life and gave me indubitable law as guidance for this life does not want it."[14] In distinction to the Molokans, Dukhobor theology asserted that the spirit of Christ passed from generation to generation embodied in their leader. That their chief was the incarnation of the Son of God gave even further impetus to the Dukhobor community not to show obedience to the tsar or the Russian state.[15] Given these religious beliefs, and the discourse of Christian identity, sectarians frequently refused military service, did not pay their taxes, may have harbored criminals and deserters, denied the authority of both spiritual and secular hierarchies, challenged the institution of serfdom, preached their faith to others, and constructed their own leadership structures with their own laws and systems of justice.

In addition to seeing them as political and social threats, state officials also viewed sectarians as a danger to the ethno-confessional unity of the Russian people, destabilizing elite definitions of Russianness. Educated circles through much of the Imperial period discerned a vital nexus between religious affiliation and ethnicity, particularly between Orthodox

18, 1893): 2; Ananii Ivanov Stollov, "Svedenie o molokanakh Tavricheskoi gubernii," *OZ*, no. 6 (1870): 301; Novitskii, *O Dukhobortsakh;* and A. I. Klibanov, *Narodnaia sotsial'naia utopia v Rossii* (Moscow, 1978), 7–55.

12. Masalkin, "Molokane," 2; and Stollov, "Svedenie," 301. The one exception to the standard Molokan relationship with state power was the Don branch of the Molokan faith. The religious teachings of the Don Molokans diverged in a number of respects from other strains of the faith, including a willingness to fulfill certain sacraments (although without priests) and a readiness to recognize state power. On the Don branch of the Molokans, see *Ispovedanie very Molokan Donskogo tolka Tavricheskoi gubernii* (Simferopol, 1875); and T. I. Butkevich, *Obzor russkikh sekt i ikh tolkov* (Petrograd, 1915), 426–32.

13. V. D. Bonch-Bruevich, ed., *Zhivotnaia Kniga Dukhobortsev,* vol. 2 of *MIIRSR* (St. Petersburg, 1909), 99, psalm 78.

14. Ibid., 84, psalm 60.

15. Skvortsov, *Zapiska,* 3–4; Gary Dean Fry, "The Doukhobors, 1801–1855: The Origins of a Successful Dissident Sect" (Ph.D. diss., The American University, 1976), 348–50; and I. Kharmalov, "Dukhobortsy: Istoricheskii ocherk," *RM* 5, no. 11 (1884): 138–61.

Christianity and Russian nationality.[16] Writing on these questions at the turn of the twentieth century, the jurist M. A. Reisner argued that nineteenth-century Russian officials and intellectuals believed that religion was the "foundation of nationality" and that each ethnic group naturally possessed its own "national religion."[17] The primordial religion for Russians was Orthodoxy, just as was Judaism for Jews and Islam for Tatars. As Leroy-Beaulieu noted, "To such Russians as would feel inclined to leave the pale of the Orthodox Church no way seems open but to drop their nationality, since their country repulses them."[18] Moreover, like many other multinational empires, Imperial Russia applied a corporatist approach to religious diversity—tolerating non-Orthodox confessions as communal groups rather than allowing freedom of conscience to individual believers. In consequence, the parameters of Russia's policies of religious toleration were broadly constructed around corporatist, national notions of religious affiliation. As deviators from their ascribed ethno-confessional community, there was little place for Russian sectarians in this approach to religious diversity.[19]

The example of the religious fracturing of Western Europe, which Russian officials viewed as perilous to state and nation, informed all tsarist deliberations over the place of sectarians in Russian society and polity. As Councilor of State Arsen'ev wrote to the Ministry of Internal Affairs, in 1833: "Are not our Old Believers similar to the Puritans and the Molokans to the Independents? And what trouble these dissenters made for England! In general haven't religious wavering and mental ferment always been the precursor of political upheavals and revolutions?" Others likened the sectarians to the Anabaptists and even the Jacobins. At the same time, officials worried that the splintering of confessional unity that the sectarians represented could easily lead to the brutality, destruction, chaos, and the "rivers of blood" that accompanied the rupture of Western Christendom in the Reformation and Wars of Religion. The experience in Western Europe impressed on Russian observers that only the elimination of religious dissent would preserve social and political sta-

16. Reisner, *Gosudarstvo*, 195. In addition to the works discussed below, see also Nicholas Riasanovsky, *Nicholas I and Official Nationality, 1825–1855* (Berkeley, 1961); Richard S. Wortman, *Scenarios of Power: Myth and Ceremony in Russian Monarchy*, Vol. I *From Peter the Great to the Death of Nicholas I* (Princeton, 1995), 379–81; Jeffrey Brooks, *When Russia Learned to Read: Literacy and Popular Literature, 1861–1917* (Princeton, 1985), 214–45; and Theodore Weeks, "Defending Our Own: Government and the Russian Minority in the Kingdom of Poland, 1905–1914," *RR* 54, no. 4 (1995): 539–51.
17. Reisner, *Gosudarstvo*, esp. 194–96; and Bobrishchev-Pushkin, *Sud*, 1–50.
18. Leroy-Beaulieu, *Empire*, 45, 508–11, quotation on 510.
19. Michael Walzer, *On Toleration* (New Haven, 1997), 14–36; Paul W. Werth, "The Limits of Religious Ascription: Baptized Tatars and the Revision of 'Apostasy,' 1840s–1905," *RR* 59, no. 4 (2000): 496–97; and Isabel de Madariaga, *Russia in the Age of Catherine the Great* (New Haven, 1981), 503–18.

bility. Notably, tsarist authorities did not pick up on the practice of external banishment (as in the case of the French Jansenists) as a means to resolve the difficulties of religious pluralism. Viewing each individual as potential revenue for the state, they opposed divesting themselves of the sectarians entirely, preferring to keep them as contributing subjects (indeed, officials were often annoyed by the flight of Old Believers and sectarians out of the country).[20]

Given Russia's corporatist and national approach to religious diversity and the sectarians' own socio-political activities, granting toleration to the sectarians was no simple matter. In addition to putting aside theological opposition to heresy, toleration required a fundamental revision of the meanings of Russianness and the foundations of state authority. Thus, despite an inclination to implement policies of religious acceptance in the Empire—whether a product of Enlightenment rationalism or mystical piety—tsarist officials did move to restrict sectarians. In this intellectual environment, Alexander I's "toleration through isolation" came to be seen as the best possible means to deal with these apostates from the Russian Church.

TOLERATION, RESTRICTION, AND ISOLATION: RELIGIOUS DISSENT IN THE REIGN OF ALEXANDER I

The reign of Alexander I (1801–25) is justifiably considered a high point of religious toleration toward non-Orthodox Christians in Imperial Russia.[21] In comparison with his predecessors, Alexander took a more lenient approach to ruling a multiconfessional society, a stance based in part on his interest in mystical Christianity. Upon ascending to the throne, in contrast to his grandmother, he was quick to extend tolerance even to sectarians—albeit on a restricted and piecemeal basis in which the majority of his early declarations were specifically directed at only one denomination, the Dukhobors. Yet his legislative activities nonetheless opened both a discursive and legislative space in which other sectarian

20. A. I. Klibanov, "Problems of the Ideology of Peasant Movements," trans. Stephen P. and Ethel Dunn, *RH* 11, no. 2/3 (1984): 168–78, quotations on 175, 177; and GARF f. 109, op. 3 (sekretnyi arkhiv), d. 1495, 1855.

21. For general discussions of religious toleration in the reign of Alexander I, see Paul Werth, *At the Margins of Orthodoxy: Mission, Governance, and Confessional Politics in Russia's Volga-Kama Region, 1827–1905* (Ithaca, 2002), 13–16; A. Vasil'ev, "Veroterpimost' v zakonodatel'stve i zhizni v tsarstvovanie imperatora Aleksandra I (1801–1825)," *Nabliudatel'* 6–8 (1896): 35–56, 257–96, 98–113; E. A. Vishlenkova, *Religioznaia politika: ofitsial'nyi kurs i "obshchee mnenie" Rossii Aleksandrovskoi epokhi* (Kazan, 1997); *Obzor,* 43–48; and E. R. "Russkii raskol i zakonodatel'stvo," *VE* 15, no. 4 (1880): 516–32.

confessions, particularly the Molokans, found greater freedom. In the process, he began the circuitous route to 1830.

Alexander's religious policies did not necessarily reflect a simple acceptance of confessional pluralism or freedom of conscience for religious minorities. During the early years of his reign, he forged a Janus-like religious policy that aimed simultaneously to carve out a legal niche in which Russian religious dissenters could exist while trying to restrict their spread and eliminate their "errors of faith." By his final years on the throne, after experimenting with a variety of policies toward the sectarians, his initial tolerance had evolved into harsher measures. On one hand, Alexander decriminalized religious nonconformity and mandated the separation of "heresy" from secular or civil crimes. Affiliation to a sectarian faith was no longer considered a criminal act in and of itself, although certain public displays of religious nonconformity were deemed criminal disturbances of the public order.[22] Indeed, Alexander granted religious dissenters civil rights not substantially less than those granted to Orthodox Russians, particularly freedom from persecution. On the other hand, Alexander also strove to prevent the growth of sectarian faiths, considering nonconformist religious beliefs to be grossly in error. However, he believed that only humane treatment and good example could bring the sectarians back into the "bosom" of the true Orthodox church. For the tsar, toleration of religious diversity was not simply an end in itself, it was also a weapon against religious dissent and the most efficient means to bring to an end the same religious pluralism he condoned.

Two other concerns lay behind this dual policy: the maintenance of public order and the fulfillment of civil and military duties by the Empire's subjects. As long as sectarians did not disrupt the "general good" and continued to meet their responsibilities as Russian subjects, Alexander did not challenge their right to exist. In practice, this meant that he increasingly upheld a juridical distinction between those sectarians who sought to spread their beliefs and those who simply adhered to a dissident faith. Nonconformists found guilty of preaching and proselytizing to Orthodox Russians faced serious criminal prosecution as threats to public order, while ordinary believers who made no effort to spread their faith were tolerated. Moreover, the government's position emphasized the importance of state obligations by requiring that leaders and disseminators of sectarian faiths be forced to carry out primarily military but also economic services useful to the state despite their status as religious criminals.

---

22. Public displays included prayer houses, public marriage or burial ceremonies, and preaching or religious discussions within earshot of Orthodox Russians.

Extending Toleration

When Alexander I became tsar in March 1801, many of his first actions concerned the fate of religious nonconformists in Russia.[23] Only one week after ascending to the throne, he ordered the return to their former homes in the New Russian provinces of all Dukhobors whom his father Paul I had summarily banished to Siberia.[24] Within a month, Alexander instructed all military and civil governors to treat Russia's sectarians in a new way. Thenceforth, when dealing with those "who have deviated from the correct faith and the rightful Holy Church" because of their "simplicity and ignorance," spiritual authorities were to replace "severity" and "coercion" with "meekness, patience and diligent insistence which alone can assuage the cruelest heart and lead them from inveterate stubbornness." The new tsar asserted that the former persecution of sectarians of his forebears (especially of his father) had accomplished little and had not "corrected" the nonconformists. Rather, it had led them to a "common bitterness" and entrenched the apostates in their false beliefs. Alexander ordered that not even "the smallest oppression" was to be used in efforts "to bring [the dissenters] to reason and point [them] on the true path." As he decreed this shift in the treatment of nonconformists, Alexander asserted that the primary concern of tsarist officials should be to ensure that the "general public order everywhere would not be disturbed."[25]

Over the course of the first twenty years of his reign, Alexander issued a series of decrees both expanding and reinforcing this original statement of religious tolerance. In November 1801, Alexander wrote to the governor of Sloboda, Ukraine, in response to a local uprising of Dukhobors. After returning from exile in Siberia, the Dukhobors burst into rebellion because of their debilitating poverty and the severe treatment they received from religious officials in New Russia, in particular the forceful nature of the priests' "admonitions." Alexander assigned the governor the task of reasserting order among the Dukhobors while also defending them from all persecution on the part of local authorities.[26] "These admonitions should in no way take on the form of interrogations,

---

23. These religious declarations formed part of a larger *oeuvre* of legislative acts that revised much of Paul I's legislation. See Allen McConnell, *Tsar Alexander I: Paternalistic Reformer* (Arlington Heights, 1970), 22–25; Marc Raeff, *Understanding Imperial Russia: State and Society in the Old Regime* (New York, 1984), 113–45; and Alexander M. Martin, *Romantics, Reformers, Reactionaries: Russian Conservative Thought and Politics in the Reign of Alexander I* (DeKalb, 1997), 15–90.
24. "O poselenii dukhobortsev v Novorossiiskom krae," *RS* 98 (May 1899): 396; Fry, "The Doukhobors," 86; and *SPChR* (1860), I:771–72, 783–89.
25. *Obzor*, 49. On Paul I's reign, see 27–43.
26. "Zapiski Moskovskogo martinista senatora I. V. Lopukhina," *RA* 52, no. 1 (1884): 87–88; and *SPChR* (1875), 17–18.

torture, and open violence to the rites of their beliefs," he ordered.[27] In a similar letter to the governor of Tambov province in 1803, Alexander I reaffirmed that "the general rule, taken by me in cases of error of this kind, consists of not doing violence to conscience and not entering into investigations of the internal profession of faith. At the same time, any external signs of deviation from the Church are not permitted, and any temptations to lure people from the Church are strictly forbidden, not as a heresy, but as a disruption of the general good and order."[28]

In 1816, Alexander I reiterated his instruction to extend tolerance to the Dukhobors. In a dispatch to the military governor of Kherson province, the tsar asked:

> Does it befit an enlightened Christian state to return those in error to the bosom of the Church through harsh and severe means, torture, exile and other similar methods? The teachings of the Savior of the world, who came to earth . . . to save the fallen, cannot be taught through violence and punishments. . . . True faith is produced by God's blessing through persuasion, edification, meekness, and, above all, good example. Severity never persuades, it only embitters. All the measures of strictness exhausted on the Dukhobors over the course of the thirty years up to 1801 not only failed to wipe out that sect, but significantly increased the number of their followers.

Even though the Dukhobors were in error in their religious beliefs, they "must feel that they exist under the protection and patronage of the laws, and only then can we reliably expect them to love and feel an attachment to the Government, and to exact their fulfillment of its laws."[29] So remarkable were Alexander's religious tactics that the French ambassador to Russia, the Comte de Noailles, wrote to Paris that the decree of December 21, 1816, "merits note for the principles of religious tolerance that it established."[30]

Alongside these declarations of tolerance, the tsar continued efforts to punish activities that threatened to disrupt the "public order." An example from Astrakhan province shows the limits of Alexander's religious tolerance. In 1802, according to official documents, Dukhobors descended "noisily, in whole crowds" into a village marketplace and "openly

27. *SPChR* (1875), 17.
28. *SPChR* (1875), 25–26 and N. Varadinov, *Istoriia ministerstva vnutrennikh del*, vol. 8, supplementary, *Istoriia rasporiazhenii po raskolu* (St. Petersburg, 1863), 63–64. Alexander again emphasized the need to approach the sectarians in Tambov with tolerance and good behavior in another letter to the governor later in 1803. See *PSZ* (1), vol. 27 (1803), no. 20904, p. 848.
29. *SPChR* (1875), 47–48.
30. Grand Duke Nikolai Mikhailovich, *Imperator Aleksandr I: opyt' istoricheskogo issledovaniia* (St. Petersburg, 1912), 2:260–61.

began to spread their depravity." Upon being sent to the local court, the Dukhobors not only refused to deny their errors but also renounced any obedience to and recognition of the state authorities. Reflecting Alexander's distinction between activist leaders and ordinary believers, the central instigators of the disturbance were exiled as criminals to the Kola Peninsula, whereas the others were granted monarchical mercy.[31]

The Origins of Isolation

The idea of sectarian segregation originated among the dissenters themselves and was later embraced by tsarist officials. Not surprisingly, religious nonconformists and tsarist authorities had quite different expectations of what isolation would mean in practice.[32] Sectarians requested isolation as a means to escape Orthodox persecution, to strengthen their economic prospects, and to evade the surveillance of state officials. In contrast, Imperial authorities saw isolation as an opportunity to restrict contact between dissenters and Orthodox Russians and to facilitate Orthodox proselytizing among the sectarians by concentrating them in one place where Church missionaries might more easily reach them. By physically separating religious nonconformists and Orthodox subjects into discrete communities, Alexander believed that he had found the best means to achieve his dual goals of toleration and restriction. Such segregation was also in keeping with the Russian belief in the close connection between nationality and religious affiliation because isolation represented the closest approximation of a new national homeland for the sectarians.[33]

The story of isolation began in 1801 when Senators I. V. Lopukhin and Iu. A. Neledinskii-Meletskii were sent to Kharkov province to investigate a series of Dukhobor complaints about their living conditions. During the investigations, Dukhobors presented Lopukhin with a petition requesting that they be amalgamated into a separate, mono-confessional colony. As he came to know these Dukhobors better, Lopukhin began to condone their faith and to sympathize with them in the face of the maltreatment local tsarist officials inflicted on them.[34] He relayed the Dukho-

31. Novitskii, *O Dukhobortsakh*, 28–29. Among numerous other examples of Alexander's severe response to religious activity that challenged social tranquility, see *SPChR* (1875), 20–24, 36–37; and *Obzor*, 46.

32. In this vein, see the discussion in GMIR f. 2, op. 7, d. 596, n.d., ll. 45–46.

33. On Russian practices of "confin[ing] the alien confessions within their historical boundaries," see Leroy-Beaulieu, *Empire*, 512.

34. On Lopukhin's religiosity more broadly, see Alexander Lipski, "A Russian Mystic Faces the Age of Rationalism and Revolution: Thought and Activity of Ivan Vladimirovich Lopukhin," *Church History* 36, no. 2 (1967): 170–89; and James H. Billington, *The Icon and the Axe: An Interpretive History of Russian Culture* (New York, 1970), 269–306.

bors' request for isolation to the tsar using language that consciously echoed Alexander's emphasis on legal treatment for nonconformists and his desire to lead them back into the Orthodox Church. First, Lopukhin argued that the formation of a Dukhobor colony would quiet sectarian unrest by removing them from the harassment and animosity of Imperial officials in the region. Second, such segregation would all but eliminate the Dukhobors' ability to spread their beliefs to others. Finally, concentrated settlements would help well-educated, moral, and patient priests in their task of bringing the Dukhobors back to Orthodoxy.[35]

Alexander agreed wholeheartedly with Lopukhin's proposal and immediately set in motion the consolidation of a separate Dukhobor colony in the recently incorporated lands of New Russia. In January 1802, the tsar granted permission for any Dukhobors in the New Russian provinces to settle together in the Molochna (or "Milky Waters") region of Melitopol district, which was then a sparsely populated part of the Empire. Alexander wrote to the Governor of New Russia that the concentration of Dukhobors, separate from other Russians, would prevent their further ruin and maltreatment "and also that I consider such separation to be the most reliable means for the extinguishing of their heresy and for the suppression of its influence on others."[36]

The terms of settlement in Melitopol district reflected a tsarist policy that was at once concerned with the welfare of the Dukhobors as Russian subjects and desirous of the termination of the sect. To facilitate their new situation, Alexander granted the Dukhobors extremely generous material conditions for settlement relative to the Empire's average peasant.[37] The Dukhobor settlers received five years of tax relief and were assigned relatively large land allotments—at least fifteen *desiatiny* per male soul, although the 1817 census indicates that they came to hold thirty-four *desiatiny* apiece. Alexander reiterated his desire that local officials "defend [the Dukhobors] from any restrictions, and work to favor their settlement." However, as part of Alexander's two-pronged religious policy, local officials were also told to ensure that these Dukhobors did not break any civil laws, in particular those pertaining to harboring illegal runaways or attracting any newcomers to their sect.[38]

---

35. "Zapiski I. V. Lopukhina," 92–96; and Novitskii, *O Dukhobortsakh*, 25.
36. *SPChR* (1875), 18, 47.
37. For details on the Dukhobors' conditions of settlement in the Milky Waters region, see John R. Staples, *Cross-Cultural Encounters on the Ukrainian Steppe: Settling the Molochna Basin, 1783–1861* (Toronto, 2003), 37–41, 68–71, 87–106; *SPChR* (1875), 18–19; Fry, "Doukhobors," 103–8; "Poselenie dukhobortsev na r. Molochnoi" *RS* 100 (October 1899): 240; Woodcock and Avakumovic, *Doukhobors*, 35–61; and Willard Sunderland, "Making the Empire: Colonists and Colonization in Russia, 1800–1850s" (Ph.D. diss., Indiana University, 1997), 138–57, 174–216.
38. *SPChR* (1875), 28–30.

By choosing isolation as the solution to religious diversity, the 1802 decree mandating a separate Dukhobor colony was a seminal first step toward the 1830 edict. However, it differed in important respects from the later legislation. Permission to settle in Melitopol district applied only to those Dukhobors already living in New Russia and was not a blanket consent for Dukhobors from the rest of Russia to move to Milky Waters. Moreover, the legislation applied only to Dukhobors and did not concern other sectarians, such as Molokans or Subbotniks, whose large populations were equally disconcerting to state officials.

Dukhobors living in other Russian provinces soon demanded inclusion in the experiment taking place in New Russia, and Alexander obligingly extended the program. In fulfilling the dissenters' demands, tsarist officials slowly moved toward a more general policy of toleration through isolation. In a mass of petitions after 1802, they requested to relocate to the Molochna region in order to unite with their co-religionists, profit from the favorable economic conditions there, and save themselves from the persecution they felt they suffered at the hands of their Orthodox neighbors and tsarist officials.[39] Alexander granted the Dukhobor request in 1804, arguing that the relocation of these sectarians would remove the causes for "discord" between the Dukhobors and Orthodox Russians, and that by settling them in one place, "the very surveillance of [the Dukhobors] would be more active."[40] The number of Dukhobors in New Russia grew rapidly in the first quarter of the nineteenth century, reaching as many as 4,100 by 1824.[41]

Over time, tsarist officials expanded, albeit inconsistently, the scope of the segregation policy beyond the Dukhobor sect, bringing other sectarians together in one prescribed place. In the 1820s, Molokan migrants (both voluntary and forced) began to settle in Melitopol district alongside the Dukhobors. In the early 1820s, for example, the Ministry of Internal Affairs received a petition from 306 Molokan families in Tambov province who wanted to be relocated to New Russia so that they could be with their religious brethren, or, in some cases, because they could not pay their annual taxes in their current location.[42] Similar policies of isolation and segregation can also be seen in the case of the Subbotniks, although with characteristics unique to the sect. Unlike Dukhobors and Molokans, Subbotniks were not sent to New Russia, but rather isolated in

39. Novitskii, *O Dukhobortsakh*, 26; and Fry, "Doukhobors," 130–31.
40. *SPChR* (1875), 27–30; and Varadinov, *Istoriia*, 65–66.
41. *SPChR* (1875), 28–31, 62–63; Varadinov, *Istoriia*, 79; Novitskii, *O Dukhobortsakh*, 26; Woodcock and Avakumovic, *Doukhobors*, 37; and Staples, *Cross-Cultural Encounters*, 38.
42. Varadinov, *Istoriia*, 129; *SPChR* (1875), 62–63, 66–67; and Staples, *Cross-Cultural Encounters*, 41. On the migration of other sectarians, see *SPChR* (1875), 44–45; and Novitskii, *O Dukhobortsakh*, 26.

the North Caucasus, particularly in Astrakhan province. Moreover, while there were voluntary migrants among the Subbotniks, their settlement in the Caucasus was more frequently a form of punishment or exile. Banishment to the Caucasian frontier frequently elicited the restrictive results desired by Russian authorities, especially conversion to Orthodoxy.[43]

As the Subbotnik example demonstrates, New Russia was not the only location in the Russian Empire where sectarians were isolated during the reign of Alexander I. In 1804, for example, Dukhobors who had been exiled to Ekaterinburg to work in the mines—and who were later moved to Irkutsk province—were not permitted to settle in New Russia because the travel distance posed too serious an obstacle. Instead, Alexander decreed that local officials should set up a Dukhobor colony in Irkutsk on the model of the one near Milky Waters.[44] Moreover, even when presented with the option, not all Dukhobors wanted to go to the Molochna colony. In 1811, for instance, as many as 4,000 Dukhobors from a variety of provinces petitioned the tsar to create a Dukhobor settlement in the recently incorporated lands of Bessarabia similar to the one in Melitopol district. Serious consideration was given to this plan before it was eventually rejected out of fear of French invasion.[45]

Assailing Alexander's Tolerance

Beginning in the 1810s, but especially in the 1820s, criticisms of Alexander I's religious policies arose from a variety of sources, including the tsar himself. While detractors proposed mutually exclusive solutions, most of them called for some combination of less tolerance and more complete isolation for sectarians. Many had grown frustrated with the tensions and contradictions that arose from Alexander's attempt to apply toleration and restriction at once. Critics also cited the inconsistency of the application of the isolation policy, since it affected sectarian denominations differently and used too many different places for segregation.

Alexander also grew impatient with the results of his policies. He found himself in constant conflict with local officials, who generally preferred to continue their previous, more oppressive approach to sectarianism. Regional officials either could not or were unwilling to recognize the distinction that Alexander made between persecuting faith and per-

---

43. GMIR f. 2, op. 7, d. 596, ll. 79–112; d. 593, 1820–40, ll. 21–29; Varadinov, *Istoriia*, 95, 99; and *SPChR* (1875), 62–63.
44. *PSZ* (1), vol. 28 (1804–05), no. 21845, pp. 1134–36.
45. Varadinov, *Istoriia*, 78; and Fry, "Doukhobors," 132–34. Apparently some Dukhobors and Molokans did clandestinely relocate to Bessarabia in the 1820s and 1830s. See Fry, "Doukhobors," 134.

secuting acts of faith that broke civil laws or threatened the social and political well-being. Despite the tsar's orders, sectarians continued to suffer
at the hands of local officials simply for professing their faith.[46] Left in
the position of watchdog, chastising officials when they ignored his
edicts, Alexander began to rethink his approach.

In the words of one Molokan, Alexander's "benevolent views towards
them and his orders in their favor have been evaded, so that some of their
families are yet separated by banishment."[47] In one case during the late
1810s, Dukhobors from New Russia complained to Alexander that twenty
of their brethren had been exiled to Siberia "not for any crimes, but only
for being Dukhobors." Alexander responded immediately, ordering that
all Dukhobors mentioned in the petition be returned from exile and settled in Milky Waters. He underscored his discontent with their banishment by demanding that Siberian officials spare no expense for their trip
back, so that no Dukhobors were lost "by exhaustion in transit."[48] In response to the evasions of local authorities, in 1818 Alexander instructed
that in the future, "when Dukhobors are uncovered, then, before they are
taken to court, before even the local administration issues any command
about prosecuting them in court," the details of the case were to be sent
to Alexander for prior review. By ordering that he become personally involved with the treatment of religious dissenters, Alexander struggled to
prevent arbitrary persecution by local officials.[49]

In addition to ignoring Alexander's relatively tolerant approach,
local officials openly protested his policies. For example, in 1816, Alexandre de Langeron, governor-general of New Russia, made clear to Alexander his vehement opposition to the policy of isolating the Dukhobors in
Melitopol district.[50] Arguing that they had lost all connections to Christianity, he demanded the dissenters' removal from Tavriia province for
leading "dissipated lives," and found them guilty of converting Orthodox
neighbors to their heresy. Alexander defended the Dukhobors' right
to exist in Melitopol and demanded proper treatment for them. For
his part, Langeron offered a more radical solution: increasing the
Dukhobors' segregation—and expanding Alexander I's policy of isolation—by moving them "to another area, where the residents are not
Christian."[51]

46. *Obzor*, 45. For similar problems under Catherine II, see E. R., "Russkii raskol," 508.
47. Quoted in Fry, "Doukhobors," 168.
48. Fry, "Doukhobors," 167–68; and *SPChR* (1875), 54.
49. *SPChR* (1875), 55. For an example where Alexander's demand for prior review halted local
prosecution of Dukhobors, see Fry, "Doukhobors," 170.
50. On Langeron's opposition to the Dukhobors, see Fry, "Doukhobors," 141–54, 164–65;
SPChR (1875), 46–49; Varadinov, *Istoriia*, 79–81; and Staples, *Cross-Cultural Encounters*, 94.
51. Quoted in Fry, "Doukhobors," 153.

In another case, M. M. Speranskii expressed his concerns about St. Petersburg's Dukhobor policy in response to the appearance of Dukhobors in Penza diocese in 1816. He found that the settlement of Dukhobors in the Molochna region represented, if not "true encouragement," at least "indifference, with a certain tinge of patronage" to the nonconformists. In the case of the Dukhobors, Speranskii found such patronage unacceptable since their doctrine was "so close to the spirit of liberty and civil equality, that the least curvature or deviation left of this line . . . could produce a very powerful shock among the people." Despite a deep disenchantment with the isolation policy, Speranskii stopped short in his letter of demanding an end to the Milky Waters settlements. However, he did underscore the problems inherent in the existing practice of giving the sectarian settlers in New Russia generous land allotments and other economic perquisites: "What differences in land, in taxes, in obligations. . . . God save us if our peasants, or particular landowners, learn of these differences."[52]

Speranskii was not the only tsarist official to voice concern that the settlement of sectarians in the Molochna area was only serving to strengthen the nonconformists' position in Russian society, even to the point of attracting Orthodox Russians to the dissenting faiths. In 1822, the governor of Tavriia province declared that the Orthodox population believed that Molokans received special state patronage. He argued that this view of Molokan privilege derived from two sources. First, both Orthodox and Molokan Russians misinterpreted the tsar's declaration of toleration for the Dukhobors in 1816, believing that the ruling not only protected all religious nonconformists from persecution, but that, through it, the state actively sought to protect sectarians and to invite "all to join the heresy."[53] Second, the large land allotments held by dissenter-settlers, relative to others in New Russia as well as to peasants elsewhere in the Empire, led people to see the religious dissent as state-sponsored.[54]

Moreover, by the mid-1820s, such high organs of government as the Ministry of Internal Affairs, the Committee of Ministers, and the State Council also protested the existing policy of isolating sectarians to New Russia, asserting that such practices had caused an eruption of new nonconformist adherents. These high-level officials believed that as soon as the

52. Speranskii's report is discussed and quoted in ibid., 155–62; and Klibanov, "Problems," 172.
53. SPChR (1875), 46–49.
54. Varadinov, Istoriia, 130. On sectarian land holdings in New Russia, see RGIA f. 379, op. 1, d. 1043, 1830–37; ll. 29–40, 54–610b, 81–820b, 123–280b, and 132–35; f. 383, op. 4, d. 3331, 1841; op. 1, d. 234, 1838; Gosudarstvennyi arkhiv Khersonskoi oblasti (GAKhO) f. 14, op. 2, d. 70, 1821–33; and Staples, Cross-Cultural Encounters, 37–41, 87–106. My thanks go to John Staples for bringing the final two RGIA references to my attention and permitting me to read his microfilm copy of the GAKhO document.

settlers in Tavriia province rooted themselves in their new homes and appre-
ciated the benefits—larger land allotments, a healthy climate, relative religious freedom, and unification with other sectarians—they concluded
that the government was looking after them. Indeed, these ministries
worried that the dissenters understood this state patronage to be not only
a conscious effort on the part of St. Petersburg to ease their lot in life, but
also an invitation for others to follow their example. Consequently, many of
those sectarians who had previously masqueraded as Orthodox by following its outward practices in order not to be exiled were no longer concerned
about the repercussions of open sectarianism. They began to declare their
faith publicly and put forward requests for transfer to Milky Waters.[55]

These state agencies were correct when they asserted that the sectarians themselves viewed Alexander's toleration as a sign of acceptance and
even encouragement. Throughout the nineteenth century and beyond,
nonconformists saw the reign of Alexander I as a golden age. In his unpublished history of the Molokans written around 1910, I. G. Vodopianov
described how the Molokans had been savagely persecuted in the late
eighteenth century, but, referring to Alexander I, that "the Blessed Tsar
granted [us] freedom."[56] Dukhobor communities described their experiences under Alexander I in a similar fashion: only during his reign "did
they begin to look on us as human beings."[57]

Alexander's religious policies of toleration and restriction also failed
to resolve the contradictions and conflicts that arose from Orthodox and
non-Orthodox Russians living together. Despite the increase in the number of dissenters sent into isolation in New Russia or the Caucasus, many
others—indeed, the majority—still remained among the Orthodox.[58]
Tensions arose in such multidenominational settings because tsarist state
policy applied different laws to people of different religious affiliations.
Such problems, in turn, provoked a demand for greater isolation of sectarians from Orthodox practitioners.

The case of Subbotniks in Aleksandrov, Astrakhan province, in the
early 1810s reflects the legal and social problems of multiconfessional liv-

55. Varadinov, *Istoriia*, 227–28.
56. GMIR f. 2, op.8, d. 237, 1910, l. 40. For descriptions of the centennial of Molokan freedom
celebrated in 1905, see N. F. Kudinov, *Stoletie Molokanstva v Rossii 1805–1905 gg.* (Baku, 1905);
"Molokanskii s"ezd v Zakavkaz'e i otmennoe k nemu vnimanie namestnika," *MO* 10, no. 11
(1905): 289–91; "Vserossiiskii s"ezd molokan," *MO* 10, no. 9 (1905): 1416; and *Otchet dukhovnykh
khristian molokan (postoiannykh) po povodu 150-ti letnogo iubileia samostoiatel'nogo ikh religioznogo
sushchestvovaniia so dnia opublikovaniia vysochaishogo ukaza gosudaria Rossiiskogo prestola Aleksandra
Pavlovicha ot 22-go iiulia, 1805* (San Francisco, 1955).
57. V. V. Vereshchagin, *Dukhobortsy i Molokane v Zakavkaz'e, Shiity v Karabakhe, Batchi i Oshumoedy
v Srednei Azii, i Ober-Amergau v Gorakh Bavarii* (Moscow, 1900), 4–6; and Novitskii, *O Dukhobori-
sakh*, 28.
58. Woodcock and Avakumovic, *Doukhobors*, 38.

ing.[59] Half of the merchants and *meshchane* in Aleksandrov were Subbotniks, causing serious problems in elections to public offices. Subbotniks were prevented from holding administrative positions because tsarist law required elected officers to swear an oath of allegiance, which the Subbotniks refused to do, and because state officials feared the possibility that they might hold positions of influence from which they could lure Orthodox subjects into error. However, in 1813, an Orthodox inhabitant of the town sent a petition to local officials requesting that Subbotniks be permitted to take part in the elections and hold public posts. The petition explained that because Subbotniks had been barred from holding elected office, the obligations and duties of all public officeholding rested solely on the Orthodox portion of the town—a grossly disproportionate burden. The petitioner believed that these extra responsibilities were not only juridically unfair, but also reduced the economic capabilities of the Orthodox inhabitants who were forced to expend a significant percentage of their energies in administration. By granting the Subbotniks freedom from duty, the existing legal setup provided the Orthodox with an unintended, yet quite material, incentive to join the Subbotniks.[60] After much interministerial discussion, the local officials decided that Subbotniks would still be prevented from holding office, but to even the playing field they would be required to pay an annual sum equal to a third of the salaries of public officials of the town.[61] Although the authorities reached a compromise here, the case of the Subbotniks in Aleksandrov reflected the pressing problems posed by the close proximity of Orthodox and non-Orthodox subjects.

The most important complaint about Alexander's policies—in the eyes of the tsar and his critics alike—was that despite his faith in the ability of tolerance to bring the sectarians back into the Orthodox fold, the number of nonconformists had in fact increased over the course of Alexander's reign.[62] Hints that the dissenter population was on the rise began to appear already in 1811 with the petition of 4,000 Tambov Dukhobors requesting to be resettled to Bessarabia—a number large enough to alarm officials.[63] These increases continued into the reign of Nicholas I, as did the government's unease and sense of impending threat from these blossoming communities. In 1826, information concerning the quantity of sectarians began to flow into the capital as a re-

59. Varadinov, *Istoriia*, 88; and GMIR f. 2, op. 7, d. 593, 1820–40, ll. 21–22.
60. *PSZ* (1), vol. 32 (1812–15), no. 25529, p. 741.
61. *SPChR* (1875), 43. These rules and regulations concerning the holding of public office were later extended to the Dukhobors. See *SPChR* (1875), 57; and Varadinov, *Istoriia*, 81.
62. *Obzor*, 47.
63. Varadinov, *Istoriia*, 78–79, 228.

sult of various efforts launched by Alexander I to collect intelligence. Rather than a decline in and geographic restriction of the number of sectarians, governors were in fact reporting an increase in the number of sectarians in the Empire, and the religious nonconformists remained widely dispersed.[64]

Reformulating Religious Policy

In the face of these growing criticisms of his religious policy, in particular of its failure to solve the problems that it set out to solve, Alexander I began to reformulate his policies toward the sectarians. The shift began in the final five years of his reign and carried over into the rule of his successor, Nicholas I. Indeed, changes in religious policy toward the sectarians that historians have generally attributed to Nicholas were in fact the progeny of a process of policy reevaluation begun under Alexander, although they were taken further with Nicholas's ideology of Official Nationality and his drive for social and political order, uniformity, and obedience.[65] Since this transformation was piecemeal, the 1820s became a time of debate and experimentation, defined by a rash of new and uncoordinated legislation and proposals. As tsarist authorities searched desperately for a new religious policy, they continued to grapple with the persistent problem of governing a multiconfessional state without endangering the putatively stable and loyal majority. With each modification, many parts of the 1830 edict (seclusion, military service, and containment) were gradually adopted as Russian policymakers unknowingly edged closer to the watershed decree.

The cornerstone of the new approach was an emphasis on increasing segregation in a single distant location as the best means to tolerate religious pluralism while protecting the preeminence of the Orthodox Church. Meanwhile, tsarist officials continued to enact restrictive policies to reduce the spread of non-conformism. While the fundamental components of Alexander's original policy remained intact, there began a subtle change in the way its tenets were emphasized that resulted in practices substantially different in tone. The imperative to convert and segregate was strengthened relative to the former approach, which treated the dissenters largely as it did Orthodox Russian subjects. If Alexander had introduced toleration with a dose of restriction, by the 1820s tsarist policy had transformed into restriction with a dose of toleration.

64. For the government's statistics on the number of dissenters in 1826 and 1827, see Varadinov, *Istoriia*, 157–80.
65. Orthodoxy occupied a prominent place, along with autocracy and nationality, in Official Nationality. See Riasanovsky, *Nicholas I*, esp. 73–183.

In that spirit, Russian officials created new obstacles to the spread of religious nonconformism and to the interaction of sectarians with Orthodox subjects. Increasing numbers of Dukhobors and Molokans were exiled to Tavriia province and many Subbotniks to the North Caucasus (and later Siberia), and disseminators of these faiths were more vigorously prosecuted in criminal court.[66] Moreover, in March of 1820, Alexander agreed to Speranskii's proposal that, due to the distance of the region from central power, Dukhobors and other schismatics in Siberia accused of disseminating their faith "could be taken to criminal court immediately." In granting this power to the local Siberian authorities, Alexander backed away from his earlier efforts to retain final authority over all affairs involving the sectarians, re-empowering local officials to take less restrained action against the nonconformists.[67]

Surveillance of all schismatics also increased dramatically in the 1820s—in part to collect information about the dissenters, in part to prevent the spread of their faiths. In addition to augmenting the financial resources available to Orthodox missionaries for supervision of sectarians, Alexander also ordered the formation of a secret committee on schismatic affairs in the final year of his life. Among the primary goals of the secret committee was the collection of information—especially demographic information—on the sectarians in the Russian Empire.[68]

After Nicholas ascended to the throne, restrictions and scrutiny accelerated. Of numerous examples, an edict of April 10, 1826 conscripted those serfs espousing the Dukhobor "heresy" into military service, with those incapable of military service exiled to Siberia for settlement. In addition, Nicholas imposed restrictions on the mobility of the Melitopol Dukhobors, denying them passports to leave their villages for work purposes and forcing them to report all short-term trips to the local police.[69]

In 1825, in the midst of these growing restrictions, and in response to the growing sense among St. Petersburg's authorities that Alexander's religious policies were failing to achieve their ends, the minister of the interior, Vasilii Sergeevich Lanskoi, proposed a new variant on the isolation

66. *Obzor*, 48; E. R., "Russkii raskol," 527–31; *SPChR* (1875), 62–63, 74–78; *PSZ* (1), vol. 40 (1825), no. 30436a, pp. 397–408; no. 30483, pp. 465–67; Varadinov, *Istoriia*, 271–77; GMIR f. 2, op. 7, d. 593, ll. 25–27; and Antoine Scheikevitch, "Alexandre Ier et l'hérésie Sabbatiste," *RHMC* 3 (1956): 223–35.

67. *SPChR* (1875), 54–55, 57–58.

68. *SPChR* (1875), 78, 80–81; Varadinov, *Istoriia*, 191; Klibanov, "Problems," 179–80; and I. P. Liprandi, "Kratkoe obozrenie sushchestvuiushchikh v Rossii raskolov, eresei i sekt kak v religioznom tak i v politicheskom ikh znachenii," in *Sbornik pravitel'stvennykh svedenii o raskol'nikakh*, vol. 2, ed. V. Kel'siev (London, 1861), 91–169. Materials from this Committee can be found in RGIA f. 1473, op. 1, especially dd. 49, 54, 55, 60, and 62. On other efforts, outside the Committee, to gather information about the Dukhobors, see RGIA f. 1284, op. 195–1826, d. 46.

69. *SPChR* (1875), 86–87; and Varadinov, *Istoriia*, 229.

model. His plan, an early form of the 1830 decree, altered the existing policy of segregation in two important ways: it proposed Siberia as the location for forced settlement and it introduced a two-tiered system of isolation, whereby those sectarians considered particularly dangerous were exiled to more distant Eastern Siberia, while those who simply professed the faith and were of "free" social status—merchants, *meshchane*, Cossacks, state and court peasants, and *odnodvortsy*—were sent to nearer Western Siberia.[70] In order to deepen the isolation of the sectarians, Lanskoi's plan stated that their settlements should house no more than 100 people per village, and that the villages be at least twenty-five kilometers from any Orthodox settlement.

The Committee of Ministers took Lanskoi's proposal seriously as an alternative to isolation in New Russia, writing to the governor-general of Western Siberia for information on available lands. In the interim, however, the tsar (by this time Nicholas I) interjected his opinion that, rather than simply banish the guilty dissenters, as Lanskoi had proposed, it would be better to enlist able-bodied sectarians into military service, while those not capable of such duties would be settled in Siberia. Nicholas's idea was to extract the maximum state benefit from the sectarian subjects. However, for five years the governors-general of both Western and Eastern Siberia failed to answer inquiries about appropriate land allotments—whether due to incompetence or their resistance to the new plan is uncertain. As a result, Lanskoi's vision for reformulating the isolation policy was stalled during the second half of the 1820s.[71]

As central authorities explored the possibilities of isolation in Siberia, the Synod proposed another geographic alternative for the isolation of nonconformists: the South Caucasus. On September 15, 1825, the Synod argued—and Alexander agreed—that Subbotnik leaders and assistants who were to be placed into military service should be sent to units in Georgia only, "on the assumption that they, not knowing the Georgian language, cannot spread their false teachings among the local inhabitants." To further increase their isolation and inhibit any proselytizing, the decree also required that Subbotnik soldiers in Georgia were neither to be relieved from duty nor granted temporary leave to visit their original homes and families. The Synod argued that separating them from their native land and "cutting them off forever from their relatives and friends would produce in the followers of the sect a fear of remaining any longer in their apostasy."[72] The Synod's belief that ethno-linguistic dif-

70. Varadinov, *Istoriia*, 228.
71. Ibid., 228–29.
72. *SPChR* (1875), 80–81; and Varadinov, *Istoriia*, 275. The practice of sending dissenters to Georgia for military service had existed prior to 1825 (involving Skoptsy and Dukhobors), but it was not widespread. *SPChR* (1875), 44, 50–51, 67, 81.

ferences would prevent transmission of the sectarians' ideas to the peoples of Georgia foreshadowed the impending debate over the general appropriateness of Transcaucasia as a place of segregation.

Dukhobors in Cossack Clothing: Choosing Transcaucasia

Although Russian officials were moving toward the 1830 edict during Alexander I's reign, the decree's final form—including the specific choice of Transcaucasia as the location to isolate sectarians, the notion of consciously using them as colonists, and the cessation of previous segregation practices in New Russia—came about through an extended process of bureaucratic negotiation—and no small amount of contingency—in which the two other geographic candidates for resettlement, the North Caucasus and Siberia, fell by the wayside. During this process, numerous proposals and counterproposals were put forward as local officials attempted to protect the interests of their regions, central authorities to solve the sectarian problem, and the Ministry of Internal Affairs to protect the dissenters' lives and livelihoods. These deliberations took place in the context of Nicholas I's developing notions of Official Nationality, with its emphasis on Orthodoxy as the heart and spirit of Russian society and polity. However, the decree was prompted by a specific problem that forced officials to take decisive action after the muddling of Alexander's later years: the appearance of Dukhobors among the Don Cossacks in the 1820s. In this way, regional issues in the Don led to the creation of a more comprehensive, Empire-wide policy regarding sectarians.

Dukhobors had been appearing with increasing regularity among the Don Cossacks since the early 1820s, if not earlier.[73] The Don leadership considered these religious dissenters a threat to the smooth running and social stability of their units. Aside from religious issues, it believed that the practice of sending pacifist nonconformists to New Russia as punishment was unintentionally creating an incentive for Cossacks to avoid military service by converting.[74] Transcaucasia and Siberia were the alternatives to New Russia then under discussion. The combination of the unpredictable twists and turns of administrative negotiations, the military requirements in the Caucasus, and the continued silence of Siberian

---

73. RGIA f. 1284, op. 195–1822, d. 10; op. 195–1824, dd. 18 and 47; op. 195–1825, dd. 7 and 61; op. 195–1827, d. 34; RGIA f. 1284, op. 195–1828, dd. 139 and 145; op. 195–1829, d. 149; GMIR f. 2, op. 7, d. 594, ll. 3–5, 75–78; d. 596, n.d., ll. 47–78, 113–31; and SPChR (1875), 69, 78, 83.

74. On Dukhobor pacifism and tsarist military service, see Nicholas B. Breyfogle, "Swords into Plowshares: Opposition to Military Service Among Religious Sectarians, 1770s to 1874," in The Military and Society in Russian History, ed. Eric Lohr and Marshall Poe (Leiden, 2002), 441–67.

officials led to the choice of the Transcaucasus as the new place of settlement for Russia's sectarians.

In 1824, Ataman Lieutenant-General Ilovaiskii reported that fifty-
seven Dukhobors had appeared in two Don *stanitsy*. Following a well-
established discourse about the Dukhobors, he described them as intransigent and stubborn in their errors and underscored the severe
threat posed by their ability to attract others to their "delusions." According to previous practices, the response of Don officials had been to
strip the "offender" of his duties and of his association with the Don
Cossacks, and to send the individual in question to the Milky Waters
Dukhobor colony as part of Alexander's isolation policies. In the 1824
case, however, Ilovaiskii argued that these earlier methods were failing
to solve the problem: "This measure, so beneficial in regards to civilian
Dukhobors, can bring about the opposite result among Cossacks who are
obligated to military service."[75] The new Dukhobor converts, Ilovaiskii
argued, were using the switch in religious affiliation as a means to escape
military service. Resettlement to Dukhobor communities in Tavriia
province provided for them all of the advantages of a quiet and bounti-
ful existence, not least by relieving them of the "cares, labors, and dangers" attached to life as a Don soldier.

Ilovaiskii confronted tsarist officials with the dilemma that the existing "punishment" might actually have the undesired effect of enticing
others to the heresy. To avoid this problem, he proposed that those Don
Cossacks discovered in the future adhering to the Dukhobor faith should
not be sent to Tavriia province, but rather resettled on the Caucasian Military Line. There they would not be able to escape military service and
"will be required . . . continually to serve with weapons in hand against
the mountain predators [and] the Dukhobor heresy on the Don will not
only weaken but will be completely destroyed. Meanwhile those infected
by [the heresy] will perform real service, for which they are being lost forever under the existing arrangement."[76] Alexander I and the Committee
of Ministers were amenable to Ilovaiskii's proposal, subject to consent
and further information from the Caucasus. They saw the Caucasian option as a means to ensure that the Dukhobors, like all subjects, would fulfill their obligation of military service to the state and that exile to the
Caucasian Line would act as a strong deterrent to other Cossacks who
might have been thinking of converting.[77]

75. RGIA f. 1284, op. 195–1825, d. 61, ll. 1–10b.
76. Ibid.; *PSZ* (2), vol. 1 (1826), no. 126, p. 188; and GMIR f. 2, op. 7, d. 594, l. 3.
77. RGIA f. 1284, op. 195–1825, d. 61, ll. 10b–2 and *PSZ* (2), vol. 1 (1826), no. 126, p. 188–89.
For an enlightening discussion of Cossack life on the Caucasian Line, see Thomas Barrett, *At the
Edge of Empire: The Terek Cossacks and the North Caucasus Frontier, 1700–1860* (Boulder, 1999).

The perilous nature of life on the Caucasian frontier was an important component of tsarist discussions over the fate of the Don Dukhobors. As all parties were well aware, service in the Caucasus was, in many respects, the equivalent of a death sentence. Whereas the average death rate per thousand troops in the Empire as a whole was 37.4 men, the rate in the Caucasus was 67 men. More significant was the fact that of these 67, only 5.8 died as a result of combat-related incidents. The remainder fell prey to widespread disease and the inhospitable climate. The traveler Robert Lyall noted that Georgia was commonly known as the "cemetery of the Russian army"—for their part, Russians often called the Caucasus "warm Siberia" or "southern Siberia."[78]

General A. P. Ermolov, commander-in-chief of Georgia and the Caucasian Region, proposed his own solution to the sectarian problem in response to Ilovaiskii's idea. While there was no doubt that the spread of Dukhobors among the Don Cossacks could no longer be tolerated, he argued, their proliferation might be even more dangerous in the Caucasian region. Because of their proximity to the border, these religious nonconformists could be neither eradicated nor restrained by the measures in use in the central provinces. Opposed to relocating them to the Caucasus region, Ermolov recommended instead that the Don Cossack Dukhobors be settled in segregated communities outside the boundary line of Russian military control, where there would be no shortage of land for settlement. In doing so, he wanted to move the Dukhobors as far as possible from the *stanitsy* of other Cossacks living in the Caucasus to prevent a replay of what was happening in the Don. He also strove to fulfill what he saw as the principal goal of resettling the Don Dukhobors: to move them to a region where, out of absolute necessity, they would be forced to defend their property and their families with arms, and through these martial activities be of benefit to the state.[79]

Ermolov's proposal prompted a mixed response in St. Petersburg. The Ministry of Internal Affairs immediately voiced deep concerns with

78. Quoted in Fry, "Doukhobors," 229–30n55; D. I. Ismail-Zade, *Russkoe krest'ianstvo v Zakavkaz'e: 30–e gody XIX–nachalo XX v.* (Moscow, 1982), 50n75; and Susan Layton, *Russian Literature and Empire: Conquest of the Caucasus from Pushkin to Tolstoy* (Cambridge, 1994), 1.

79. RGIA f. 1284, op. 195–1825, d. 61, ll. 13–130b. Ermolov's decision here stands in contrast to his earlier opinions on the matter of sectarians in Transcaucasia. In fact, he had been among the first tsarist officials to raise objections to the settlement of sectarian Cossacks in Tavriia province. In 1817, presaging Ilovaiskii, Ermolov had argued that the exile of Dukhobors from the Caucasian Cossacks to New Russia would act as an enticement to others to join the sectarians. Instead, Ermolov found that there were sufficiently small numbers of sectarians among the Caucasian Cossacks that they posed little threat. He even went so far as to assert that they could be permitted to conduct their own religious services according to their conscience. See GMIR f. 2, op. 7, d. 594, l. 6. On Ermolov more generally, see Michael Whittock, "Ermolov: Proconsul of the Caucasus," *RR* 18, no. 1 (1959): 53–60; and A. P. Ermolov, *Biograficheskii ocherk* (St. Petersburg, 1912).

his plan, fearing that the Dukhobors would either enter into secret, sub-
versive interactions with the neighboring "mountaineers" or move
abroad, since there was nothing to prevent them from abandoning Russia.[80] In contrast, the State Council, the Committee of Ministers, and
Nicholas I all sided with Ermolov's plan to settle the Don Dukhobors beyond the Caucasian Line, noting that it fulfilled two purposes. The constant
contact with the mountaineers would force them to defend themselves
and the grim fate of these Dukhobors would restrain other Don Cossacks
from joining the sect. Moreover, added the Committee of Ministers, the
idea that they would run away was without foundation since the Dukhobors would have nowhere to go, other than to the mountaineers, who,
the Committee of Ministers felt, would surely attack them.[81]

In the discussions that followed Ermolov's proposition, Ober-Eger-
meister Pashkov, chair of the Department of Laws of the State Council,
expressed the most detailed and critical view of the Dukhobors.[82] His virulent dislike for the Dukhobors and his open desire for their eradication
is in stark contrast to the more moderate positions most of his colleagues
took up. Yet his was a voice of influence that even the tsar came to agree
with on many fronts. Pashkov argued that the Dukhobors posed an enormous threat to "Church, Throne, and Fatherland" because they con-
cealed themselves behind a veil of respectability and modesty, a mask with
which they were able to trap the weak of faith and spread their heresy.
Pashkov cited the provincial statistics that demonstrated a rapid spread
of the Dukhobors' faith, concluding that none of the measures taken to
stem this growth appeared to be working. Finding the antisectarian measures far too lenient, he demanded nothing short of the annihilation of
the Dukhobor communities.

Pashkov supported Ermolov's proposal as the best means to correct
the moral evil that the Dukhobors represented, to subdue them by fos-
tering obedience to state power and law, and to protect Orthodox people. He cited five reasons in support of Ermolov's plan. First, finding
themselves suddenly among hostile people, the Dukhobors would be required to defend themselves. In doing so, not only would they complete
their service for the state, but, more important, they would "come themselves to understand the necessity and benefit of the institutions of government power and with full obedience to them will soon realize that no
community can exist without a head and authorities."[83] Second, Dukho-

80. *PSZ* (2), vol. 1 (1826), no. 126, pp. 189–90. The Ministry of Finance also opposed Ermolov's
proposal.
81. RGIA f. 1284, op. 195–1825, d. 61, l. 19; and *PSZ* (2), vol. 1 (1826), no. 126, p. 190.
82. The following discussion is drawn from RGIA f. 1284, op. 195–1825, d. 61, ll. 20–21ob; *PSZ*
(2), vol. 1 (1826), no. 126, pp. 190–92.
83. RGIA f. 1284, op. 195–1825, d. 61, ll. 20ob–21.

bor exile outside the Caucasian region would prevent any means for them to spread their "spirit of depravity," which was deeply harmful to the "good health" of the Empire. Third, exile would serve as a "moral lesson" for those who might think of attaching themselves to the heresy. Fourth, the exile of the Dukhobors would not only separate "evil" subjects from "good" ones, it would also clear the central provinces of "unruly and audacious" sectarians and thereby permit obedient Orthodox subjects to "enjoy a peaceful tenure in the homes of their ancestors." Finally, the Dukhobors would spare Orthodox subjects the risks inherent in settling in the forbidding Caucasian region. Pashkov's arguments contain the first articulation of the idea that the settlement of sectarians in Transcaucasia, in addition to isolating the Orthodox faithful from contagion and ridding the central provinces of their influence, would also assist in achieving the goal of colonizing the newly conquered territories.

Pashkov concluded by refuting potential objections to his analysis. He noted that, as the Dukhobors were not known for great military feats, it could be argued that settling them so close to the wild mountain peoples so "skilled in the arts of war" would be tantamount to meaningless mass slaughter. In response, he asserted that "necessity itself will be their teacher." However, Pashkov added, somewhat heartlessly, "Is it not more useful to the government to occupy the border, which demands strict defense, with a group of people who by their spirit and rules are dangerous to the general good, than have such people support the interior of the state? The loss of evil-doers who are intransigent and unable to leave their anarchic heresy should not be considered a loss for the state."[84]

Almost as an afterthought, Pashkov added an opinion that broadened the application of the plan to send all Dukhobors to the Caucasus. He wrote that, in the event that too few Dukhobors be found among the Don Cossacks to populate the territory beyond the Caucasian Line, Dukhobor settlers from other provinces should be chosen to fill out the complement. Nicholas agreed to Pashkov's addendum and ordered the exile to the Caucasus of those merchants, lower-middle class, *odnodvortsy*, and state and appanage peasants who belonged to the Dukhobor and Molokan sects.[85]

The policymaking process took yet another turn when Ermolov discovered how many Dukhobors would be resettled. Finding the amount far too small—only eighty-six Dukhobor men, among whom only twenty-four were actually serving at the time—he began to backpedal on his proposal to settle sectarians beyond the Caucasian line. Ermolov had

84. Ibid., l. 210b.
85. Ibid., ll. 37–370b, 51; and RGIA f. 1284, op. 195–1826, d. 46.

assumed that there would be sufficient Dukhobors exiled from the Don Cossacks to form their own separate *stanitsa,* a group strong enough to defend itself. He wrote to the Ministry of Internal Affairs that it was no longer feasible to settle them according to his initial plan: "To settle them separately in the vicinity of the local mountain people would mean to give them up as sacrifices the first time that the mountaineers attacked." Since he also felt that it was not possible to settle Dukhobors among Cossacks on the Caucasian Line for fear of religious contagion, he recommended that the Don Dukhobors be exiled to Siberia. Ermolov was no longer willing to take on the extra responsibility—and the drain on resources—that protecting the exposed Dukhobors would entail.[86]

While the Don Cossack Ataman repeatedly and desperately voiced his concern over the ongoing presence of Dukhobors in his fighting force, the command in the Caucasus shifted from Ermolov to General I. F. Paskevich.[87] Paskevich further complicated the question of resettling the Don Dukhobors by bringing to the table a new proposal—one that earmarked not the Caucasian Line but Transcaucasia as the location for sectarian resettlement.[88] No matter what level of supervision and surveillance was imposed, he argued, settling the Don Dukhobors just outside the Caucasian Line would inevitably involve interaction between them and the Line Cossacks. Rather than resolving the Dukhobor problem, it would simply shift it from the Don region to the Caucasus, especially because the Dukhobors would find it relatively easy to spread their false teachings among the Caucasian Cossacks.

The danger of heretical contagion was augmented, Paskevich continued, because Russia's southern border was unstable and likely to be pushed farther and farther south with every Russian military success. Under these conditions, Dukhobor settlements located just outside the boundary of the Caucasian region would soon find themselves in the middle of southward-moving Cossack villages and defense systems. The Dukhobors could be relocated along with the movement of the frontier, but Paskevich did not endorse this option, finding it disruptive both for the Dukhobors and for the regional administrators. Instead, Paskevich

86. RGIA f. 1284, op. 195–1825, d. 61, ll. 29–30, 530b–540b. It is unclear how much of Ermolov's proposal was genuine concern for the sectarians, how much was simply a desire to be rid of them as a problem, and how much it was fear of the vast resources that would be necessary to expend in order to help keep them alive. In other discussions about Russian settlement, Ermolov had noted an absence of free state land and raised the specter of the potentially fatal climate. Khachapuridze, *K istorii,* 140–41.
87. On the frequent correspondence of the Don officials concerning the continued presence of Dukhobors in their ranks and the lengthy silence in response to these entreaties, see RGIA f. 1284, op. 195–1825, d. 61, ll. 740b–77, 79–800b, 82–84, 85–86, 102, 111–12; and op. 195–1828, d. 139.
88. RGIA f. 1284, op. 195–1825, d. 61 ll. 46–460b and GMIR f. 2, op. 7, d. 596, ll. 70–72.

proposed that the Don Dukhobors be settled in Georgia or another Transcaucasian province. There the language and cultural barriers would deprive them of the opportunity to preach their "dogma." At the same time, Paskevich also envisioned that the sectarians would serve as an important barrier to attack by "predators." Paskevich informed the Don Ataman that resettlement of the Dukhobors would have to be postponed until suitable land for their settlement was found.

The choice of the exact location in Transcaucasia for settlement was left to N. M. Sipiagin, the military governor in Tiflis, the tsarist administrative center in the Caucasus. While Paskevich had suggested that the Dukhobors be settled in Georgia, Sipiagin found this location undesirable because of the potential spread of the sectarian faiths among Orthodox peoples. Dialogue between Christian groups was inevitable, he believed, even between ones as culturally distinct as Georgians and Russian sectarians. So Sipiagin reported to Paskevich that he could find no better place for settlement of the Dukhobors than the lands of the former Talysh khanate in the southeastern part of Transcaucasia. As further justification for this proposal, Sipiagin added, prophetically, that the climate of Talysh would in all likelihood kill off many of the sectarians until they became accustomed to it.[89]

Paskevich made one final adjustment to Sipiagin's proposal when he wrote to the Ministry of Internal Affairs about the arrangements for sectarian settlement. Rather than the Talysh khanate, as Sipiagin recommended, Paskevich now listed the destination as the Karabakh and Shirvan regions of the so-called Muslim Provinces. With the exception of Russian military personnel and administrators, there were no Orthodox subjects in the vicinity. Paskevich argued that it would be difficult for sectarians to enter into any kind of relationship with the various inhabitants of these regions because of cultural, linguistic, and religious differences. Moreover, the population density in the Karabakh province, for example, was less than four people per square kilometer and the mountains made travel difficult.[90]

During all of the discussions over the fate of the Don Dukhobors, Siberia was also being vetted as a potential location for the settlement of the religious dissenters, as Lanskoi and later Ermolov proposed. However, despite repeated missives from central authorities requesting information on the possibility of sectarian settlement, Siberian authorities maintained their silence. Existing documents do not reveal whether this was a stalling tactic on the part of local officials to prevent the movement

---

89. GMIR f. 2, op. 7, d. 596, ll. 73–74; and d. 594, l. 4.
90. GMIR f. 2, op. 7, d. 596, ll. 77–78.

of sectarians into their jurisdiction or simply a result of the long and un-reliable lines of communication. Whatever the reason, the result was the same. On May 18, 1828, after repeated requests for information, the Ministry of Internal Affairs finally gave up on waiting for Siberia to respond, abandoning any thoughts of using Siberia as a repository for the sectarians. From that point on, Transcaucasia became the sole candidate for the sectarians' new home, and migration to New Russia was terminated.[91]

More than any other agency, the Ministry of Internal Affairs acted as the voice of support for the Dukhobors. The State Council believed that the loss of the Dukhobors could not be considered a loss for the state, and Sipiagin justified settling the Dukhobors in the Muslim Provinces of Transcaucasia because more of them would be likely to die because of the climate. By contrast, the Ministry repeatedly called for better treatment for the Dukhobors. In June 1828, it wrote to Paskevich that the recent peace conducted with Persia facilitated the process of finding greater "means and comforts" for the sectarian settlers who were, after all, to provide an important service to the state. In a discussion of the choice of land for resettlement, the Ministry reminded Paskevich to pick a location "so that they are settled as much as possible in the most advantageous place for the continuation of service and for the protection and provisioning of their families, together with distance [to impede] the conversion of others to their religion."[92]

TOLERATION, ISOLATION, AND COLONIZATION

The road to the 1830 edict underscores the importance of religious forces to the construction of the tsarist empire and indicates important continuities in the religious policies of Alexander I and Nicholas I. Indirectly and unexpectedly, Alexander's inclinations to "toleration through isolation" led ultimately to Russian colonial settlement in the South Caucasus. His introduction of restricted tolerance evolved into the practice of segregation after the Dukhobors' request for a separate settlement. Dissatisfaction with Alexander's initial policies led Russian officials to reformulate their treatment of sectarians in the early 1820s. In the ensuing bureaucratic debates over what path to follow, the contours of the 1830 rescript began to take shape. However, only with the ascension of Nicho-

91. RGIA f. 1284, op. 195–1825, d. 61, ll. 88–89ob; and PSZ (2), vol. 5:2 (1830), no. 4010, p. 169. For the repeated efforts to obtain a response from Siberia, see RGIA f. 1284, op. 195–1825, d. 61, ll. 48, 50–51, 59.
92. RGIA f. 1284, op. 195–1825, d. 61, ll. 90–93ob, quotation on 93ob. See also GMIR f. 2, op. 7, d. 596, ll. 75–76.

las I and the spread of Dukhobors among the Don Cossacks did tsarist administrators hit upon a broadly accepted revision of their religious policy: enhanced segregation of sectarians in the distant and dangerous periphery of Transcaucasia, where the dissenters might usefully take on the role of colonists.

Even though tsarist authorities did come to see the sectarians as "model" colonial settlers over the succeeding decades, their potential contribution as colonizers was a minor factor in sending them to the region. Indeed, the decision to relocate Russians to the Transcaucasus was far more an effort to rid the interior provinces of people for whom tsarist Russia could find no place within its national, corporate framework of religious affiliation. Before 1830, officials generally saw the sectarians as valueless people whose likely demise in Transcaucasia from the climate or indigenous peoples would represent no great loss, and whose grudging existence could only serve the state by sparing the lives of Orthodox Russians.

Such "accidental" colonialism was characteristic of one branch of tsarist social engineering before the Great Reforms that attempted to exploit the Empire's borderlands as a safety valve to release social, political, and religious tensions. This type of state-sponsored, Slavic movement to the imperial "periphery" had a long pedigree in Russian history, including the banishment of Old Believers, witches, criminals, and political dissidents, and also had corollaries in West European expansion, such as the British and French practice of banishing convicts overseas.[93] Such exploitation of the borderlands demonstrates an understanding of frontier regions as somehow distinct from the imperial core. Here tsarist officials showed little concern for the demographic fate of the periphery, and were generally only troubled by the status of the central regions.[94]

93. G. F. Fel'dshtein, *Ssylka: ocherki eia genezisa, znacheniia, istorii i sovremennogo sostoianiia* (Moscow, 1893), esp. 147–85; Alan Wood, "Crime and Punishment in the House of the Dead," in *Civil Rights in Imperial Russia*, ed. Olga Crisp and Linda Edmondson (Oxford, 1989), 215–33; Robert O. Crummey, *The Old Believers and the World of Antichrist: The Vyg Community and the Russian State, 1694–1855* (Madison, 1970), 3–38; Roy R. Robson, *Old Believers in Modern Russia* (DeKalb, 1995), 21–23; Valerie Kivelson, "Patrolling the Boundaries: Witchcraft Accusations and Household Strife in Seventeenth-Century Muscovy," *Harvard Ukrainian Studies* 29 (1995): 302–23; and Mark Bassin, "Turner, Solov'ev, and the 'Frontier Hypothesis': The Nationalist Signification of Open Spaces," *JMH* 65, no. 3 (1993): 473–511. For comparison, see David Eltis, ed., *Coerced and Free Migration: Global Perspectives* (Stanford, 2002); A. G. L. Shaw, *Convicts and the Colonies: A Study of Penal Transportation from Great Britain and Ireland to Australia and other parts of the British Empire* (London, 1966); Alice Bullard, *Exile to Paradise: Savagery and Civilization in Paris and the South Pacific, 1790–1900* (Stanford, 2000); Timothy J. Coates, *Convicts and Orphans: Forced and State-Sponsored Colonizers in the Portuguese Empire, 1550–1755* (Stanford, 2001); and Michael Heffernan, "French Colonial Migration," in *The Cambridge Survey of World Migration*, ed. Robin Cohen (Cambridge, 1995), 33–38.

94. Note that in the late nineteenth century the ethnic makeup of borderland regions became extremely important to military statisticians. Peter Holquist, "To Count, to Extract, and to Exter-

The mass movement of undesirable populations also reflects a certain type of tsarist population politics that endeavored to create ideal societies (defined in various ways, in this case religiously) by physically *removing* unwanted groups. In this social-engineering structure, the "utopia" would be created in the center by purging to the periphery those considered obstacles to the envisioned ideal world. The drive for a more perfect core was a prominent feature of the tsarist period and it would reappear in Soviet Russia, for example in the special settlements in the north.[95] That said, the safety-valve usage of the borderlands stands in marked contrast to a second, simultaneous pattern of tsarist "utopian" social engineering in the borderlands—efforts to build vibrant, economically and militarily productive societies on the frontier, such as the peopling of New Russia under Catherine II, the military colonies, and the pre-reform resettlement of state peasants from "land-starved" regions. In this vision, the periphery was to be *connected* to the core—the ideal society would be forged in both places at once, with significant mutual influences.[96]

The protracted deliberations about the place of sectarians in Russian society and polity that led up to the 1830 statute also offer a clear example of the contingent and often haphazard policymaking process of early nineteenth-century Russia. This new era in religious and colonial policy was forged through the triangular interaction of central decisionmakers, local authorities, and the sectarians themselves, each group with entirely different demands and goals. The initiative for policies frequently originated from below, urged on by events in the periphery. Decisions evolved not so much from the implementation of a preconceived vision but rather from the twists and turns of bureaucratic bargaining, in which the terms and geographic locale of sectarian segregation were repeatedly renegotiated among numerous competing proposals—and often in the absence of sufficient information. Local officials resorted to evasion of

minate: Population Statistics and Population Politics in Late Imperial and Soviet Russia," in *A State of Nations: Empire and Nation-Making in the Age of Lenin and Stalin,* ed. Ronald Grigor Suny and Terry Martin (New York, 2001), 111–44.

95. Lynne Viola, "The Other Archipelago: Kulak Deportations to the North in 1930," *SR* 60, no. 4 (2001): 730–55.

96. Roger Bartlett, *Human Capital: The Settlement of Foreigners in Russia, 1762–1804* (Cambridge, 1979); Marc Raeff, "In the Imperial Manner," in *Catherine the Great: A Profile,* ed. Raeff (New York, 1972), 197–246; Sunderland, "Making the Empire"; Sunderland, "Peasants on the Move: State Peasant Resettlement in Imperial Russia, 1805–1830s," *RR* 52, no. 4 (1993): 472–85; Charles Steinwedel, "Resettling People, Unsettling the Empire: Migration, Colonization, and the Challenge of Governance, 1861–1917," in *Peopling the Periphery: Russian Settlement in Eurasia from Muscovite to Soviet Times,* ed. Nicholas B. Breyfogle, Abby Schrader, and Willard Sunderland (forthcoming); Alfred Rieber, "Colonizing Eurasia," in ibid.; Richard Pipes, "The Russian Military Colonies, 1810–1831," *JMH* 22 (1950): 205–19; and Francois-Xavier Coquin, *La Sibérie: Peuplement et immigration paysanne au XIXe siècle* (Paris, 1969).

central policies they found inconvenient or inappropriate. Choices made to solve one problem often had unexpected and unwanted ramifications in other areas.

While Russia's sectarians could not have been aware of the extensive deliberations leading to 1830, their lives were forever changed by them. Although small numbers of Russians had moved to Transcaucasia before 1830, the decree opened the door to unprecedented geographic mobility, including both the heart-rending relocations that accompanied exile and the ever-hopeful, voluntary migration of dissenters in search of better lives.[97] Throughout the remainder of the nineteenth century, but especially in the 1830s and 1840s, many thousands of sectarians chose to uproot themselves from central Russia for the perils and possibilities of the South Caucasus.

97. On pre-1830 migrants, see Ismail-Zade, *Russkoe,* 34–35; and A. Iunitskii, "Sektantskiia gnezda na Kavkaze (v predelakh Bakinskoi gubernii)," *KhCh,* no. 1 (January–February, 1895): 142–46.

2

TO A LAND OF PROMISE

Sectarians and the Resettlement Experience

State officials regarded sectarian relocation as a means to regulate their multiconfessional empire and to harness population movement for state benefit; for the settlers themselves, migration meant something very different. For them, resettlement was understood in the personal terms of material well-being and religious self-expression—a process saturated with aspirations, social ramifications, cultural meanings, and life-altering consequences. Migration was inevitably a momentous event. It required leaving behind everything and everyone that these Russians had ever known and traveling—often on foot—to a part of the world that was very different from their homelands. Whereas state officials saw sectarian relocation in corporatist terms—the movement of often undifferentiated categories of people—the nonconformists understood the experience not only as their communal fate as sectarians, but also as a personal voyage. Yet, for all the differences, state and sectarian existed in a symbiotic dynamic: if tsarist Russia wanted to create an ideal society in the central provinces by ridding itself of dissenters, then many sectarians were just as happy to rid themselves of tsarist Russia by leaving for the potential "utopia" of the Caucasian borderlands.

Resettlement to the South Caucasus took three forms: forced exile by government or court order; the legal, voluntary decision to migrate of individuals, families, or communities of sectarians; and the unauthorized flight of those who had been denied official permission to relocate. Given the absence or unreliability of official statistics, it is difficult to discern with any accuracy the total number of sectarians who resettled to Transcaucasia, but it is clear that the vast majority went voluntarily, whether legally or illegally.[1] Settlers came from a variety of different, often land-

1. Official statistics vary widely and do not include all of the clandestine migrants. Studying various villages in what was then Erevan province, I. V. Dolzhenko found that of 343 families, 284 (82.8 percent) arrived voluntarily, 56 (16.3 percent) were exiled, and 3 families (0.9 percent) ar-

poor, provinces, particularly Tambov, Tavriia, Voronezh, Orenburg, Sara-tov, Samara, Astrakhan, the North Caucasus, and the Don Region.[2] While overwhelmingly peasant in social make-up, they also included merchants, *meshchane,* and *odnodvortsy.* State peasants dominated the ranks of rural migrants because the 1830 decree gave permission only to that category of peasants to resettle to Transcaucasia voluntarily. A significant number of serfs did make their way to Transcaucasia, but they did so either through exile or unlawfully, as they had no legal right to relocate. Transcaucasia was officially open only to sectarian settlers, but many Orthodox Russians, noting that sectarian religious affiliation afforded geographic mobility, uprooted themselves and joined the sectarians heading south— some by converting to a sectarian faith, others illicitly.

Whereas exiles had little choice, voluntary migrants based their decision to confront the challenges and uncertainties of cross-continental migration on a variety of mutually influential motives. Religious concerns were a primary motivation: the promise of greater spiritual freedom, an escape from religious persecution, or the apocalyptic expectation of the imminent arrival of Christ's kingdom on earth. Settlers were also animated by the prospects of a better material life on the frontier, the desire either to escape unpleasant family circumstances or perhaps to join relatives already in the South Caucasus, and the tantalizing possibility of avoiding military service.[3]

With their future lives at stake, settlers became leading actors in the drama of resettlement—both to their benefit and their ruin. State officials went to great lengths to micromanage their movement. Yet, due to bureaucratic inefficiencies, incompetent planning, and the challenges of controlling so many people in so vast a territory, their regulations were less government initiatives than an uncoordinated reaction to sectarian activities. If anything, the story of relocation to the southernmost frontier reveals much about the space between, around, and within the laws and administrative structures of state power where individuals and collectives might negotiate niches for themselves.

---

rived illegally, although the latter number is undoubtedly far too low. I. V. Dolzhenko, "Pervye russkie pereselentsy v Armenii (30–50–e gody XIX v.)," *VMU, Seriia IX, Istoriia* 29, no. 3 (1974): 60.

2. GMIR f. 2, op. 7, d. 594, ll. 61, 67–71; and Dolzhenko, "Pervye," 59.

3. In general, scholars of Russian migration to the periphery before the Great Reforms have privileged the economic origins of resettlement, such as famine, a desire for land, and utopian legends of a land of milk and honey. I. V. Dolzhenko, *Khoziaistvennyi i obshchestvennyi byt russkikh krest'ian vostochnoi Armenii (konets XIX—nachalo XX vv.)* (Erevan, 1985), 18–39; François-Xavier Coquin, *La Sibérie: Peuplement et immigration paysanne au XIXe siècle* (Paris, 1969); David Moon, *Russian Peasants and Tsarist Legislation on the Eve of Reform: Interaction Between Peasants and Officialdom, 1825–1855* (London, 1992), 23–61; and K. V. Chistov, *Russkie narodnye sotsial'no-utopicheskie legendy XVII–XIX vv.* (Moscow, 1967), 237–326.

The resettlement process elicited inconsistent and conflicting attitudes of state officials toward sectarians. At least in some quarters, the extermination of the sectarians was one prominent objective of the 1830 decree. In the actual course of relocation, however, rather than letting them perish, Russian authorities frequently came to the rescue of nonconformists who experienced hardship and deprivation in transit. In part, this contradiction between policy and practice reflects an inherent tension in the 1830 edict between eliminating the sects and fulfilling service obligations to the state. To say the least, dead or starving sectarians made poor servitors. At the same time, decisions to provide support to sectarians rested on individual officials. Coming face to face with the human suffering of migrants, local and regional officials were more likely than their central counterparts to provide aid to the sectarians, since the latter group, regarding the sectarians from afar, saw them less as people and more as an abstraction.

EXILING THE HERETICS

Tsarist officials exiled Russian sectarians to Transcaucasia from 1830 to the end of the nineteenth century, most of them before 1860.[4] The frequency and form of exile varied from denomination to denomination. Most Dukhobors who relocated to the Transcaucasus were exiled in entire communities, either from the Don Cossacks in 1830 or from the Molochna region from 1841 to 1845. By contrast, Molokans and Subbotniks were more frequently exiled as individuals or in small groups, trickling into Transcaucasia almost continually. Tsarist law offered those designated for exile the option of converting as a way to remain in the central provinces, and in fact a small percentage did prefer Orthodoxy to forcible resettlement.[5]

Officially, the Russian state exiled sectarians to Transcaucasia as punishment for such "crimes against faith" as "spreading their heresy and attracting others to it, and also for temptations, unruly behavior, and insolence toward the Orthodox Church and its priesthood."[6] According to the letter of the law, it was not a crime in and of itself to be a sectar-

---

4. RGIA f. 1284, op. 222-1897, d. 65, ll. 13-22; op. 200, d. 15, 1843; op. 218, d. 14, 1878; op. 196-1834, d. 71; f. 1149, op. 6t.-1866, d. 108; f. 398, op. 53, d. 17201, 1889; f. 381, op. 2, d. 808, 1849; ORRGB f. 648, k. 46, d. 2, ll. 19-20; and I. Ia. Orekhov, "Ocherki iz zhizni zakavkazskikh sektatorov," *Kavkaz*, no. 135 (June 16, 1878): 1.
5. See for example, RGIA f. 1284, op. 195-1825, d. 61, l. 184; *PSZ* (2), vol. 5:2 (1830), no. 4010, p. 169; and Nicholas B. Breyfogle, "Heretics and Colonizers: Religious Dissent and Russian Colonization of Transcaucasia, 1830-1890" (Ph.D. diss., University of Pennsylvania, 1998), 284-89.
6. *PSZ* (2), vol. 5:2 (1830), no. 4010.

ian.[7] In practice, however, the vague wording of the law allowed for a great deal of latitude for local priests or administrators to implement the laws as they saw fit. It was never entirely evident exactly what actions could be construed as "spreading," "tempting," or "converting" an Orthodox subject to some form of sectarianism. All overt manifestations of sectarian rites and practices—such as public marriage and burial ceremonies, or the existence of sectarian prayer houses—were expressly illegal, but prayer meetings in private homes and Subbotnik circumcision, for example, were more ambiguous manifestations of belief. Although not explicitly forbidden, such practices were frequently punished anyway.[8] Moreover, it was never exactly clear whether attempts to spread heresy had to be successful in order to be prosecuted, any more than whether a sectarian father could be convicted for teaching his faith to his children.[9] The practical effect of these ambiguities was to make sectarian faith per se grounds for exile.

Secular and spiritual officials alike took advantage of the power of exile to settle personal scores and rid themselves of unwanted sectarians. In one 1835 effort to intimidate sectarians, Nicholas I let authorities in Tambov exile ten innocent Molokans each time an Orthodox person converted and the Molokans as a group refused to name the "seducer."[10] Similarly, the circumstances surrounding the exile of the Molokan I. E. Podkovyrov in 1889 highlight the instrumental uses of banishment.[11] Podkovyrov was an affluent peasant who lived in the Don military region. In a bitter memoir, he recounted how one night he gave shelter to two Cossacks as a gesture of kindness to weary travelers. Local officials, who generally disliked Podkovyrov, quickly accused him of converting his guests to the Molokan faith. In court, the Cossacks testified that Podkovyrov could not have converted them since they had been Molokans for years, and the case was dismissed. However, local religious authorities, unhappy with the decision, brought a new trial against Podkovyrov with new witnesses. In this example of double jeopardy, he was found guilty, stripped of his rights, and punished with exile to Transcaucasia. Podkovyrov was imprisoned, treated harshly, and, as with so many exiles, made the trip south on foot and under guard, in manacles and special prisoner's clothing.[12] Only after the enactment of the religious toleration

7. In addition to the discussion in chapter 1, see *SPChR* (1875), 181; and GARF, f. 109, op. 3 (sekretnyi arkhiv), d. 1495, 1855.
8. For one attempt to clear up this confusion, see *PSZ* (2), vol. 18:2 (1843), no. 17218.
9. RGIA f. 383, op. 4, d. 3175, 1841–42.
10. *SPChR* (1875), 140–41.
11. GMIR f. 2, op. 8, d. 300, n.d.
12. On the procedure for moving the exiles to Transcaucasia in general, see GMIR f. 2, op. 7, d. 594, l. 13.

laws of 1905 was Podkovyrov able to return to his place of birth and to his family.

Podkovyrov wrote two songs about his trial and exile that reveal the human dimension of forcible resettlement.

SONG NO. 1 (MAY 15, 1889)
They called us to trial.
Before the court we stood.
Judges asked us questions,
Punished us in our cases,
Read the decision
For the third time:
Exile us to Transcaucasia.
Our heads and legs lost their nerve
And all our limbs grew weak.
Black crows attacked us,
Pecked at us on the road.
Then some people fought,
And others shed tears,
Many growled like lions,
And many cried and sobbed.
Children, give me help.
I will subdue all the troubles in my heart.
My heart beats in me,
From my eyes tears flow.
In shackles they chained us
And to Transcaucasia they drove us.

SONG NO. 2 (SEPTEMBER 18, 1889)
They drove us to Transcaucasia
Took the shackles from our legs
The sergeant took us over
And gave us to a caravansary.
I walked around the town.
I looked all around me
And was happy
That I had received freedom.
On the second and third day I walked around
On the fourth, I went out,
But I did not find pleasure
My happiness flew away;
All spiritual sweetness.
Tired, I sat down
And sang this song:
Late, late in the evening
All the people were resting

And having been cruelly locked up alone
In deep, dreary silence
A sorrowful prisoner, breathing heavily
Past midnight I sit without sleep.
A farewell song I sing
At the prison window.
Fly wild winds
To my beloved homeland
Carry news about me.
What has happened here to me.
Let my friends know
That my turn to suffer has come.
Let them not wait for me
In my homeland ever.
Such a day will not come
That I will be in my homeland.
My life withers with sadness
In a country of alien tribes.
They banished me to Transcaucasia
They chained my freedom to the mountains of the Caucasus,
Deprived me of my kin and friends,
And abandoned me alone here
Stole me from my wife and children.
For them I have died forever
Amen.[13]

Podkovyrov's songs express the personal helplessness and frustration of banishment. While he laments the violent treatment by the police and court officials, he reserves the most space to relate the spiritual anguish of being torn away in shackles from friends, family, and his native land, without any expectation of seeing them again. His use of imagery strengthens the impact of the songs. Officials who escorted the exiles on the journey are described as "black crows" who "pecked" at them, angry convicts as growling lions. Moreover, Podkovyrov reminds us that exile was both a group and individual tragedy. His first song describes events in the communal terms of "us" and "we." At times the exiles appear to act as if they possess one mind and body ("our heads and legs lost their nerve"). Once in Transcaucasia, the point of view shifts to the first person, and the sense of personal loss and suffering overshadows the group misfortune. The wind offers his only connection to family, friends, and homeland. Despite being freed from his shackles upon arrival, and initially feeling that his problems were over, Podkovyrov soon discovers that

---

13. GMIR f. 2, op. 8, d. 300, n.d., ll. 1–10b.

his woes remain. Even with a certain physical liberty, his spirit remains "chained to the mountains of the Caucasus."[14]

Of the many instances of forcible group exile to Transcaucasia, the state-enforced resettlement of Dukhobors from Melitopol district in Tavriia province was the largest. Almost 5,000 Dukhobors were banished between 1841 and 1845, migrating in five different parties over the four-year period.[15] Reflecting the intolerance for religious difference characteristic of Nicholas I's reign, central ministries and legislative organs saw the exile as an opportunity for the "annihilation" and "eradication of the dangerous Dukhobor sect." They anticipated that the threat of exile would be incentive enough to cause a mass conversion to Orthodoxy of Dukhobors eager to avoid the South Caucasus. If not, officials predicted that banishment to the Caucasus would so segregate them on the Empire's periphery as to threaten the future of the sect.[16]

The impetus for this mass movement centered officially around state charges of heinous crimes committed by the Dukhobors between the 1810s and 1830s. The 1841 declaration informing the sectarians of their banishment listed many of their alleged transgressions:

> And for all the mercy and good deeds that [Alexander I] showered on you, [he] demanded only that you live in peace and harmony among yourselves and not violate state laws and decrees. [Yet] hardly had you settled on the land allotted for you, when in the name of your faith, and with the command, or consent, of your false leaders and teachers, you began—and continue to this day—to murder people, torture them tyrannically, shelter deserters and vagabonds, hide crimes committed by your religious brethren, and disobey and scorn the power and commands of state and Tsar. . . . [For these crimes] you can no longer remain here and must be sent to such a place where you will be deprived of the means to bring harm to those around you.[17]

From the moment the charges were made, there began a heated debate over their veracity that continues to this day. Not unexpectedly,

14. My thanks to Gabriella Safran for her help in translating and interpreting these songs. Podkovyrov's experiences are echoed in the story of a Baptist exile. See "V tiur'me i v ssylke. Zapiski baptista E. N. Ivanova," in *MIIRSR*, vol. 1, ed. V. D. Bonch-Bruevich (St. Petersburg, 1908), 41–47.

15. For full details of the migration see SSC'SA f. 4, op. 2, d. 2430, 1839–47; RGIA f. 383, op. 4, d. 3212, 1841–43; f. 384, op. 2, d. 977, 1841; f. 565, op. 4, d. 13676, 1842–45; *AKAK* vol. 9:1, docs. 19, 29, 35, 38, 43, 44, and 48; vol. 9:2, docs. 510, 516, 523, and 526; John R. Staples, *Cross-Cultural Encounters on the Ukrainian Steppe: Settling the Molochna Basin, 1783–1861* (Toronto, 2003), esp. 87–106; and Gary Dean Fry, "The Doukhobors, 1801–1855: The Origins of a Successful Dissident Sect" (Ph.D. diss., The American University, 1976), 286–307.

16. RGIA f. 383, op. 4, d. 3212, 1841–43, l. 1; *SPChR* (1875), 256; and Staples, *Cross-Cultural Encounters*, 95–96.

17. PJBRMA, file 758, l. 1. Graphic descriptions of the alleged crimes can be found in ibid., file 399, and Staples, *Cross-Cultural Encounters*, 96–101.

Dukhobors denied them vociferously, but even the state officials involved in the case were plagued by uncertainty. In the most recent contribution to this dispute, John Staples argues that while some of the crimes probably were committed, they nowhere approximated the quantity and savage quality suggested by the declaration, and that the Dukhobors were far from the evil and criminal community depicted in the indictment. In the end, whether the charges were true or not is a somewhat moot point, because tsarist officials proceeded against the Dukhobors as if the accusations were valid.[18]

While the crimes served as the official rationale for banishment, three other overlapping and mutually influential factors played at least some role in bringing about the decision to exile the Dukhobors: the corruption and greed of local officials, diminishing regional isolation from the rest of the Empire, and land allotment problems in the Molochna region. First, a variety of sources suggest that the Dukhobors were the victims of a small number of local officials who, whether for personal profit or religious hatred, concocted the criminal charges.[19] Second, tsarist officials moved the Dukhobors from New Russia to Transcaucasia—that is, closer to the periphery—as an immediate means to decrease interdenominational contact. As New Russia became increasingly integrated into the core of the Russian Empire, the region's population more than tripled from 1803 to 1844, bringing in many Orthodox migrants. As a result, the Dukhobors' religious segregation had diminished sharply, and with it the original rationale for concentrating the nonconformists in the Molochna region.

Tied in with the question of religious segregation was the third factor, a burgeoning land crisis in New Russia. Indeed, if the sole reason for the banishment of the Dukhobors to Transcaucasia had been to reinforce isolation, then one would expect tsarist authorities to have exiled the Molokans from New Russia as well—something that did not occur. From 1832 through 1834, settlers in the Molochna area suffered the fall-out of terrible droughts and poor harvests. They also faced the dilemma of diminishing land holdings thanks to government-sponsored migration from land-poor central provinces designed to relieve those regions. The Dukhobors held a significantly larger share of land than their neighbors,

18. Staples, *Cross-Cultural Encounters*, 93–105. See also Aylmer Maude, *A Peculiar People: the Doukhobors* (New York, 1904), 121–26; Fry, "The Doukhobors," 270–83, 300–303, 351; Peter Malov, *Dukhobortsy, ikh istoriia, zhizn' i bor'ba*, vol. 1 (Thrums, BC, 1948), 23–24; and George Woodcock and Ivan Avakumovic, *The Doukhobors* (Toronto, 1968), 49–60.

19. Staples, *Cross-Cultural Encounters*, 94–95, 103–5; PJBRMA, file 392; Anna Filibert, "Neskol'ko slov o Molokanakh v Tavricheskikh stepiakh," *OZ*, no. 6 (1870): 293–94; Moritz Wagner, *Der Kaukasus, und das Land der Kosaken*, quoted and translated in a review in *The Westminster and Foreign Quarterly Review* 50, no. 1 (1849): 272.

FIGURE 1. Terpenie, a Dukhobor village in the Molochna region, Tavriia province, c. 1817. British Columbia Archives I-61634, published with permission.

which, when combined with their religious difference, made them obvious targets for expropriation. Thus, land pressures in the Molochna area were relieved by moving the Dukhobors out and giving their holdings to Orthodox Russians, Mennonites, and occasionally Molokans.[20] With the proclamation of the exile decree, the Dukhobors were given a month to choose between forcible relocation or, if they wished to remain in New Russia, conversion to Orthodoxy. Reflecting Dukhobor faithfulness (and the failure of state hopes for a mass movement to Orthodoxy), only 248 out of more than 5,000 converted and remained behind.[21] Yet, if they were unwilling to convert, they certainly did not migrate happily. In one petition, echoing Podkovyrov, the Dukhobors lamented that they were being "torn from our homes and the land which we, over dozens of years and with great difficulty obtained, and spilling tears in comprehension of our fate, must set out on a journey, a long journey, and settle in a barren climate on infertile land, impoverished, brought almost to the sacrifice of our lives, comforted only by the knowledge that we are guiltless."[22]

20. Staples, *Cross-Cultural Encounters*, 87–106; Fry, "The Doukhobors," 186–93, 283–86; GMIR f. K1, op. 1, d. 6, 1890; RGIA f. 379, op. 1, d. 1043, ll. 29–40, 54–61ob, 81–82ob, 123–280ob, and 132–35; f. 383, op. 4, d. 3331, 1841; op. 1, d. 234, 1838; *PSZ* (2), 5:2 (1830), no. 4010, art. 12. For the uses put to Dukhobor land following their departure, see RGIA f. 383, op. 5, d. 4319, 1842–48 and *SPChR* (1875), 309–10. On later Transcaucasian Dukhobor efforts to retrieve some of the value of the land taken from them in New Russia, see GMIR f. K1, op. 1, d. 5, 1865–67 and RGIA f. 1284, op. 221–1886, d. 44.
21. Staples, *Cross-Cultural Encounters*, 96.
22. Quoted in ibid., 104.

The petitioners were not wrong, relocation did mean suffering and hardships. Despite the fact that tsarist authorities knew about the proposed exile from 1839, they often waited until the last minute before informing a Dukhobor community of its deportation. The German zoologist Moritz Wagner noted while traveling in Russia that because the Dukhobors "had to sell their little possessions in all haste in order to begin their pilgrimage to the Caucasus, they fell into the hands of usurers and cheats, who gave them scarcely a tenth part of the value; and not a few official personages made handsome profits on the occasion."[23] The Dukhobors, like Podkovyrov, were escorted by military detachments while in transit; as one exile described it, they were "driven . . . at the point of the bayonet."[24]

VOLUNTARY SETTLERS: MOTIVES FOR MIGRATION

Whereas the cases of exile underscore the human tragedies caused by Russia's religiously based population politics, by far the majority of sectarians who resettled to Transcaucasia did so voluntarily. Sectarians chose to migrate for many reasons, usually involving some combination of negative influences at home and perceived positive benefits at their destination.[25] The types of knowledge a would-be sectarian migrant possessed, and the manner in which such information was obtained, were crucial factors in motivating resettlement. While potential settlers could judge their present state of affairs accurately, they might know very little about life on the frontier, as the available information was fragmentary and, unbeknownst to them, unreliable. Descriptions of the South Caucasus came frequently through rumors, legends, or exaggerations that were spread through the preaching of a few particularly charismatic personalities, and often painted entirely contradictory pictures of what awaited. This is not to intimate that sectarians went blindly to their fate. Even as they were influenced by hearsay, sometimes they knew a great deal about what awaited them in Transcaucasia. A constant flow of information was provided by government officials and documents, sectarian scouts who traveled to Transcaucasia to choose lands, correspondence of family

---

23. Wagner is quoted in *Westminster and Foreign Quarterly Review*, 271–72. See also RGIA f. 384, op. 2, d. 977, 1841.
24. Joseph Elkinton, "The Doukhobors: Their Character and Economic Principles," *Charities* 13, no. 10 (1904): 252; and Xavier Hommaire de Hell, *Travels in the Steppes of the Caspian Sea, The Crimea, The Caucasus* (London, 1847), 81.
25. On the interaction of push and pull factors elsewhere in the Russian Empire, see Moon, *Russian Peasants*, 23–61.

members already in situ, and migrants who had returned from the Transcaucasus, either permanently or seasonally. So while many potential
migrants based their decisions on hardly any information about Transcaucasia at all, certain of them relocated south with a remarkably clear
idea of what to expect.[26]

Legal restrictions on religious life and extralegal persecution were
principal motivations for migration. Sectarians voluntarily departed for
Transcaucasia in an effort to free themselves from a web of officially mandated limitations to the fulfillment of their spiritual lives, which expanded markedly in the 1830s and 1840s under Nicholas I.[27] Both
spiritual and secular authorities redoubled their efforts to weaken the dissident faiths, restrict their spread, and convert sectarians to Orthodoxy.[28]
Public manifestations of their teachings—such as prayer houses, prayer
meetings, public preaching of their faith "in earshot of Orthodox people" and attempts to convert an Orthodox subject—were punished more
often and more severely.[29] Officials also introduced systems intended to
"preempt" future sectarian growth. State power became progressively
invasive in the daily lives of sectarian communities through aggressive police surveillance and intervention, intelligence-gathering to discover
who sectarian leaders were (in order to exile them) and how their religious communities functioned, and frequent arrests and decrees of exile, with the arrestees often locked up in monasteries and subjected to
admonitions and high-pressure conversion efforts by Orthodox priests.[30]
Orthodox primary schools were built in communities with sectarian inhabitants, whose children were required to attend.[31] Marriages between
Orthodox and sectarians were forbidden, and, although this was not officially sanctioned in all cases, Molokan children were sometimes taken

---

26. For comparison, see Willard Sunderland, "Peasant Pioneering: Russian Peasant Settlers Describe Colonization and the Eastern Frontier, 1880s–1910," *JSH* 34, no. 4 (2001): 896–901.

27. V. D. Bonch-Bruevich, a Bolshevik and ethnographer of sectarian life, noted that the number
of decrees against sectarians increased dramatically during the reign of Nicholas I. From 1730 to
1801 there were 12 such decrees, 59 under Alexander I, 495 under Nicholas I, and 189 under
Alexander II (1855–73). V. D. Bonch-Bruevich, *Izbrannye sochineniia*, vol. 1, *O religii, religioznom
sektantstve i tserkvi* (Moscow, 1959), 304. Sectarians experienced these laws as persecution, and
that was certainly a significant part of the intent. Yet such laws also represented a rationalization
and codification of rights, responsibilities, and restrictions that was broadly characteristic of
Nicholas I's reign. Fry, "The Doukhobors," 1–2, passim; *SPChR* (1875), 318–19; *Rossiiskoe zakonodatel'stvo X–XX vekov*, vol. VI, *Zakonodatel'stvo pervoi poloviny XIX veka* (Moscow, 1988), 160–73,
217–21, 335–41; and Michael Stanislawski, *Tsar Nicholas I and the Jews: The Transformation of Jewish Society in Russia, 1825–1855* (Philadelphia, 1983).

28. *SPChR* (1860), II:267–68, 281–84, 289–90, 333–35, 345, 496–97; *SPChR* (1875), 140–41,
144–46, 154–56, 189–91, 236–37, 397–98; and *PSPRVP*, 740–41, 889.

29. *SPChR* (1875), 124, 189–91.

30. *SPChR* (1860), II:295–96, 321–27, 333–35, 345, 415–17; *SPChR* (1875), 140–41, 151–52,
217, 267–68, 397–98, 469–70; and ORRGB f. 648, k. 46, d. 2, ll. 19–20.

31. *SPChR* (1860), II:312–13.

from their parents, baptized into Orthodoxy without consent, and raised in Orthodox families.[32] Moreover, whereas sectarians had previously enjoyed the right to purchase substitutes from other faiths when their brethren were conscripted into military service, new laws in the 1830s and 1840s required that a replacement come from within the same sect. Designed to ensure that sectarians suffered the afflictions of conscription at least as much as Orthodox Russians, the law was particularly galling because these conformists explicitly eschewed violence and military service on ethical and theological grounds.[33]

Sectarians of all denominations—particularly serfs—moved to Transcaucasia in order to escape oppressive and extralegal treatment by secular and religious officials.[34] Sectarian sources recount vast numbers of incidents involving severe and arbitrary treatment by landlords, priests, and local officials: beatings, torture, sexual assault, the stockade, exile into penal servitude, disproportionate and unfair conscription into military service, and aggressive demands for bribes.[35] The accuracy of sectarian sources requires special comment because their narratives of maltreatment are often extreme and embellished. While it is true that they cannot always be believed to the letter, they still offer a vivid illustration of the sectarians' sense of their place within Orthodox Russian society. Over the course of their existence, and coupled with a larger Christian sense of persecution, sectarian communities developed an acute sense of victimization and martyrdom at the hands of the Orthodox. Indeed, even tsarist officials themselves realized that the unnecessary mistreatment of sectarians had brought about a culture of persecution in these communities.[36]

According to a Molokan saying, "The priest betrays and the policeman tortures." Indeed, when Orthodox priests failed to convert sectarians through admonitions or incarceration, Molokans record that the clerics

32. *Ibid.*, II:290–94; *SPChR* (1875), 153–54, 210, 433; and RGIA f. 1284, op. 197–1837, d. 63.
33. *SPChR* (1875), 202–3, 229–30, 266; *SPChR* (1860), II:348; *PSZ* (2), vol. 18:2 (1843), no. 17446; and RGIA f. 1268, op. 1, d. 433, l. 25. Most sectarians did serve out their military duties but they remained uncomfortable with the requirement. See my "Swords into Plowshares: Opposition to Military Service among Religious Sectarians, 1770s to 1874," in *The Military and Society in Russia, 1450–1917*, ed. Eric Lohr and Marshall Poe (Leiden, 2002), 441–67.
34. GMIR f. K1, op. 8, d. 470, l. 2; and I. V. Dolzhenko, "Russkie begletsy v Zakavkaz'e (k istorii formirovaniia russkoi diaspory v 1830–1850-e gody)," *EO*, no. 1 (1995): 54.
35. In addition to the examples discussed below, see also RGIA f. 383, op. 30, d. 149, 1832–39, l. 16; GMIR f. 14, op. 3, d. 1962, 1902, ll. 1–2; f. 2, op. 8, d. 237, 1910, l. 40; d. 300, l. 2; I. E. Petrov, "Seleniia Novo-Saratovka i Novo-Ivanovka Elisavetpol'skogo uezda," *IKOIRGO* 19, no. 1 (1907–08): otd. 1, 226; E. R., "Russkie ratsionalisty," *VE* 16, no. 7 (1881): 286; and Maude, *Peculiar People*, 121–26.
36. *SPChR* (1875), 402–3. In this example, state authorities were concerned that local practices of incarcerating sectarians for long periods of time while they waited for trial, even when the charges were minimal, were causing feelings of intense persecution and abuse among the nonconformists.

often asked civil authorities and landowners to beat and intimidate them into performing Orthodox rites.[37] Dukhobor peasants in Tambov province were flogged for their refusal to follow Orthodox practices until, "discolored with black-blue bruises and wales . . . [they] could hardly stand on their feet," and a few of them were knouted to death.[38] Molokans relate that the clergy called them "heathens," coerced them to bow before icons and kiss crosses, and forcibly baptized their children—all of which were against the tenets of their faith—and mercilessly beat the sectarians if they refused.[39] One Molokan history describes the abuse Molokan serfs were forced to endure: "To crown his [the landlord's] malice, he forced them to milk pigs and to nurse pedigree dogs and bear cubs at their own breast."[40] Another account describes how the serfs "ran away from landowners who with every possible means exhausted [them] with harsh work."[41]

In one anomalous, incredible story recorded by the Molokan N. M. Anfimov, a particularly enraged noble decided to punish a Molokan for his faith by hanging him up on a cross with express orders not to take him down until the noble decreed he could be removed. As the tale goes, the noble was distracted from the case of the suffering Molokan when one of his best hunting dogs became sick and had to be taken to town for medical treatment. Some days later, the noble returned, only to be confronted by the now-dead Molokan still hanging on the cross. To add insult to injury, the priest opposed the request of the deceased's family that he be buried according to the practices of their faith. The landowner was forced to resort to beatings and violence in order to quell the protests on the part of a Molokan community outraged by the Orthodox funeral.[42]

Internal Synodal documents corroborate sectarian claims of mistreatment. For instance, in a review of grievances by religious dissenters in Saratov province, the Synodal investigator found that the complaints of persecution arose both from their own "fanaticism" and from "the stern actions of certain priests that were sometimes incongruous with good sense." The report concluded with a reminder that in their everyday interactions with sectarians, including efforts to restrict them, repre-

37. *Spirit and Life—Book of the Sun. Divine Discourses of the Preceptors and the Martyrs of the Word of God, the Faith of Jesus, and the Holy Spirit, of the Religion of the Spiritual Christian Molokan-Jumpers*, ed. Daniel H. Shubin, trans. John Volkov (n.p., 1983), 12–13, 18.
38. Maude, *Peculiar People*, 124–25. Another case of local priests and officials "oppressing" sectarians by "torturing two [Dukhobors] with lashes and knouts" is found in GMIR f. 2, op. 7, d. 594, l. 6.
39. GMIR f. K1, op. 8, d. 516, ll. 10b–2; RGIA f. 1284, op. 197–1837, d. 63.
40. *Spirit and Life*, 14.
41. N. M. Leont'ev, "Dukhovnye khristiane sela Ivanovki, Geokchaiskogo u. Bakin. g. (Svedeniia dlia nastol'nogo kalendaria dukhovnykh khristian," *DKh* 4, no. 1 (1909): 18.
42. GMIR f. 2, op. 8, d. 234. n.d.

sentatives of Orthodoxy were not to step outside the boundaries of the law.[43]

In addition to the willful actions of civil and ecclesiastical officials, sectarians also exercised their option to relocate in response to mutual "unpleasantness" that sectarians shared with their Orthodox neighbors.[44] Disagreeable relations between adherents of different faiths in multiconfessional villages are reflected by the frequency with which Orthodox villagers allowed sectarians to leave their commune. As a general rule, communes were reluctant to permit their members to move out because their loss reduced the number of agricultural laborers available and, at times, increased the tax and recruitment burden for those who remained. Nonetheless, many communities believed that liberating themselves from the confrontations and disturbances of a tense multiconfessional situation was well worth the economic setbacks that the absence of the sectarians would create.[45]

If legal restrictions and extralegal maltreatment were not motivation enough, most migrants realized that Transcaucasia offered a chance at relative religious autonomy. Its distance from the central authorities and the region's recent incorporation into the Empire meant that the local administration lacked the men and resources to govern the region effectively—there was a particular shortage of Russian Orthodox priests to pursue conversion—which would leave sectarian settlers largely unhindered by outside interference.[46] Chief Administrator of the Caucasus Baron G. V. Rosen wrote to the Ministry of Internal Affairs in the 1830s that "to prohibit them [from practicing their religion] is impossible in Transcaucasia since they all resettled here voluntarily, and at their own expense, from central provinces with the expectation that they would not encounter any prohibition in the fulfillment of their rites."[47] Writing of their own experiences, one Molokan explained that he and his coreligionists "arrived from within Russia to this wild Transcaucasia with its many tribes for calm and quiet so that they could praise the name of God unimpeded."[48] This is not to say that settlers escaped entirely the interference of state and Orthodoxy—examples abound of their dashed ex-

43. RGIA f. 797, op. 11, otd. II, st. 1, d. 28271, 1841–42, ll. 1–2, 60b. See also f. 1284, op. 197–1837, d. 63.
44. RGIA f. 383, op. 30, d. 149, 1832–39, ll. 4, 16.
45. See, for example, RGIA f. 379, op. 1, d. 1151, 1831–34, ll. 21–210b; f. 383, op. 30, d. 149, 1832–39, l. 340b; and f. 1284, op. 200–1843, d. 508, ll. 7–70b.
46. RGIA f. 1268, op. 1, d. 650, 1844, ll. 250b–26; f. 797, op. 24, otd. III, st. 1, d. 96, 1854–58, ll. 26–33, passim; f. 796, op. 442, d. 951, 1883, ll. 19–20, 300b–31; d. 1124, 1886, ll. 61–630b; GMIR f. K1, op. 8, d. 516, l. 40b; Sh-v, "Privol'noe," Kaspii, no. 79 (July 30, 1882): 2–3; and A. Iunitskii, "Sud i delo nad al'ty-agachskimi skoptsami na Kavkaze," TV, no. 20 (May 14, 1892): 318.
47. RGIA f. 1284, op. 197–1837, d. 143, ll. 1–10b. See also f. 1284, op. 221–1886, d. 75, l. 3.
48. GMIR f. 2, op. 8, d. 324, ll. 1–10b.

pectations—but the frontier did provide relative religious liberty. Understandably, they moved with the aspiration to benefit from it.[49]

Quests for liberty of spiritual practice and freedom from persecution were not the only religious factors that drew sectarians to the southern frontier. Equally important were the widespread reports in the early 1830s of the imminent end of the world and the coming of God's thousand-year kingdom.[50] Such speculation, which appeared widely in 1832 and predicted the apocalypse in 1836, was stimulated by the circulation of a book entitled *The Triumphant Tale of the Christian Faith (Pobednaia povest' khristianskoi very)*. The spread and varying content of the rumors, however, had more to do with the sermons of traveling preachers than with sectarians reading the book themselves.[51] The first of these was the Molokan Nikitin Ivanov from Tavriia province. Having read *The Triumphant Tale,* he abandoned his life in the Molochna region and set off for the borders of Persia, where he thought the commencement of the thousand-year kingdom of Christ would take place. Traveling through towns and villages where Molokans lived, he preached of Christ's impending arrival in the south. While only a few of his listeners actually took to the road with him, he planted the belief that Christ's kingdom would begin in 1836. The idea spread rapidly among Molokans, who began to preach that "the time of the triumph of spiritual Christians over heathens has come; soon the heavenly redeemer will appear and on the holiday of Easter gather together from north to east all his chosen people, from where He will rule with them for one thousand years . . . and this time is close, since signs of the coming of Christ have already appeared."[52]

Inspired by the message of these sermons, Molokans often did not wait for Christ to gather them together but set off immediately. The question that remained was where the exact site of the New Jerusalem would be. Some said Tavriia province, others Persia, and a third group—the majority—pointed to the Transcaucasus, often specifically Mount Ararat. In 1833, long wagon trains stretched from various provinces to the Caucasus as Molokans hurried to meet God in His promised land. As future citizens of the New Jerusalem, they went to the new land in exultation and joy, often singing psalms and spiritual songs, thereby attracting attention

49. RGIA f. 1284, op. 198–1838, d. 66; and GMIR f. 14, op. 3, d. 1962, 1902.
50. Unless otherwise noted, the following discussion draws from "Istoricheskiia svedeniia o Molokanskoi sekte," *PS* (November 1858): 294–309; August von Haxthausen, *Studies on the Interior of Russia,* ed. S. Frederick Starr, trans. Eleanore L. M. Schmidt (Chicago, 1972), 154–55; N. M. Nikol'skii, *Istoriia russkoi tserkvi* (Riazan, 1930), 207; and Orekhov, "Ocherki," no. 135, 1. The two best general studies of utopian legends are Chistov, *Russkie narodnye,* esp. 237–326; and A. I. Klibanov, *Narodnaia sotsial'naia utopiia v Rossii XIX vek* (Moscow, 1978), esp. 19, 140–210.
51. The role of charismatic leaders was notable in providing the impetus to resettle outside of a purely religious context as well. RGIA f. 379, op. 1, d. 1151, 1831–34, l. 29.
52. "Istoricheskiia svedeniia," 297–98.

and other crowds to their entourage. The Orthodox author of an article in *Pravoslavnyi sobesednik* continues the story: "Of those Molokans who either personally had not decided to leave their native land, or who were held back from resettlement by the government or their nobles, many sold their homes, ceased farming and waited impatiently for the heavenly redeemer. Even Orthodox peasants, in the midst of whom lived Molokans, were among the agitation. . . . Many Orthodox were so weak of faith that, joining the Molokan heresy, they left behind their homeland and property, and together with the wandering heretics went in search of the promised New Jerusalem."[53]

When 1836 finally did arrive, Molokan enthusiasm for resettlement grew stronger. Even the unmasking of several false prophets in the interim had not dampened their hopes for the Second Coming. Quite the opposite, Orthodox Russians complained that Molokans were invading their churches during services, throwing rocks, shooting at icons, and generally disrupting worship.[54] A number of false Christs appeared at the appointed moment for His coming, and Molokans ecstatically collected to listen to their sermons. One Christ convinced his listeners to stop all work, devote themselves to singing and prayer, put on their holiday clothes, and go to Transcaucasia, but only after bringing him their money and possessions. On the way, some felt distress over the houses and possessions that they had left behind and turned back, whereupon they demanded the return of their money and voiced doubts about his divinity. To calm these fears, the Christ convincingly carried out the miracle of bringing a woman back to life. The doubters fell to their knees in tears, asking for forgiveness. The trek to the Promised Land resumed.[55]

While religious motivations were the most important inducements, sectarians also chose to move to the South Caucasus for economic reasons. In tandem with the laws restricting sectarian religious activities, a spate of legislative obstacles impeded their ability to prosper.[56] Laws confined sectarian travel and landownership to within a radius of thirty kilometers from their official place of residence.[57] New legislation forbade

53. Ibid., 302.
54. Ibid., 304.
55. Expectations of the coming kingdom of God did not end in 1836. There are a number of recorded incidents of sectarians in Transcaucasia leaving behind their possessions, debating what clothes to wear to meet Christ, and then heading off to various parts of the region in order to be there for the opening of the thousand-year kingdom. See, for example, A. Dunaev. "Molokane sekty obshchikh," in *Russkie sektanty, ikh uchenie, kult i sposoby propagandy,* ed. M. A. Kal'nev (Odessa, 1911), 65–68; and S. Kolosov, "Russkie sektanty v Erivanskoi gubernii," *PKEG na 1902* (Erevan, 1902): otd. IV, 146.
56. On these laws in general, see "Istoricheskiia svedeniia," 309–10; and GMIR f. 2, op. 7, d. 594, ll. 40–41.
57. *SPChR* (1875), 121–22, 156–57, 254–55, 267–68. For an example of the occasional exceptions to these travel restrictions, see ibid., 305.

nonconformists from registering in a merchant guild. Sectarians who were already merchants could remain so, but they were prohibited from moving to a higher guild and their children were denied the right to inherit that social designation.[58] In a similar vein, government decrees banned sectarians from transferring their registration from one commune to another—an act designed to thwart efforts to move from a rural to an urban *soslovie*, but which also applied to movement from one urban commune to another.[59] Finally, tsarist officials passed legislation that prohibited Orthodox Russians from living with or working for sectarians, and vice versa, and Molokan and Dukhobor *odnodvortsy* were outlawed from owning serfs.[60]

These laws were more than mere paper restrictions in the lives of Russia's sectarians, and as such they provided a strong impetus to resettle to Transcaucasia. Historian I. V. Dolzhenko goes so far as to assert that the state passed the 1835 law preventing sectarians in a peasant *soslovie* from registering in an urban one precisely to push rich trading sectarians south.[61] This was certainly the result in the case of Timofei Petrov, a Molokan *meshchanin* from Tambov province, who complained in his petition for resettlement of the severe limitations placed on his business activities because of his faith. He described how existing legislation (and the treatment by officials) denied him passports for work-related trips out of town and prohibited him either to hire or interact with Orthodox workers.[62]

In tandem with these legal restrictions, downturns in their economic fortunes also sparked sectarian resettlement. The 1830s in Russia were a time of failed harvests, famine, the rampant spread of cholera, and increasing landowner exactions from serfs.[63] Testimony of the sectarians themselves fills in the picture of misery, lamenting such problems as land insufficiency and poor harvests.[64] Molokan *odnodvortsy* from Tavriia province asked for permission to resettle "because in our village of Astrakhanka there are no forests whatsoever, the water supply is insufficient and failed harvests are common; quite the opposite is true in the Trans-

58. *SPChR* (1875), 189–91. Sectarians were also forbidden from receiving the title of honored citizen. See ibid., 149.
59. *SPChR* (1875), 189–91.
60. *SPChR* (1875), 156–57, 189–91, 307–8, 367; *PSZ* (2) vol. 17:2 (1842), no. 15543; and vol. 22:2 (1847), no. 21006.
61. Dolzhenko, "Pervye," 60.
62. RGIA f. 1284, op. 205–1850, d. 166, ll. 2–20b. See also f. 381, op. 1, d. 23160, 1842, ll. 1–10b; and f. 1284, op. 200–1845, d. 36.
63. Moon, *Russian Peasants*, 23–61; R. E. McGrew, *Russia and the Cholera, 1823–1832* (Madison, 1965); François-Xavier Coquin, "Faim et migrations paysannes en Russie au XIXe siècle," *RHMC* 11 (April–June 1964): 127–44; and Staples, *Cross-Cultural Encounters*, 88–90.
64. GMIR f. 2, op. 7, d. 594, l. 49; RGIA f. 383, op. 30, d. 149, 1832–39, ll. 49–490b; and f. 1268, op. 10, d. 254, 1860, ll. 20b–3.

caucasian provinces where everything is extremely abundant."[65] In her study of the first Russian settlers in Armenia, Dolzhenko draws upon an array of statistical work on the impoverishment of peasants in the central provinces—and especially the problem of land shortage—in order to explain the desire of peasants to move.[66] In the standard work on the history of religious sectarianism in Russia in the nineteenth century, A. I. Klibanov adds the argument that only poorer state peasants chose to resettle in an effort to improve their economic situation, although the evidence Klibanov presents is insufficient. Unlike their poorer neighbors, wealthier peasants had much to lose and little to gain from resettling. Moreover, richer peasants could increase their wealth not only by cheaply buying up the land and immovable property migrants left behind, but also by giving credit at usurious rates to the settlers as aid for their trip.[67]

Sectarians, especially Molokans, heard that a land of plenty waited for them in Transcaucasia. As one nineteenth-century commentator described, rumors began to circulate "of faraway Caucasian lands [that] were filled with the most unbelievable notions about the new Promised Land: about a land of milk and honey, about heavenly manna, occurring there with a thickness of one and a half *arshin* [approximately forty inches], about forests filled with every sort of fruit tree and teeming with game. . . . In a word, these secret places, in their opinion, had been chosen by God himself for persecuted people."[68] In fact, rumors did not have to depict a Shangri-la in order to prompt sectarians to resettle. The simple fact that they had somewhere else to go where they would be accepted was often enough. For instance, a rumor that induced some sectarians to migrate was "that this being a new region, settlement would be permitted to any newcomer."[69]

While the sectarians did not find their utopia in Transcaucasia, they did encounter greater economic opportunities than their coreligionists in the central provinces. Large numbers of sectarians, particularly Subbotniks, migrated to Transcaucasia specifically to take advantage of these possibilities.[70] The central government passed a series of laws during the 1830s and 1840s that served to equalize the status of sectarians in

65. RGIA f. 379, op. 1, d. 1151, 1831–34, ll. 1–10b.
66. Dolzhenko, "Pervye," 60; and idem, "Russkie begletsy," 53–55. For comparison, see Willard Sunderland, "Peasants on the Move: State Peasant Resettlement in Imperial Russia, 1805–1830s," *RR* 52, no. 4 (October 1993): 477–78; and Coquin, "Faim et migrations," 127–37.
67. A. I. Klibanov, *Istoriia religioznogo sektantstva v Rossii (60–e gody XIX v.–1917 g.)* (Moscow, 1965), 148.
68. Orekhov, "Ocherki," no. 135, 1. Ellipses in the original. On the prevalence of rumors of "faraway lands," see Chistov, *Russkie narodnye*, 237–340.
69. RGIA f. 1268, op. 1, d. 650, 1844, l. 8.
70. *AKAK* vol. 8, docs. 43 and 48; *PSZ* (2) supplement to vol. 12 (1837), no. 10093a, pp. 1–2; *SPChR* (1875), 200; and GMIR f. 2, op. 7, d. 593, 1820–40, ll. 24–27.

Transcaucasia with Orthodox Russians.[71] Among these rights were official sanction for business trips within the South Caucasus (1836), and
the right for Molokans to travel for trade and work to Persia (1843).[72]
Moreover, in 1846 sectarians in the South Caucasus were permitted—in
stark contrast to the situation of their brethren elsewhere in the Empire—to hire and be hired by Orthodox people as long as the nonsectarian party was not ethnically Russian (for example, Georgian Orthodox
was allowed).[73]

In addition to religious and economic issues, family factors also impelled Russian sectarians to embark for Transcaucasia. In certain instances, sectarians migrated to escape disagreeable family situations,
especially as a form of de facto divorce. In one case, a young Molokan
woman fled her home in Astrakhan province in order to escape her Orthodox husband who had been abusing her because of her Molokan
faith. She secretly migrated with an uncle who was legally resettling to
Transcaucasia. Upon her arrival, she changed her name, remarried—
this time to a fellow Molokan—and began her life anew. Later, this young
woman's mother, also a Molokan, requested official permission to join
her daughter after the mother's husband had abandoned her for a new
wife in Tavriia province.[74] In similar fashion, among the Dukhobors banished from the Don Cossacks in 1830, seventeen married women elected
to break ties with their husbands, choosing instead to resettle south with
their children.[75]

Equally important in prompting sectarians to resettle was the appeal
of joining family members who had already moved south. Much has been
written about the centrality of the family to Russian peasants, and the resettlement of sectarians to Transcaucasia supports these notions. The
family foundation was frequently challenged by a confluence of tsarist
religious and resettlement policies, leaving peasants in the untenable situation of surviving without familial support systems. Reunion in Transcaucasia was seen as a solution to these problems. Moreover, even if the
desire to unite with relatives (or friends, fellow villagers, and coreligionists, for that matter) did not play a role in the decision to move, these people almost always acted as conduits in the resettlement process. For those
peasants wishing to escape their predicament—and this was especially
the case for those who were contemplating running away—relatives on

71. These laws and decrees are discussed in chapter four, sectarian economic success in chapter
three.
72. RGIA f. 381, op. 1, d. 23322, 1846, ll. 2–20b; f. 1284, op. 200–1842, d. 476, ll. 2–20b, 50b,
7, 15; f. 1268, op. 1, d. 433, 1843–48, ll. 18–180b; and *SPChR* (1875), 335.
73. RGIA f. 381, op. 1, d. 23322, 1846.
74. GMIR f. 2, op. 7, d. 594, ll. 46–47. See also RGIA f. 1268, op. 6, d. 233, 1852, ll. 1–10b.
75. GMIR f. 2, op. 7, d. 596, l. 120.

FIGURE 2. A Molokan woman in the South Caucasus, c. 1865. From V. V. Vereshchagin, *Dukhobortsy i Molokane v Zakavkaz'e, Shiity v Karabakhe, Batchi i Oshumoedy v Srednei Azii, i Ober-Amergau v Gorakh Bavarii* (Moscow, 1900), 27.

the frontier provided both a geographic destination and the comforting prospect that someone would take them in once they arrived.[76] In one 1841 incident, two women from Tambov province requesting resettlement to Transcaucasia explained that their husbands had been exiled there in 1839 for supporting the Molokan faith and spreading it to their children. The petitioners were left with the children "without any means for subsistence, so that we are deprived of practically any daily sustenance and shelter," a situation that prompted them to petition for permission to move before ruin overtook them completely.[77]

Not all cases of families desiring reunification involved members of the same faith, and there were a substantial number of petitions for re-settlement to Transcaucasia from Orthodox family members who had been left behind. In one instance, an Orthodox husband whose wife and children were Molokans who had requested to go to Transcaucasia along

---

76. In addition to the cases cited below, see also GMIR f. 2, op. 7, d. 594, ll. 46–47, 49; RGIA f. 1268, op. 8, d. 275, 1856, l. 2; f. 1284, op. 197–1837, d. 37, l. 4; and f. 379, op. 1, d. 1151, 1831–34, ll. 1–10b.

77. RGIA f. 383, op. 4, d. 3175, 1841–42, quotation is on ll. 1–10b. For a similar case, see OR-RGB f. 648, k. 46, d. 2, ll. 48–49.

with other coreligionists, applied to move with them since he wished to remain "forever inseparable" from his wife.[78] In another incident, in 1836, an Orthodox former soldier named Drobshev requested permission to join his family—father, mother, wife and four children, all Molokans originally from Orenburg province—in the Transcaucasus. According to his petition, Drobshev was born to Orthodox parents and he married an Orthodox woman before leaving for military service. While serving his term, the family converted to the Molokan faith and practiced in secret for many years to avoid persecution. They resettled to Transcaucasia for unstated reasons and informed Drobshev of their actions by letter. When his military term came to an end he wished to join them even though he was still Orthodox. His request was allowed, reflecting a state policy of the time that placed the sanctity of the family ahead of complete sectarian isolation and hence did not seek to split families because of differences in faith.[79]

Sectarians also saw migration as a means to avoid military service, which their religious beliefs could only tolerate at best. There was no military conscription in Transcaucasia until 1887, and there were plentiful rumors that application for resettlement meant freedom from army duty.[80] Echoing one such rumor, a Molokan woman explained that she and others had moved to Transcaucasia, "as a result of an appeal by Prince M. S. Vorontsov who promised a fifty-year reprieve from military service."[81] However, despite these expectations for immediate liberation from enlistment, the laws regarding resettlement were designed specifically to enforce the fulfillment of such duties by not allowing anyone to migrate who was in line for call-up.[82] As a result, many simply fled clandestinely to avoid service. E. T. Klyshnikov, a Tambov peasant, took flight

78. RGIA f. 1284, op. 197–1837, d. 37, l. 4.

79. RGIA f. 1284, op. 197–1837, d. 33. With the prevalence of multiconfessional families and the complexities of the state's religion-based resettlement project, tsarist officials in the 1830s and 1840s hotly debated the question of what to do with sectarians who wished to resettle or were designated for banishment but whose families contained Orthodox members. From 1830 until 1846, tsarist officials generally utilized a "pro-family" policy designed to keep the family intact as much as possible. The law prevented sectarians with Orthodox family members from migrating to Transcaucasia, although on certain occasions Orthodox relatives were permitted to relocate along with their sectarian kinsmen. After 1846, in an effort to enhance isolation, Russian legislation granted sectarians in multiconfessional families the option to split the family and leave their Orthodox relations behind. See RGIA f. 1284, op. 195–1825, d. 61, ll. 169, 175–76ob, 180–80ob, 186–87; op. 200–1843, d. 15, l. 2; op. 202–1847, d. 118; f. 383, op. 30, d. 149, 1832–39, ll. 8–9; op. 4, d. 3175, 1841–42; f. 381, op. 1, d. 23401, 1846–47; *SPChR* (1875), 216–17, 376–77; and GMIR f. 2, op. 7, d. 594, l. 80.

80. RGIA f. 379, op. 1, d. 1151, 1831–34, ll. 12–120b, 370b; and Breyfogle, "Swords into Plowshares."

81. Leont'ev, "Dukhovnye khristiane," 18.

82. RGIA f. 1284, op. 200–1843, d. 15, l. 4. For comparison, see Sunderland, "Peasants on the Move," 476.

to Transcaucasia in 1840 in order to escape military service, which he considered against his religious principles.[83]

Finally, a chain reaction to news of successful resettlement was itself a stimulus to sectarian migration. In one series of events, 206 Molokans from Orenburg province received permission to resettle in 1832. Once the news spread, another petition for resettlement appeared from 602 Molokans, and then another from 104. The second two petitions explicitly cited the fulfillment of foregoing requests as impetus for their efforts.[84]

UNAUTHORIZED MIGRATION

In addition to the thousands of Russian sectarians who migrated to Transcaucasia voluntarily and legally, many others did so clandestinely without permission. These runaways and vagabonds—part of a long-standing Russian tradition of peasant flight—included a large percentage of serfs and army deserters.[85] Although Transcaucasia had been demarcated solely for sectarian settlement, runaways included both Orthodox and nonconformist Russians, especially Molokans and Subbotniks.

The underlying reasons for illegal resettlement to Transcaucasia were much like those for lawful, voluntary resettlement. However, there were numerous legislative and social restrictions that left some determined migrants little choice but to resettle without authorization. After all, the overwhelming majority of the population was denied the legal option of moving to the South Caucasus. According to the 1830 edict (and later amendments), resettlement was designated almost exclusively for state peasants (among rural dwellers), leaving serfs with only illegal migration options. Similarly, Orthodox subjects generally did not have the right to migrate to Transcaucasia, even though the appeal of a better life could be as strong for them as it was for many sectarians. Draftees unhappy with the terms of their military service, especially in the Caucasian borderlands, had little choice but to desert. Without the right to resettle, scores of Russians simply picked up and left for the frontier.[86]

Even those sectarian migrants who were eligible for legal resettlement

83. GMIR f. K1, op. 8, d. 470, l. 1.

84. RGIA f. 383, op. 30, d. 149, 1832–39, l. 16. See also RGIA f. 379, op. 1, d. 1151, 1831–34, ll. 1–10b.

85. Petrov, "Seleniia," 228; and Dolzhenko, "Russkie begletsy," 54–55. On peasant flight more generally, see Jerome Blum, *Lord and Peasant in Russia from the Ninth to the Nineteenth Century* (Princeton, 1961), 266–68, 309–10, 552–54, 559; and Moon, *Russian Peasants*, 23–61.

86. RGIA f. 1268, op. 10, d. 254, 1860, ll. 1–20b, 4; op. 1, d. 433, 1843–48, ll. 46–46ob; and SSCSA f. 240, op. 1, d. 457, 1860.

faced countless bureaucratic hurdles, any one of which could dash their hopes. At various stages of the petition process, the family; the commune; the Spiritual Consistory; local, regional and central administrations; or the Transcaucasian authorities could deny or delay resettlement for any number of reasons. Factors barring or retarding migration included familial or communal opposition to losing an individual's economic contribution, nonfulfillment of military service, having an Orthodox family member, not being up to date on tax payments, the absence of available land or a poor harvest year in the Transcaucasus, economic problems in provinces along the migration route, the fear on the part of authorities that an application approval would spark a mass of similar petitions or even conversions from nearby Orthodox Russians, and the purely arbitrary or capricious decisions of administrative bodies at various levels. Denied at any step, would-be migrants often took matters into their own hands and set off for Transcaucasia.[87]

While it is difficult to determine with any accuracy the number of runaway settlers to the South Caucasus—as statistics reveal only those who were found out—there are specific periods in which sudden floods of clandestine migrants appeared in Transcaucasia.[88] The first such time was in the 1830s, when religious and economic factors impelled large numbers of Russians to pick up and leave their homes for the periphery.[89] The second mass influx of illegal migrants occurred during and after the Crimean War (1853–1856). These included army deserters who wanted neither to fight nor to return to their official places of habitation and peasants from the interior provinces who accompanied military caravans to the South Caucasus, enticed by rumors of a more Edenic land in which to live.[90] By far the majority of these civilians were given permission to do so as part of the war effort. Others, however, took advantage of the size of the caravans, as well as the inevitable disorder of wartime, to make their way to Transcaucasia surreptitiously. With the end of the war, some moved to the Ottoman Empire, while "the remainder dispersed through [Transcaucasia] and, working as day laborers, went from place to place and were able to support their existence in that way."[91]

87. See, for example, RGIA f. 1284, op. 196–1831, d. 136, ll. 36–360b; op. 205–1850, d. 166; op. 197–1837, d. 63; f. 381, op. 1, d. 23297; 1844–45, ll. 13–130b, 17–170b; op. 1, d. 23160, 1842; and f. 383, op. 4, d. 3175, 1841–42.
88. Dolzhenko "Pervye," 60; idem, "Russkie begletsy," 65; RGIA f. 1268, op. 1, d. 650, 1844, l. 8; d. 342, 1842–49, ll. 16–170b; op. 10, d. 254, 1860; and Petrov, "Seleniia," 228–29.
89. See the discussion above in the section "Motives for Migration" and RGIA f. 1268, op. 10, d. 254, 1860, ll. 20b–4.
90. Petrov, "Seleniia," 228; and RGIA f. 1268, op. 10, d. 254, 1860. In addition, the rumor spread widely among army reserves during the Crimean War that they were going to be freed from their army status. When they discovered that they were not in fact going to be released from service, many of these reservists fled to the Transcaucasus. Dolzhenko, "Russkie begletsy," 55.
91. RGIA f. 1268, op. 10, d. 254, 1860, ll. 1–20b.

Deserters and runaways, whatever their faith, tended to go directly to sectarian villages because, as essentially the only ethnic Russians in the region outside of administrators and military personnel, their settlements provided the sole option for illegal migrants to find shelter, provisions, and work. As one nineteenth-century observer noted, the runaways found there "not only safe and secure shelter, but also a full guarantee from any administrative prosecution."[92] Indeed, the clandestines also discovered that they could register quasi-legally in a sectarian village. Nonconformists in Transcaucasia compiled the official census registers themselves and often forged these lists to include family members who had never existed, or who had died. "For an agreed-upon price, [they] began to take vagabonds and deserters into their community in the places on the lists that were not actually filled, calling them by forged names."[93] Along with a change in official identity, such registration frequently also required a shift in religious affiliation to a sectarian faith, if the runaway was Orthodox. A commission investigating clandestine settlers commonly found families in which a "grandfather" would be younger than his son or grandson, or in which close family members (spouses, brothers) would not know each other. In one case, investigators discovered 135 empty places in the false family registers that the villagers had not yet succeeded in selling to vagabonds.[94]

Two case studies illustrate the process and outcomes of clandestine migration. In 1833, authorities uncovered runaway serfs and church peasants from Tambov among the Molokan settlers of Karabakh. They had secretly made their way to Transcaucasia by blending in with parties of exiled Molokans already en route. "Desiring to legalize their situation, they appealed in Karabakh to the Molokan commune with the entreaty that they take them into their sect." The Molokans agreed to the plea based on Isaiah 21:14, which describes the giving of water and bread to travelers in flight, and also because the village elder had secured the cooperation of the local police officer to register those in the community without passports in return for 100 rubles per registrant.[95] In another incident, runaways, deserters, and criminals were found in the villages of Topchi and Alty-Agach in Shirvan province, where they were involved in a number of illegal activities. In addition to living there without permission, they were making their own coins, forging documents, and receiv-

92. Petrov, "Seleniia," 228; SSC'SA f. 239, op. 1, d. 806, 1857; f. 240, op. 1, d. 375, 1859–60; d. 457, 1860; and Dolzhenko, "Russkie begletsy," 58.

93. RGIA f. 1268, op. 10, d. 254, 1860, ll. 50b, 110b–12; GMIR f. K1, op. 8, d. 470, l. 1; and Petrov, "Seleniia," 229–30

94. SSC'SA f. 239, op. 1, d. 806, 1858, ll. 310b–32; f. 240, op. 1, d. 375, 1859–60; f. 4, op. 2, d. 631, 1847; RGIA f. 1268, op. 10, d. 254, 1860, ll. 6–60b; and Dolzhenko, "Russkie begletsy," 59.

95. GMIR f. 2, op. 7, d. 594, ll. 22–23.

ing money from state sources in Tiflis based on false documents they had created.[96]

Runaways could also "legalize" themselves in the region by buying forged documents bearing another name in urban markets. This approach, however, was much riskier than buying one's way onto sectarian village registers. High rates of illiteracy among the runaways meant that vagabonds were unable to read what was actually printed on the documents they were obtaining, often with unwanted results. One vagabond, Ivan Vasil'ev, bought a passport in a bazaar in Tiflis that had already expired. However, Vasil'ev did not suffer from this mistake because the local Georgian authorities were having an equally hard time reading Russian documents.[97]

So great was the surge of illegal migrants to Transcaucasia during the Crimean War that the viceroy, Prince A. I. Bariatinskii, set up a commission in 1858—the first of two—to examine and resolve the problem. The investigators uncovered an intricate system of harboring runaways as well as villages that were almost entirely composed of illegal settlers, such as Novo-Ivanovka in Elisavetpol district. Beginning in the early 1850s, nine families of clandestine migrants settled in the location of the future village. As one later ethnographer described the origins of the village, "Out-of-the-way wooded thickets, the complete absence of even Tatar villages nearby turned this small Molokan village into the primary center to which runaways and deserters began to flock, and bit-by-bit they founded two contiguous villages—Baglydzha and Ak-Kilisa, later turned into Novo-Ivanovka."[98]

Although desertion and flight were patently illegal, the perpetrators frequently did not suffer harsh consequences when caught and were almost always permitted to remain in Transcaucasia.[99] This is not to say that there was no punishment at all. Even when allowed to settle in Transcaucasia, many runaways were brought to trial with a potential penalty of corporal punishment.[100] Nonetheless, tsarist officials were primarily interested in punishing those people who enabled illegal migration, not the migrants themselves. In fact, by the mid-1850s tsarist authorities had taken to granting amnesty to runaways, allowing them and their families

96. Ibid., ll. 23–25. For another case, see ibid., ll. 26–27.
97. Dolzhenko, "Russkie begletsy," 57.
98. Petrov, "Seleniia," 228; SSC'SA f. 240, op. 1, d. 490, 1860–62, ll. 1–4; and d. 457, 1860. Other villages composed primarily of clandestine migrants included Samisi (Tiflis district) and Privol'noe (Borchalo district). RGIA f. 1268, op. 10, d. 254, 1860, ll. 8–9; and SSC'SA f. 240, op. 2, d. 317, 1858–63, ll. 160b–17.
99. Unlike in the North Caucasus, officials in Transcaucasia took no extraordinary measures to curb illegal flight. RGIA f. 1268, op. 1, d. 342, 1842–49, ll. 10–140b, 16–170b, 25–250b.
100. RGIA f. 1268, op. 1, d. 650, 1844, l. 8; GMIR f. 2, op. 7, d. 593, 1820–40, ll. 30–31; d. 594, ll. 27, 47; and SPChR (1875), 213–14.

to register in Transcaucasia without penalty or prosecution (except for police surveillance and certain minor restrictions). Hundreds of clandestine migrants took advantage of these amnesties to come forward, declare themselves, and embrace the opportunity to stop hiding and settle themselves legally in Transcaucasia. Only in the case of military service were central tsarist authorities determined to ensure that the runaway completed his obligations to the fullest—whether for a deserter to finish out his term, or for a clandestine migrant to be subject to the draft. Yet even here, local officials were often quite lax about tracking down and returning deserters to service.[101]

There were four primary reasons that state officials chose to permit runaways to stay in Transcaucasia. By increasing the number of Russians in the South Caucasus, runaways fulfilled important economic and imperialist functions that administrators were loath to disrupt. As one government report put it, "All those Molokans registered under a false name work in the transport trade, in the fields making hay and growing grain, and also work as artisans. Overall, they are a hard-working and beneficial people." Another report added, "The deprivation of so sizable a number of good workers would be felt by the economy of the region." By allowing runaways to stay, state officials were beginning to see these "harmful" people as colonists—a process that would expand during the nineteenth century.[102] In addition, serf owners in the central provinces often did not want their runaway serfs returned to them because, as religious dissenters with a history of flight, they considered them doubly dangerous and unreliable. The law also required that the commune or landowner cover the expense of transporting their runaways back to the interior, a cost they were often quite willing to forego.[103] Furthermore, there were so many clandestines that punishing them posed a serious logistical problem. In one case alone, tsarist agents would have been obliged to apply punishments to well over 700 people at once.[104] Finally, local officials feared a violent reaction from the sectarians if they were to push too hard on this issue.[105]

101. RGIA f. 1268, op. 10, d. 254, 1860, ll. 30b–29; d. 115, 1865; and Dolzhenko, "Russkie begletsy," 62–64.
102. Respectively, SSC'SA f. 239, op. 1, d. 806, 1858, l. 32 and RGIA f. 1268, op. 10, d. 254, 1860, ll. 150b–16. On state efforts to increase the presence of Russian settlers in Transcaucasia as part of their process of imperial integration, see chapter four; GMIR f. K1, op. 8, d. 470, l. 2; and Dolzhenko, "Russkie begletsy," 62.
103. GMIR f. 2, op. 7, d. 594, ll. 23–24; RGIA f. 1284, op. 196–1834, d. 106, ll. 3–4, 9–11; E. R., "Russkie ratsionalisty," 285; SPChR (1875), 133–34; and AKAK vol. 9:1, doc. 28, p. 27.
104. RGIA f. 1268, op. 10, d. 254, 1860, ll. 130b–150b; and SSC'SA f. 240, op. 1, d. 457, 1860, ll. 820b–83, passim.
105. GMIR, f. 2, op. 7, d. 594, ll. 24–25; and "Russkie begletsy," 61.

ON THE ROAD

The actual experience of resettlement to Transcaucasia varied as widely as the settlers' reasons for migrating. Initial efforts on the part of state agents to manage the population movement were chaotic because of the vast distances within the Empire, the often incompetent bureaucrats who ran local affairs and interpreted laws in their own fashion, a marked absence of the needed resources, and the vagaries of the Russian climate. To be fair, the structure of resettlement did undergo a process of reform and rationalization, particularly in 1842 and 1843, that not only made it more efficient but also resulted in fewer deaths on the part of migrants.[106] However, despite their pretensions to complete control, state administrators simply could not envisage and then prepare for every conceivable permutation of the sectarians' needs, desires, and actions. Settlers repeatedly took matters into their own hands when they sensed that events were not proceeding to their advantage—sometimes to their benefit, sometimes not—in an effort to force the hand of the state and to bring about certain desired outcomes. State officials were left trying to manage a social process that constantly surged beyond their control.[107]

Certain sources depict joyous sectarians going to Transcaucasia, happily singing psalms and basking in the expectation of the coming kingdom of Christ and their promised place within it. "While on the road," other settlers were said to "enjoy complete freedom, stay in unrestricted apartments and visit their religious brethren who also receive them into their homes for visits," spreading their faith as they went.[108] More common, however, were stories of great hardship and suffering. Most groups arrived in Transcaucasia exhausted, ragged, and starving.[109] The journey generally took at least six months, but could last more than a year if the migrants were caught off-guard by a harsh winter and forced to stop on the way.[110] Official settlers moved in large groups; adults walked the entire distance, while children rode in wagons if the group was lucky enough to have some. Families were transformed during those months: mothers gave birth, some migrants died, some fell in love, livestock per-

---

106. Compare, for example, the differences in resettlement practice between the regulations of December 13, 1832, December 14, 1842, and May 2, 1843, as well as the efforts to reform the latter rules later that year. *SPChR* (1875), 113–15, 328–35; RGIA f. 1263, op. 1, d. 791, 1832, ll. 2920b–97; f. 1284, op. 200–1843, d. 15; and *AKAK* vol. 9:2, doc. 515.

107. In his "Peasants on the Move," Willard Sunderland finds the reactive role of tsarist officials to be characteristic of pre-reform resettlement in general. *SPChR* (1875), 403–4.

108. *SPChR* (1875), 403–4.

109. *Spirit and Life*, 19–20; RGIA f. 1263, op. 1, d. 791, 1832, ll. 2920b–97; f. 379, op. 1, d. 1043, 1830–37, ll. 910b–940b; f. 381, op. 1, d. 23401, 1846–47; f. 1284, op. 202–1847, d. 118; and op. 200–1843, d. 15.

110. RGIA 1284, 196–1831, d. 136, 1831–43, l. 130.

ished or, as the only available food, was consumed. Some settlers underwent a change of heart about resettlement and took the only action
that would let them return to their original homes: conversion to
Orthodoxy.[111]

The sectarians followed one of two prescribed routes. The original
and primary itinerary took migrants from their home province through
Stavropol, where settlers from different points of origin were put into
larger groups for the trip through the Caucasus Mountains. The settlers
then traveled via Vladikavkaz and Tiflis to Shusha, where they were dispersed to their specific places of settlement in the region.[112] Timing was
critical for this route—the settlers had to reach Stavropol between April
and May. An early arrival meant that they would not have "warm shelter"
as they neared the mountains, depriving "their horses of sufficient pasturage"; a late arrival meant that they would traverse the mountains in
May or June, "when the melting snow can be very difficult. . . . For new
settlers from Russia, travel through Transcaucasia in July and August is
highly ruinous because of the local heat which burns away the grass in
the steppe area."[113] Moreover, if they arrived too late in Transcaucasia,
the sectarians found themselves unable to sow winter crops, which they
desperately needed to survive their initial months. However, to reach
Stavropol by May required settlers to set off in late winter or early spring,
when the roads were awash in mud from the thaw and "the land was without fodder for the horses or oxen that were pulling their wagons."[114] In
response to all of the problems posed by this first route, a second itinerary into Transcaucasia was created leading down the east side of the Caucasus through Astrakhan, Kizliar, Derbent, and Shemakha to their final
place of residence. The migrants were to pass through Kizliar in August
so that they could arrive in their new homes in September, "when the heat
ends in Transcaucasia and the ground fodder once again begins to
appear."[115]

Whereas state officials, in theory, provided exiled sectarians with provisioning during their migration, tsarist law, especially in the 1830s, re-

111. GMIR f. 2, op. 7, d. 594, ll. 75–77; RGIA f. 1284, op. 195–1825, d. 61, ll. 199–990b; Breyfogle, "Heretics and Colonizers," chapter 5.
112. GMIR f. 2, op. 7, d. 594, ll. 4, 13; SPChR (1875), 114.
113. AKAK vol. 9:2, doc. 515, p. 600.
114. Ibid. and SPChR (1875), 330.
115. AKAK vol. 9:2, doc. 515, p. 600; and D. I. Ismail-Zade, "Russian Settlements in the Transcaucasus from the 1830s to the 1880s," in The Molokan Heritage Collection, vol. 1, ed. Ethel Dunn
and Stephen P. Dunn (Berkeley, 1983), sec. 3, p. 61. The second route was particularly appropriate since the majority of sectarians came to live in eastern Transcaucasia. After the mid-1840s,
the Stavropol route was used for exiled sectarians and those voluntary migrants to be settled in
the Georgian region. The remainder (the majority) relocated to Transcaucasia along the Kizliar
route.

quired voluntary settlers to pay their own way and provide for all their possible needs while in transit.[116] Lacking experience in accumulating sufficient resources, however, voluntary migrants frequently began their travels unprepared for the arduous task ahead of them. At the same time, these settlers often found themselves unexpectedly impoverished even before they left. When selling their immovable and unwanted property before embarking, they almost always received well below market value for the goods because buyers realized that migrants would sell cheaply for fear of having to abandon the belongings altogether.[117] The settlers' incapacity to provide for themselves forced authorities to intervene in order to prevent mass starvation.[118] Baron Rosen noted in 1833 that "sectarians, while on the road through the Caucasian Line, are often in a condition of extreme need and require provisions of bread." Indeed, Rosen negotiated a temporary cessation in the resettlement process in 1833 and 1834 because poor harvests in the Caucasus had caused "a painful insufficiency" of foodstuffs available to the already ravaged sectarians in transit. To buy the grain the migrants needed was "only possible at extremely high cost."[119] Moreover, although state laws required that local officials along the route grant food and shelter to banished sectarians, the exiles frequently complained that they rarely received the promised goods, leaving them hungry and destitute.[120]

In the face of these devastating outcomes and the weighty obstacles to successful resettlement, the settlers endeavored to take actions that would help to ensure success by controlling the time, manner, and location of resettlement. In 1833, Orenburg Molokans demanded permission for immediate migration so that they would have time to sow crops and cut hay in their new place of residence.[121] One group of petitioners, revealing how they conceived of the potential dangers that lay ahead, urged to be allowed to migrate in the company of another group of sectarians "in order that [we] will run no danger marching through wild, Asiatic places."[122] Dukhobors asked to be settled in areas where they could remain close to Shusha and other towns in order to foster trade.[123] Other settlers also requested specific towns in which to settle.[124]

Despite their efforts to shape the terms of their relocation, migrants

116. *SPChR* (1875), 114.
117. Orekhov, "Ocherki," no. 135, 1.
118. See, for example, RGIA f. 384, op. 2, d. 1288, 1842–45.
119. RGIA f. 1284, op. 196–1831, d. 136, ll. 95, 118–180b, 130; and f. 379, op. 1, d. 1043, 1830–37, ll. 1380b–39.
120. GMIR f. 2, op. 7, d. 596, n.d., ll. 121–22.
121. RGIA f. 383, op. 30, d. 149, 1832–39, l. 4.
122. RGIA f. 1284, op. 197–1837, d. 9, ll. 3–4.
123. RGIA f. 379, op. 1, d. 1043, 1830–37, l. 710b; and f. 1268, op. 10, d. 49, 1861.
124. RGIA f. 1263, op. 1, d. 791, 1832, ll. 287–880b; and f. 381, op. 1, d. 23160, 1842, ll. 8–80b.

were by no means unified or steadfast in their resettlement plans when faced with the harsh realities or confused reports surrounding relocation—a fact that complicated state efforts to manage their movement.[125] The oscillating migration agenda of Molokans from Astrakhanka in Tavriia province spotlights this logistical chaos. In their initial petition, the Molokans asked to send scouts to Transcaucasia to begin the process of selecting and preparing land. A few months later they wrote again, saying that since the time of the first petition they had received correspondence from coreligionists living in the South Caucasus who assured them that the land there was "definitely suitable." They were now willing to resettle without sending prior representatives, and in fact preferred not to since it would waste time that could be better used in planting grain and preparing housing in their new homeland. Further, the petitioners noted that the number of potential migrants was growing significantly. Despite the opinions voiced in the second letter, scouts did in fact make a trip to Transcaucasia and returned disillusioned. The would-be migrants then officially revoked their desire to resettle, stating that the land was not suitable and that "by their [Molokan] way of life, they cannot live with the indigenous population."

Not all Astrakhanka Molokans agreed with this evaluation of the prospects of frontier life, however, and the list of resettlement applicants continued to grow to more than a thousand, from roughly 200. At this stage, the number had become so large that the commune was on the verge of blocking their movement altogether, as the departure of all these people would have left the community bereft of taxpayers and military recruits, which would have confronted those remaining behind with the possibility of ruination. Dissension continued to grow in the Molokan ranks. Further petitioners charged that the scouts had inaccurately labeled the land unusable because they had not actually gone to the specific plots designated for them. Moreover, two pessimistic scouts had disregarded the opinion of a third, who found the conditions perfectly acceptable. Confusion continued to reign as Molokans wavered in their desire to resettle. All the while, local authorities struggled in vain to ascertain which of those Molokans who at any particular moment evinced a desire to move met the state's criteria for resettlement, to prevent those who did not meet the requirements from leaving on their own, and to set up the necessary support structures for successful migration.

In other cases, even before receiving permission for migration, it was common for sectarians to stop sowing their fields; to sell their houses, possessions, grain stores and livestock; and to live in rented rooms, bivouacs,

---

125. The following discussion is drawn from RGIA f. 379, op. 1, d. 1151, 1831–34. ll. 1–50.

or specially prepared wagons. As a result, they reached the point where they could no longer provide for themselves in their current location—often, multiple families were living in one hut. They took this potentially ruinous path for a combination of reasons: They felt certain of receiving future consent for resettlement, they were excited at the prospect of moving, and, most important, they were trying to bend the will of the state by presenting their departure as a fait accompli. Trying to force the state's hand in this manner was a risky, albeit common, gambit, especially after the government implemented specific laws in 1838 that denied permission to those who stopped sowing or sold their property in advance of official resettlement permission. However, in the face of complete misery, state officials usually had little option but to yield to the sectarians' designs and grant them the right to immediate relocation.[126]

The experiences of Orenburg Molokans serve as an example not only of the general confusion surrounding early resettlement endeavors but also of another ploy used by settlers—simply setting off on their own after obtaining general permission to relocate but prior to the official go-ahead to begin traveling.[127] In 1833, the governor of Saratov sent the Ministry of Internal Affairs unexpected reports of 170 Molokan *odnod-vortsy* from Orenburg who, having received permission to resettle to Transcaucasia, had been held up in Saratov province by the onset of cold weather and poor harvests. They were having great difficulties continuing on their way, especially because there were many young children in their company. News of the Molokans' movement to Saratov province came as a complete surprise to the authorities in Orenburg, as they had not given them permission to take to the road and had explicitly told the would-be migrants not to set off by themselves. The officials were deeply annoyed that they had set out at such an inauspicious time of year.[128] The Molokans entreated the local Saratov authorities to let them remain there until the arrival of spring made further progress possible. The Ministry agreed to this, but under the strict condition that they be watched closely in order to prevent any spread of their faith. They rented apartments and bought grain from the inhabitants of the village of Tiagloe, and waited out the winter.

Reports from the Caucasus the next spring showed that the harvest had failed, and the Ministry of Finance ordered that the erstwhile settlers

---

126. RGIA f. 381, op. 1, d. 23160, 1842, ll. 2–160b; f. 383, op. 30, d. 149, 1832–39, ll. 160b–17, 30–300b. For comparison, see Sunderland, "Peasants on the Move," 480.

127. The following discussion is drawn from RGIA f. 383, op. 30, d. 149, 1832–39, especially ll. 19–220b, 47–61, 71–730b, and 95–980b.

128. RGIA f. 383, op. 30, d. 149, 1832–39, ll. 9, 22–220b. The issue of the timing of resettlement was a focal one in discussions between Transcaucasian and central officials. RGIA f. 379, op. 1, d. 1043, 1830–37, ll. 90–900b.

should now stay in Tiagloe until such time as there was a good harvest. However, the Saratov governor had already sent the Molokans on their way before word arrived to hold them there. He had hastened them on their journey after complaints by the bishop that their presence was acting as a temptation to the Orthodox and that there had been conversions to the heresy.[129] The confusion did not end when the Orenburg Molokans finally arrived in Transcaucasia: since there had been no official permission to begin the journey, and since some had decided at the last minute to remain in Orenburg province, authorities had little idea how many Molokans the South Caucasus was to expect. In the event, Transcaucasian officials reported that 1147 Molokans had arrived from Orenburg, a great many more than was anticipated. Without accurate lists, there was no way of knowing who was actually permitted to be there and how the taxes for these resettlers were to be divided between Transcaucasia and Orenburg province, especially since those migrants who had made it were devastated by the journey.

The process of resettlement aggravated fault lines within families. Once again, the Orenburg Molokans in the 1830s serve as a prime example. In their attempts to compile a list of those Molokans desirous of and eligible for resettlement, Orenburg officials discovered families undergoing power struggles and fragmentation. For instance, families divided between those who wished to migrate and those who wished to stay put—a fracture that tended to split along confessional lines. In one case, a Molokan woman who had intended to follow her father to Transcaucasia was forced to remain with her husband since the latter did not wish her to go. In another case, a Molokan man began to have doubts about his convictions and decided to remain in his home village, even though his father, wife, and children—also Molokans—planned to resettle. In another incident, a man wanted to resettle but was prevented from doing so by his wife and children, who converted to Orthodoxy and wished to stay behind. Similarly, three wives converted to Orthodoxy and decided to remain in the Orenburg area despite their husbands' continued intention to relocate. These cleavages created tension, to be sure, but also opportunities for escaping unwanted family situations. For state officials, such circumstances complicated their efforts to control the process of resettlement, as they were forced to weigh the sanctity of the family versus the imperative to isolate sectarians, not to mention what they would do with children who were not old enough to decide for themselves.[130]

Resettlement was not necessarily a one-way ticket for sectarians. Many

---

129. A. I. Klibanov demonstrates the enormous impact that these travelers had upon the spiritual lives of the Orthodox villagers and on the spread of Molokanism. Klibanov, *Narodnaia,* 149–59.
130. RGIA f. 383, op. 30, d. 149, 1832–39, ll. 31–41; and f. 1284, op. 198–1838, d. 87.

retained ties to their original places of residence in the central provinces, and some went back and forth. Indeed, recently settled Molokans often petitioned to be allowed to leave their new homes in order to work temporarily in the central provinces and maintained contact with relatives who remained behind. Moreover, migration could be temporary, with individuals staying a few years in Transcaucasia and then returning.[131]

The unauthorized migration of Aleksei Gus'kov and his family illustrates that resettlement did not necessarily mean a permanent break with the village of origin.[132] The Gus'kov clan moved between Orenburg province and Transcaucasia multiple times in the 1830s and 1840s. In 1842, the family was found guilty of leaving its place of residence in Orenburg province without proper papers and for twice converting from Orthodoxy to Molokanism. Under questioning, Gus'kov related that while he was away working in a nearby town, he heard news that another peasant from his village had abducted his wife and son. (There is some question whether the wife and son simply left freely with this other man.) Gus'kov immediately demanded and received permission—and proper papers—from his commune to go after them. For unexplained reasons, at the county center the clerk took away his papers and held him for thirteen days before Gus'kov escaped, whereupon he found his wife and daughter in Astrakhan.[133] But instead of returning to their Orenburg village, the family made for the town of Shemakha in the Transcaucasus with the intention of joining relatives who had been sent there for settlement. Akulina, his wife, corroborated this story, adding that she had left Orenburg with the express purpose of joining her coreligionists and relatives living in Transcaucasia, and that she and the abductor had engaged in no sexual relations. During the investigation that accompanied their arrest in 1842, more information about the family's past came to light. In 1835, they had left their home in Orenburg province without official permission and lived in the Transcaucasian village of Alty-Agach until 1836. There they stayed with Gus'kov's mother, who had been exiled for converting Orthodox subjects to the Molokan faith. In 1836, however, for unexplained reasons they procured false papers and set off for their former home in the Russian interior. Along the way, they were apprehended, punished, and returned to their official Orenburg place of residence. In the 1843 proceedings, Gus'kov escaped punishment for his vagabondage by converting to Orthodoxy, and he and his family settled in Transcaucasia.[134]

---

131. GMIR f. 2, op. 7, d. 597, l. 2; and Dolzhenko, "Russkie begletsy," 56–57. For broad patterns, see Coquin, "Faim et migrations," 136–37; and Sunderland, "Peasant Pioneering."
132. The case is found in RGIA f. 1284, op. 200–1843, d. 508.
133. At this juncture the abductor disappears from the story without explanation.
134. See also the story of Petr Bezzubtsov's family in RGIA f. 1284, op. 204–1849, d. 799.

MIGRATION AND ITS POSSIBILITIES

The incorporation of Transcaucasia into the Russian Empire and the state's decision to isolate sectarians there opened a wide vista of opportunities for Russia's religious dissenters. Perhaps most important, this nexus of religious and imperial policies granted sectarians mobility. Resettlement to Transcaucasia was both an individual and group experience. State legislation made large-scale resettlement possible by setting sectarians apart in a shared legal category. Orthodox Russians who desired to move to Transcaucasia were often required at some point to take up sectarian affiliation and collective identity. However, the migrants also understood the journey in individual terms. Sectarians from different social backgrounds and branches of Christianity relocated for a variety of reasons, each reflecting personal choices and exigencies as they struggled to remedy hardships that threatened them and to realize their dreams and aspirations. The process of resettlement was very chaotic and, as often as not, the settlers did not find what they were looking for. Families collapsed, communities fell into disagreements, and the road to Transcaucasia proved perilous and capricious. Despite state laws and administrative structures governing the migration process, these Russian subjects largely took matters into their hands and forced state officials into a reactive role. They petitioned to migrate on their own terms, took to the road on their own schedule, and moved back and forth between the interior and Transcaucasia in order to profit from both regions. When prevented from realizing the option to resettle to Transcaucasia, both sectarian and Orthodox subjects migrated there clandestinely.

The process of resettlement had significant ramifications for the religious life of nonconformist communities throughout Russia, often strengthening their faiths. By making conversion to Orthodoxy a means for a sectarian to escape relocation, the resettlement process served as a weeding-out process in which only the most devoted and faithful made the move. While on the road, migrants might spread their beliefs over a wider area and recruit others to join them in the South Caucasus. In addition, migration brought together members of these different sects in one location. By providing a concentrated territory from which to act, resettlement expanded the possibilities for spiritual growth and doctrinal standardization.

If the sectarian settlers left their homes with certain expectations in mind, empire-building and a colonial mission was not among them. This absence of imperialist designs was a significant characteristic of peasant colonialism across the Empire.[135] Unlike Russian missionaries, soldiers,

135. Sunderland, "Peasant Pioneering," 909–10.

traders, and administrators, the religious dissenters did not go to the borderlands to bring civilization to those perceived as lacking it, to proselytize, to defend the strength of the Empire, to Russify the colony, or to develop its economic relationship with the metropole. Russian religious policy populated the Transcaucasus with Russians who felt little or no attachment to Russian state power—at least initially—and who had their own agendas in migrating to the frontier. Exiles in particular were filled with antagonism and bitterness over the years of mistreatment by officialdom and, unlike the voluntary settlers, often wanted nothing more than to return to their former homes.

Dukhobors, Molokans, and Subbotniks arrived in Transcaucasia as outcasts unwanted in the central provinces and as migrants in search of a better life on the frontier, including being part of Christ's New Jerusalem. However, their appearance in the borderlands set in motion a series of processes that nobody at the time foresaw. Vibrant "new worlds" were created in the South Caucasus through the formative interactions of the settlers with the environment, local tsarist authorities, and the peoples of the South Caucasus.

PART 2

LIFE ON THE SOUTH CAUCASIAN FRONTIER

3

"IN THE BOSOM OF AN
ALIEN CLIMATE"

Ecology, Economy, and Colonization

Arriving in 1830 in the South Caucasus, the Dukhobors exiled from the Don Cossacks encountered widespread hunger, soaring death rates, and economic destitution. Tsarist officials had prepared for their arrival by selecting lands in Karabakh province, constructing fifty mud huts "with spacious outer entrance halls," and stockpiling wood, wheat, millet, and barley for each family. Despite their good intentions, however, the authorities made grave errors. Shaba-Kishliak, the first location for the Dukhobors, was in a valley that proved inaccessible to wheeled transport and lacked sufficient pastureland for the settlers' livestock. Worse yet, weakened and destitute from the journey, the Dukhobors were greeted by the debilitating heat of August. The "murderous" high temperature and humidity were exacerbated by the fact that the huts built for them were based on winter housing for nomads, which was designed expressly to maximize heat retention. Cholera and other fevers spread widely through the community.

The result was, as one official put it, "wholesale death." Between August 20 and September 20 alone, twenty-two of the 265 Dukhobor exiles succumbed to the climatic conditions (8.3 percent); by March 1831, the death toll had mounted to fifty-eight. Poor harvests in the first few years only made matters worse. In 1831 in particular, agricultural produce was entirely insufficient and the Dukhobors had no choice but to petition the administration for wheat on credit so that they would have something to sow for 1832. Witnessing the human disaster, local tsarist officials struggled to alleviate their situation: they moved the exiles to a different location—which proved no safer—and requested funds to buy livestock and provisions for each Dukhobor family. However, the appeal for food aid was denied by higher authorities, who were little concerned about Dukhobor mortality and preferred to channel resources elsewhere.[1]

The Don Dukhobors were but the first in a long line of sectarian migrants who, upon their arrival in Transcaucasia, suffered physical and economic devastation. This narrative of distress—all too real and enduring—represents the first in a varied and complex set of interactions between the new Russian colonists and the South Caucasian environment. Despite a very difficult period in the first years after relocation, most settlers adapted successfully and went on to become extremely wealthy, often more prosperous than they could have become in the central provinces. In this interface of Russian colonization and the South Caucasian ecology, the environment transformed the colonists much more profoundly than they changed it.[2] Over the long term, the migrants responded to the new ecological challenges by modifying their economic practices, particularly by complementing their settled grain agriculture with an emphasis on market-oriented livestock raising, the carting trade, and a multiplicity of artisanal, industrial, and commercial ventures.

This is not to say that the relationship between people and place was not reciprocally influential, only to argue that the balance of influence was uneven. In ways that were both intentional and unintentional, the Russian migrants did refashion the landscape and biodiversity of the region through their agricultural practices, their building of infrastructure, and their importation of a spectrum of heretofore unfamiliar, usually domesticated plants and animals. The settlers' collective ability to induce environmental change in the Transcaucasus was sharply limited, however, especially because they represented a very small percentage of the population. Over time, the Russian colonists' presence and economic development had only a limited impact on the ecology of the region.

The evolving and mutually transformative interactions between the sectarian migrants and the South Caucasian environment are an important component of the settlers' daily experiences on the periphery of the Empire, offering a case study of the connections among religiosity, borderland settlement, and peasant economic activity. In addition, the confrontation between settlers and environment is also crucial to understanding the meanings and consequences of Russian empire-building in

1. GMIR f. 2, op. 7, d. 596, ll. 113, 121, 123–24, 128; d. 594, ll. 67, 70–71, 75–78; RGIA f. 1284, op. 195–1825, d. 61, ll. 145–47, 151–52; AKAK vol. 8, doc. 60, pp. 81–82; and vol. 10, doc. 293, pp. 285, 287. Quotation in chapter title is from A. F. Liaister, "'Pryguny' v Erivanskoi gubernii (stranichka iz istorii religioznykh iskanii russkogo cheloveka)," PKEG na 1912 g. (Erevan, 1912): Literaturnyi otdel, ch. II, 1.
2. While I argue here that Transcaucasia's ecology fundamentally changed the sectarian communities, I do not wish to indicate some sort of environmental determinism or absence of human agency.

the region. The manner in which colonists altered the environment directly affected how indigenous peoples experienced the imperialist presence; the "colonization" of the settlers by the Transcaucasian environment complicated Russian conceptions of civilizational hierarchies and imperial power relations.

This story is also important because of its comparative dimension. The historiography of other imperial contexts has drawn attention to the potential linkages between environment and empire.[3] These works suggest that the formation of empires transformed ecosystems just as it affected such human systems as politics and culture—and, indeed, these environmental changes in turn regularly modified human systems. Colonist-induced ecological transformations, often in tandem with such socio-economic changes as the introduction of market relations, influenced the well-being—even the very survival—of indigenous peoples.[4] As a contiguous rather than an overseas empire, the Russian case offers a fruitful perspective for exploring the interconnections of empire and ecology, and a new vantage point for the writing of environmental history.[5]

INITIAL TRAGEDIES

The opening years of settlement proved devastating for the Molokans, Dukhobors, and Subbotniks. Entering unprepared into a foreign environment, they endured disease, debilitating heat, undrinkable water, unsuitable soil and climate for their accustomed crops, and economic deprivation. The long and arduous trip, along with the inexperience and incompetence of local administrators, only exacerbated the migrants' suffering. Having sold off most of their property for almost nothing, and having taken with them only what was deemed absolutely necessary, they

---

3. Tom Griffiths and Libby Robin, eds., *Ecology and Empire: Environmental History of Settler Societies* (Seattle, 1997); Alfred Crosby, *Ecological Imperialism: The Biological Expansion of Europe, 900–1900* (1986; repr. New York, 1996); Jared Diamond, *Guns, Germs and Steel: The Fates of Human Societies* (New York, 1999); Richard Grove, *Green Imperialism: Colonial Expansion, Tropical Island Edens and the Origins of Environmentalism, 1600–1860* (New York, 1995); and William Cronon, George Miles and Jay Gitlin, "Becoming West: Toward a New Meaning for Western History," in idem, ed. *Under an Open Sky: Rethinking America's Western Past* (New York, 1992), 11–12.

4. William Cronon, *Changes in the Land: Indians, Colonists, and the Ecology of New England* (New York, 1983); and Richard White, *The Roots of Dependency: Subsistence, Environment, and Social Change among the Choctaws, Pawnees, and Navajos* (Lincoln, 1983).

5. These questions have been understudied in the case of tsarist history. For recent exceptions, see Thomas Barrett, *At the Edge of Empire: The Terek Cossacks and the North Caucasus Frontier, 1700–1860* (Boulder, 1999); David Moon, "Peasant Migration and the Settlement of Russia's Frontiers, 1550–1897" *HJ* 40, no. 4 (1997): 859–93; and idem, "Agricultural Settlement and Environmental Change on the Open Steppes of Southeastern European Russia in the Nineteenth Century," in *Peopling the Periphery: Russian Settlement in Eurasia from Muscovite to Soviet Times,* ed. Nicholas B. Breyfogle, Abby Schrader, and Willard Sunderland (forthcoming).

arrived with few resources to establish themselves in their new place of settlement.[6]

With its extensive mountain ranges, alpine meadows, and subtropical lowlands slotted between the Black and Caspian Seas, the South Caucasus encompassed a wide variety of topographies and climatic zones. Substantial variations in temperature, humidity, rainfall, and soil type characterized the region, with areas both hospitable and inhospitable to human habitation. Annual rainfall might vary from less than 200 mm in some locales to as much as 3200 mm in others; depending on the area, mean January temperature ranged from −12° to 3° Celsius, and mean summer temperature from 18° to 26° Celsius.[7]

For the first settlers in the 1830s, tsarist authorities set aside land of low elevation that was deemed "uninhabited" in the former khanates of Karabakh, Talysh, and Shirvan, then part of what Russian officials labeled the "Muslim Provinces." This site was chosen because tsarist officials believed that the sectarians would be isolated there from Orthodox subjects and unable to spread their heresies among their Muslim and Armenian neighbors. They also considered the lowland regions of Transcaucasia to be the most appropriate place for settled farming because of their "warm climate, water, fertile soil and quite large and flat land plots."[8]

Given their failure to carry out any preliminary surveys of the region, the administrators did not appreciate why these lands had traditionally been unpopulated. As the settlers quickly discovered, the location chosen for them became a killing zone in summer because of the oppressive heat, the insufficient and polluted drinking water, and the proliferation of malaria, cholera, and other diseases.[9] One Russian author writing at the end of the nineteenth century described the Lenkoran district before the Russians' arrival as "completely barren, without forest, without people, and an extremely unhealthy place."[10] The indigenous peoples of the region—primarily nomads—had long ago learned to use such low-lying

6. I. Ia. Orekhov, "Ocherki iz zhizni zakavkazskikh sektatorov," *Kavkaz*, no. 135 (June 16, 1878): 1; RGIA f. 384, op. 2, d. 1288, 1842–45, ll. 20b, 16; and f. 379, op. 1, d. 1043, 1830–37, ll. 1380b–390b.

7. N. A. Gvozdetskii, *Kavkaz: Ocherk prirody* (Moscow, 1963).

8. A. N. Iamskov, *Environmental Conditions and Ethnocultural Traditions of Stockbreeding (the Russians in Azerbaijan in the 19th and early 20th Centuries)* (Moscow, 1988), 3; "O russkikh pereselentsakh v Zakavkazskom krae," *Kavkaz*, no. 32 (April 22, 1850): 127; and A. I. Masalkin, "Iz istorii zakavkazskikh sektantov. Ch. III. Sektanty, kak kolonizatory Zakavkaz'ia," *Kavkaz*, no. 333 (December 16, 1893): 2.

9. SSC'SA f. 240, op. 1, d. 1428, 1865–67; GMIR f. 2, op. 7, d. 597, l. 4; RGIA f. 1268, op. 2, d. 533, 1847–48, ll. 1–20b; "O russkikh," 127; D. A. Kistenev, "Ekonomicheskii byt gosudarstvennykh krest'ian Lenkoranskogo uezda, Bakinskoi gubernii," in *MIEB*, vol. 7 (Tiflis, 1887), 568; Orekhov, "Ocherki," no. 135, 2; Masalkin, "Kolonizatory," 2; Iamskov, *Environmental Conditions*; and Gary Dean Fry, "The Doukhobors, 1801–1855: The Origins of a Successful Dissident Sect" (Ph.D. diss., American University, 1976), 248.

10. "Vliianie malarii na kolonizatsiiu Kavkaza," *KK* 54 (1899): otd. II, 57.

areas only for winter habitation, taking to the mountains as the snow receded in spring to escape the summer heat. Unfortunately for the sectarians, fully twelve of their first nineteen villages were founded in low-lying places.[11] Poor planning and execution on the part of the officials entrusted with the task of settling the migrants exacerbated the climatic devastation. All too often, administrators allotted insufficient land with soil unsuitable for growing grain or settled the sectarians "in places without water and . . . on land which later, it became known, belonged to nobles."[12] As a result, the settlers suffered from disease and hunger, and the death rates were high by almost any standard of comparison.[13] While mortality statistics are not entirely reliable—no two sets of numbers agree—they offer a rough portrait of the devastation. Between 58 and 67 percent of sectarian settlers in Karabakh province died in the first three to seven years. The village of Topchi lost between 42 and 50 percent of its initial contingent from 1834 to 1838, while Alty-Agach and Dudakchi each lost 20 percent of their migrants.[14]

The fate of the settlers in Topchi in the former Shirvan khanate illustrates the human tragedy behind these statistics. For Molokans who began to arrive in this village in 1834, Topchi was a "place from Hell" where they "had to endure much, and carry a great deal on their shoulders in the name of their faith." The "severe climate" killed as many as eight people a day from May through October every year, and after twelve years they had buried more than 2,000 people, piling twelve coffins into each grave. Whole families died together, and widows and orphans multiplied rapidly.[15] Every year the Topchi Molokans unsuccessfully petitioned local tsarist authorities for permission to move elsewhere to escape the terrible toll of their new environment. Predicting that "we will unavoidably all be killed next year," these petitions described "devastation" from a

11. "O russkikh," 127.
12. RGIA f. 1268, op. 2, d. 533, 1847–48, ll. 1–20b; and f. 381, op. 1, d. 23300, 1844, l. 2.
13. Orekhov, "Ocherki," no. 135, 2; and *Ocherk sel'skogo i lesnogo khoziaistva Lenkoranskogo uezda, Bakinskoi gubernii* (Baku, 1914), 34. On high mortality among Russians settling in other parts of the Empire and European colonial settlers elsewhere in the non-European world, see Thomas Barrett, "Lines of Uncertainty: The Frontiers of the North Caucasus," *SR* 54, no. 3 (1995): 583; Robert Hughes, *The Fatal Shore: The Epic of Australia's Founding* (New York, 1987), esp. 84–128; Edmund Sears Morgan, *American Slavery, American Freedom: the Ordeal of Colonial Virginia* (New York, 1975), 101; and Philip D. Curtin, *Death by Migration: Europe's Encounter with the Tropical World in the Nineteenth Century* (Cambridge, 1989).
14. *AKAK* vol. 10, doc. 293, p. 285; vol. 8, doc. 60, p. 82; GMIR f. 2, op. 7, d. 594, ll. 67, 70–71, 77.
15. There is little agreement among the sources regarding the specific number of fatalities in Topchi. However, all these statistics agree on high death rates and indicate a reduction in the mortality rate over time. GMIR f. 2, op. 8, d. 324, n.d., ll. 1–10b; d. 237, 1910, l. 43; f. 2, op. 7, d. 594, ll. 67, 70–71, 77; d. 597, l. 10; RGIA f. 383, op. 30, d. 149, 1832–39, ll. 680b–69; f. 381, op. 1, d. 23300, 1844; *AKAK* vol. 8, doc. 60, p. 82; SSC'SA f. 4, op. 2, d. 397, 1846–47, ll. 7–70b; and N. M. Leont'ev, "Dukhovnye khristiane sela Ivanovki, Geokchaiskogo u. Bakin. g.," *DKh* 4, no. 1 (1909): 18–19.

"malignant" climate, "swampy" land, "harmful water," and "disease-ridden place." As one Molokan petition lamented in 1835, the spread of "this fatal sickness" meant that "not even one person remained in a completely healthy state" and that "the collection of the harvest remains unfinished because [we] are simply unable to carry out the work as a result of the sickness."[16]

The unlucky settlers to Topchi only escaped their living nightmare by personally prostrating themselves before Viceroy M. S. Vorontsov in 1846 as he passed near the village. One Molokan author recounts the incident in dramatic terms.

> The entire community, both old and young, went out to the road to ask the Viceroy to grant them permission to relocate to a new place, with an easier climate. When Vorontsov rode up to them, the weather was rainy, and all the elders, wives and children who stood by the road on the steppe, fell down onto bended knee in the mud. They cried: "Your eminence, our father, have pity on us, we are all sick, we are dying from fever. We bury every day three, five, eight corpses. Move us to another climate."[17]

According to a journalist on the scene, in response to the sight of the destitute Russian settlers, Vorontsov declared: "Oh God, what horrors." He quickly granted them permission to move to an area in Tiflis province that the Molokans named Vorontsovka in honor of their savior.[18]

If the settlers in the southern and eastern regions suffered from heat, disease, and foul water, the Dukhobors who were exiled to Akhalkalaki district in Tiflis province between 1841 and 1845 suffered from long winters, deep snow, frosts, hail, and "rocky and mountainous soil." The land chosen for them was on a plateau 8,000 feet above sea level—a location known as the "Wet Mountains." Reporting in 1844 on their condition, one tsarist official found them "condemned to death by starvation" because at that elevation "not even barley grows and the snow does not recede until the end of May." The Dukhobors themselves complained frequently that they suffered "failed harvests because of the cold climate,"

16. SSC'SA f. 4, op. 2, d. 397, 1846–47, ll. 6–70b; RGIA f. 383, op. 30, d. 149, 1832–39, ll. 680b–690b, 71Bob–72; GMIR f. 2, op. 7, d. 597, 1835–40, l. 10; d. 596, ll. 124–27; d. 594, ll. 4–5; N. Kalashev, "Selenie Ivanovka, Lagichskogo uchastka, Geokchaiskogo uezda, Bakinskoi gubernii," SMOMPK, vol. 13 (Tiflis, 1892), otd. II, 238; and I. Ia. Orekhov, I. Ia. "Ocherki iz zhizni zakavkazskikh sektatorov," Kavkaz, no. 136 (June 17, 1878): 1. The Molokan village of Alty-Agach, located not far from Topchi, also suffered in its first few years of existence. See RGIA f. 381, op. 1, d. 23300, 1844, l. 10b; GMIR f. 2, op. 7, d. 597, ll. 4, 7–8; and S. I. Pokhilevich, "Selenie Alty-Agach, Shemakhinskogo uezda, Bakinskoi gubernii," SMOMPK, vol. 1 (Tiflis, 1881), 89–90.
17. GMIR f. 2, op. 8, d. 237, 1910, l. 43. For a different version of this story, although with the same basic outlines, see GMIR f. 2, op. 8, d. 324, ll. 1–2.
18. Orekhov, "Ocherki," no. 136, 1; SSC'SA f. 4, op. 2, d. 397, 1846–47, ll. 6–70b; and Leont'ev, "Dukhovnye khristiane," 18–19.

FIGURE 3. Mountains looking northeastward from the Delizhan Pass, Erevan province, c. 1897. From Esther Lancraft Hovey, "The Old Post-Road from Tiflis to Erivan," *National Geographic Magazine* 12, no. 8 (August 1901): 302.

large hail, and heavy rainfall, and that many families found themselves "in terrible need."[19]

In contrast, Molokan and Subbotnik migrants to Erevan province did not suffer such a tragic fate.[20] Erevan province more closely approximated the environmental conditions they knew from their former homelands. Also, by the mid-1840s, when migration to this region started, the authorities were more experienced in discerning what was necessary to ensure a successful settlement. After some settler input in the selection

19. RGIA f. 381, op. 1, d. 23300, 1844, ll. 1–10b; f. 1284, op. 200–1844, d. 19, ll. 2–20b; SSC'SA f. 244, op. 3, d. 100, 1869, ll. 20–200b, 42, 54–540b, 70; d. 42, 1863–70, ll. 20b–3; f. 239, op. 1, d. 85, 1850–57, ll. 1–10b; f. 222, op. 1, d. 6, 1847, l. 6; A. M. Argutinskii-Dolgorukov, "Borchalinskii uezd, Tiflisskoi gubernii v ekonomicheskom i kommercheskom otnosheniiakh," in *RTKE* (Tiflis, 1897), 41; "O russkikh," 127; Kh. A. Vermishev, "Ekonomicheskii byt gosudarstvennykh krest'ian v Akhaltsikhskom i Akhalkalakskom uezdakh, Tiflisskoi gubernii," in *MIEB*, vol. 3: 2 (Tiflis, 1886), 23, 41; Petr Nikolaevich Malov, *Dukhobortsy, ikh istoriia, zhizn' i bor'ba*, vol. 1 (Thrums, BC, 1948), 23–24; and S. A. Inikova, "Vzaimootnosheniia i khoziaistvenno-kul'turnye kontakty kavkazskikh dukhobortsev s mestnym naseleniem," in *Dukhobortsy and Molokane v Zakavkaz'e*, ed. V. I. Kozlov and A. P. Pavlenko (Moscow, 1992), 45.

20. RGIA f. 1268, op. 5, d. 359, 1851, ll. 80b–10; I. V. Dolzhenko, "Pervye russkie pereselentsy v Armenii (30–50-e gody XIX v.)," *VMU, Seriia IX, Istoriia* 29, no. 3 (May–June 1974): 58–61; N. D. Dingel'shtedt, *Zakavkazskie sektanty v ikh semeinom i religioznom bytu* (St. Petersburg, 1885), 1–3; and Liaister, "'Pryguny,'" 1–6.

of lands, authorities chose to place the incoming sectarians in six villages near Lake Gokcha, approximately 6,500 feet above sea level. The Erevan Molokans and Subbotniks found the soil conducive to grain production and pasturing and were able to recreate many of their traditional economic activities without enduring the death rates their coreligionists elsewhere did. One contemporary observer claimed, with some exaggeration, that the settlement region in Erevan province was "not a bit inferior to Swiss meadows" with their "thick layers of black earth," "fertile alpine meadows," and "perfect pastureland." The settlers found that "wheat, rice, barley, German wheat, potatoes . . . ripen here after all" and that, aside from the sometimes harsh winters, "the sectarians experience marvelous mountain air, perfect water, and a soft climate." Moreover, the Erevan settlers consciously chose the upper plateau in order not to be settled in the sweltering and unhealthy lowlands just to their south, which, despite long summers and their bounty of "grapes, rice, and cotton," promised similar traumas as had devastated their brethren to the east.[21] Still, sectarians in Erevan province did not entirely escape the difficulties of early settlement, suffering also from long winters, snow, a short growing season, and ferocious storms. It took them many years, even in these relatively good climatic circumstances, to establish their communities and begin productive work on their new lands.[22]

As these different examples indicate, the experiences of the initial settlement years, while often similar in harshness, varied temporally and geographically. Settlers arriving in Transcaucasia from the late 1840s onward tended to fare better than those who arrived in the 1830s or early 1840s.[23] Moreover, those located at middle to high altitudes generally managed better than those located closer to sea level. Settlers in Erevan or Elisavetpol provinces enjoyed better health in their early years than those in Baku or Tiflis provinces.[24]

CONFRONTING DISASTER: SHORT-TERM RESPONSES, ON-GOING PROBLEMS

The sectarian settlers took three types of immediate action to mitigate these difficult conditions.[25] They sent a flurry of petitions to state officials pleading for aid; they frequently moved within Transcaucasia, both

21. Liaister, "'Pryguny,'" 1–3; Dingel'shtedt, *Zakavkazskie sektanty*, 1–2; Dolzhenko, "Pervye," 58; idem, *Khoziaistvennyi i obshchestvennyi byt russkikh krest'ian vostochnoi Armenii (konets XIX–nachalo XX vv.)* (Erevan, 1985); 18–39; and "O russkikh," 128.
22. RGIA f. 384, op. 1, d. 1288, 1842–45, ll. 21, 300b, 34.
23. A. I. Serebriakov, "Sel'skoe khoziaistvo v Elisavetpol'skom uezde," *ZKOSKh*, no. 5/6 (1861): 101.
24. "O russkikh," 127.
25. RGIA f. 381, op. 1, d. 23300, 1844, l. 2.

legally and clandestinely, searching out more habitable locations; and they secured the right to return to the Russian interior by converting to Orthodoxy—or simply by leaving. While only a minority of the settlers chose conversion, their choice nonetheless reflects how the environmental impact of Transcaucasia, in tandem with tsarist laws, influenced the migrants' religious lives by causing many to switch official religious affiliation.

Destitute and sick, settlers demanded that state agents take measures to keep them alive and facilitate their resettlement. Such sectarian lobbying efforts did prompt officials to concern themselves with how to avoid such rates of mortality in the future, to make the settlement process less punitive, and perhaps even to elicit some benefit from their presence in the Transcaucasian colony.[26] Faced with immediate problems, tsarist officials provided the settlers with money, loans, and tax relief. They also rendered assistance by giving or loaning grain seed, livestock, agricultural implements and tools, houses and housing supplies, wood, and foodstuffs.[27] This short-term assistance reached such a level that, in 1844, one state administrator lamented the hemorrhaging of treasury funds necessary to feed the Dukhobors settled in the Wet Mountains.[28]

In addition to this interim support, state officials also strove to regularize the resettlement process for the long term. By the early 1840s, they began to consider more carefully factors such as climate, soil quality, access to safe water, and the location and quantity of the lands they would allot to the sectarians.[29] In 1846 and 1847, Viceroy Vorontsov founded the Commission for the Organization of Settlement in Transcaucasia to facilitate resettlement, and his administration also passed a series of laws that gave the migrants a host of work-related perquisites to help them survive the environment.[30] These actions on the part of the regional government did not always solve the problems, however, because local officials frequently ignored orders. Many, for instance, arbitrarily allotted the settlers less land than they were supposed to receive.[31]

To evade the travails of settlement in "the most God-forsaken places with unhealthy climates," the settlers also moved multiple times from vil-

26. RGIA f. 381, op. 1, d. 23300, 1844, ll. 20b–30b; f. 1268, op. 2, d. 533, 1847–48; f. 383, op. 30, d. 149, 1832–39, ll. 69–690b, 71Bob–72; GMIR f. 2, op. 7, d. 597, 1835–40, l. 10; d. 596, ll. 124–27; d. 594, ll. 4–5; and Orekhov, "Ocherki," no. 135, 2; no. 136, 1.

27. RGIA f. 1268, op. 1, d. 666, 1844–45; op. 2, d. 171, 1846, ll. 2–3; f. 1284, op. 200–1843, d. 15, l. 76; op. 196–1834, d. 71, ll. 1–10b; f. 379, op. 1, d. 1043, 1830–37, ll. 710b–72, 1380b–390b; SSC'SA f. 222, op. 1, d. 6, 1847, l. 3; f. 240, op. 2, d. 233, 1853–61, l. 165; GMIR f. 2, op. 7, d. 594, ll. 75–76; d. 596, ll. 113–16, 121; and Masalkin, "Kolonizatory," 2.

28. RGIA f. 381, op. 1, d. 23300, 1844, l. 10b.

29. Ibid., ll. 2–30b; RGIA f. 1268, op. 2, d. 533, 1847–48, ll. 1–20b, 11; f. 379, op. 1, d. 1043, 1830–37; and AKAK vol. 9:2, doc. 532, pp. 629–30.

30. "O russkikh," 127; RGIA f. 1268, op. 2, d. 533, 1847–48; d. 865, 1848–52, l. 30b; op. 6, d. 177, 1852, ll. 1–10b; and the discussion in chapter four.

31. GMIR f. 2, op. 7, d. 597, ll. 4–7.

lage to village within Transcaucasia before finally arriving at a place where they could survive.[32] Generally, they arrived in lowlands and then progressed up to mountain areas "where the land and climate were more suitable."[33] For instance, Molokans who settled in Dudakchi in 1832 moved after seven years to another location, Bazar-Chai, "because of a burning climate and insufficient amount of land." They relocated once again in 1840 when they suffered "failed grain harvests and extreme cold." They lived temporarily in Karabulagh and then in 1842 settled permanently in the village of Borisy, a full decade after they first stepped foot in the region.[34] Tsarist authorities were reluctant to permit such wanderings despite the unforgiving climate and the existence of legal provisions that sanctioned relocation under specific conditions. Even after numerous petitions, many sectarians remained—at least legally—locked in their designated points of settlement.[35]

The officials' decision to ignore the settlers' cries for relocation reflects the dominant negative perception of the sects of the day, and the partly punitive reasons for segregating them in Transcaucasia. As one administrator later lamented the settlers' initial treatment, the colonists suffered "from the lack of concern of the local powers, and the [authorities] gave the majority of the unhappy settlers as sacrifices to the location."[36] While most settlers did eventually gain official permission to resettle, those who were denied often took matters into their own hands, roaming Transcaucasia in search of a better site.[37] The migrants also attempted to mitigate the harsh ecological conditions through seasonal relocation—both legally and illegally—in an effort to take advantage of whatever paid work they could find. Most commonly, Russian migrants went to work as wage laborers in the fields of their indigenous neighbors, a strategy that saved many of them from suffering or death.[38]

32. "O russkikh," 127; Orekhov, "Ocherki," no. 135, 2; N. A. Abelov, "Ekonomicheskii byt gosudarstvennykh krest'ian Elisavetpol'skogo uezda Elisavetpol'skoi gubernii," MIEB, vol. 7 (Tiflis, 1887), 14, 21, 24; RGIA f. 1268, op. 1, d. 363, 1842; GMIR f. K1, op. 8, d. 470, l. 2; f. 2, op. 7, d. 597, l. 7; and Leont'ev, "Dukhovnye khristiane," 18–19.

33. One nineteenth-century commentator described this movement from lowlands to high in epic, essentializing terms: "The lowlands with their fevers and artificially irrigated fields in which ripen grapes, cotton, rice and maize, could not attract the attention of the Russian colonizer, who has been accustomed from the time of Riurik only to the old wooden plow." Masalkin, "Kolonizatory," 2.

34. SSC'SA f. 240, op. 1, d. 1428, 1865–67, l. 5. There are many examples of this initial mobility in Transcaucasia. See RGIA f. 1268, op. 2, d. 533, 1847–48, ll. 10b–2; AKAK vol. 10, doc. 293, p. 284; Abelov, "Elisavetpol'skogo uezda," 24; and "O russkikh," 128.

35. RGIA f. 1284, op. 200–1843, d. 15, l. 76; Argutinskii-Dolgorukov, "Borchalinskii uezd," 41; and "O russkikh," 127–28.

36. RGIA f. 381, op. 1, d. 23300, 1844, ll. 1–10b.

37. RGIA f. 1268, op. 2, d. 533, 1847–48, ll. 1–20b; f. 1284, op. 200–1843, d. 15, l. 76; GMIR f. 2, op. 7, d. 597, ll. 4, 10; Dolzhenko, "Pervye," 58; I. E. Petrov, "Seleniia Novo-Saratovka i Novo-Ivanovka Elisavetpol'skogo uezda," IKOIRGO 19, no. 1 (1907–1908): otd. 1, 226–27; and Kalashev, "Selenie Ivanovka," 238–41.

38. RGIA f. 1284, op. 200–1842, d. 476, ll. 2–20b, 7, 15, passim; f. 1268, op. 1, d. 433, 1843–

Movement within Transcaucasia proved a double-edged sword, however. On the one hand, it granted the settlers a potentially new lease on life. On the other hand, frequent relocation, often through a series of sites, exacerbated many of their economic problems by preventing them from setting down roots and beginning agricultural cultivation in earnest. Vorontsov himself complained that "running into the same discomforts in the new places of settlement, they sink into despondency, become unaccustomed to work, and give themselves up to vagrancy and dissolute behavior."[39] Moreover, the very prospect of relocation was itself the source of further traumas. One official noticed that, soon after settling in Alty-Agach, the Molokan community fractured into two groups. One concentrated on building an infrastructure—erecting houses, sowing fields, and accumulating grain stores—while the other demanded relocation and refused to do anything at all to set themselves up in the village. As a result, the relocation contingent suffered greater economic problems and higher rates of disease and death than did the other group.[40]

The settlers' final escape option was to return to the central Russian provinces. Conversion to Orthodoxy was the only lawful way open to sectarians in Transcaucasia to receive permission to go back to their homelands, and in its efforts to terminate dissenting faiths, the government offered generous terms for converts.[41] The environmental difficulties, combined with such legal incentives, proved an important motivation for sectarians to switch religious affiliation rather than to endure continued starvation and deprivation.[42] In fact, tsarist officials realized early in the settlement process that the hardships of life on the Transcaucasian frontier were more effective than missionary efforts in bringing the sectarians back to the "bosom" of Orthodoxy.[43] That many Dukhobor exiles from the Don Cossacks converted in order to be able to leave Transcau-

48, ll. 18–18ob; A. I. Serebriakov, "Sel'skoe khoziaistvo v Elisavetpol'skom uezde," ZKOSKh, no. 1/2 (1862): 52, 56; and the discussion in chapter five.

39. RGIA f. 1268, op. 2, d. 533, 1847–48, ll. 1–20b; f. 381, op. 1, d. 23300, 1844, l. 2; and AKAK vol. 10, doc. 293, p. 287.

40. GMIR f. 2, op. 7, d. 597, l. 7.

41. PSZ (2), vol. 5:2 (1830), no. 4010; vol. 22:2 (1847), no. 20889; RGIA f. 1284, op. 196–1835, d. 73; op. 196–1833, d. 33; f. 1268, op. 2, d. 279, 1846–47; f. 381, op. 1, d. 23279, 1844, ll. 6–8; op. 2, d. 2014, 1858; f. 383, op. 30, d. 149, 1832–39, ll. 67–670b; GMIR f. 2, op. 7, d. 594, ll. 34–35; and Nicholas B. Breyfogle, "Heretics and Colonizers: Religious Dissent and Russian Colonization of Transcaucasia" (Ph.D. diss., University of Pennsylvania, 1998), 284–89.

42. See for example, RGIA f. 1284, 196–1835, d. 73, l. 1; op. 196–1833, d. 33, esp. ll. 1–10b, 3–40b, 5–50b; f. 1268, op. 10, d. 156, 1861; f. 383, op. 30, d. 149, 1832–39, ll. 67–670b; f. 381, op. 1, d. 23279, 1844, ll. 2–20b; op. 2, d. 2014, 1858–59; GMIR f. 2, op. 7, d. 594, n.d., ll. 34–35, 67–68; AKAK vol. 8, doc. 60, p. 82; I. L. Segal', "Russkie poseliane v Elisavetpol'skoi gubernii (statistichesko-etnograficheskii ocherk)," Kavkaz, no. 43 (February 16, 1890): 3; and Breyfogle, "Heretics and Colonizers," 281.

43. RGIA f. 1268, op. 2, d. 279, 1846–47, ll. 1–2; "K voprosu o zakavkazskikh sektantakh," Kavkaz, no. 84 (April 18, 1881): 2; and Segal', "Russkie poseliane," no. 42, 3.

casia immediately—50 of the 266 arrivals took up Orthodoxy—emboldened the Chief Administrator of the Caucasus, I. F. Paskevich, to conclude in 1831 that "the climate of their present place of settlement exerts
a large influence on their conviction to leave behind their errors and
harmful heresy."[44]

Not unexpectedly, such environment-induced shifts in religious affiliation to Orthodoxy were not always permanent. The "religious remorse"
of the 1830 Dukhobor converts in Karabakh was permanent only for a
handful, once they had returned to the comforts of the central provinces.
When authorities realized that they had once again left the Orthodox
fold, they banished the recidivists back to Karabakh without right of return.[45] Moreover, despite all of the hardships of the frontier and the material benefits of conversion, only a minority of settlers chose conversion
and return. Thus, despite the substantial denominational switching practiced by the settlers, faith won out over material circumstances much
more than the government hoped.[46]

Whatever short-term actions the settlers took, however, the unfamiliar and threatening environmental conditions continued in succeeding
decades to bedevil those who remained in the region, albeit to a lesser
degree. The lack of usable water, wood, and soil posed a serious obstacle
for the sectarians that threatened their very survival and restricted the development of their economy.[47] Disease and illness, while less devastating
to the population than in the early years of settlement, remained an ongoing problem for both the settlers and their livestock, especially malaria
and other unspecified "fevers" that "gravely tell on the health of the Russian population."[48] Extreme temperatures routinely punished the
colonists, particularly in Lenkoran district, where the summers were "burning hot, dry, with a dry haze," and in the long, cold winters of the Wet

44. RGIA f. 379, op. 1, d. 1043, 1830–37, ll. 19–190b; f. 1284, op. 196–1835, d. 46, ll. 14–160b;
op. 195–1825, d. 61, ll. 211–13; *AKAK* vol. 7, doc. 415, p. 466. Since 58 of the settlers had died
by March of 1831, the 50 converts (45 in some sources) represented an even larger percentage
of the living population (approximately 25 percent). GMIR f. 2, op. 7, d. 596, n. d., l. 124.
45. GMIR f. 2, op. 7, d. 596, ll. 130–31; and d. 594, l. 5.
46. See RGIA f. 383, op. 4, d. 3212, 1841–43, ll. 64–65, 680b, 70–71; f. 1284, op. 200–1844, d.
19, ll. 2–3; f. 565, op. 4, d. 13676, 1842–45, l. 34; and f. 384, op. 4, d. 977, 1841.
47. S. Kolosov, "Russkie sektanty v Erivanskoi gubernii," *PKEG na 1902 g.* (Erevan, 1902): otd. IV,
151; *AKAK* vol. 10, doc. 293, p. 286; V. V. Vereshchagin, *Dukhobortsy i Molokane v Zakavkaz'e, Shiity v Karabakhe, Batchi i Oshumoedy v Srednei Azii, i Ober-Amergau v Gorakh Bavarii* (Moscow, 1900),
4; Serebriakov, "Sel'skoe khoziaistvo," (1861), 156; SSC'SA f. 244, op. 3, d. 100, 1869, ll. 20–210b,
54–540b, 70; and Vermishev, "Ekonomicheskii byt," 23.
48. "Ocherk sel'skogo," 34; SSC'SA f. 222, op. 1, d. 55, 1849; RGIA f. 1268, op. 2, d. 1021, 1848–
53, ll. 34–340b; f. 560, op. 26, d. 86, 1894, l. 43; Kalashev, "Selenie Ivanovka," 248–56; "Vliianie
malarii," 49–67; Kistenev, "Ekonomicheskii byt," 568; Argutinskii-Dolgorukov, "Borchalinskii
uezd," 93; Il'ia Zhabin, "Selenie Privol'noe, Bakinskoi gub., Lenkoranskogo uezda," in *SMOMPK*,
vol. 27 (Tiflis, 1900), otd. II, 43; *AKAK* vol. 10, doc. 293, p. 287; K. Gorskii, "Marazinskaia sel'skaia
shkola," *Kavkaz*, no. 130 (1871): 2; and "Khronika," *Kavkaz*, no. 212 (September 22, 1883): 1; no.
213 (September 23, 1883): 1; no. 224 (October 7, 1883): 1; and no. 234 (October 19, 1883): 1.

Mountains.[49] Settlers often found themselves and their crops battered by winds and hail (of potentially "Homeric" proportions), and the rain veered unhelpfully between extremes, causing floods and droughts.[50] The animals and insects of the region, especially locusts, mice, bears, and boars, often devoured crops.[51]

Together, these climatic, pathogenic, and animal adversaries caused the settlers extraordinary problems and transfigured their social and economic structures. On one level, these ecological realities had a negative effect on the "health and natural growth of the population." Such was the case in Lenkoran district, where the immigrant Russian population, as the "alien" entrants into a preexisting ecology, grew more slowly and suffered higher death rates than the neighboring Azerbaijani and Talysh communities.[52] On another level, these forces of nature resulted in sizable monetary losses and hindered them from establishing a viable economy. For example, the Russian population of Elisavetpol province in the 1880s lost an estimated 569,847 rubles because of environment-related disruptions to their economic activities.[53]

ADAPTING TO THE NEW ENVIRONMENT

Given all these challenges, Russian settlers found themselves with little choice but to modify their economic practices to conform to the demands that the environment of their adoptive homeland imposed on them. They changed the way they tilled the soil, planting different types of crops and, with the help of new agricultural technologies, cultivated them in new ways, and sold a greater percentage on the market. More significantly, without abandoning grain agriculture, they diversified their economic practices in order to avoid too great a reliance on the production of cereals and vegetables. They focused increasingly on animal hus-

49. Zhabin, "Privol'noe," 43; Gorskii, "Marazinskaia shkola," 2; Kistenev, "Ekonomicheskii byt," 568; "Ocherk sel'skogo," 34; Argutinskii-Dolgorukov, "Borchalinskii uezd," 93; SSC'SA f. 244, op. 3, d. 100, 1869, ll. 20–210b, 54–540b, 70; Vermishev, "Ekonomicheskii byt," 23; L. P. Zagurskii, "Poezdka v Akhaltsikhskii uezd v 1872 godu," ZKOIRGO, no. 8 (1873): art. 16, 74; Pokhilevich, "Selenie Alty-Agach," 91.
50. Segal', "Russkie poseliane," no. 41, 3; Zagurskii, "Poezdka," 74; SSC'SA f. 244, op. 3, d. 100, 1869, ll. 20–210b, 54–540b, 70; Vermishev, "Ekonomicheskii byt," 23; and Argutinskii-Dolgorukov, "Borchalinskii uezd," 107–8; Pokhilevich, "Selenie Alty-Agach," 90–91; "Sel. Slavianka," Kaspii 14, no. 100 (May 13, 1894): 3; and "Ocherk sel'skogo," 13.
51. Segal', "Russkie poseliane," no. 41, 3; I. Ikoteli, "Iz sela Slavianka, Elisavetpolsk. uezda (urozhai i polevyia myshi)," KSKh, no. 139 (September 5, 1896): 2378; RGIA f. 1268, op. 2, d. 171, 1846, ll. 2–3; Serebriakov, "Sel'skoe khoziaistvo," (1861), 155–56, 160.
52. Kistenev, "Ekonomicheskii byt," 568; "Ocherk sel'skogo," 34; and RGIA f. 1268, op. 2, d. 1021, 1848–53, ll. 34–340b.
53. Segal', "Russkie poseliane," no. 41, 3.

bandry, particularly sheep for the wool market, and also tried such nona-gricultural endeavors as the transportation trade and various artisanal and commercial ventures.[54] In the long term, these adaptations ensured survival and eventually even prosperity. To be sure, the sectarian settlers altered their economic practices reluctantly, remaining committed to grain agriculture whenever possible. Moreover, communities did not transform their economies in the same ways, varying along three axes. They diverged according to the specific location of settlement, especially altitude; the type of religious community; and the settlers' original location in the central provinces, which affected the differing economic practices that they brought with them.[55]

Diversified economies encompassing various agricultural and nonagricultural activities were characteristic of nineteenth-century Russian peasant society throughout the Empire, particularly in the borderland regions. In this respect, the variety of sectarian economic activities in the South Caucasus is not a great surprise, and they fit into the broader patterns of peasant subsistence. However, the settler example does represent a different economic structure in two ways. First, many of the economic endeavors they embraced, especially the transport trade, were specific to the South Caucasus. Second, and more important, in comparison to the other Russian peasants, for whom grain cultivation comprised the primary economic endeavor (despite forays into handicrafts and trade), a substantially larger percentage of sectarian households relied on nonagricultural activities and commercial livestock for the better part of their incomes, which in turn meant they were more frequently involved in market interactions. In this regard, the South Caucasian settlers were economically distinct from the majority of Russian peasants.[56]

Remaking Farming Practices

Since many of their former staple crops did not produce sufficient harvests in Transcaucasia, the colonists modified their agricultural activities to correspond as best as possible to the new environment. They concentrated on the grains and vegetables that did succeed, adopted local crops (or local variants of familiar crops), took up certain indigenous agricultural practices, and altered the timing of their sowing and harvesting to

54. See for example ibid.; Iamskov, *Environmental Conditions*, 3–4; Vermishev, "Ekonomicheskii byt," 1–284; Abelov, "Elisavetpol'skogo uezda," 1–140; and A. Kalantar, "Merinosy v Zakavkaz'e," *KSKh*, no. 206 (December 18, 1987): 839–41. On the diversification of peasant economic activity in general, see David Moon, *The Russian Peasantry, 1600–1930: The World the Peasants Made* (New York, 1999), 118–55.
55. Masalkin, "Kolonizatory," 3.
56. Moon, *Russian Peasantry*, 118–55, esp. 121 and 148; and idem, "Peasant Migration," 876, 893.

match the South Caucasian growing seasons. These changes were not one-time events, nor were they always successful, but they were part of an ongoing process of agricultural adaptation and experimentation. Indeed, as one observer wrote, after more than a generation of settlement in Elisavetpol district, "agriculture cannot yet establish itself and almost every year undergoes changes."[57]

Through trial and error, sectarians focused their attentions on familiar crops that would grow. Despite the relatively good quality of the land on which they were settled, the Molokans of Vorontsovka found that wheat became "drunk" as a result of a certain weed that was common in rainy years. "The grain taken from such fields . . . is almost always unsuitable for use. It produces the most extreme foolish effects, giddiness, and the loss of use of one's limbs." Moreover, wheat sown in the "lower and flat locations . . . topples over and does not produce ears." So the Molokans reoriented their agricultural activities to focus on cultivating oats, rye, flax, and root crops instead.[58] The Dukhobors of Akhalkalaki district found that, of the staple crops they knew, they could produce only barley because wheat and rye perished under the severe conditions.[59] Settlers in Elisavetpol district channeled their energies to planting flax and hemp for oil since sesame and palmcrist would not grow.[60]

Russian migrants also attempted to grow some of the grains, fruits, and vegetables favored by indigenous inhabitants, with mixed results depending on their settlement locations. Settlers in Elisavetpol district noticed that lands near Lake Gokcha and in the Kursk valley produced a greater harvest than what they were able to reap. Assuming that these disparities derived from the type of wheat being cultivated, the colonists purchased supplies of these grains to sow on their own lands in the hope of more abundant harvests. "But these experiments . . . were extremely unsuccessful. The wheat taken from the plain either froze or gave a scanty harvest of rye, and the Lake Gokcha sort was sterile."[61] For their part, the Vorontsovka Molokans attempted to set up orchards in their villages to grow native fruits. However, the climatic difficulties of their place of settlement—high elevation, winds, hail, late frosts—diminished the successes of their endeavors.[62]

In addition to changing the crops they used, Russian migrants also

57. Serebriakov, "Sel'skoe khoziaistvo," (1861), 156–57.
58. Orekhov, "Ocherki," no. 136, 2.
59. SSC'SA f. 244, op. 3, d. 100, 1869, l. 54.
60. Segal', "Russkie poseliane, no. 41, 3. See also Pokhilevich, "Selenie Alty-Agach," 92; and Serebriakov, "Sel'skoe khoziaistvo," (1861), 155–56
61. Serebriakov, "Sel'skoe khoziaistvo," (1861), 156–57.
62. Argutinskii-Dolgorukov, "Borchalinskii uezd," 40–41. See also SSC'SA f. 240, op. 1, d. 1429, 1865–67; and Pokhilevich, "Selenie Alty-Agach," 92.

tried to vary the way in which they sowed and harvested, again with uneven outcomes. Dukhobors from Efremovka in Akhalkalaki district described how they "tried to soften this climate by sowing seeds early, but
these efforts produced only straw." Their brethren in Kars territory embraced what they called "'Turkish" agricultural practices—"plow deeper,
sow earlier"—because the summer heat dried the top layers of soil, and
crops planted too late were subject to the effects of frosts in late August.[63]

Opting for Livestock

Many communities of settlers also began to focus more on livestock
breeding, particularly of sheep, cattle, and horses, but also including
such activities as beekeeping and fishing.[64] The varying ecologies of
Transcaucasia proved generally more suitable for animal husbandry,
long a staple activity of Transcaucasia's Muslim nomads as well as of the
settled Armenian and Georgian populations. Molokans and Dukhobors
from the Molochna region had developed extensive livestock-rearing enterprises (especially sheep) prior to their migration and they were able
to build upon these economic experiences in the South Caucasus.[65]
With increased livestock specialization came greater commercialization
(and substantial profits), as settlers produced not simply for their own
consumption but increasingly to sell in regional or even international
markets.

The nonconformist migrants initially turned to rearing livestock in response to the unproductive conditions for tilling the soil, but over the
decades this economic orientation became more a matter of capitalizing
on sizable profit opportunities, making many Dukhobors and Molokans
extremely wealthy.[66] In the early years after resettlement, as one observer
documented, the Akhalkalaki Dukhobors "complain: 'Grain does not
grow and frost kills everything,' . . . [which] forced them, whether they
wanted to or not, to change their economy and to take up livestock rearing." Similarly, one Dukhobor from Rodionovka explained that "given
our pitiable situation we familiarized ourselves with livestock ranching as
much as we could, and that, somehow, is our existence and economy."[67]

63. SSC'SA f. 244, op. 3, d. 100, 1869, l. 54; and Inikova, "Vzaimootnosheniia," 50.
64. On the relative importance of animal husbandry among Russian peasants in the empire's periphery, see Moon, "Peasant Migration," 876.
65. A. I. Klibanov, History of Religious Sectarianism in Russia (1860s–1917), ed. Stephen Dunn, trans.
Ethel Dunn (New York, 1982), 183; Anna Filibert, "Predislovie k stat'e 'Neskol'ko slov o molokanakh v Tavricheskoi gubernii,'" OZ, no. 6 (June 1870): 292–93; and John Staples, Cross-Cultural Encounters on the Ukrainian Steppe: Settling the Molochna Basin, 1783–1861 (Toronto, 2003),
69–71.
66. Segal', "Russkie poseliane," no. 41, 3; and George Woodcock and Ivan Avakumovic, The
Doukhobors (Toronto, 1968), 64.
67. Vermishev, "Ekonomicheskii byt," 18–50, 124; Malov, Dukhobortsy, 23–24; Inikova, "Vza-

In contrast, by the 1860s, Molokans in Elisavetpol district made a conscious choice to "concentrate all of their attention on [animal husbandry], so in harmony with local conditions, and make livestock rearing the foundation of their economy."[68]

Some settlers also reoriented their activities toward highly profitable beekeeping. In Vorontsovka, the Molokans developed an elaborate beekeeping business with many hives, cultivation of various types of nectarous plants for the bees, and an up-to-date library of beekeeping books and journals. When a new apiary system was demonstrated in these journals, the Molokans were quick to try it out, building frames in many different designs to see which would work best in their location.[69] By the late 1880s, the villages of Mikhailovka and Slavianka in Elisavetpol province kept as many as 1300 bee huts between them.[70]

When grain agriculture failed, settlers near lakes and rivers turned their attention to fishing.[71] Villagers from Rodionovka caught as many as 6,000 fish on one "good" fishing trip, and the Akhalkalaki Dukhobors together secured more than 25,000 pounds of trout each year from the district's rivers and lakes. Fishing became so important for their survival that they aggressively lobbied local officials both to expand their fishing rights and to protect them when threatened by other Transcaucasians laying claim to the water's bounty.[72]

Beyond Agriculture

In addition to restructuring their agriculture, settlers regularly abandoned agrarian pursuits altogether to escape an environment that they

---

imootnosheniia," 45; *AKAK* vol. 10, doc. 98, p. 123; Kalantar, "Merinosy," no. 206, 839–41; SSC'SA f. 244, op. 3, d. 100, 1869, ll. 20–21ob, 54–54ob; and Zagurskii, "Poezdka," 74. For the similar example of the Vorontsovka Molokans, see Orekhov, "Ocherki," no. 136, 2; A. D. Eritsov, "Ekonomicheskii byt gosudarstvennykh krest'ian Borchalinskogo uezda Tiflisskoi gubernii," in *MIEB*, vol. 7 (Tiflis, 1887), 367–534; and Argutinskii-Dolgorukov, "Borchalinskii uezd," 1–323. The settlers in Elisavetpol province provide other fruitful examples. See Serebriakov, "Sel'skoe khoziaistvo," (1861), 101 and (1862), 51; and A. Kalantar, "Merinosy v Zakavkaz'e," *KSKh*, no. 207 (December 25, 1897): 864.

68. Serebriakov, "Sel'skoe khoziaistvo," (1862), 16; Kalantar, "Merinosy," no. 206, 841 and no. 207, 864; Segal', "Russkie poseliane," no. 42, 3; Abelov, "Elisavetpol'skogo uezda," 74–80; D. Mikhailidis, "Iz sela Slavianki, Elisavetpol'skogo uezda," *KSKh*, no. 16 (March 31, 1894): 285–86; and Serebriakov (1862), 6.

69. Argutinskii-Dolgorukov, "Borchalinskii uezd," 40.

70. Segal', "Russkie poseliane," no. 41, 3; Masalkin, "Kolonizatory," 2; Serebriakov, "Sel'skoe khoziaistvo," (1862), 32; and S. Buniatov, "Pchelovodstvo russkikh pereselentsev Borchalinskogo uezda," *KSKh*, no. 138 (August 28, 1896): 2356–57.

71. SSC'SA f. 239, op. 1, d. 85, 1850–57, ll. 1–10b.

72. Vasilii Perevalenko, "Pis'mo iz Akhalkalaki (9 Apr. 1852 g.)," *ZV* (April 9, 1852): ch. neofitsial'naia, 79; Zagurskii, "Poezdka," 67; and SSC'SA f. 239, op. 1, d. 85, 1850–57. On Molokan and Subbotnik fishing enterprises, see SSC'SA f. 239, op. 1, d. 764, 1857; N. B., "Ozero Gokcha (iz vospominanii o zakavkazskom krae)," *Kavkaz*, no. 61 (1861): 328–30; P. Paul', "Iz sel. Elenovki, Erivanskoi gubernii (o vliianii russkikh na korennoe naselenie Novobaiazetskogo uezda)," *KSKh*, no. 169 (April 3, 1897): 230; Liaister, "'Pryguny,'"4; and "O russkikh," 127–28.

saw as dangerous and capricious. They branched out into many fields, becoming carters, artisans, owners of small industries, domestic servants, traders, wage laborers, and proprietors of summer retreats for the Russian colonial elite. In some villages, nonagricultural endeavors came to predominate: in Nikitino in 1857, for example, only 22 of 67 household heads (33 percent) gained their livelihood from agriculture.[73] These other activities ensured immediate survival and produced a more consistent and usually larger income over time. Indeed, as their economies began to stabilize and nonagricultural practices generated substantial enrichment, the settlers looked increasingly for other opportunities for their economic energies.

The most important of these shifts in economic practice was the colonists' entry into the transportation trade: carting freight and humans on their wagons and sleighs both within Transcaucasia and into Russia, Turkey, and Persia.[74] While the transport trade provided the majority of sectarian communities with a significant income, it made certain individuals extremely wealthy.[75] For some villages, work as carters was seasonal, accomplished in between the sowing and harvesting periods; for others, it became a more or less full-time endeavor for male members of the community. In Elenovka in Erevan province, "Each spring the household head hurries to sow the fields, and in the fall to harvest the crops, so that he can head off on the easy work of carting. The population uses this collateral occupation for two-thirds of the year, carrying out the carting of loads from Akstafa to Erevan and back."[76] In contrast, the Molokan villages of Golovino and Delizhan in Elisavetpol province were "exclusively occupied with [carting] because the land allotted to them is entirely unsuitable for cultivation."[77]

The settlers' entry into the transportation trade was greatly facilitated by a technological advantage in the style of wagons that they brought with them from Russia. In contrast to the two-wheeled *arba* that had predom-

73. V. I. Kozlov, ed., *Russkie starozhily Zakavkaz'ia: Molokane i Dukhobortsy* (Moscow, 1995), 78.
74. Abelov, "Elisavetpol'skogo uezda," 99; Serebriakov, "Sel'skoe khoziaistvo," (1861), 103; RGIA f. 1268, op. 2, d. 865, 1848–52, ll. 3–4; op. 9, d. 367a, 1857–58, l. 10b; SSC'SA f. 4, op. 2, d. 792, 1848–51, l. 820b; "Alty-Agach," *Kaspii* 14, no. 115 (June 1, 1894): 3; and D. I. Ismail-Zade, *Russkoe krest'ianstvo v Zakavkaz'e: 30-e gody XIX–nachalo XX v.* (Moscow, 1982), 78.
75. Vermishev, "Ekonomicheskii byt," 41.
76. Z. Nikitin, "Iz sel. Elenovki, Novobaiazetskogo uezda," *KSKh*, no. 66 (March 30, 1895): 1151–52. For similar patterns in neighboring Semenovka and Konstantinovka, see also Masalkin, "Kolonizatory," 3.
77. Serebriakov, "Sel'skoe khoziaistvo," (1861), 103. See also Zagurskii, "Poezdka," 74; SSC'SA f. 244, op. 3, d. 100, 1869, l. 70; Perevalenko, "Pis'mo," 79; V. P. Bochkarev, "Karsskaia oblast'," in *RTKE* (Tiflis, 1897), 369; Liaister, "'Pryguny,'" 18; Kozlov, ed., *Russkie starozhily*, 82; Argutinskii-Dolgorukov, "Borchalinskii uezd," 41; and A. G. Dekonskii, "Ekonomicheskii byt gosudarstvennykh krest'ian v Shushinskom i Dzhebrail'skom uezdakh, Elisavetpol'skoi gubernii," in *MIEB*, vol. 4: 1 (Tiflis, 1886), 232.

inated in the region prior to the settlers' arrival, the Russians moved
goods and people on a four-wheel, deep-bed, two-axle wagon originally
of German design. Although the large wagons were less maneuverable in
the mountain passes, they were more stable than the *arby* and able to
carry larger loads over longer distances. As a result, the Russian colonists
quickly found that they could take over a large part of the regional market for transporting goods and people.[78]

Carting work affected the gender and social structures of sectarian villages. The economic emphasis on conveyance, with large numbers of
men away on the road, left women responsible for traditionally male agricultural tasks.[79] Carting brought sectarian men into contact with the different rhythms of urban life and the distinct cultures and peoples in the
region, influences from which they inevitably brought back into their
home villages. Moreover, the younger generation often evinced little desire to work in the fields, preferring instead to make their living in the
more profitable and worldly carting trade.[80]

The sectarians' work as carters brought them significant fame and a
reputation in the region for their skill and reliability in transporting
goods. Reputedly, "local merchants preferred [them] to all other transporters."[81] As another observer noted, "Almost all of the Caucasus knows
the inhabitants of Vorontsovka as tireless carters. . . . In Vladikavkaz, Erevan, Aleksandropol, Kars, and Tiflis, one constantly can see the heavily
laden wagons of the Vorontsovka villagers, either conveying merchant
goods or supplying their abundant reserves of hay, oats, and potatoes to
the market."[82]

In addition to transport work, the sectarians also engaged in artisanal,
handicraft, industrial, and commercial ventures. As one commentator
declared, "Placed in an impossibly severe location, distanced from markets, they were required to produce everything themselves. . . . The present situation taught them all of the artisan trades."[83] Indeed, the settlers
worked as carpenters, woodcutters, haymakers, blacksmiths, masons, tai-

78. Segal', "Russkie poseliane," no. 40, 3; Serebriakov, "Sel'skoe khoziaistvo," (1861), 102; Zagurskii, "Poezdka," 73; Inikova, "Vzaimootnosheniia," 49; and Ismail-Zade, *Russkoe,* 78. Cossacks
in the North Caucasus also played vital roles in the transport trade but used the native *arba.*
Thomas Barrett, "Crossing Boundaries: The Trading Frontiers of the Terek Cossacks," in *Russia's
Orient: Imperial Borderlands and Peoples, 1700–1917,* ed. Daniel R. Brower and Edward J. Lazzerini
(Bloomington, 1997), 239–40.
79. Perevalenko, "Pis'mo," 79. Thomas Barrett notes a very similar phenomenon among the Terek
Cossacks. Since military responsibilities kept the men out of the villages for long stretches, women
took on more responsibilities and relatively greater social power. Barrett, *Edge of Empire,* 129–45.
80. Nikitin, "Iz sel. Elenovki," 1151–52.
81. Bochkarev, "Karsskaia oblast'," 368–69.
82. Argutinskii-Dolgorukov, "Borchalinskii uezd," 38–39; and Serebriakov, "Sel'skoe khoziaistvo,"
(1862), 56.
83. Vermishev, "Ekonomicheskii byt," 41.

lors, coopers, bakers, joiners, shoemakers, stove-makers, wheel-makers, and other skilled craftsmen.[84] They also built and managed water mills for oil and flour, brick and tile factories, and workshops to make plows, wagons, riding tackle, and even bicycles.[85] The village of Privol'noe in Lenkoran district, for instance, was involved in a wide spectrum of market-oriented manufacturing activities, including eleven tile factories, two mills for producing oil, and four water mills for grinding flour.[86]

The sectarians profited from their state-granted right to own commercial ventures, particularly shops, taverns, and postal stations. As Russian settlers, state officials preferentially allocated such contracts to them, and the sectarians either ran these undertakings themselves or sold the rights to their indigenous neighbors. The village of Karabulagh in Shusha district contained as many as twenty shops that the Molokans rented to their neighbors for "a significant profit."[87] Similarly, in 1856, the villagers of Elenovka petitioned the viceroy for permission to open a tavern in their village to sell drinks and supplies. The Subbotniks were eager to take advantage of the travelers who frequently came through their village because of its location along a primary road and designation as a postal station.[88]

The sectarians also supported themselves through two other nontraditional economic means: domestic service and the provision of holiday homes for tsarist elites settled in Transcaucasia's towns. Many Molokans and Subbotniks, particularly women and young girls, worked as domestic servants for tsarist bureaucrats and quickly monopolized the laundry business in Erevan. They went both permanently and seasonally to urban centers "where there exists a strong and constant demand for domestic servants in private homes."[89] Meanwhile, Konstantinovka near Lake Gokcha in Erevan province, like numerous other sectarian villages, served as a *dacha* location to which Russian administrators went every year to evade the "heat, dust and gnats" of summertime Erevan. The villagers rented part or all of their houses to officials on holiday, and moved into the shed or squeezed themselves into a corner of the hut. The administrators' annual escape to Konstantinovka prompted certain villagers to build separate two- or three-room houses specifically for the purpose of

84. "O russkikh," 127; Zhabin, "Privol'noe," 49–50; Serebriakov, "Sel'skoe khoziaistvo," (1861), 102; RGIA f. 1268, op. 9, d. 367a, 1857–58, l. 10b; op. 2, d. 865, 1848–52, ll. 3–40b; SSC'SA f. 4, op. 2, d. 792, 1848–51, ll. 82–820b; and B. "Ozero Gokcha," 330.
85. SSC'SA f. 4, op. 2, d. 629, 1847–52; and Serebriakov, "Sel'skoe khoziaistvo (1861), 170.
86. Zhabin, "Privol'noe," 50–51.
87. Dekonskii, "Ekonomicheskii byt," 232. See also SSC'SA f. 240, op. 2, d. 25, 1859–67.
88. SSC'SA f. 239, op. 1, d. 637, 1856–57, and the discussion in chapter four.
89. The quotation is from Kolosov, "Russkie sektanty," 154. See also B., "Ozero Gokcha," 330; Petr Egorov, "Zakavkazskaia dorozhnaia zapiski 1851 goda: doroga ot Tiflisa do Shemakhi i g. Elisavetpolia," RI, no. 218 (October 11, 1857): 903; and Vermishev, "Ekonomicheskii byt," 41.

renting to those officials who wanted more space or privacy. The sectarians' economy increasingly came to rely on this extra infusion of cash, as "the villagers of Konstantinovka waited with impatience [each year] for the officials to come from Erevan for the summer."[90]

Preserving the Economic Fabric

Ultimately, there were limits to the natural world's ability to shape and mold the settlers' socio-economic practices. Indeed, the colonists' response to inhospitable environmental conditions was also characterized by a determination to stick with their familiar economic ways when adaptation was not absolutely necessary.[91]

When the sectarians had some choice over their place of settlement—primarily in the case of Erevan province—they sought out those locations that most closely approximated the climatic and ecological characteristics of the Russian lands they had left behind. In such places, as A. F. Liaister put it, "the settler can immediately employ in his work all of his Great Russian agricultural inventory and systems of agriculture, nothing new is necessary to learn and there is no need to forget anything they have known before. Such is the nature of the Russian person, not being inclined to innovation."[92] Moreover, Russian ethnographers underscored that settlers' villages were constructed with similar housing styles to their former homes, and in a similar layout. Travelers to the sectarians' settlements found themselves "forgetting the thousands of kilometers they had traveled from central Russia" when they looked upon the very familiar scenes of the Russian villages.[93] Of course, reflections on the unchanging nature of peasant agriculture were a standard trope in educated Russian circles and symptomatic of their cultural constructions of the peasantry, and must be read critically. In parallel, such pronouncements also reflect an imperialist vision of Russian settlers bringing a fixed, superior civilization to the people there. Yet, as David Moon has shown, Russian peasant migrants throughout Eurasia did tend to choose regions where the environment differed as little as possible from their homes, and in this regard the South Caucasian sectarians were not unusual.[94]

Contemporary observers repeatedly noted how the Russian settlers remained attached to grain production and continued their loyalty to the

90. Masalkin, "Kolonizatory," 3; "O russkikh," 128; Kolosov, "Russkie sektanty," 148; Pokhilevich, "Selenie Alty-Agach," 90; James Bryce, *Transcaucasia and Ararat* (1896; repr. New York, 1970), 178; M. G., "Putevye zametki," *Kaspii* 2, no. 109 (October 8, 1882): 3.
91. Serebriakov, "Sel'skoe khoziaistvo," (1861), 101.
92. Liaister, "'Pryguny,'" 4; Segal', "Russkie poseliane," no. 40, 3; and Dingel'shtedt, *Zakavkazskie sektanty*, 2.
93. Liaister, "'Pryguny,'" 2.
94. Moon, "Peasant Migration," 874.

FIGURE 4. The village threshing floor at Elenovka, Erevan province, c. 1897. From Esther Lancraft Hovey, "The Old Post-Road from Tiflis to Erivan," *National Geographic Magazine* 12, no. 8 (August 1901): 308.

livestock and staple vegetables (such as cabbage, red beets, potatoes, and cucumbers) that they had brought with them.[95] Such was the case with the Akhalkalaki Dukhobors who, "despite conditions completely impossible for growing grain, . . . continue to sow barley and wheat in order to have 'their bread,' and in this way they carry out the cherished dream of every peasant."[96] Discussing the Pryguny community in Erevan province, Liaister noted that although many of their number underwent profound changes in their economic endeavors as a result of the unfamiliar climate, "the majority have remained as before—typical *khlebobory* [strugglers with grain], living on the land . . . and only dreaming of working the land."[97]

Moreover, settlers frequently held firm to agricultural practices that they had developed while in the Empire's central provinces. In livestock breeding, they continued traditional animal husbandry practices (with certain modifications) and did not appropriate the indigenous ways of look-

95. Abelov, "Elisavetpol'skogo uezda," 82; and Serebriakov, "Sel'skoe khozaiastvo," (1862), 5–10.
96. Vermishev, "Ekonomicheskii byt," 124. Elsewhere in Transcaucasia, see *AKAK* vol. 10, doc. 293, p. 287; Zhabin, "Privol'noe," 47–48; and Abelov, "Elisavetpol'skogo uezda, 80.
97. Liaister, "'Pryguny,'" 18. For similar sentiments, see also Masalkin, "Kolonizatory," 2.

ing after the livestock. Rather than a nomadic or semi-nomadic lifestyle, the Russians organized their livestock ranching along transhumant lines, pasturing near their villages or in stalls during cold weather. Russian settlers also tended to feed their livestock on hay or other food reserves during the winter months, rather than allow them to pasture freely, the most common practice among the indigenous population.[98]

MODIFYING THE ENVIRONMENT

The transformative influences between people and place in the South Caucasus were not solely unidirectional. The Russian migrants also left their mark on the region's environment in a perpetual, mutually reactive system. In their efforts to rebuild their economies in a new context and to tame and transform the hostile climate to their needs, they made incursions into Transcaucasia's preexisting ecology (particularly through infrastructure building and "species shifting").[99] And yet, the settlers' environmental impact in Transcaucasia was comparatively minor, subtle, and geographically restricted to locales proximate to the settlers' villages. Neither extensive nor long-lasting, the colonists' imprint did not enduringly change the South Caucasian environment.[100]

Infrastructure and Environment

The settlers occupied themselves with gaining access to water, cutting down trees to make way for fields and villages, building mills and industrial workshops, and carving out access roads from their new villages to markets and towns. In opening new paths through the mountains, the sectarians brought the imprint of humanity to lands that had previously felt only a light human touch.[101] By building dams and redirecting rivers to supply power to water mills, they flooded previously dry land, which affected both terrestrial and aquatic life.[102] When they dug irrigation ditches and laid pipes in order to bring water to their villages, they reshaped the contours of the landscape and redirected the flow of rivers to

98. Serebriakov, "Sel'skoe khozaiastvo," (1862), 16; Iamskov, *Environmental Conditions;* and Kalantar, "Merinosy," no. 207, 864.
99. The term "species shifting," defined as "the movement of alien organisms into ecosystems from which they were once absent," is taken from Cronon et al., "Becoming West," 11. On Russian peasant alterations of the Eurasian environment generally, see Moon, "Peasant Migration," 859–93.
100. In comparison, see Barrett, *Edge of Empire,* 57–83; Moon, "Agricultural Settlement"; and Crosby, *Ecological Imperialism.*
101. Bochkarev, "Karsskaia oblast'," 368–69; and Serebriakov, "Sel'skoe khoziaistvo," (1862), 39.
102. SSC'SA f. 4, op. 2, d. 629, 1847–52

suit their needs, depriving certain areas of water in order to saturate others.[103]

Deforestation was a widespread outcome of the settlers' arrival, although it was far less extensive than elsewhere in Russia or in other European colonial contexts, and it was often surpassed by indigenous tree cutting.[104] Sectarian wood felling tended to be localized and to radiate outward from a village center, although in some regions a substantial loss of wooded areas did directly affect the climate and fauna. In regions with low forest density, the settlers sometimes threatened to extinguish woodlands entirely, prompting state conservation efforts. Settlers cut down trees to make way for fields and pastureland; to use as fuel; to build their houses, barns, sheds, and fences; and to sell in money-making ventures. The village of Golovino in Elisavetpol district entered into an active lumber business in an effort to expand their economic foundation, selling wood in Erevan and producing significant deforestation. In fact, the Golovino villagers were so successful in their lumber enterprise that state officials intervened in an effort to make the profitable venture their own. In 1869, they took forest land that had previously been designated for Golovino use and declared it the property of the forestry commission in order to "bring significant revenues to the treasury."[105]

When Molokans first arrived to settle Alty-Agach in Shirvan district in 1835, they found a large forested area in which to build their new homes. Over the first few years, the sectarians denuded tracts of this woodland to make way for their village and agricultural fields, dramatically changing the preexisting bionetworks. These largely unsustainable activities brought on a wood shortage by the early 1860s, particularly after state agents stepped in to restrict cutting, in part for wood conservation and in part to ensure sufficient supplies of wood for the state's needs. Additionally, while the surrounding forest had earlier been home to a variety of animal species—among them deer, antelope (*dzheirany*), wild boar, bears, martens, foxes, and badgers—this biodiversity was substantially reduced, a process also exacerbated by settler hunting.[106] The woodcutting of settlers in Elisavetpol province had other significant effects on the local environment. The disappearance of tree cover on the hills increased soil erosion, which in turn exacerbated the migrants' problems with crop production and further pushed them to rely on livestock rearing. More-

103. SSC'SA f. 222, op. 1, d. 26, 1847–50, for example.
104. Barrett, *Edge of Empire*, 57–83; Moon, "Peasant Migration," 874; Sh-v., "Privol'noe," *Kaspii* 2, no. 79 (July 30, 1882), 2; and Michael Williams, "Ecology, imperialism, and deforestation," in *Ecology and Empire*, 169–84.
105. SSC'SA f. 240, op. 1, d. 290, 1859–62; and "O russkikh," 127. For Akhalkalaki Dukhobor deforestation for economic profit, see ORRGB f. 369, k. 45, d. 4, 1953, ll. 40–41.
106. SSC'SA f. 240, op. 1, d. 1024, 1863–65; and Pokhilevich, "Selenie Alty-Agach," 91–92.

over, contemporary observers blamed the sectarians' deforestation for a decrease in precipitation in the flatland areas around their villages, which in turn lowered water levels in nearby rivers and negatively affected harvests for all inhabitants.[107]

The settlers' mills and factories produced changes in the preexisting ecology. In one incident, the villagers of Elenovka constructed a water mill in their village with state assistance. The dam and canals that they built to collect water raised the level of the locality's primary river, the Zanga, altering its flow and velocity. They also created a new lake—albeit, because of the dam's poor construction, one that leaked—and used canals to add new river tributaries. In consequence, the postal road that ran near the river frequently became flooded and impassable. At the same time, the fields and meadows of two neighboring Armenian villages were inundated, leaving them unusable for the inhabitants.[108]

Similarly, colonist efforts to overcome problems of water supply also caused significant changes in the local ecology. Aided by government financing and planning, they constructed aqueducts, artificial lakes, and elaborate irrigation systems and rerouted and combined rivers, all of which altered the region's water dynamics. Their efforts at redirecting water flow placed greater strains on the region's water supplies and depleted aquifers. The villages (and state coffers) suffered the ongoing expenses of attaining water and building elaborate water conveyance systems.[109]

The stories of two villages in Baku province, Ivanovka and Marazy, demonstrate the effects of settler endeavors to solve serious water problems. Despite plentiful annual rainfall, the villagers of Ivanovka found themselves in a constant battle to obtain sufficient water because there were no rivers or lakes in the immediate vicinity of their settlement. In order to provide water for their animals, the villagers constructed ponds in the village that captured rain. For the human inhabitants, the closest source of potable water was three kilometers away, and villagers were required to load barrels onto wagons and cart them back and forth over the steep terrain. In times of drought, both humans and animals in Ivanovka obtained water from the nearest irrigation ditch. "Seeing that the population suffers from an insufficiency of water, which in the summer is hardly enough for the first-line needs of survival," the Baku governor oversaw the construction of an expensive aqueduct system that siphoned

107. Iamskov, *Environmental Conditions*, 4; and Serebriakov, "Sel'skoe khoziaistvo," (1861), 128–29.

108. SSC'SA f. 4, op. 2, d. 629, 1847–52, ll. 90b–10, 170b.

109. Kistenev, "Ekonomicheskii byt," 568; "Ocherk sel'skogo," 34; and RGIA f. 1268, op. 4, d. 196, 1850, l. 4. For comparison, on tsarist irrigation in Central Asia, see Muriel Joffe, "Autocracy, Capitalism and Empire: The Politics of Irrigation," *RR* 54, no. 3 (1995): 365–88.

FIGURE 5. Dukhobor women carrying water, early 1890s. British Columbia Archives G-02819, published with permission.

off water from the river Akhokh-chai for Ivanovka and transported it over a distance of more than twenty-five kilometers.[110]

From the moment of their settlement in Transcaucasia, the Molokans in Marazy complained to the administration about a drastic insufficiency of water.[111] They were initially required "to transport water in barrels for one and a half [kilometers] from the wells belonging to the nomads of the Marazy area."[112] Efforts on the part of tsarist officials beginning in the late 1840s to remedy the problem repeatedly resulted in failure. Initially, the viceroy ordered that the Molokans themselves be made re-

110. Kalashev, "Selenie Ivanovka," 247–48; and M. G., "Putevye," 3. Securing a sufficient quantity of water also represented a vexing problem for the settlers of the aptly named Sukhoi Fontan (Dry Fountain) (Erevan province) who had been "settled in a waterless desert." Kolosov, "Russkie sektanty," 151.
111. SSC'SA f. 4, op. 2, d. 406, 1846–57; d. 1953, 1846–57; f. 222, op. 1, d. 26, 1847–50; and Gorskii, "Marazinskaia shkola," 2.
112. SSC'SA f. 222, op. 1, d. 26, 1847–50, l. 20b.

sponsible for searching out and drilling new artesian wells, but this tactic did not work because even "when the instruments were given to them, they did not have any understanding whatsoever of the arts of water supply."[113] Convinced that the Molokans would not be able to resolve the problem themselves, local officials contracted a series of artisans and engineers—initially a contingent of Persians, then Azerbaijanis, then Greeks from Turkey—each of whom failed to bring water to the village. Finally, a second Azerbaijani work crew solved the problem, ending the costly comedy of errors.

State agents, Molokans, and contractors toiled over many years to erect an aqueduct from distant water springs (as far as seven kilometers from the village) that would be channeled together into a stone fountain in the middle of Marazy. On the second attempt, the watercourse included over 20,000 pipes, extensive ditches, and multiple support structures. When this effort proved fruitless and Marazy's fountain remained dry, they attempted to augment the volume of flowing water by adding other springs via thousands of new pipes and a series of land bridges to support them. However, these later additions were placed in parts of the foothills where waters from the heavy autumn rains and the spring thaw flooded the terrain and buffeted the piping, requiring it to be repaired annually. Moreover, while the plan called for the pipes to travel underground through a mountain shortcut, the artisans found themselves required to circumnavigate the mountain on the outside, thereby greatly increasing the amount of piping necessary for the job. After a number of years, water finally flowed into Marazy, but with success came other problems. The village's fountain and five stone collecting troughs, built many years earlier, were too small to handle the quantity of water then running into the village. The water spilled out from the fountain, producing a sea of mud all around it and "a little lake not far away. . . . In the lake, one can water livestock, but it is unsuitable for the village and in this way the majority of the water is lost without any benefit for the village."[114]

"Species Shifting"

The settlers' importation of organisms new to the region affected Transcaucasia's ecological structures through three paths: the Russian cultivation of imported plants and animals; the adoption by Transcaucasian inhabitants of the previously alien species for their own agricultural use; and both planned and unplanned interbreeding of livestock. However, despite certain immediate and palpable consequences, the shifting of or-

113. SSC'SA f. 4, op. 2, d. 1953, 1846–57, l. 10b.
114. SSC'SA f. 222, op. 1, d. 26, 1847–50, l. 590b.

ganisms to Transcaucasia created change in the region's ecosystems only on a relatively restricted scale. In their new context, the "Russian" organisms had difficulties surviving and were often assimilated into the mass of the existing gene pool. Since these animals and plants were domesticated and consciously cultivated, they did not, as far as the sources indicate, multiply outside of human control.

The sectarians transported a series of vegetables and grains that had not been cultivated to any significant degree in the region before their arrival, introduced different varieties of already existing crops (such as wheat and flax), and brought a variety of alien animal species and breeds. Imported plants and animals placed new types of demands on the terrain, and by bringing under cultivation land that had previously grown wild, Russian settlers also displaced pre-existing wild plants with newly imported domesticated ones. Incoming animals expanded the region's biodiversity and altered the gene pool of existing domesticated breeds, usually through intentional interbreeding.[115]

Of equal importance to Transcaucasia's ecological structures was the way in which indigenous communities in the region also began, in small measure, to domesticate and cultivate "Russian" vegetables, grains, and livestock. Contemporaries noted how potatoes, beets, carrots, cabbage, and wintercress all became part of the repertoire of vegetables cultivated by Armenians and Azerbaijanis in Elisavetpol province. Russian observers considered this spread of "Russian" vegetables and crops to be a symbol of Russia's civilizing of the region, reflecting their assumption that Russian vegetables were themselves somehow superior to the varieties that the native peoples had traditionally grown.[116]

The story of the merino sheep that the Dukhobors brought into Transcaucasia in the early 1840s exemplifies the nature of the sectarians' ecological impact on the South Caucasus. In New Russia, the Dukhobors had become accustomed to breeding the fine-fleeced merino (or "Spanish") variety of sheep. Certain of them continued to do so in the South Caucasus, particularly the Dukhobors in Elisavetpol province, who took to sheep-rearing with great determination. In comparison with the other breeds found in Transcaucasia, merino sheep produced a finer quality of wool—although in lesser quantities—which fetched a higher price on

115. Argutinskii-Dolgorukov, "Borchalinskii uezd," 93; "O russkikh," 127; Segal', "Russkie poseliane," no. 40, 3; Serebriakov, "Sel'skoe khoziaistvo," (1861), 159–60; and (1862), 5–6; RGIA f. 932, op. 1, d. 83, n.d., ll. 5aob–5bob; SSC'SA f. 4, op. 2, d. 792, 1848–51, l. 82; and AKAK vol. 12:1 (1893), doc. 18, p. 37.

116. Segal', "Russkie poseliane," no. 40, 3; and Serebriakov, "Sel'skoe khoziaistvo," (1861), 160; and (1862), 5–6. See also Kolosov, "Russkie sektanty," 151; Petrov, "Seleniia," 247; Inikova, "Vzaimootnosheniia," 49; and N. I. Grigulevich, "Osnovnye komponenty pitaniia russkikh starozhilov, azerbaidzhantsev i armian," in Dukhobortsy i Molokane, 60–88.

the market. When Viceroy Vorontsov became actively interested in developing the sheep-farming business in Transcaucasia in the 1840s and 1850s, Russian state officials consciously increased the number of merino sheep through a special commission.[117]

The settlers' neighbors, particularly Armenians, "initially looked upon the new breed highly skeptically, but later, convinced by the breed's profitability and advantageousness, they so valued its quality that in the village of Chardakhlu, for example, they completely parted with the indigenous breed and began rearing only the merino sheep." The Dukhobor practice of hiring local residents to shepherd their flocks further spread the merinos into the herds of the non-Russian Transcaucasians by demonstrating their potential for profit up close. At the same time, pasturing different varieties of sheep together also facilitated the process of natural interbreeding and thereby transformed the gene pool of the region's sheep.[118]

In addition to such unintentional mixing, planned crossbreeding by settlers, local sheep herders, and Vorontsov's special commission produced marked consequences. They strove to engineer sheep with wool whose quality would approach that of the merino and would be both sturdy enough to survive the region's conditions and better adapted to the traditional practices of sheep-rearing that Armenians and Muslims practiced in the region.[119] In the estimation of one contemporary analyst, "The mixing of the Spanish variety with the indigenous variety of sheep has formed a mixed breed that presents in middle degrees the characteristics of its parents. The wool is longer than the Spanish variety and finer than the indigenous breed. In durability, the mixed-blood sheep also has a bit of both parents. The settlers are completely satisfied with this mixed sheep."[120] The tsarist state was also actively involved in such genetic engineering. In 1848, Viceroy Vorontsov had a hundred female sheep and seven rams transported from New Russia to Transcaucasia in order to form a new breed that would be the foundation of active wool production in the region. The imported sheep were interbred with the indigenous variety at a special breeding center near Tiflis.[121]

The settler-imported Cherkess cows similarly affected the region's biodiversity.[122] Characterized by their larger size and gray color, these cows

117. Kalantar, "Merinosy," no. 206, 839–41 and no. 207, 864; Segal', "Russkie poseliane," no. 42, 3; Mikhailidis, "Iz sela," 285–86; Vereshchagin, *Dukhobortsy i Molokane*, 20; *AKAK* vol. 10, p. 835; and Abelov, "Elisavetpol'skogo uezda," 93.
118. Kalantar, "Merinosy," no. 206, 839 and no. 207, 865–66; and Mikhailidis, "Iz sela," 285–86.
119. Abelov, "Elisavetpol'skogo uezda," 93.
120. Serebriakov, "Sel'skoe khoziaistvo," (1862), 27.
121. Kalantar, "Merinosy," no. 206, 839–40.
122. On similar processes with horses, see Zagurskii, "Poezdka," 74.

were known for their relatively higher milk production (albeit with lower fat content), and the bulls for their great strength and stamina. Since Cherkess cattle required greater care and attention than local breeds, settlers embarked on a project of interbreeding with local varieties, introducing Cherkess genetic characteristics into the region. The colonists found that combining the bull of the indigenous varieties with the Cherkess female produced a mixed breed offspring with the durability of the father and the height of the mother. As A. I. Serebriakov noted, "The latter quality is extremely important to the settlers because they cultivate livestock not only for work but also to sell as meat."[123]

Despite their significant environmental impact, grains, vegetables, and even animals introduced by the Russians often experienced difficulties surviving, let alone flourishing, in the unfamiliar climate of Transcaucasia. Even with their interbreeding efforts, the Dukhobors' merino sheep proved to be susceptible to temperature extremes, suffered frequently from various diseases endemic to the region, and required a great deal more care, supervision, and expense to look after than did other types of sheep. Moreover, the wool of merino sheep could be shorn only once a year, as opposed to twice in the case of the indigenous breeds, thereby reducing its profitability despite the higher price per pound. Russian efforts to rear merino sheep also foundered on an absence of markets for their product. While the cheaper, lower quality wool would be bought by any number of local consumers, the market for merino wool was more restricted and often found only abroad. The costs of transport, to England for example, made the farming of this type of sheep in the South Caucasus less tenable.[124]

As a result of these and other impediments, the numbers of animals and plants that the Russians brought to Transcaucasia dwindled over time. Settlers frequently turned their attention to local varieties of grains, vegetables, and livestock. The majority of Russian colonists came to use one of the indigenous varieties of sheep, with only a select few retaining an allegiance to the merino variety they had imported. Thus, Dukhobors settled in Akhalkalaki district abandoned their merino sheep in favor of indigenous breeds. Only their brethren in Elisavetpol district remained committed to this strain. By 1853, Vorontsov's breeding center was closed down and the remaining merino sheep were given to the Elisavetpol Dukhobors.[125]

123. Serebriakov, "Sel'skoe khoziaistvo," (1862), 15–16; Abelov, "Elisavetpol'skogo uezda," 90–91; and Segal', "Russkie poseliane," no. 42, 3.
124. Kalantar, "Merinosy," no. 206, 840; Abelov, "Elisavetpol'skogo uezda," 93; Serebriakov, "Sel'skoe khoziaistvo," (1862), 18–19, 25–27; and Zagurskii, "Poezdka," 70.
125. Kalantar, "Merinosy," no. 206, 839–41; Serebriakov, "Sel'skoe khoziaistvo," (1862), 25–27. On Cherkess cattle, see ibid., 15–16.

Moreover, many natives who incorporated Russian grains, vegetables or livestock into their agricultural practices later abandoned them in favor of more traditional and reliable plants and animals. Soon after making a transition to merino sheep, many of the Caucasian sheep herders encountered the same difficulties in rearing the merino in Transcaucasia as the Russians.[126] In addition, merino sheep never entirely took hold among the indigenous population because their meat was less palatable than the local varieties and therefore brought a lower price.[127] Similarly, "Russian" crops and vegetables never came to take on the importance in indigenous agricultural practices that they did for the Russian settlers.[128]

The lasting impact of interbreeding was also constrained because of the relatively small number of alien animals compared to the native ones. Over time, as a result of an absence of further infusions of nonnative species, the genetic characteristics of sheep and cattle brought from Russia tended to be drowned out. For instance, after the first burst of merino sheep in the region in the 1840s and 1850s, no new merino sheep were introduced in the area. For those merino sheep that were interbred with other breeds, the mixed bloodlines caused alterations in the merino wool and body structure. The quantity and quality of wool on the imported merino sheep deteriorated and decreased. Folds and wrinkles on the sheep's body that had been a prominent characteristic of the sheep when they first arrived began quickly to smooth out. "Perfect flocks of merino sheep, strong of skin and productive in their wool" rapidly disappeared. Similarly, mixed breeding with other breeds of sheep resulted in animals that produced fifteen pounds of wool per head as opposed to thirty pounds of wool from the purebred animal.[129]

LAND OF OPPORTUNITY

The present condition of the settlers is one that one can . . . consider to be fairly prosperous. The disarray that they endured in the earlier times from long periods of not being allotted land, and from settlement in places that were unsuitable and unhealthy, have now stopped. Some of them swell with prosperity and work in different kinds of industry, in addition to agriculture.[130]

126. These difficulties in acclimatizing the merino sheep to the region were increased by the very different approaches to sheep herding carried out by the indigenous inhabitants (especially the nomadic Muslims) in comparison with the Russian settlers: nomadic pasturing and open field grazing versus transhumant livestock herding with winter pens and feeding.

127. Serebriakov, "Sel'skoe khoziaistvo," (1862), 26–27.

128. Abelov, "Elisavetpol'skogo uezda," 83.

129. Mikhailidis, "Iz sela," 285–86; Kalantar, "Merinosy," no. 207, 864; Serebriakov, "Sel'skoe khoziaistvo," (1862), 25–26; and Zagurskii, "Poezdka," 70.

130. SSC'SA f. 4, op. 2, d. 792, 1848–51, ll. 81–81ob.

> The richest of the settlers in Transcaucasia are without argument
> the sectarians.[131]

The environment that had caused the Russian colonists so much pain and suffering at the outset ultimately became the context for economic opportunity. Gaining steadily from the 1850s onwards, and certainly by the 1870s, the majority of sectarian communities attained extraordinary economic success and, with it, an enviable standard of living.[132] The levels of wealth varied from one village to another, with some settlements remaining relatively poor, and their communities became increasingly socially stratified. Nonetheless, the settlers began to live very well overall and, for Russian peasants, in relative luxury. Three factors were especially important for the sectarians' economic success: their adaptations to the environment, the opportunities offered on the frontier (particularly through government contracts), and the socio-religious characteristics of their communities. Of these, the first two were more important for sectarian enrichment, and only in tandem with the influences and possibilities of the "periphery" did their religious characteristics help generate prosperity.

Nineteenth-century statisticians and bureaucrats, as well as Soviet-era historians, meticulously documented the sectarians' burgeoning wealth, and some of these statistics are worth citing to indicate the degree of the settlers' enrichment.[133] A. I. Klibanov, a leading Soviet historian of the sectarians, concluded from 1899 statistics that the Dukhobors of Akhalkalaki district, while comprising only sixteen percent of the population, enjoyed 35 percent of the land, 20 percent of the cattle, 43 percent of the sheep and goats, and 70 percent of the horses. Whereas average landholding in the district was 2.32 *desiatiny* per soul, each Dukhobor held 5.07.[134] The wealth of certain settler communities was evident in their vast livestock holdings. As early as 1862, the village of Slavianka, with a population of 240 families, possessed 420 horses, 2,045 cattle and 5,116 sheep (of which 1,100 were merino). By the late 1880s, the Slavianka commune's herds included as many as 40,000 merino sheep, and the annual revenue from their wool-producing efforts reached as high as

131. Masalakin, "Kolonizatory," 2–3.
132. Orekhov, "Ocherki," no. 135, 1; Kistenev, "Ekonomicheskii byt," 551; Liaister, "'Pryguny,'" 1–2, 18; Serebriakov, "Sel'skoe khoziaistvo," (1862), 51; Mikhailidis, "Iz sela Slavianki," *KSKh*, no. 5 (January 13, 1894), 88–89; and RGIA f. 1268, op. 10, d. 170, 1860, ll. 150b–16.
133. For full information, see Segal', "Russkie poseliane," nos. 40, 41, 42, and 43: 3; Orekhov, "Ocherki," nos. 135, 136, 143, 145: 1–2; Klibanov, *History*, 105–225; Dolzhenko, *Khoziaistvennyi*, esp. 40–106; Ismail-Zade, *Russkoe*, 64–88; and the detailed economic statistics found in *MIEB* and *RTKE*.
134. Klibanov, *History*, 113.

40,000 rubles.[135] The Dukhobor settlers collected a communal savings fund that may have reached a million rubles. While many Subbotnik and Molokan villagers had tens of thousands of rubles in savings, certain Baku Molokans became individual millionaires from various trade, manufacturing, and transport enterprises, as well as from involvement in the burgeoning oil industry.[136]

Visible signs of the settlers' wealth and economic achievements emerged in the appearance of their villages. As one source recounts, in the Molokan-Subbotnik villages of Konstantinovka and Elenovka, "crooked peasant huts became stone houses, stone and sod roofs became wood and metal."[137] Similarly, an observer in 1897 noted that in Molokan Vorontsovka "small huts . . . are quickly replaced with beautiful one- and two-story houses with large windows and decorated with balconies and other trappings of urban life. The architecture of the houses, the mass of shops, the lively movement on the streets, and in particular the internal furnishings of the houses, make one forget that one is in a village with 272 households, more than 100 [kilometers] from the nearest city."[138]

The sectarians' expanding wealth became apparent in growing social stratification, leading to cleavages within their communities.[139] Some villagers became large landowners and others profitably rented state-owned land as a commercial agricultural venture.[140] The wealth of some villagers was also visible in the employment of hired hands, usually non-Russians. Paid laborers allowed the settlers to focus their attention on other trade and industrial affairs that were less physically burdensome and more profitable.[141] A number of well-off settlers had such large cash stores that they were constantly in search of new investment opportunities and commercial ventures.[142]

The colonists' growing economic strength is also shown by the ap-

135. Orekhov, "Ocherki," no. 136, 2; Masalkin, "Kolonizatory," 2–3; Serebriakov, "Sel'skoe khoziaistvo," (1862), 51–52; Kalantar, "Merinosy," no. 207, 864; Mikhailidis, "Iz sela," (March 31, 1894), 285–86; and GARF f. 102, op. 3, 1895, d. 1053, ch. 1, l. 185.

136. Samed-bek Mekhmandarov, "V molel'ne u dukhovnykh (prygunov)," Kaspii 3, no. 109 (September 25, 1883): 4; Kaspii 2, no. 59 (May 30, 1882): 2; and no. 76 (July 23, 1882): 1; RGIA f. 1287, op. 38, d. 3035, 1895–1907, ll. 50b–6; GARF f. 102, 3 d-vo, op. 1885, d. 59, ch. 37, ll. 2–20b; and GMIR f. 2, op. 8, d. 237, 1910, ll. 45–46.

137. Masalkin, "Kolonizatory," 3. The same changes were also witnessed elsewhere, see Orekhov, "Ocherki," no. 136, 1; and Vermishev, "Ekonomicheskii byt," 41.

138. Arguitinskii-Dolgorukov, "Borchalinskii uezd," 38. Translation is from Klibanov, History, 198. See also figure 15 in chapter 6.

139. See, for example, Arguitinskii-Dolgorukov, "Borchalinskii uezd," 39; Klibanov, History, 125–40; and A. I. Masalkin, "K istorii zakavkazskikh sektantov: I. Molokane," Kavkaz, no. 306 (November 18, 1893): 2–3.

140. SSC'SA f. 240, op. 1, d. 964, 1863–67. Such was also the case of the village of Vorontsovka, which was able by degrees to buy 14,000 desiatiny of land from surrounding nobles.

141. Arguitinskii-Dolgorukov, "Borchalinskii uezd," 39; SSC'SA f. 4, op. 2, d. 629, 1847–52; and Mekhmandarov, "V molel'ne," 4.

142. See the case of Samodurov in SSC'SA f. 4, op. 2, d. 1010, 1849.

pearance of mechanized agricultural tools to aid in developing market-oriented grain production. They either imported or themselves constructed different types of modern plows built on international designs. Simultaneously, they began to incorporate mechanical harvesters, threshers, sorters—modern machinery that was only just beginning to appear in peasant villages in other parts of the Empire. In 1897, A. M. Argutinskii-Dolgorukov noted that of the Vorontsovka Molokans:

> The working of the fields is carried out here almost exclusively with improved equipment. At a time when many villages still plow with the ancient wooden plows, in Vorontsovka there are as many as 160 plows of the Guenier, Howard and Ransolls systems, around ten threshers with horse-drawn carts, a great many cornhuskers and sorters, hayers, harvesting machines, and much else which other villages cannot expect to have for decades. Recently in Vorontsovka there have appeared four shops issuing on the spot plows with improved systems. Vorontsovka supplies many villages, even distant ones, with these plows.[143]

Another sign of the increasing Vorontsovka prosperity was the many subscriptions to a variety of newspapers, journals, and professional periodicals dealing with agricultural practices, tools, and machines.[144]

The sectarians' enrichment was so dramatic that it demands explanation. The relationship that developed between the settlers and their new environment helped to bring about this shift from destitution to riches. Innovation was rewarded, and the imperative to change economic practices in the face of otherwise dire consequences turned out to be a long-term blessing. Those settlers who embraced, however involuntarily, new forms of livelihood—particularly the rearing of livestock; the transportation trade; and the growth of industrial, artisanal, and trade activities—and who began to specialize and become involved in market relations were, unsurprisingly, the ones who prospered. Thus, certain villages found themselves able to build expansively and rapidly; others, while not poor, were unable to move beyond the confines that a reliance on crop agriculture placed on them.[145]

The source of the sectarians' success can also be found in the opportunities and economic possibilities that the South Caucasus provided them as a borderland in the Russian Empire. As "Russian" colonists in a Russian imperial holding, the sectarians received higher levels of state as-

---

143. Argutinskii-Dolgorukov, "Borchalinskii uezd," 99–100. Translation is from Klibanov, *History*, 197–98.
144. Argutinskii-Dolgorukov, "Borchalinskii uezd," 39–40.
145. Masalkin, "Kolonizatory," 2; Argutinskii-Dolgorukov, "Borchalinskii uezd," 39; and M. G., "Putevye," 2.

sistance: more land than their non-Russian neighbors and than they could have had in black-earth provinces.[146] The imperial presence of Russian administrators and military personnel in the region's urban centers generated an immediate demand for the settlers' goods and services. These officials preferred to consume their traditional foods and the sectarians became the obvious providers of such "Russian" vegetables, grains, and meats.[147] Likewise, the appearance of Russian elites created a demand for domestic servants and summer retreats, which Molokans, Subbotniks, and Dukhobors fulfilled very profitably. The settlers were also paid handsomely for other services, such as providing horses, beds, and board for traveling administrators or housing postal stations in their villages. Tsarism's various wars in the region provided substantial economic opportunities for the settlers. In particular, participation in the Russo-Turkish War of 1877–78 produced enormous wealth for the sectarians through the fulfillment of military contracts.[148]

The migrants also opportunistically filled certain niches in the local economic structures, often exploiting the advantage of different types of technology available to them from Russia or abroad, such as the example of the carts, already mentioned. Transcaucasia apparently suffered from a dearth of mills and brick factories, and Molokans and Subbotniks regularly stepped in to fill the manufacturing void.[149] By the end of the nineteenth century, the Molokans of Vorontsovka operated four separate workshops that made plows, which peasants in the region eagerly purchased because of their modern, international design; their durability; and the ease with which they could be brought back to Vorontsovka for repairs. Moreover, the Vorontsovka blacksmiths had introduced certain alterations to the standard designs in order to accommodate the region's soil and topographical peculiarities. Vorontsovka metalworkers also took advantage of their skills to manufacture Swift-style bicycles that were sold in Tiflis.[150]

The settlers' success depended also on cultural and religious teachings that embraced work, eschewed a profligate or wasteful lifestyle, and espoused sobriety and mutual self-help. Molokans, Dukhobors, and Subbotniks—each in their own way—had socio-cultural and religious conceptions of labor that helped to fuel their economic achievements and allowed them to take advantage of the opportunities presented them in

146. Klibanov, *History*, 182.
147. Argutinskii-Dolgorukov, "Borchalinskii uezd," 93; and Segal', "Russkie poseliane" no. 41, 3.
148. See chapter four and Nicholas B. Breyfogle, "Caught in the Crossfire? Russian Sectarians in the Caucasian Theater of War, 1853–56 and 1877–78," *Kritika* 2, no. 4 (2001): esp. 733–36.
149. SSC'SA f. 4, op. 2, d. 1010, 1849; d. 629, 1847–52; RGIA f. 1268, op. 9, d. 367a, 1857–58, l. 10b; "O russkikh," 127; and Serebriakov, "Sel'skoe khoziaistvo," (1861), 102.
150. Argutinskii-Dolgorukov, "Borchalinskii uezd," 40, 99–100.

Transcaucasia.[151] Nineteenth-century commentators found that a "hard-working lifestyle," "industry and diligence," and highly developed structures of communal assistance lay at the foundation of the Akhalkalaki Dukhobors' religious beliefs and material well-being. They quote the Dukhobors as saying that "work is the cleansing of the body and the soul." Only such a strong love of and faith in labor could help them face the ecological and economic "adversities [that] rained down on them from all sides."[152] Similarly, for religious reasons, Molokans were disinclined to embrace "the comfortable life." Instead, they pushed themselves into their work and away from any excess or overt display of wealth. Sectarians were, as another observer wrote, "the most hard-working people in the entire Transcaucasian region."[153]

Certain scholars have attempted to link the religious sources of sectarian success to Max Weber's theory of the Protestant work ethic. Such comparative efforts are "neither precise nor fruitful," to adopt Robert Crummey's description of these theories in the case of Old Believer prosperity. Molokans, Dukhobors, and Subbotniks shared little with the special doctrines of the Calvinists that Weber saw as crucial to the origins of modern capitalism. However, it does appear that the sectarian communities shared certain religious tenets and social practices that made them successful economically. In particular, much like the Vyg Old Believers, the sectarians were pariah groups who tended to turn inward and work together as a community, providing vital economic and social support to each other.[154]

Evidence of the religious roots of sectarian economic success is seen in the fact that Orthodox peasants who lived next to sectarians under similar climatic and geographic conditions, or who took over nonconformist land after exile, rarely approximated the sectarians' success. Indeed, when Orthodox peasant colonists began to migrate into Transcaucasia in the 1880s and 1890s, they were generally unable to repeat the dissenters' material triumphs.[155] Moreover, sectarian economic success in Transcaucasia had corollaries across the Empire. In Tavriia, Tambov, Riazan, and

151. T. B. Koval, "Tiazhkoe blago": Khristianskaia etika truda (Moscow: 1994), 241–78; Staples, Cross-Cultural Encounters, 68–69; and V. Grigor'ev, "Molokane Ranenburgskogo uezda," RM, no. 5 (July 1884): 40–58.
152. Vermishev, "Ekonomicheskii byt," 40–41; and Zagurskii, "Poezdka," 67, 74.
153. Serebriakov, "Sel'skoe khoziaistvo," (1862), 52, 55–56; RGIA f. 1284, op. 223–1896, d. 76 gr. B, l. 470b; and SSC'SA f. 4, op. 2, d. 792, 1848–51, l. 82.
154. Robert O. Crummey, The Old Believers and the World of Antichrist: The Vyg Community and the Russian State, 1694–1855 (Madison, 1970), 135–58; Max Weber, The Protestant Ethic and the Spirit of Capitalism, trans. Talcott Parsons (New York, 1992); idem, The Sociology of Religion, trans. Ephraim Fischoff (Boston, 1991); Koval, "Tiazhkoe blago"; and Donald Nielsen, "Sects, Churches and Economic Transformations in Russia and Western Europe," IJPCS 2, no. 4 (1989): 493–522.
155. Grigor'ev, "Molokane," 54–57; D. Z. Eliseev, "Vnutrennee obozrenie," Sovremennik, no. 3 (1865): 57–59; and chapter four.

Nizhegorod provinces and along the Amur, for example, these religious communities enjoyed similar prosperity—a fact that indicates cross-geographical socio-religious characteristics that led to enrichment. However, the exceptional communal wealth of Molokans and Dukhobors in Tavriia and the Amur also reinforces the significance of the two other causes of prosperity in the South Caucasian case. Often for environmental reasons, these nonconformists in southern Ukraine and eastern Siberia became actively involved in commercial livestock breeding and market-oriented production, particularly through mechanization. They also embraced nonagricultural activities such as textile factories, flour milling, lumber, various trading enterprises, and even a steamship line. Additionally, while there were certainly wealthy sectarians in the central provinces, their extraordinary economic success was most marked in the borderland regions of the Empire. As Russian settlers on the frontier, they gained certain advantages—such as access to land, government contracts, relative social and political freedom, and special state treatment—that helped them to thrive, just like the sectarian-settlers in the South Caucasus.[156]

ECOLOGY AND EMPIRE

Life on the frontier transformed the settlers' communities in a multiplicity of ways, creating "new worlds" as it destroyed old patterns. In the mutual interactions between the South Caucasian environment and sectarian migrants, the settlers adapted to fit the local ecological structures much more than the reverse. Initially, local ecological systems impoverished, infected, and killed many of them, ravaging their communities to such an extent that a significant number of migrants chose to abandon their sectarian religious affiliation in return for the right to escape back to the more familiar climes of the internal Russian provinces. For those who remained, the climate, land, flora, and fauna forced the sectarians to reformulate their economic practices in novel directions. In tandem with other factors, these changes in economic activity generated extraordinary long-term prosperity for many of these settler communities.

The story of the sectarian settlers demonstrates that the South Caucasus, like Siberia and other imperial frontiers, proved to be a land of opportunity for Russian peasants. Indeed, it highlights the significance of borderland regions as leading, dynamic spaces in the economic devel-

156. Klibanov, *History*, 181–203; K. Litvintsev, "Amurskie sektanty: molokane i dukhobory," *KhCh*, no. 11/12 (1887): 549–52; "Dukhovnye khristiane molokane na Amure," *Molokanin* I, no. 1 (1910): 35–38; Filibert, "Predislovie," 292–97; Staples, *Cross-Cultural Encounters*, 68–71; Grigor'ev, "Molokane," 40–58; and Ethel Dunn, ed., *A Molokan's Search for Truth: The Correspondence of Leo Tolstoy and Fedor Zheltov* (Ottawa, 2001), viii, 150–54.

opment of nineteenth century Russia.[157] While the sectarians' religious culture played a discernable role in their success, a greater cause of their enrichment was the possibilities offered them—even forced upon them— on the Empire's periphery. Moreover, the standard characterization of a relatively unchanging peasantry, which was then buffeted by the forces of industrialization in the late imperial period, while perhaps appropriate for some of the central Russian provinces, largely does not apply in the South Caucasus. Russian peasants were not necessarily locked into certain economic practices, and those who moved away from a reliance on grain agriculture were most likely to become wealthy.[158]

The outcomes of the meeting between settlers and environment are important to understanding the forms and effects of the tsarist imperial project in Transcaucasia overall, as well as the South Caucasian peoples' experience of Russian empire-building. In this imperial context, ecological and economic acculturation occurred primarily on the part of the settlers, and it was the imperial holdings that changed the colonists more than the other way around. The case of the settlers and their relationship to Transcaucasia reflects in many respects the relatively light touch of Russian colonialism in the South Caucasus. While the disruptions that Russian migration caused to the indigenous communities were certainly significant, from a comparative environmental perspective their fate could have been much worse.[159] Additionally, the local ecosystems were not enduringly altered; "ecological imperialism," to use Alfred Crosby's term, was not an active force accompanying Russian military, administrative, and population imperialism in the region. The South Caucasian environment absorbed the incursion of these human migrants with only minimal changes. Only the settlers who came in line with the ecological structures and transformed their economic activities survived and, later, thrived.[160]

The absence of a large-scale transformation of the region's ecology

157. Donald Treadgold, *The Great Siberian Migration: Government and Peasant in Resettlement from Emancipation to the First World War* (Princeton, 1957); and Alfred J. Rieber, *Merchants and Entrepreneurs in Imperial Russia* (Chapel Hill, 1982).

158. In this way, the Transcaucasian sectarians stand in contrast to the general "durability" of peasant economic activity, caused itself by the possibility of migration. See Moon, "Peasant Migration," 893.

159. I am thinking here particularly of the impact on native Americans, Australian Aborigines, and New Zealand's Maoris. White, *Roots of Dependency*; Cronon, *Changes in the Land*; Crosby, *Ecological Imperialism*, esp. the chapter on New Zealand; Michael J. Heffernan and Keith Sutton, "The Landscape of Colonialism: The Impact of French Colonial Rule on the Algerian Rural Settlement Pattern, 1830–1987," in *Colonialism and Development in the Contemporary World*, ed. Chris Dixon and Michael J. Heffernan (London, 1991), 121–52; and, in the Siberian case, Moon, "Peasant Migration," 877. See also chapter five.

160. On the defining impact on Russian colonization of the difficulties of the Eurasian environment generally, see M. K. Liubavskii, *Obzor istorii russkoi kolonizatsii s drevneishikh vremen i do XX veka* (Moscow, 1996).

also had significant symbolic meaning for tsarist imperialists. Like their counterparts in Western Europe, Russian officials and observers took "pride in environmental control."[161] They frequently linked the settlers' economic transfiguration of the South Caucasus with Russia's civilizing project—the colonists developed Russian crops, livestock, and economic practices, which were all considered superior to the native varieties. Yet in their efforts to subdue, control, and manipulate the South Caucasian territory for the Empire's benefit, Russian officials and settlers could do little but watch as the conquered territory in turn "conquered" the colonists. The Transcaucasian lands dictated the terms of its encounter with Russian colonists—both to the settlers' detriment and benefit— forcing the migrants to adapt to it, rather than the reverse. The settlers' early ecological accommodations proved disconcerting and destabilizing to tsarist notions of imperialist hierarchy. Only with the sectarians' later prosperity did tsarism's sense of cultural superiority reappear.

The relationship between the sectarians and the South Caucasian environment provides an insightful point of comparison with similar processes in other parts of the tsarist empire, and it expands our understanding of the linkages of empire and ecology in other geographic and temporal contexts. Recent scholarship on the human-environment interaction in Imperial Russia has highlighted the degrees to which Russian peasant settlers modified the Eurasian steppe as they expanded their zones of settlement south and east. On one level, the experiences of the sectarian colonists in Transcaucasia fit easily into the long-term trends of peasant migration. As David Moon has asserted in his survey of peasant migration, "this pattern of adapting to the environment, and altering it to suit to the needs of peasant farming and other activities, was repeated across large parts of the expanding Russian state."[162] On another level, however, the Transcaucasian case stands distinct from other contexts in the tsarist empire. It indicates that Russian colonization was not necessarily accompanied by marked environmental change—although this was the case more often than not— and the environment might modify the peasants more than the reverse. Yet despite, or perhaps because of, the sectarian settlers' limited ecological impact, they ultimately attained considerable wealth. In contrast, Thomas Barrett finds that the Terek Cossacks, just across the mountains in the North Caucasus, altered the region's ecology, as part of both military and socio-economic activities, through extensive deforestation that produced

161. John M. MacKenzie, "Empire and the Ecological Apocalypse: the historiography of the imperial environment," in *Ecology and Empire*, 216–18; Patricia Seed, *Ceremonies of Possession in Europe's Conquest of the New World, 1492–1640* (New York, 1995), 16–40; and Willard Sunderland, "The 'Colonization Question': Visions of Colonization in Late Imperial Russia," *JGO* 48, no. 2 (2000): 210–32.
162. Moon, "Peasant Migration," 874.

flooding and disease. In the end, he argues, the "lands mastered the Cossacks," but only after the Cossacks had "unwittingly practiced eco-warfare against [themselves]."[163]

Not unexpectedly, colonial Transcaucasia was not a site for the sort of biological invasion that accompanied Europeans into the Americas, Australia, or New Zealand. There is no indication that the sectarian-settlers brought with them the "weeds, feral animals, and pathogens" that came "often without help and even despite European actions" and so transformed these other continents by pushing out native species and grabbing their territory.[164] The Transcaucasian case did not feature any examples of the uncontrolled spreading of a species that were witnessed in Western European white settler colonies—and which have become an increasing environmental concern in recent times with accelerating globalization.[165]

This fundamental difference was the result of at least three different factors. First, the organisms that accompanied the Russian settlers were domesticated plants and animals that were imported consciously and expanded into the South Caucasus under humanity's restrictive control. Second, in contrast to these other imperialist holdings, the South Caucasus was not separated from central Russia by a water barrier. Trade routes through Eurasia had long brought different species from various regions into contact with each other. As a result, the contiguous nature of the tsarist empire took away the ecological advantage so important to European expansion in the Americas, Australia, and New Zealand. Third, in comparison to these other lands, the sectarian settlers moved to Transcaucasia in sufficiently small numbers that their presence did not cause the environmental trauma often required to cause the rapid replacement of "native" species by nonnative ones.[166] Of course, the reverse was also true: one of the reasons that that their numbers remained small was that their presence did not wreak havoc on the preexisting environment to make possible greater Russian migration.

The limited environmental impact of the sectarian settlers in Transcaucasia adds to our understanding of the relationship between empire and ecology worldwide. First, it supports the recent historiographical tendency to see environmental history (and imperial-ecological history) as

163. Barrett, *Edge of Empire*, 58 and 77. Such was also the case in Siberia; see Moon, "Peasant Migration," 876–77. On deforestation internationally, see Michael Williams, "Ecology, Imperialism, and Deforestation," 169–84.

164. Crosby, *Ecological Imperialism*, 148.

165. On the unintended spread and dominance of alien organisms, see for example John Reeds, "Hull of a Problem," *Geographical* 71, no. 10 (1999): 26–33; R. D. Bowman, "Messing About with *Bufo Marinus*," *Origins: Current Events in Historical Perspective* I, no. 2 (1993): 44; and Alexandre Meinesz, *Killer Algae*, trans. Daniel Simberloff (Chicago, 1999).

166. Crosby, *Ecological Imperialism*, 145–70.

something more complex than a "purely destructive" or apocalyptic phenomenon.[167] Second, the Transcaucasian case compels us to rethink Crosby's assertion that "the migrant Europeans could reach and even conquer, but not make colonies of settlement of these pieces of alien earth until they became a good deal more like Europe."[168] Crosby argues that in the "Neo-Europes" that the Americas, Australia, and New Zealand became, Europeans could quickly and easily control the land, without significant change in their economic activities. Yet, despite the fact that the sectarians did not "conquer" the region in an environmental sense, they not only sank deep roots and lived there through the end of the Soviet period, but they also thrived economically.

167. Tom Griffiths, "Ecology and Empire: Towards an Australian history of the World," in *Ecology and Empire*, 9; and Peregrine Horden and Nicholas Purcell, *The Corrupting Sea: A Study of Mediterranean History* (Oxford, 2000), 338–41, passim.
168. Crosby, *Ecological Imperialism*, 172. William Cronon, George Miles, and Jay Griffin have added, "Europeans thrived best where their organisms did." Cronon et al., "Becoming West," 12.

4

HERETICS INTO COLONIZERS

Changing Roles and Transforming Identities
on the Imperial Periphery

In a report to Alexander III in 1890, A. M. Dondukov-Korsakov, then chief administrator of the Caucasus, exhibited an inconsistent attitude toward the sectarians in Transcaucasia, seeing them simultaneously as dangerous nonconformists and laudable Russian colonists.[1] On one hand, he relayed his very positive estimation of the sectarians' economic, political, and military role in tsarist empire-building: "Despite their isolated situation among nationalities alien to them and the unfavorable climatic and soil conditions, they all attained considerable material well-being, through which they showed their perfect qualities as colonizers and greatly contributed to the economic success of the country." The combination of economic activities, vital assistance to Russian forces during the Russo-Turkish War of 1877–78, and "significance in the process of Russifying the southern borderlands" led Dondukov-Korsakov to conclude that "one can only meet with approval the idea of settling in the newly incorporated Kars territory up to 10,000 Russian sectarian souls from Transcaucasia."

In the very same document, however, Dondukov-Korsakov raised fears of the dangers that their religious beliefs posed to the state, arguing that all possible measures should be taken to prevent sectarian proselytism or public manifestations of their faith. For him, this was particularly true in those cases where, under the guise of religious teachings, sectarians were actually preaching political content that was "threatening to the existing state order of our Fatherland." He feared that the spread of sectarian theology would be a corrupting influence "on the Russian element that serves as our political strength in this borderland." In response to this threat, he proposed an enlargement of the presence of Orthodoxy in

1. RGIA f. 932, op. 1, d. 319, 1890, ll. 5–50b.

Transcaucasia through an aggressive policy of building churches, increasing the number of trained Russian priests—as opposed to Georgian Orthodox priests—and expanding the quantity and scope of state schools, which would bring enlightenment to the sectarian population.

Of particular note is Dondukov-Korsakov's contradictory notion of "Russian." In one passage he called the sectarians "Russians," remarked on their Russifying potential, and underscored their significant imperialist contributions. In the very next paragraph, he worried about their impact on the "Russian element" in the borderlands, as if the dissenters comprised a people distinct from "Russians."

Dondukov-Korsakov's ambivalent report illustrates the ways in which frontier life altered the position of sectarians in Russian polity and society. The document also indicates how ethnic, religious, and state identities formed a triangular nexus of mutually constituting categories in tsarist Russia, and how the meanings of "sectarian" and "Russian" changed on the southern periphery.[2] The tsarist practice of banishing "undesirables" to the borderlands forced local officials to use as colonizers precisely those people who did not feel much sense of colonial mission and held no stake in Russian state power. Efforts to refashion such outcasts into colonists proved transformative, not only for the settlers but also for Russian imperialism.

The sectarians' resettlement expanded the possible roles available to them as subjects of the realm. In these multi-ethnic provinces, nonconformists accounted for the majority of those people whom state authorities considered "Russian" and, by extension, loyal and dependable. In the absence of other Russians, tsarist officials came to rely on these religious dissenters to govern and defend the region. The banished nonconformists ironically became quasi-representatives of state power, taking on indispensable administrative, economic, and military functions in the imperial enterprise. The fate of Russia's imperialist project and geopolitical endeavors in the South Caucasus became intricately linked to the internal development of the sectarians' communities there.

As the Dondukov-Korsakov report indicates, migration also profoundly altered the characterizations of state officials toward the sectarians, as well as of the dissenters toward the state and themselves. Alongside official categorizations of religious dissenters as "pernicious heretics"

---

2. My understanding of identity draws from the scholarship of community psychology and its examination of "sense of community," commonly defined by four elements: "membership," "influence," "integration and fulfillment of needs," and "shared emotional connection." David W. McMillan and David M. Chavis, "Sense of Community. A Definition and Theory," *Journal of Community Psychology* 14, no. 1 (1986): 8–20. See also Peter Sahlins, *Boundaries: The Making of France and Spain in the Pyrenees* (Berkeley, 1989); and Rogers Brubaker and Frederick Cooper, "Beyond 'Identity,'" *Theory and Society* 29, no. 1 (2000): 1–47.

arose a second, contradictory state label: the "model Russian colonist." By demonstrating that they could be contributing subjects of empire, the activities of the sectarian settlers had a profound impact on their political categorization as loyal subjects and on their ethnic identity as Russians. Indeed, membership in the Russian national community in the nineteenth century—with its attendant privileges and obligations—was constructed on two primary planes, and sectarians experienced an evolution in status in both areas. One was political and imperial, in which officials classified, and strove to create, "subjects"—whatever their ethnicity, language, or religion—based on their positive contributions to pan-imperial *Rossiia*. Another was ethnic, in which Russian (*russkii*) identity was defined variously according to language, culture, blood, and often religious affiliation. These two planes sometimes intersected, sometimes competed with each other.

The sectarians' sense of self-identity followed a similar trajectory, although state and sectarian frequently did not agree on what constituted a "Russian" or "loyal" subject. With their resettlement to South Caucasia, the nonconformist settlers began to forge bonds of identity with earthly communities—although their religious affiliation and spiritual separateness continued to play a vital part in their sense of self. In multicultural Transcaucasia, the sectarians' own identification with Russian ethnicity was enhanced by day-to-day interactions with ethno-cultural "others." Moreover, in their new role of frontier "colonists," the sectarians found themselves both invested in and able to influence the Russian state, especially in times of war. Their sense of identification as Russians and Russian subjects grew alongside their religiously derived self-definitions.

Thus, in the eyes of state officials and of the sectarians themselves, settlement on the frontier fostered new, fluid, and often competing notions of identity. Simultaneously, there existed socially and politically inclusive and exclusive characterizations, and the boundaries of the sectarians' identity were negotiated and renegotiated around the two tropes of "Russian colonist" and "pernicious heretic." The relations between state and sectarian became a reinforcing spiral in which evolving state definitions of sectarians brought about a reformation in sectarian self-identity as regarded the state. These new forms of sectarian identification then propelled even further shifts in the state's categorizations, and so the mutually influential relations continued. This manner of fashioning identities—however contextual and impermanent they may have been—and the tension between self-understanding and external labeling, produced outcomes and parameters of their own. In an empire such as Russia that attempted to impose a system of rigid categories on an extremely heterogeneous population, and that applied different systems of laws to different classification groups, the struggle over labels and identities was of paramount importance to the outcomes of everyday life. Moreover, as they endeavored to carve a niche for themselves, sectarians frequently used discursive strategies that exploited the "Russian colonist" category in order to underscore their membership and influence in Russian society.

SECTARIANS IN THE SERVICE OF EMPIRE

Once on the frontier, the so-called "most pernicious" sectarians began, wittingly and unwittingly, to perform administrative, economic, military, and Russification functions, proving themselves to be not only indispensable but also superlative contributors to the building of empire. Indeed, the presence of Russian peasant colonists in the South Caucasus—albeit sectarian—facilitated tsarist empire-building efforts in important ways. However, although officials began to set out specific imperialist roles for them, the nonconformists never became state bureaucrats and did not simply follow state dictates. Rather, they supported Russian state power as quasi-independent agents with their own agendas and, as much as possible, to their own benefit. When their interests did not coincide with those of the imperial tsarist state, they either withdrew their assistance or provided it grudgingly.[3]

The sectarians helped to enforce Russian notions of legality through their actions as unofficial police agents. In some cases, they were conscripted to carry out a specific law enforcement task; in others, they simply took matters into their own hands extralegally when they felt that they had been treated unlawfully. One Molokan from Alty-Agach in Baku province relates how Molokans frequently chased after robbers and bandits who had stolen their possessions. When they captured thieves, they turned them over to the tsarist police, thereby aiding these officials in their jobs.[4] This work, however necessary, did not come without its perils, as Aleksei Dobrynin, *starshina* of Vorontsovka in Tiflis province, discovered when "predators" stole four horses from the village's stables in March 1849. Under Dobrynin's leadership, a posse of armed Molokan villagers set off to chase after the thieves, finally catching up with them just as the sun began to set. The three armed robbers opened fire on their

3. For a comparison of the divergent agendas of "state colonialism," "settler colonialism," and "civilizing colonialism," see John Comaroff, "Images of Empire, Contests of Conscience: Models of Colonial Domination in South Africa," in *Tensions of Empire: Colonial Cultures in a Bourgeois World*, ed. Ann Laura Stoler and Frederick Cooper (Berkeley, 1997), 178–91. In the Russian case, see Daniel Brower, *Turkestan and the Fate of the Russian Empire* (London, 2003), esp. 126–51.

4. GMIR f. 14, op. 3, d. 1962, 1902, l. 14. See also RGIA f. 1268, op. 1, d. 433, 1843–48, ll. 51–510b; ORRGB f. 369, k. 42, d. 2, 1950, l. 402; SSC'SA f. 16, op. 1, d. 10631, 1854–58; and f. 239, op. 1, d. 45, 1849–52, ll. 44–450b.

pursuers, wounding one. Undeterred, with guns blazing Dobrynin rushed the thieves, seized one of them, recovered the stolen horses, and later handed their new captive over to the police. In the official report of the incident, Viceroy Prince M. S. Vorontsov noted that "this courageous and entirely new act of the Russian settlers had such a strong influence on the predators that since then neither Russian settlers, nor neighboring Armenians have been subjected to their attacks and robbery."[5]

The sectarian migrants also provided certain forms of infrastructural support to Russia's governance of Transcaucasia. Their communities often housed local administrative structures and personnel because tsarist officials considered Russian villages to be more appropriate locations for such governing facilities than native ones. For example, the Molokan village of Ivanovka in Baku province possessed the district's police station, medical office, communal court, and forest administration office.[6] The settlers also expedited the movement of men and information along official communication routes. Sectarian villages provided stopping points for tsarist officials traveling through the region and supplied the horses and wagons these officials used on the road.[7] In addition, as discussed earlier, sectarians offered widely lauded support systems for the imperial administration on other levels, such as domestic and holiday services.[8]

Sectarian villages figured prominently in the development of the postal system. In the 1840s, Armenians ran most of the postal stations, but local officials repeatedly voiced their preference for Russians as postal workers. They did so for reasons of perceived ethnic loyalty and in the hope of reducing the significant costs of maintaining the postal network. In the late 1840s, authorities even floated the idea of creating a *soslovie* of postal peasants from among the sectarians to increase the number of stations controlled by Russian settlers. The centrality of the sectarian villages to the postal structure is illustrated by the case of the Molokans of Nikolaevka in Shemakha (later Baku) province. In 1847, the villagers petitioned regional authorities to be moved to another location, citing great economic suffering because of insufficient land. In response, local authorities stressed that the village could not be relocated because

5. RGIA f. 1268, op. 3, d. 438, 1849, ll. 1–10b. Vorontsov was so impressed that he requested permission to award Dobrynin with the honored cloth caftan as encouragement for other settlers to react similarly to the attacks of robbers in the future. Vorontsov's request was denied because all public honors and decorations were forbidden by law (February 13, 1837) to members of those sects considered most pernicious. See also SSC'SA f. 222, op. 1, d. 60, 1849, ll. 47–58, passim; and f. 239, op. 1, d. 45, 1849–52, ll. 17–19, 46–47ob, 57–63ob.
6. N. Kalashev, "Selenie Ivanovka, Lagichskogo uchastka, Geokchaiskogo uezda, Bakinskoi gubernii," *SMOMPK*, vol. 13 (Tiflis, 1892), otd. II, 243–44.
7. GMIR f. K1, op. 1, d. 4, 1886; SSC'SA f. 222, op. 1, d. 42, 1848; and ORRGB f. 369, k. 42, d. 2, 1950, l. 447.
8. See chapter three.

FIGURE 6. The village of Semenovka, Erevan province, c. 1897. From Esther Lancraft Hovey, "The Old Post-Road from Tiflis to Erivan," *National Geographic Magazine* 12, no. 8 (August 1901), 303.

it contained a postal station. Rather than move the station to one of the surrounding Muslim villages, officials decided instead to reduce the taxes and obligations of the Russian settlers substantially, in order to maintain their presence in the communication structure.[9]

Contemporary observers heaped high praise on the sectarians for fulfilling the economic component of the state's imperialist goals.[10] Their domination of the transportation industry, at least until the appearance of the railways in the 1870s, increased both the frequency of trade as well as the quantity of goods that passed through the region. This expansion of commerce represented an important aspect of Russian plans to develop the "colony" in economic terms by strengthening the trade links between Russia and "the East" through the conduit of Transcaucasia.[11] The location of the settlers' villages—often along transportation

9. SSC′SA f. 4, op. 2, d. 792, 1848–51; d. 748, 1848–51, l. 13; f. 222, op. 1, d. 1, 1847–50; RGIA f. 1268, op. 2, d. 772, 1848; d. 865, 1848–52, ll. 3–30b; and f. 1284, op. 221–1888, d. 73.

10. A. I. Masalkin "Iz istorii zakavkazskikh sektantov. Ch. III, Sektanty, kak kolonizatory Zakavkaz′ia," *Kavkaz*, no. 333 (December 16, 1893): 3; and RGIA f. 1268, op. 9, d. 367a, 1857–58, ll. 1–10b.

11. *AKAK* vol. 10, doc. 97, p. 120; vol. 12:1 (1893) doc. 18, p. 38; and RGIA f. 381, op. 2, d. 2014, 1858, ll. 22–230b.

routes—facilitated the passage of goods by providing rest stops for merchant caravans. The settlers also maintained the roads in functioning condition during winter snows and *rasputitsa*.[12]

Tsarist officials considered the sectarian settlers to be "industrious people and excellent farmers" who "spread different, previously unknown types of agriculture" and fostered industrial development.[13] Indeed, a member of an 1856 state expedition remarked that land "put into the hands of the conscientious Dukhobors becomes plowed and pasture land, with communal uses and important results for the region that would never come about in the hands of the indigenous population."[14] Officials also noted with appreciation various industrial and commercial ventures, such as Russian-style flourmills, tile factories, stores, and taverns, which they considered to be of significant value to the development of the region's economy.[15] Particularly important in the eyes of tsarist administrators and other Russian observers was the impact that the sectarians had in the artisanal sphere. Viceroy Vorontsov noted that Transcaucasian towns had lacked sufficient numbers of artisans and workers, so that the local administration was obliged to conscript military personnel to perform basic economic functions. In order to solve this acute problem, he worked at length to increase the sectarian artisanal presence.[16] Later, Viceroy Prince A. I. Bariatinskii was happy to report that the nonconformists "increased the number of artisans, of which hitherto there had been a complete insufficiency."[17]

The sectarians further contributed to the imperialist state's agenda of civilizational "uplift" of the non-Russian population. According to Russian officials and indigenous (especially Georgian) nobles, the colonists acted as "positive examples for the nomadic peoples of the region to fol-

12. N. B., "Ozero Gokcha (iz vospominanii o zakavkazskom krae)," *Kavkaz*, no. 61 (1861): 30; and RGIA f. 1284, op. 218–1881, d. 34, ll. 8–160b. *Rasputitsa* is the time of year during which the roads were impassable, usually from mud.

13. RGIA f. 381, op. 1, d. 23297, 1844–45, ll. 23, 52–53, 580b–59, 1320b–33; f. 384, op. 3, d. 1149, 1846–51, ll. 96, 970b–98; "Iz signakhskogo uezda (kor. Kavkaza)," *Kavkaz* 31, no. 15 (February 1, 1877): 3; and Vartan Gregorian, "The Impact of Russia on the Armenians and Armenia," in *Russia in Asia: Essays on the Influence of Russia on the Asian Peoples*, ed. Wayne S. Vucinich (Stanford, 1972), 183–84.

14. Quoted in S. A. Inikova, "Vzaimootnosheniia i khoziaistvenno-kul'turnye kontakty kavkazskikh Dukhobortsev s mestnym naseleniem," *Dukhobortsy i Molokane v Zakavkaz'e*, ed. V. I. Kozlov and A. P. Pavlenko (Moscow, 1992), 48.

15. SSC'SA f. 4, op. 2, d. 629, 1847–52; d. 792, 1848–51, l. 82; *AKAK* vol. 12:1 (1893), doc. 18, p. 38; and chapter three.

16. RGIA f. 1268, op. 2, d. 865, 1848–52, ll. 1–13; op. 6, d. 177, 1852; f. 381, op. 1, d. 23470, 1848, ll. 1–8; and GMIR f. 2, op. 8, d. 237, 1910, l. 71.

17. *AKAK* vol. 12:1 (1893), doc. 18, p. 38. See also N. B. "Ozero Gokcha," 330; T. B. "U beregov Kaspiia (tri goda nazad), ch. II Baku," *Kavkaz*, no. 3 (1881): 1; and SSC'SA f. 4, op. 2, d. 792, 1848–51, ll. 82–820b. There is some hyperbole in these declarations to be sure, since the South Caucasus was not devoid of artisans, as official records indicate. George Bournoutian, ed. and trans., *Russia and the Armenians of Transcaucasia, 1797–1889: A Documentary Record* (Costa Mesa, 1998), 112–13.

low"—this despite their religious nonconformity.[18] Administrators also believed that a Russian presence in the region would bring to the indigenous peoples what they saw as desperately needed European agricultural techniques, implements, and tools. In fact, tsarist authorities in 1847 generated a plan to settle Russian sectarians into Armenian villages, assuming that in such mixed communities "the Armenians can gradually adopt from the settlers the best modes of economic production and house construction, and can learn the Russian language." In two districts alone, forty-four Armenian villages voiced their willingness to have the sectarian colonists join their villages. In the end, however, only a small number of such mixed villages actually came into existence. While insufficient land allotments was a crucial issue, equally important was the Russian settlers' general preference to live in separate communities where they might conduct their religious lives unencumbered. Thus, while sectarians served imperial interests, they often refused to take on tasks that conflicted with their own aspirations.[19]

In tandem with their administrative, economic, and "civilizing" roles, tsarist officials noted another significant sectarian contribution to Russian imperialism: the biological "Russification" (*obrusenie*) of the South Caucasus.[20] As ethnic Russian colonists, their existence in the region— the very presence of their Russian bodies—acted as the glue of imperial integration by physically linking center and periphery, "in political terms, acting to consolidate Russian dominion there and to bring about the merging of the region with the empire."[21] One author in the official publication *Kavkazskii Kalendar* of 1880 underscored what he saw as Russia's much more successful imperialist tactics of colonization in comparison to those by the British. "British power in India is founded not upon the settling of the English in the region, but on the weakness and internal discord among the native population; on an exaggerated notion of British wealth and might. . . . Nothing similar to this is taking place in the Caucasus. This land is being gradually and naturally colonized by the Russian population."[22]

18. RGIA f. 381, op. 1, d. 23297, 1844–45, ll. 23, 280b–29, 52–53, 580b–59, 1320b–33.
19. Quoted in I. V. Dolzhenko, *Khoziaistvennyi i obshchestvennyi byt russkikh krest'ian vostochnoi Armenii (konets XIX—nachalo XX vv.)* (Erevan, 1985), 30.
20. Russification took on a variety of forms in different parts of the Russian Empire. On administrative and cultural Russification, see E. C. Thaden, ed., *Russification in the Baltic Provinces and Finland* (Princeton, 1981); Theodore R. Weeks, *Nation and State in Late Imperial Russia: Nationalism and Russification on the Western Frontier, 1863–1914* (DeKalb, 1996); Austin Jersild, *Orientalism and Empire: North Caucasus Mountain Peoples and the Georgian Frontier, 1845–1917* (Montreal & Kingston, 2002); and Ronald Suny, "Eastern Armenians under Tsarist Rule," in *The Armenian People from Ancient to Modern Times*, vol. II, *Foreign Dominion to Statehood: the Fifteenth Century to the Twentieth Century*, ed. Richard G. Hovannisian (New York, 1997), 128–30.
21. RGIA f. 381, op. 1, d. 23297, 1844–45, ll. 1320b–33.
22. Quoted and translated in Firouzeh Mostashari, "The Politics of Colonization: Sectarians and Russian Orthodox Peasants in Nineteenth Century Azerbaijan," *Journal of Central Asian Studies* 1,

However, while contemporary state officials saw the dissenters as the human anchor of empire, in retrospect it is clear that sectarian settlement also had the opposite impact on the course of Russian imperialism: as an obstacle to a broader policy until the late nineteenth century of Orthodox Russian colonization. On every occasion when tsarist authorities considered relocating Orthodox Russians into Transcaucasia, local officials barred such an action unless the Orthodox settlers could be located at a great distance from the dissenters. In this way, the sectarian presence in Transcaucasia acted as a dam blocking large-scale Russian migration until the late 1880s.[23] As Vorontsov wrote in April 1850, the settlement of Orthodox Russians in Transcaucasia "is not only premature, but even dangerous to a certain degree, because the coming together of Orthodox with the sectarians who are found here would be harmful for Orthodoxy and would spread the schism among Russian Orthodox settlers. Such a rapprochement is one of the primary reasons why sectarians are sent from Russia to Transcaucasia."[24]

Perhaps most important, the sectarians provided invaluable support to tsarist military operations in Transcaucasia.[25] Caught in the frontlines—and sometimes behind enemy lines—the aspirations of these Russian borderland colonists and the tsarist empire-building enterprise became inextricably intertwined. They did not enlist or fight because of their pacifist religious beliefs and because the inhabitants of Transcaucasia were exempt from military conscription until 1887. Nonetheless, the nonconformists played active roles in the military encounter by constructing and running infirmaries, providing food and other supplies, billeting troops in their villages, and, most significant, transporting provisions, weapons, and personnel.[26] In some instances the sectarians paid dearly for their assistance, both in human life and in material well-being;

no. 1 (1996): 17. See also Peter Holquist, "To Count, to Extract, and to Exterminate: Population Statistics and Population Politics in Late Imperial and Soviet Russia," in *A State of Nations: Empire and Nation-Making in the Age of Lenin and Stalin,* ed. Ronald Grigor Suny and Terry Martin (New York, 2001), 119–20; A. P. Liprandi, *Kavkaz i Rossiia* (Kharkov, 1912); and Jersild, *Orientalism,* 126–44.

23. Before 1890, some Orthodox Russian peasants did migrate to the Transcaucasus, but they did so inconsistently, in very small numbers, and to regions far away from the sectarians. These Orthodox migrants frequently proved incapable of successfully setting up permanent, economically viable settlements. See RGIA f. 1268, op. 4, d. 363, 1850–55; d. 13, 1850; and *AKAK* vol. 12:1 (1893), doc. 18.

24. *AKAK* vol. 10, doc. 42, p. 47; and RGIA f. 384, op. 3, d. 1149, l. 950b. See also RGIA f. 1268, op. 4, d. 363, 1850–55, ll. 4–40b.

25. I explore this topic in greater detail elsewhere. See my "Caught in the Crossfire? Russian Sectarians in the Caucasian Theater of War, 1853–56 and 1877–78," *Kritika: Explorations in Russian and Eurasian History* 2, no. 4 (2001): 713–50 and my "Swords into Plowshares: Opposition to Military Service among Religious Sectarians, 1770s to 1874," in *The Military and Society in Russia, 1450–1917,* ed. Eric Lohr and Marshall Poe (Leiden, 2002), 441–67.

26. RGIA f. 932, op. 1, d. 318, 1889, l. 100b.

in others, they benefited financially and in terms of the invaluable good-will of tsarist officials. The extent of the sectarians' assistance increased as the century progressed, although they aided Russian forces as much as possible as independent agents with their own goals in mind.[27]

The Alty-Agach Molokans became an integral component of Russian military efforts against Caucasian "mountaineers" from the 1830s to 1850s. In a memoir, one Molokan related how, almost immediately after their arrival in the 1830s, Russian armies began to use the village as a staging point for their engagements. The army leadership forced sectarian hosts to provide the soldiers with beds, food, and drink, and to transport the army's supplies and equipment. As the memoirist recalls: "on [our] shoulders they moved on to the theater of war." The Molokans were far from content with this arrangement. While they chafed against the need to supply the armies from their own food stores, they were particularly aggrieved by the restrictions on the practice of their faith that the presence of so many Orthodox Russians entailed. Both military leaders and the Orthodox priests who came along with the soldiers were afraid that the Molokans' religious beliefs would adversely affect the fighting forces. In consequence, they stringently forbade the Molokans from practicing their faith—even in the privacy of their own homes or in forests far away from the village. They searched out, captured, and severely beat with birch rods any Molokans found praying in a non-Orthodox manner. That the Orthodox extended the beatings to women and even young girls incensed the settlers even further. Although the Molokans ended up providing valuable assistance to the Russian military effort against the mountaineers, their interaction with the soldiers understandably left them wondering "in what way were these oppressors any better then the Turkish *bashi-buzuki?*"[28]

The dissenters were more willing and increasingly able assistants during the Crimean War (1853–56) and the Russo-Turkish War (1877–78). With a marginal infrastructure for the requirements of war, the tsarist army found itself in desperate need of extra resources in both conflicts, and they turned to the Russian colonists to provide it. Indeed, the supply lines were so tenuous during the wars that, without the aid of the sectarians, the outcome might well have been much worse. As one soldier wrote about the Russo-Turkish War, "If not for the Molokans and

27. While not discussed here, Molokans also provided various forms of support to military endeavors during World War I. See RGIA f. 821, op. 133, d. 213, 1915, l. 1; *Otchet komiteta po okazaniiu pomoshchi ranenym voinam pri Bakinskoi Obshchin Dukhovnykh Khristian (Molokan) c 7-go Sentiabria 1914 g. po 28-oe Fevralia 1915 g* (Baku, 1915); V. V. Ivanov, "Na pomoshch ranenym voinam," *Baptist*, no. 15/16 (1914): 17–18; and S. E. Il'in, *Moia Zakavkazskaia Rossiia* (Moscow, 1998), 126.
28. GMIR f. 14, op. 3, d. 1962, 1902, ll. 1–5. A *bashi-bazouk* was a Turkish irregular soldier. The term was used colloquially in Russian to denote a bandit, brigand, or cutthroat.

Dukhobors, if not for [their] cumbersome wagons, the fate of the Russian army in Asian Turkey would be very bad. One needs to consider the wagons supplied by these banished peoples to be equivalent to Cossack squadrons."[29]

During the Russo-Turkish War, Dukhobors, Molokans, and Subbotniks supplied their most extensive and sustained wartime assistance.[30] In terms of transport support, Dukhobors "consistently and efficiently" maintained from 400 to 600 wagons for military use, and as much as half of the Dukhobor male population worked as army carters at some point during the war.[31] State sources reveal that in 1876, even before the outbreak of the war, Aleksei Zubkov, the Dukhobor *starshina*, voluntarily sent out as many as 400 wagons with drivers to help transport military personnel, goods, and equipment closer to the border. Once the war began, the Dukhobors were vigorous in providing a variety of support services to the military. When cavalry units became stuck en route because snowdrifts or *rasputitsa* made roads impassable, they cleared the roads and then brought wagons to carry the equipment and facilitate the soldiers' journey. The Dukhobor transport team was particularly important in the battle for Ardagana. When the Russian soldiers were close to running out of provisions, the Dukhobors braved the battle zone to bring needed food and supplies from the stores in Akhalkalaki. Moreover, Molokans and Dukhobors alike brought the wounded and sick from the battlefield to hospitals—"all kinds of mutilated and blood-stained corpses," in the words of one Dukhobor—and carted the dead away to be buried—sometimes the bodies were piled in huts until the spring thaw permitted digging the ground.[32]

In addition to transport work, Molokans, Dukhobors, and Subbotniks also provided other important functions during both wars. They supplied

29. Sergei Studzinskii, "U nashikh kavkazskikh raskol'nikov (Ocherk)," *Slovo*, no. 1 (February 1878): 124. See also V. L. Velichko, *Kavkaz: Russkoe delo i mezhduplemennye voprosy* (Baku, 1990, rpt. 1904), 203.

30. In addition to the examples cited below, see also: RGIA f. 932, op. 1, d. 319, 1889, l. 5; I. Ia. Orekhov, "Ocherki iz zhizni zakavkazskikh sektatorov," *Kavkaz*, no. 136 (June 17, 1878): 1; M. N-n, "Dukhobory v Dukhobor'e," *Obzor*, no. 159 (June 17, 1878): 3; I. E. Petrov, "Dukhobory Elizavetpol'skogo uezda," *IKOIRGO* 18, no. 3 (1905–1906): 178; Studzinskii, "U nashikh," 119, 124; GARF f. 579, op. 1, d. 2580, 1913, l. 3; and Kh. A. Vermishev, "Ekonomicheskii byt gosudarstvennykh krest'ian v Akhaltsikhskom i Akhalkalakskom uezdakh, Tiflisskoi gubernii," in *MIEB*, vol. 3:2 (Tiflis, 1886), 41.

31. N-n, "Dukhobory," 3; RGIA f. 1284, op. 218–1881, d. 34, ll. 8–12; and "Smert' Dukhoborcheskogo kantslera," *MO* 5, no. 1–6 (1900): 485.

32. RGIA f. 1284, op. 218–1881, d. 34, ll. 8–100b, 130b–160b; ORRGB f. 369, k. 45, d. 4, 1953, l. 40; k. 42, d. 2, 1950, ll. 405–7; k. 43, d. 1, 1950, l. 813; Svetlana A. Inikova, "Istoriia patsifistskogo dvizheniia v sekte dukhoborov (XVII–XX vv.)," in *Dolgii put' Rossiiskogo patsifizma*, ed. T. A. Pavlova (Moscow, 1997), 128; Petr Nikolaevich Malov, *Dukhobortsy, ikh istoriia, zhizn' i bor'ba*, vol. 1, (Thrums, BC, 1948), 26; N-n, "Dukhobory," 2–3; Vasilii A. Potapov, *V plenu u razboinikov: rasskaz* (n.p., 1936), 32; Studzinskii, "U nashikh," 124; and Orekhov, "Ocherki," no. 136, 1.

temporary housing to large numbers of Russian troops as they moved to and from the front.[33] The Dukhobors were also instrumental in Russian efforts to track down Turkish deserters who had come across the Russian border.[34] In addition to food aid, the sectarians also supplied equipment and animals that Russian soldiers used for carting and riding. During the Russo-Turkish War, for instance, Akhalkalaki Dukhobors sold to the Russian army bulls, draught horses, and cavalry horses (complete with saddle). Molokans supplied an "enormous" quantity of wagons, Arabian horses, and bulls that Russian military personnel used for transport.[35]

Finally, the sectarians contributed vital medical assistance to Russian troops. Medical military units often rented buildings in Dukhobor villages to care for the sick and wounded before sending them on the long trip back into central Russia. When typhus went on a rampage through other military hospitals during the Russo-Turkish War, as many as 1,500 soldiers were evacuated to the village of Gorelovka, where they were not only housed in "comfortable quarters" but also fed precious meat specially supplied by the Dukhobors to help them recover. Other Dukhobor villages constructed an infirmary at their own cost in order to help the sick and wounded. At the same time, the Transcaucasian Dukhobor community gave 1,000 rubles to the Red Cross Society for its efforts in helping the sick and injured.[36]

While the sectarians' aid to the Russian forces was a great boon to the Russian military, for the colonists themselves it was a mixed blessing, although on balance the benefits far outweighed the costs. On one hand, the involvement of Dukhobors, Molokans, and Subbotniks as noncombatants provided them with an unprecedented opportunity to enrich themselves through direct state payments for their services, and their coffers swelled dramatically. On the other hand, the settlers—whose villages were positioned right at the conflagration between Ottoman and tsarist forces—paid for their contributions in many ways, including loss of property, exposure to hostage taking, and widespread illness, injury, and death.

33. "Eshche o Dukhoborakh," *Obzor,* no. 237 (September 6, 1878): 2; ORRGB f. 369, k. 42, d. 2, 1950, l. 402; k. 45, d. 4, 1953, ll. 40–41; Studzinskii, "U nashikh," 119–24; and Orekhov, "Ocherki," no. 136, 1.
34. RGIA f. 1284, op. 218–1881, d. 34, l. 15.
35. Ibid., ll. 10, 150b; ORRGB f. 369, k. 45, d. 4, 1953, ll. 40–41; GARF f. 579, op. 1, d. 2580, 1913, l. 3; I. E. Petrov, "Seleniia Novo-Saratovka i Novo-Ivanovka Elisavetpol'skogo uezda," *IKOIRGO* 19, no. 1 (1907–1908): otd. 1, 228; Studzinskii, "U nashikh," 119–24; Orekhov, "Ocherki," no. 136, 1; and V. D. Bonch-Bruevich, ed., *Raz"iasnenie zhizni khristian i Byl u nas, khristian, sirotskii dom (dve dukhoborcheskiia rukopisei),* vol. 2 of *MIIRS* (Christchurch, UK, 1901), 21.
36. RGIA f. 1284, op. 218–1881, d. 34, ll. 10–100b; ORRGB f. 369, k. 42, d. 2, 1950, ll. 406–7; k. 45, d. 4, 1953, l. 41; "Eshche," 1–2; Inikova, "Istoriia," 128; and Bonch-Bruevich, *Raz"iasnenie,* 21.

The sectarians made an especially handsome profit from the Russo-Turkish War. Dukhobors earned as much as 1.5 million rubles from their contracts with the Russian army, and "many rich [Dukhobors] found their beginnings specifically in the war period."[37] While there are no comparative figures available for Molokan gains, it is clear that they too were greatly enriched.[38] Although they provided some of their support for free, the settlers were paid handsomely for much of their carting work. For instance, during the movement of two grenadier units through the Borzhomi pass in the Russo-Turkish War, the Dukhobors were richly reimbursed for their loan of 1,200 wagons and drivers.[39] Likewise, the soldier Sergei Studzinskii noted that the Molokans were also making a sizable profit from wartime transport: "They feed themselves with transport, keep themselves and their families in what they need, and even put some away in the money box. A good wagon in peace time costs approximately 300 rubles, and now the price approaches 400 rubles."[40]

Many Dukhobors also made their fortune supplying livestock, horses, foodstuffs, and services to the army. One Dukhobor described the scene in his villages during the Russo-Turkish War as follows:

> [The soldiers] bought up everything from us: eggs, milk, butter, vegetables, sauerkraut that we prepared in large quantities, potatoes, baked bread, and chicken. Everything was sold to the soldiers coming through the village. Those who spent the day or passed the night, paid well for everything: for the samovars, the bath, a place to spend the night, and for sheets. Many of our sisters worked as domestics for the soldiers. The officers bought from us large amounts of smooth woolen cloth, towels, linen, all homespun. They really liked our attire, especially women's apparel, which they bought for their domestics as a present. And from all of this, many among us became rich.[41]

Indeed, realizing the revenue potential of the wartime situation, "the more enterprising of them" went up into the hills to buy livestock, especially sheep, from their non-Russian neighbors for resale to the army. Quartermasters paid handsomely for these herds, and certain Dukhobors pocketed "legendary amounts of money." Dukhobor livestock traders cut out new swaths of pastureland in the hills, where they could fatten up the

37. Vermishev, "Ekonomicheskii byt," 41; Inikova, "Istoriia," 128; ORRGB f. 369, k. 45, d. 4, 1953, ll. 40–41; "Smert'," 485; and "Akhalkalakskii uezd (ot nashego korrespondenta)," Kaspii 14, no. 25 (January 25, 1894): 3.
38. A. M. Argutinskii-Dolgorukov, "Borchalinskii uezd, Tiflisskoi gubernii v ekonomicheskom i kommercheskom otnosheniiakh," in RTKE (Tiflis, 1897), 39.
39. RGIA f. 1284, op. 218–1881, d. 34, ll. 10–100b.
40. Studzinskii, "U nashikh," 123–24.
41. ORRGB f. 369, k. 45, d. 4, 1953, l. 41.

herds before selling them. Others strove to take advantage of the wartime situation by increasing their harvest in order to sell the excess crops.[42] During the Crimean War, the villagers of Elenovka requested permission to open a tavern and supply store in their village in order to take advantage of the profits from the increased traffic of soldiers and other travelers through their village.[43]

All of these benefits did not come without a price. Particularly in the Crimean War, they suffered enemy assaults, abductions, attacks by neighboring Azerbaijanis, evacuations, economic disruptions, casualties, and deaths.[44] The settlers' own actions—their active engagement in the military process and conscious decision to support Russian power—also brought illness and loss of property on themselves. In terms of property, the constant use of so many wagons and horses during 1877 and 1878 caused frequent breakdowns and animal deaths.[45] Some settlers contracted disease or were wounded, and approximately 140 Dukhobors died. Sectarians became casualties by coming too close to the range of rifle and artillery fire. Others were infected by the typhus that sectarian drivers carried back from the front into their settlements or that spread through the settler communities because of billeting sick Russian soldiers.[46] Sectarians also endured poor treatment on the part of the Russian soldiers who were temporarily billeted in their villages. Especially during the Crimean War, they often would not pay for services rendered or, worse yet, plunder the village for whatever valuables they could carry away with them.[47]

FROM "PERNICIOUS SECTARIANS" TO "RUSSIAN COLONIZERS"

The attitudes of tsarist officials toward the sectarians changed drastically after their resettlement to Transcaucasia—an evolution in labeling that

42. Ibid., l. 40; RGIA f. 1284, op. 218–1881, d. 34, l. 10; and Vermishev, "Ekonomicheskii byt," 41.
43. SSC'SA f. 239, op. 1, d. 637, 1856–57, ll. 1–10b.
44. Breyfogle, "Caught in the Crossfire?"; SSC'SA f. 240, op. 2, d. 233, 1853–61; d. 317, 1860–63; AKAK vol. 12:1 (1893), doc. 18, p. 38; RGIA f. 1268, op. 9, d. 367a, 1857–58, l. 10b; op. 14, d. 77, 1869–70, ll. 1–10b; ORRGB f. 369, k. 42, d. 2, 1950. ll. 402–4, 407; Zakharii Nikitin, "Iz sel. Elenovki, Novobaiazet. uezda (Proiskhozhdenie Elenovki i khoziaistvennyi byt naseleniia)," KSKh, no. 126 (1896): 2170; Orekhov, "Ocherki," no. 136, 1; Petrov, "Seleniia," 228; and N-n, "Dukhobory," 2–3.
45. RGIA f. 1284, op. 218–1881, d. 34, ll. 9–90b.
46. Ibid.; Vermishev, "Ekonomicheskii byt," 41; ORRGB f. 369, k. 43, d. 1, 1950, l. 813; k. 42, d. 2, 1950, l. 407; Potapov, V plenu, 32; James Wright, Slava Bohu: The Story of the Doukhobors (New York, 1940), 36–37; and N-n, "Dukhobory," 2–3.
47. Nikitin, "Iz sel. Elenovki," (1896), 2170; and "Eshche," 2.

reflects the fertile possibilities that the frontier provided for the transformation of identity. During the opening decades of the nineteenth century, both secular and religious authorities branded the nonconformists not only as heretical pariahs but also as political and strategic threats. A large body of legislation restricting the activities of the sectarian population reflected these beliefs, as did extralegal oppression. Once in Transcaucasia, however, a new classification—the "Russian colonist"—appeared alongside "pernicious heretic," as tsarist bureaucrats came to see the sects as colonizers and representatives of Imperial Russia's interests in the borderlands. In the words of contemporaries, state officials began to view the sectarians "not as exiles, but rather as the first pioneers of the future extensive colonization of an untamed region" and as model colonists who raised "high the banner of Russian culture" in the southern borderlands.[48] This metamorphosis in categorization was a transition of discourse that carried with it significant policy ramifications. The new labeling paved the way for a whole spectrum of benefits and opportunities for the Transcaucasian dissenters, and significantly reduced the legal restrictions and oppression that their brethren continued to face in the interior provinces. However, despite this advent of the pioneer identity, the previous characterization as threatening religious dissenters did not disappear. As the nineteenth century progressed, the "Russian colonist" and "dangerous heretic" labels competed for prominence in the minds of tsarist officials, a divide that was expressed in the policies they created.

The change in attitude toward the sectarians did not take place immediately. The uninterested reception of local officials in the 1830s to the arrival of religious nonconformists reflects the preexisting conception of threatening sectarians and disloyal subjects. Although he provided some limited aid to the destitute dissenters, Chief Administrator of the Caucasus Baron G. V. Rosen pleaded with the Ministry of Internal Affairs in the early 1830s to cease any further settlement of sectarians to the provinces under his governance. He argued that the relocation of such pernicious nonconformists generated no benefit, either for the state or for the region. The settlers, he contended, hindered the indigenous inhabitants in their nomadic migrations and ended the possibility of allowing Turkic peoples or tribes from Persia to settle in the Russian Empire. He forcefully asserted that the concentration of such an unreliable population in so strategically vital an area could be harmful to the

---

48. For the "first pioneers" quotation, see Masalkin, "Kolonizatory," no. 333, 2; and S. Kolosov, "Russkie sektanty v Erivanskoi gubernii," *PKEG na 1902* (Erevan, 1902): otd. IV, 143–55. For the imagery of the banner, see Ilarion Dzhashi, "Obshchestvo Slavianskoe, Elizavetpol'skoi gubernii i uezda," *SMOMPK*, vol. 27 (Tiflis, 1900), otd. 2, 31; and A. K. Borozdin, *Russkoe religioznoe raznomyslie* (St. Petersburg, 1907), 175.

Empire. For Rosen, the danger derived from the "ingrained prejudice" of sectarians and "their natural fervor and struggle for self-interest." These characteristics would negatively affect the indigenous populations, particularly Azerbaijanis and Persians, who were "only just becoming accustomed to order" by inhibiting the development of their devotion to the government. The result would be reluctance on the part of the local inhabitants to contribute voluntarily to the administration of the region and to the support of Russia's armies in times of need. Moreover, in the debates over the resettlement process that took place between Rosen and the Ministry of Internal Affairs, the threat of sectarian contagion remained a primary topic of concern. Rosen argued that the settlement of sectarians in Transcaucasian towns posed a danger to the Russian armed forces stationed in those urban centers because the settlers would spread the antistate content of their religious dissent.[49]

The Ministry disagreed with Rosen, however, downplaying the negative implications of sectarian resettlement in the region and leaving the policy of resettlement in place. Since the sectarians would be settled in small villages far away from each other, reasoned the Ministry, they would never reach a sufficient concentration to have any meaningful impact on the defense or administration of the region. However, while local and central officials disagreed on the degree of potential harm, they agreed on the premise that the resettlement in Transcaucasia would only bring about benefit to the internal provinces from which they were being purged. Even in the Ministry's relatively optimistic estimation, the dissenters would not be contributors to the imperial enterprise—they simply would do no significant damage to it.[50]

Similar views to Rosen's were heard from Commandant Orlovskii, who was placed in charge of sectarian settlement in Shirvan province in the early 1830s. Setting up the new arrivals turned into a debacle that resulted in misery for the sectarians. Orlovskii attempted to explain his own mistakes by writing to superiors that the fault lay with the Molokans, describing them as "extremely disloyal" people who provided refuge for runaways and vagabonds and who, despite being well-off people, begged aid from the treasury. In doing so, he was no different from the many other administrators of the time who consciously manipulated the existing "pernicious heretic" identity for their own ends.[51]

49. RGIA f. 1263, op. 1, d. 791, 1832, ll. 287–910b; and *SPChR* (1875), 152–53, 181–82. On Rosen's overall views on tsarist imperialism in the South Caucasus and his opposition to administrative and cultural "Russification," see Laurens Hamilton Rhinelander, "The Incorporation of the Caucasus into the Russian Empire: The Case of Georgia, 1801–1854" (Ph.D. diss., Columbia University, 1972), 191–215.
50. RGIA f. 1263, op. 1, d. 791, 1832, ll. 296–97.
51. GMIR f. 2, op. 7, d. 597, 1835–40, ll. 4, 6. No initials are given for Orlovskii in the report.

The paradigms that defined the relationship between state authority and Transcaucasian sectarians soon changed, however, during the viceroyship of M. S. Vorontsov (1844–54). In the multi-ethnic and multi-confessional Transcaucasus, state attitudes toward the resettled sectarians metamorphosed from identifying religious nonconformity as the primary essence of these people to spotlighting their Russian ethnicity and the enormous service that sectarians could provide for state power on the Empire's frontier. Although Georgian, Armenian, and Azerbaijani elites filled the ranks of tsarist officialdom, Russian authorities were often driven by an ethnic logic that considered Russians to be inherently more reliable than non-Russians, even if the Russians were not Orthodox.[52] Moreover, when the sectarians began to fulfill administrative, economic, and military goals in ways that far exceeded initial expectations, the categorization of the religious dissenters as political liabilities lost its immediacy. Russian authorities began to realize that these non-Orthodox Russians could be productive, contributing, and loyal subjects of the Empire.

The transformation also had much to do with the character of Viceroy Vorontsov. His biographer, Anthony Rhinelander, describes how "Vorontsov would look for the strength of a particular group even though it might not appear to fit into a traditionally reliable category."[53] The viceroy had come to know the Molokans and Dukhobors during his tenure as governor-general of New Russia, and he had witnessed their contributions to the development of the Molochna region. In Transcaucasia, Vorontsov began to see the sects as a crucial component of the Russian efforts, and the characterization of sectarian-settlers as "dangerous heretics" faded into the background. That said, Vorontsov continued simultaneously to see them as distinct and inferior subjects because of their religious nonconformity. For the good of the Empire, he advocated their continued segregation from Orthodox Russians.

The shift in the views of Russian authorities can be seen in the following 1845 quotation from the Caucasus Committee, which argued that the settlement in Transcaucasia of Russian sectarians was "extremely beneficial, both in the political sense, acting to consolidate Russian dominion there and to integrate the region into the Empire, and especially in the economic sense, strengthening as much as possible the territory's industrial activity and spreading different, previously unknown, forms of

---

52. Ronald G. Suny, "Russian Rule and Caucasian Society in the First Half of the Nineteenth Century: The Georgian Nobility and the Armenian Bourgeoisie," *NP* 7, no. 1 (Spring 1979): 53–78; and Jersild, *Orientalism.*
53. Anthony L. H. Rhinelander, *Prince Michael Vorontsov: Viceroy to the Tsar* (Montreal and Kingston, 1990), 86.

agriculture."[54] Vorontsov agreed wholeheartedly with this evaluation as well as with the need to increase the Russian presence in the area. In an 1848 report, the viceroy lauded the sectarian settlers: "The settlement here of an agricultural population brings to the region unquestionable benefit; a fact of which I am more convinced every day. This is especially true of the Molokans who carry out transport of a variety of sorts and provide the indigenous peoples with an example of how to work the land and a variety of artisanal activities."[55]

This change in attitudes was not simply an intellectual evolution, it also produced concrete legislative results that, in turn, tended to reinforce the revised views about sectarians. Vorontsov instituted a series of polices that greatly extended the privileges accorded to sectarian migrants in the South Caucasus.[56] He did so in an effort to attract more dissenters to the region, to smooth the transition they would have to undergo, and "as much as possible to ameliorate the condition of the Russian migrants settled in Transcaucasia." As D. I. Ismail-Zade, historian of Russian settlement in the Transcaucasus, has asserted, "The broadening of their rights lifted them from the category of the persecuted and gave them the status of that portion of the Russian population which, from the tsarist viewpoint, was to become the bulwark of the regime in the borderlands."[57]

In 1847, Vorontsov set up the Commission for the Organization of Settlements in Transcaucasia. In contrast to the views of his predecessors, who had attributed the initial difficulties of the settlers to their "laziness" and "fanaticism," Vorontsov put the blame on the inactivity and total disregard of the local Chamber of State Properties, "who, in designating lands for settlement, did not think about the climate of the location, the quality and specific quantity of lands, and also did not have positive certification that the allotted land truly belonged to the treasury." In the process, the words he used to describe the sectarians—"Russian migrants"—underscores that he was not viewing them solely as religious or social deviants.[58] In 1848, Vorontsov successfully lobbied for voluntary

54. AKAK vol. 10, doc. 97, pp. 119–20. Reflecting the original intent of the 1830 decree, the Caucasus Committee added that a further benefit of increasing the Russian presence in Transcaucasia was that it would "deprive [the sectarians] of the means to spread their schism among the Orthodox people of the internal provinces." Quotation on 120.
55. RGIA f. 1268, op. 2, d. 865, 1848–52, ll. 3–30b.
56. In addition to the discussion that follows, see also Vorontsov's activities in my "Colonization by Contract: Russian Settlers, South Caucasian Elites, and the Dynamics of Nineteenth-Century Tsarist Imperialism," in Extending the Borders of Russian History: Essays in Honor of Alfred J. Rieber, ed. Marsha Siefert (Budapest, 2003), 143–66.
57. D. I. Ismail-Zade, "Russian Settlements in the Transcaucasus from the 1830s to the 1880s," in The Molokan Heritage Collection, vol. 1, ed. Ethel Dunn and Stephen P. Dunn (Berkeley, 1983), section 3: 58–65, quotation on 64.
58. RGIA f. 1268, op. 2, d. 533, 1847–48, ll. 1–20b; and d. 1021, 1848–53, ll. 50b–14.

FIGURE 7. Women and children of Elenovka, Erevan province, c. 1897. From Esther Lancraft Hovey, "The Old Post-Road from Tiflis to Erivan," *National Geographic Magazine* 12, no. 8 (August 1901): 304.

settlers to Transcaucasia to receive an eight-year tax holiday from the moment of their arrival, a significant increase from the three-year reprieve they had previously enjoyed.[59] He also strove to improve the health of the settlers, providing funds to hire medical personnel to tend to the settlers and reduce the appalling death rate.[60]

As a means to facilitate their material conditions and their new roles as colonizers, Vorontsov also organized for Transcaucasian sectarians to receive economic opportunities and benefits not available to their brethren in the interior provinces. These included not only freedom from economic restrictions but also significant financial investment in their trade and industrial projects.[61] A decree issued in January 1846 made the Transcaucasus an exception to the law that "more pernicious" sectarians were not permitted to live with, hire, or work for Orthodox people—a painfully restrictive law for sectarians in the internal Russian provinces. Law-

59. *SPChR* (1875), 400–401.
60. RGIA f. 1268, op. 2, d. 1021, 1848–53, ll. 34–35.
61. Of numerous examples, see SSC'SA f. 4, op. 2, d. 629, 1847–52; d. 1010, 1849; f. 222, op. 1, d. 6, 1847; and d. 26, 1847–50.

makers agreed with Vorontsov that in Transcaucasia sectarians should be permitted to interact in these ways with Georgian Orthodox inhabitants. Reflecting ongoing concerns about the spread of religious dissent, however, this exception specifically forbade sectarians from hiring, being hired by, and living with Orthodox subjects of Russian descent. In making his case to central authorities, Vorontsov minimized the threatening component of the sects' identity, confident that the nonconformist faiths would not spread because of the linguistic and cultural differences between Russian sectarians and Orthodox Georgians.[62]

Vorontsov also made efforts to enhance the sectarians' role in the imperial enterprise by increasing their presence in Transcaucasia's towns. In doing so, he normalized the identity and status of religious dissenters in comparison to Orthodox Russians. When Vorontsov came to office, existing legislation restricted sectarian urban settlement to those towns populated primarily by Muslims and Armenians as a means to ensure their segregation from the Orthodox Russian administrators and military personnel, who tended to be clustered in metropolitan areas. In 1848, however, Vorontsov lobbied successfully to increase the number of towns in which sectarians could register officially. Sectarian settlement in Transcaucasian towns "would little by little create a lower-middle class urban society," he wrote, adding that "the formation here of an urban *soslovie* would not simply be beneficial, but is absolutely necessary, and the sooner the better." He considered the settlement of Russian sectarians to be the best means by which to accomplish this urbanization process and thereby to strengthen Russia's imperial presence.[63]

To support his request to expand the sectarians' urban presence, Vorontsov noted that one consequence of the permission to allow sectarians in Transcaucasia to work for Georgian Orthodox people was that the dissenters would temporarily hire themselves out to work for urban dwellers in a variety of towns. He reported that such interaction had not led to the spread of the sectarians' beliefs among Orthodox Russians. Indeed, Vorontsov entirely de-emphasized the "pernicious heretic" characterization. He also noted that sectarians in the "Muslim" towns of Shemakha province were relatively prosperous. They worked as "transporters and artisans and greatly facilitated the inhabitants of those towns in the acquisition of necessary goods."

62. RGIA f. 381, op. 1, d. 23322, 1846; and f. 1268, op. 2, d. 566, 1847–48, ll. 11–12, passim. See chapter two for a discussion of the role of legal restrictions on economic activity as an impetus for migration, and chapter three for examples of state economic assistance to the settlers.
63. RGIA f. 1268, op. 2, d. 865, 1848–52, ll. 1–13; op. 6, d. 177, 1852; f. 381, op. 1, d. 23470, 1848, ll. 1–8; and GMIR f. 2, op. 8, d. 237, 1910, l. 71.

"RUSSIAN COLONISTS" VERSUS "PERNICIOUS DISSENTERS," 1850S-1880S

By the end of Vorontsov's rule in 1854, two competing visions of the place of the Transcaucasian sectarians in the Russian imperial enterprise existed—one inclusive, one exclusive. During the following decades, the tension between these two tropes resulted in an ambivalent understanding of the sectarians' place in the Russian Empire, one that was manifested in Dondukov-Korsakov's report. The dual constructs of "Russian colonist" and "pernicious sectarian" existed together uneasily, each attaining preeminence in different contexts and at different times. From the perspective of the government, the sense of the sectarians as superlative colonists and unsurpassed representatives of Russia in the borderlands remained a dominant one, gaining strength with the sectarian contributions to the Russo-Turkish War. Yet the characterization of the politically dangerous sectarian, having been downplayed by Vorontsov, revived under his successors. These two characteristics existed concurrently and often with no great sense of contradiction in the minds of central and regional administrators from the 1850s to the 1880s. Through this period, both administrators and settlers manipulated and drew on these two identity categories in their interactions with each other.

Long-standing antipathy within officialdom toward sectarians remained, as did the central concerns of 1830 to constrict, if not eliminate, the religious, political, and social threats that nonconformity represented.[64] However, three additional processes during the second half of the nineteenth century stimulated renewed concern among officials over religious identities: first, the formation of new subsects (such as the Pryguny and Obshchie) and other sectarian activities in the Transcaucasus; second, the spread in Russia of sectarian groups drawing their religious origins from Western Protestantism, especially the Baptists, Shtundists, and other Evangelical Christians; and third, a transformation in the perspective of the central authorities regarding the importance of Orthodoxy to Russia that accompanied the ascension of K. P. Pobedonostsev to the role of synodal over-procurator.

Although he saw the sectarians as a vital colonizing element, in 1858 Viceroy Prince A. I. Bariatinskii voiced concern over the presence of nonconformists in Transcaucasia, especially their tendency to break into subsects (here he was referring primarily to the Pryguny).[65] Directly linking religious affiliation to disloyal state identity, he described the Pryguny as

---

64. See, for example, RGIA f. 1268, op. 9, d. 367a, 1857–58, ll. 2–20b; f. 384, op. 3, d. 1149, 1846–51, ll. 97–99.
65. RGIA f. 1268, op. 9, d. 367a, 1857–58.

"an absurd, anti-societal sect" that "destroys communal life and weakens respect for and obedience to authorities."[66] More generally, he saw all sectarians as inferior state servants—Orthodox Russians being superior—noting their fanaticism, their lack of "hard rules in their faith," their latent harmful influence on neighboring Muslim inhabitants, the possibility that the sectarians would leave Russia for Turkey, and the threat of the potential seduction of Russian soldiers into religious error—especially deserters, who often found shelter in sectarian villages.[67] In an effort to break sectarians from their religious "errors," he proposed an enormous tax break lasting twenty-five years for all Transcaucasian sectarians who converted to Orthodox Christianity. While Bariatinskii's proposal was a huge jump from the existing laws, which mandated only a three-year tax reprieve for converts, it fell far short of the lifetime respite from taxes granted to Muslim converts to Orthodoxy. Nonetheless, Bariatinskii argued, the conversion of a sectarian to Orthodoxy was far more important to the health of the Empire than the conversion of a Muslim because the sectarians were Russians.[68]

Despite all of these criticisms, however, the Ministry of State Domains was reluctant to grant Bariatinskii's petition and disagreed over the need for conversion at all. In challenging the viceroy's assertions, the Ministry argued that sectarians were excellent colonists and a boon to the region, and also that since the end of the 1830s regional leaders had repeatedly requested increases in the rate of sectarian resettlement, a pattern inconsistent with the premise that sectarian identity posed an urgent problem. This line of thinking and the final result, that new tax incentives for conversion were not granted, reflects how strongly the "Russian colonist" identity of sectarians had taken hold among central state officials, even as it was being destabilized by authorities at the local level.[69] It is remarkable to consider that it had been only a few decades since the central administration had jettisoned the sectarians out to the periphery as pariahs—a process during which the Ministry of State Domains had done precious little to ensure their survival—and yet here was the very same ministry lauding their colonial contributions. Additionally, the disagreement between Bariatinskii and the Ministry of State Domains illuminates the degree to which central and local administrators frequently clashed over the needs and trajectories of tsarist colonialism and religious policy.

---

66. RGIA f. 381, op. 2, d. 2014, 1858, ll. 170b–18. On the Pryguny in general, see SSC'SA f. 5, op. 1, d. 183, 1865; d. 776, 1868; RGIA f. 1268, op. 9, d. 481, 1857; and N. D. Dingel'shtedt, *Zakavkazskie sektanty v ikh semeinom i religioznom bytu* (St. Petersburg, 1885).
67. RGIA f. 381, op. 2, d. 2014, 1858, ll. 30b–4, 170b–18, 23–230b.
68. Ibid., l. 40b. For the broader context of tsarist population politics in the region in which Bariatinskii was making his decisions, see Peter Holquist, "To Count," 116–19.
69. RGIA f. 381, op. 2, d. 2014, 1858, ll. 22–310b.

The appearance in the late 1860s of Shtundists, Baptists, and Pash-kovites in various parts of the Russian Empire and especially of Baptists in Transcaucasia after 1877 had the effect of undermining the valuation of South Caucasian sectarians as loyal and contributing members of the state community.[70] Inspired by Western Protestantism, the rapid spread of these new sects was considered exceptionally dangerous to the well-being of the Russian state, as it threatened the accepted meaning of Russianness at its very core, especially the link between Russian ethnicity and Orthodox religion.[71] Dukhobors, Molokans, and Subbotniks were separate religious phenomena, but the eruption of Baptists and Shtundists tainted all religious dissenters in the eyes of tsarist authorities.

In the mid-1880s, in the context of deteriorating Russian-German relations, the Exarch of Georgia, like many others, described the Baptists as a grave threat not only to the Orthodox Church, but also to the state, because Shtundists and Baptists "are ready enemies of Russia and allies of Protestant Germany." (He was quick to emphasize that the Baptists were an even greater menace than Polish Catholicism.) "Infection" by these foreign faiths, he continued, destroyed "all sympathy for the Russian people" and for its ideals, legends, and folk beliefs. Such saturation, "with hate both for Orthodoxy and for Russian nationality," would result in secular marriages and the destruction of family structures. In addition to the ravaging of Russianness, the Exarch maintained, the beliefs of these Baptists also spawned "tremendous revolutionary power."[72] Chief Administrator in the Caucasus A. M. Dondukov-Korsakov continued in this vein, asserting that such foreign sects separated a Russian person from his "native Orthodoxy." By converting to German Protestantism, Russians extinguished in themselves any sympathy for the Russian people, their way of life, and their social and religious beliefs. "In a word, it makes them non-Russian."[73]

In addition to this general unease, the presence of Baptists in the Transcaucasus presented special problems to the administrators of the region. For Dondukov-Korsakov, such deformity of the Russian character

---

70. On the history of these groups in general, see Heather Coleman, "The Most Dangerous Sect: Baptists in Tsarist and Soviet Russia, 1905–1929" (Ph.D. diss., University of Illinois at Urbana–Champaign, 1998); Sergei I. Zhuk, "Russia's Lost Reformation: Peasants and Radical Religious Sects in Southern Russia and Ukraine, 1830–1905" (Ph.D. diss., Johns Hopkins University, 2002); A. I. Klibanov, *Istoriia religioznogo sektantstva v Rossii (60–e gody XIX v.—1917 g.)* (Moscow, 1965), 187–285; and Andrew Blane, "Protestant Sects in Late Imperial Russia," in *The Religious World of Russian Culture*, vol. II, ed. idem (The Hague, 1975), 267–304.
71. On the views of central tsarist authorities concerning the threat of these new religious movements, see A. Iu. Polunov, "Gosudarstvo i religioznoe inakomyslie v Rossii (1880–nachalo 1890-kh godov)," in *Rossiia i reformy: Sbornik statei*, vol. 3, ed. M. A. Kolerov (Moscow, 1995), 126–41.
72. RGIA f. 1284, op. 221–1885, d. 74, ll. 110b–120b.
73. RGIA f. 1284, op. 221–1886, d. 75, l. 4, passim; and *Sektanty Kavkaza* (Tiflis, 1890).

represented a severe security risk to the Russian Empire in the southern borderlands. The threat derived in part from the conversion of Molokans to the "foreign" Baptist faith: the very social foundation of Russian colonialism in Transcaucasia was being swayed into the reviled "German faith." To explain Molokan conversion, Tsarist officials mentioned that sectarians lacked the anchor of Orthodox teachings to keep them from deviating into "heresies." Further, Molokans were "generally very receptive to any form of rationalistic religious teachings, and they zealously read and spread forbidden books containing religious false-teachings."[74] While only a small number of Molokans actually did join the Baptists, the appearance of Protestant faiths in Russia made all Transcaucasian sectarians suspect. It reinvigorated the idea shared by both secular and religious central authorities, that membership in the Orthodox Church was a prerequisite for Russian ethnicity and faithful service to the larger Russian Empire (*Rossiia*).[75]

Third, Pobedonostsev's assumption of the position of over-procurator—followed in short order by the ascension of his pupil Alexander III to the throne—heralded a shift in the relationship between state power and non-Orthodox Christians in the Empire. In the spirit of the Great Reforms, his predecessors had moved to tolerate a degree of religious nonconformity, as seen in the laws of 1858, 1864, 1874, and 1883.[76] The result had been a policy toward religious dissenters characterized by benign indifference at worst and conciliatory acceptance at best, in which religious faith in and of itself, was not considered an offense. In stark contrast, Pobedonostsev vehemently believed, in the words of the historian Alexander Polunov, that "a vital society can be united solely by one power (autocracy) and one faith."[77] He argued that politics could not be sepa-

---

74. RGIA f. 1284, op. 221–1885, d. 74, ll. 14–140b.

75. While very real in their minds, the Transcaucasian authorities' fears of mass conversion to the "de-Russianizing German faith" appear to have been overstated. See GMIR f. K1, op. 8, d. 516, n.d.; d. 470, 1925; f. 14, op. 2, d. 104, n.d.; RGIA f. 1284, op. 221–1882, d. 44; op. 221–1886, d. 75, ll. 6–60b; op. 221–1885, d. 74, ll. 70b–8; and my "Heretics and Colonizers: Religious Dissent and Russian Colonization of Transcaucasia, 1830–1890," (Ph.D. diss., University of Pennsylvania, 1998), 271–347.

76. *SPChR* (1875), 609–17, 672–82; *PSZ* (3), no. 1545 (May 3, 1883), 219–21; V. I. Iasevich-Borodaevskaia, *Bor'ba za veru. Istoricheko-bytovye ocherki i obzor zakonodatel'stva po staroobriadchestvu i sektantstvu v ego posledovatel'nom razvitii* (St. Petersburg, 1912), 1–108; N. L. Solov'ev, *Polnyi krug dukhovnykh zakonov* (Moscow, 1907), 18–44; and Peter Waldron, "Religious Toleration in Late Imperial Russia," in *Civil Rights in Imperial Russia*, ed. Olga Crisp and Linda Edmondson (Oxford, 1989), 109–11.

77. Polunov, "Gosudarstvo," 130; idem, *Pod vlast'iu ober-prokuratora. Gosudarstvo i tserkov' v epokhu Aleksandra III* (Moscow, 1996); idem, "Politicheskaia individual'nost' K. P. Pobedonostseva" *VMU Seriia 8, Istoriia*, no. 2 (1991): 42–48; and D. K. Burlaka and S. L. Firsov, eds., *K. P. Pobedonostsev: Pro et Contra* (St. Petersburg: 1996), esp. 80–275, which is a reprint of Pobedonostsev's *Moskovskii Sbornik*. For a critique of Pobedonostsev's "one state/one nation/one religion policy," in which I. V. Tregubov argued that "Orthodoxy cannot guarantee the welfare of Russia," see GARF f. 124, op. 5, d. 267, 1896, ll. 4–50b.

rated from morality and spirituality, and that religion was irrevocably tied to nationality: "Our enemies are cutting us off from a mass of Russian people and making them into Germans, Catholics, Muslims and others, and we are losing them for the Church and for the Fatherland forever."[78] With these new currents of central policy, the sectarians of Transcaucasia found themselves increasingly besieged for their religious nonconformity. State officials characterized them as threats to Fatherland, society, and Russian nationality, and developed policies based on those principles.

Despite the revival of the "pernicious sectarian" characterization, with its unease concerning the loyalty of sectarians to the state, the "model colonist" trope retained much of its power. Not only did a deep acceptance of the sectarians' role as colonizers and representatives of the Russian Empire in the borderlands persist, but their colonist identity exerted a strong influence on tsarist colonial and ethnic policy in the region. Tiflis governor G. D. Shervashidze voiced many of these views in an 1895 report concerning the Dukhobors:

> Resettled among so unpropitious conditions, enduring deprivation and dire straits, they, thanks to persistent work and a prudent lifestyle, not only attained material well-being, but forced the surrounding population to respect them. . . . Stretched out over three provinces among the poor native peoples, their flourishing villages were pleasing oases. From the political perspective, they represented staging points for Russian affairs and influence in the region.[79]

Such positive estimations of the sectarians were hardly restricted to official circles; voices of praise rang out also among Russian nongovernmental elites, journalists, and ethnographers. The settlers' exploits had begun to enter the collective consciousness and to change the opinions of educated Russians about the place of religious nonconformity in Russia. The statistician V. P. Bochkarev in 1897 opined: "With the exception of their religious deviation from Orthodoxy, in all other remaining relations they remain devoted to the interests of the Fatherland to the point of self-sacrifice, which they demonstrated more than once during the wars with Turkey in 1855 and 1878."[80]

Earlier in the century, Bariatinskii presaged Shervashidze's positive

78. Quotation is from a letter to E. F. Tiutcheva, December 20, 1881. The letter is reprinted in Aleksandr Polunov, ed., "K. P. Pobedonostsev v 1881 godu (Pis'ma k E. F. Tiutchevoi)," in *Reka vremen, kniga pervaia, gosudar'–gosudarstvo–gosluzhba* (Moscow, 1995), 185.
79. Shervashidze is quoted in Borozdin, *Russkoe,* 175.
80. V. P. Bochkarev, "Karsskaia oblast'," in *RTKE* (Tiflis, 1897), 368. See also I. P. Iuvachev (Miroliubov), "Zakavkazskie sektanty," *IV* 95 (February 1904): 597; Studzinskii, "U nashikh," 124; N-n, "Dukhobory," 2–3; and Velichko, *Kavkaz,* 203.

perspective. In 1857, less than a year before his attack on the Pryguny and his proposal of twenty-five years of tax amnesty to converts, Bariatin-skii reported to the Caucasus Committee that the settlement of Russian sectarians in Transcaucasia "has been highly beneficial for the growth of agriculture and industry here," pointing to their seminal contributions during the Crimean War. As a result of this approving estimation, Baria-tinskii argued to increase the number of Russian settlers in the region and lamented the lack of state land on which to settle them. In order to increase the possibilities of settling more Russian sectarians in Transcau-casia, Bariatinskii lobbied successfully to have them settle on unoccupied parcels of land owned by local nobles. This was a highly irregular request because the settlers were officially state peasants and therefore could not legally be settled on privately owned land. Indeed, Vorontsov had pro-posed this as a solution to the land crisis in the 1840s and 1850s, but the minister of state domains, P. D. Kiselev, turned him down because of the incongruities, from a *soslovie* perspective, of state peasants inhabiting land owned by nobles. However, by 1858, the desire to increase the Rus-sian population in Transcaucasia had grown to such a degree that both Bariatinskii and authorities in St. Petersburg were willing to increase the influx of sectarians and allow them to make their new homes on noble land.[81]

Viceroy Grand Duke Michael Nikolaevich (1862–82) was a particu-larly staunch supporter of the sectarian settlers, especially in light of their contributions to tsarist military endeavors during the Russo-Turkish War.[82] The Grand Duke lauded their colonial activities on numerous oc-casions, such as in a report from the late 1860s: "Time and experience have demonstrated that the settlement of Russian settlers brings great benefit to the region in economic and industrial respects. Especially im-portant is their settlement near our borders both for political as well as for military goals. For, each settlement strengthens the Russian element there and increases convenient means of conveyance, so important dur-ing wartime."[83]

His official characterization of sectarians as effective colonizers pro-duced numerous economic and social benefits for the dissenters. The Molokans of Vorontsovka in Tiflis province profited from the viceroy's

81. RGIA f. 1268, op. 9, d. 367a, 1857–58, ll. 1–28; and *AKAK* vol. 12:1 (1893), doc. 18, p. 37–42. The relations between settlers and South Caucasian landowners is discussed in chapter five and my "Colonization by Contract."

82. Breyfogle, "Caught in the Crossfire?"; and GMIR f. 2, op. 8, d. 237, 1910, l. 50.

83. RGIA f. 1268, op. 14, d. 77, 1869–70, ll. 1–10b. In his 1867 review of the region, Senator Prince Bagration-Mukhranskii made almost identical comments about the great military, eco-nomic, and political importance of the sectarian settlers in Transcaucasia. See Orekhov, "Ocherki," no. 136, 1.

positive estimation of them in their efforts to buy land from the Georgian noble on whose property they had been settled. In the mid-1840s, the village of Vorontsovka had been established on land belonging to Prince Makarii Orbeliani based on a contract due to expire in 1871. Unhappy with the structure of the agreement—especially the requirement to pay quitrent and the insecurity of their property situation—the Vorontsovka Molokans declared their intention in 1869 to migrate upon the termination of the contract to the North Caucasus, where they believed they could acquire their own land. Grand Duke Michael made his dissatisfaction with this prospect plain: "Such a disappearance of so considerable a Russian population from an area which has both political as well as strategic importance would have extremely unfavorable consequences."[84]

Reflecting this "colonist" classification of sectarians, the Chief Administration of Transcaucasia made wide-ranging efforts to keep the Molokans in Vorontsovka. It proposed that the settlers buy from Orbeliani 8,000 *desiatiny* of land they had been using. However, an enormous chasm existed between Orbeliani's asking price, which was based on the land value, and the amount that the sectarians could afford to pay. In their efforts to keep the settlers in place, tsarist officials negotiated the price down from twenty rubles per *desiatina* to seven, but even then the Molokans did not have the 56,000 rubles necessary to purchase the land. So the local authorities granted a loan to make up the difference, a plan that Grand Duke Michael supported in no uncertain terms. Again, he pointed to the "great importance" of Russian settlements so near the border and to the benefit that would result from transforming these Russian peasants into private proprietors. In the final result, Vorontsovka's Molokans received 32,000 rubles in an interest-free loan to be repaid over a fifteen-year period and were also given 8,000 rubles as a one-time gift. Tsarist officials so valued the sectarians' imperialist functions that they were willing to go to great lengths to retain and strengthen the "Russian colonizers" in the region, to the point that the Molokans had to pay only 16,000 rubles for land that had originally been valued at 160,000 rubles.[85]

Moreover, as a reward for their activities during the Russo-Turkish War, Grand Duke Michael set aside for sectarians the choicest land allotments in the newly conquered Kars territory, thereby permitting many of them to benefit materially from Russia's war gains.[86] Indeed, so indis-

84. RGIA f. 1268, op. 14, d. 77, 1869–70, ll. 10b–2.
85. Ibid., ll. 1–210b; RGIA f. 1284, op. 221–1885, d. 22, ll. 1–50b; and Orekhov, "Ocherki," no. 136, 1.
86. ORRGB f. 369, k. 42, d. 2, 1950, ll. 407–10; RGIA f. 932, op. 1, d. 319, 1890, ll. 5–50b; Inikova, "Istoriia," 128; Bochkarev, "Karsskaia oblast'," 325–519; RGIA f. 932, op. 1, d. 298, 1882;

pensable did he consider the Dukhobors' and Molokans' contributions to the military effort that he traveled to Dukhobor villages personally to thank them for their help and to pay honor to the elders who had led the way. Additionally, he petitioned the Ministry of Internal Affairs to allow him to grant the Dukhobors' *starshina*, Aleksei Zubkov, "hereditary honored citizen" status in reward for his community's exemplary contributions during the war. Russian law forbade the awarding of such an honor to the members of any sect designated "most pernicious," but the viceroy appealed fervently for an exception. He described the Dukhobors' assistance to the Russian war effort and argued that the "fulfillment of service demonstrates to the government their exemplary moral qualities—qualities of which I am personally aware." Here, as a result of their efforts on behalf of the Russian military cause, the viceroy was requesting something relatively radical: that the state treat sectarians as equals of Orthodox Russians, if only in this one case. The Ministries of the Interior, Justice, and War all concurred with this plan to reduce the legal barriers between different religious groups. Only the Synod's opposition prevented Zubkov from receiving the award.[87]

As well as being a heartfelt enunciation of their official appreciation, declarations of praise and acts of appreciation to the sectarians not unexpectedly also had a utilitarian component. By lauding and rewarding their actions, tsarist officials hoped to ensure that these Russian settlers would continue to provide such services in the future. For instance, following the Dukhobors' assistance to the carabineers during the Crimean War, both Viceroy Bariatinskii and the High Commander, Lieutenant-General Prince Vasilii Osipovich Bebutov, personally thanked the sectarians for their "zeal" and for the free transportation they had provided. They hoped that their official gestures of appreciation "would serve as encouragement for them in the future and also as an example for other Russian settlers." In a similar vein, following the Russo-Turkish War, Mikhail Nikolaevich believed that official recognition of the Dukhobor efforts was absolutely necessary because he feared that without such praise the Dukhobors would in future lose interest in the needs of the Russian state.[88]

As a result of their growing reputation as unmatched colonizers and despite any concerns over their religious nonconformity, tsarist officials

d. 333, 1884; d. 306, 1882; f. 796, op. 442, d. 1612, 1896, ll. 78–790b; ORRGB f. 369, k. 42, d. 2, 1950, l. 70; and Petrov, "Dukhobory," 178.

87. RGIA f. 1284, op. 218–1881, d. 34, ll. 100b–12, 14–15, 23–30, passim. Similar cases can be found in RGIA f. 1268, op. 3, d. 438, 1849; and f. 1284, op. 222–1902, d. 70.

88. SSC'SA f. 240, op. 2, d. 233, 1853–61, ll. 160b–17, 57–570b; RGIA f. 1284, op. 218–1881, d. 34, ll. 100b–12; and f. 1268, op. 3, d. 438, 1849.

began to use the sectarians as colonists in Central Asia and Siberia. In fact, in general discussions of Russian colonization throughout Eurasia in the late nineteenth century, sectarians "stood at the top of the empire's settler hierarchy."[89] Local officials in the Transcaspian region argued that "Molokans represent an extremely appropriate element for the Russian colonization of the region," and Molokan families did move there during the late 1880s and early 1890s. Here, Molokan hopes to escape to escape land shortages in Transcaucasia dovetailed with the wishes of tsarist authorities to enhance the Russian presence in the area.[90]

Even when Orthodox Russians began to move into Transcaucasia in the late 1880s, local officials repeatedly lamented that their skills as colonizers paled in comparison with the abilities and achievements of the sectarians—an assessment that further solidified the perception of sectarians as outstanding colonists. Unlike the sturdy, adaptable, economically successful nonconformists, reports indicate that Orthodox settlers drank too much, were poor farmers, and frequently returned to the interior provinces after a short time.[91] Ethnographer I. E. Petrov captured the prevailing views among both tsarist officials and Russian commentators:

> In the history of Russian colonization in the Caucasus, sectarians played an extremely visible role. Even the most fervent opponents of sectarianism cannot but recognize them as excellent colonizers of the region, who with their impeccable sober lives, well-designed economy, highly regarded comfortable circumstances, won respect among the cultured indigenous population. . . . Instinctively, the student of Russian colonization in the Caucasus makes the parallel between the sectarians and today's settlers, and without any choice, sadly has to realize that the palm of primacy . . . must be given, not to the present-day settlers, but to the sectarians.[92]

Lieutenant-General A. N. Kuropatkin even argued that "by the solid construction of their villages, the way that they carry out their economic ac-

89. Willard Sunderland, "The 'Colonization Question': Visions of Colonization in Late Imperial Russia," *JGO* 48, no. 2 (2000): 223; and Charles Steinwedel, "Resettling People, Unsettling the Empire: Migration, Colonization, and the Challenge of Governance, 1861–1917," in *Peopling the Periphery: Russian Settlement in Eurasia from Muscovite to Soviet Times,* ed. Nicholas B. Breyfogle, Abby Schrader, and Willard Sunderland (forthcoming).

90. RGIA f. 1284, op. 221–1888, d. 73, quotation on ll.1–10b; A. N. Kuropatkin, *Soobrazheniia nachal'nika Zakaspiiskoi oblasti po voprosu o pereselenii v Zakaspiiskuiu oblast' dukhoborov-postnikov* (n.p., n.d.), appendices 1–5; Masalkin, "Kolonizatory," no. 333, 3; and RGIA f. 821, op. 133, d. 93. On Siberia, see A. I. Klibanov, *History of Religious Sectarianism in Russia (1860s–1917),* ed. Stephen Dunn, trans. Ethel Dunn (New York, 1982), 184–96; and Iu. V. Argudiaeva, *Krest'ianskaia sem'ia u vostochnykh slavian na iuge Dal'nego Vostoka Rossii (50-e gody XIX v.–nachalo XX v.)* (Moscow, 1997).

91. See for example, GARF f. 102, 3 d-vo, op. 1884, d. 88, ch. 2, ll. 3–60b; RGIA f. 560, op. 26, d. 86, 1894, ll. 700b–71; "O pereselentsakh v Karsskoi oblasti," *Kavkaz,* no. 22 (August 1, 1890): 2; and *AKAK* vol. 12:1 (1893), doc. 18, p. 40.

92. Petrov, "Seleniia," 247.

tivities, their friendly, harmonious lives, mutual help, and hard-working ethic, the Dukhobors . . . constituted a dependable colonizing element and could serve as a useful example for the population around them . . . not only the indigenous peoples but also the [Orthodox] Russian population in the area."[93]

The "model colonist" typology continued into the twentieth century, with important repercussions for the role of sectarians in the Empire. Around the turn of the century, elections to the Lenkoran town duma at times returned a larger percentage of Muslims than Russian law permitted. In consequence, the governor stepped in and appointed Molokans to fill the excess seats. The choice of Molokans rested consciously on their Russian ethnicity and their classification as loyal subjects. This was especially true at the end of the nineteenth century when tsarist opinion of Armenians—who, as Christians, had been Russia's traditional support in eastern Transcaucasia—had taken a negative turn because of the rise of Armenian nationalist-separatist groups. The consequence of this politics of ethnic categorization permitted the Molokans a much larger representation in governing bodies than their percentage of the population demanded.[94]

The change in the state identification of the sectarians illuminates ways in which events on the periphery affected other areas of the Empire, including the central provinces. The dissenters' success as colonizers influenced the structure of Russian colonialism throughout the Empire, as both local and central officials often pushed for sectarians to act as the advance guard of settlement in diverse parts of the Empire, and in the process spread the geographic range of their religious communities. Moreover, the praise and acceptance that was extended to the dissenters in Transcaucasia—the realization that these non-Orthodox Russians could be productive, contributing, and loyal subjects of the Empire—affected the place of sectarian Christians throughout the Empire, expanding the parameters of religious toleration in Russia, even if that toleration was not shared by all officials and commentators. Indeed, legislation that was applied to the Transcaucasian dissenters in an effort to facilitate their colonizing efforts often came later to be granted to non-Orthodox Russians elsewhere.

At the same time, the ultimately ambivalent approach of tsarist officials to the sectarians also manifested itself in a reformulation of the

93. Kuropatkin, *Soobrazheniia*, 15, 40.

94. *Vsepoddanneishii otchet o proizvedennoi v 1905 godu po vysochaishchuiu poveleniiu senatorom Kuzmin-skim revizii goroda Baku i Bakinskoi gubernii* (St. Petersburg, 1906), 359. On changing tsarist perspectives on the Armenian population, see RGIA f. 1287, op. 38, d. 3471, 1898–1907; and Ronald Grigor Suny, *Looking Toward Ararat: Armenia in Modern History* (Bloomington, 1993), 31–93.

meanings of religious dissent. In 1889, Dondukov-Korsakov renewed a proposal that Mikhail Nikolaevich had originally tendered in 1866 for an alteration in the resettlement laws that would end the exile of particularly zealous sectarians to the South Caucasus while still permitting voluntary resettlement. Both leaders worried about the "extremely harmful influence" that exiles had not only on the Orthodox population but also on the remaining nonconformists who were otherwise excellent colonists. Here, in contrast with the early nineteenth century, when all religious dissenters were lumped together in the same negative category, Mikhail Nikolaevich and Dondukov-Korsakov were redefining the "sectarian" label by differentiating between the majority that could be considered loyal and contributing subjects (equal with or even better than other subjects) and a smaller group of bad apples who actively spread their "heresy" and needed to be treated more harshly than banishment to the South Caucasus entailed.[95]

SECTARIANS VIEW TSARIST AUTHORITY

The sectarians' own sense of their place within Russian society and polity underwent transformations similar to the changes in official characterizations. Molokans, Dukhobors, and Subbotniks arrived in Transcaucasia as self-defined outsiders in the tsarist state. In the early nineteenth century, they considered themselves true Christians, claimed spiritual descent from the early Christian fathers, and compared themselves favorably to a corrupt and misguided Orthodox Church. Although the specific religious beliefs and practices varied from sect to sect, generally they saw themselves as people chosen by God and found communal identity with God's world, not with any earthly state or ethnic community.

Once in Transcaucasia, however, the sectarians' feelings of membership in, and their influence on, the Russian Empire grew rapidly. Official persecution receded, state authorities treated sectarian settlers as colonists, and the dissenters found new roles and opportunities to serve along with the attendant benefits. Flanking their religious identity appeared a sense of state affiliation and a willingness to voice such an identification (especially among Molokans). Thus, like tsarist elites, sectarians also possessed both dissenter and colonizer self-identities. However, whereas state categories dealt in the sharp parameters of "us" and "them," individual self-definition did not. Sectarians possessed a whole spectrum of self-

---

95. RGIA f. 398, op. 53, d. 17201, 1889; f. 1149, op. 6t-1866, d. 108; f. 396, op. 1, d. 1270, 1897, ll. 70b–11, passim; and Kuropatkin, *Soobrazheniia*, appendix 2, 1.

definitional identities and affiliations, of which only one was manifest at any given moment.[96]

The sectarians' enunciation of commonality with tsarist interests may have reflected the internalization of an identification with state power or a conscious, instrumental manipulation of a discourse of loyalty—or some combination of the two: many did in fact see themselves as part of a larger Russian state and ethnicity while simultaneously realizing the benefit that could be derived from voicing such loyalties at appropriate moments. However, even if entirely mercenary in intent, such declarations of integration with the larger imperial polity were, in and of themselves, a fundamentally new behavior for the sectarians, one that joined them in novel ways to a pan-imperial conversation of support for tsar, government, and Fatherland. Indeed, prior to their relocation to Transcaucasia, these nonconformist communities voiced a bond with the tsarist state, whether strategic or heartfelt, only on scattered occasions.

Particularly from the 1850s onward, sectarians in the South Caucasus came to associate themselves with the Russian state along with their emphasis on being God's people. For instance, on the occasion of the visit of Alexander II to Tiflis in 1871, Vasilii Emel'ianov Shubin, a Prygun, wrote songs in praise of the Emperor.

> We, natural sons of Russia
> Will sing these verses
> And with thundering voices praise
> And glorify the Emperor!
> The Emperor is a great Tsar,
> Ruler of all Russia
> Anointed by God our Father!
> We are ready to make all sacrifices for you.
> To take up arms against enemies
> For the Tsar, all Russian people are ready.
> We are your faithful subjects
> And you are Autocrat of us all
> We praise you out of love
> And wish you health.[97]

96. For a discussion of different levels of interpersonal systems, see Jim Orford, "Theories of Person-in-Context" in *Community Psychology: Theory and Practice* (New York, 1992), 26–29. Eric Hobsbawm makes a similar argument in his discussion of national identity: "Men and women did not choose collective identification as they chose shoes, knowing that one could only put on one pair at a time. They had, and still have, several attachments and loyalties simultaneously, including nationality, and are simultaneously concerned with various aspects of life, any of which may at any one time be foremost in their minds, as occasion suggests." E. J. Hobsbawm, *Nations and Nationalism Since 1780: Programme, Myth, Reality*, 2nd ed. (Cambridge, 1992), 123.
97. Quoted in N. D. [Nikolai Dingel'shtedt], "Pryguny (Materialy k istoriia obruseniia Zakavkazskogo kraia)," *OZ*, no. 10 (1878): 410–14.

Similarly, on the ascension of Alexander III to the throne, Molokans and Subbotniks from numerous communities wrote to the tsar expressing their "heavy and sad feelings" at the "martyr's death" of Alexander II and their "true subject happiness" for the reign of the new monarch.[98] Vocalization of their sense of integration in the state community continued into the twentieth century. Molokans in Kars territory in 1908, for example, expressed to local officials their "true subject love" to Russia and their "devotion and readiness to champion with might and main the defense of Tsar and dear Rus."[99]

The new self-identification grew up in part from the state's more tolerant treatment of sectarians in Transcaucasia after the mid-1840s. As one Russian journalist described the transformation in a newspaper article in 1868, "From the time that local police powers terminated their strict surveillance of, and interference in, the religious affairs of the sectarians, the dissenters no longer have cause to nourish any hostile feelings toward the government because they no longer suffer any constraints on their conscience.... From this, it is not surprising that Molokans genuinely reject the liberal points of their founders' teachings."[100] Indeed, a lawyer representing Dukhobors in a court case in 1889 declared that "from [the 1840s] to the present moment, [they] have felt themselves to be citizens completely equal in rights to the surrounding population, enjoying goodwill and patronage on the part of the existing powers in general."[101]

Additionally, the perquisites and privileges that they received as "Russian colonists" increased sectarian manifestations of respect for earthly authority. In 1884, when the Molokans of Vorontsovka had paid off the treasury loan that they had received in order to buy the land from Prince Orbeliani, they wrote to thank the tsar for his financial help. The letter reflects both the transition in their views toward the state as well as a desire to be seen by tsarist authorities as loyal subjects. In gratitude for the monetary aid the Molokans organized a celebration during which they prayed for the tsar

> so that God will not take away his blessing from the venerable house of the Russian Throne, and so that God inalienably will crown with wisdom . . .

98. RGIA f. 1284, op. 220–1882, d. 32, ll. 1–10b; *Kaspii* 3, no. 65 (June 10, 1883): 2; *Kaspii* 1, no. 95 (December 9, 1881): 2; *Kaspii* 2, no. 113 (October 17, 1882), 2; A. I. Masalkin, "K istorii zakavkazskikh sektantov: II Subbotniki," *Kavkaz*, no. 307 (November 19, 1893): 22; and RGIA f. 821, op. 133, d. 213, 1915, l. 2.

99. *Karsskii oblastnoi s"ezd dukhovnykh khristian 1-go, 2-go i 3-go iiunia 1908 g v sel. Vladikarse, Karsskogo uchastka i okruga* (Kars, 1908), 4–5.

100. K. S-A., "Russkie raskol'niki, poselenye v Bakinskoi gubernii," *Kavkaz*, no. 10 (January 24, 1868): 3. See also GMIR f. 2, op. 8, d. 237, 1910, ll. 50, 71.

101. SSC'SA f. 244, op. 3, d. 573, 1888, l. 49.

his Majesty the Emperor Alexander Aleksandrovich III so that we under his blessed regal patronage will live in peace and quiet. And [we pray] so that the Almighty God with His powerful hand will threaten all the Tsar's enemies who make an attempt upon the peaceful life of Russia. . . . Long live the Russian Tsar!! Each soul, putting his hand to his chest, reverently pours out ardent prayers to God about the blessed Russian Tsar![102]

While the Vorontsovka Molokans praised the tsar in their letter of thanks, they were also sure to underscore that they used Molokan rites and prayers, not Orthodox ones. Thus, even though the Molokans now showed greater deference and respect for the tsar, the transition to loyal servitors did not lead them to abandon their religious beliefs and practices.[103]

Participation in Russia's war efforts, whether to their benefit or detriment, helped to foster close ties between the sectarians and the Russian state. The clash of empires and the incursions of enemy armies into their villages forced choices on the settlers. Faced with the alternatives of Russian or Ottoman sovereignty, the nonconformists chose to align themselves with Russian ethnicity, a pan-Christian alliance, and the protections of Russian political and military power—a sense of affiliation with Imperial Russia that lasted well beyond the end of the wars. Passing through the Molokan village of Vorontsovka during the Russo-Turkish War, the soldier Studzinskii found the inhabitants hungry for information from the front: "One female member of the family asked: 'Will we drive away the Turks?' When she heard that the Turks were holding their ground, she was overcome with feelings of regret."[104] Dukhobors took pride in their contributions to the Russian military enterprise. Describing their services and exploits, one Dukhobor was "carried away by a . . . feeling of patriotism" and declared with self-satisfaction that "'Muhtar Pasha, they say, learned about all these services of ours and long grieved, regretting that he did not destroy us all at the beginning.'"[105]

Not unexpectedly, the sectarians frequently utilized a discourse of state loyalty when petitioning to attain various goals. For example, when Molokans from a variety of locales in the South Caucasus approached the government in the late 1890s and early 1900s with requests for permission to build prayer houses—long forbidden under tsarist law—the petitioners focused on the Molokans' record as loyal subjects in the Caucasus and promised even greater dedication in the future, "carrying to God heartfelt prayers about the health of You and Your August Family."

102. RGIA f. 1284, op. 221–1885, d. 22, ll. 1–30b.
103. For similar cases, see *Kaspii* 3, no. 65 (June 10, 1883): 2; and *Kaspii* 1, no. 95 (December 9, 1881): 2.
104. Studzinskii, "U nashikh," 123.
105. N-n, "Dukhobory," 3.

In one case, Molokan supplicants from Nizhnie Akhty in Erevan Province argued that they deserved the right to build a communal prayer house "because they have lived in Transcaucasia for fifty years and have been good subjects of the Tsar, have done nothing blameworthy and will continue to be true subjects of the Tsar."[106] Similarly, in 1913, petitioners from the village of Vorontsovka wrote to the Viceroy, I. I. Vorontsov-Dashkov, in an effort to free their preacher and spiritual leader, who had been arrested for spreading the Molokan faith. In their appeal, they underscored the assistance that their forefathers supplied the Russian Empire both during the Russo-Turkish War and during the Azerbaijani-Armenian violence of 1905.[107]

In tandem with these public expressions of their state identification, sectarian communities also became more willing and reliable in the fulfillment of their subject obligations, as their military, administrative, and economic service suggests.[108] Discussing this new relationship with state power one newspaper asserted: "all Russian sectarians constitute the most obedient and peaceful population."[109] In 1878, moreover, governors' reports from across the region all noted no antagonistic relations between sectarians and either the local authorities or Orthodox priesthood. Quite the opposite, the conduct of sectarians was "industrious" and "exemplary," and they had accorded state officials full respect and obedience.[110] A police file discussing Erevan province in 1883 relates: "Russian sectarian-Molokan settlers . . . remain devoted to the government and preserve their Russian distinctiveness."[111]

However, their newfound sense of affiliation with the Russian state did not eclipse their feelings of religious difference. The nonconformists held dual identities of state association and theologically based sectarian disenchantment from state power. Even when they prayed for the tsar, they did so as Molokans, Dukhobors, and Subbotniks, as the example of the Vorontsovka Molokans demonstrate. The settlement of sectarians in separate, isolated communities in Transcaucasia—left, for the most part,

106. RGIA f. 1284, op. 222–1905, d. 35, l. 30b; op. 221–1889, d. 92, l. 2; op. 222–1899, d. 114, ll. 5–50b; and Nicholas B. Breyfogle, "Prayer and the Politics of Place: Molokan Church-Building, Tsarist Law, and the Quest for a Public Sphere in Late Imperial Russia," in *Sacred Stories: Religion and Spirituality in Modern Russian Culture*, ed. Heather Coleman and Mark Steinberg (Bloomington, forthcoming).
107. GMIR f. 2, op. 8, d. 196, 1913, ll. 1–10b. See also SSC'SA f. 222, op. 1, d. 44, 1848–52, l. 64; GARF f. 102, 5 d-vo, op. 1901, d. 509, l. 490b; and f. 579, op. 1, d. 2580, 1913, ll. 3–30b.
108. A. I. Masalkin, "K istorii zakavkazskikh sektantov: I Molokane," *Kavkaz*, no. 306 (November 18, 1893): 2; and V. M. Skvortsov, *Zapiska o dukhobortsakh na Kavkaze* (n.p., 1896), 10–11.
109. S-A., "Russkie," 3. See also GMIR f. 2, op. 8, d. 237, 1910, ll. 50, 71.
110. RGIA f. 1268, op. 24, d. 231, 1879–80, ll. 300b–31, 1570b–58, 2160b, 674–740b; CRCR 1895–09–20a, ll. 80–800b; Orekhov "Ocherki iz zhizni zakavkazskikh sektatorov," *Kavkaz*, no. 143 (June 25, 1878): 1; and Kuropatkin, *Soobrazheniia*, 19.
111. GARF f. 102, 3 d-vo, op. 1884, d. 88, ch. 2, l. 200b.

FIGURE 8. A Molokan presbyter in the South Caucasus, c. 1865. From V. V. Vereshchagin, *Dukhobortsy i Molokane v Zakavkaz'e, Shiity v Karabakhe, Batchi i Oshumoedy v Srednei Azii, i Ober-Amergau v Gorakh Bavarii* (Moscow, 1900), 23.

to their own devices with their own communal leaders and systems of justice—bolstered the bonds of their socio-religious identity. Sources note constant religious discussions and debates among the settlers, and their faith remained the center of their daily lives. The Molokans' frequent intraregional conferences to hash out points of theology and spiritual practice and the birth of new religious movements from among the Molokans such as the Pryguny and Obshchie attest to the vitality of their religious life.[112] That they had not strayed far from their earlier tenets is witnessed in the manuscript "About the Molokan Sect," seized by police from a Molokan house in 1901. It read in part, "The foundation of the moral life of a true Christian should be complete independence from any human laws and coercion. Spiritual Christians have no need of earthly power and human laws which they are obliged to fulfill and especially those which are at variance with the teachings of the word of God, such as: serfdom, wars, military service, oaths."[113]

---

112. Of many examples, see GMIR f. 2, op. 8, d. 324, n.d.; d. 237, 1910; and Kolosov, "Russkie sektanty," 143–55.

113. GARF f. 102, 5 d-vo, op. 1901, d. 509, l. 46.

RUSSIANS OR NON-RUSSIANS: RELIGIOUS AND ETHNIC IDENTITY IN THE IMPERIAL CONTEXT

In Transcaucasia, the settlers' ethnic identification also underwent profound changes, just as state identity did, producing multiple, contested understandings of a sectarian's ethnicity. These transformations illustrate that political loyalty and contributions to the imperial enterprise could be one constituent element, along with language, religion, culture, blood, and history, in the way that tsarist elites defined the ethnic boundaries of "Russianness." In addition, these alterations also reflect how ethnic, religious, and state identity categories were mutually constitutive and interdependent. Because of the links between Orthodox Christianity and Russian ethnicity, elite Russians tended to classify sectarians in the internal provinces first of all by their religious dissent as non-Russians, or at best dubious Russians. By placing these religious dissenters in the midst of the multi-ethnic Transcaucasian frontier, however, their ethnicity as Russians came into bold relief. The writings of Russian intellectuals that romanticized and essentialized the inhabitants of the Caucasus as "other" enhanced this process of defining the parameters of Russianness.[114]

There was a strong sense among administrators and other observers that the sectarian settlers were ethnically and culturally Russian. Tsarist anthropologists journeyed to the sectarians' villages to examine, among a myriad of other physical characteristics, their height, eye color, hair color, and even the age when beards first appeared, in an investigation of the impact on "Great Russians" of living in Transcaucasia.[115] Indeed, the term "Great Russian" (both *velikorussy* and *velikorossiane*) appeared frequently in published works on the Transcaucasian sectarians.[116]

Not only was their "Russianness" spotlighted by Transcaucasia's multiethnic backdrop, but the sectarians' growing state identity as "colonizers" also fundamentally altered the parameters of what "Russian" denoted to state authorities (as well as influencing what "religious sectarian" signified). The evolution from "heretics" to "colonizers" derived from official assumptions about identity: that ethnic Russians made the most reliable subjects. During the nineteenth century, events in the South Caucasus

114. Susan Layton, *Russian Literature and Empire: Conquest of the Caucasus from Pushkin to Tolstoy* (Cambridge, 1994); idem, "Nineteenth-Century Russian Mythologies of Caucasian Savagery," in *Russia's Orient: Imperial Borderlands and Peoples, 1700–1917*, ed. Daniel R. Brower and Edward J. Lazzerini (Bloomington, 1997), 80–100; Jersild, *Orientalism;* and Katya Hokanson, "Literary Imperialism, Narodnost' and Pushkin's Invention of the Caucasus," *RR* 53, no. 3 (1994): 336–52.
115. A. I. Ivanovskii, "K antropologii zakavkazskikh velikorussov," *Russkii antropologicheskii zhurnal* 6, no. 1/2 (1905): 141–58.
116. See, for instance, Petrov, "Seleniia," 247; Orekhov, "Ocherki," no. 136, 1; Kolosov, "Russkie," 150–51; and Borozdin, *Russkoe,* 175.

prompted tsarist officials to see the reverse as equally true: that as model colonists, the sectarians could still be considered Russian despite their non-Orthodoxy. As tsarist officials came to embrace sectarians as loyal, contributing settlers, the state discourse that had once anathematized their religious identity lost some of its force in the advent of ethnic labels that lauded their Russianness. For instance, on reading a report of one incident in which Molokans serving in an unofficial militia had fought off an attack by "bandits" as they escorted arrested Azerbaijanis to court, Nicholas I corrected the nomenclature of lower bureaucrats: "it does not follow to call them sectarians, but simply Russian settlers."[117] This statement—in many respects unexpected given the importance of Orthodoxy and Official Nationality to Nicholas's reign—was an expression of the tsar's definition of Russianness as partly based on contributions to state power, and of the acceptance of Transcaucasian sectarians into the "Russian" fold.

Perceived differences in ethnicity—based on language, culture, and blood—among various groups in Transcaucasia played an important role in defining the scope of activities that state policy permitted to sectarians in their new home. Policymakers based their initial decision to settle the sectarians in the eastern part of Transcaucasia rather than in Georgia on the belief that Muslims of various communities and Russians were so distinct linguistically and culturally that there could be no possibility of social interaction and, by extension, of the sectarians spreading their faith.[118] In debates over whether the sectarian settlers could be permitted to register as inhabitants of Transcaucasian towns, official characterizations of the dissenters as Russians were of paramount importance. Baron Rosen argued that sectarians could be located in towns with Muslims and Armenians because of the cultural and linguistic chasms between them.[119] A similar ethnic logic was at work in decisions to settle dissenters on lands belonging to Georgian nobles. Prince Vorontsov asserted that the settlement of sectarians so close to Georgian serfs "categorically cannot have any harmful consequences . . . because of the sharp differences in way of life, customs, and ideas that exist between Russian and Georgian peasants."[120] Ethnic considerations were also at the forefront of Vorontsov's decision to allow sectarians to work for and hire Orthodox Georgians, because he believed that no harmful results to Orthodox Christianity were likely because of the differences in language

---

117. RGIA f. 1268, op. 1, d. 433, 1843–48, ll. 51–51ob.
118. See the discussion in chapter one.
119. RGIA f. 1263, op. 1, d. 791, 1832, ll. 287–98; f. 379, op. 1, d. 1043, 1830–37, ll. 720b–730b; *AKAK* vol. 8, doc. 34, p. 34; and GMIR f. 2, op. 7, d. 594, ll. 17–18.
120. *AKAK* vol. 10, doc. 42, p. 47.

and "in the peculiarities of the moral and spiritual formation of each people."[121]

Sectarian self-identity shifted in similar ways to state classifications of them. In the new context of Transcaucasia, day-to-day interaction with ethnically and culturally distinct neighbors solidified their identification as Russians. In the public expression of their sense of self, ethnic descriptors separating a Russian "us" from a non-Russian "them" were layered on top of the discourse of "true Christians" and "God's people." Sharing the vocabulary of state authorities—whether knowingly or not is unclear—sectarians described their new neighbors as "uncivilized," "wild," and "Asian."[122] Molokans saw themselves as ethnically and culturally distinct from their new neighbors, describing them as "strange and baffling creatures of Asiatic and Mohammedan stock" who carried knives and guns and whose language and customs were incomprehensible to the colonists.[123] In 1847, Molokans from all over Transcaucasia met in the village of Borisy to ensure "that here among multi-tribal Asian peoples we Molokans would not lose our faith nor our Russian nation."[124] In 1908, other Molokans underlined how, despite all trials and tribulations of life on the frontier, they had "remained Russian in blood and in spirit."[125] Indeed, the sectarian colonists frequently described themselves as "Russians" in correspondence with state authorities.[126] The sense of "us" and "them" hardened because of the initially antagonistic relations between Russian settlers and their South Caucasian neighbors, which were filled with stories of theft, vandalism, violence, murder, and rape.[127]

However, as with their "state" identity, the ethnicity of sectarians in Transcaucasia—whether self-labeled or state-categorized—remained ambivalent as the nineteenth century progressed. State officials were increasingly inclined to see sectarians as "Russians" even if the dissenters at times eschewed that label in favor of a religious self-categorization and flip-flopped between describing themselves as Russian and not. Dukhobors frequently denied their "Russianness," preferring an ethno-religious self-designation. The Dukhobor author S. F. Rybin noted that the Dukhobors "have turned their sect into a nation. When they meet an unknown person they ask: and who might you be? I am a Dukhobor, one answers.

---

121. RGIA f. 381, op. 1, d. 23322, 1846; f. 1268, op. 2, d. 566, 1847–48.

122. See, for example, GMIR f. K1, op. 8, d. 470, 1925, l. 2; RGIA f. 1284, op. 197–1837, d. 9. ll. 3–4; and f. 379, op. 1, d. 1151, 1831–34, l. 23.

123. *Spirit and Life—Book of the Sun. Divine Discourses of the Preceptors and the Martyrs of the Word of God, the Faith of Jesus, and the Holy Spirit, of the Religion of the Spiritual Christian Molokan-Jumpers*, ed. Daniel H. Shubin, trans. John Volkov (n.p., 1983), 20.

124. GMIR f. 2, op. 8, d. 324, n.d., l. 1.

125. *Karsskii oblastnoi s"ezd*, 4–5.

126. RGIA f. 383, op. 30, d. 149, 1832–39, ll. 69–690b, for example.

127. These antagonistic relations are discussed at length in chapter five.

Ah, a Dukhobor. And I thought you were Russian. It turns out that the Dukhobors are not Russians, but Dukhobors."[128] Shifts in self-labeling reflected, on one hand, a self-understanding that simultaneously embraced both ethnic and religious descriptive categories and, on the other hand, the conscious manipulation of each type of identification at appropriate moments, particularly taking up the mantle of Russian ethnicity to achieve desired ends. In one instance, Molokan petitioners emphasized that they were "native Russian people" in order to legitimate their requests for permission to relocate.[129]

Similarly, there was not always a consensus among state officials about whether the Transcaucasian religious nonconformists were "Russian," and, more generally, what constituted "Russian" in an ethnic sense. In certain contexts, state representatives and journalists asserted steadfastly that sectarians were Russians—in doing so, they underscored that cultural, linguistic, and political factors could be sufficient to define what "Russian" was. In others, they included Orthodox Christianity as a necessary component, such as the case of the Baptists discussed above. Not unexpectedly, in the case of the Transcaucasian sectarians, secular elites tended to downplay religious affiliation as a component of Russian ethnicity, while Orthodox clerics and publicists assumed that to be Russian required also being Orthodox.

Military personnel in particular voiced their steadfast vision of religious dissenters as ethnic Russians, concerned as they were with perceived loyalty and fighting strength on the borders. In a 1908 report, Colonel Andrievskii noted that "sectarians comprise the overwhelming majority [of the civilian Russian population]. However, that fact does not have any special importance, since on the Asian frontier each Russian person is a source of strength."[130] Governor Shervashidze echoed this ethnic assessment in 1895: "The Caucasus administration considered [the Dukhobors] Russian people, Russian by blood and by soul."[131]

In contrast, illustrating the views of religious authorities in general, the Orthodox priest Ioann Vostorgov wrote in 1903 of the Molokan desire to emigrate to America: "Something painful is felt in this striving to leave the Motherland. . . . With the conversion to sectarianism a Russian person loses patriotic feeling. It is a strange affair, but to the question: 'Are you Russian?' he never gives an affirmative answer, but declares: 'No

128. Quoted and translated in Klibanov, *History*, 110.
129. GARF f. 579, op. 1, d. 2580, 1913, ll. 3–3ob.
130. General'nogo shtaba polkovnik Andrievskii, *Voenno-geograficheskoe i statisticheskoe opisanie Kavkazskogo voennogo okruga* (Tiflis, 1908), 71. I thank Peter Holquist for bringing this to my attention. See also Kuropatkin, *Soobrazheniia*, 41.
131. Shervashidze is quoted in Borozdin, *Russkoe*, 175.

I am a Molokan.' From this comes the ease with which sectarians decide to emigrate." By linking the Molokans' denial of ethnicity in favor of confessional identity and their rejection of Russia (*Rossiia*) implicit in the desire to emigrate—a doubly damning combination—Vostorgov strove to discredit the sectarians in the eyes of both the state and public opinion. His story also served to entrench the view, both for himself and for the reader, that adherence to the Orthodox faith was a prerequisite for being both Russian and a loyal subject.[132]

Tsarist labeling as dissenters or Russians conflicted at times with the nonconformists' sense of self, producing significant legislative outcomes that affected everyday life for these religious communities. Such was especially the case for the Subbotniks, who saw themselves as "Jews"—and not as Russians or Christian sectarians, as officials and publicists tended to characterize them.[133] Indeed, elite Russians generally refused to accept such assertions of self-identity, downplaying in the process the importance of Orthodox religion in defining Russianness, as the following quotation from a Kars newspaper reporter illustrates.

> Coming from the Russian family, belonging to her in spirit and in flesh, having left at one time from their shared religion and taken up the laws of Moses, Subbotniks should not be permitted to merge with the Jewish nation which is entirely foreign to them in ancestry . . . since the separation of them from the Russian people who are tied to them by blood . . . would castrate the feeling of national self-love, and . . . would tear them away from the united body. . . . By necessity Russian sectarians are separated from the Empire's governing Church. But the law does not separate them from the nation, and by placing them in the situation of *raskol'niki*, it joins them to the Russian family, and prohibits only the further spread of their newly adopted faith (or heresy from the Orthodox point of view) which is considered dangerous for society and the interests of the dominant religion.[134]

These different interpretations of what it meant to be Russian came into conflict over the question of synagogues for Subbotniks. Indeed, it mattered greatly which category they were placed in because tsarist law specifically forbade sectarians from building prayer houses. In contrast,

132. Ioann Vostorgov, "Puteshestvie vysokopreosviashchenneishogo Aleksiia, ekzarkha Gruzii, po Karskoi oblasti, Erivanskoi i Tiflisskoi guberniiam," *Polnoe sobranie sochinenii*, vol. 4 (1916; repr. Moscow, 1995), 125.
133. Masalkin, "Subbotniki," 2; N. St-v, "Obychai i zakon v brachnykh delakh subbotnikov," *Kars*, no. 41 (October 8, 1891), 3; T. B., "U beregov Kaspiia (iz putevykh zametok i vospominanii). Tri goda nazad. Ch. VII, v Lenkorane," *Kavkaz*, no. 58 (March 14, 1881), 2–3; RGIA f. 1284, op. 222–1893, d. 81, ll. 22–220b; and Breyfogle, "Heretics and Colonizers," 196–99.
134. St-v, "Obychai," 3.

Jews, as representatives of an officially recognized non-Russian religious faith, were entitled to places of worship. In the nineteenth century, Subbotnik places of worship were repeatedly closed because of their "Russian" and "sectarian" labels, despite extensive Subbotnik efforts to define themselves as Jews. This struggle between the demands of individuals and communities to define their own identities and the efforts of state authorities to categorize their subjects according to other criteria indicates the intricate interaction among religious, ethnic, and state identities. It also reflects how freedom of individual conscience remained inaccessible to Russian subjects who were ascribed a place in the tsarist state's corporatist approach to religious pluralism.

THE TRANSFORMATIVE FRONTIER

The Transcaucasian frontier provided the sectarians with new opportunities and roles as members of the Russian state. The settlement of Russian agrarian colonists in the Empire's periphery not only "Russified" the region, but it also installed essential support structures that the Russian imperialist regime could call upon in the absence of necessary infrastructure. In so doing, the sectarians became an influential third force in defining the empire-building process, alongside state officials and local peoples. Policymakers certainly did not foresee this systemic function when they originally decided to send sectarians to Transcaucasia, but they grew to be extremely grateful for it. In this way, Russia's control over its peripheral regions and its expansion into adjacent territory were linked to the presence of these Russian colonists and their activities in support of the imperialist project.

However, they should not be understood simply as another arm of the state. While they might fulfill indispensable imperialist roles, the sectarian settlers did so primarily when their interests and material needs overlapped with those of the state (or when the state forced them), not solely or necessarily out of a sense of commonality with tsarist aspirations. Rather than fight in the Russian army, for instance, they provided a military infrastructure which was in line with their nonviolent religious tenets and which granted them financial opportunities. As the Dukhobor oppositional movement discussed below shows, the settlers' own agenda did not always coincide with the state's goals, and they could as easily challenge state authority in the borderlands as support it.[135]

The Transcaucasian frontier also supplied fertile soil for the growth

---

135. See chapters six and seven.

of new sectarian identities, both in terms of sectarian self-definition and the external labeling of state officials.[136] The "Russian colonist" appeared next to the "oppositional sectarian," often in tension, often not. The dissenters' frontier societies were vibrant, switching rapidly from one self-identification to the other, as were the labels that state authorities imprinted on them. In the process, the content and meanings of such categories as "sectarian," "Russian" and "loyal subject" were open to definition, redefinition, and cynical manipulation. While in certain contexts sectarian religious identification (whichever faith it might be) precluded a sense of community with the state, in other circumstances, sectarians took up the mantle of state servitors—with it attendant benefits—and were lauded by state officials as model subjects. Moreover, in the first scenario, state officials considered sectarians politically pernicious and functionally outside of the fold of loyal and acceptable subjects by virtue of their nonconformist religion. In the latter context, their much-praised state service altered the meaning state authorities attributed to sectarianism by pushing most of the negative connotations into the background, although never entirely.

These fledgling state characterizations and self-definitions affected the relations between government and nonconformist, both in the formation of policy and in the willingness of sectarians to perform state service. From the viceroyship of Vorontsov onwards, state officials viewed the sectarians both as "model colonists" and "dangerous fanatics," and state policy flowed inconsistently from these dual labels. Thus, Prince Bariatinskii could both laud the sectarians as Russian pioneers and demand more of them for the region while also lobbying to increase the benefits of conversion to Orthodoxy because the nonconformists were "disobedient to authority."

Such incongruities reflect a larger struggle in Russian governance between ideology and practice—in this case, between assumptions about the innate desirability of Orthodox Russians and the experiential realization of the sectarians' superior performance. They also reflect how practice could moderate ideology; how lived experience complicated and altered the state's efforts to map Russia's complex social hetero-

136. Colonial or frontier regions in other geographic and temporal contexts also allowed for transformations of official labeling and communal identity. See, for example, Alice Bullard, *Exile to Paradise: Savagery and Civilization in Paris and the South Pacific, 1790–1900* (Stanford, 2000); Alan Lester, *Imperial Networks: Creating Identities in Nineteenth-Century South Africa and Britain* (London, 2001); and the four articles in the forum "The Formation of Ethnic Identities in Frontier Societies, *Journal of World History* 4, no. 2 (1993): 267–324. However, the sectarian experience should be contrasted with the absence of change in identity among Orthodox settlers in Siberia. See Willard Sunderland, "Peasant Pioneering: Russian Peasant Settlers Describe Colonization and the Eastern Frontier, 1880s–1910s," *JSH* 34, no. 4 (2001), 911–12.

geneity. Despite ingrained official opposition to their religious identity, the dissenters' colonizing contributions modified state policies toward them in Transcaucasia. Such inconsistencies further demonstrate the fundamental importance of geographic location in tsarist Russia. By privileging Transcaucasian sectarians, tsarist labeling and actions were contingent on where in the Empire a dissenter lived—a fact which highlights the regional diversity of experience among Russian subjects in the nineteenth century. Such regionalism is simultaneously seen in the way that local and central authorities often characterized the sectarians quite differently.[137]

In Imperial Russia, religious, ethnic, and state affiliations were webs of constructed and coded meaning that existed in dynamic and mutually influential interaction.[138] Scholars have traditionally discerned a vital nexus between Orthodox Christianity and Russian ethnicity. Yet not all subjects of the Empire who were considered, or who considered themselves, to be "Russian" adhered to the Orthodox faith.[139] The interrelations of confessional, ethnic, and state identity among the Transcaucasian nonconformists belie any simple connection between Russian nationality and Orthodox religion. Under one set of conditions, the classification of Transcaucasian sectarians as "Russian" was based on a combination of linguistic, cultural, and racial criteria that made their "Russianness" unproblematic. Yet in other circumstances, identification as "sectarian" problematized and de-stabilized their Russianness, moving religious dissenters outside the boundaries of who was Russian. Moreover, in this triangular interaction of religious, ethnic, and state identifications, the last was often the determining one. In the case of these sectarians, performance of political loyalty was a significant factor in constructing the boundaries of Russian ethnicity as a social category. Both state agents and the nonconformist colonists came to see the "sectarians" as "Russians" in great part because of their contributions to the tsarist imperial enterprise and their loyalty to the Russian state.

Growing state affiliation also changed the valence that both officials and sectarians attached to their religious dissent, making it much more acceptable to secular tsarist administrators. While ethnic factors increased in importance in defining nationality in Europe as the nine-

137. Notably, the ethnicity of an individual official (whether Russian, Georgian, Baltic German, Armenian, Azerbaijani, or other) does not appear to have been a determining factor in how state authorities classified the sectarians.

138. The image of the web is from Clifford Geertz, "Thick Description: Toward an Interpretive Theory of Culture," in *The Interpretation of Cultures* (New York, 1973), 5.

139. Nor, for that matter, were all Orthodox believers also Russian, producing its own complications of identification. Paul Werth, *At the Margins of Orthodoxy: Mission, Governance, and Confessional Politics in Russia's Volga-Kama Region, 1827–1905* (Ithaca, 2002).

teenth century progressed, the case of the Transcaucasian sectarians demonstrates that religious identity remained an important factor in the construction of communal identity in late Imperial Russia. In particular, while the Russian state (excluding the Synod) increasingly mapped its population on ethnic grounds, the sectarians continued to define themselves in religious terms even as they added new ethnic and state understandings to their communal self-definition.[140]

140. Hobsbawm, *Nations*, 102. Charles Steinwedel, "To Make a Difference: the Category of Ethnicity in Late Imperial Russian Politics, 1861–1917," in *Russian Modernity: Politics, Knowledge, Practices*, ed. David Hoffmann and Yanni Kotsonis (Basingstoke, 2000), 67–86.

5

FRONTIER ENCOUNTERS

Conflict and Coexistence between Colonists
and South Caucasians

In his influential book, *The Middle Ground*, Richard White notes that the history of the interaction between Europeans and Native Americans in the colonial era has traditionally been limited in its approaches and findings. "Indians are the rock," he writes, "European peoples are the sea, and history seems a constant storm. There have been but two outcomes: The sea wears down and dissolves the rock; or the sea erodes the rock but cannot finally absorb its battered remnant, which endures. The first outcome produces stories of conquest and assimilation; the second produces stories of cultural persistence." While not discounting the veracity of these narratives, White goes on to argue that "the tellers of such stories miss a larger process and a larger truth. The meeting of sea and continent, like the meeting of whites and Indians, creates as well as destroys. Contact was not a battle of primal forces in which only one could survive. Something new could appear."[1]

White's depiction of the limitations of the conventional historiography of early America also characterizes recent scholarship on the interactions between Russians and non-Russians in the tsarist empire. It too has depicted cultural contact in dichotomous, conflicting terms of Russian ascendancy and indigenous response, a Russian sea crashing wave after wave upon the rocky shores of its borderlands. As a recent study contends, "The cultural and social encounter was inherently unequal. . . . Those who held the instruments of political power also controlled the terms in which that communication took place."[2] Nineteenth-century

---

1. Richard White, *The Middle Ground: Indians, Empires, and Republics in the Great Lakes Region, 1650–1815* (New York, 1991), ix.
2. Daniel R. Brower and Edward J. Lazzerini, eds., *Russia's Orient: Imperial Borderlands and Peoples, 1700–1917* (Bloomington, 1997), xvii.

Russian authorities shared some of these perspectives. Behind the perception of sectarians as model Russian colonizers lay the assumption that the dissenters would act as conduits of Russian cultural norms and economic practices—in other words, of civilization in general—to Transcaucasia's native peoples. From the perspective of Russian administrators, such socio-cultural transference would move in one direction only (from Russian to native) and it would be progressive, lifting the indigenous peoples up the civilizational hierarchy.[3]

In contrast to this "collision" narrative, the frontier encounters between sectarian settlers and Armenians, Azerbaijanis, Georgians, and the wide variety of other indigenous peoples in the region suggest a very different story, one much closer to White's notion of creation as a primary characteristic of colonial contact. For many of the Russian dissenters, this was their first experience living near non-Slavic peoples.[4] For their part, native Transcaucasians had come to know Russians as soldiers, but the sectarians' migration was their first encounter with Russians as civilian, nonconformist neighbors. In this relatively unregulated region of the Russian Empire, these disparate peoples were left to negotiate the boundaries of a space in which to interact; to delineate modes of interconnection suitable for their new, shared context; and to construct mutually beneficial economic relationships and patterns of survival. In their daily negotiations, rather than the unequal subjugation of one party by the other, no single group consistently played a predominant role, and the Russian colonists were not necessarily privileged in the encounter. The forces of acculturation and accommodation altered both settlers and locals, proving especially transformative for the Russians. In the process, "new worlds" were created even as all communities simultaneously reinforced old social and cultural patterns.[5]

The meeting of sectarians and local Transcaucasians produced five forms of interaction which evolved in contradictory and often unpredictable directions: land disputes, partial "enserfment," violent clashes, economic bonds and mutual aid, and, to a lesser degree, socio-economic and cultural exchange. First, the settlement of sectarians in South Cau-

3. I. V. Dolzhenko, *Khoziaistvennyi i obshchestvennyi byt russkikh krest'ian vostochnoi Armenii (konets XIX—nacholo XX vv.)* (Erevan, 1985), 30; Willard Sunderland, "Russians into Iakuts? 'Going Native' and Problems of Russian National Identity in the Siberian North, 1870s–1914," *SR* 55, no. 4 (1996): 806–25; idem, "An Empire of Peasants: Empire-Building, Interethnic Interaction, and Ethnic Stereotyping in the Rural World of the Russian Empire, 1800–1850s," in *Imperial Russia: New Histories for the Empire*, ed. Jane Burbank and David Ransel (Bloomington, 1998), 175–76, 180–81, 184; and Yuri Slezkine, *Russia and the Small Peoples of the North* (Ithaca, 1994).
4. Molokans and Dukhobors in New Russia had encountered non-Slavs through their contacts with Mennonites and Nogays, and similar patterns can be seen among the sectarians in Siberia.
5. Willard Sunderland finds similar patterns elsewhere in the Russian Empire. See his "Empire of Peasants," 181–85.

casia disrupted previous patterns of land use and valuation and produced struggles with local inhabitants over land allotments. Second, communities of dissenters settled on land owned by Caucasian notables, entering into uneven contracts with these native elites that left them in a subordinate position. Third, in response to what the settlers saw as the brutality and banditry of Transcaucasian Muslims and in a reversal of their religious tenets, groups from these formerly pacifist communities turned to violent reprisals.[6] Fourth, the growth of mutual assistance and intricate, collectively beneficial economic relations—a "frontier exchange economy"—also characterized native-sectarian interrelations.[7] Finally, economic interactions led to the growth of reciprocal influences. They developed first and foremost through the exchange of agricultural practices, implements, and subsistence strategies. From there, they expanded —albeit slowly and fitfully—into other realms as peoples swapped languages and cultural practices along with goods and services.

The sectarians settled near a large number of distinct peoples and communities, and their mutual interactions varied depending on the ethnicity, religious affiliation, social status (peasant, landowner or merchant), and economic lifestyle (settled farmer, nomad, or urban trader) of the indigenous people involved, as well as the beliefs and practices of the different sectarian groups.[8] While violence coexisted with economic interactions and mutual support throughout the period under investigation, the patterns of interaction changed over time. As day-to-day contacts created both tensions and bonds, settlers and natives constantly made and remade both themselves and their cross-cultural interactions.[9] Conflict predominated in the wake of initial contact because the settlers had abruptly upset the existing structures. As relations calmed through

6. For a discussion of the parameters of Molokan and Dukhobor pacifism, see my "Swords into Plowshares: Opposition to Military Service among Religious Sectarians, 1770s to 1874," in *The Military and Society in Russia, 1450–1917*, ed. Eric Lohr and Marshall Poe (Leiden, 2002), 441–67.

7. Daniel H. Usner, Jr., *Indians, Settlers and Slaves in a Frontier Exchange Economy: The Lower Mississippi Valley before 1783* (Chapel Hill, 1992).

8. On this rapidly evolving ethnic "salad bowl," see N. G. Volkova, "Etnicheskie protsessy v Zakavkaz'e v XIX–XX vv." in *KES*, vol. 4, ed. V. K. Gardanov (Moscow, 1969), 3–54; Tadeusz Swietochowski, *Russian Azerbaijan, 1905–1920: The Shaping of a National Identity in a Muslim Community* (Cambridge, 1985), 7–8; and John F. Baddeley, *The Russian Conquest of the Caucasus* (London, 1908), xxi–xxxviii.

9. See Marshall Sahlins for a persuasive argument about the relationship between "structure and event": "Every reproduction of culture is an alteration, insofar as in action, the categories by which a present world is orchestrated pick up some novel empirical content." Sahlins, *Islands of History* (Chicago, 1985), 136–56, quotation on 144. In this vein, see also White, *Middle Ground*, 52, where he argues that "the result of each side's attempts to apply its own cultural expectations in a new context was often change in culture itself. In trying to maintain the conventional order of its world, each group applied rules that gradually shifted to meet the exigencies of particular situations. The result of these efforts was a new set of common conventions, but these conventions served as a basis for further struggles to order or influence the world of action."

a series of compromises, economic exchange and mutually supportive relationships came to the foreground. This is not to say that fighting disappeared entirely, nor that the ties of mutual assistance and trade did not exist from the outset, because both persisted in different forms throughout the nineteenth century. In contrast, conflicts over land were a constant aspect of settler-native contacts during the entire period of this study.

MARKING BOUNDARIES AND DISPUTING LAND

The sectarians' settlement in Transcaucasia altered the region's human ecology and destabilized existing systems of landownership and usage. Bitter land conflicts resulted from the fact that nonconformists often settled on lands already in use by indigenous Transcaucasians. For natives relying on settled agriculture, this practice reduced the amount of land they could put under cultivation. For nomads, the Russians' settled lifestyle disrupted long-standing patterns of migration and pasturing. In both cases, Russian settlement caused suffering and aroused anger. In clashes over real estate, sectarians and natives took matters into their own hands in an effort to resolve what they felt were unfair situations. They occupied and used lands allotted to others, allowed their livestock to trample crops, and openly fought over access to land. Both settlers and Transcaucasians (especially Armenians) turned to state authorities as an arbiter, and on occasion tsarist officials intervened to resolve the differences. Local inhabitants objected particularly to the larger allotments of land that Russians received. As population pressures increased over the course of the nineteenth century, the flurry of appeals by Transcaucasians to remedy inequalities grew more frequent and ardent. At the same time, sectarians insisted in their own petitions that whatever the differences in the apportionment of land, even they did not have sufficient land to feed themselves adequately.[10]

Conflicts over land distribution and demarcation were complicated by the peculiarities of Transcaucasian agricultural structures, which varied enormously within regions and among ethnic groups. Rural dwellers in Transcaucasia occupied a full spectrum covering settled, semi-nomadic, and nomadic; although nomadism was more common further east toward the Caspian Sea. Serfdom was prevalent in Georgia until 1871, while other forms of lord-peasant relations and Church-peasant ties existed

---

10. For general discussions of land allotments, Russian colonization, and inter-ethnic conflict, see David Moon, "Peasant Migration and the Settlement of Russia's Frontiers, 1550–1897," *HJ* 40, no. 4 (1997): 882–86; and Sunderland, "Empire of Peasants," 182–83.

elsewhere. The incorporation of these regions into the Russian Empire had deep repercussions for the socio-economic structure, expanding the power of the Georgian nobles while disrupting the relationships between peasants and *beks* (high-ranking dignitaries of noble origin, in the so-called Muslim Provinces of eastern Transcaucasia.[11]

Eastern Armenia, subsequently Erevan province, serves as an example of this socio-economic complexity.[12] At the time of incorporation in 1828, the Armenian minority of the population was almost exclusively settled, living as farmers or practicing various trades and professions. The region's Muslims were divided ethnically among Persians, Azerbaijanis, Turks, and Kurds: the Persians were almost exclusively a settled population, the Azerbaijani and Turkish inhabitants ranged from settled to semi-nomadic and nomadic, and the Kurds were primarily nomadic. The nomads used more than half of the land in the region. In contrast, as discussed in chapter 3, sectarians were state peasants who practiced settled agriculture and local livestock pasturing, among other pursuits.

There has been disagreement, both among commentators at the time and also among scholars more recently, over the nature of Russian state policy regarding land distribution during colonization. Soviet historians in particular have discussed Russian settlement in Transcaucasia within strict exploiter/exploited parameters. G. A. Orudzhev, for example, points to "the flagrant infringement of the land rights of native peasants. Tsarist colonizers, when settling Russian peasants in Azerbaijan, robbed land from the local inhabitants and with every act aroused clashes between the Azerbaijani and Russian peasants."[13]

While there is no doubt that tsarist imperialists often embarked on aggressive land appropriations, the intentions of tsarist colonization policy

11. The most valuable socio-economic and land use information (divided by region) is found in the seven-volume series *MIEB* (1885–87). See also V. D. Mochalov, *Krest'ianskoe khoziaistvo v Zakavkaz'e k kontsy XIX v.* (Moscow, 1958); Ronald Grigor Suny, "'The Peasants Have Always Fed Us': The Georgian Nobility and the Peasant Emancipation, 1856–1871," *RR* 38, no. 1 (1979): 27–51; idem, *The Making of the Georgian Nation*, 2nd ed. (Bloomington, 1994), 63–112; Swietochowski, *Russian Azerbaijan*, 17–23; and George Bournoutian, "The Ethnic Composition and the Socio-Economic Condition of Eastern Armenia in the First Half of the Nineteenth Century," in *Transcaucasia: Nationalism and Social Change*, ed. Ronald Grigor Suny (Ann Arbor, 1983), 69–86.
12. Bournoutian, "Ethnic Composition."
13. G. A. Orudzhev, "Iz istorii obrazovaniia russkikh poselenii v Azerbaidzhane," *Izvestiia Akademii Nauk AzSSR: Istoriia, Filosofiia, Pravo*, no. 2 (1969): 21. See also O. E. Tumanian, *Ekonomicheskoe razvitie Armenii*, 2 vols. (Erevan, 1954), 1:41–42; Dolzhenko, *Khoziaistvennyi*, 29–33; A. N. Iamskov, *Environmental Conditions and Ethnocultural Traditions of Stockbreeding (the Russians in Azerbaijan in the 19th and early 20th Centuries)* (Moscow, 1988), 5; A. I. Klibanov, *History of Religious Sectarianism in Russia (1860s–1917)*, ed. Stephen Dunn, trans. Ethel Dunn (New York, 1982), 122; Stephen F. Jones, "Russian Imperial Administration and the Georgian Nobility: The Georgian Conspiracy of 1832," *SEER* 65, no. 1 (1987): 65–66; and Firouzeh Mostashari, "Tsarist Colonial Policy, Economic Change, and the Making of the Azerbaijani Nation: 1828–1905" (Ph.D. diss., University of Pennsylvania, 1995), 332–39.

involved a complex mixture of concern for and maltreatment of the Transcaucasian peoples. There was no consistent privileging of the settlers because they were still religious dissenters and pariahs even if they were ethnically Russian. Also, Russian imperialists in this case do not appear to have acted on the *res nullius* or *terra nullius* principles Europeans in other colonial settings used to justify appropriation of land. Although varying in their application from one imperial power to another, these legal concepts rationalized European denials of native property rights, arguing instead that lands that were not being employed productively, or that could be exploited more efficiently, belonged to no one and were therefore open for the taking by the first person to put them to proper economic use.[14] Moreover, in many cases regional authorities were genuinely concerned about the economic welfare of the indigenous population and they did not automatically take land to give to the Russian settlers. Already in 1832, Baron G. V. Rosen voiced his apprehension that the settlement of sectarians in Transcaucasia would "constrain the indigenous inhabitants in regards to their nomadic encampments and pastures."[15] In an 1843 report, state authorities made clear that if the sectarians were to be settled in Transcaucasia, then it was to be done on empty land without causing any "inhibition" or "restriction" of the native population.[16] Indeed, while discussing the absence of lands for Russian settlement in the late 1850s, Viceroy A. I. Bariatinskii asserted that "fairness demands designating free lands primarily to the native peasants, of whom a large number are suffering from an extreme insufficiency of land."[17]

Despite some degree of concern for the welfare of Transcaucasia's indigenous peoples—one partly motivated by fear of disorder—officials frequently did put the interests of the sectarians first. They allotted more land per family to Russian settlers than was the regional norm, arguing that as newcomers they needed more help to survive, and this land often came from indigenous inhabitants.[18] On some occasions, tsarist authorities did not realize that the native peoples had any claims to land allotted to settlers because of misunderstandings (and incompetence) in

14. Anthony Pagden, *Lords of all the World: Ideologies of Empire in Spain, Britain, and France, c. 1500–c. 1800* (New Haven, 1995), 73–86; and Patrick Wolfe, *Settler Colonialism and the Transformation of Anthropology: The Politics and Poetics of an Ethnographic Event* (London, 1999), 26–27.
15. RGIA f. 1284, op. 196–1831, d. 136, l. 90b. See also SSC'SA f. 4, op. 2, d. 748, 1848–51, ll. 13–130b, passim.
16. RGIA f. 932, op. 1, d. 83, l. 47. See also RGIA f. 1268, op. 9, d. 367a, 1857–58, l. 10b; and I. V. Dolzhenko, "Pervye russkie pereselentsy v Armenii (30–50-e gody XIX v.)," *VMU Seriia IX Istoriia*, no. 3 (1974): 58–59.
17. *AKAK* vol. 12:1 (1893), doc. 18, p. 38; RGIA f. 1263, op. 1, d. 791, ll. 287–910b; and SSC'SA, f. 240, op. 2, d. 188, 1858–59. See also RGIA f. 1268, op. 2, d. 772, 1848.
18. RGIA f. 381, op. 1, d. 23300, 1844, ll. 2–20b.

surveying the region. More often, however, the Russian dissenters were given land that had knowingly been taken from local inhabitants. Even if official policy endorsed the settlement of Russian peasants on land that officials considered unoccupied, there was not always a sufficient amount of such unused land to meet the needs of the settlers.[19] In such cases, native land was confiscated, especially if local authorities believed the land was not being exploited in the ways they desired—preferring sedentary farming over nomadic pasturing. The indigenous population was moved elsewhere, usually without its consent and to its great anger, and was awarded tax benefits and direct grants from the treasury's coffers in order to defray the relocation costs.[20] For instance, in order to provide what Russian officials believed to be sufficient amounts of land, Dukhobors in Akhalkalaki district were granted parcels from neighboring Armenian communities—but on the condition that it be done without harming or antagonizing the inhabitants of these villages.[21]

The settlement of Russians in permanent villages also did much to disrupt long-standing patterns of nomadic migration, especially in eastern Transcaucasia.[22] In the mid-1830s, Molokan families settled in Topchi and Alty-Agach and "actively set to the construction of dwellings, started vegetable gardens near their homes and sowed fields (some more than 70 *desiatiny*) with millet (primarily), flax, oats, peas and hemp."[23] Although the land that they had been given was defined as treasury land, local inhabitants previously had used it for farming and pasturing their flocks. Soon after the arrival of the sectarians, nomads from the Shirvan

19. Throughout the nineteenth century, officials debated furiously exactly how much occupied or unoccupied land there was in Transcaucasia, how to define habitable or inhabitable land, and how much land each type of people needed in order to survive.

20. Dolzhenko, "Pervye," 59; SSC'SA f. 240, op. 1, d. 1228, 1864; and Vartan Gregorian, "The Impact of Russia on the Armenians and Armenia," in *Russia and Asia: Essays on the Influence of Russia on the Asian Peoples*, ed. Wayne Vucinich (Stanford, 1972), 183–84. On the importance of inadequate land exploitation as justification for land appropriations, compare Pagden, *Lords*, 76–86.

21. *AKAK* vol. 10, doc. 98, p. 123. See also SSC'SA f. 244, op. 3, d. 100, 1869; and Dolzhenko, "Pervye," 63.

22. Russian administrators in the nineteenth century subscribed to a hierarchy of humanity in which settled peoples were considered more civilized than nomads. In the demarcation of lands throughout the Empire, officials generally paid little attention to nomadic needs and hoped to encourage them to adopt a settled lifestyle. For comparison, see Sunderland, "Russians into Iakuts?" esp. 808–11; Daniel Brower, "Kyrgyz Nomads and Russian Pioneers: Colonization and Ethnic Conflict in the Turkestan Revolt of 1916," *JGO* 44, no. 1 (1996): 41–53; Virginia Martin, *Law and Custom in the Steppe: The Kazakhs of the Middle Horde and Russian Colonialism in the Nineteenth Century* (Richmond, Surrey, 2001); Dov Yaroshevski, "Attitudes towards the Nomads of the Russian Empire under Catherine the Great," in *Literature, Lives, and Legality in Catherine's Russia*, ed. A. G. Cross and G. S. Smith (n.p., 1994); and Michael Khodarkovsky, *Where Two Worlds Met: The Russian State and the Kalmyk Nomads, 1600–1771* (Ithaca, 1992).

23. The discussion that follows is drawn from GMIR f. 2, op. 7, d. 597, 1835–40. See also SSC'SA f. 4, op. 2, d. 748, 1848–51; and f. 222, op. 1, d. 60, 1849, ll. 4–40b.

and Kubin regions appeared and settled themselves on or near the lands designated for the Molokans. The Kubin nomads not only let their herds graze on Molokan meadows but also trample and devour the settlers' sown grain. Seeing the devastation caused by the neighboring nomads, Russian arrivals the following year refused to settle in these villages. The sectarians petitioned Chief Administrator Rosen, claiming that they had not received appropriate protection from the local commandant, named Orlovskii, and demanded reimbursement for their losses.

There was deep disagreement among Russian officials over whom to blame for the hostility between the natives and the Alty-Agach and Topchi settlers. Some found fault with the nomads, who had "harmed the Molokans in all possible ways." In contrast, when Rosen sent one of his administrators, a man named Petrusevich, to resolve the land disputes, the agent reported that the boundaries of the land designated for the Molokans had not been clearly demarcated. As a result, the Molokans, "being too lazy to clear their lands of blackthorns and shrubs," seized possession of other strips of land that were not designated for them. Petrusevich ordered the return of the land the Molokans had seized, compensating the Molokans with an additional allotment of 1,000 *desiatiny*. However, Petrusevich did not blame the Molokans alone. "Over the course of three years already," he reported, the nomads "provoked a fight over their fields and hayfields, using the latter without permission of the local administration." As a result, Rosen decided that the only way to prevent further conflict was to establish permanent mediation between the settlers and the nomads. He stationed a Cossack captain in the Molokan villages every year during the time between the sprouting of the grain's shoots until its harvest, for the purpose of defending the fields from the nomads' herds. In addition, he made the local Muslim notables fully responsible for any future destruction of the Molokans' crops.[24]

All of these land redistribution practices caused hardships for the natives and engendered a sense of maltreatment. They also produced ongoing conflicts between locals and Russians concerning land quality, the establishment of land norms, and the distribution of meadows, watering holes, forests, and pastureland. Illegal use, or even seizure, of land and livestock was an almost daily occurrence.[25] Russian villagers of Sukhoi-Fontan in Erevan province regularly engaged in "skirmishes" with nomadic Azerbaijanis who encroached upon their lands and attempted to drive their livestock through the village's cultivated allotments. Indeed, when they went to their fields, they did so armed not only with the nec-

24. GMIR f. 2, op. 7, d. 597, 1835–40, ll. 5–7.
25. Dolzhenko, "Pervye," 63.

essary agricultural tools but also "with guns in their hands," which they used to attack the Azerbaijanis who threatened to destroy their crops.[26]

Similarly, the Dukhobor village of Rodionovka in Tiflis province complained that armed Muslims attacked them as they cultivated their allotted land, damaged their crops, and chased away their herds. In 1884, the villagers petitioned the authorities to request that people "of another nationality and religion" who were more "conscientious" than the Muslims be settled next to them in order to end the struggle.[27] Furthermore, there were frequent conflicts between the Dukhobors of Gorelovka and Spasskoe in Tiflis province and their Armenian neighbors over access to allocated state lands. In 1864, the Dukhobors used force to expel shepherds from nearby Satkha who were pasturing their flocks on meadowland that the settlers claimed. Soon thereafter, the Armenians reasserted their rights to use these treasury lands and drove out the Dukhobors and their herds.[28]

The reconstruction of land arrangements to make space for the colonists also produced an unrelenting flood of petitions and complaints to the administration. The grievances of local inhabitants centered on the larger land holdings of the Russian sectarians and their preferential taxation rates.[29] Georgians, Armenians, and Azerbaijanis were incensed that the settlers might receive as much as six times the land that they did—despite which the sectarians incessantly complained about insufficient land.[30] There were numerous petitions from Armenians living in the village of Makravank in Erevan province complaining to the administration about a land shortage. In 1866, they insisted that "the Molokan village Konstantinovka has so much land that they are not in a position

---

26. S. Kolosov, "Russkie sektanty v Erivanskoi gubernii," *PKEG na 1902 g.* (Erevan, 1902): otd. IV, 151. See also SSC'SA f. 17, op. 1, d. 4042, 1899; f. 239, op. 1, d. 45, 1849–52, ll. 26–27; f. 222, op. 1, d. 60, 1849; f. 240, op. 1, d. 684, 1860–61; K. Gorskii, "Marazinskaia sel'skaia shkola," *Kavkaz*, no. 130 (1871): 2. Such armed agriculture formed part of a larger pattern of Russian expansion into the steppe. See Michael Khodarkovsky, *Russia's Steppe Frontier: The Making of a Colonial Empire, 1500–1800* (Bloomington, 2002), 8; Daniel Brower, *Turkestan and the Fate of the Russian Empire* (London, 2003), 126–51; and Sunderland, "Empire of Peasants," 182–83.

27. SSC'SA f. 17, op. 1, d. 1828, 1884, ll. 1–10b; f. 240, op. 1, d. 1034, 1863; f. 239, op. 1, d. 45, 1849–52, ll. 11–110b; f. 5, op. 1, d. 1454, 1870; and S. A. Inikova, "Vzaimootnosheniia i khoziaistvenno-kul'turnye kontakty kavkazskikh dukhobortsev s mestnym naseleniem," in *Dukhobortsy i Molokane v Zakavkaz'e*, ed. V. I. Kozlov and A. P. Pavlenko (Moscow, 1992), 48.

28. Inikova, "Vzaimootnosheniia," 48; SSC'SA f. 244, op. 3, d. 42, 1863–70; and d. 100, 1869. Russian peasants frequently approached state officials in Erevan with complaints that neighboring Armenian villagers were illegally seizing their lands. See Dolzhenko, "Pervye," 63; SSC'SA f. 4 op. 2, d. 410, 1846–47; and d. 748, 1848–51.

29. In addition to the examples below, see SSC'SA f. 4, op. 2, d. 410, 1846–57; GARF f. 102, 5 d-vo, op. 1901, d. 509, l. 510b; and Gregorian, "Impact of Russia," 184.

30. Gregorian, "Impact of Russia," 184; SSC'SA f. 240, op. 1, d. 1428, 1865–67; f. 244, op. 3, d. 100, 1869; *AKAK* vol. 10, doc. 98, p. 123; N. A. Abelov, "Ekonomicheskii byt gosudarstvennykh krest'ian Elisavetpol'skogo uezda, Elisavetpol'skoi gubernii," in *MIEB*, vol. 7 (Tiflis, 1887), 14; and the articles in *MIEB* and *RTKE* in general.

to sow it all, and as a result they farm out their land to us for prices that are very profitable for them."[31] Other petitions decried any redistricting of land that reduced native access to agricultural terrain. In 1866, the inhabitants of the village of Nizhnaia Akhta requested the return of land that had been taken from them: "As a result of [Molokan] settlement, our agricultural land, which is fertile and close to the village, was cut off and given to them. We were left only with land that is rocky and far away in the Akhmagan Mountains."[32]

Russian colonization policies did not necessarily need to be aggressively exclusionary for indigenous inhabitants to feel imperial oppression, particularly as exaggerated stories of Russian intentions proliferated throughout the region. In one case in the late 1840s, rumors spread rapidly through Shemakha province that as many as 40,000 new Russians were coming to colonize the area—rather than the few hundred who were actually scheduled to arrive—and that these settlers were to be given not only the best pasturing land from Muslim nomadic communities but also even the very houses of urban and rural Azerbaijanis in the area. Confronted with the possibility of dispossession and Russian demographic invasion, many families petitioned for permission to emigrate to Persia or the Ottoman Empire.[33]

RUSSIAN SETTLERS AND LOCAL ELITES

The interactions over land between Russian settlers and Transcaucasians depended a great deal on the social status of the latter group. The settlement of sectarians on property belonging to local landowning elites—especially Georgians but also Armenians and Azerbaijanis—produced interethnic relations quite different than when the natives were peasants or nomads.[34] For one thing, the practice of settling sectarians on estate lands violated tsarist law. Russian dissenters who relocated to Transcaucasia, whatever their original social designation in the interior provinces, were juridically considered state peasants upon their arrival on the frontier.[35] Tsarist regulations required state peasants to live on state land and to pay taxes solely to the treasury. Nonetheless, beginning in 1841, Trans-

31. Dolzhenko, "Pervye," 64; Inikova, "Vzaimootnosheniia," 47; and SSC'SA f. 244, op. 3, d. 42, 1863–70.

32. Dolzhenko, "Pervye," 63.

33. SSC'SA f. 4, op. 2, d. 748, 1848–51.

34. I discuss this theme in greater depth elsewhere. See my "Colonization by Contract: Russian Settlers, South Caucasian Elites, and the Dynamics of Nineteenth-Century Tsarist Imperialism," in *Extending the Borders of Russian History: Essays in Honor of Alfred J. Rieber*, ed. Marsha Siefert (Budapest, 2003), 143–66.

35. A small number of sectarian settlers either remained upon their resettlement or later became *meshchane* and merchants in Transcaucasia.

caucasian officials permitted some settlement of Russian sectarians on land belonging to local notables on an ad hoc basis, but only on uncultivated land, so as not to aggravate the condition of those Georgian or Azerbaijani serfs and bonded peasants who already lived on the estates. After multiple entreaties from regional administrators, in 1858 St. Petersburg agreed to a general policy of such settlement on noble lands.[36]

Settling sectarians on the property of notables did not mean "enserfment" in a strict sense of the word, but the landowners gained many of the same benefits. The dissenters retained their official status as state peasants and entered into contracts with the landowners defining the rights and responsibilities of each side. Writing to the Caucasus Committee in 1857, Bariatinskii endorsed a region-wide policy of settlement on private lands as mutually profitable for settlers and owners both. He claimed that "in the future, this example can act as a good influence for the spread of mutual agreements and transactions between peasants and landowners, both in this region and in the internal provinces," thereby holding up the case of Russian settlers and Transcaucasian nobles as a model for the rest of the Empire to follow.[37]

The practice of settling sectarians on the lands of Transcaucasian notables had its origins in five factors. First, and perhaps most important, Russian colonists settled on private lands because the local gentry desired it. Representatives from such Georgian noble families as the Chavchavadzes, Dadianis, and Orbelianis approached the regional administration with proposals to settle sectarians on their lands.[38] They recognized the profits and benefits that could be derived from placing Russian peasants on their property, such as cultivating unused areas and increasing the rents they received. For their part, sectarian settlers were willing to settle on noble lands because they hoped to enhance their economic opportunities and escape unpromising locations. Third, as part of the tsarist policy of strengthening their control by increasing the number of ethnic Russians in the region, officials settled the incoming sectarians on the properties of the local elites in an effort to provide adequate land to support all the dissenters who wanted to relocate to Transcaucasia. Lacking sufficient treasury land while not wanting to appropriate land from local peasants and nomads, tsarist officials—especially Viceroys Prince M. S. Vorontsov and Bariatinskii—turned to the unused land of notables.[39] Fourth, sectarians found themselves living on private lands because of

36. Breyfogle, "Colonization by Contract," 144–52; RGIA f. 1268, op. 9, d. 367a, 1857–58; f. 381, op. 1, d. 23297, 1844–45; f. 384, op. 3, d. 1149, 1846–51; AKAK vol. 10, doc. 95, p. 118; and vol. 12:1 (1893), docs. 18 and 22, pp. 39–41, 49.
37. RGIA f. 1268, op. 9, d. 367a, 1857–58, l. 40b.
38. RGIA f. 381, op. 1, d. 23297, 1844–45; RGIA f. 1268, op. 1, d. 866, 1845–46; AKAK vol. 10, docs. 95 and 97, pp. 118–23.
39. AKAK vol. 10, docs. 42, 95, and 97, pp. 46–47, 118–23; and SPChR (1860), II:417–30.

changing tsarist policy toward local elites. In 1841, for instance, land belonging to Muslim notables in eastern Transcaucasia was confiscated as part of a state-sponsored "Russification" effort to weaken the elites and provide state-owned land for the Russian colonists to live on. In 1842, tsarist policy shifted away from this practice and the property was returned to the original owners, leaving recently settled Russians inhabiting lands belonging to Muslim notables.[40] Finally, sectarians found themselves on the property of indigenous landowners as a result of the inability of tsarist administrators to demarcate land boundaries in Transcaucasia. Dissenters settled on land that tsarist officials had initially labeled state-owned, designations that local landowners later disputed. For example, in 1843 Molokans in Aleksandropol district settled on land that administrators claimed as treasury property. However, the Orbeliani family soon challenged the state for ownership and after a protracted court battle regained possession in 1853.[41]

The actual agreements negotiated between settlers and nobles varied dramatically from case to case in almost every respect: the settlers' dues and obligations, what the sectarians received in return, the type and duration of the contract, whether and how the contract might be amended or voided, and whether the settlers were allowed to move or travel from the lands. Despite their heterogeneity, the content of these accords indicates what each side hoped to receive from such arrangements. The evidence suggests that the nobles were most concerned to ensure a constant flow of lucrative rents without incurring any of the costs or frustrations of having to manage the settlers' communities directly. For their part, the sectarians wanted the best possible package of land and obligations, the freedom to move from lands when they wanted, the opportunity to take advantage of other economic opportunities (especially in the carting trade and milling), and the protection of the state from exploitation. Required to approve these contracts, state officials were not shy about intervening in the process. They changed conditions and wording in order to ensure that the deals were detailed and fair to all involved—in fact, they were very solicitous about defending the rights of the colonists.[42]

The Russian state-peasant settlers obtained a variety of benefits from the contracts. Most important, they were granted land on which to settle

40. RGIA f. 1268, op. 15, d. 86, 1870, l. 1; and *AKAK* vol. 10, doc. 293, p. 287. For a discussion of the shifts of tsarist policy toward local elites more broadly, see Swietochowski, *Russian Azerbaijan*, 12–13; and L. H. Rhinelander, "Russia's Imperial Policy: The Administration of the Caucasus in the First Half of the Nineteenth Century," *CSP* 17 (1975): 218–35.

41. RGIA f. 1268, op. 9, d. 367a, 1857–58, ll. 9–90b.

42. See, for example, SSC'SA f. 240, op. 1, d. 1709, 1867, ll. 7–70b; op. 2, d. 317, 1858–63, l. 7; RGIA f. 381, op. 1, d. 23297, 1844–45, ll. 61–62, 135–420b; f. 1268, op. 15, d. 86, 1870, l. 10b; and f. 384, op. 3, d. 1149, 1846–51, ll. 940b–950b.

and work, certain rights to use nearby forests for wood, occasionally the use of any industrial enterprises already on the land (such as mills, taverns, or general stores), and frequently the protection of the landowner in the event that others tried to seize their allotted land. The contracts of certain settlers even included promises of relief from payment of dues in the initial years of settlement and of direct aid in the event of poor harvests. In addition, some colonists received the option of engaging in a variety of economic endeavors, including building and operating gristmills selling lumber, owning taverns and stores, mining coal and minerals, and fishing.[43] In the case of an 1845 agreement with Prince David Dadiani, settlers received land that could serve a variety of purposes (from viticulture to grain growing, haymaking, and pasturage) but to a limit of ten *desiatiny* per adult male. In order to help the settlers in their first years of habitation, Dadiani offered to supply each family with a two bulls, two cows, two pigs, general provisions for the first two years, and an exemption from rents during the first year.[44]

The specific advantages sought by the landowners varied widely. Rents paid in cash diverged in amount, sometimes calculated per household (anywhere from one to twenty-four rubles per year), sometimes as a lump sum from the community (from 200 to 330 rubles per year).[45] Many nobles required payment in kind, which might include wheat, barley, wood, beeswax, and honey.[46] Other nobles preferred a combination of rents and service: for example, Talysh-bek Begliarov negotiated successfully for 10 percent of the total harvest, as well as two workdays annually per settler.[47] Contracts might include any number of other service obligations in addition to working the noble's land. Nina Ivanova Loris-Melikova requested an annual payment of eight silver rubles and two full carts of wood per household, the latter to be delivered directly to her house in Tiflis; she also retained the right to build herself a summer house in the Molokans' village.[48]

Contracts also varied in form and duration, lasting from seven to thirty years. At the end of each contract, both sides had the opportunity to rene-

43. SSC'SA f. 240, op. 1, d. 1709, 1867, ll. 1–3; op. 2, d. 317, 1858–63, ll. 3–50b; and RGIA f. 1268, op. 9, d. 367a, 1857–58, ll. 9–150b.
44. RGIA f. 381, op. 1, d. 23297, 1844–45, ll. 600b, 139–390b.
45. RGIA f. 1268, op. 9, d. 367a, 1857–58, ll. 9–150b; op. 15, d. 86, 1870, ll. 10b–2; SSC'SA f. 240, op. 1, d. 1709, 1867, ll. 10b–2, 7–9; op. 2, d. 317, 1858–63, ll. 3–4.
46. AKAK vol. 10, doc. 293, p. 287; SSC'SA f. 240, op. 2, d. 317, 1858–63, ll. 3–30b; and op. 1, d. 1709, 1867, ll. 10b–2.
47. AKAK vol. 10, docs. 97 and 293, pp. 120 and 287; and RGIA, f. 381, op. 1, d. 23297, 1844–45, ll. 1390b–40.
48. SSC'SA f. 240, op. 2, d. 317, 1858–63, ll. 3–5. As discussed in chapter three, it was not uncommon for nobles and administrative elites to escape the summer heat of urban areas by renting houses in the sectarian mountain villages. See also SSC'SA f. 240, op. 1, d. 1709, 1867, l. 20b.

gotiate on the same or different terms, or they could agree to go their separate ways. Whereas most pacts were written, prior to 1858 the agreements governing the sectarians living on the land of Princess Maria Orbeliani and Princes Ivan and Makarii Orbeliani were entirely verbal. In the case of Ivan and Makarii, the settlers found that the landowners' demands changed arbitrarily from year to year. In response to settler complaints concerning these unilateral alterations, Bariatinskii required that all agreements after 1858 exist in written form and be approved by the government.[49]

Whatever the specific terms of the contracts binding sectarians and Transcaucasian landowners, many local elites strove to obtain the economic benefits of a servile economy without assuming the associated responsibilities. Georgian and Armenian nobles often required agents from the Ministry of State Domains to act as middlemen to avoid the potential complications of direct interaction with the settlers. For instance, the Orbeliani family in Erevan province required that "in enforcing the collection of these moneys, and in all other situations, the Princes Orbeliani should have no direct relations with the peasants." As it did not want the nobility to have too much control over the state peasants, the government was all too happy to comply with this wish.[50]

Both before and especially after the legislation of 1858, the practice of Russian state-peasant settlement on the lands of Caucasian nobles created both exciting opportunities and painful frustrations for settlers, nobles, and state officials alike. Their ongoing interactions tell a great deal about the lived experience of Russian colonialism in the South Caucasus. Significantly, the documentary sources indicate that these relations were dominated by socio-economic tensions characteristic of tenant-landowner relations and were generally devoid of ethnic or confessional considerations.[51] Moreover, these peasant-noble contacts show how the tsarist state managed its multi-ethnic empire. Rather than the unmitigated champion of any one side, tsarist officials frequently found themselves in the role of mediator between the Russian peasants and the Caucasian nobles, charged with arbitrating the terms of the contracts when disputes arose and rights were violated.

49. SSC'SA f. 240, op. 2, d. 317, 1858–63, ll. 10b, 40b; op. 1, d. 1709, ll. 1–6; RGIA f. 381, op. 1, d. 23297, 1844–45, l. 142; f. 1268, op. 9, d. 367a, 1857–58, ll. 9–150b; and op. 15, d. 86, 1870, l. 10b.

50. RGIA f. 1268, op. 9, d. 367a, 1857–58, l. 11; and f. 381, op. 1, d. 23297, 1844–45, ll. 140–400b. See also RGIA f. 1268, op. 15, d. 86, 1870, l. 10b. Not all nobles tried so hard to keep the sects at arm's length. There were cases where nobles were willing, even eager, to interact directly with the sectarians so that they might wield more thorough control. AKAK vol. 10, doc. 97, p. 120; and RGIA f. 381, op. 1, d. 23297, 1844–45, ll. 60–63.

51. That social-status power hierarchies proved prominent in this case contrasts with the "ethnic-religious conflict" that Vartan Gregorian highlights as an important aspect of the relations between Armenian peasants and Azerbaijani landowners. Gregorian, "The Impact of Russia," 183.

The landowners generally embraced the opportunity to have Russian settlers work their lands even though some felt that sectarians did not always make the best tenants. In contrast, the sectarians themselves were ultimately almost universally dissatisfied by the economically "burdensome" nature of the contracts.[52] In the late 1840s and early 1850s, Molokans in the villages of Novo-Saratovka and Vorontsovka in Tiflis province "feared enslavement from the Orbelianis and began to look for a new place to live that would be on state-owned land."[53] Many Vorontsovka villagers did depart for Elisavetpol district. Those who stayed behind remained disgruntled about their economic situation and repeatedly voiced their unhappiness to tsarist authorities. The Molokans found the payment of quitrent to be economically disadvantageous and were particularly frustrated by the economic "insecurity of their property situation" that resulted from "dependence" on a landowner who held the power to change the terms of their rental agreement.[54]

The contracts that Transcaucasian landowners and the sectarians entered into governing land usage and remuneration belie any simple categorization of the power relationships between colonizer and colonized in Transcaucasia. In this instance, socio-economic power structures overshadowed the ethnic hierarchies of colonial power systems, often to the detriment of the Russian peasant colonists. At the same time, the settlement of colonists as renters of noble lands presents two conflicting aspects of Russian imperialist policy. On one hand, especially after 1842 Russian policy in Transcaucasia tried to enlist the support of local elites in Russia's empire-building project both by granting them privileges and ceasing to antagonize them.[55] On the other hand, tsarist authorities wanted to increase the presence of ethnic Russians in the region, because they considered Russians the most loyal subjects and because they wanted to reduce future reliance on non-Russians. When the drive to increase the number of Russians in the region required the state to settle Russian colonists on private land, one aspect of the Russian imperialist agenda overshadowed another. Since tsarist authorities considered the native

52. *AKAK* vol. 10, doc. 293, p. 287. Some settler communities did find their economic status rise. See Breyfogle, "Colonization by Contract," 157.

53. I. E. Petrov, "Seleniia Novo-Saratovka i Novo-Ivanovka Elisavetpol'skogo uezda," *IKOIRGO* 19, no. 1(1907–1908): otd. 1, 226. See also RGIA f. 1268, op. 9, d. 367a, 1857–58, ll. 130b–14; *AKAK* vol. 10, doc. 98, p. 123; and Inikova, "Vzaimootnosheniia," 45.

54. As discussed in chapter four, state authorities intervened in this case in order to keep the sectarians in the village. See RGIA f. 1268, op. 14, d. 77, 1869–70; and I. Ia. Orekhov, "Ocherki iz zhizni zakavkazskikh sektatorov," *Kavkaz*, no. 136 (June 17, 1878): 1.

55. Ronald Grigor Suny, "Russian Rule and Caucasian Society in the First Half of the Nineteenth Century: The Georgian Nobility and the Armenian Bourgeoisie, 1801–1856," *NP* 7, no. 1 (1979): 60; Anthony L. H. Rhinelander, *Prince Michael Vorontsov: Viceroy to the Tsar* (Montreal and Kingston, 1990), 146–84; and Mostashari, "Tsarist Colonial Policy," 332–402.

elites to be of higher social standing than the Russian colonists—and, therefore, the recipients of certain prerogatives—the settlers entered into uneven relationships with indigenous notables. By settling the sectarians on landowner property under such contracts, tsarist officials placed the same Russian colonists they considered the advance guard of "Russification" in an economically subordinate position to Transcaucasian elites.[56]

PACIFISTS INTO PACIFIERS: VIOLENCE AND COLONIAL CONTACT

The memoirs of sectarian settlers, as well as official documents and the writings of contemporary ethnographers and journalists, are filled with incidents of robbery, attack, murder, kidnapping, rape, and other forms of violent treatment perpetrated by indigenous Transcaucasians and Turkish "brigands" on the Russian colonists. Sectarians clearly distinguished among the region's different native peoples, laying blame for the maltreatment primarily at the feet of the so-called "Tatars" and other Muslim peoples from Persia and the Ottoman Empire. In contrast, there is not a single mention in the sources of Georgians assaulting colonists despite their regular interaction with the Russian settlers. Armenians were considered "deft fleecers and exploiters of the simple Russian population" who at times turned to theft and violence to get their way. The Dukhobors of Slavianka in Elisavetpol province, for one, claimed that Armenians "never missed the opportunity to short-change and swindle" them.[57]

The causes of what Russians perceived as Muslim violence have produced a variety of explanations. Russian officials and other contemporary commentators attributed acts of theft and violence to the Muslim mountain culture.[58] As one administrator expressed the prevailing interpretation, in Transcaucasia "the murder of humans has been carried out on the road of life since the dawn of time, and the land is soaked to the depths with human blood from many wars."[59] In his October 1844 report

---

56. Although not discussed here, the same patterns can be seen on a political level in the interactions between settlers and the large number of indigenous Caucasians who occupied the lower and middle ranks of tsarist administration in the region, and therefore governed over the Russian settlers. See chapters 6 and 7.

57. GARF f. 102, 3 d-vo, op. 1884, d. 88, ch. 2, ll. 9–90b; V. V. Vereshchagin, *Dukhobortsy i Molokane v Zakavkaz'e, Shiity v Karabakhe, Batchi i Oshumoedy v Srednei Azii, i Ober-Amergau v Gorakh Bavarii* (Moscow, 1900), 21; SSC'SA f. 17, op. 1, d. 4042, 1899; and f. 240, op. 1, d. 1428, 1865–67.

58. See I. Ia. Orekhov, "Ocherki iz zhizni zakavkazskikh sektatorov," *Kavkaz*, no. 135 (June 16, 1878): 2; GMIR f. 2, op. 7, d. 489, 1928, l. 1; and op. 8, d. 352, 1935, l. 12.

59. GMIR f. 2, op. 7, d. 489, 1928, l. 1.

on the conditions of the sectarians, a tsarist official named Gageimeister noted that "the theft of livestock is a common affair among the Tatars, but their stealing from each other comprises a system of collective responsibility. Russians are not accustomed to such a form of self-regulation and the state hardly wishes them to become used to such a manner of settling affairs."[60] Archives contain hundreds of nineteenth-century police reports detailing acts of robbery and violence on the part of Muslims, indicating that the dissenters were by no means the sole targets of such crimes.[61] In that light, Russians generally understood Muslim acts of hostility toward the sectarians as the result of a primordial violence that would have existed with or without the sectarians' presence. Yet the appearance of the settlers in Transcaucasia unmistakably altered the form and intensity of the antagonism because it directly threatened the economic existence of settled farmers and especially nomads.

Moreover, in categorizing the Transcaucasian peoples in this manner, Russian sectarians were mirroring with remarkable clarity a discourse widespread in Russia about the Transcaucasian peoples. Georgians were considered a weak, feminine, lazy, non-threatening people; Armenians wily, commercial types and rootless traders—some Russians called them "Caucasian Jews"; and Muslims an uncivilized, naturally martial people.[62] With this in mind, there is some reason to doubt whether Muslims really were the sole source of violent attack—especially in the early years of settlement—as it is certainly possible that the accusations arose from Russian cultural expectations of Islamic aggression.

Whatever the origins of the violence and whoever the perpetrators, both sectarians and Russian officials believed that the violence originated from Azerbaijanis, Turks, and other Muslims, and that such people were inherently predisposed to armed robbery and warlike behavior. Colonists and administrators took action within the parameters of such assumptions. Despite their religious prohibitions, members of the sectarian com-

60. RGIA f. 381, op. 1, d. 23300, 1844, l. 20b.
61. See, for example, RGIA f. 1268, op. 9, d. 100, 1857–58; d. 74, 1858; op. 10, d. 46, 1859; d. 62, 1860–61; d. 44, 1861; d. 46, 1862; d. 32, 1863; and d. 28, 1866. For comparison, see Moshe Gammer, *Muslim Resistance to the Tsar: Shamil and the Conquest of Chechnia and Daghestan* (London, 1994), 18–21; and Virginia Martin, "Barīmta: Nomadic Custom, Imperial Crime," in *Russia's Orient*, 249–70.
62. Susan Layton, *Russian Literature and Empire: Conquest of the Caucasus from Pushkin to Tolstoy* (Cambridge, 1994), esp. 175–212; Ronald Grigor Suny, *Looking Toward Ararat: Armenia in Modern History* (Bloomington, 1993), 31–51; Seymour Becker, "The Muslim East in Nineteenth-Century Russian Popular Historiography," *CAS* 5, no. 3/4 (1986): esp. 32–33; Austin Lee Jersild, "From Savagery to Citizenship: Caucasian Mountaineers and Muslims in the Russian Empire," in *Russia's Orient*, 101–14; Sunderland, "Empire of Peasants," 185–90; and Gammer, *Muslim Resistance*, 25–26. However, as Susan Layton has pointed out, the meanings attributed by different Russians to the images of these peoples were not always uniform. See her "Nineteenth-Century Russian Mythologies of Caucasian Savagery," in *Russia's Orient*, 80–100.

munities at times embraced violent tactics as a deterrent, meeting hostility with even greater hostility. In so doing, they accommodated themselves to what they perceived as the prevailing form of interpersonal and inter-group relations.

Sectarians were no strangers to violence. In the central provinces, they regularly suffered the verbal and physical assaults of local officials, landlords, priests, and neighboring Orthodox villagers, and some nonconformists had been forced to serve in the military before resettlement. In addition, Molokans and Dukhobors routinely made distinctions among different kinds of violence and killing, accepting bloodshed as self-defense but not as aggression.[63] However, the use of force they described the Muslims as perpetrating in the South Caucasus—bands on horseback attacking villages and taking hostages, highway brigandage, murder—represented something new and unfamiliar. The settlers attached different meanings to the violence in Transcaucasia, feeling initially overwhelmed and easily victimized by what they saw as an unfathomable culture of criminality.

Sources yield a multitude of examples of Azerbaijani violence toward sectarians. The painter V. V. Vereshchagin, who visited Dukhobor and Molokan villages in the 1860s, quotes a Slavianka Dukhobor saying that Muslims "robbed you in broad daylight, seized you, tied your hands behind your back and held a knife to your throat, all the while others carried off your horses," often killing Dukhobors in the process.[64] Journalist I. Ia. Orekhov described how Molokans in Baku province had been settled "between half-wild indigenous people who are hostile and envious," gangs of whom "would conduct open attacks on their settlements" and carry off children from the settler communities as hostages.[65] Sectarians also complained of similar treatment by Turkish subjects who frequently rode across the porous border—too long, mountainous, and poorly guarded to act as any sort of obstacle—attacked and stole from farmers and shepherds in the fields, forayed into villages, and then crossed back to the safety of their own country with as much booty as they could carry. These incursions often threatened to become international incidents, although ultimately there was little tsarist authorities could do other than petition the Turkish ambassador. A number of sectarians spent many years in Ottoman villages as captive servants.[66]

63. Breyfogle, "Swords into Plowshares," 449–65.
64. Vereshchagin, *Dukhobortsy i Molokane*, 21 and 4. See also I. E. Petrov, "Dukhobory Elisavet-pol'skogo uezda," *IKOIRGO* 18, no. 3 (1905–1906): 176; SSC'SA f. 240, op. 2, d. 233, 1853–61; and f. 17, op. 1, d. 1828, 1884.
65. Orekhov, "Ocherki," no. 135, 2. See also *Spirit and Life—Book of the Sun. Divine Discourses of the Preceptors and the Martyrs of the Word of God, the Faith of Jesus, and the Holy Spirit, of the Religion of the Spiritual Christian Molokan-Jumpers*, ed. Daniel H. Shubin, trans. John Volkov (n.p., 1983), 20.
66. Of many examples, see SSC'SA f. 5, op. 1, d. 1454, 1870; f. 244, op. 3, d. 100, 1870; RGIA f.

The attacks and robberies depicted in the sources threatened everything from life and limb to material and psychological well-being. One Dukhobor story tells of the particularly gruesome demise of one of their brethren who, while returning from a trip to Tiflis, was hacked to death with an axe for his money and left in pieces by the roadside.[67] Similarly, one November night in 1856, two Molokans, Evstrat and Ivan Sherbakov from Shemakha (later Baku) province, were on their way home from Tiflis in their wagons when they were met on the road by five armed Azerbaijanis. Realizing that the bandits intended to rob them, the Molokans drove their horses forward at full speed. The Azerbaijanis made chase, firing their rifles and brandishing their sabers. In the melee, one Molokan horse was slashed by a sword and the other horse was struck by a bullet. The injured horses pulled up and the Molokans were forced to surrender to the robbers. And robbery was not confined to the roadways: bands of thieves fearlessly entered sectarian villages, breaking into houses to steal property—often with the owners inside. When settlers went after bandits to retrieve property and captives, they frequently came face to face with armed Azerbaijani villagers who repulsed their efforts and protected the thieves.[68]

Rape was another, not uncommon, form of violence that sectarians confronted. In one incident, three Azerbaijanis reportedly intent on rape confronted some Dukhobor women coming home from the fields. The women successfully fought back and, as they were not far from the settlers' village, the attackers took off through the fields where they encountered two other Dukhobor women. Isolated from their coreligionists, these Dukhobors were less fortunate and despite a struggle eventually succumbed to the attackers.[69]

Theft and banditry caused the sectarians material losses and took a substantial psychological toll. In 1847 and 1848 alone, 58 horses and cattle were stolen from the villagers of Vorontsovka and Novo-Saratovka, as well as property with a total value of 1,573 rubles; the Ormashen commune reportedly suffered losses from robbery of up to 1,767 rubles.[70] In terms of the mental impact, Dukhobors described the terror in which they lived. "You head off somewhere and don't know whether [the

1268, op. 3, d. 438, 1849; Vasilii A. Potapov, V plenu u razboinikov: rasskaz (n.p., 1936); and M. N-n, "Dukhobory v Dukhobor'e," Obzor, no. 159 (June 17, 1878): 3.
67. ORRGB f. 369, k. 42, d. 2, 1950, l. 398.
68. RGIA f. 1268, op. 9, d. 100, 1857–58, ll. 18, 86; SSC'SA f. 222, op. 1, d. 60, 1849; f. 239, op. 1, d. 45, 1849–52; and f. 240, op. 1, d. 1428, 1865–67.
69. SSC'SA f. 222, op. 1, d. 60, 1849, ll. 5–50b. See also GMIR f. 14, op. 3, d. 1962, 1902, ll. 13–14.
70. Inikova, "Vzaimootnosheniia," 46; I. V. Dolzhenko, "Istoriia pereseleniia i osnovaniia russkikh selenii v Zakavkaz'e," in Russkie starozhily Zakavkaz'ia: Molokane i Dukhobortsy, ed. V. I. Kozlov (Moscow, 1995), 33; SSC'SA f. 222, op. 1, d. 60, 1849, l. 47; and f. 239, op. 1, d. 45, 1849–52, ll. 21–250b, passim.

"Tatars"] are waiting for you in back. And you arrive home, and not even necessarily from a long trip, and you say to yourself: Thank you God! Night is approaching quietly and there was no theft in the village. Everyone thanks God, and maybe tomorrow, somehow we will survive."[71] Indeed, Dukhobors were so concerned with attacks and robberies that they developed incantations (to be read three times while walking around the house) to protect their families and property, "and with these prayers the people saved themselves."[72]

The initial response of the sectarians was to turn to the state for protection. On many occasions they petitioned the local and regional authorities with complaints of mistreatment by their new neighbors. However, the sectarians often found the response of state officials to be ineffectual and their stories relate their frustration with the authorities. After attacks or robberies, Molokan villagers from Alty-Agach frequently captured the thieves and presented them, along with an official accusation, to the police for punishment. Despite such initiative, the Molokans generally found that the police would set these "Tatar-thieves" free almost immediately, making their efforts irrelevant.[73] Vereshchagin heard similar grievances from the Dukhobors about the state's ineffectual approach. In the face of Azerbaijani attacks, they lamented, there was nowhere to turn for justice, especially not the court system. As one Dukhobor related: "They pull you into court in the very middle of the work day. They summon you, and in the town they say to you that the thieves involved in your case have not been found—and you sign, brother, on this piece of paper to say that you are content—and there the affair comes to an end."[74]

There were three reasons for the failure to prosecute. First, representatives from various indigenous groups maintained a strong presence among tsarist officialdom in Transcaucasia, both at the regional level in Tiflis and especially as local administrators, policemen, and low-level bureaucrats. They tended not to have any sympathy for the sectarian interlopers.[75] In the police report for Kars territory for 1883, the author

71. Vereshchagin, *Dukhobortsy i Molokane*, 21. On fear of attack, see also Sergei Studzinskii, "U nashikh kavkazskikh raskol'nikov. (Ocherk)," *Slovo*, no. 1 (February 1878): 122–23; N-n, "Dukhobory," 3; and "Alty-Agach. (Ot nashego korrespondenta)," *Kaspii*, no. 115 (June 1, 1894): 3.

72. Quoted and translated in Svetlana Inikova, *Doukhobor Incantations Through the Centuries*, trans. and ed. Koozma Tarasoff (Ottawa, 1999), 76–80.

73. GMIR f. 14, op. 3, d. 1962, 1902, l. 14. This is not to say that the sectarians received no state aid in tracking down thieves or attackers. See SSC'SA f. 222, op. 1, d. 60, 1849, ll. 47–58.

74. Vereshchagin, *Dukhobortsy i Molokane*, 21. See also SSC'SA f. 239, op. 1, d. 45, 1849–52, ll. 20b, 13.

75. N. D. [Nikolai Dingel'shtedt], "Pryguny (Materialy k istoriia obruseniia Zakavkazskogo kraia)" *OZ*, no. 10 (1878): 381–83; Rhinelander, *Prince Michael Vorontsov*, 169–84; and Swietochowski, *Russian Azerbaijan*, 10–17. For comparison, see Stephen Velychenko, "Identities, Loyalties and Service in Imperial Russia: Who Administered the Borderlands?" *RR* 54, no. 2 (1995): 188–208.

vented his frustration about the selection of Armenian administrators in the region. He found them to be untrustworthy, given to nepotism and favoritism, and adherents to "that cult, which deliberately, consistently and finely develops an ill will, . . . one can even say hatred, towards all those who carry a Russian name and to Russian people in general."[76] Second, some Russian authorities in the region initially did not want the sectarians to settle in Transcaucasia, so they often ordered local officials to do what they could to eliminate the nonconformists.[77] Finally, and most important, the failure of state officials to secure the existence of Russian settlers in the region derived from their powerlessness to do so. Not only had there been little time after conquest to build Russian administrative structures in Transcaucasia, but the tsarist empire was also still many years from fully controlling the region even militarily, due both to internal opposition and the attacks of external forces from Turkey and Persia.[78]

The response of the authorities to Dukhobor complaints of Muslim attack in 1847 reveals the problems facing tsarist officials in their efforts to control the region. In order to put an end to the banditry of both "neighboring and foreign" Muslims, from which the Dukhobors suffered "incessantly," Vorontsov sent orders to establish a line of "permanent residential pickets" that would run from the town of Akhalkalaki to the Armenian village of Shestony. They were to be composed of inhabitants from local Muslim villages, since there was no one else available to perform the policing tasks. Ordered to secure the passage from Akhalkalaki to Aleksandropol, they were also entrusted with guaranteeing the safety of the Dukhobors from robbers and were required to take responsibility in case of attacks from Azerbaijani co-villagers. Thus, state policy placed representatives of the very people the Dukhobors considered to be their attackers in positions responsible for their defense. However, the affair took an unexpected turn when, despite these direct orders, the local official from Akhalkalaki district recruited members of the Dukhobor community, rather than Azerbaijanis, for these crime-control efforts. The Dukhobors complained bitterly, and unsuccessfully, that they were being ordered to take up policing activities, since it contradicted their religious teachings and diverted them from economic activities. Thus, the state's eventual response to Dukhobor complaints of attack was to assign them the task of their own defense.[79]

In the face of constant attack and an unresponsive and/or impotent

76. GARF f. 102, 3 d-vo, op. 1884, d. 88, ch. 2, ll. 80b–90b.

77. In this regard, see chapter four as well as GMIR f. 2, op. 7, d. 597, 1835–40; and N. D., "Pryguny," no. 10, 382.

78. Jones, "Russian Imperial Administration," 53–76; Swietochowski, *Russian Azerbaijan*, 9; Firouzeh Mostashari, "Tsarist Colonial Policy"; Baddeley, *Russian Conquest*; and Gammer, *Muslim Resistance*.

79. *AKAK* vol. 10, docs. 98 and 100, pp. 123–24.

state, at least some Molokans and Dukhobors across Transcaucasia could see no other solution but to take matters into their own hands. Despite the tenets of their faiths, both of which forbade violence and killing, the settlers started to meet their attackers on their own violent terms. In so doing, they not only underwent a profound change in religiosity but also fulfilled General Ermolov's prediction that, once in the Caucasus, they would be forced to take up arms and defend themselves, their property, and their families.[80] Discussing the need to compromise their ethical stance, the Dukhobor Petr Malov relates how his forebears' "immense farms and large number of livestock represented a constant temptation for the bellicose native population, and raids and robberies did not diminish but became more frequent. They found it necessary to protect their property and thus, little by little, the Dukhobors began to acquire their own weapons. On that soil, bloody dramas were often performed and even murders occurred on both sides."[81]

The Dukhobors "ceased to forgive the Tatars for their insults" and began to fight back.[82] Dukhobor communities formed detachments of armed and uniformed "Cossacks" who defended their coreligionists and provided permanent bodyguards to Dukhobor leaders (see Figure 9).[83] Soviet historian A. I. Klibanov describes the Dukhobors' militarization in the following terms: "Mounted Cossacks, armed with sabers, daggers and revolvers, under the command of local chiefs, existed in a number of Dukhobor villages, carried out military training and were subordinate to the overall command of 'the sergeant-major.' "[84] Moreover, Dukhobors began to try native suspects in their own courts rather than in state ones. In doing so, they ensured that the reprisals meted out to their persecutors would be as stern as their collective conscience would allow.[85] The Dukhobors also began to fortify their farms in order to provide protection for their communities. Svetlana Inikova, an ethnographer and Dukhobor expert, notes that the construction of barns and sheds changed as a result of the violence that the Dukhobors encountered in Transcaucasia. On a visit to the Dukhobor communities in the 1980s, she observed that barns from the mid-nineteenth century were built with metal grates as a way of turning them into defense-ready fortresses. Sim-

80. See chapter one.
81. Petr Malov, *Dukhobortsy, ikh istoriia, zhizn' i bor'ba*, vol. 1 (Thrums, BC, 1948), 25–26; SSC'SA f. 5, op. 1, d. 1454, 1870; f. 244, op. 3, d. 100, 1870; and RGIA f. 1268, op. 3, d. 438, 1849.
82. Petrov, "Dukhobory," 176.
83. B. N. Terletskii, "Sekta Dukhoborov," in *Russkie sektanty, ikh uchenie, kult, i sposoby propagandy*, ed. M. A. Kal'nev (Odessa, 1911), 10–11; and Aylmer Maude, *A Peculiar People: the Doukhobors* (New York, 1904), opposite 222.
84. Klibanov, *History*, 122–23.
85. Terletskii, "Sekta Dukhoborov," 10–11.

FIGURE 9. Dukhobor "Cossacks," early 1890s. British Columbia Archives C-01939, published with permission.

ilarly, sheds had windowless walls, and the only windows were on the roof—a design that was typical of Azerbaijani dwellings of the time.[86]

Other sectarians told similar stories. When Molokans from Alty-Agach complained to Vorontsov about Muslim violence, he is said to have replied, "Is it really possible that you cannot cope with the Tatars your-

86. Inikova, "Vzaimootnosheniia," 46.

selves?" In the wake of this rebuke, the Molokans began to take matters into their own hands. In memoirs, Molokans describe hunting down and castrating Azerbaijanis who they felt were guilty of "dishonoring" their women. They also relate how they would "shoot Tatars like hares" in cases of vandalism or when a Russian had been injured or murdered.[87] Similarly, Orekhov reported in the 1870s that "the most somber rumors about the settler-Molokans reign in the midst of the surrounding indigenous people. The Molokans, the natives say, burn thieves—their enemies— should they happen to fall into the Molokans' hands. One hears such a variety of stories with the most unbelievable contents." The indigenous population asserted that the Molokans resorted frequently to blood reprisals and savage punishments—in short, "the law of lynching."[88] Another Russian journalist asserted in 1871 that the sectarians showed very little compassion toward those of other faiths: "Their toughness stands in sharp relief in the struggle for life and death with the neighboring Tatars. They do not even consider the latter to be people and they strive to exploit them in all possible ways."[89]

In their efforts to ensure their own security, the sectarians received a modicum of state support. The understaffed tsarist officials in the region not only granted permission to the sectarian settlements to arm themselves and form paramilitary bands for their own defense, but even helped them acquire weapons. On Vorontsov's orders, small groups of armed guards were recruited from among the settlers in order to protect villagers from robbery, theft, and attack.[90] Officials found it inexpensive to support such militias, which ranged from three to ten people in size. They needed only to supply weapons, salaries being considered unnecessary because the recruits were on temporary assignment.[91] In 1854, local officials, unable to defend the Dukhobors in Elisavetpol district during the Crimean War, sold them 913 rifles from the Tiflis artillery garrison at reduced prices, loaned other guns without charge for long periods, and supplied the powder for free. Once tsarist officials had done this for the Dukhobors, other Russian settlers began to request weapons from the state under these terms, reflecting their ongoing distancing from their religious tenets of nonviolence.[92]

Sectarian sources reveal little about how they reacted or gave meaning to these changes in their behavior and morals. The adoption of violent tactics represented such a direct challenge to their religious beliefs

87. GMIR f. 14, op. 3, d. 1962, 1902, ll. 13–14.
88. Orekhov, "Ocherki," no. 135, 2.
89. K. G., "Obshchii vzgliad na vnutrenniuiu zhizn' russkikh sektantov v zakavkazskom krae," Kavkaz, no. 141 (1871): 2. See also GMIR f. K1, op. 8, d. 470, 1925, l. 9.
90. RGIA f. 1268, op. 3, d. 438, 1849, ll. 1–10b.
91. AKAK vol. 10, doc. 100, p. 124.
92. SSC'SA f. 16, op. 1, d. 10631, 1854–58; and Inikova, "Vzaimootnosheniia," 46.

that they could hardly have come about without considerable debate. Yet contemporary sources give no indication of spiritual struggles or soul-searching within the sectarian communities. Only in the last quarter of the nineteenth century does discussion of this question turn up in the sectarians' own writings—first with the appearance of the Baptists in Transcaucasia in the late 1870s, and then with the Dukhobor pacifist movement from 1894 to 1899.[93]

Sources do not make concrete distinctions between the Molokans and Dukhobors in terms of the frequency and forms of violence, and there are no references to the Subbotniks in discussions of settler violence. What is clear, however, is that in their use of force, Dukhobors and Molokans did not simply appropriate the local forms of violence, but rather shifted from nonviolence to violence within their own cultural framework. Instead of appropriating Azerbaijani models, they reacted with structures of aggression more typical of Russian culture—a pattern not dissimilar to the violence between Europeans and native peoples in North America.[94] They resorted to weapons whose design was originally Caucasian, in part because these were the weapons most readily available to them. Yet, in response to kidnapping, highway robbery or theft of livestock, for example, there is no indication that the settlers ever committed these specific crimes in retribution—a response that the Azerbaijanis may have expected within their cultural system.[95] Although they described their actions as defensive and prompted only by the Azerbaijani attacks, the sectarians generally reacted with extreme measures and frequently with greater violence than had been done to them. Descriptions of burning culprits alive, castrating rapists, hunting criminals, and setting upon thieves in large numbers to inflict beatings all reflect an approach to violence that was preemptive as much as retaliatory, hoping to ward off future mistreatment through the use of excessive force to spread fear. One cannot but notice the similarity of the justification of force presented by General Ermolov: "I desire that the terror of my name should guard our frontiers more potently than chains and fortresses, that my word should be for the natives a law more inevitable than death. Condescension in the eyes of Asiatics is a sign of weakness, and out of pure humanity I am inexorably severe. One execution saves hundreds of Russians from destruction, and thousands of Mussulmans from treason."[96]

93. See chapters six and seven.
94. Thomas S. Abler, "Scalping, Torture, Cannibalism, and Rape: An Ethnohistorical Analysis of Conflicting Cultural Values in War," *Anthropologica* 34 (1992): 3–20. I thank Robert Johnson for bringing this article to my attention.
95. For comparison, see Gammer, *Muslim Resistance;* Martin, "Barīmta"; and Swietochowski, *Russian Azerbaijan,* 16–17.
96. Quoted in Baddeley, *Russian Conquest,* 97.

The manner in which settlers applied violence was channeled by ethnic factors. Whereas the nonconformists took up arms against those natives who insulted, attacked, or robbed them, they took no similar actions toward Orthodox Russians who caused them injury in other ways. Writing at the beginning of the twentieth century, one Molokan author from Alty-Agach lamented that the Molokan community never considered imposing force on those Orthodox Russians who lived in their village and persecuted the Molokans for their faith. Rather than meet the Orthodox attacks with an eye for an eye, they succumbed meekly to the actions of Russian soldiers and priests who commandeered food and lodging, chased Molokan women, and aggressively prevented the Molokans from gathering for prayer services on the Sabbath.[97]

Yet if the sectarians were driven by ethnic considerations in their violent treatment of indigenous Azerbaijanis and, on occasion, Armenians, they did not develop a specifically racial sense of difference, as can be seen in other contexts of European imperialism.[98] In particular, they did not articulate an ideology of racial domination based on theology, such as in the case of the Boer settlers in South Africa. Boers justified their oppression of Africans and their belief that "eternal servitude was the divine calling of blacks" by referring to the biblical story of Ham—"a slave of slaves shall he be to his brothers" (Genesis 9:24). In general, Russian sectarians developed no such divinely inspired explanation to vindicate their treatment of Transcaucasia's Muslims. The one partial exception was the Pryguny. On describing the thousand-year kingdom of God, their leader Maksim Rudometkin envisioned the Muslims as their eternal subordinates: "They themselves will be our servants and breadwinners forever and their wives will be the servants and wetnurses of our children, everywhere with bows to them to the earth."[99]

The sectarian adoption of violence had two primary consequences. First, the armed militias of sectarian villages came to take on important roles in the administration of the Transcaucasus. By protecting themselves, the sectarians provided an unofficial armed force that aided in implementing Russian law and maintaining peace and Russian sovereignty on the frontier. Second, the colonists' use of force began to "tame" what

97. GMIR f. 14, op. 3, d. 1962, 1902, ll. 9–14.

98. See for example, Dane Kennedy, *Islands of White: Settler Society and Culture in Kenya and Southern Rhodesia, 1890–1939* (Durham, 1987), 148–66; and Ann Laura Stoler and Frederick Cooper, "Between Metropole and Colony: Rethinking a Research Agenda," in *Tensions of Empire: Colonial Cultures in a Bourgeois World,* ed. idem (Berkeley, 1997), 1–56.

99. Quoted and translated in Klibanov, *History,* 166. On the Boers, see John Comaroff, "Images of Empire, Contests of Conscience: Models of Colonial Domination in South Africa," in *Tensions of Empire,* 180–81; and Andre Du Toit, "No Chosen People: The Myth of the Calvinist Origins of Afrikaner Nationalism and Racial Ideology," *AHR* 88, no. 4 (1983): 920–52.

the sectarians described as the "hideous" and "disgraceful" behavior of the Muslims.[100] Official sources indicate that over the course of the nineteenth century, the rate and degree of violence and theft toward sectarians dropped so much that the authorities no longer considered it to be a problem. Whereas official reports from the first thirty years of the Russian sectarian presence in Transcaucasia are filled with comments about the difficult relations between them and the natives, police reports from the 1880s mention hardly any conflict at all. For instance, the governor's report for Elisavetpol province for 1878 and the political reviews of Baku province for 1884 and 1887 describe the relations between sectarians and native peoples as "good," "amicable," and "peaceful," with only rare misunderstandings.[101]

The settlers became widely respected for their ability to defend themselves. Natives no longer saw them as potential victims and, in some cases, openly feared them. A contemporary analyst reported that "the local inhabitants . . . are frightened of [the Russians], because in cases of attack, the theft of livestock, etc., all the commune acts like one person, energetically pursuing and prosecuting the violator of property."[102] Another Russian commentator added: "For the simple Tatar the word 'urus,' which they use to call any Russian, is united with a . . . respect and deference in their interactions with him, although the right to that respect was paid for dearly by [the sectarians] through struggle."[103]

It bears noting that tsarist officials and Russian commentators also attributed the reduction in violence and theft to a very different source: to moral forces as well as aggressive measures. Reflecting their views of Russians as civilizing agents, they asserted that the cultural values and social practices of the nonviolent, antimilitarist sectarians—their "good morals"—began to influence those around them. Discussing the Russian sectarians in Erevan province, journalist S. Kolosov asserted that the sectarians' "peaceful morals and the absence of the habit of carrying daggers or revolvers . . . have an effect on the spiritual way of life of the indigenous population, which sees that a Russian person behaves with confidence and trust towards other people, expects from them humane relations rather than attack, and looks upon the surrounding population not as enemies . . . but as upon his brothers. All of this deeply

100. GMIR f. 14, op. 3, d. 1962, 1902, ll. 13–14.
101. See RGIA f. 1268, op. 24, d. 231, 1879–80, l. 158; GARF f. 102, 3 d-vo, op. 1885, d. 59, ch. 37, l. 2; op. 1887, d. 9, ch. 36, l. 2; and "V 'Russkom Kur'ere,'" *Kaspii* 2, no. 59 (May 30, 1882): 2.
102. A. G. Dekonskii, "Ekonomicheskii byt gosudarstvennykh krest'ian v Shushinskom i Dzhebrail'skom uezdakh, Elisavetpol'skoi gubernii," *MIEB*, vol. 4: 1 (Tiflis, 1886), 232.
103. A. I. Masalkin, "Iz istorii zakavkazskikh sektantov. Ch. III, Sektanty, kak kolonizatory Zakavkaz'ia," *Kavkaz*, no. 333 (December 16, 1893): 3.

affected the morality of the native peoples."[104] Similar voices echoed throughout Transcaucasia, describing the restraining and peaceable influences of the sectarians on those around them and asserting that the settlers' economic success instilled respect for the Russian settlers and their achievements.[105]

The belief of tsarist officials in the pacifying effect of the sectarians on their neighbors—whatever its cause—affected colonial policies in Transcaucasia. In 1848, a tsarist official proposed to construct a Molokan village at a specific location in Erevan province "for the prevention of plundering and robberies on the part of nomadic inhabitants."[106] Similarly, in the late 1880s, the governor of Baku came to the conclusion that the best means to confront the crime problem in Kubin district would be to settle Russians in the area. As such, he ordered the settlement of twenty Molokan families "as an experiment" into a part of the region that was particularly violent, and where Russian soldiers had engaged in pitched gun battles with the local "robbers." The experiment was reportedly a "shining" success and crime rates in the region dropped dramatically.[107]

Although assaults and thefts were much reduced, they by no means disappeared altogether. Violence remained a central component of the relations between settlers and natives, although the quantity and the quality of the violence changed. From the 1860s into the twentieth century, there were periodic reports of neighboring Azerbaijanis stealing Russian livestock and conducting roadside killings and of Lezgins openly attacking Russian communities. Starting in 1905, there were reports of Armenians attacking Molokan communities.[108] In particular, the sectarian villagers in Novo-Saratovka and Novo-Ivanovka in Elisavetpol province complained that their horticulture suffered at the hands of Azerbaijani robbers. According to the contemporary commentator I. E. Petrov, nomads in the process of moving their herds through Transcaucasia often took advantage of the lack of serious supervision of the gardens to chop down trees and otherwise ruin the gardens of Molokans. It was also not

104. Kolosov, "Russkie sektanty," 152.
105. Inikova, "Vzaimootnosheniia," 49; "Iz Signakhskogo uezda (kor. Kavkaza)," *Kavkaz*, no. 15 (February 1, 1877): 3; Masalkin "Kolonizatory," no. 333, 3; I. Ia. Orekhov, "Ocherki iz zhizni zakavkazskikh sektatorov," *Kavkaz*, no. 143 (June 25, 1878): 1; Kh. A. Vermishev, "Ekonomicheskii byt gosudarstvennykh krest'ian v Akhaltsikhskom i Akhalkalakskom uezdakh, Tiflisskoi gubernii," in *MIEB*, vol. 3:2 (Tiflis, 1886), 42–43; A. N. Kuropatkin, *Soobrazheniia nachal'nika Zakaspiiskoi oblasti po voprosu o pereselenii v Zakaspiiskuiu oblast' dukhoborov-postnikov* (n.p., n.d.), 15; and Petrov, "Seleniia," 247.
106. Quoted in Tumanian, *Ekonomicheskoe razvitie*, 1:41.
107. RGIA f. 560, op. 26, d. 86, 1984, ll. 700b–71; and *Kaspii* 2, no. 59 (May 30, 1882): 2.
108. SSC'SA f. 17, op. 1, d. 4042, 1899; GARF f. 102, oo d-vo, op. 1907, d. 100, t. 1, ch. 2, ll. 131–320b; T. B., "U beregov Kaspiia (iz putevykh zametok i vospominanii). Tri goda nazad. Ch. IX, V Malorusskoi kolonii," *Kavkaz*, no. 75 (April 4, 1881): 1; "Sel. Slavianka," *Kaspii* 14, no. 243 (November 11, 1894): 3; and "Selenie Semenovka," *Tiflisskii listok* 18, no. 158 (July 13, 1895): 1.

uncommon for the local Azerbaijanis to unearth the trees and carry them to their own homes, where they would replant them in an effort to cultivate orchards as the Molokans had. The Molokans frequently caught these thieves and forcibly exacted payment of a few rubles for each tree. The practice of stealing trees was so common that there were middlemen who would sell the Azerbaijanis trees from the Molokans' orchards at prices well below what they would be forced to pay if they were caught stealing the trees.[109]

ECONOMIC RELATIONSHIPS AND BONDS OF MUTUAL RELIANCE

In addition to violent conflicts and land tensions, colonists and Transcaucasians also entered into mutually beneficial economic relationships. After their arrival in Transcaucasia, especially in the 1830s and 1840s, the sectarians could not have survived their initial trials without the direct assistance and employment opportunities offered by their neighbors. Over the course of the century, however, the forms of aid and support changed markedly. The settlers and natives became intertwined in increasingly elaborate bonds of reciprocal assistance and intricate trade networks that worked for the economic benefit of all parties. Moreover, as the sectarians became more prosperous, it was the indigenous Caucasians who benefited from and, increasingly, relied on the material benefits that the Russian settlers had to offer. Despite these close ties, in comparison with other European settler colonies, the sectarian colonists neither depended on native labor through exploitation and economic domination (such as in Kenya and Rhodesia) nor attempted to replace native production with their own (such as in Australia).[110] The growth of economic bonds was facilitated by a process of economic specialization in which settlers and natives took on different economic functions and filled complementary niches.[111]

Indigenous Transcaucasians provided invaluable assistance to the newly arriving, usually destitute, Russian settlers, although not always willingly. Orders issued by local tsarist officials obliged the native peoples to

109. Petrov, "Seleniia," 241, 247. There is no mention of the ethnicity of the middlemen. On blurring distinctions between "crime" and "trade" in the North Caucasus, see Thomas Barrett, "Crossing Boundaries: The Trading Frontiers of the Terek Cossacks," in *Russia's Orient*, 227–48.
110. Sunderland, "Empire of Peasants," 183; Kennedy, *Islands of White*; Wolfe, *Settler Colonialism*; and Donald Denoon, *Settler Capitalism: The Dynamics of Dependent Development in the Southern Hemisphere* (Oxford, 1983).
111. On comparative economic specialization and the relations between Russian settlers and natives in the North Caucasus, see Barrett, "Crossing Boundaries," 227–48.

supply any number of services. They built temporary dwellings to shelter the new arrivals, sowed fields for the settlers before they arrived, billeted the sectarians while they set themselves up, provided seed for future sowing, prepared wood for fuel and for the construction of houses, and donated wheat and other foodstuffs—both directly and, through taxation, indirectly.[112] For example, when the Dukhobors came to Transcaucasia in the early 1830s, the Tiflis military governor Strekalov ordered the local inhabitants to sow the land allotted to the Dukhobors before the settlers' arrival and, later, to harvest the crops with their own livestock and tools. When it proved too difficult for the Dukhobor settlers to access their lands because the lack of roads prevented wheeled transport, the state officials agreed to move them elsewhere. While the settlers were waiting for their new homes to be built, they were billeted with local inhabitants in nearby villages—a common practice.[113]

In a similar vein, initial economic setbacks suffered by the majority of sectarians during their first few years in their new homes frequently meant that the settlers were forced to turn to the indigenous peoples for material aid necessary for survival. Molokan settlers to Vorontsovka in Tiflis province suffered severe economic hardship during their first few years there, despite the region's rich agricultural promise. In response, they hired themselves out to neighboring Armenians as farm workers. Without the payment for this work, the settlers would certainly have starved, and such employment became a pattern.[114] Indeed, in the first twenty years of Russian settlement, the majority of sectarians found themselves with no other economic alternative than to supplement their own agricultural activities with work for their neighbors. Local authorities quickly saw that the sectarians would suffer unbearable deprivation without the supplementary work in the natives' fields, so they loosened restrictions on sectarian movement and labor in order to facilitate such economic opportunities.[115]

Beginning in the late 1840s and early 1850s, economic relations between the groups shifted markedly as Russians and Transcaucasians entered into a variety of economic arrangements. Most notably, the patterns of hiring began to equalize. Rather than working for others only, Russian settlers began to look for paid laborers from among the local inhabitants to help run their increasingly profitable agricultural ventures. Transcau-

112. See RGIA f. 1284, op. 196–1831, d. 136, ll. 37–370b, 830b–84; op. 195–1825, d. 61, ll. 142–420b; and GMIR f. 2, op. 7, d. 596, l. 121.
113. GMIR f. 2, op. 7, d. 594, l. 76. After the first few waves of sectarian arrivals, however, the practice of housing Russian settlers in native villages ceased; instead they were placed with their coreligionists during the period of acclimatizing. Dolzhenko, "Pervye," 61.
114. Orekhov, "Ocherki," no. 136, 2.
115. RGIA f. 381, op. 1, d. 23322, 1846; SPChR (1875), 359; and chapter four.

casians found the settlers to be a source of material benefit—the Dukhobors in Akhalkalaki district frequently employed Armenians as laborers in their fields and Armenians, Kurds, and Azerbaijanis as shepherds. Indeed, Russians widely considered nomads to be the best shepherds available in the region and regularly hired them over their coreligionists to look after their flocks.[116]

Colonists and natives rented land and livestock from each other. Subbotniks from Erevan province focused their economic energies on the transport trade and leased their allotments to neighboring Armenians for cultivation.[117] Russians also "leased alpine land in summer and lowlands in winter from aborigines" in order to pasture their flocks.[118] In other cases, sectarians rented land to grow crops, such as in the case of the Molokans of Marazy, who rented a large amount of unused land that belonged to the neighboring nomads for the very low price of two rubles per *desiatina*.[119] The Dukhobors preferred to raise horses, which they considered more profitable, but they still needed the oxen they hired from Armenians to plow the rocky soil in the region.[120]

Sectarian-local interactions included other economic relations. Since many sectarian and native villages were mixed together in a single rural community, people of different ethnicities were required to make certain economic decisions together.[121] Armenians and Georgians frequently set up inns or taverns in the settlers' villages to profit from the traffic—military, bureaucratic, and merchant—that came through the colonists' villages. In addition, the sectarians used the regional market extensively, entering regularly into contact and various contracts with the region's inhabitants.[122] Through their dominance of the transportation industry, the settlers forged agreements with Georgians, Armenians, Azerbaijanis, and Kurds—merchants, artisans, and peasants—to move produce all over Transcaucasia.[123] Many Subbotniks from the village of Privol'noe in Baku province sold bread as well as other products to Azerbaijani agents from a nearby village. The Muslim traders would then take these products to be sold in Baku and bring the money back to the Russians after

116. Inikova, "Vzaimootnosheniia," 50; Iamskov, *Environmental Conditions*, 5–6; Masalkin, "Kolonizatory," no. 333, 3; and SSC'SA f. 4, op. 2, d. 1953, 1846–57.

117. "'Subbotniki' v Erivanskoi gubernii," *PKEG na 1912 g.* (Erevan, 1912), literaturnyi otdel, ch. III, 9.

118. Iamskov, *Environmental Conditions*, 5–6; and Dolzhenko, "Pervye," 64.

119. T. B., "U beregov Kaspiia (iz putevykh zametok i vospominanii). Tri goda nazad. Ch. X, Ot Baku do Tiflisa," *Kavkaz*, no. 85 (April 19, 1881): 2.

120. Inikova, "Vzaimootnosheniia," 50.

121. D. I. Ismail-Zade, *Russkoe krest'ianstvo v Zakavkaz'e: 30-e gody XIX–nachalo XX v.* (Moscow, 1982), 61. The exception to this rule was the Dukhobors, who were administratively separate.

122. Orekhov, "Ocherki," no. 136, 2.

123. Dolzhenko, "Pervye," 65.

receiving a percentage of the profits.[124] In Elisavetpol province, sectarians themselves marketed their surplus production to nearby villages and local towns.[125]

In the closing decades of the nineteenth century, the development of small-scale factories and other manufacturing work among the sectarian communities broadened the range of economic contacts with Transcaucasians. For instance, the villages of Novo-Ivanovka and Novo-Saratovka both started enterprises that produced glazed tiles and construction lumber. These products were used not only by the Russian villagers but also by the surrounding Armenians and Azerbaijanis, who provided a strong demand for their house construction.[126] Moreover, early in the twentieth century, Russians and indigenous inhabitants began to enter into joint ventures. In 1903, for instance, a Molokan and an Armenian started a pig-farming enterprise in the Novo-Ivanovka area—an even more surprising union because of the Molokans' long-standing prohibition of the consumption of pork.[127]

Soviet historians portrayed the economic relations between the local population and the sectarians as a form of class and colonial exploitation.[128] In contrast, commentators of the time evaluated these socio-economic relations very differently. Writing in the late nineteenth century, the statistician Kh. A. Vermishev noted very good relations between the Dukhobors and their native farm hands. Indigenous farm workers found that once they had gained the trust of their sectarian bosses, they could count on the Dukhobors in times of trouble for help, including loans of money or food. The Dukhobors maintained a large store of both funds and grain in their "Orphan Home" (*sirotskii dom*)—an institution whose purposes included the provision of help to the needy in their communities. From this reserve, they frequently granted interest-free loans to their coreligionists, a practice that soon expanded to the surrounding population as well. However, according to Vermishev, the Dukhobors quickly realized that their neighbors were taking advantage of this privilege, so they raised the interest rate to a very reasonable five to ten percent, still well below the going rate of twenty percent.[129] In times of harvest failure, the Dukhobors of Kars territory would give their neighbors grain from their communal stores free of charge.[130]

124. Il'ia Zhabin, "Selenie Privol'noe, Bakinskoi gub., Lenkoranskogo uezda," in *SMOMPK*, vol. 27 (Tiflis, 1900), otd. II, 49, 51.
125. I. L. Segal', "Russkie poseliane v Elisavetpol'skoi gubernii (statistichesko-etnograficheskii ocherk)," *Kavkaz*, no. 41 (February 14, 1890): 3. See also Gorskii, "Marazinskaia shkola," 2.
126. Petrov, "Seleniia," 242.
127. Ibid., 236.
128. See especially Klibanov, *History*, 122.
129. Vermishev, "Ekonomicheskii byt," 42–44; and Petrov, "Dukhobory," 176. On the Orphan Home, see chapter six.
130. V. P. Bochkarev, "Karsskaia oblast'," in *RTKE* (Tiflis, 1897), 370.

Assistance from the sectarians came not only in times of poor harvest, but also during other natural disasters. The 1899 case of Dukhobor aid following a severe earthquake in Tiflis province is typical of the mutual aid that developed among the different peoples of Transcaucasia. Twenty-one villages were affected, most of them Armenian. Despite living more than one hundred kilometers from the affected area, many Dukhobors appeared on the scene to help out. They provided 130 wagons and horses and worked ceaselessly to transport victims to medical aid. They did so without asking for payment, saying that as Christians they were obligated by conscience to help in any way they could.[131]

Although never to the same degree as in the first few decades, the sectarians did continue to benefit from the aid and support of those around them. For instance, when the water reserves in the village of Marazy dried up in 1865, Azerbaijanis from a village approximately two kilometers away gave the Molokans permission to use their water. As the sectarians were exceptionally slow to reestablish their water supply, this developed into a quasi-permanent arrangement.[132]

TECHNOLOGY TRANSFER, CULTURAL EXCHANGE

As part of these ever-expanding economic relationships and bonds of mutual assistance, settlers and local Transcaucasians entered into a process of appropriation and exchange involving economic techniques, technology, and, to a smaller degree, cultural practices. Nineteenth-century Russian commentators and state officials praised the sectarians' "Russification" of the local economy through the introduction of Russian agricultural practices and products, as well as their "civilizing" of the local peoples through the example of their morality, honesty, sobriety, work ethic, and prosperity.[133] One journalist, describing Tiflis province, noted that the Molokans' "strict morals, settled life, hard work, economic success, internal harmony, [and] few crimes . . . have had a charming effect on our Georgians."[134] Only a few scattered voices demurred. One official argued that "the closed nature of the sectarians' lives impedes their rapprochement with, and useful influence on, the neighboring native peoples."[135] Whether the sectarians were successful as a civilizing force or

131. GARF f. 102, 3 d-vo, op. 1899, d. 4365, ll. 48–54ob.
132. Gorskii, "Marazinskaia shkola," 2.
133. In addition to the examples discussed below, see Petrov, "Seleniia," 247; P. Paul', "Iz sel. Elenovki, Erivanskoi gubernii (o vliianii russkikh na korennoe naselenie Novobaiazetskogo uezda)," KSKh, no. 169 (April 3, 1897): 230; Orekhov, "Ocherki," no. 143, 1; Kuropatkin, Soobrazheniia," 15; and "Iz Signakhskogo uezda," 3.
134. "Iz Signakhskogo uezda," 3; and Masalkin "Kolonizatory," no. 333, 3.
135. GARF f. 102, 3 d-vo, op. 1884, d. 88, ch. 2, ll. 200b–21.

not, Russian narratives of acculturation in the nineteenth century depicted the process as a one-way street: from Russian to Transcaucasian. A. I. Masalkin, a journalist for the newspaper *Kavkaz*, described the imperial hierarchy in unambiguous terms: "[the sectarians] have adopted nothing from the indigenous peoples, who stand in every respect poorer and lower than the sectarians."[136]

Contrary to these claims, the reality of settler-native contact did not follow such a simple trajectory. The flow of influences was by no means unidirectional. As Richard White has described in the North American context, each group became "more like [the other] by borrowing discrete cultural traits. . . . Different peoples, to be sure, remained identifiable but they shaded into one another."[137] In nineteenth-century Transcaucasia, the primary channel of appropriation and transference between settlers and Caucasians was an economic one. There is evidence of a significant transfer of agricultural implements, production methods, subsistence strategies, livestock, and foodstuffs between natives and sectarians.

Moreover, in terms of the degree of appropriation, the minority of Russian voices who saw the communities as too separate for any meaningful cultural exchange were closer to the mark. Not unexpectedly, social, cultural, and religious systems proved more impervious to reformation than economic ones. While the sectarians were indisputably transformed through the assimilation of various Transcaucasian cultural practices, the extent of such "nativization" was much less marked when compared with other borderland regions of the Russian Empire, such as Siberia and the North Caucasus. "Russification" was also relatively less apparent despite significant sectarian influences on the local populations.[138] The principal exception to this characterization was in the arena of language acquisition, in which some Russians, Azerbaijanis, Armenians, and Georgians living in the same region spoke up to four languages.

Writing about agricultural changes in Erevan province, Kolosov asserted that Armenians and Azerbaijanis learned truck farming from the sectarian example: "Before the settlement of Russians, the indigenous population sowed very few beets and carrots, and did not plant potatoes

---

136. Masalkin, "Kolonizatory," no. 333, 3.
137. White, *Middle Ground*, x–xi.
138. In his exploration of the North Caucasus, Thomas Barrett argues that "the boundaries between colonist and native, between Cossack and 'enemy,' indeed between Russia and 'the Orient,' could be rather loose and at times nonexistent." Barrett, "Crossing Boundaries," 229. See also idem, "Lines of Uncertainty: The Frontiers of the North Caucasus," *SR* 54, no. 3 (1995): 578–601; Sunderland, "Russians into Iakuts?" 806–25; and John Mack Faragher, "Americans, Mexicans, Métis: A Community Approach to the Comparative Study of North American Frontiers," in *Under an Open Sky: Rethinking America's Western Past*, ed. William Cronon, George Miles, and Jay Gitlin (New York, 1992).

at all. The Russians widely spread the culture of these plants and now in many places the natives are introducing vegetable gardens." The author asserted that the annual production of potatoes for Novobaiazet and Aleksandropol districts alone was 629,700 hectoliters, whereas in the 1830s none had been grown at all.[139] Other commentators throughout Transcaucasia echoed Kolosov in describing the appearance of vegetable farming among the native population and of traditional Russian produce in particular.[140]

Indigenous Transcaucasians reportedly took from the sectarians the use of certain agricultural implements and a variety of other economic practices. For instance, Armenians and Azerbaijanis in Erevan province adopted scythes, pitchforks, harrows, threshing blades, and rakes of Russian design. In imitation of the Russians, Transcaucasians also began to replace oxen—which they used both for field work and transportation— with the horses preferred by Russian settlers. Moreover, according to one author, "Native villagers on the banks of lake Gokcha were completely unfamiliar with the fishing method of using large nets," a system they then adopted from the Russians. The Transcaucasians also learned from the Russians a process of curing fish by drying them—a trade that proved very profitable for the locals.[141]

The sectarians also facilitated the growth of commercial farming among local Transcaucasian farmers, not only by introducing crops that Russians in Transcaucasia and the central provinces would buy, but also by facilitating the transport of these and other goods throughout the region.[142] As the century progressed, Armenians and Azerbaijanis began to copy the sectarians' wagon design and entered into the transport trade themselves in competition with the settlers. Not only would they transport goods for less money than the Russians, they also would work as drivers throughout the summer when many of the sectarians reverted to field work. This indigenous appropriation of settler carts in the South Caucasus contrasts with the reverse process in the North Caucasus, where Cossacks adopted the local *arba* to such a degree that state officials worried about the impact that this dependency on local technology would have on the Cossacks' ability to perform their military duties.[143]

Russian settlers also adopted local agricultural techniques and culti-

139. Kolosov, "Russkie sektanty," 151.
140. See Petrov, "Seleniia," 247; Segal', "Russkie poseliane," no. 40, 3; Inikova, "Vzaimootnoshe-niia," 49; and N. I. Grigulevich, "Osnovnye komponenty pitaniia russkikh starozhilov, azerbaid-zhantsev i armian," in *Dukhobortsy i Molokane*, 60–89.
141. Paul', "Iz sel. Elenovki," (1897), 230.
142. Inikova, "Vzaimootnosheniia," 49.
143. Kolosov, "Russkie sektanty," 151; N. B., "Ozero Gokcha (iz vospominanii o Zakavkazskom krae)," *Kavkaz*, no. 61 (1861): 330; Paul', "Iz sel. Elenovki," (1897), 230; Petrov, "Seleniia," 245; and Barrett, "Crossing Boundaries," 239–40.

FIGURE 10. Dukhobor children, c. 1895, in front of typical building with sod roof. British Columbia Archives C-01454, published with permission.

nary practices. Dukhobors, for example, were quick to take up the local design for a thresher (made from wood, stones, and pebbles) that replaced the stone thresher they brought with them from New Russia. However, sectarians continued to use the traditional, heavier Russian plow instead of the lighter plow favored by indigenous farmers.[144] Settlers underwent an even greater degree of acculturation in the arena of food and drink. Russians borrowed a variety of dairy products and processes from their Azerbaijani neighbors and introduced to their diet an array of local fruits and vegetables. Although the sectarians integrated Azerbaijani foods, dishes, and modes of food production into their diet, they attached different cultural valences to these foods than they did to Russian cuisine. The more culturally meaningful the meal, the more likely that traditional Russian dishes would predominate. Whereas daily tables would feature a much greater variety of local foodstuffs and dishes (such as pilaf, shashlyk, and dolma), funeral repasts continued to be dominated by such Russian staples as cabbage soup, noodles, meat, potatoes, tea, and sweets.[145]

144. Inikova, "Vzaimootnosheniia," 49–50; Segal', "Russkie poseliane," no. 41, 3; and chapter three.
145. N. I. Grigulevich, *Cultural and Ecological Peculiarities of the Traditional Diet of the Russians in Azerbaijan* (Moscow, 1988); idem, "Osnovnye komponenty pitaniia," 60–89; and idem, "Pitanie kak odin iz osnovnykh pokazatelei adaptatsii pereselentsev," in *Russkie starozhily,* 183–208.

Much as settlers and locals exchanged their economic implements and practices, so too did architectural styles evolve. Sectarians generally constructed their houses and villages in a style that approximated their homes in central Russia but with certain differences that reflected the influence of Transcaucasia's environment and peoples. Settler dwellings in South Caucasia were more likely to be made out of stone than the traditional Russian wood—often difficult to obtain in the region—and were designed with relatively flatter roofs than peasant housetops in the internal Russian provinces. At times, they also appropriated certain defensive aspects of Azerbaijani construction, as mentioned earlier.[146] The impact of the Russian settlers on the architecture of the surrounding population was perhaps even more keenly felt. P. Paul approvingly noted the appearance of houses with windows and tile roofs in those indigenous villages located near Russian settlements, as opposed to the "shanties" with one opening in the roof that they had used before.[147]

In order to conduct trade and to negotiate their differences, Russian settlers were required to learn a variety of the local languages. Indeed, the very large difference in population size between the settlers and the natives left the lion's share for learning new modes of communication to the sectarians. The ethnographer N. Kalashev reported that in the village of Ivanovka, the Russian settlers spoke very fluent Azerbaijani as a result of their "constant interactions" with their Azerbaijani and Armenian neighbors. Indeed, Kalashev was particularly surprised to find that conversations among Russians were sometimes conducted in a local tongue even when no natives were present. In the process of learning these languages, many Armenian and Azerbaijani words passed into the sectarians' Russian vocabulary, especially words dealing with economic and agricultural topics.[148] Similarly, indigenous people who lived near sectarians learned to speak Russian. Petrov asserts that it was not uncommon, in the last few decades of the nineteenth century, to find Muslim nomads in the mountains speaking such a pure, vernacular Russian that "if it was not for his clothes, you could think that in front of you stood a Great Russian peasant from Tambov or Saratov province."[149]

There were distinct limits to cross-cultural assimilation, however.[150]

146. Orekhov, "Ocherki," no. 136, 1; and Inikova, "Vzaimootnosheniia," 46.
147. Paul', "Iz sel. Elenovki," (1897): 230. See also Kolosov, "Russkie sektanty," 151–52; and Petrov, "Seleniia," 247.
148. N. Kalashev, "Selenie Ivanovka, Lagichskogo uchastka, Geokchaiskogo uezda, Bakinskoi gubernii," SMOMPK, vol. 13 (Tiflis, 1892), otd. II, 274. On Russians learning to speak local languages, see also Kolosov, "Russkie sektanty," 154; Vereshchagin, Dukhobortsy i Molokane, 36–37; Inikova, "Vzaimootnosheniia," 52; and Ismail-Zade, Russkoe, 86–88.
149. Petrov, "Seleniia," 247.
150. See the similarities with the multiconfessional Molochna region in Sunderland, "Empire of Peasants," 183–84.

Despite the mutual appropriation of languages and of certain economic technologies, Russians and the native Georgians, Azerbaijanis, and Armenians remained distinct and noninfluential in most of their social and cultural practices. During the nineteenth century, settlers and natives perceived each other as both ethnically and religiously different. Dukhobors, for instance, maintained their religiously based sense of distinctiveness throughout their tenure in Transcaucasia, believing themselves to be "chosen people." Upon their arrival in the 1840s, they found extremely strange the local population's clothing, external appearance, oxen-drawn wagons, and methods of plowing.[151] This sense of difference and distinction was not one-way by any means. Transcaucasians initially looked upon the Dukhobors as murderers and criminals whom they "avoided like lepers."[152]

Sectarians and South Caucasians lived isolated from each other in separate geographical and cultural communities. They maintained traditional structures of village governance and justice, divided domestic labor in their own ways, and raised their children according to long-standing cultural practices. They continued to celebrate different holidays separately and utilized distinct ceremonial forms, to name but a few fundamental distinctions. In contrast with other regions in the Russian Empire and other European settler colonies, there are few documented cases of interethnic sexual relations or marriage between sectarians and Transcaucasians. Discussing the Russian settlers of Eastern Armenia, I. V. Dolzhenko states that "marriages to non-believers were forbidden" by the sectarian communities—a rule that appears to have applied equally to both Christian and Muslim Transcaucasians. Unlike many other colonial settings, the dissenter communities in South Caucasia maintained a numerical balance between the sexes, many having migrated as families, which left few searching elsewhere for sexual partners or spouses.[153]

There were certain exceptions to this physical separation. Male Russian sectarians traveled throughout the region as wagon drivers and were exposed to a whole spectrum of different ways of life. In particular, while the clothing of sectarian women tended to undergo only internally generated changes, male settlers more often dressed in borrowed indigenous

151. Inikova, "Vzaimootnosheniia," 51–52. See also Kuropatkin, Soobrazheniia, 15 on Dukhobor "isolation" and "arrogance."

152. Vermishev, "Ekonomicheskii byt," 42.

153. Dolzhenko, "Pervye," 66. For an exception to endogamous marriage practices, see RGIA f. 1268, op. 3, d. 443, 1849–50. For comparison, see Sunderland, "Russians into Iakuts?" 806–25; Moon, "Peasant Migration," 880; Donald Treadgold, The Great Siberian Migration: Government and Peasant in Resettlement from Emancipation to the First World War (Princeton, 1957), 241; W. Bruce Lincoln, The Conquest of a Continent: Siberia and the Russians (New York, 1994), 84–86; Kennedy, Islands of White, 174–79; Stoler and Cooper, "Between Metropole"; and White, Middle Ground, 60–75.

FIGURE 11. Dukhobor family in Slavianka, Elisavetpol province, c. 1912. British Columbia Archives F-04016, published with permission.

styles.[154] In addition, as time progressed, it was more common to find small numbers of non-Russians living in sectarian villages as laborers, tavern or inn owners, or local officials.[155] However, these were minor exceptions that serve to reinforce the rule that, while they might interact and acculturate on the economic plane, their domestic lives remained isolated from each other.

Particularly in the area of religion, there was very little overlap between the Russian dissenters and the indigenous Transcaucasians and no marked exchange of beliefs or practices.[156] The lack of religious accul-

154. Dolzhenko, "Pervye," 65; Kalashev, "Selenie Ivanovka," 275; Kolosov, "Russkie sektanty," 154; and S. A. Inikova, "Istoriia i simvolika dukhoborcheskogo kostiuma," *Zhivaia starina*, no. 1 (1994): 29–36. Compare Faragher, "Americans, Mexicans, Métis," 104.
155. Petrov, "Seleniia," 231–32, 243; and Orekhov, "Ocherki," no. 136, 2.
156. For general statements of this trend, see GMIR f. 2, op. 7, d. 545, 1893, l. 21; and *Sektanty Kavkaza. Stat'ia* (Tiflis, 1890), 4.

turation supported the initial assumptions of tsarist policymakers, that sectarian settlement in Transcaucasia would produce only scattered instances of interethnic conversion because of significant cultural differences.[157] Exceptions found in the archives include an Armenian man who took on the Molokan faith and a Dukhobor woman who unsuccessfully petitioned the authorities for the right to change her faith to Armenian-Gregorian.[158] The explosion of the Prygun branch of the Molokans into Transcaucasia also attracted a small number of Armenians into the faith. According to contemporary commentators, the dynamism and magnetism of the Prygun leader Maksim Rudometkin and the ecstatic nature of the religious ceremonies were so forceful as to draw non-Russians to the prayer services.[159]

Conversion by Georgian Orthodox or Muslims to a sectarian faith or the reverse was almost unheard of. There is a brief mention in the annual report of the Exarch of Georgia for 1883 that Georgians were being tempted by the allure of the sects—especially Molokans and Baptists—living nearby. The author notes that the propaganda of the sectarians was succeeding primarily because they were able to propagandize the young Georgians who were brought into sectarians' homes to work as servants. This "vacillation" in faith was something new, the Exarch argued, because "from time immemorial the mass of the people were solid in their faith in Orthodoxy." Only three years later, however, in the report for 1886, the Exarch reported that despite these temptations and a certain wavering in their faith, "sects do not appear among the Georgians."[160]

FRONTIER ENCOUNTERS

The types and tenor of the on-the-ground interactions of sectarian settlers and Armenians, Azerbaijanis, and Georgians are essential to a broader understanding of Russia's presence in Transcaucasia and the meanings of the frontier to Russian history. Especially in rural areas, the native peoples interacted with sectarians more frequently than with Russian state agents. Indeed, for many Transcaucasians, the sectarians came to represent both Russia and Russians. Writing about his travels through

---

157. RGIA f. 379, op. 1, d. 1043, 1830–37, l. 19.

158. For the former, see GMIR f. 2, op. 7, d. 594, n.d., l. 23. For the latter, see RGIA f. 1268, op. 3, d. 443, 1849–50.

159. On the appearance of Armenians in Prygun prayer services, see N. D. "Pryguny," no. 10, 387; Kolosov, "Russkie sektanty," 145; John K. Berokoff, *Molokans in America* (Whittier, CA, 1969), 13–31; and Dunaev, "Sekta Prygunov" in *Russkie sektanty, ikh uchenie,* 190, for a photo of an Armenian Prygun.

160. RGIA f. 1268, op. 9, d. 367a, 1857–58, ll. 4–40b; f. 796, op. 442, d. 48, 1862, l. 140b; d. 208, 1866, l. 150b; d. 365, 1871, l. 19; d. 951, 1883, ll. 26–260b; and d. 1124, 1886, l. 53.

Transcaucasia, the essayist Petr Egorov remarked that "the indigenous peoples call all Russian peasants 'Molokans.'"[161] How Transcaucasians experienced Russian imperialism on a daily basis was defined in great part by their relationships with the nonconformist colonists.

In these interactions, Transcaucasia was more than simply an arena of imperial dominance and native resistance. It was not always clear in which direction the power between "colonizer" and "colonized" flowed, and it was more often the locals who dictated the terms of the relationship. The combination of the extreme difference in numbers between the two groups—a small drop of sectarians in a sea of Transcaucasians—the unfamiliar terrain and the fact that the sectarians did not always receive advantageous treatment from state officials meant that the settlers accommodated and acculturated to the Transcaucasians' world as much as, if not more than, the other way around. Moreover, in the settlement of dissenters on the lands of native elites and in the widespread presence of indigenous peoples in official positions of administration and governance, the Russian peasant settlers were often thrust into a position socially and politically subordinate to the colonized Caucasian peoples.

Through the interactive, and unpredictable interrelations of settlers and Caucasians, the Transcaucasian frontier also provided a fertile space for the germination among Russians of new social and cultural systems not possible in central Russia. In particular, the nonconformists underwent a fundamental change in their religiosity, accepting violence as a means of resolving differences and transforming from pacifists into "pacifiers."

In the end, despite mutual accommodations, profound transformations, and growing socio-economic bonds, sectarians and South Caucasians remained relatively isolated from each other and unchanged by their meetings. Cross-ethnic, cross-confessional, or cross-social ties were rare in this Empire borderland. This was particularly noticeable in comparison with other Russian frontiers (such as the North Caucasus and Siberia) and especially with colonial situations elsewhere (such as North America and Africa). Even in Southern Rhodesia and Kenya, where the white settlers struggled to erect impermeable cultural and racial boundaries between themselves and the native peoples, the Europeans remained in "intimate daily" interactions with Africans because of the inseparability of their common economic fate.[162] The separation of sectarians and South Caucasians resulted in great part from the fact that the Russian colonists were religious dissenters. The nonconformists remained

161. Petr Egorov, "Zakavkazskiia dorozhnyia zapiski 1851 goda: doroga ot Tiflisa do Shemakhi i g. Elisavetpolia," RI, no. 217 (October 10, 1857): 817.
162. Kennedy, Islands of White, 148–66.

consciously separate from the natives, cherishing their newfound isolation and independence (from Russians and non-Russians alike) and interacting with their neighbors primarily on an economic level.

The sectarian communities changed through encounters with their new ethno-confessional neighbors, the region's environment, and state officials and imperialist agendas. However, the southern frontier, with its less-regulated spaces, also gave the sectarians the opportunity and impetus to reformulate their religious identities and practices. It is to one such process of religious refashioning, and a dramatic pacifist movement that accompanied these spiritual shifts, that I turn in the next two chapters.

PART 3

THE DUKHOBOR

MOVEMENT

6

FROM COLONIAL SETTLERS TO
PACIFIST INSURGENTS

The Origins of the Dukhobor Movement, 1887–1895

In mid-1895, Dukhobor settlers in the South Caucasus erupted in a pacifist opposition movement that emphatically challenged the legitimacy of tsarist authority and permanently transformed Russian colonialism in its southern provinces. Beginning in the late 1880s, a majority of Dukhobors embarked on a religious revival that embraced an exacting and radical religiosity and sundered their community into antagonistic factions. In a manifestation of a burgeoning nonviolent ideology, one branch of this dissenter community categorically refused military service. Those Dukhobors already in the army ceased fulfilling these obligations, refused to follow orders, and returned their weapons to their officers, declaring that "they serve only God and their faith forbids them to kill people."[1] Others in line for conscription or in the reserves contemptuously threw their draft tickets at the feet of Russian officials and denounced all secular authority: "There is one tsar, in heaven, there should be no tsar on earth."[2]

The Dukhobors' oppositional movement reached its peak on the night of June 28, 1895, when Dukhobor communities in three Transcaucasian provinces erected huge bonfires into which they threw all of their personal weapons. This public display of pacifism was consciously designed to make a lasting impression, to spread their message of nonviolence, and perhaps even to bring upon themselves a certain martyrdom. The scene was something to behold. In preparation, the Dukhobors collected wagonloads of firewood, gallons of kerosene, piles of coal, and,

---

1. V. G. Chertkov and A. K. Chertkova, *Dukhobortsy v distsiplinarnom batal'one*, vol. 4 of *MIIRS* (Christchurch, UK, 1902), 44.
2. Quoted and translated in Andrew Donskov, "On the Doukhobors: From Imperial Russian Archival Files," *CES* 27, no. 3 (1995): 254.

where wood was scarce, heaps of dung-cakes. Each male brought his weapons personally "so that he could be done with his sin himself."[3] Once the fuel was sparked at midnight, "flames and smoke [rushed] from the ground to heaven" and "lighted the Caucasian mountains."[4] For miles around, towers of fire colored the night sky. The heat was overpowering, forcing the crowds of Dukhobors to stand back from the blaze and causing guns to discharge their bullets. The unintentional volleys of gunfire threatened those who might come in their path and startled neighbors both near and far from their sleep. Curious and alarmed, Caucasians, tsarist officials, and those Dukhobors who had not embraced the new ideas came to witness the conflagration, unsure exactly what was unfolding. Well into the next day—for some, even the day after—the thousands of Dukhobors who congregated for the event sang psalms and prayed with joy in their hearts. "We have burned evil," they declared with tears of exaltation at the righteousness of their actions.[5]

The Dukhobors' opposition movement represents a turning point in the history of Russian colonization of the South Caucasus. By its end, the world that the sectarian settlers had created during the nineteenth century was all but washed away. Their "insurgency" fundamentally altered the relationship between Russian state authority and the nonconformists—a reversion from "colonizers" to "heretical pariahs" in both official characterizations and self-conceptions. It also enduringly transformed the Dukhobors' socio-economic structures, their religious foundations, and their interactions with their Caucasian neighbors. Although a minority branch of the Dukhobors held firmly to the community's more moderate religious practices and relations to the state, so great was the impact of the activities of the radical majority that all Dukhobors in Transcaucasia—indeed, all sectarian colonists, Molokans and Subbotniks included—could not but be affected.

Tsarist authorities responded to the Dukhobors' insubordination with severity in an effort to pound them and their pacifist message into submission. Some officials went even further, administering brutal punishments arbitrarily and illegally. The authorities meted out beatings, arrests, gang rapes, and sentences of imprisonment and exile. They appropriated Dukhobor possessions, enforced economic penalties, dragged them through multiple court trials, and impressed the conscientious objectors into the dreaded penal battalions. In the final event, approxi-

3. N. S. Zibarov, *O sozhzhenii oruzhiia dukhoborami* (Purleigh, 1899), 5.
4. Respectively, GMIR f. 2, op. 7, d. 509, n.d., l. 3; and d. 489, 1928, l. 5.
5. GMIR f. 2, op. 7, d. 509, n.d., l. 3. For descriptions of the arms burning, see also Zibarov, *O sozhzhenii*, 5–6; ORRGB f. 369, k. 42, d. 2, 1950, ll. 447–49; k. 43, d. 1, 1950, ll. 585–86; and P. I. Biriukov, *Dukhobortsy. Sbornik statei, vospominanii, pisem, i drugikh dokumentov* (Moscow, 1908), 41–50.

mately one-third of the Dukhobor population found itself with little option but to emigrate to Canada (1898–99) in the hope of finding a more accepting state in which to live.[6]

Tsarist authorities feared that the Dukhobor "movement" would spread beyond the sectarians' community: to other religious dissenters in Transcaucasia, to the indigenous South Caucasian peoples, and to the peasants of the central provinces.[7] Not without reason, officialdom was also alarmed because the Dukhobors' activities intersected with opposition movements among educated society and revolutionary groups. The efforts and publications of the Bolshevik V. D. Bonch-Bruevich and especially Leo Tolstoy and his followers made the Dukhobors' case a cause célèbre for pacifists, and a public relations debacle for the autocracy, both in Russia and abroad. In the wake of the Dukhobors' rejection of tsarist militarism, other dissenting Christian communities in Russia, particularly the Molokans, were emboldened, albeit in less dramatic ways, to voice their opposition to conscription.[8] Shock waves from the Dukhobors' nonviolent uprising continued to resonate until the end of the tsarist regime in debates over religious toleration and draft policy, with the 1895 case often invoked as a cautionary tale.[9] In the early years of the Soviet period, Bolshevik leaders rewarded the Dukhobors for their anti-tsarist activities with a formal, albeit brief, release from military duties.[10]

The story of the Dukhobor oppositional movement illuminates broad patterns of political, imperial, and social development in late Imperial Russia. It stands out as one of the most important manifestations of religious pacifism in all of Russian history. It expands our understanding of peasant resistance to tsarist power, underscoring the religious roots of many such struggles. At the same time, the Dukhobors' experiences highlight the significance of local officials in defining the practice of tsarist governance—in applying and altering central policy directives—and the problems faced by Russia's modernizing state as it attempted to extend its direct authority onto a diverse multicultural society.

6. On Dukhobor experiences in Canada, see George Woodcock and Ivan Avakumovic, *The Doukhobors* (Toronto, 1968); and Koozma J. Tarasoff, *Plakun Trava: the Doukhobors* (Grand Forks, BC, 1982).

7. GARF f. 102, 3 d-vo, op. 1895, d. 1053, ch. 1, ll. 513–130b.

8. GMIR f. 2, op. 8, d. 356, n.d.; RGIA f. 1284, op. 222–1900, d. 69; and GARF f. 102, 5 d-vo, op. 1901, d. 509, 1901–2. On the Molokans, see the final chapter.

9. Joshua A. Sanborn, *Drafting the Russian Nation: Military Conscription, Total War, and Mass Politics, 1905–1925* (DeKalb, 2003), 187; and A. Kartashev, "K voprosu o religioznoi svobode," *Strana*, no. 117 (1906): 1, clipped in GKP, box 106.

10. Aleksandr Etkind, "Russkie sekty i Sovetskii kommunizm: proekt Valdimira Bonch-Bruevicha," *Minuvshee: istoricheskii al'manakh* 19 (Moscow, 1996): 275–319; A. I. Klibanov, *Religioznoe sektantstvo i sovremennost'* (Moscow, 1969), 188–208; Bruno Coppeters and Alexei Zverev, "V. D. Bonch-Bruevich and the Doukhobors: on the conscientious-objection policies of the Bolsheviks," *CES* 27, no. 3 (1995): 72–90; and Sanborn, *Drafting*, 183–99.

Moreover, the story of the Dukhobor movement is inextricably embedded in the multi-ethnic colonial situation of the South Caucasus. That Russia's own agents of empire were taking a stand against the regime threatened the stability of Russian imperialist goals in the South Caucasus. If the imperial power could not restrain its own peasant colonists, how could it expect to manage the subjugated indigenous peoples? Tsarist officials believed that a great deal was riding on the question of whether they would be able to reassert control, and the high stakes affected the form and intensity of the response. The Dukhobors' activities also impinged on the peoples of the Caucasus, dragging them into the conflict in a number of ways. In particular, the prominent roles that non-Russian officials played in suppressing the Dukhobors' movement, with its inversion of the ethnic hierarchy of colonial power, speaks eloquently to the multi-ethnic, pan-imperial nature of tsarist governance at the turn of the century.[11]

THINGS FALL APART, 1887–1895

Both the Dukhobors' opposition to Russian authority and the state's severe and decisive reaction were an about-face from the mutually supportive relations that had existed during the preceding decades when tsarist officials considered them to be "model Russian colonists" who had "raised high the banner" of Russian imperialism in the region.[12] Indeed, the need to explain this transformation from colonizers to pacifist insurgents gripped tsarist authority at the time. As E. Taranovskii, a deputy chief of police in Akhalkalaki district, wrote in September 1895, "Over the course of many years . . . the Dukhobors were always considered the best people in Transcaucasia. They willingly fulfilled military service. What could possibly be the reason that they at the present moment have become bad people?"[13]

To answer Taranovskii's question, one must examine the convergence of three processes. First, beginning in 1887, the Dukhobor community underwent fierce internal struggles over leadership, control of the com-

---

11. On this theme, see Austin Jersild, *Orientalism and Empire: North Caucasus Mountain Peoples and the Georgian Frontier, 1845–1917* (Montreal and Kingston, 2002).
12. See, for example, ORRGB f. 369, k. 44, d. 1, 1950, ll. 162–64, 175–76; k. 42, d. 2, 1950, ll. 406–7; RGIA f. 1284, op. 218–1881, d. 34; SSC'SA f. 244, op. 3, d. 573, 1888, l. 49; A. K. Borozdin, *Russkoe religioznoe raznomyslie* (St. Petersburg, 1907), 175; A. N. Kuropatkin, *Soobrazheniia nachal'nika Zakaspiiskoi oblasti po voprosu o pereselenii v Zakaspiiskuiu oblast' dukhoborov-postnikov* (n.p., n.d.), 15, 40; and Nicholas B. Breyfogle, "Caught in the Crossfire? Russian Sectarians in the Caucasian Theater of War, 1853–56 and 1877–78," *Kritika: Explorations in Russian and Eurasian History* 2, no. 4 (2001): 713–50.
13. CRCR 1895–09–20a, l. 81.

munity's wealth, and their religious beliefs and practices—these added up to a profound spiritual metamorphosis that forever altered Dukhobor religion, society, and culture. The internal chaos and escalating conflict of this schism, in turn, was a primary cause of the deteriorating relations with state power. The majority branch of the Dukhobor community embraced a more radical religiosity, stricter in its doctrinal opposition to temporal powers. State authorities intervened in this community at war with itself, often in a good-faith effort to mediate, but the attempt left each side even more outraged by the other.

Second, the shift in Dukhobor-state relations was a result of Empire-wide changes in governing practice that formed part of the diverse reform measures of Alexander II and Alexander III. These changes included efforts at institutional standardization; administrative and cultural Russification (and, with it, Orthodoxization); the enactment of a more invasive modernizing state; and halting steps in the direction of equal treatment of the Empire's diverse communities of subjects.[14] Like many peasant communities in Europe, Dukhobors resented these new governing structures as they threatened their traditional ways of life, religious freedom, and independence. Indeed, these central policies can be seen as one variant of the "internal colonialism" that existed in a variety of forms in Imperial and Soviet Russia, and could be seen throughout Europe during the second half of the nineteenth century.[15] However, in the case of the sectarian settlers, the processes of internal state-building actually took place in a colonial holding. This meeting of internal and external imperialism transformed the dynamics of both and changed the

14. Francis William Wcislo, *Reforming Rural Russia: State, Local Society, and National Politics, 1855–1914* (Princeton, 1990); W. Bruce Lincoln, *The Great Reforms: Autocracy, Bureaucracy, and the Politics of Change in Imperial Russia* (DeKalb, 1990); Edward Thaden, ed., *Russification in the Baltic Provinces and Finland, 1855–1914* (Princeton, 1981); and Ronald Suny, "Eastern Armenians under Tsarist Rule," in *The Armenian People from Ancient to Modern Times*, vol. II, *Foreign Dominion to Statehood: the Fifteenth Century to the Twentieth Century*, ed. Richard G. Hovannisian (New York, 1997), 128–30.

15. On state actions toward, and views of, the Russian peasantry as "internal colonialism," see Stephen Frank, *Crime, Cultural Conflict, and Justice in Rural Russia, 1856–1914* (Berkeley, 1999), 1–50, 307–17; and Lynne Viola, *Peasant Rebels under Stalin: Collectivization and the Culture of Peasant Resistance* (New York, 1996), 3, passim. The "internal colonialism" argument is found most pervasively in the historiography of modern France. For the classic study, see Eugen Weber, *Peasants into Frenchmen: The Modernization of Rural France, 1870–1914* (Stanford, 1976). For counterarguments, see Charles Tilly, "Did the Cake of Custom Break?" in *Consciousness and Class Experience in Nineteenth-Century Europe*, ed. John M. Merriman (New York, 1979), 17–44; and James R. Lehning, *Peasant and French: Cultural Contact in Rural France During the Nineteenth Century* (New York, 1995). On internal colonialism, see also John Stone, "Internal Colonialism," in *Ethnicity*, ed. John Hutchinson and Anthony D. Smith (New York, 1996), 278–81; and M. Hechter, *Internal Colonialism: the Celtic Fringe in British National Development, 1536–1966* (Routeledge and K. Paul, 1975). On peasant opposition to central state intrusions, see (of many examples) Peter Sahlins, *Forest Rites: The War of the Demoiselles in Nineteenth-Century France* (Cambridge, MA, 1994); and Caroline Ford, *Creating the Nation in Provincial France: Religion and Political Identity in Brittany* (Princeton, 1993).

stakes of the encounter. Here, tsarist efforts at state-building (and to a degree nation-building), rather than knitting the people of the Russian Empire together, shattered many of the preexisting bonds not only within and among communities but also between communities and tsarist state power.

Finally, these two other processes were compounded by the illicit actions of a handful of local administrators. Their corruption, brutality, and incompetence tipped the delicate balance at decisive moments in the relations between state and settlers. Independently, each of these factors was detrimental to the relationship between Russian state power and the South Caucasian Dukhobors. Together, however, they caused unbridled mutual antagonism. Every new government demand, every attempt to intervene in the internal dynamic of their communities, and every act of cruelty or fraud brought the Dukhobors one step closer to outright disrespect for and opposition to the tsarist state. With the growing chaos of the Dukhobors' communal relations, the rise of radical factionalism, the refusal to fulfill state obligations, and the ongoing threat of economic collapse, state officials became ever more frustrated. The result was a spiral of increasing conflict—by 1895, the bonds that had united the Dukhobors and the tsarist state, and the Dukhobor community internally, had frayed almost to nothing.

SCHISM AND THE SUCCESSION STRUGGLE

The transformation of the Dukhobor community and the breakdown of relations with state power began with the death of the Dukhobors' longtime leader Luker'ia Vasil'evna Kalmykova in December 1886. Kalmykova was loved passionately by the Dukhobors for her twenty-two years of leadership, and she was widely respected by tsarist officialdom. Her demise opened an enormous emotional, spiritual, and political void, and set off a leadership crisis among the Dukhobors because she had died without any direct descendants and without officially designating a successor.[16] For generations, the leadership of the Dukhobor community had been handed down through the Kalmykov line. (Somewhat unusually, Kalmykova had inherited the reins of power from her husband Peter Kalmykov because they had no children.) This blood inheritance had both religious and political importance because the Dukhobor faithful believed that their leader was the reincarnation of Christ, and that the spirit of Christ

16. GMIR f. 2, op. 7, d. 494, 1914, ll. 1–2; CRCR 1895–09–20a, ll. 740b–75; and "Pogrebenie Dukhoborcheskoi prorochitsy—Lukerii Kalmykovoi," MO 1, no. 1 (1896): 93.

FIGURE 12. Luker'ia Vasil'evna Kalmykova, Dukhobor leader from 1864 to 1886. British Columbia Archives C-01444, published with permission.

passed hereditarily from generation to generation, from leader to leader. Kalmykova's lack of children left the Dukhobors not just without a leader but without a living Christ to guide them.[17]

At stake in the leadership crisis was more than the reins of communal power, however—it also carried profound material repercussions. The Dukhobor leader traditionally administered the so-called Orphan Home, which comprised communal moneys, land, livestock, and buildings worth a fortune—more than one million rubles in cash alone, according to some estimates.[18] Located in Gorelovka, the Orphan Home also held an

---

17. Nicholas B. Breyfogle, "Building Doukhoboriia: Religious Culture, Social Identity and Russian Colonization in Transcaucasia, 1845–1895," *CES* 27, no. 3 (1995): 30–32; and "Sel. Slavianka," *Kaspii* 14, no. 172 (August 11, 1894): 3.

18. The Orphan Home was composed of buildings, money capital, grain stores, and livestock that

important symbolic place in the Dukhobor psyche as the physical and spiritual core of their community. Thus, in addition to political preeminence in the community and Christ-status, Kalmykova's successor would also become de facto heir to these riches and have access to the cultural capital associated with a vital religious site.

Two competing factions quickly arose to lay claim to the mantle of leadership. On one side, there was a group of elite Dukhobors led by Aleksei Zubkov who pressed the candidacy of Kalmykova's brother Mikhail Gubanov. Zubkov, known as the "Dukhobor Bismarck" for his twenty-four years as the Akhalkalaki Dukhobors' *starshina,* was widely respected both inside and outside of the Dukhobor community. Zubkov, Gubanov, and others had ruled as an oligarchy for much of Kalmykova's reign and wanted to avoid the possibility of losing their privileged positions and control of the Dukhobor wealth. Moreover, since Gubanov was a blood relative of Kalmykova, he could claim the mantle by appealing to the traditions of hereditary succession.[19]

The other aspirant to power was the young Peter Vasil'evich Verigin, who had been a favorite of Kalmykova's in the last years of her reign, working as her personal secretary and, according to some rumors, living as her lover and successor-in-training. He came from a wealthy and powerful family from the distant village of Slavianka, and his popularity grew rapidly in the community. Verigin's candidacy was championed by his relatives, who publicly declared him to be the son of Peter Kalmykov (from an extramarital affair with Verigin's mother) and, therefore, the direct blood heir of the Christ-leadership. Both Slavianka's midwife at the time and recent Dukhobor authors have questioned his mother's claims (certainly such declarations sit uneasily with reports of Verigin's sexual relationship with Kalmykova). Nevertheless, their truth is of less consequence than what Dukhobors then believed to be true. The notion of Verigin as a biologically direct descendant of the Christ lineage spread widely.[20]

---

were collected from the Dukhobor community annually. The wealth was distributed by the sectarians' leader to those families or individuals in need and often loaned at no interest to Dukhobors, South Caucasians, and even state officials in the region. On the structure, content, and value of the Orphan House, see V. D. Bonch-Bruevich, ed., *Raz"iasnenie zhizni khristian i Byl u nas, khristian, sirotskii dom (dve dukhoborcheskiia rukopisei),* vol. 2 of *MIIRS* (Christchurch, UK, 1901), 19–20; idem, ed., *Pis'ma Dukhoborcheskogo rukovoditelia Petra Vasil'evicha Verigina,* vol. 1 of *MIIRS* (Christchurch, UK, 1901), ix–xiii; V. Ol'khovskii [V. D. Bonch-Bruevich], "K istorii russkogo dukhoborchestva," *Obrazovanie* 14, no. 9 (1905): 28–31; ORRGB f. 369, k. 43, d. 1, 1950, ll. 11, 14; H. F. B. Lynch, "Queen Lukeria of Gorelovka," *Harper's New Monthly Magazine* 93, no. 553 (1986): 39–41; and Breyfogle, "Building Doukhoboriia," 32–34. In addition to Figure 15, for photographs of buildings and property belonging to the Orphan Home in Gorelovka, circa 1925, see BCA C-01618, C-01676, C-01677, C-01678, and C-01679.

19. On Zubkov, see "Semrt' dukhoborcheskogo kantslera," *MO* 5, no. 1/6 (1900): 481–87.

20. RGIA f. 1291, op. 50, d. 23, 1906, ll. 12–130b; GARF f. 102, 3 d-vo, op. 1895, d. 1053, ch. 1, ll. 5400b, 596–97; ORRGB f. 369, k. 42, d. 2, 1950, l. 13; k. 45, d. 4, 1953, l. 42; M. Tebenkov, "Dukhobortsy, ikh uchenie, organizatsiia i nastoiashchee polozhenie," *RS* 27, no. 8 (1896): 290;

FIGURE 13. Peter Vasil'evich Verigin, leader of the Large Party. From Aylmer Maude, *A Peculiar People: The Doukhobors* (New York, 1904), plate II.

Verigin's rapid increase in popularity came especially from the ranks of young Dukhobors. Many sources point to Verigin's good looks and winning physical presence as a factor that drew others to him. His vow to free the Dukhobors from military service was understandably of particular interest to the young Dukhobor men, who became subject to conscription after it was introduced in Transcaucasia in 1887.[21] Verigin further invigorated his campaign through his public conduct and manner of speech. Tsarist sources describe how, following the death of Kalmykova, he trav-

Peter Brock, ed., "Vasya Pozdnyakov's Doukhobor Narrative," *SEER* 43, no. 100 (1964–65): 163; Bonch-Bruevich, *Raz"iasnenie*, 22; and Tarasoff, *Plakun Trava*, 17–20.

21. RGIA f. 797, op. 57, otd. II, st. 3, d. 268, 1887–91, l. 1; f. 1291, op. 50, d. 23, 1906, l. 130b; Tarasoff, *Plakun Trava*, 14; and "Smert'," 485–86.

eled around various Dukhobor settlements "pretending to be a prophet and even, as was the case at one meeting, Christ."[22]

The leadership crisis quickly became intertwined with a larger debate over the future spiritual direction of the Dukhobor faith. Verigin picked up on a nascent mood among the Dukhobors in favor of religious renewal, and he advocated a fundamentally different spiritual future than Zubkov and his supporters offered. A growing number of Dukhobors had come to feel that their community had made too many compromises since arriving in the South Caucasus, concessions that challenged the very essence of what it meant to be a Dukhobor. They had strayed from their pacifist roots, both in the everyday interactions with their neighbors and in the assistance they offered the tsarist war effort against the Ottoman Empire. They had also become extremely wealthy, which introduced social stratification into a community that had been known for its social equality, emphasis on communal welfare, and rejection of material concerns. Their involvement in the Crimean and Russo-Turkish wars, and the riches they earned from these contracts, led them to lament their moral compromises, as this excerpt from one unnamed Dukhobor demonstrates:

> And we began to forget the beliefs of our ancestors and began to live like everyone else and not like natural Dukhobors. Alcoholism, smoking, idling, revelry, rich weddings, carousing in neighboring towns, all appeared among us. We even went to Tiflis and there carried on disgracefully. We threw money about. . . . Our dear Lushechka [Kalmykova] was hurt by this. Many times she went to the people and implored them to stop, not to go to ruin, to return to the confession of our ancestors, to break from a dissipated life, from drunkenness, from rowdiness, and from fights (which earlier we never had among us) in which they beat each other unmercifully, almost to death. But nothing helped. Money, wealth, and self-conceit divided us. The poorer and more modest began to stand firm . . . and often grumbled about those who, like spiders, had sucked their fill of someone else's good, and began to live life in a completely unseemly manner.[23]

After an intense period of lobbying efforts, smear campaigns, and political maneuvers, the Dukhobor community fractured into two groups

22. RGIA f. 797, op. 57, otd. II, st. 3, d. 268, 1887–91, l. 1; f. 1291, op. 50, d. 23, 1906, l. 120b; Brock, "Vasya Pozdnyakov's," 163–64. I discuss these and other factors leading to his popularity at length in my "Rethinking the Origins of the Doukhobor Arms Burning, 1887–1893," in *The Doukhobor Centenary in Canada: A Multi-Disciplinary Perspective on their Unity and Diversity*, ed. Andrew Donskov, John Woodsworth, and Chad Gaffield (Ottawa, 2000), 59–62.

23. ORRGB f. 369, k. 45, d. 4, 1953, ll. 41–42. See also "Pis'mo dukhobortsa Vasiliia Potapova k P. I. Biriukova," in *MIIRSR*, vol. 1, ed. V. D. Bonch-Bruevich (St. Petersburg, 1908), 159; and SSC'SA f. 240, op. 2, d. 25, 1859–67.

FIGURE 14. Main street of Gorelovka, Tiflis province, 1893. From H. F. B. Lynch, "Queen Lukeria of Gorelovka," *Harper's New Monthly Magazine* 93, no. 553 (1896): 37.

supporting Verigin and Zubkov. Somewhere between two-thirds and three-quarters of the Dukhobor population supported Verigin as the next leader.[24] His supporters came to be known initially as the Veriginite, or Large Party, while those who threw their support behind Zubkov belonged to the Gorelovka, or Small Party. Despite his numerical support, Verigin's ascension to power was incomplete. While he might hold the reins of political power by virtue of majority support, the Small Party blocked his efforts to take possession of the Orphan Home, as should have been the leader's prerogative. Zubkov retained control over this seat of Dukhobor power because of the structure of tsarist inheritance laws and the fact that they already physically controlled the building as a holdover from Kalmykova's days.[25]

24. Breyfogle, "Rethinking," 57–63, 65, 73. The actual number of households supporting each group varied regionally and also shifted over time. For instance, whereas almost all the Dukhobors in Kars came to support Verigin, the village of Slavianka (Elisavetpol province) split much more evenly: 171 households for the Large Party and 131 for the Small. Tebenkov, "Dukhobortsy," no. 8, 292–93; RGIA f. 1291, op. 50, d. 23, 1906, ll. 130b–14; ORRGB f. 369, k. 42, d. 2, 1950, l. 445; and GARF f. 102, 3 d-vo, op. 1895, d. 1053, ch. 1, l. 5970b.

25. Breyfogle, "Rethinking," 59, 65; and ORRGB f. 369, k. 43, d. 1, 1950, ll. 12–13.

Animosity between the two parties quickly escalated to open confrontation.[26] As early as the spring of 1887, police in Elisavetpol district noted that "the religious fanaticism of the two warring parties [in Slavianka] had developed to such a degree and enveloped all aspects of communal and family life."[27] In Gorelovka, at the funeral repast in honor of Kalmykova in January 1887, "discord appeared between the two parties to the point of large-scale dissension," as one Dukhobor related.[28] From that point forward, Verigin ordered Large Party members to cut off all contact with any Dukhobors who did not recognize his leadership. Small and Large Party Dukhobors refused to attend communal prayer meetings together. Members of opposing parties ceased greeting or bowing to each other, a previously "sacred Dukhobor custom" and symbol of mutual respect. The factions began to work the fields and pasture their flocks separately. Large Party leaders forbade their opponents to bury their dead in the communal Dukhobor cemeteries. Indeed, on May 28, 1889, a funeral in Slavianka province became so contentious and chaotic that "the active interference of the police" was needed to restore the peace.[29]

Signs of the fissure within the community appeared in many confrontations between the two parties. The conflict led to political machinations, as each party struggled to elect its representatives to positions of authority in village and Dukhobor councils.[30] Moreover, acrimonious court battles over possession of the Orphan Home dragged on from 1887 to 1893. These legal struggles greatly exacerbated the already poor relations and drained the coffers of both factions. At the heart of the litigation was the question over whether the Orphan Home had been the individual property of Kalmykova or the communal property of all Dukhobors. Zubkov argued that Gubanov was the direct blood heir of Kalmykova and that the Orphan Home, as individual property, should pass to living relatives under tsarist law. In contrast, the Large Party believed as an article of faith that the property was communally owned and only entrusted to the leader for management; as such, it should be passed as communal holdings to the next leader. On December 14, 1887, the

26. In an exception to this statement, Kars Dukhobors appear initially to have been unaffected by the schism's factional bile. Breyfogle, "Rethinking," 73; and GARF f. 102, 3 d-vo, op. 1895, d. 1053, ch. 1, ll. 186–86ob.

27. GARF f. 102, 3 d-vo, op. 1895, d. 1053, ch. 1, l. 5790b.

28. GMIR f. K1, op. 1, d. 628, n.d., l. 1.

29. Brock, "Vasya Pozdnyakov's," 165; Tebenkov, "Dukhobortsy," no. 8, 293; ORRGB f. 369, k. 42, d. 2, 1950, ll. 26, 446, 566; GARF f. 102, 3 d-vo, op. 1895, d. 1053, ch. 1, l. 184; and "Sel. Slavianka," (August 11, 1894): 3.

30. See, for example, the 1887 incident known as the Gorelovka "putsch." RGIA f. 797, op. 57, otd. II, st. 3, d. 268, 1887–91, l. 2; f. 1291 op. 50, d. 23, 1906, ll. 14, 150b–160b; Brock, "Vasya Pozdnyakov's," 165; ORRGB f. 369, k. 42, d. 2, 1950, ll. 19–20, 306; GMIR f. 2, op. 7, d. 954, n.d., l. 1; V. D. Bonch-Bruevich, ed., *Rasskaz dukhobortsa Vasi Pozdniakova*, vol. 3 of *MIIRS* (Christchurch, UK, 1901), 9–10; Bonch-Bruevich, *Raz"iasnenie*, 23; and Breyfogle, "Rethinking," 69–70.

FIGURE 15. Summer pavilion (*Besedka*) of Dukhobor leader Luker'ia Vasil'evna Kalmykova in Gorelovka, 1893. The building was part of the Orphan Home. From H. F. B. Lynch, "Queen Lukeria of Gorelovka," *Harper's New Monthly Magazine* 93, no. 553 (1896): 38.

Tiflis regional court found in favor of Gubanov, upholding his inheritance of individual property from his sister. Outraged and dumbfounded, the Large Party charged the Small Party of stealing the Orphan Home and violating Dukhobor tenets. Certain that local authorities knew of the Orphan Home's collective status Veriginites were baffled that the court had ignored sworn testimony from neighboring Armenians, Azerbaijanis, and Georgians, who asserted that the property was indeed owned in common by all Dukhobors, a conclusion based on years of contact with the colonists. In consequence, members of the Large Party brought a series of lawsuits against Gubanov, the decisions of which went in both directions. In 1893, however, the Large Party decided to abandon the legal challenges, and the property remained in Gubanov's hands.[31]

31. GMIR f. K1, op. 1, d. 19, 1887; d. 8, 1889–95, doc. 27; d. 24, 1887–97; ORRGB f. 369, k. 42,

Among the most intense points of conflict were the pitched battles over control of the Troitskoe farmstead's livestock that took place in 1887 and 1888. As part of his claims to the Orphan Home, Gubanov also declared his entitlement to certain lands, livestock, and buildings found in the nearby village of Troitskoe that had earlier been loaned to the Orphan Home for the use of the whole community. In response to Gubanov's declaration of ownership of the farmstead's herds, in July 1887 more than 200 Large Party Dukhobors assembled in the fields to capture all of the livestock, which they believed properly belonged to them—including as many as 2,000 sheep and an unspecified number of horses and cows. A violent standoff ensued between the two sides, requiring police intervention.[32]

Since party divisions did not fall neatly along family lines, the schism also provoked "a bitter condition in our family situation, and among related families it produces strong discords and arguments." Husbands and wives annulled their marriages, parents abandoned their children, and children fled their parents.[33] Vasia Pozdniakov describes how an order from Verigin to cease and desist all contact between parties shattered existing families: "Many families were separated and hundreds of children were left without attendance."[34] In this context, the personal quickly became the political. After his wife abandoned him and the Small Party to join the Veriginites, the Spasskoe village elder wantonly used his authority to antagonize Large Party adherents as retribution for his personal loss.[35]

Family strife reached such a point that Large Party Dukhobors in Gorelovka petitioned the government in 1889 for permission "to completely separate" from the Small Party. As part of this process, they sought to split up families, terminate their "mixed" marriages, and relocate to live with their like-minded party members. State authorities initially denied the request, deciding that the Dukhobors' case did not constitute an exemption to the Empire's general marriage laws.[36] During the early 1890s, however, the tensions and antagonisms intensified so much that both the Small and Large parties decided that they could no longer tol-

d. 2, 1950, ll. 26–27, 35–36; RGIA f. 1291, op. 50, d. 23, 1906, ll. 230b–24; and SSC'SA f. 244, op. 3, d. 573, 1888.

32. SSC'SA f. 244, op. 3, d. 573, 1888; GMIR f. K1, op. 1, d. 24, 1887–91, ll. 6–60b, passim; Ol'khovskii, "K istorii," 29–30; RGIA f. 1291, op. 50, d. 23, 1906, l. 16; and ORRGB f. 369, k. 42, d. 2, 1950, ll. 19, 23–25.

33. GMIR f. K1, op. 1, d. 8, 1889–95, doc. 56, ll. 1–10b. See also GARF f. 102, 3 d-vo, op. 1895, d. 1053, ch.1, l. 184; Brock, "Vasya Pozdnyakov's," 165; ORRGB f. 369, k. 42, d. 2, 1950, l. 567; k. 43, op. 1, 1950, ll. 586–88 and 813–14; and GMIR f. 2, op. 7, d. 484, n.d., ll. 1–2.

34. Brock, "Vasya Pozdnyakov's," 165.

35. ORRGB f. 369, k. 42, d. 2, 1950, l. 567.

36. GMIR f. K1, op. 1, d. 8, 1889–95, docs. 55, 56.

erate cohabitation. In 1893, the local administration agreed to their entreaties to sever the two sides into distinct rural communities on an official basis. As part of the process of administrative redistricting, Small Party adherents relocated to Gorelovka and Large Party followers migrated to other villages, often swapping houses with each other. Husbands and wives of different parties moved away from each other, at times remarrying once they arrived in their new location.[37] Children usually went with their mothers.

DISINTEGRATING STATE-DUKHOBOR RELATIONS

As the community spiraled into ever more extreme divisions and internecine confrontation, Russian officials were drawn into the melee and relations between the Large Party and the state degenerated. For many generations, the Dukhobor community had existed as a relatively independent entity. In return for their colonial services, payment of taxes, fulfillment of obligations, and respect for tsarist authority, the state at all levels had left the Dukhobors alone to govern their communities as they wished. Indeed, both Dukhobors and tsarist officials had come to see the Dukhobor community as a "state within a state," labeling their lands "Dukhobor'e," as if it were a national homeland.[38] The schism brought the Russian state decisively into the midst of the Dukhobors' community, however. Getting involved usually meant choosing a side, and state authorities most frequently came down on the side of the Small Party, although many of the Large Party petitions were taken seriously and fulfilled.

Both Large and Small Party Dukhobors actively sought to utilize state power to their advantage in their conflicts, dragging the government into their troubles whether it wanted to be involved or not. During the struggle that took place at Kalmykova's funeral repast, for example, Zubkov and the Small Party blocked Verigin's assumption of power by enlisting the aid of the district police officer, Metsatunov. Zubkov, who was held in great respect by the authorities, informed Metsatunov that Verigin posed

37. ORRGB f. 369, k. 42, d. 2, 1950, ll. 35, 563–64; M. Tebenkov, "Dukhobortsy, ikh uchenie, organizatsiia i nastoiashchee polozhenie," *RS* 27, no. 9 (1896), 495; SSC'SA f. 17, op. 1, d. 3244, 1892, ll. 1–20b. Similar Large Party efforts to split the Slavianka rural community in Elisavetpol province came to a different conclusion, with the request denied. See RGIA f. 1291, op. 50, d. 23, 1906, ll. 19–200b.
38. "Dukhobor'e," *ES* 11: 1 (St. Petersburg, 1893), 253; GARF f. 102, 3 d-vo, op. 1891, d. 44, ch. 51, ll. 4–40b; Kuropatkin, *Soobrazheniia*, 12; "Smert'," 486; and Polkovnik General'nogo shtaba Andrievskii, *Voenno-geograficheskoe i statisticheskoe opisanie Kavkazskogo voennogo okruga* (Tiflis, 1908), 57–58. There was no equivalent geographic designation for Molokans or Subbotniks.

a dire threat to "communal safety," and was "disturbing the peace and considered himself a prophet." Fearing an outbreak of serious violence, the police arrested Verigin and other "ringleaders," much to the outcry of the Large Party.[39]

Zubkov's decision to enlist the support of the state to arbitrate the schism represented a profound shift in Dukhobor practice. That one of the community's leading figures had invited state officials into the midst of their internal affairs generated enormous anger and frustration, a fact noted by Tiflis governor G. D. Shervashidze in an 1895 report:

> This appeal of the Dukhobors for the intervention of the administration in the community's affairs—the first in the course of half a century—astonished everyone in the extreme. Correctly evaluating the meaning of these events for their sect, the Dukhobors were gripped by agitation and bitterness. "Our own Zubkov wanted to trample the fatherland and sold us out," they said in despair. And from that time, Aleksei Zubkov, who had received special honor and respect among the Dukhobors over the preceding 25 years . . . became in the eyes of the majority of Dukhobors a symbol of treachery and apostasy . . . for such an alteration to the sacred traditions of the sect.[40]

The *starshina*'s actions opened a new period in Dukhobor history in which both factions courted the tsarist state to tip the balance of the power struggle in their direction. Indeed, parallel to Zubkov, representatives of the Large Party repeatedly petitioned different branches of the tsarist government in an effort to enlist official support for their cause, specifically to have Verigin legally recognized as Kalmykova's successor and proprietor of the Orphan Home.

Tsarist officials also became enmeshed in the Dukhobors' quarrels because they wanted to maintain public order and to assist those who were suffering as a result of the conflicts. When matters got out of hand at the 1887 funeral repast and in the conflict over the Troitskoe farmstead, tsarist police stepped in to try to calm the situation, although they only succeeded in escalating tensions.[41] Additionally, the disruption of family life was so severe that tsarist authorities found themselves compelled to intervene in order to prevent widespread destitution among jettisoned

39. ORRGB f. 369, k. 42, d. 2, 1950, ll. 14c, 16; k. 43, d. 1, 1950, ll. 13–14; RGIA f. 1291, op. 50, d. 23, 1906, ll. 14–150b; f. 797, op. 57, otd. II, st. 3, d. 268, 1887–91, l. 10b; Tebenkov, "Dukhobortsy," no. 8, 291–92; and GMIR f. 17, op. 1, d. 628, n.d., l. 1. For similar actions in August 1887, see ORRGB f. 369, k. 42, d. 2, 1950, ll. 21–22; and Breyfogle, "Rethinking," 67–68.
40. Tebenkov, "Dukhobortsy," no. 8, 291; "Smert'," 486; and Breyfogle, "Building Doukhoboriia," 26.
41. RGIA f. 1291, op. 50, d. 23, 1906, ll. 16–160b; f. 797, op. 57, otd. II, st. 3, d. 268, 1887–91, ll. 2–20b; and ORRGB f. 369, k. 42, d. 2, 1950, ll. 5, 20, 306.

wives. Court officers distributed to these women writs of execution providing spousal support of fifteen rubles per month. It was not uncommon during these years for these wives to enter their former villages under police escort to collect their monthly due. The police would aid the wife in assessing the value of the husband's property, and in cases where he could not pay—or refused to—the entire community was held liable.[42] Similarly, tsarist authorities also ordered wives who had willingly abandoned their husbands and children to return to their former homes and renew their parental responsibilities, even if their husbands had beaten them for choosing a different party.[43] The differing treatment of the male and female cases highlights the state's conceptions of gender structures within the family—males could substitute money for their familial duties, but females could not.

State officials were often drawn into the fray quite reluctantly. Many tsarist officials initially took a stance of noninterference in the Dukhobors' internal affairs based on the prevailing central policy toward sectarians. Such noninvolvement tended to help the Small Party's cause, however, and Veriginites took this nonengagement as a sign of partisanship. Such was the case when local authorities took no action on the inheritance of the Orphan Home, allowing regular tsarist law to take its course. In a report on the 1887 events in Dukhobor'e, the head of the Caucasian civilian administration, Peshchurov, asserted that nonintervention in the Dukhobor schism was the best way to maintain the general order and to reduce tensions. He declared that the recently passed law of May 3, 1883—an effort to extend certain civil rights to schismatics and sectarians in the Russian Empire—legally barred local officials from intervening in the internal affairs of religious nonconformist communities, except when local officials considered such actions necessary for "the prevention and suppression of actions which tend to the disruption of communal order and decorous behavior."[44] As a result, in the Orphan Home case, Peshchurov believed that no special mediation was necessary from the Russian government. The property should be passed on according the "general order established by the laws concerning property," which had the legal consequence of allowing Gubanov to inherit the Dukhobors' communal wealth. Thus, without intent of malice, the state's hands-off approach to internecine struggle was understood by the Large Party Dukhobors as an indication of the state's antagonism toward them.[45]

42. ORRGB f. 369, k. 42, d. 2, 1950, l. 26.
43. Brock, "Vasya Pozdnyakov's," 165; and ORRGB f. 369, k. 42, d. 2, 1950, ll. 561–63.
44. PSZ (3), vol. 3 (1886), no. 1545, pp. 219–21. Quotation from RGIA f. 1291, op. 50, d. 23, 1906, l. 15.
45. RGIA f. 1291, op. 50, d. 23, 1906, ll. 15–150b; and CRCR 1895–09–20a, ll. 75–77.

As local authorities were drawn ever deeper into the Dukhobors' internal conflicts, the increasingly antistate activities of the Large Party prompted them to respond with arrest, exile, police surveillance, restrictions on movement (through denial of passports), and village occupation. Although these government measures were intended to reduce the hostilities, they had exactly the opposite effect, prompting vociferous Veriginites to complain about a long list of state injustices. In the immediate aftermath of an 1887 confrontation in Gorelovka, tsarist police arrested between thirty and forty Dukhobor elders considered "instigators" or "agitators."[46] Soon thereafter, in an effort to put an end to the disturbances and to prevent contact between Verigin and his followers, the Transcaucasian authorities exiled Verigin and five other Large Party leaders to the Russian far north for a period of five years under police surveillance; Verigin to Shenkursk in Archangel province, the others to Olonets province.[47] State officials considered Verigin a primary culprit for the "terrible hatred" that was playing itself out between the parties: he had worsened the conflict through his continued proclamations of being a "prophet" and "the Tsar of Tsars," his claims to leadership and to the Orphan House, and his unbending requirement that Dukhobors throughout Transcaucasia show obedience only to him.[48] One report of the Elisavetpol province administration feared that his continued presence "could have the most ruinous consequences and his exile from the boundaries of the province represents the only measure that can pacify the population."[49]

In practice, however, the exile of Verigin and the other leaders only aggravated the Large Party Dukhobors. They blamed Small Party "slander" and the selfish machinations of Zubkov and Gubanov for the banishment.[50] They simply could not understand a government that would "exile the innocent" for their faith in God.[51] For Veriginite Dukhobors, "this exile of people respected by the Dukhobor community undermined in the end the trust of the Dukhobors in the people who held power, and surrounded the exiles with an aura of martyrdom, only increasing their moral influence on the community."[52]

46. ORRGB f. 369, k. 42, d. 2, 1950, l. 20; GMIR f. 2, op. 7, d. 954, n.d., ll. 10b–2; RGIA f. 1291 op. 50, d. 23, 1906, l. 160b; RGIA f. 797, op. 57, otd. II, st. 3, d. 268, 1887–91, ll. 2–20b; and Bonch-Bruevich, *Rasskaz*, 11.
47. RGIA f. 797, op. 57, otd. II, st. 3, d. 268, 1887–91, ll. 2–3; f. 1291 op. 50, d. 23, 1906, ll. 160b–17; and ORRGB f. 369, k. 42, d. 2, 1950, l. 23.
48. Tebenkov, "Dukhobortsy," no. 8, 293; and RGIA f. 1291, op. 50, d. 23, 1906, ll. 14–140b.
49. GARF f. 102, 3 d-vo, op. 1895, d. 1053, ch. 1, l. 1830b.
50. Ibid., l. 1790b.
51. ORRGB f. 369, k. 42, d. 2, 1950, l. 305.
52. Pavel Ivanovich Biriukov and Vladimir Chertkov, *Polozhenie dukhoborov na Kavkaze v 1896 godu i neobkhodimyia sredstva oblegcheniia ikh uchasti* (London, 1897), 19.

Large Party Dukhobors also bristled at measures to prevent their contacting the exiled Verigin. Officials were concerned that Verigin would
continue to lead the Dukhobors from afar, spreading his ideas and orders
through intermediaries. They also wanted to limit, if not stop, the dispersal of money to Verigin that his followers collected in order to assist
him in his place of exile. To accomplish these tasks, tsarist agents increased police surveillance of Verigin, monitored his correspondence,
moved him to even more remote locations (from Shenkursk to Kola in
1890, back to Shenkursk in 1892, and then to Obdorsk in 1894), extended the term of his original five-year exile, scrutinized and followed
the "middlemen" who regularly visited Verigin, and demanded sworn
statements from Dukhobor elders that they would report to the police
any contact with these go-betweens. They also restricted access to passports for those Dukhobors wishing to travel to visit either Verigin or their
family members who had been arrested or sent into exile.[53] Government
measures to restrict movement and contact were generally unsuccessful,
and Dukhobors carried on a brisk correspondence with Verigin. He received a steady stream of visitors who traveled back and forth from Transcaucasia to carry news, letters, and supplies. However, the government
policy of separating Verigin from his followers did have the unintended
result of granting a select few influential Dukhobors, especially Vasilii Verigin and Ivan Konkin, a great deal of power in carrying, transforming,
and sometimes radicalizing Verigin's words.[54]

In addition to arrest and exile, tsarist officials strove to restore communal peace by deploying military detachments to Gorelovka. The occupation force was initially stationed there as a deterrent against
"assaults" on the Orphan Home and as a buffer between the Small and
Large parties.[55] However, the soldiers soon began to take punitive action
toward the Large Party, generating enormous anger from these Dukhobors.[56] Conflict occurred in part because of the troops' own irresponsi-
ble behavior and in part because Russian soldiers were required to obtain
their own provisioning from the villages in which they were deployed. Initially, Small Party Dukhobors supplied the troops in Gorelovka. However,
in what appears to have been the result of a Small Party effort to reduce

53. SSC'SA f. 17, op. 1, d. 3358, 1893; Tebenkov, "Dukhobortsy," no. 9, 496; RGIA f. 1291, op.
50, d. 23, 1906, ll. 17–18ob; ORRGB f. 369, k. 42, d. 2, 1950, ll. 34–35; Biriukov, Dukhobortsy,
34–35.
54. GMIR f. 2, op. 7, d. 263, 1891; d. 379, 1893; Bonch-Bruevich, Pis'ma; Chertkov and Chertkova,
Dukhobortsy, 45; "Selo Slavianka," Kaspii 14, no. 115 (June 1, 1894): 3; and "Sel. Slavianka," Kaspii
14, no. 202 (September 21, 1894): 3.
55. RGIA f. 1291, op. 50, d. 23, 1906, l. 160b; and GMIR f. 2, op. 7, d. 954, n.d., l. 2.
56. RGIA f. 1291, op. 50, d. 23, 1906, l. 160b; ORRGB f. 369, k. 42, d. 2, 1950, ll. 20, 305–18;
GMIR f. 2, op. 7, d. 954, n.d., ll. 2–4; Bonch-Bruevich, Rasskaz, 10; and Breyfogle, "Rethinking,"
71–72.

their burden, the occupation troops soon turned to the surrounding Dukhobor villages with demands for food. Not unexpectedly, Large Party Dukhobors opposed the idea of feeding the very troops who were there to prevent them from gaining control of the Orphan Home. In village after village, soldiers dispatched to obtain provisions met with the same response from Dukhobor elders: "I didn't request you. You are not necessary to me. Whoever you are necessary to, let him feed you."[57]

In Bogdanovka, Orlovka, and Troitskoe, each community banded together to refuse Prince Machabeli, the leader of the occupation force, the provisions he requested. The troops responded by grabbing whatever they wanted. In Troitskoe, the soldiers seized as many as 2,000 cattle and 500 pedigree sheep. They ate some of these provisions themselves, and others they sold for cash to buy vodka and "small foodstuffs." When villagers came out to question the soldiers' conduct, Machabeli ordered the complaining Dukhobors to be beaten back with rifle butts. To make matters worse, the district administrator, Prince Sumbatov, had the dissenting villages occupied by a detachment of Cossacks as punishment. The Cossacks treated the villagers in an equally harsh manner, taking food willfully and beating with whips those Dukhobors who showed even passive resistance.[58]

The Dukhobors also balked when tsarist officials tried to designate starshiny for their villages on a unilateral basis. The splits within the Dukhobor communities made the election of a starshina difficult since the factions could not agree on a candidate, and the minority Small Party feared that they would fall under the Large Party's control. In an effort ·to avoid administrative breakdown, local authorities put their own choice for starshina in place. These government-appointed communal leaders were almost exclusively non-Russian in ethnic origin—mostly Armenians and Azerbaijanis—and some already held local administrative posts in the police or local civil administration.[59]

In one case, when the squabbling Small and Large Parties of the Slavianka commune could not agree upon a starshina, tsarist officials appointed a series of Armenians to enforce tsarist authority. Veriginites saw the appointments of these external starshiny as an imposition of state authority in the internal affairs of their communities; railed against the use of non-Russians, whom they found to be culturally ill-equipped to make decisions for this religious community; and complained bitterly about the

57. ORRGB f. 369, k. 42, d. 2, 1950, l. 307.
58. Ibid., ll. 20, 307–8; and Bonch-Bruevich, Rasskaz, 10. See also the events in Orlovka. GMIR f. 2, op. 7, d. 954, n.d., ll. 2–3.
59. While the examples below discuss cases of Armenian starshiny, Dukhobor communities were also likely to be governed by an Azerbaijani starshina. ORRGB f. 369, k. 42, d. 2, 1950, l. 561; and CRCR 1895–09–20a, l. 78.

requirement to pay 700 rubles each year for the *starshina*'s salary. Relations strained to the breaking point with the second appointee who, according to the Veriginites, began openly to "implement terrible measures" against them. They confronted him, saying, "We say to you, *starshina*, that you do not serve us, and we will not pay you your salary." As part of a recurring pattern, the authorities stepped in to force the Dukhobors to pay, confiscating livestock and property, appraised it below the market value, and then took that money to pay the Armenian *starshina*. Then they sold the livestock to neighboring Armenian and Muslim peasants at much higher prices, often pocketing the difference. The result, not unexpectedly, was further disillusionment with the tsarist state: "Looking at all of these un-Godly situations, our conscience led us to refuse their regime and to negate their rule of law, and we began to fulfill the law of the ruling God, Jesus Christ."[60]

COLONIZING THE COLONISTS: THE END OF INDEPENDENCE

The rapidly deteriorating relationship between the Large Party Dukhobors and the tsarist administration in the early 1890s was helped along by a series of Empire-wide changes in administrative practice that the Dukhobors found to be invasive in their daily affairs and a direct challenge to the autonomy to which they had become accustomed. These changes were initially unrelated to the schism, and some of them were even designed to provide the Dukhobors with rights more equal to Orthodox Russians. They involved government efforts to make the law and administrative practice more standardized and uniform—a process that was common to modernizing polities in Europe in the late nineteenth century. In the Dukhobors' case, these state practices included registration of births, deaths, and marriages in metrical books, state-sponsored health care programs, schools, the requirement that the Dukhobors contribute to emergency communal grain storage and capital reserves, and, most important, the extension of mandatory military service to the Dukhobors.

In mandating new socio-political demands, cultural norms, and administrative integration on a minority community in a borderland region of the Empire, these state actions toward the Dukhobors, in many respects, constituted one branch of the larger Russification process of Alexander III's reign that many Caucasian elites themselves opposed.

60. ORRGB f. 369, k. 42, d. 2, 1950, ll. 446–47, 452; d. 1, 1950, ll. 59–60; and GARF f. 102, 3 d-vo, op. 1895, d. 1053, ch.1, l. 1840b. See also CRCR 1896–04–23c, ll. 3790b–81.

Here, however, tsarist policy was Russifying the "Russians," which Dukhobors, not unexpectedly, resented. Although these particular Russian sectarians had earlier been considered exemplary colonists, the broad shifts in governance that characterized the post-emancipation period included an evolution in tsarist thinking that streamlined the definition of "Russian." Russians now had to be of a certain type, take on certain prescribed behaviors, and accept state presence in their daily lives if they were to be included in the national polity.[61]

Of the new state obligations, the most onerous from the Dukhobors' perspective was by far the imposition of mandatory military service. Although Russia had shifted to a system of universal conscription in 1874, the draft was not introduced to inhabitants of the Transcaucasus until 1887 (or, in Kars territory, 1890).[62] Freedom from the draft was especially important to the Dukhobors because, like Molokans and other Christian communities, they were doctrinally opposed to acts of violence.[63] Although the Dukhobors did not immediately refuse to serve in the army, as they would in 1895, the demands of universal conscription generated frustration and unease.

Other state demands also angered the Dukhobors and intensified the antagonism between the state and Dukhobor communities. Large Party Dukhobors saw as intrusive the government's new request for registration in metrical books, just as was required of the Orthodox population. Prior to a law of April 19, 1874, Dukhobors and other sectarians had been denied inclusion in such registers. Without official records, the dissenters were reduced to second-class subjects who could not receive many of the rights and privileges that the state reserved for Orthodox Russians. In particular, barring sectarians from registering their marriages meant that their unions were juridically seen as "cohabitation," without any of the rights that applied to married couples and their families. The state's extension of the registers to sectarians during the Great Reform era was part of an agenda of greater toleration that more nearly equalized their civil rights with those of Orthodox Russians, and aimed, more ominously from the Dukhobor perspective, to keep track of the sectarians for the new military recruitment system.[64]

61. On peasant opposition to these changes generally, see Christine Worobec, *Peasant Russia: Family and Community in the Post-Emancipation Period* (DeKalb, 1991). On Russification and its opponents, see Ronald Grigor Suny, *Looking Toward Ararat: Armenia in Modern History* (Bloomington, 1993), 15–78; Thaden, *Russification;* and Theodore Weeks, *Nation and State in Late Imperial Russia: Nationalism and Russification on the Western Frontier, 1863–1914* (DeKalb, 1996).
62. RGIA f. 932, op. 1, d. 318, 1889, l. 100b. On conscription generally, see Sanborn, *Drafting.*
63. Nicholas B. Breyfogle, "Swords into Plowshares: Opposition to Military Service among Religious Sectarians, 1770s to 1874," in *The Military and Society in Russian History,* ed. Eric Lohr and Marshall Poe (Leiden, 2002), 441–67.
64. *SPChR* (1875), 609–17, 672–82; *PSZ* (3) vol. 3 (1886), no. 1545, pp. 219–21; V. I. Iasevich-

Despite the state's more benign intentions, Large Party Dukhobors were wary of providing such precise recordings about their communities and were willing only to submit annual "short notations." They feared a loss of their beloved independence and worried what the state would do with the information. Initially, Transcaucasian officials applied the 1874 law only sparingly, if at all.[65] However, in the late 1880s and early 1890s, for reasons that are unclear, regional administrators began to enforce compliance to a much greater degree. In December of 1889, the Kars military governor ordered the local police to ensure the completion of official registers among all sectarians despite Dukhobor refusals.[66] In early 1895, when tsarist authorities appeared in the village of Rodionovka in Akhalkalaki district to retrieve the metrical books, the Dukhobors refused to provide this information, asserting that they registered themselves not in government lists "but in the Living Book." No threat, not even exile, could persuade the Dukhobors to comply with this registration.[67]

The Dukhobors were equally angered at government public-health initiatives in their communities. On a number of occasions in the 1880s and 1890s, state officials interceded in Dukhobor communities during outbreaks of disease such as cholera and diphtheria in an effort to restrict the spread of the maladies and to reduce mortality rates. However, in the process, they threatened traditional Dukhobor medical practices and were often forced to disregard Dukhobor beliefs and mores that might further spread certain communicable diseases, the prime example of this being the practice of kissing a corpse as part of the funeral ceremony. Dukhobors construed government medical assistance as a conscious effort to infiltrate their communities, take away their autonomy, and rob them by forcing them to purchase expensive and unknown medicines.[68]

Similarly, the expansion of state-sponsored schooling also elicited dissatisfaction. Large Party Dukhobors almost universally refused to enroll their children, fearing that tsarist education taught blind allegiance to

Borodaevskaia, *Bor'ba za veru. Istorichesko-bytovye ocherki i obzor zakonodatel'stva po staroobriadchestvu i sektantstvu v ego posledovatel'nom razvitii* (St. Petersburg, 1912), 1–108; N. L. Solov'ev, *Polnyi krug dukhovnykh zakonov* (Moscow, 1907), 18–44; Peter Waldron, "Religious Toleration in Late Imperial Russia," in *Civil Rights in Imperial Russia*, ed. Olga Crisp and Linda Edmondson (Oxford, 1989), 103–20; and Nicholas B. Breyfogle, "Prayer and the Politics of Place: Molokan Church-Building, Tsarist Law, and the Quest for a Public Sphere in Late Imperial Russia," in *Sacred Stories: Religion and Spirituality in Modern Russian Culture*, ed. Heather Coleman and Mark Steinberg (Bloomington, forthcoming).

65. ORRGB f. 369, k. 42, d. 1, 1950, ll. 67–68.

66. RGIA f. 1284, op. 222–1891, d. 39. The sudden enforcement of the 1874 rules here was likely linked to the extension of military service to Kars territory in 1890.

67. ORRGB f. 369, k. 42, d. 2, 1950, l. 494.

68. ORRGB f. 369, k. 42, d. 2, 1950, ll. 33–34; d. 1, 1950, l. 68; CRCR 1985–09–20b, ll. 82 and 83ob; and "Khronika," *Kavkaz*, no. 212 (September 22, 1883): 1; no. 213 (September 23, 1883): 1; no. 224 (October 7, 1883): 1; no. 234 (October 19, 1883): 1.

the tsar and was saturated with Orthodox Christianity. They also opposed formal schooling because of a general opposition to the written word that was a cornerstone of their religious beliefs. Rather than recognizing the written scriptures, they instead esteemed the "Living Book" that was transmitted orally over the generations and carried in the "hearts and souls of people." The Dukhobors had reason to be uneasy about the schools, for tsarist officials in the Caucasus clearly regarded such institutions as tools of integration and assimilation that would break down Dukhobor particularities and help to draw them into a state-defined national culture.[69]

Finally, the Dukhobors' rejection of the formation of an emergency agricultural fund is a telling example of how the expansion of state power into their lives led to disillusionment with the tsarist government. From the early 1870s, Dukhobor communities—like all villages in Transcaucasia—had been required by law to maintain storehouses to keep excess grain "for the aversion of poverty or hunger during an unfruitful harvest due to natural causes or from sudden poverty."[70] Tsarist authorities noted that until the early 1890s, the Dukhobors had "fulfilled correctly" the state's demands to supply a portion of their grain for emergency uses, and the Dukhobors administered these granaries themselves, independent of government interference.[71] However, around 1890, state officials ordered two changes in the existing system in an effort to improve it. First, they demanded that grain reserves from different communities around the region be amalgamated into one large communal storehouse that local officials—rather than the individual communities—would administer and that would serve a variety of communities in the region. Second, tsarist authorities also decided that Transcaucasian peasants should, when possible, substitute cash payments in place of contributions of grain in order to create a capital fund for emergencies that the local officials would administer for a fee.[72]

Dukhobors of the Large Party vehemently refused to pay into this centralized emergency fund. Verigin saw it as an infringement on his powers as the Dukhobors' supreme leader and as a bold attempt to homogenize and dismantle the Dukhobors' distinct society. Moreover, through the Orphan Home, the Dukhobors had for generations maintained their own fund for disaster relief and welfare for the poor, and they saw no

---

69. GMIR f. 2, op. 7, d. 545, 1893, l. 39, passim; and GARF f. 102, 3 d-vo, op. 1895, d. 1053, ch. 1, ll. 545–46, 551ob–52.

70. "O sel'skikh zapasnykh khlebnykh magazinakh v Akhaltsiskom uezde," *Tiflisskii vestnik*, no. 31 (1875): 3; "Obshchestvennye sel'skokhoziaistvennye kapitaly," *Kaspii* 14, no. 17 (January 22, 1894): 2. On this same process in Siberia, see "Gosudarstvennye sberegatel'nye kassy," *Irkutskie gubernskie vedomosti*, no. 8 (February 19, 1897): 8–9.

71. ORRGB f. 369, k. 44, d. 1, 1950, ll. 190–91.

72. ORRGB f. 369, k. 42, d. 2, 1950, ll. 27–33; GMIR f. 14, op. 2, d. 3, 1898; and "O sel'skikh zapasnykh," 3.

need for an official communal bank.[73] Voicing their aggravation, one Large Party petition of June 8, 1892, entreated the Tiflis governor to exempt them from the capital fund requirement and to return to the Dukhobors the money that local officials had already collected from them. They argued that "to make payments to state institutions of their spare capital" violated the tenets of their faith, which forbade them from accepting "government surveillance in their affairs concerning the storage of their communal funds." They gave notice that "they would prefer to die than to agree to something that was against their conscience." Notably, Dukhobor petitioners were primarily concerned to maintain their communal monies separate from those of their indigenous neighbors, and to administer such a fund without outside involvement. Dukhobor sources indicate that Tiflis governor Shervashidze realized that Large-Party revulsion against an encroaching Russian state was the crux of the matter; they quote him as saying that "they request the return of the communal capital fund to them, but this is not the most important thing for them. . . . For them what is most important is not to have any contact with us."[74]

Although the Russian state had embarked on a reduction of local autonomy and heterogeneity, they did demonstrate flexibility in the application of their new administrative structures. When push came to shove in the early 1890s, with the Dukhobors evincing a determination not to bend to new demands, central officials were willing to back off. In the case of the metrical books, for example, when the Kars governor attempted to force compliance despite categorical Dukhobor refusals, the minister of the interior intervened, asserting that such registration was voluntary and should be left to the discretion of the sectarian communities.[75] The Dukhobors won similar concessions in the case of the agricultural emergency funds. After years of "pestering" the local administration and refusing, according to Shervashidze, with "obstinacy" and "stubbornness" to carry out the obligation, the Dukhobors were not only relieved of their responsibility to fulfill the state order for contributions to the capital fund, but tsarist officials also returned to the Veriginites part of the money that they had been forced to pay. According to Dukhobor sources, the minister of state domains said that "it is necessary to render assistance voluntarily, but if someone does not want it then there is no need to force them."[76]

73. ORRGB f. 369, k. 44, d. 1, 1950, ll. 190–91; and k. 42, d. 2, 1950, ll. 27–33, 36–37.
74. ORRGB f. 369, k. 42, d. 2, 1950, ll. 36–37; SSC'SA f. 17, op. 1, d. 3245, 1892; and Tebenkov, "Dukhobortsy," no. 9, 496–97;
75. RGIA f. 1284, op. 222–1891, d. 39.
76. Dukhobors had paid between 12,000 and 14,000 rubles in cash into the communal capital fund. SSC'SA f. 17, op. 1, d. 3245, 1892, l. 17; ORRGB f. 369, k. 42, d. 2, 1950, ll. 36–37; and Tebenkov, "Dukhobortsy," no. 9, 497.

These concessions did little to mitigate the Dukhobors' frustration with the state's modernizing tendencies. However, they do reflect the state's elasticity in its dealings with its subjects, even while the subjects themselves felt the state to be heavy-handed and invasive. That said, the Dukhobor success had potentially ominous repercussions for Russian imperial control in the region. As Shervashidze related in his report of 1895, "The Dukhobors loudly celebrated the return of their agricultural monies as a true victory over the government and, in contrast to a half century of tradition, they even started openly to propagandize among the surrounding indigenous population: 'act like us,' the Dukhobors said, 'and then they will begin to fear you.'"[77] Tsarist authorities—including Georgian nobles like Shervashidze—felt the stakes to be high in their efforts at administrative modernization and uniformalization. Problems in implementing these changes on the Russian peasant population, while serious throughout the Empire, posed an especially heightened threat in the imperial borderlands, where, officials feared, opposition of the Russian colonists could unravel the whole imperial tapestry. If the Russian settlers refused to be "Russified," how could tsarist agents expect to apply Russification policies to the non-Russian population?

CORRUPTION AND BRUTALITY: THE DECISIVE ROLE OF LOCAL OFFICIALS

The developing schism and the confrontations over state-building in Dukhobor communities were causing a meltdown in Large Party-tsarist relations. However, the corrupt, arbitrary, and frequently brutal manner in which certain local officials carried out central directives, or intervened in communal conflicts, made an already delicate and deteriorating situation worse.[78] In incident after incident, the actions of a small number of local administrators proved decisive, not only in ratcheting up the rancor of the schism but also in turning the fissures between Russian state power and the Veriginites into veritable chasms. Notably, while Armenians, Georgians, and Azerbaijanis played central roles in the forceful imposition of tsarist will on the Dukhobor colonists during these years, Dukhobor sources give little indication that they thought of their tormentors in ethnic or religious terms. Instead, they saw them as corrupt agents of a dishonest and shameful state; the "savagery" was a "tsarist"

---

77. Tebenkov, "Dukhobortsy," no. 9, 497.
78. Official corruption was by no means unique to the South Caucasus. See, for example, Frank, *Crime*, 91–92; and Dmitrii Ivanovich Rostislavov, *Provincial Russia in the Age of Enlightenment: The Memoir of a Priest's Son*, ed. and trans. Alexander Martin (DeKalb, 2002), esp. 53–81.

phenomenon, not a result of uncivilized or alien Caucasians.[79] The extent of corruption in official ranks remains impossible to discern with any exactness because of wide discrepancies in the stories told by state- and Dukhobor-generated sources.[80] Whatever the case, Large Party Dukhobors considered payoffs to be an inextricable part of the government system, and rumors of official corruption circulated widely. The feeling that the state's arbitration could be bought off greatly damaged whatever faith existed in the institution of government.

Veriginite Dukhobors were convinced that Zubkov had paid the Akhalkalaki district administrator, Prince Sumbatov, between 10,000 and 15,000 rubles in 1887 to settle the inheritance in Gubanov's favor and to exile Verigin. Reputedly, Sumbatov used this money to buy large tracks of land in Borchalo district, where he quickly retired into a life of luxury.[81] Dukhobors also accused Sumbatov's successor, D'iachkov-Tarasov, of graft. Indeed, a local police officer, Malinovskii, reported that his superior took bribes, doing so "on any and every possible occasion: for passports, for the release of arrestees, and for the cessation of legal affairs, etc."[82] When the relatives of exiled Dukhobors requested permission either to resettle with or just to visit their banished family members, they were told that passports for such trips were strictly forbidden. However, it became clear that by offering foodstuffs or money to D'iachkov-Tarasov, these passports could easily be obtained. The wife of Large Party leader Dmitrii Lezhebokov, for instance, is reputed to have paid twelve pounds of butter, eight carts of hay, and six carts of *kiziak* (pressed dung used as fuel) in return for a passport to be with her husband.[83] Dukhobors also reported paying D'iachkov-Tarasov as much as several hundred rubles per arrestee to have their relatives released from prison. In one case, the district administrator received 500 rubles in return for the release of seventeen Dukhobors who had been arrested for an incident at the Troitskoe farmstead. There are even indications that officials began to arrest Dukhobors as a moneymaking venture.[84] Moreover, state investigations into D'iachkov-Tarasov's tenure as district administrator found that he used the emergency agricultural reserves as his personal savings account.

79. GMIR f. 14, op. 2, d. 3, 1898; ORRGB f. 369, k. 42, d. 2, 1950, ll. 27–33, 733–39; and d. 1, 1950, ll. 65–69.
80. GARF f. 102, 3 d-vo, op. 1895, d. 1053, ch. 1, ll. 180–800b; and CRCR 1895–09–20a, ll. 77–770b.
81. ORRGB f. 369, k. 42, d. 2, 1950, ll. 21–22, 305; Bonch-Bruevich, *Rasskaz*, 9; CRCR 1895–09–20a, ll. 76–760b.
82. GARF f. 102, 3 d-vo, op. 1895, d. 1053, ch. 1, ll. 180–800b.
83. Other passports cost between 200 and 500 rubles. Bonch-Bruevich, *Rasskaz*, 11; idem, *Raz"iasnenie*, 14; GARF f. 102, 3 d-vo, op. 1895, d. 1053, ch. 1, l. 1800b; ORRGB f. 369, k. 42, d. 2, 1950, ll. 23, 36; and GMIR f. 14, op. 2, d. 3, 1898, ll. 9–10.
84. ORRGB f. 369, k. 42, d. 2, 1950, l. 25; Bonch-Bruevich, *Raz"iasnenie*, 14.

Dukhobors estimated that they lost as much as 50,000 rubles as a result of these acts of embezzlement.[85]

Other Large Party sources asserted that almost all of the local administrators, including police and court officials, received some form of payment in return for their assistance in the conflict. Vasia Pozdniakov contended that after Kalmykova's death, the Small Party spent the extraordinary sum of half a million rubles to buy off the officials of Tiflis province alone. The bribery reputedly reached as far as the Tiflis governor, who was supposed to have received a carriage with horses valued at 8,000 rubles. According to another Dukhobor, the chief administrator of Kars territory received "a thousand rubles from a man who applied for a certificate excusing his son from military service."[86]

As a result of both real and perceived corruption and exploitation, the Dukhobors became deeply disillusioned with Russian "law" and tsarist rule in general. "What is the use of a law if it can be bought?" they appealed.[87] As one Dukhobor author related, "Then we saw Russian law. Before we had thought that these signatures and seals were like the laws of God. But for exactly fifty rubles, he had sold the law and . . . it was obvious that Russian law is not God's law, but the law of money. And that there is no truth in that situation. Then we stopped serving such falsehoods."[88] Moreover, some Dukhobors considered their increasing reluctance to pay bribes as one of the causes of the government's "illegality and oppression" toward them:

> When we lived according to our fleshly lusts, and served our own pleasure and lived in compliance with those around us, the Caucasian officials liked us; especially when we gave to every government official in our towns every kind of bribe. But when [we] began to accomplish the will of God and to serve only the Lord, at the same time ceasing to give bribes, the officials immediately changed their opinion about us, and now they say, "You are criminals against the Emperor." But if the Emperor knew who were the real criminals against the law, he would put them under a special judgment.[89]

85. CRCR 1895–09–20a, l. 770b; 1895–09–20b; ORRGB f. 369, k. 42, d. 2, 1950, ll. 36–37; Tebenkov, "Dukhobortsy," no. 9, 497. D'iachkov-Tarasov's treatment of the Dukhobors is in many ways unexpected given his generally favorable estimation of their work as Russian colonists. See Lynch, "Queen Lukeria," 37.

86. Bonch-Bruevich, Rasskaz, 9, 11–12; Vladimir Tchertkoff [Chertkov], Christian Martyrdom in Russia: Persecution of the Spirit-Wrestlers (or Doukhobors) in the Caucasus (London, 1897), 65; and Kuropatkin, Soobrazheniia, 21. Sources do not indicate whether the governor to whom they refer was Grosman or Shervashidze, who replaced Grosman in 1888.

87. Tchertkoff, Christian Martyrdom, 65.

88. GMIR f. 14, op. 2, d. 3, 1898, ll. 9–10. See also GARF f. 102, 3 d-vo, op. 1895, d. 1053, ch. 1, l. 180.

89. Tchertkoff, Christian Martyrdom, 66; and Bonch-Bruevich, Raz"iasnenie, 24.

In addition to corruption, the Large Party Dukhobors were also disgusted by the brutality and violence that local tsarist representatives used in their efforts, on the one hand, to enforce central directives of the modernizing state such as health measures and the agricultural fund and, on the other hand, to restore order or punish the Dukhobors as a result of the schism. The Dukhobors' persecution stories were certainly carefully constructed to elicit a strong reaction, and they must be read with caution. Nonetheless, other sources from both state and nonstate observers corroborate much of what the Large Party recounted, and even if some of it is hyperbole, the stories clearly reflect Dukhobor perspectives on the confrontation.

On numerous occasions, when the Dukhobors refused to pay into the communal capital fund, local officials responded with staggering violence. In one incident, Dukhobor elders were called into the town of Akhalkalaki to be punished. When they continued to refuse to pay, the district police officer, Prince Solomon Petrovich Chavchavadze, tied their hands together to form a line and then he—along with Cossacks and Muslim irregular soldiers—beat them with fists, sticks, whips, or the flat sides of swords until blood streamed down their swollen and lacerated faces. D'iachkov-Tarasov then ordered a military occupation of the Dukhobors' villages with the dual purpose of forcibly confiscating property as payment for the fund and of demonstrating tsarist might. The military occupation was carried out by between fifty and a hundred Muslim and Armenian policemen and military irregulars led by Chavchavadze. The occupation force descended upon one Dukhobor village after another where, in the words of a Dukhobor observer, they "behaved disgracefully." Housed in Dukhobors' huts, the occupiers seized barley and hay from grain bins to feed their horses and appropriated butter, milk, eggs, chickens, and other livestock for themselves. Indeed, they added insult to injury when they forced the Dukhobors to sit by and watch while the state agents feasted on freshly slaughtered livestock "day and night" around a huge cooking fire. The occupiers also passed the time of day by racing the Dukhobors' horses. When the Dukhobors attempted to intercede, the occupiers quickly turned violent, beating them with sticks and lashes for as long as it took to quell the Russian colonists. In the process, many Dukhobor elders were arrested and subjected to all manner of indignities. Following the arrest of a certain Ivan Ivin, a rope was tied around his right hand and he was forced to run behind a mounted Georgian military escort for more than three hours.[90]

90. GMIR f. 14, op. 2, d. 3, 1898, ll. 6–7; ORRGB f. 369, k. 42, d. 2, 1950, ll. 31–33; and k. 43, d. 1, 1950, l. 814.

In addition to these illegal practices of intimidation, the occupation forces went from hut to hut confiscating sheep, cows, horses, and other possessions in order to collect the moneys due to the communal capital fund. Tsarist officials invited neighboring Armenian villagers to appraise and buy the appropriated goods at auction. The Dukhobors' property was almost always sold at a value much lower than the market rate—anywhere from one-fifth to one-twentieth of the actual value. Of that meager amount, as much as half went straight into the pocket of the local officials, the remainder fulfilling the Dukhobors' outstanding communal fund debt.[91]

Such incidents notwithstanding, only a very small minority of officials was so outlandishly corrupt or brutal, and official treatment of the Veriginites was by no means limited to such horrific forms. Many of the Large Party's complaints were indeed taken seriously by various tsarist authorities who showed great concern for the social health of the community. At the end of 1892, Shervashidze removed D'iachkov-Tarasov from office for corruption in response to Dukhobor complaints.[92] Behind the scenes, other tsarist officials lobbied to reverse the Small Party's usurpation of the communal wealth. In 1890, the administrator of state properties for Tiflis province argued in intraministerial correspondence that since the Troitskoe farmstead was state-owned land that had earlier been allotted for the Troitskoe villagers' use, it could not belong to Gubanov. To this he added the more general argument that "the seizure of this land by one of the Dukhobors to the direct detriment of the interests of the entire community cannot be tolerated."[93] Similarly, Shervashidze did what he could to intervene in the court proceedings to ensure that the Troitskoe land be returned to the villagers, since he considered Gubanov's appropriation of the land to be "undoubtedly a transgression both of the interests of the treasury and the inhabitants of the village of Troitskoe."[94] In fact, Dukhobor sources assert that none other than the former viceroy, Grand Prince Mikhail Nikolaevich, intervened on their behalf in the court proceedings and arranged to have the property title transferred.[95] Yet these good intentions and actions on the part of the local administration did little to change the Dukhobors' views of the state as violent and corrupt and of its laws as unworthy of respect.

91. ORRGB f. 369, k. 42, d. 2, 1950, ll. 20, 36–37, 307–8, 738–39; GMIR f. 2, op. 7, d. 954, n.d., ll. 2–3; and Bonch-Bruevich, *Rasskaz*, 10. The Dukhobors' refusal to embrace state-sponsored medical care met with a similar response. See ORRGB f. 369, k. 42, d. 2, 1950, ll. 33–34; and d. 1, 1950, l. 68.
92. ORRGB f. 369, k. 42, d. 2, 1950, l. 34.
93. GMIR f. K1, op. 1, d. 24, 1887–94, ll. 16–180b.
94. SSC'SA f. 244, op. 3, d. 573, 1888, l. 75.
95. Bonch-Bruevich, *Rasskaz*, 12; idem, *Raz"iasnenie*, 24; RGIA f. 1291, op. 50, d. 23, 1906, l. 150b; and Breyfogle, "Rethinking," 66.

NEW DUKHOBORISM

In the context of the schism and the collapsing relations between Large-Party Dukhobors and Russian state power, the followers of Verigin embarked on a profound religious transformation that led them to embrace a more radical religiosity—the New Dukhoborism. Beginning in late 1893 and gathering steam through 1894 and into 1895, this spiritual renewal had wide-ranging repercussions, taking the earlier conflicts to new and more extreme levels. It split the Veriginite Dukhobors into two factions—thereby producing a third party—and further antagonized dealings among all the parties of this fracturing community. It pushed the Dukhobors' relationship with the Russian state to the breaking point, bringing the Dukhobors to open defiance of state power. Additionally, it hurt the region's economic situation and further dragged neighboring Caucasian peoples into Dukhobor affairs in many ways.

Through his "lieutenants," the exiled Verigin sent word to the Large Party in Transcaucasia that the time had come to live more exactly—and exactingly—according to traditional Dukhobor tenets, as taught in their psalms and Living Book, "because many Dukhobors today consider themselves Dukhobors only because they wear a blue peaked cap." The new religious teachings contained twelve points that combined certain original tenets with a reformulation of long-standing Dukhobor beliefs. The precepts fell broadly into four categories: social and religious life, gender and sexuality, socio-economic communalism, and relations to temporal power.[96]

In terms of religious and social practices, Dukhobors were to give up meat, tobacco, and alcohol and tea, each of which was, in its own way, leading the Dukhobors in a sinful life. Verigin also called for a return to nonviolence, which prompted the appeal for vegetarianism ("in order to eat meat or fish it is necessary to kill a living creature") and enjoined them not to take part in military service.[97] He ordered weekly prayer meetings and the "need to abolish all holidays, except Sunday, because they are only useful for popular drunkenness and gluttony. For God, one should celebrate everyday in the cleanness of one's own heart."[98] On the gender front, Verigin opposed the traditional payment of a bride price because it treated the woman as chattel. At the same time, women were com-

---

96. GMIR f. 17, op. 1, d. 628, n.d., l. 2; RGIA f. 1291, op. 50, d. 23, 1906, ll. 23–230b; Tebenkov, "Dukhobortsy," no. 9, 498; and *Vsepoddanneishii otchet ober-prokurora sviasheishego Sinoda K. Pobedonostseva po vedomstvu pravoslavnogo ispovedaniia za 1894 i 1895 gody* (St. Petersburg, 1898), 231–32.
97. "Otryvok iz vospominanii N. I. Dudchenko," in Bonch-Bruevich, *Pis'ma*, 155; and ORRGB f. 369, k. 42, d. 2, 1950, l. 37.
98. GMIR f. 17, op. 1, d. 628, n.d., l. 2.

manded no longer to leave their villages to go to town because Verigin considered it "unbecoming." There were also sexual prohibitions, including a moratorium on new marriages, a ban on producing children (married couples were to "live as brothers and sisters"), and the demand for sexual abstinence for both married and unmarried Dukhobors. There is disagreement in the sources as to the intent of these restrictions on sexuality. According to some documents, Verigin ordered these changes because he believed that only through physical purity could the Dukhobor faithful achieve spiritual purity and everlasting life. In other records, abstinence from intercourse, marriage, and childbirth are given a more utilitarian explanation. The Large Party leadership realized that they were about to undergo persecution for their beliefs and would be resettled to a "far-away region." They wanted to stop the birthing process to ensure that the community was not burdened with the care of "suckling babies" during their ordeal.[99]

Five of the new tenets dealt with the evils of property and material possessions, indicating that the Dukhobors should embrace communalism and socio-economic equality and avoid the pursuit of profit. Each household head was to give away at least half of his wealth to a common fund; all movable property was to be divided among rich and poor or given to strangers; Dukhobors were to pay the debts of the poor; and agricultural land was to be worked collectively and the fruits of the land dispersed equally. Finally, the tenets of the New Dukhoborism also included an instruction to change their relationship with tsarist state power. Verigin asserted that the Dukhobors should no longer provide horses to traveling administrators, should no longer pay bribes to the government, and "should be careful what [they] say" when contacted by officials.

There is disagreement in the sources regarding the origins of the tenets of the New Dukhoborism. Not unexpectedly, Verigin indicated that the ideas were those of God, communicated through him as the living Christ, which all true Christians should follow. In contrast, contemporary observers and recent historians emphasized the importance of Tolstoy's moral teachings on Verigin. "Exile," George Woodcock and Ivan Avakumovic write, "became Verigin's University." He talked at length with other sectarians, political exiles, and Tolstoyans, studying Tolstoy's philosophy, especially *The Kingdom of God is Within You*. Verigin then merged long-standing Dukhobor beliefs, such as communalism and pacifism, with Tolstoy's emphasis on vegetarianism and sexual purity, with certain radical socialist ideas thrown into the mix. While this conventional in-

99. *Vsepoddanneishii otchet*, 232; RGIA f. 1405, op. 521, d. 445, 1895–97, ll. 324ob, 327–27ob; f. 1291, op. 50, d. 23, 1906, ll. 23–23ob; GARF f. 102, 3 d-vo, op. 1895, d. 1053, ch. 1, ll. 598ob–99; Brock, "Vasya Pozdnyakov's," 168; and Tebenkov, "Dukhobortsy," no. 9, 498.

terpretation posits Tolstoy as indirect mentor and Verigin as student—placing the peasant Dukhobors in the traditional position of vessels for elite ideas and influence—Josh Sanborn has recently argued quite the opposite. Verigin was the consummate politician, Sanborn asserts, consciously manipulating Tolstoy by tailoring his new principles to attract the attention of the writer and his followers. The Dukhobor leader realized that the Large Party required publicity if their pacifist opposition was to succeed, which Tolstoy could—and did—provide. Moreover, while giving Verigin due credit, state officials and contemporary journalists also believed that whatever Verigin may have said, it was his lieutenants, especially Ivan Konkin, who brought about the sea change in the Dukhobor communities. Indeed, some argue that Konkin, when transporting Verigin's instructions back from exile, injected his own ideas into the Dukhobor community, using Verigin's name to give them legitimacy.[100]

Other sources indicate that the Dukhobor rank and file thought up and introduced this shift in spiritually sanctioned social practices without assistance from their leaders or any outsiders. The sense of having strayed from the true path of the Dukhobor faith since arriving in Transcaucasia had only increased during the travails following Kalmykova's death. "Our conscience began to speak to us," one Dukhobor declared.[101] Indeed, the animosity and conflict that had characterized the preceding years—both between the two parties and between tsarist officials and the Large Party—had infected the Dukhobors with a self-described "moral illness." The Large Party Dukhobors "gathered together and discussed that they lived in hatred . . . and they needed to return to a better life, and they were frightened of where their fear would lead them, and how much the hatred had hardened everyone."[102]

The origins of the New Dukhoborism can also be found in a confluence of other factors. Vasia Pozdniakov, a Dukhobor who eventually fell out with Verigin's leadership, indicates that millenarian expectations of the glories of the next world helped induce the Large Party Dukhobors to embark on their religious changes: "Verigin's intimates were telling the Dukhobors 'to pray to God with awe and expect at every moment the coming of Verigin, and a time when he will clear all the Dukhobors and

---

100. RGIA f. 1291, op. 50, d. 23, 1906, l. 20; and GARF f. 102, 3 d-vo, op. 1895, d. 1053, ch. 1, ll. 541, 598; Brock, "Vasya Pozdnyakov's," 167; Josh Sanborn, "Pacifist Politics and Peasant Politics: Tolstoy and the Doukhobors, 1895–99," *CES* 27, no. 3 (1995): 52–71; Biriukov, *Dukhobortsy*, 35; idem, *Dukhoborets Petr Vasil'evich* Verigin (Geneva, 1903); Chertkov and Chertkova, *Dukhobortsy*, 45; Woodcock and Avakumovic, *Doukhobors*, 84–97; and "Sel. Slavianka," (September 21, 1894): 3.
101. ORRGB f. 369, k. 42, d. 2, 1950, l. 38; GMIR f. 2, op. 7, d. 483, n.d., l. 13; and Biriukov, *Dukhobortsy*, 34.
102. Bonch-Bruevich, *Rasskaz*, 12–13; and "Otryvok," 153–54.

separate the believers from the unbelievers; and grant to the believers an everlasting joy and condemn the unbelievers to destruction.'"[103] For their part, state officials understood the New Dukhoborism as a further stage in the ongoing battle between the Large Party and the Small Party: the new religious teachings were a conscious effort to open up further spiritual differences between the two parties, "with the goal to distinguish them from the opposing side" and "uncouple the hostile parties."[104] Finally, part and parcel of the decision to embrace the new teachings was the burgeoning confrontation with Russian state power. For some Dukhobors, the shift in religious beliefs and practices represented not only a movement toward spiritual truth and purity, but also a means "to prepare for conflict with the government."[105] Some state officials saw the New Dukhoborism as a conscious effort to antagonize the tsarist administration and provoke a conflict: "The Dukhobors knew in advance that their actions, without fail, would bring on them cruel oppression," through which crucible they would be spiritually purified to enter a golden future of God's glory.[106]

Whatever the causes of the new religiosity and whoever originated and spread the ideas, it is worth noting that this sort of religious revival was not unique to the Dukhobors in late Imperial Russia, but formed part of a much broader religious awakening among a spectrum of unconnected spiritual communities involving many of the same beliefs and practices that the Veriginites espoused. The link between spiritual purity and true Christianity, on the one hand, and celibacy, teetotalism, forswearing of tobacco, vegetarianism, communalism, serving the poor, and nonviolence, on the other, appeared (in differing combinations and formulations) in such disparate late-Imperial religious movements as Mari Orthodox monasticism, various "Orthodox heresies," Father John of Kronstadt and his followers, Baptists, Skoptsy, and Old Believers, to name but the merest handful. Of course, many of these ideas had long lineages in Eastern Christianity, and Verigin was reflecting these traditions in the New Dukhoborism.[107]

103. Brock, "Vasya Pozdnyakov's," 166.

104. RGIA f. 1291, op. 50, d. 23, 1906, ll. 20–210b.

105. GMIR f. 17, op. 1, d. 628, n.d., l. 2.

106. "Otryvok," 158.

107. J. Eugene Clay, "Orthodox Missionaries and 'Orthodox Heretics' in Russia, 1886–1917," in *Of Religion and Empire: Missions, Conversion, and Tolerance in Tsarist Russia*, ed. Robert P. Geraci and Michael Khodarkovsky (Ithaca, 2001), 38–69; Nadieszda Kizenko, *A Prodigal Saint: Father John of Kronstadt and the Russian People* (University Park, 2000); Laura Engelstein, *Castration and the Heavenly Kingdom: A Russian Folktale* (Ithaca, 1999); Heather Coleman, "The Most Dangerous Sect: Baptists in Tsarist and Soviet Russia, 1905–1929" (Ph.D. diss., University of Illinois Urbana–Champaign, 1998); Paul W. Werth, *At the Margins of Orthodoxy: Mission, Governance, and Confessional Politics in Russia's Volga-Kama Region, 1827–1905* (Ithaca, 2002); Ronald D. Leblanc, "Vegetarianism in Russia: the Tolstoy(an) Legacy," *The Carl Beck Papers*, no. 1507 (May 2001); Roy Robson, *Old*

The call to heed these new teachings and tenets had a profound impact on the Dukhobors' social practices, cultural beliefs, and everyday life. Hearing their leader's recommendations, Veriginites gathered together in heated meetings to discuss the foundations of their faith and the ways in which they should translate Verigin's demands into everyday action and behavior.[108] As one observer noted, 1894 was "the most intense year in their intellectual lives," a year during which they hashed out questions of morality, socio-economic practice, and relations with temporal power. By early 1895, many had embraced the New Dukhoborism, while others had split from their brethren, unable to accept the new religious convictions and social practices.[109]

One result was a second schism within the Dukhobor community, this time splitting the Large Party into two relatively equal parts. Those who transformed their religious practices, came to be known as the Fasters (*postniki*) (or the "Third" or "White" Party). The remaining group was known as the "Butchers" (*miasniki*) or the Middle Party, because they occupied the middle ground religiously and politically between the Small Party and the Fasters.[110] The Middle Party continued to revere Verigin as its leader and to demand the return of the Orphan Home to their community's control, but was "unwilling to take the radical steps of the Fasters."[111] They would not become vegetarians, were uncomfortable with the idea of relinquishing their material possessions, and voiced a greater willingness to submit to the demands of the administration, realizing "their position of relative weakness" compared to the government— although they still opposed military service and state schooling. In response to the Fasters' increasingly radical religiosity, the Middle Party's chief, A. F. Vorob'ev, appealed to the governor neither to confuse the two factions nor to hold the Middle Party responsible for the actions of the Fasters, whom he considered dangerously radical and on a collision course with the government.[112]

The effects of the New Dukhoborism varied geographically from one Dukhobor community to another.[113] In the villages of Bashkichet, Ka-

---

Believers in Modern Russia (DeKalb, 1995); Robert O. Crummey, *The Old Believers and the World of Antichrist: The Vyg Community and the Russian State, 1694–1855* (Madison, 1970); Irina Paert, *Old Believers, Religious Dissent and Gender in Russia, 1760–1850* (Manchester, 2003); and Eve Levin, *Sex and Society in the World of the Orthodox Slavs, 900–1700* (Ithaca, 1989).
108. RGIA f. 1291, op. 50, d. 23, 1906, ll. 20, 210b; and Tebenkov, "Dukhobortsy," no. 9, 497.
109. "Otryvok," 158.
110. ORRGB f. 369, k. 42, d. 2, 1950, l. 38.
111. GARF f. 102, 3 d-vo, op. 1895, d. 1053, ch. 1, ll. 1170b–18.
112. Ibid., ll. 1770b–78, 5510b–53, 5670b; Tebenkov, "Dukhobortsy," no. 9, 497–98; Brock, "Vasya Pozdnyakov's," 167; and RGIA f. 1291, op. 50, d. 23, 1906, l. 230b.
113. Bonch-Bruevich, *Rasskaz*, 12; RGIA f. 1291, op. 50, d. 23, 1906, ll. 20–200b; and ORRGB f. 369, k. 42, d. 2, 1950, l. 37.

raklis, and Ormashen, for example, the majority of Dukhobors found the new religious requirements too difficult to maintain, despite their many efforts. Initially, outward changes were visible among them: many stopped smoking, drinking, and paying a bride price, among other commandments. However, after a few months, "tension" could be felt in the villages: "They wanted to smoke a little, drink every now and again, but felt awkward in front of each other." Finding it necessary to conceal such activities, "the atmosphere became all the more unbearable," and, little by little, they returned to their former ways.[114]

Elsewhere, the new religiosity found more fertile soil and Dukhobors came to embrace vegetarianism, abstain from alcohol, reduce sexual activity, produce no children, scorn material possessions, and move toward communalism, both in production and distribution. In terms of the latter process, "those who were rich began to feel their inequality as a burden and they began to help the poor." Fasters gave money away, forgave debts, paid off the debts of those brethren who owed others, and collected funds for a new Orphan Home, which again amounted to several hundred thousand, if not over a million, rubles.[115] They also began to labor in the fields and in their workshops as a unit, with all produce apportioned equally.[116]

However, "even this did not unburden their consciences, and they decided to divide their property equally, beginning in the summer of 1894."[117] Fasters began to see "the division of property" as an "evil" which contradicted the commandments to love your neighbor as yourself and to do unto others what you would have others do unto you. Both rich and poor brought their money, livestock, and other material possessions to one place and handed it over to community elders, emptying their deposits from the Akhalkalaki treasury bank in the process.[118] V. I. Popov gave away 43,340 rubles of what he called "accursed money," and was exhilarated by his newfound feelings of liberty. "When I brought it in a bag—silver, gold, paper bills—and when I flung it down on the table, I said, take it for the communal fund, give it where you want, and so I felt relieved: I felt freedom, exactly as if a rock of some sort was cast off from me. From then on I have lived a brotherly life, with everyone together, I toil with my own strength and joyfully I began to live in the light."[119] Not

114. "Otryvok," 156–57.
115. Quotation from Bonch-Bruevich, *Rasskaz*, 12–13. See also ORRGB f. 369, k. 42, d. 2, 1950, l. 452; RGIA f. 1291, op. 50, d. 23, 1906, ll. 21–210b; and "S. Slavianka," *Kaspii* 14, no. 45 (February 25, 1894): 3.
116. ORRGB f. 369, k. 42, d. 2, 1950, ll. 38c, 40; Bonch-Bruevich, *Rasskaz*, 13; and GARF f. 102, 3 d-vo, op. 1895, d. 1053, ch. 1, l. 554.
117. Bonch-Bruevich, *Rasskaz*, 12–13; ORRGB f. 369, k. 42, d. 2, 1950, l. 452; RGIA f. 1291, op. 50, d. 23, 1906, ll. 21–210b; and GARF f. 102, 3 d-vo, op. 1895, d. 1053, ch. 1, ll. 544–440b.
118. ORRGB f. 369, k. 42, d. 2, 1950, l. 38c; Bonch-Bruevich, *Rasskaz*, 13; Tebenkov, "Dukhobortsy," no. 9, 498; and GARF f. 102, 3 d-vo, op. 1895, d. 1053, ch. 1, ll. 5530b–54.
119. ORRGB f. 369, k. 42, d. 2, 1950, l. 39; and k. 43, d. 1, 1950, l. 585.

unexpectedly, there were some Dukhobors who, when confronted with the reality of giving up their wealth and possessions, refused to do so. They often argued that such actions would "indulge sloth," and a small number of Dukhobors demanded their money returned when they could not bear the loss.[120]

Despite these shifts, the Fasters were not fully satisfied. They felt that they continued to hold too much wealth as a community, especially in comparison to their non-Russian neighbors. Feeling that the riches threatened the future morality of their religious movement, they sold off or gave away vast amounts of property to their neighbors. "And we . . . all began to help them with money and clothes and we even gave livestock to the Armenians, Tatars, and others."[121] The Dukhobors Ozerov and Orekhov unloaded 2,000 rams, 10 milk cows, 10 pairs of bulls, and 20 horses; another personally gave away 20,000 rubles.[122] In Elisavetpol province, local officials witnessed the Dukhobors dispensing with their fine-fleeced merino sheep for as little as one to four rubles a pair.[123] Word spread quickly through the region that the Dukhobors were unloading their property. Their neighbors came with requests for money or property, and the Fasters "did not turn anyone down, and for this everyone praised God and was very thankful."[124]

The transformation of their social and economic structures had a profound impact on the Dukhobors' spiritual and material well-being. One Faster noted that "after all these decisions and actions, we began to live more happily and easily, and our moral illness . . . began to pass."[125] Another concurred: "When we all started to do this, then we felt ourselves to be completely different people, newly born into the light of God. We became so happy and merry in our souls."[126] That said, the Dukhobors' inversion of economic practices and social relations had substantial material ramifications for their communities. They brought hardship and relative poverty on themselves by terminating many of the activities that had made them so wealthy in preceding decades and giving away vast amounts of their material possessions.[127]

Equally important, the Fasters' religious revival directly affected the livelihood of those outside of their community. In some cases, their phil-

120. Bonch-Bruevich, *Rasskaz*, 13; RGIA f. 1291, op. 50, d. 23, 1906, l. 230b; and ORRGB f. 369, k. 42, d. 2, 1950, l. 38c.
121. Bonch-Bruevich, *Rasskaz*, 13–14.
122. GARF f. 102, 3 d-vo, op. 1895, d. 1053, ch. 1, ll. 544–440b.
123. RGIA f. 1291, op. 50, d. 23, 1906, l. 21; Tebenkov, "Dukhobortsy," no. 9, 498; and "Selo Slavianka," (June 1, 1894): 3.
124. ORRGB f. 369, k. 42, d. 2, 1950, l. 452.
125. Bonch-Bruevich, *Rasskaz*, 13.
126. ORRGB f. 369, k. 42, d. 2, 1950, l. 40. The dark-light imagery appears in many sources. See, for example, GARF f. 102, 3 d-vo, op. 1895, d. 1053, ch. 1, ll. 1800b–81.
127. ORRGB f. 369, k. 42, d. 2, 1950, l. 452; and GARF f. 102, 3 d-vo, op. 1895, d. 1053, ch. 1, l. 5400b.

anthropy enriched the neighboring Caucasian population. In others, the Dukhobors' activities hurt the natives' economic situation and the vibrancy of the region's economy more generally. The Fasters sowed only the amount of grain that they felt necessary for their community, thus reducing the quantities of produce available for purchase.[128] Having sold off or given away their merino sheep, the Dukhobors no longer provided wool to the market, and these sizable revenues disappeared. They ceased hiring neighboring Armenians and Azerbaijanis, in part because they no longer had anything for them to do in their new stripped-down economy and in part because they believed that using the labor of another human was improper.[129] Moreover, Fasters stopped their work as carters, disrupting the regional transportation network of which they were an important component. The director of the nearby Kedabek copper-smelting factory complained to the governor that they were depriving him of the transportation base that he needed to get his product to market.[130] Similarly, one Armenian from Akhalkalaki reported that the cessation of the Dukhobors' wagon transport resulted in a loss of 30,000 rubles in annual revenues.[131]

The Transcaucasian administration became desperately concerned by the Dukhobors' new religious teachings and saw their results as "extremely undesirable to state interests," both economically and politically. On one hand, the sudden arrival of the new teachings breathed life into the intracommunal ferment that state authorities had believed was relatively under control. Official reports—however inaccurate—indicated that the hostilities between the Small and Large Parties, while by no means gone, were declining in intensity in 1893 as the events of the late 1880s receded into the past. On the other hand, the tenets of the New Dukhoborism clearly enunciated a disinclination to obey the state. The authorities were particularly unnerved because they discerned among the Dukhobors the influence of Tolstoy's ideas and the strengthening of "communist tendencies and sectarian fanaticism" that linked these religious dissenters with the revolutionary movement that was plaguing Russian leaders in St. Petersburg.[132]

Moreover, the appearance of the new religious teachings "led to the breakdown of the material well-being of whole groups of the population, who until this time had been significantly superior to their neighbors

128. GARF f. 102, 3 d-vo, op. 1895, d. 1053, ch. 1, l. 598.
129. ORRGB f. 369, k. 42, d. 2, 1950, l. 38c.
130. RGIA f. 1291, op. 50, d. 23, 1906, l. 21; GARF f. 102, 3 d-vo, op. 1895, d. 1053, ch. 1, l. 598; and ORRGB f. 369, k. 42, d. 2, 1950, l. 38c.
131. CRCR 1895–09–20a, ll. 80–800b.
132. RGIA f. 1291, op. 50, d. 23, 1906, ll. 22, 24.

(both indigenous and sectarian) in the level of their economic well-being."[133] Tsarist officials were consequently worried that the changes in Dukhobor activities would have an adverse long-term effect on the region's economy, and that they were about to be saddled with caring for whole villages of destitute Dukhobors.[134] The fact that the Fasters' activities were involving the non-Russian peoples as well, by giving away property and forgiving debts, meant that the Dukhobors' threat might expand beyond their own communities to the indigenous population.

The concern of state officials was by no means unwarranted. From autumn 1894 and into the opening months of 1895, the antagonism and disrespect of the Fasters toward the tsarist state became ever more extreme. The burgeoning antistatism of the late 1880s and early 1890s turned into a religiously based "open defiance of government power and refusal of state service." They destroyed portraits of the tsar, refused to perform the orders of administrative personnel, and acted "insolently" toward tsarist officials.[135] Specifically, the Fasters refused to swear the required oath of allegiance to the new tsar Nicholas II, following the lead of the exiled Verigin, who asserted: "I am a Dukhobor, our Tsar is Christ and we are citizens of the whole world."[136] They withheld taxes and denied the state's right to tithe them, arguing that "the land belongs to God."[137] Additionally, in stark contrast to preceding decades, the Fasters no longer provided administrative support to state officials (such as wagons and horses for traveling officials) and refused to maintain the regime's roads.[138] In October 1894, the chief administrator for the Caucasus region noted that inhabitants of the village of Slavianka "were spreading among the local Dukhobors false teachings and social-communist ideas and actively carrying out antistate agitation, openly inciting the people to nonfulfillment of state orders and evasion of fulfilling transportation, road, and even military duties."[139]

Moreover, Fasters turned down all positions of state authority (such as *starshina*) that they had previously held willingly. For example, in March 1895, the Spasskoe rural community chose Andrei Popov, a resident of

133. Ibid., l. 22.
134. GARF f. 102, 3 d-vo, op. 1895, d. 1053, ch. 1, l. 5400b.
135. Ibid., ll. 185, 1860b–87.
136. GMIR f. 2, op. 7, d. 489, 1929; f. 17, op. 1, d. 628, n.d., l. 2; RGIA f. 1291, op. 50, d. 23, 1906, l. 2400b; and Woodcock and Avakumovic, *Doukhobors*, 93–94.
137. ORRGB f. 369, k. 42, d. 2, 1950, l. 41; and GARF f. 102, 3 d-vo, op. 1895, d. 1053, ch. 1, l. 185. Peoples of the Steppe voiced similar arguments in their struggles with Russian power. See Michael Khodarkovsky, *Russia's Steppe Frontier: The Making of a Colonial Empire, 1500–1800* (Bloomington, 2002), 175.
138. RGIA f. 1291, op. 50, d. 23, 1906, ll. 24–2400b; CRCR 1895–09–20a, l. 7900b; Biriukov, *Dukhobortsy*, 39–40; Kuropatkin, *Soobrazheniia*, 13.
139. RGIA f. 1291, op. 50, d. 23, 1906, ll. 23, 24–2400b.

Orlovka, to be the *starshina*. However, Popov refused to take on this official position and its obligations, calling such work a "roguish affair." Instead, he declared his willingness to "serve only God and not the Sovereign because 'the Sovereign is unrighteous and all affairs are resolved unjustly.'" He asserted that he did not wish "to do violence to anyone and . . . to give orders to my brothers," feeling that his time would be better spent working for his keep rather than passing "time idly" in administrative work.[140]

The Large Party Dukhobors also refused thenceforth to carry out the state obligation of helping to capture, guard, or transport criminals and prisoners.[141] In one incident of May 1895, when the Fasters were ordered to help officials apprehend thieves and protect the roads from robbers, many refused outright while those who went on the posse did so without any weapons (except for whips).[142] Those Dukhobors who refused this state service did so for two reasons. They attempted not to commit violence of any sort. As the elder V. I. Popov declared, "We hastily will fulfill everything that is not against God's law. But that (that is catch the robber) we cannot do . . . because we cannot kill a person, as it is said in the law of God."[143] They also argued that, as unarmed pacifists, they were not willing to allow themselves to be killed when the task was not for "truth." Popov told the *starshina*, "The thief is not a turkey; they are all armed and we cannot carry weapons in our hands because we consider it to be a sin, and we cannot kill people."[144]

Frustrated and afraid of potential ramifications, the tsarist state—in the form of the Georgian governors of Tiflis and Elisavetpol provinces, Shervashidze and Nakashidze—replied to the refusals of service and the possibility of economic collapse as they had done before: with beatings, imprisonment, and exile.[145] In doing so, the Georgians' actions underscore the significant role played by South Caucasians in response to the Dukhobors' challenge to Russian state power. Lieutenant-General Nakashidze petitioned to have Verigin moved to an even more distant part of the Empire where he would not be able to remain in contact with his followers. He also called for the exile of other Dukhobor leaders like Ivan

140. ORRGB f. 369, k. 42, d. 2, 1950, l. 40; Bonch-Bruevich, *Rasskaz*, 14–15; RGIA f. 1291, op. 50, d. 23, 1906, l. 240b; Biriukov, *Dukhobortsy*, 39; and Chertkov and Chertkova, *Dukhobortsy*, 9.

141. GARF f. 102, 3 d-vo, op. 1895, d. 1053, ch. 1, l. 185; Bonch-Bruevich, *Rasskaz*, 14; Chertkov and Chertkova, *Dukhobortsy*, 8; and CRCR 1895–09–20a, ll. 790b–80.

142. ORRGB f. 369, k. 42, d. 2, 1950, ll. 494–97; Chertkov and Chertkova, *Dukhobortsy*, 9; and CRCR 1895–09–20a, l. 790b.

143. ORRGB f. 369, k. 42, d. 2, 1950, l. 41.

144. Ibid., ll. 494–96, quotation on 496; Biriukov, *Dukhobortsy*, 39; and Kuropatkin, *Soobrazheniia*, 13.

145. RGIA f. 1291, op. 50, d. 23, 1906, l. 23; Chertkov and Chertkova, *Dukhobortsy*, 9; and ORRGB f. 369, k. 42, d. 2, 1950, l. 41.

Konkin, who had been instrumental in bringing the new teachings to the Dukhobors. As a result, in August of 1894, Verigin was relocated to Obdorsk in Tobol'sk province with an extension of his sentence, and Konkin was sent for five years to Archangel province.[146]

The refusal of the Dukhobors to help with criminals elicited a more extreme reaction from Shervashidze. Dukhobor memoirs relate that the governor became extremely aggravated at their "refusal to serve the Russian tsar" and ordered them beaten severely: "'You sons of bitches,' he threatened, 'I will put you in shackles.'" V. I. Popov replied that they would serve God alone because the "earthly tsar only bribes." Worse yet, in an effort to force Popov's hand and punish him for his recalcitrance, Shervashidze sent two squadrons of Cossacks to Popov's village where, having threatened Popov with this possibility, they took Popov's son into custody and beat him, and then took property and money from Popov's house.[147]

ON THE PRECIPICE

> We served like children serving their parents because we expected protection from the sovereign and from the government, and we thought that the law of the sovereign approached the law of God. At this time, instead of protection, we have received from the Russian government our contemporary ruin, because they made us into criminals for the truth, took away our property and chased us out of our own homes.
>
> *Anonymous Dukhobor, in Bonch-Bruevich,* Raz"iasnenie, *21.*

After decades of mutually supportive interaction and an acceptable modus vivendi, the relationship between the Dukhobors and tsarist authority in the South Caucasus began its sharp deterioration almost immediately after the death of Kalmykova. The internecine power struggle destroyed the peaceful cohesiveness that had long defined the Dukhobor community, with each party savagely certain of the righteousness of its cause. At each moment of contact between tsarist officials and the Veriginites, the subjects increasingly lost faith in the state, finding it to be arbitrary, corrupt, morally bankrupt, violent, and unnecessarily invasive in their communal lives. In parallel fashion, Dukhobor unrest sapped tsarist officials of any sympathy they might once have had. From 1887 to 1895, authorities ratcheted up their measures against the Dukhobors, and official patience with the Dukhobor machinations was wearing ever thin-

146. RGIA f. 1291, op. 50, d. 23, 1906, ll. 210b–220b.
147. ORRGB f. 369, k. 42, d. 2, 1950, ll. 41–43, 494–503.

ner. A spiraling change in the relations between state and Dukhobors developed: with each state intrusion, the Dukhobors became more antigovernment in their religiosity, and with each opposition to the implementation of tsarist policy, state officials became increasingly anti-Dukhobor.[148] Both sides stood on the precipice of a tragic conflagration.

The radical religious awakening of the Dukhobors in the years leading up to the burning of weapons represents an example of the possibilities and transformations of life on the imperial periphery. After their resettlement, the interactions of Dukhobor colonists with tsarist officials, the peoples of Transcaucasia, and the region's environment helped to bring about the changes in social and religious practice that Large Party Dukhobors came to see as moral failures in need of renovation. At the same time, the Dukhobor story underscores the vibrancy and diversity of Russian religiosity in the late nineteenth century, and the tendency of "sectarian" communities (including Molokans, Subbotniks, as well as Dukhobors) to splinter over time into subsects in their search for religious truth.

The communal schism and breakdown of state-Dukhobor relations highlight the ways in which local, relatively peripheral processes (such as the leadership struggle and religious reformation movement of a sectarian community) intersected with Empire-wide transformations (administrative standardization and cultural Russification, for example) to produce historical outcomes of profound and enduring resonance. In particular, the Dukhobors' experience demonstrates the importance of local authority figures. Whatever policy intent the central authorities may have had with the marriage registers or the grain reserves, for example, local authorities determined the actual outcomes of these laws. The corruption and brutality of a small number of these local officials—especially D'iachkov-Tarasov—dramatically changed the course of events, pushing the Dukhobors into an ever more uncompromising stance.

The origins of the Dukhobor opposition movement also illustrate the often unconquerable hurdles that the modernizing tsarist state confronted in its multi-ethnic, multicultural empire—problems that ultimately destabilized the polity.[149] In part, the intent of administrative reform efforts after midcentury was the application of standardized laws to the multiplicities of peoples and regions of the Empire, and the breaking down of particularistic barriers and divisions. Given the attendant en-

---

148. ORRGB f. 369, k. 42, d. 1, 1950, ll. 59–69; d. 2, 1950, ll. 18–38, 446–52; k. 44, d. 1, 1950, ll. 161–271; GARF f. 102, 3 d-vo, op. 1895, d. 1053, ch. 1, passim; and GMIR f. 14, op. 2, d. 3, 1898.

149. Theodore Weeks also notes this tendency of multi-ethnicity to disrupt modernization and administrative rationalization in the western borderlands. Weeks, *Nation*, esp. 131–92.

croachment of state power into the lives of its subjects, however, the very people these changes were supposed to help were themselves often uninterested or even opposed. Efforts at state-building in tsarist Russia tended to produce its opposite: state-unraveling. The Dukhobors were Russians and had for decades functioned as indispensable agents of tsarist imperialism. Yet their religious distinctiveness came to the foreground in the face of the homogenizing efforts of the late-imperial tsarist state, and they experienced their own version of the "Russification" process. In opposing these new governing structures, the Dukhobors were Russian colonists rebelling against the colonizing force of the metropole, which brought foreign and unwanted political and social structures into their midst. In this way, the patterns of Dukhobor resistance form part of a longer continuum of peasant and "frontier" opposition to state intrusions into the society and governance of traditionally more autonomous rural and borderland communities.[150] Of course, Russia was far from alone in this regard, as (among many examples) Breton resistance to French state policies at the turn of the century, or the North-West Rebellion in nineteenth-century Canada, suggest.[151]

150. Of many examples, see Marc Raeff, "Pugachev's Rebellion," in *Preconditions of Revolution in Early Modern Europe,* ed. Robert Forster and Jack Greene (Baltimore, 1970), 161–202; Khodarkovsky, *Russia's Steppe Frontier,* 172; Paul Avrich, *Russian Rebels, 1600–1800* (New York, 1972); Viola, *Peasant Rebels.*

151. Ford, *Creating the Nation;* and Thomas Flanagan, *Riel and the Rebellion: 1885 Reconsidered,* 2nd ed. (Toronto, 2000).

7

PEASANT PACIFISM AND
IMPERIAL INSECURITIES

The Burning of Weapons, 1895–1899

The centerpiece of the New Dukhoborism—and the most aggravating for tsarist authorities—was the Fasters' embrace of strict nonviolence, which in 1895 culminated in their refusal of military service and public burning of weapons. With these defiant measures, the conflict between tsarist authority and the Large Party Dukhobors came to a head. For the Dukhobors, it was the zenith of their religious transformation and their rejection of tsarist power—and it remains so to this day. For both doctrinal and utilitarian reasons, the oppositional Dukhobors turned primarily to nonviolent civil disobedience as their "weapon" against state power. Tsarist officials responded initially to their pacifism with violence and banishment, which ultimately led to extensive human suffering, the permanent dismemberment of their communities, and the emigration of more than seven thousand Dukhobors from the South Caucasus at the end of the nineteenth century.

The Dukhobors' explosion of religious pacifism and the state's forceful response throws into bold relief questions of militarization, empire-building, identity, and religious structures in late Imperial Russia. In particular, the Dukhobors' nonviolent opposition movement reflects the very complex—and tenuous—place of pacifists in Russia's modernizing polity and the fate of those who would stand against the agendas of expanding state power. In the post-reform period, both civilian and especially military authorities linked citizenship, loyalty, and membership in the national community with the universal male requirement to accede to military conscription and participate in state-sponsored violence. In this context, the Dukhobors' antimilitary stance posed a threat to the burgeoning national polity that Russian military authorities were seeking to construct.[1] The Fasters' intersections with other pacifist groups in Russian society—such as Molokans and Tolstoy and his followers, to name but a few—only heightened the perceived menace and urgency.[2]

Indeed, tsarist officials were faced with the increasingly difficult problem of deciding what to do with these pacifist opponents of the Russian state. In the wake of the weapons bonfire, they lamented the loss of their model colonists and wondered how to restore the status quo ante. The Dukhobors' pacifist civil disobedience proved a difficult obstacle for tsarist authority. While the state routinely turned to force to put down other peasant and worker uprisings over the course of the nineteenth century, Russian officials found that such applications of violence to resolve the Dukhobor problem did not have the intended effect of bending the population into submission. As other government authorities in such faraway places as British India and the American South would soon discover, responding to nonviolence with violence often failed to produce the desired result, and might instead reveal the naked power of state authority in all of its brutality and bankruptcy.

In addition, the Dukhobor pacifist movement introduced significant changes in the state categorization of the Dukhobors, as well as their own self-understanding. If the decades after migration witnessed a change in Dukhobor identification wherein "ethnic Russian," "loyal subject," and "model colonist" labels joined preexisting religious characterizations, the 1890s witnessed a further shift in these identifications. Dukhobors increasingly saw themselves in religious terms, as a Christian community who stood outside the realm of temporal power and who shared bonds of humanity with all people regardless of ethnicity or nationality. Meanwhile, state officials began to see the Dukhobors, or at least the Fasters, as political threats, as they had in the first third of the nineteenth century. However, unlike the preceding decades, the Dukhobors still remained ethnically "Russian" in official views, despite their religious nonconformity and opposition to state power.

REFUSING MILITARY SERVICE

The Large Party's pacifist ideology flowed from Verigin's religious teachings and was considered a return to a past golden age of nonviolence. As one Dukhobor described the process, "We began to think and talk things

1. Joshua A. Sanborn, *Drafting the Russian Nation: Military Conscription, Total War, and Mass Politics, 1905–1925* (DeKalb, 2003), esp. chapter 5.
2. On Tolstoy and pacifism, see Peter Brock, *Freedom from War: Nonsectarian Pacifism, 1814–1914* (Toronto, 1991), 185–220. I discuss contemporaneous Molokan pacifism in the final chapter.

over and we saw that we had not yet parted with evil. We owned weapons. A thief would come and I would kill him, and that is a sin. Love the Lord; love those close to you. And we decided to burn our weapons, not to serve in the military or any other government service that would demand violence on those close to us. The sword of God should be our weapon."[3] Their pacifism also derived from their increasing distrust of state power and their belief that legitimate authority came only from God: "We wish to fulfill the will of the emperor," one Dukhobor explained, "but he teaches people to kill and my soul does not want that . . . because the Savior commands (that is, forbids) people to kill, and I believe in the Savior, I am fulfilling the will of God."[4] Thus, if the tsarist state linked violence with political belonging, the Dukhobors were trying to sever that link, rejecting a polity that required violence of them.

The first act of their pacifist drama was the refusal of military service. From 1887 to 1895, Dukhobors had reluctantly sent their sons into the army despite their long-standing belief that war and military service were sins.[5] As the newly conscripted young men left for their assignments, Dukhobor elders told them, "When it comes time to fight, do not shoot at people."[6] Covert "everyday resistance" soon changed into overt opposition, however. In a series of defiant acts involving many hundreds of young Dukhobors stretching from 1895 to 1898, those already in military service handed over their weapons to their commanders (or simply threw them away) and refused to obey orders, declaring that they would no longer kill or fight.[7] Those Dukhobors not on active duty (reserves, militia, or in line for the draft) returned their military papers to Russian officials in a series of tense incidents.[8]

3. ORRGB f. 369, k. 42, d. 2, 1950, l. 40.

4. V. G. Chertkov and A. K. Chertkova, *Dukhobortsy v distsiplinarnom batal'one*, vol. 4 of *MIIRS* (Christchurch, UK, 1902), 8.

5. GMIR f. 2, op. 7, d. 489, 1928, l. 3; and Nicholas B. Breyfogle, "Swords into Plowshares: Opposition to Military Service Among Religious Sectarians, 1770s to 1874," in *The Military and Society in Russia, 1450–1917*, ed. Eric Lohr and Marshall Poe (Leiden, 2002), 441–67.

6. ORRGB f. 369, k. 42, d. 2, 1950, l. 18.

7. Chertkov and Chertkova, *Dukhobortsy*, 5–8, 44–50; RGIA f. 1291, op. 50, d. 23, 1906, ll. 240b–25; Joshua A. Sanborn, "Non-Violent Protest and the Russian State: the Doukhobors in 1895 and 1937," in *The Doukhobor Centenary in Canada: A Multi-Disciplinary Perspective on their Unity and Diversity*, ed. Andrew Donskov, John Woodsworth, and Chad Gaffield (Ottawa, 2000), 84–87; ORRGB f. 369, k. 42, d. 2, 1950, ll. 40–41; and Vladimir Tchertkoff [Chertkov], *Christian Martyrdom in Russia: Persecution of the Spirit-Wrestlers (or Doukhobors) in the Caucasus* (London, 1897), 65–69. Easter 1895 is generally taken as the date for the beginning of the refusal of service, although there are indications that it began in 1894 in small measure. See George Woodcock and Ivan Avakumovic, *The Doukhobors* (Toronto, 1968), 109.

8. "Otryvok iz vospominanii N. I. Dudchenko," in *Pis'ma Dukhoborcheskogo rukovoditelia Petra Vasil'evicha Verigina*, vol. 1 of *MIIRS*, ed. V. D. Bonch-Bruevich (Christchurch, UK, 1901), 155; V. D. Bonch-Bruevich, ed., *Rasskaz dukhobortsa Vasi Pozdniakova*, vol. 3 of *MIIRS* (Christchurch, UK, 1901), 15; Chertkov and Chertkova, *Dukhobortsy*, 7; and GMIR f. 2, op. 7, d. 489, 1928, l. 5.

Each refusal of service was accompanied by a forceful declaration linking their refusal of violence with a denial of state authority. Matvei Lebedev, the first Dukhobor conscript to manifest his pacifism, asserted: "I do not wish to serve the Sovereign; I will serve only the one God. I want to obey the Sovereign [but] if the law demands things that are against my religious beliefs, then I cannot fulfill the demand of that law. Thus, for example, I cannot kill anyone, either in wartime or peacetime, even if they were to shoot at me. For my faith I am prepared to endure any physical torment."[9] In another incident, forty-four reserve and militia soldiers gathered together in the street; according to official sources, they threw their military documents to the ground, "explaining that they exclusively serve the Heavenly King and fulfill only His will, and do not wish to serve and obey the Sovereign Emperor because he is a killer and teaches the killing of people."[10]

Tsarist authorities were angered by these actions and concerned that the Dukhobors' defiant pacifism would spread to Russian Orthodox soldiers and peasants in the central provinces, other sectarian communities (particularly the Molokans), or the many indigenous peoples in the South Caucasus who were already manifesting national independence movements and a restiveness in response to Russia's imperial presence.[11] Officials were particularly worried about real and perceived contacts with Tolstoyans, socialists, and other oppositional intellectuals.[12] Rumors spread like wildfire that many Caucasians were following the Dukhobors' example, heightening official fears of a region-wide disruption of military activities. Moreover, Dukhobors in strategic areas such as Kars territory on the Turkish border were opposing service and thereby putting the very boundaries of the Empire at risk.[13]

The army initially responded with admonitions, arrests, threats, and physical punishment. In one fairly typical case, tsarist officers flogged recalcitrant soldiers "with thorny rods" so mercilessly that the thorns lodged themselves deep in the ruptured flesh of their backs: "The blood splattered in all directions; the prickles entered into the flesh, and when they were pulled out, bits of flesh fell down."[14] Beaten to within an inch

9. Chertkov and Chertkova, *Dukhobortsy*, 44–45.
10. RGIA f. 1291, op. 50, d. 23, 1906, ll. 25–250b.
11. Chertkov and Chertkova, *Dukhobortsy*, 9 and 53; A. K. Borozdin, *Russkoe religioznoe raznomyslie* (St. Petersburg, 1907), 203–4; and A. N. Kuropatkin, *Soobrazheniia nachal'nika Zakaspiiskoi oblasti po voprosu o pereselenii v Zakaspiiskuiu oblast' dukhoborov-postnikov* (n.p., n.d.), 13.
12. GARF f. 102, 3 d-vo, op. 1895, d. 1053, ch. 1, ll. 513–130b, 518; and John Woodsworth, ed. and trans., *Russian Roots and Canadian Wings: Russian Archival Documents on the Doukhobor Emigration to Canada* (Manotick, Ont., 1999), 102.
13. P. I. Biriukov, *Dukhobortsy: Sbornik statei, vospominanii, pisem, i drugikh dokumentov* (Moscow, 1908), 37–38; and Sanborn, "Non-Violent Protest."
14. Tchertkoff, *Christian Martyrdom*, 52.

of their lives, they were thrown into cold, dark cells and left to suffer in hunger, only to have the process repeated. Others were beaten to death. When these harsh measures failed, as they regularly did, the tsarist military tried the survivors in courts-martial and dispatched them to the Ekaterinograd disciplinary battalion as punishment, where the physical and mental torture continued.[15]

THE BURNING OF WEAPONS AND AFTER

As Large Party soldiers and conscripts made their stand against military service, the remainder of the Dukhobor community also demonstrated their commitment to nonviolence. In three of the four centers of Dukhobor habitation in the South Caucasus—Akhalkalaki and Elisavetpol districts, and Kars territory—the Fasters simultaneously brought together all the personal weapons in their possession to be ignited in a huge bonfire that would purge violence from their communities. The burning of weapons was a symbolic, purifying, and legendary act for the Dukhobors and a watershed in the relations between the Dukhobors and the state. Having lost all patience with the Dukhobor community because of the discontent of the preceding years, certain local authorities took advantage of the arms burning to unleash savagery on the Dukhobors. The brutality of regional officialdom unnerved government leaders in St. Petersburg, ultimately provoking a crisis of conscience.

The communal decision to reduce their weapons to ashes evolved seamlessly out of the New Dukhoborism, with its opposition to violence.[16] However, the burning of weapons was not simply a purging of "evil" and an act of truth for God. It was also calculated to have a wider impact beyond the confines of their communities. On one hand, it was designed as a kind of public relations event intended to publicize their nonviolent faith. Dukhobor sources make clear that it was important for them actually to destroy their weapons because, "if we were simply to throw them away somewhere, this event would not be visible to everyone." Indeed, "we decided to burn the weapons so that it would be well known not only

---

15. About three hundred Dukhobors who refused their reserve military positions, and another thirty who were already in active service, were incarcerated in disciplinary (or penal) battalions. Chertkov and Chertkov, *Dukhoborlsy;* CRCR 1896-02-27g, ll. 370-710b; P. I. Biriukov and Vladimir Chertkov, *Polozhenie dukhoborov na Kavkaze v 1896 godu i neobkhodimyia sredstva oblegcheniia ikh uchasti* (London, 1897), 9; Peter Brock, ed., "Vasya Pozdnyakov's Doukhobor Narrative," *SEER* 43, no. 100 (1964-65): 168-69; Tchertkoff, *Christian Martyrdom,* 50-56; Biriukov, *Dukhobortsy,* 35-40. On the penal battalions in general, see Peter Brock and John L. H. Keep, *Life in a Penal Battalion of the Imperial Russian Army: The Tolstoyan N. T. Iziumchenko's Story* (York, UK, 2001).
16. GMIR f. 2, op. 7, d. 509, n.d., l. 1; ORRGB f. 369, k. 42, d. 2. 1950, ll. 40-41; and Biriukov, *Dukhobortsy,* 42.

in our region but also in all Russia and even Europe."[17] On the other hand, it was also clear to many Dukhobors that such an activity, no matter how innocuous or peaceable in their own minds, would likely provoke some reaction on the part of the authorities. Great sacrifices would be necessary from "brave people," they argued, "but the bonfire must be lit." For some Dukhobors, they hoped that a major conflict with the state would act as a final, apocalyptic confrontation between Good and Evil that would propel the faithful to the golden future of God's world that Verigin promised.[18]

With slight regional variations, the actual burning of weapons was carried out similarly at the three different sites across the South Caucasus.[19] That said, the outcomes of the pacifist demonstration varied dramatically according to the personal inclinations of local officials. For example, tsarist agents left the Kars Dukhobors more or less alone to carry out their project, and "the burning of weapons took place without the slightest conflict with them." Local authorities meted out relatively minimal retribution, arresting approximately 185 Dukhobors they considered to be the ringleaders or who had refused military service. In fact, one source reports that the Kars Dukhobors were so disappointed in the restrained state reaction that they did what they could to exacerbate the situation, but the local official, an Azerbaijani, would not respond to their efforts to manufacture an incident.[20]

The Dukhobors in Elisavetpol province met greater intervention and more extensive punishment. The tsarist police consciously waited for the Dukhobors to finish their prayers before intervening so as not to disturb a religious event. Following the burning of weapons, the police and armed military contingents began to round up those Dukhobor elders considered responsible. Aiding in this process were the Small Party Dukhobors, who collected evidence of wrongdoing and spread rumors about the Fasters' activities. When the police demanded to know why they had burned their weapons and were returning their military documents, the Dukhobors replied that as "Christians . . . we cannot be killers of our brothers according to the commandments of God. We cannot serve two sovereigns, that is the Lord God and you." Police officers ordered beat-

17. N. S. Zibarov, *O sozhzhenii oruzhiia dukhoborami* (Purleigh, UK, 1899), 4; and Joshua Sanborn "Pacifist Politics and Peasant Politics: Tolstoy and the Doukhobors, 1895–99," *CES* 27, no. 3 (1995): 52–71.

18. GMIR f. 2, op. 7, d. 489, 1928, l. 5.

19. Zibarov, *O sozhzhenii*, 5–6; Biriukov and Chertkov, *Polozhenie*, 9; GMIR f. 2, op. 7, d. 489, 1928, ll. 5–6; d. 509, n.d., 1. 3; Woodsworth, *Russian Roots*, 55–58; CRCR 1895–11–29d, ll. 2200b–21; and 1895–09–20a, ll. 79–790b.

20. Biriukov and Chertkov, *Polozhenie*, 8–9; GMIR f. 2, op. 7, d. 489, 1928, ll. 5–6; d. 510, n.d., l. 1; Woodcock and Avakumovic, *Doukhobors*, 100; GARF f. 102, 3 d-vo, op. 1895, d. 1053, ch. 1, ll. 567–670b; and Biriukov, *Dukhoboртsy*, 41–42.

ings of the more recalcitrant offenders and imprisoned approximately one hundred Dukhobors, although they were quickly permitted to return to their home villages.[21]

In contrast, the Dukhobors of Akhalkalaki district not only faced extensive government interference in their efforts to burn the weapons but, tragically, felt the full punitive force of the savagery of local officials and military personnel. Watching Veriginite preparations, Small Party members began to worry about all the armaments and ammunition they saw being collected. Thinking that the Large Party was planning an attack on them and the Orphan Home—or possibly using this prospect as a pretext—they informed the authorities that an armed assault was imminent and they needed protection. As a result, while the Dukhobors were praying and burning their weapons on the first night, the night of the 28th, the local police ordered in tsarist troops—three companies of the 153rd Baku infantry regiment and two squadrons of the First Uman Cossack regiment. The soldiers and Cossacks came to "pacify the rebellious villages" and "both to prevent the impending disorders among the Dukhobors and to quell them once they in fact arise."[22]

Led by Esaul Praga, who played the role of villain in this drama, the Cossacks occupied the village of Bogdanovka. As Praga related in his official report, "There, by order of the police, the division spread itself out in the homes of the rebellious inhabitants and used violence in their activities. . . . Almost in every house it was necessary either to beat them or to threaten them with the lash [because the Dukhobors] scolded the officers . . . [and] impudently renounced tsarist power and the government."[23] At sunrise on the morning of the 30th, a government agent came to the praying Dukhobors ordering them to appear at nine o'clock the same morning in Bogdanovka, where the local police officer lived and to which the Tiflis governor was traveling. They replied that they were in the midst of a religious service and would not come until they had finished praying: "If the governor wants to see us, then let him come to us, there are thousands of us and he is only one person."[24] After another entreaty to have the Dukhobors report as ordered, Praga's Cossacks arrived on horseback, charging the crowd of Fasters to break up the prayers.[25]

An orgy of violence followed, as the Cossacks set off at full gallop with

21. ORRGB f. 369, k. 42, d. 2, 1950, ll. 447–50; GMIR f. 2, op. 7, d. 509, n.d., ll. 1–4; and Biriukov and Chertkov, *Polozhenie*, 9.
22. Woodsworth, *Russian Roots*, 56; and CRCR 1895-11-29d, ll. 319–28.
23. CRCR 1895-11-29d, ll. 2190b-21.
24. Biriukov, *Dukhobortsy*, 45.
25. CRCR 1895-11-29d; Woodsworth, *Russian Roots*, 69–72; Biriukov, *Dukhobortsy*, 45–47; and Zibarov, *O sozhzhenii*.

cries and whoops, slashing their way into the crowd with sabers and whips: "They beat us to such a point that it was impossible to tell who was whom since the faces were so abused and covered in blood, pieces of skin, and flesh hanging from faces. The ground darkened from all the blood."[26] To save each other, the Dukhobors took turns moving from the middle of the pack to the front and then back again. When the Cossacks tried to separate the men from the women, the latter would not move. They feared that such a separation would allow the Cossacks to kill or abuse the men, believing that they could use their subordinate gender position and perceived physical inferiority as a protective wall for the rest of the community. Nonetheless, the Cossacks turned their energies on the women, beating "the scarves off the women's heads." One woman, voicing the feelings of many of the beaten Dukhobors, told the Cossacks that they were not "defenders" but "thieves."

Finally, Praga and his Cossacks cowed the Dukhobors sufficiently to move them to Bogdanovka. On the way, the Dukhobors sang psalms and prayed, which Praga went to great lengths to stop.[27] Upon their arrival in the village, he tried to have the Dukhobors doff their hats as a sign of submission to Governor Prince G. D. Shervashidze, but they refused. In answer to Shervashidze's question, "Will you obey the government?" they replied, "If this is it, then we do not wish to."[28] A number of the young Dukhobor men approached the governor and threw their reserve and militia papers at his feet. The policemen that were with Shervashidze grabbed staves from Armenians standing nearby and began to beat these Dukhobors, and the Cossacks joined with whips. The governor is reputed to have ordered that "every Dukhobor without exception will bare his head and bow not only to state officials, but also to every single Cossack. . . . Above all, the impudent outburst against the government must be stopped."[29]

One police officer reported the results: "Many Dukhobors were severely beaten by the Cossacks, and some were severely injured when they were trampled under horses."[30] The sources set forth a terrible chronicle of physical abuse and suffering, some of which was rumor and exaggeration, but a great portion of which was verified in later investigations conducted by tsarist officials, members of educated society, and the Dukhobors themselves. Indeed, Cossack violence in this case formed part of a larger pattern of behavior in the South Caucasus in late Imperial Rus-

26. Zibarov, O sozhzhenii, 7–9, quotation on 8; and GMIR f. 2, op. 7, d. 489, 1928, l. 6.
27. Zibarov, O sozhzhenii; and CRCR 1895–11–29d, ll. 221ob–22ob.
28. Woodsworth, Russian Roots, 70.
29. Quoted in Sanborn, "Non-Violent Protest," 90.
30. Woodsworth, Russian Roots, 71; Zibarov, O sozhzhenii, 12–14; and CRCR 1895–11–29d.

sia, in which they unleashed shocking cruelty against various groups considered opponents of the regime and public order.[31]

Dukhobor memoirs relate that Shervashidze became so enraged that he ordered the reservists shot for their insubordination.[32] Lined up to be executed, the Dukhobors were reportedly only saved—in one version of events—by the intervention of a Muslim local administrator, Mustafa Bek Prince Skopinskii. "It is forbidden to shoot!" he cried. "There is no such law that permits the killing of people. There is the court and it cannot be done without the court." That they had been saved by a Muslim noble from the hands of a Georgian governor was not lost on the Dukhobors— the colonial-civilizational hierarchy had been inverted. Caucasian Muslims who had long been the bane of the Dukhobors' existence had now become their saviors, the protectors of legality and due process. The Russian state, which only a few years earlier the sectarians had seen as their benefactor and the bringer of order to the region, was now the purveyor of unwarranted violence and destruction.[33]

To make matters worse, the Cossacks immediately began an occupation of the Dukhobor villages that was to make earlier occupations seem tame by comparison. For five days the Cossacks rampaged through the Dukhobor villages with the intention of restoring tsarist control on the disloyal subjects.[34] Unlike the infantry squadron, which set up a systematic structure for receiving supplies, the Cossacks took food and property haphazardly and in far greater quantities than they needed—"*whatever they required and whatever they desired*," as one tsarist report decried.[35] The Cossacks also made their presence felt through savage beatings, to the point that the regular infantry soldiers were required to intervene to protect the Dukhobors.[36] While the regular soldiers received the respect of the Dukhobor population, the violent excesses of the Cossacks irreversibly transformed the state in the eyes of the Dukhobors, leaving them, in the words of Dukhobor Nikolai S. Zibarov, a participant in the Akhalkalaki arms burning, asking "Where is there a law in the Russian Empire that permits such an outrage."[37]

31. Gr. Startsev, "Letuchie otriady," *Strana*, no. 117 (1906): 2, clipped in GKP box 106; "Lenkoran," *Kaspii* 1, no. 32 (July 10, 1881): 3; and "Lenkoran," *Kaspii* 1, no. 45 (August 9, 1881): 3. See also a similar incident in Kazan province, described in Robert P. Geraci, *Window on the East: National and Imperial Identities in Late Tsarist Russia* (Ithaca, 2001), 38.
32. Elsewhere, Shervashidze claims in contrast that he intervened to stop the excesses of Praga and the Cossacks. Woodsworth, *Russian Roots*, 60–61.
33. GMIR f. 2, op. 7, d. 489, 1928, ll. 6–7. This story is one of a number of variants of the end of the stand-off between the Dukhobors and tsarist power. See also Woodcock and Avakumovic, *Doukhobors*, 102.
34. Woodsworth, *Russian Roots*, 62 and 71; and Zibarov, *O sozhzhenii*, 15.
35. Woodsworth, *Russian Roots*, 63. Italics in original.
36. Ibid., 58.
37. Zibarov, *O sozhzhenii*, 15.

In addition to the continued beatings and acts of theft, female Dukhobors also endured sexual assault and gang rape by the Cossacks.[38] There is a disagreement among the documents as to the extent of the sexual assaults and the number of women involved: state officials confirmed four cases; Dukhobors documented fourteen. It is very likely, however, that many more suffered and were unwilling to report it, whether within their community or to tsarist authorities.[39] In one incident, Cossacks in groups of twenty to thirty men sexually assailed the women of the village of Bogdanovka over a two-day period in their efforts to exert control, a spree that only ended when the outraged governor intervened. As one official report stated, "The criminal activity took the following forms: several Cossacks would break into a house at night, drag the women into another room; while some of the Cossacks stood guard and kept the men at bay with whips, the rest took turns raping the women, leaving them in an unconscious state." According to Dukhobor sources, the Cossacks ordered Dukhobor elders to bring them women to rape and were beaten when they refused. Some women were able to fight off attempted rapes and to escape the villages. Such was the case of two women who broke from their captors, hid under a dung heap in a barn, and then made their way to safety in a nearby Armenian village.[40]

For the victims, the response of local officials to these complaints of rape added insult to injury. When some of the women approached the local police for protection and justice, they were turned away. Such was the case for Fedosia Soprikina, who was raped along with her daughter, the latter so brutally that she was unable to move from her bed for days. A police report notes that "although the complainant's words were completely supported by her external appearance and the marks of rape on her body, still, Police Chief Markarov did not find it possible to accept such a complaint. . . . He told the complainant that 'since the Dukhobors do no wish to obey the government, complaints from them will not be heard.'"[41]

While it is difficult to reconstruct the Cossacks' mindset when they raped these women or the meanings that the Dukhobors attributed to such traumas, these gang rapes linked gender, violence, and political belonging. On one level, the Cossacks connected their assaults with tsarist authority and Orthodox Christianity, exclaiming during the attacks, "Where

38. CRCR 1895–09–16c, ll. 67–670b; Woodsworth, *Russian Roots*, 49–50, 71; Tchertkoff, *Christian Martyrdom*, 58–64, 70; and "Dokumenty ob izbienii i iznasilovanii kozakami dukhoborcheskikh zhenshchin," in Bonch-Bruevich, *Rasskaz*, 31–40.
39. Woodsworth, *Russian Roots*, 64–67; and "Dokumenty," 40.
40. Woodsworth, *Russian Roots*, 55, 65–66; and "Dokumenty," for Dukhobor accounts of group rape.
41. Woodsworth, *Russian Roots*, 50.

FIGURE 16. Dukhobor women in traditional dress, mid 1890s. British Columbia Archives C-06344, published with permission.

is your God? Why does he not help you?"[42] In addition, violence and masculinity were linked in Russian military culture, and the Dukhobors were refusing to accept their male role as soldiers. The Cossacks' raping spree demonstrated very clearly what the Dukhobors were giving up in that decision: pacifism resulted in an inability to protect the women of their communities from attack. That the Cossacks frequently left the men within earshot of their sexual assaults underscores their conscious use of rape as a statement to the entire community that nonviolence meant powerlessness. At the same time, the Cossacks fortified their own masculinity, both by acting as military servitors and by demonstrating their dominance over the community through female rape.[43] The rapes and the refusal of the local police to investigate also reflect how the Dukhobors' decision not to fulfill the government demand of military service placed all Dukhobors outside the boundaries of Russian society and polity, leaving them open for attack and unworthy of state protection.

42. Bonch-Bruevich, *Pis'ma*, 90; and Tchertkoff, *Christian Martyrdom*, 60.
43. Sanborn, *Drafting*, esp. chapter four. For an exploration of the relationship among military actions, gender, and rape, see Alexandra Stiglmayer, ed., *Mass Rape: the War Against Women in Bosnia-Herzegovina* (Lincoln, 1994).

In response, Dukhobor women strove to escape their physical torments by emphasizing their spiritual purity and superiority over the rapists. "I shall remain alive, thou shalt perish," one woman told her attackers, reminding them that the Dukhobors would be saved in the next life. Others prayed to God asking Him to forgive the Cossacks for their actions. The women also strove to use gender and familial norms to protect themselves. Such was the case with another woman who tried to defuse the Cossacks' aggressive masculinity by assuming a maternal persona: "Spare me, an old woman," she said. "Take whatever you like but do not insult us; I am really like a mother to you all."[44]

The Dukhobors' suffering did not end with the Cossack occupation. Within five days, Shervashidze ordered all unrepentant Fasters from Akhalkalaki district to be separated from their coreligionists and exiled internally within Transcaucasia. As many as 4,128 Dukhobors (439 households) were banished to Georgian, Ossetian, or Imeretian communities as far as 400 kilometers from their original homes, with two or three families placed in each village.[45] These Large Party Dukhobors were offered the option to remain in their homes if they expressed remorse and swore allegiance to the tsar, but only a handful were willing to accept such terms. In the process, the Dukhobors blamed what they considered an inappropriately invasive state for their fate: "if they had been left alone to fulfill their law by themselves," there would not be any need for them to leave their homes.[46] Once again, regional variations are important to the story. Dukhobors from Kars territory and Elisavetpol province were not subjected to internal banishment and continued living in their home villages with only minimal disruption to their daily lives.

With the forcible migration, Shervashidze had several goals in mind. Certainly, it was designed as a punishment for the Veriginites' affront to tsarist power. At the same time, the policy was intended as a heavy-handed threat to induce repentance and, as the Tolstoyan Aylmer Maude notes, "to oblige them to abandon their principles by the practical threat of slowly exterminating them should they refuse to submit."[47] It was also a prophylactic measure to prevent any further collective action on the part of the Akhalkalaki Fasters by physically isolating them one from another and cutting them off from the outside world. Here the local authorities were once again, as they had in the 1830s and 1840s, using the local population's different ethnicity, culture, and language as a human buffer to

44. Tchertkoff, *Christian Martyrdom*, 60, 62.
45. GMIR f. 2, op. 7, d. 489, 1928, l. 7; CRCR 1895–09–20a, l. 780b; GARF f. 102, 3 d-vo, op. 1895, d. 1053, ch. 1, l. 525; and Biriukov and Chertkov, *Polozhenie*, 9–10.
46. Zibarov, *O sozhzhenii*, 18.
47. Quoted in Woodcock and Avakumovic, *Doukhobors*, 105–6. See also Tchertkoff, *Christian Martyrdom*, 87.

segregate the Dukhobors from other Russian people. That said, although the loss of Dukhobor life does not seem to have worried the local officials greatly, it does not appear to have been their intention to exterminate the Dukhobors outright. Be that as it may, Fasters and their supporters did understand their internal banishment as a conscious form of genocide. Witnessing these events, the Tolstoyans Pavel Biriukov and Vladimir Chertkov asked rhetorically: "Can it really be that the Russian state wants to annihilate these people for not fulfilling a demand that goes against their conscience?"[48]

PICKING UP THE PIECES

In the years before emigration, both state officials and Dukhobors of all parties attempted to figure out what to do after the arms burning and the ensuing orgy of violence. In the end, however, the collision of Large Party Dukhobors and the tsarist government became increasingly untenable for both sides. While Small Party Dukhobors carried on much as they had before, Veriginites made efforts on three fronts: they strove to stay alive, to remain steadfast in their nonviolent dissent and the other tenets of the New Dukhoborism, and to find some sort of resolution that would allow them to live in keeping with their religious beliefs and practices. With their semi-autonomous state within a state now a memory, they increasingly realized that there was little place for them in the new Russian polity, even on the edge of empire. For their part, tsarist officials took a variety of measures to reintroduce calm and normalcy in the wake of the arms-burning debacle: end the Fasters' movement and prevent its spread, punish the community's leaders and instigators, investigate the incident and punish the criminal actions of officials, and find some workable long-term solution. Throughout, Tolstoyans, other oppositional intellectuals, and religious communities from around the world became actively involved in the Dukhobor case, providing aid to the pacifists and spreading word of the Dukhobors' plight both within the Empire and abroad.

To suppress the Dukhobors' resistance and to punish those who had opposed the government, officials in the Caucasus initially maintained and expanded many of the policies of repression used from 1887 to 1895, including internal exile, wide-ranging imprisonment (especially of leaders), extensive police surveillance, prohibition of public gatherings, a standing requirement to comply with state orders, and bans on Dukhobors leaving their villages.[49] Those who refused military service contin-

48. Biriukov and Chertkov, *Polozhenie*, 12.
49. Woodsworth, *Russian Roots*, 76–77, 84–85; GMIR f. 2, op. 7, d. 489, 1928, l. 8; ORRGB f. 369, k. 42, d. 2, 1950, l. 450; and Biriukov and Chertkov, *Polozhenie*, 10–11.

ued to be sent to disciplinary battalions in order to punish them for their disloyalty through all manner of torturous treatment.[50] Government officials brought in Orthodox priests and missionaries to admonish the Dukhobors to return to their former compliance with tsarist power and, if possible, to convert them. They also opened schools and even Orthodox churches in Dukhobor settlements.[51]

The authorities also resorted both to censorship and to the suppression of communication among Dukhobors, oppositional intellectuals, and the international community. They hoped to reduce public knowledge about—to hide—the Dukhobors' defiance of power and what high-level authorities increasingly came to see as their own embarrassingly savage response. At the same time, silence would allow officials "to starve them into submission without public discredit," as George Woodcock and Ivan Avakumovic have argued.[52] Official directives forbade Russian periodicals from mentioning the Dukhobors or their arms burning and strictly punished violators of these regulations. In 1898, the police closed down *Russkie vedomosti* for publicizing the Dukhobor predicament and collecting money to help them. They even demanded the names and addresses of those who had donated to the fund, although the editors refused to hand them over. When Tolstoyans became involved in publicizing the Dukhobors' sufferings in pamphlets in Russia and newspapers throughout Western Europe, they were immediately banished, some internally, others externally. Only Tolstoy's great fame saved him from a similar fate.[53] Moreover, tsarist officials also took measures to prevent the Dukhobors from becoming martyrs. When Veriginites died in internal exile from the challenging conditions, the communities placed memorial markers above their graves. State officials immediately cut them down, fearing that they would act as symbols of Christian suffering and encourage other Dukhobors. Nonetheless, as one Dukhobor recorded, "We felt that the memory of these martyrs will remain forever in our souls and hearts."[54]

The government also took pains to block the spread of Dukhobor resistance to the indigenous peoples of the South Caucasus. The governor of Elisavetpol province, Prince Nakashidze, argued that if the government did not soon resolve the problem permanently and forcefully, then the "leniency could bring about new disorders that would have an ex-

50. GMIR f. 2, op. 7, d. 489, 1928, l. 7; CRCR 1896–02–27g, ll. 370–710b; Chertkov and Chertkova, *Dukhobortsy;* Biriukov and Chertkov, *Polozhenie,* 11; and Woodsworth, *Russian Roots,* 74–75.
51. Zibarov, *O sozhzhenii,* 24; GMIR f. 2, op. 7, d. 503, n.d.; d. 489, 1928, l. 7; V. M. Skvortsov, *Zapiska o dukhobortsakh na Kavkaze* (n.p., 1896).
52. Woodcock and Avakumovic, *Doukhobors,* 108; and Andrew Donskov, "On the Doukhobors: From Imperial Russian Archival Files," *CES* 27, no. 3 (1995): 256.
53. P. I. Biriukov, ed., *Svobodnoe slovo,* no. 1 (Purleigh, UK, 1898), 175; Woodcock and Avakumovic, *Doukhobors,* 107–12; and Sanborn, "Non-Violent Protest," 91.
54. GMIR f. 2, op. 7, d. 510, n.d., ll. 8–9.

tremely demoralizing influence on the local population, witnessing the weakness of the authority of state power."[55] Both Russian and Caucasian authorities believed that the indigenous peasants held the Dukhobors in very high esteem, seeing them as "the best people," and therefore were very likely to be influenced by the sectarians' ideology. State agents reported widespread proselytism on the part of Dukhobors "trying to destroy the meaning of authority" among the local population. In response, state officials spread fear of the Dukhobors throughout the indigenous communities, saying that the Fasters were "heretics" and "witches" who would "tempt you" into sinful and illegal acts. Moreover, administrators met personally with Caucasian leaders to inform them about the origins of the disorders—placing the blame squarely on the Dukhobors, naturally—and to emphasize that the "disobedient [Dukhobors] will be punished"—as would they, were they to mimic the Fasters' path.[56]

St. Petersburg also sent agents and missionaries to Transcaucasia to uncover why events had turned so horribly violent, to assign blame for the debacle, and to take actions that might help prevent a future reoccurrence.[57] There was a strong sense in the capital that something had gone terribly awry. Then minister of the interior, I. N. Durnovo, "was particularly struck by the illegal actions permitted by the military squadrons summoned to calm the disturbances and the inaction in respect thereof on the part of the representatives of the local administration," and he ordered these probes to ensure "that the guilty parties be held criminally responsible."[58] The investigative agents uncovered a variety of explanations for the events. For some, following a standard trope about peasant agency, the fault lay with the Dukhobors themselves and especially with certain "ringleaders" who had led the mass of otherwise good Dukhobors astray. Cut off the head, they argued, and a pliant Dukhobor body could be salvaged. For many others, the cause was found in the intervention of Tolstoy and his followers (particularly Biriukov, Chertkov, and Ivan Tregubov) and other oppositional intellectuals. Still others blamed certain local officials—such as Praga, D'iachkov-Tarasov, and even Shervashidze—who, in the view of investigators, had acted outside the law and brutalized an otherwise good and loyal people into an unyielding opposition.[59]

St. Petersburg officials also believed that the Dukhobors had become frustrated with the state because local officials tended to be Transcauca-

55. CRCR 1896–04–23c, l. 3810b.
56. Kuropatkin, *Soobrazheniia*, 15–16; GMIR f. 2, op. 7, d. 510, n.d., l. 2; and Donskov, "On the Doukhobors," 258.
57. Woodsworth, *Russian Roots*, 54–67; GMIR f. 2, op. 7, d. 489, 1928, ll. 7–8; d. 503, n.d.; and CRCR 1895–09–20a, ll. 740b–81.
58. Woodsworth, *Russian Roots*, 54.
59. GARF f. 102, 3 d-vo, op. 1895, d. 1053, ch. 1, ll. 548–49; Woodsworth, *Russian Roots*, 17–18, 100; and CRCR 1895–09–20a, ll. 750b–81.

sians. As Durnovo argued, "the local police . . . consisting mainly of non-Russians (Georgians and Armenians) do not enjoy the favor and trust of the purely Russian Dukhobor population."[60] As such, the state found scapegoats for the breakdown in authority in these Caucasian officials. From that point forward, the central administration strove to increase state supervision of the Dukhobors, assigning "specially chosen police . . . consisting of reliable Russian Orthodox people."[61] Some Russian officials working in Transcaucasia shared this view of the central administrators. For example, E. Taranovskii, a deputy chief of police in Tiflis province, saw the natives' domination of positions of authority as a primary cause of the Dukhobors' opposition to state power:

> I have been in the Caucasus since 1878 and . . . with the exception of D'iachkov-Tarasov, the administration of Akhalkalaki district was comprised and is composed exclusively of indigenous peoples—Armenians, Imeretians, and Georgians—to whom the Dukhobors related and relate not especially trustingly. At the present time, a Muslim Warrant Officer of the police, Mustafa Palavandov, has been designated the state *starshina* in Dukhobor'e. Permit me to think that the Tiflis governor, Prince Shervashidze, knew little about the Dukhobors and his opinion of them was formed solely through reports from the bureaucrats of the Akhalkalaki administration.[62]

While the state took measures to punish, evoke repentance, cover up, and investigate, the majority of Large Party Dukhobors remained firm in their faith, despite their sufferings.[63] As soon as the exiled Verigin heard of the arms burning, he wrote to them that "it was necessary . . . to suffer with Christ. Though the body might be harmed, the spirit was invulnerable. Therefore, at all costs the faithful must remain steadfast in refusing to obey the government."[64] Shervashidze quoted others who were even more strident in the immovability of their faith, as in this example: "Until you return [the Orphan Home] to us, we will not quiet down, we will not leave the government alone, and we will give no one any peace. It would be better to slaughter us all. Whether you want to or not, you will need to shoot us. We would sooner die than to agree to something that is against our conscience."[65]

The Fasters embraced their martyrdom as a sign of their righteousness

60. Woodsworth, *Russian Roots*, 18. Azerbaijanis should also be added to this list.
61. Ibid., 79. Indeed, tsarist officials in St. Petersburg did what they could to take the Dukhobors out of the control of local jurisdictions—for instance, by preventing local courts from trying cases concerning the Dukhobors. CRCR 1896–04–23c, ll. 379–790b.
62. CRCR 1895–09–20a, ll. 770b–78.
63. GMIR f. 2, op. 7, d. 556, 1896, ll. 7–10; and Tchertkoff, *Christian Martyrdom*, 87.
64. Woodcock and Avakumovic, *Doukhobors*, 105.
65. Quoted in Kuropatkin, *Soobrazheniia*, 14.

in the eyes of God. They, like Christ, were suffering for virtue and truth: "The unblemished tsar is Jesus of Nazareth. Who wanted to kill Christ— wasn't it Herod? Wasn't it the royal governor Pilate that crucified the Savior? In the same way, they crucify verity and truth, and us."[66] Moreover, their unwavering stance in the face of government torments was also connected to their sense of millenarian destiny. If they could endure the trials of this period, then a glorious future awaited, as prophesied by one of their early leaders, Savelii Kapustin, and reemphasized by Verigin: "The virtues of the community shall overcome the kingdom of this world, which is drawing near to its end. Then shall the Dukhobors be known to all mankind, and Christ Himself shall reign as king. . . . Only after they have passed through great tribulations shall this honor be done to the Dukhobors."[67]

Indeed, during the events of 1887 through 1895, the Large Party's self-understanding underwent a fundamental reorientation. A religious identity not unlike their Christian discourse of the early nineteenth century returned in the 1890s as the uppermost factor in their communal identification. In 1896, at Verigin's behest, his followers renamed themselves "The Christian Community of Universal Brotherhood." Verigin contacted the tsarina to inform her of this name change, explaining that "the word 'Dukhobortsy' is incomprehensible for outsiders. From this point forward we will call upon the Spirit of God in order to struggle against carnal weakness and sin, and the name 'Christian Community of Universal Brotherhood' will more clearly speak to the fact that we look at all people as brothers, according to the testament of our Lord Jesus Christ."[68]

In this process, the Dukhobors' sense of identification with the tsarist state and Russian ethnicity, which had grown stronger during their decades in Transcaucasia, all but disappeared. They self-consciously placed themselves outside the fold of the Russian people, instead claiming a spiritual identity that transcended all temporal power and a cross-ethnic bond with all humans as children of God. To Shervashidze, Veriginites declared: "No, we do not consider ourselves Russian subjects, we will not submit to disgraceful laws."[69] Police records report Fasters saying: "We are pilgrims, we are striving [to reach] our heavenly fatherland, and we do not cherish or wish to defend an earthly [fatherland]. . . . The Russian emperor, the Persian Shah, the Turkish Sultan, are equally dear to us as brethren, they are all God's creation. . . . We do not recognize a

66. Donskov, "On the Doukhobors," 254.
67. Quoted in Woodcock and Avakumovic, *Doukhobors*, 88.
68. Bonch-Bruevich, *Pis'ma*, 91–94; and Woodsworth, *Russian Roots*, 88.
69. Quoted in Sanborn, "Non-Violent Protest," 85.

fatherland on earth, all people are our compatriots."[70] Moreover, Fasters also negated their Russian ethnicity. In response to Shervashidze's question "Are you Russian?" the answer was "No, we are Dukhobors."[71]

As they waited for the coming glories and held fast to their revitalized religious identities, the impact of dispersal to Georgian and Imeretian villages devastated the Dukhobors. Many died, succumbing to heat, hunger, malnutrition, and a range of diseases—dysentery, fever, dyspepsia, and eye disease, especially hemeralopia.[72] According to Biriukov and Chertkov, in 1896 there were 106 deaths in Signakhi district out of 100 Faster families, in Gori district 147 people perished of 190 families, and the 100 families in Tioneti district suffered 83 deaths.[73] To make matters worse, state officials often took advantage of the Dukhobors' dispersal to abuse them. Despite the many deaths, both they and Georgian peasants barred the Dukhobors from burying their dead in local cemeteries, or else they demanded payment for burial plots that the Fasters could not afford.[74] In addition, the division of the Dukhobor community into smaller groups further cleaved families. In the case of Zibarov, a particularly vindictive official designated his five-year-old son as a head of household and then sent the two "households" to different villages. More commonly, a wife would choose not to join her husband in internal exile, thereby splitting the family.[75]

The dispersal to Georgian villages also had a tremendous impact on the Dukhobors' material well-being, with destitution quickly becoming widespread.[76] They had little time to sell whatever immovable property they had left after the antimaterialism of the New Dukhoborism. "Dwellings and property were abandoned, grain was left standing in the fields, livestock was sold for nothing," as one official described the process.[77] In the opinion of many Fasters, their misery was a conscious plan on the part of the local administration to hurt them and to line the pockets of both officials and Small Party Dukhobors.[78] The economic conditions and regulations in exile exacerbated the suffering. The dispersed Dukhobors were not allotted any land in the Georgian villages on which to grow food. "The authorities do not think about how we are to feed our chil-

70. GARF f. 102, 3 d-vo, op. 1895, d. 1053, ch. 1, translation from Donskov, "On the Doukhobors," 254.

71. ORRGB f. 369, k. 44, d. 1, 1950, l. 133.

72. Tchertkoff, *Christian Martyrdom*, 79, 82.

73. Biriukov and Chertkov, *Polozhenie*, 10; GMIR f. 2, op. 7, d. 982, 1899; d. 489, 1928, l. 7; d. 510, n.d., ll. 2–9; Woodsworth, *Russian Roots*, 84.

74. Tchertkoff, *Christian Martyrdom*, 80–81, 84; and Woodsworth, *Russian Roots*, 74.

75. Zibarov, *O sozhzhenii*, 20–21, 25–26; GMIR f. 2, op. 7, d. 557, 1895, ll. 1–4; and d. 510, n.d., ll. 2–8.

76. Of many examples, see Tchertkoff, *Christian Martyrdom*, 72.

77. Kuropatkin, *Soobrazheniia*, 21; and Woodsworth, *Russian Roots*, 72.

78. Zibarov, *O sozhzhenii*, 16–17.

dren," one complained. "Or do they want to starve us to death?"[79] To make matters worse, the exiles were not permitted to travel from their place of banishment, thereby ruling out any possibility of carting work or trade.[80] The Fasters' economy also suffered because they did not know how long or under what conditions they would remain in the Georgian villages: "Evidently the Government desires to keep them in this state of material uncertainty," Chertkov contended, "so that they may be obliged by sheer force of hunger to fall in with the proposals of the Government."[81]

The exiles responded to their increasingly grave economic situation in three ways. First, they lived primarily off the help of local villagers through payment for day labor. Second, they survived on what was left of their savings and on the Large Party's communal funds, which had been collected in place of the Orphan Home moneys after the split with the Small Party.[82] Third, the exiles took matters into their own hands, scrounging what work and provisions they could. Some found employment around the railway line in Gori region; others disobeyed the prohibitions and traveled to find work; and still others rented land from nobles and villagers in order to be able to grow at least some food. Some Fasters simply took what they needed from the lands of local Georgian nobles—chopped down noble-owned forests for fuel and used pastureland and other arable lands without payment. In one reported incident, "settlers in the Tioneti region killed a forester for not allowing the Dukhobors to help themselves to the government forest."[83]

Representatives of the exiled Dukhobors met in December 1896 to try to figure out what to do about their material difficulties. They noted happily that money was beginning to come in from people outside their communities, such as Quakers in England and sympathizers in Moscow and St. Petersburg. However, these funds were insufficient for their survival and their savings had almost run out. In an effort to help themselves, they decided to try to unite the exiled families in order to reduce their dispersion and to concentrate their resources and human power.[84]

The Dukhobors' interactions with the Georgians and Imeretians among whom they were banished comprise an important part of the nar-

---

79. Woodsworth, *Russian Roots*, 74.
80. Zibarov, *O sozhzhenii*, 23; and Tchertkoff, *Christian Martyrdom*, 85.
81. Tchertkoff, *Christian Martyrdom*, 86–87; and Biriukov and Chertkov, *Polozhenie*, 12.
82. GARF f. 102, 3 d-vo, op. 1895, d. 1053, ch. 1, ll. 5510b–5400b.
83. ORRGB f. 369, k. 43, d. 1, 1950, l. 823; "Nekotoroe vliianie Dukhobor na mestnye obychai," *KSKh*, no. 198 (October 23, 1897): 678–79; Tchertkoff, *Christian Martyrdom*, 86; GARF f. 102, 3 d-vo, op. 1895, d. 1053, ch. 1, ll. 525–28; and Donskov, "On the Doukhobors," 255.
84. GMIR f. 2, op. 7, d. 556, 1896, ll. 7–10; Polkovnik General'nogo shtaba Andrievskii, *Voenno-geograficheskoe i statisticheskoe opisanie Kavkazskogo voennogo okruga* (Tiflis, 1908), 61–62; and Tchertkoff, *Christian Martyrdom*, 82, 85–86.

FIGURE 17. Dukhobor exiles in Georgia before emigrating, 1898. British Columbia Archives C-01649, published with permission.

rative of the Dukhobor movement. They also offer insight into the functioning of the tsarist multi-ethnic empire and highlight the varied impacts of Russian colonialism on the indigenous population. Significantly, the exiled Dukhobors acted differently toward their new neighbors based on social status, showing disdain for native elites and urging an equality of wealth and help for the poor. As part of their faith, they proclaimed, "The land is God's, it is created for all equally. Possession is robbery. . . . The princes and the landowners have robbed the people, seizing so much land."[85]

The relations between the exiles and Georgian peasants (and, when Dukhobors were later sent to Baku province, Azerbaijanis) were initially mixed. When the Fasters arrived, some locals ignored them, others received them "cordially" and "felt sorry for them," while "the rougher ones oppressed them—stole their horses and other property." Over time, however, the Dukhobors' actions appear to have won over the support of the majority of villagers. As part of their Christianity, the exiles acted with "kindness" toward the poorer Georgians and Azerbaijanis. Shervashidze

85. Donskov, "On the Doukhobors," 254, 258.

noted that they "offered financial aid and help through their physical labor to poor families of the peasant population, for which they [sought] no remuneration, or they restrict[ed] themselves to receiving the most pitiful compensation for tilling the ground." They gave generously many of their possessions, such as kitchen utensils and clothing, in an effort to relieve poverty. In one case, the Dukhobors took what little money they had and bought clothes in the local town to distribute to the village's destitute. Of course, these religiously inspired acts of charity further exacerbated their already tenuous economic situation.[86] In addition, while state officials interpreted the Dukhobors' kindnesses and communalism as a form of revolutionary proselytism, for the Fasters it was more a matter of living according to their Christian beliefs.

As a result, Georgian peasants began to help the Dukhobors in whatever ways they could. They gave exiles good rooms in their huts for no rent. They paid the Dukhobors as much as they could, and as much as the Dukhobors would allow, for the Fasters' work in their fields. The fact that local peasants tended to see the Dukhobors as sturdy and accomplished workers only helped to increase the number of Georgian peasants willing to hire them as labor.[87] Reports of Georgian landowners indicate that there was a coming together of the local peasants and the banished sectarians: "In general the native Georgians, having come to know the [Dukhobors], do not know why these righteous people are being exterminated, are indignant against the authorities, and are doing their best to help and protect the sufferers, though this 'best' is more valuable spiritually than materially, for it is so little they can do, owing to their own poverty and subjection."[88]

Initially, the Georgian nobles in the region welcomed the arrival of the exiled Dukhobors as "a great blessing of the state toward local landownership . . . [and] a cheap, useful work force" because "the Dukhobors [were] famous as most excellent workers." However, the exiles proved a great disappointment. The Fasters refused to work on the nobles' lands, even for high wages, preferring to work for free for the village poor. They took property from nobles without compunction and used their lands without payment. All the while, the Dukhobors sold or gave away their own property and livestock to the Georgian peasants, even when a noble might offer five times as much to purchase the same property. The Dukhobors also "showed open scorn for the titles of the nobles, beks, and princes, attempting to demean the prestige of the landowners in the eyes

86. GARF f. 102, 3 d-vo, op. 1895, d. 1053, ch. 1, ll. 525–28; Donskov, "On the Doukhobors," 258; Tchertkoff, *Christian Martyrdom*, 83–84; and GMIR f. 2, op. 7, d. 510, n.d.
87. GARF f. 102, 3 d-vo, op. 1895, d. 1053, ch. 1, ll. 525–28; "Nekotoroe vliianie," 678–79; and Tchertkoff, *Christian Martyrdom*, 83.
88. Tchertkoff, *Christian Martyrdom*, 84.

of the peasant indigenous peoples." In consequence, a large segment of the nobles and Georgian intelligentsia began to look down upon the Fasters. Significantly, the chasm that developed between these groups because of divergent social views also prevented a linkage between, on one hand, those Georgian nobles who might oppose tsarist rule and, on the other hand, the Dukhobors and their Russian elite supporters (Tolstoyans, socialists, and anarchists). If any cross-ethnic oppositional movement was to develop, it would only be between the Fasters and Georgian peasants, and even here a regional opposition movement did not develop, despite boiling peasant discontent.[89]

While most tsarist officials and Russian observers worried about the potential transference of the Dukhobor opposition movement to the indigenous people, there were those who saw the banishment of Dukhobors into Georgian villages as an important opportunity to spread Russian economic and cultural practices to the "natives" and once again raise their civilizational level. Most interestingly, it was often not Russian but Georgian intellectuals who continued to see the Dukhobors as Russian colonists and carriers of superior practices—a fact that reflects the integration and cooperation of Georgian elites in the tsarist empire.[90] One Georgian wrote in 1897, even after all the unrest of the Dukhobor movement: "Dukhobors, being more cultured than the indigenous inhabitants, in many things naturally serve as an example for better economic activity." This observer noted multiple ways in which the dispersed Dukhobors continued to serve their colonialist functions, especially enhancing the economic potential of the region. Despite their poverty-stricken condition, the Dukhobors brought with them new agricultural techniques (particularly ways of harvesting grain), new crops, a needed expertise in horses, and their exemplary work ethic. Fasters plowed under meadows that had been left unused, which increased overall agricultural output. The author also remarked on the Dukhobors' influence on Georgian gender structures, claiming that local peasants adapted the Dukhobor practice of having women work in the fields alongside men. As a result, mirroring proposals from earlier decades, this commentator called for the permanent settlement of these Dukhobors in the region and the allotment of free treasury land to them—this despite their official designation as seditious.[91]

89. GARF f. 102, 3 d-vo, op. 1895, d. 1053, ch. 1, ll. 525–28; and Kenneth W. Church, "From Dynastic Principality to Imperial District: The Incorporation of Guria into the Russian Empire to 1856" (Ph.D. diss., University of Michigan, 2001).
90. Austin Jersild, *Orientalism and Empire: North Caucasus Mountain Peoples and the Georgian Frontier, 1845–1917* (Montreal and Kingston, 2002).
91. "Nekotoroe vliianie," 678–79.

MIXED RESULTS, FAILING POLICIES

The state's efforts to punish and quell the Dukhobors' opposition movement had mixed results. There are indications that these harsh measures, combined with the physical and spiritual exhaustion of many Dukhobors, did lead to a reduction in tensions. More characteristic, however, was an ongoing intransigence on both sides and a mounting sense among tsarist officials that their pacification policies were failing. Opposition persisted, the use of force to suppress the pacifist resistors was proving counterproductive, and the Dukhobor movement was continuing to connect with both indigenous peoples and Russia's elite opponents of the regime. As a mutually acceptable solution appeared increasingly unlikely, both Dukhobors and government began to look for other resolutions to the conflict.

There was some good news for the state. Certain reports from 1896 and 1897 indicated that many Fasters were beginning to soften their views, seek some sort of accommodation with tsarist power, and even voice a desire to resume their pre-schism life. Reporting in 1897, the chief administrator of the Caucasus, G. S. Golitsyn, noted a reduction in hostility among the Dukhobors in Slavianka in the year following the arms burning. He pointed to the arrests and trials of "influential leaders" as one of the primary causes, as well as their extreme material destitution. He also emphasized that "the mutual spiritual struggle between equally strong parties, and the morally sobering family influence of sensible co-villagers who belong to the [Small] Party, began already a year ago to have a pacifying influence on the mutinous part of the Elisavetpol Dukhobors."[92] Indeed, Golitsyn reported that the majority "belong to the class of moderate Fasters, who are willing to make compromises with the ruling authorities, except as regards military service."[93] Many Veriginites, including those returning from prison or the penal battalions, began to express regret at their "past stupidities and mistakes" and "anger and frustration against their leaders, who they believe led the Slavianka Dukhobors astray." The chief administrator also noted "conversions" from the Large Party to the Small, and he even dared to hope that all Dukhobors would soon rejoin the Small Party.[94]

In addition, Golitsyn reported a very significant change in the mood of Fasters generally. Since Easter of 1896, Golitsyn noted, the Fasters had once again begun to bow before members of other parties, to visit their homes, and "to render each other mutual services and help, something

92. GARF f. 102, 3 d-vo, op. 1895, d. 1053, ch. 1, ll. 5410b–42.
93. Donskov, "On the Doukhobors," 256.
94. GARF f. 102, 3 d-vo, op. 1895, d. 1053, ch. 1, ll. 545 and 597.

that they did not permit for many years."[95] He related that the Veriginites were also beginning somewhat to soften their stance on eating meat and drinking alcohol, and once again were building up their economic strength. Whereas in the preceding year they had only planted one-third of their land, in 1897 they had planted almost all of it. Those with any extra money were moving back into the livestock business, buying cows and rams; others were returning to carting work. Many of these Fasters were now attending communal meetings, following the *starshina*'s directives, and fulfilling state obligations such as fixing roads or helping in the transport of mail.[96]

Quiet also reigned among the Dukhobors in Akhalkalaki, in great part because of the dampening impact of ten years of mutual conflict and the exile of the "mutinous" Dukhobors. Police reports indicate a certain rapprochement between the Small and Middle Parties, who together lobbied government officials against the return of the internally exiled Fasters to their original homes. They feared that a return would lead to another outbreak of conflict and once again disturb the peace and order of the communities. Of course, Small and Middle Party Dukhobors also had material reasons to keep their coreligionists away: they had appropriated the property and land of the banished Fasters, and had no desire to return it.[97]

That said, in 1897, Golitsyn still did not believe that matters had returned sufficiently to the status quo ante for the state to claim victory or let down its guard. "Energetic measures" continued to be necessary "to destroy the insolent and impossible relations toward the Higher Authorities, state institutions and law, which have appeared on the side of the mutinous Dukhobors." Despite repeated requests from the commune, he refused to permit the Slavianka Dukhobors to elect their own *starshina*, fearing that it would only reignite factional conflict. He also pushed the importance of tsarist schools as tool of integration and pacification of the Dukhobors.[98]

Golitsyn was not wrong to remain wary. While there were some hints of a reduction in enmity, antagonism among the Dukhobor factions nonetheless remained, particularly in fights over religious truth and over control of political and economic power within their communities.[99] In April 1896, members of the Small Party in Slavianka reported to the governor that if strict measures were not taken against the Large Party, they would be forced to mete out "blood reprisals."[100] Moreover, among the

95. Ibid., ll. 542ob–43.
96. Ibid., ll. 543–44.
97. Ibid., ll. 551ob–53.
98. Ibid., ll. 545–46ob, 554ob.
99. Ibid., ll. 567ob–68ob.
100. CRCR 1896–04–23c, l. 381.

Kars Dukhobors, factional struggles between the Fasters and Butchers remained an everyday affair. State officials noted that the Fasters manipulated family structures in their attempts to enlist members, consciously luring wives from husbands and children from parents—the presumed weaker links in the family chain—in order to increase the number of former Butchers in their ranks. Fasters also used their numerical majority to help attract others to their side by orchestrating the distribution of village lands and apportionment of taxes in such a way that it benefited those who came over to their cause.[101] In addition, state officials saw in the Large Party Dukhobors' reproductive cycle signs of an unabated commitment to extremism. State authorities noted with unease that between 1894 and 1897 there had not been a single marriage among the Faster Dukhobors in Slavianka and that the number of their "countable births" had also dropped to almost zero as they readied "to meet Christ, according to Verigin's sayings."[102]

In tandem with the ongoing factionalism and infighting, state reports also indicate that many Dukhobors remained steadfast in their opposition to conscription, "refused to serve the tsar and Fatherland . . . [and] recognize[d] as tsar only the One Lord God, who they must serve."[103] State efforts in 1896 to force the Slavianka Dukhobors to pay the salary of their Armenian *starshina* ended in violence.[104] Among the Kars Dukhobors, opposition and antagonism remained especially virulent. Golitsyn reported: "The majority decisively and in the most extreme expressions negate the High Authority of the Holy Special Sovereign, and do not recognize either the administration, or laws, or state institutions, preaching social-communistic views on property, land, taxes, etc." They continued to refuse military billeting, did not make the required payments to the local guard, avoided paying taxes, refused to reveal information to the government about who was next in line for conscription, and ignored the orders of the local authorities to provide horses for military use.[105] Furthermore, reports of the religious authorities were filled with apocalyptic warnings that the Dukhobors were having a very undesirable impact on the Orthodox population in the militarily sensitive Kars territory.[106] The extremism among Kars Dukhobors resulted from the

101. GARF f. 102, 3 d-vo, op. 1895, d. 1053, ch. 1, ll. 549–50, 567–68ob.
102. Ibid., ll. 598ob–99; and Brock, "Vasya Pozdnyakov's," 168 and 172–73 for the decision to rescind the chastity order.
103. CRCR 1896–04–23c, ll. 378–82.
104. Ibid., ll. 379ob–82. See also *Vsepoddanneishii otchet ober-procurora sviateishego Sinoda K. Pobedonostseva po vedomstvu pravoslavnogo ispovedaniia za 1896 i 1897 gody* (St. Petersburg, 1899), 151; and Biriukov and Chertkov, *Polozhenie,* 11.
105. GARF f. 102, 3 d-vo, op. 1895, d. 1053, ch. 1, ll. 547ob–49, 551ob, 567–68ob; and *Vsepoddanneishii otchet, 1896 i 1897,* 151.
106. RGIA f. 796, op. 442, d. 1612, 1896, ll. 78–79ob.

numerical predominance of the Fasters in their villages, with many Faster leaders coming from or living in the region. The Kars communities also served as a focal point for Dukhobor organization, especially Terpenie, which, with Gorelovka under Small Party control, was designated the new Dukhobor Zion and site for a new Orphan Home.[107]

The Fasters' opposition endured despite the violence of the Russian state, and their pacifist civil disobedience not only challenged the moral underpinnings of government authority but forced officialdom to rethink its policies. Such was particularly the case with the penal battalions where Dukhobor soldiers were sent for their conscientious objection—although the Dukhobors scattered in Georgian villages posed similar problems.[108] Both Dukhobor and tsarist sources indicate that the sectarians suffered horrific torture, beatings, and other maltreatment at the hands of battalion commanders. Nonetheless, such violence had little impact on the Dukhobor movement. "We must endure," the Fasters insisted, "because God himself our Lord Jesus Christ endured and gave to His followers an example of the strength of God. And if we die for Christ, then we will live with Christ. We should hardly be surprised with the trials that we are undergoing, but quite the opposite, we should be joyful that we are honored to share the sufferings of our Lord Jesus Christ."[109] Moreover, the Dukhobors' endurance prompted Tolstoy and Tolstoyans to engage in a writing campaign to free the Dukhobors, directly contacting the leaders of the disciplinary battalions to beg a more Christian mercy.[110]

The minister of the interior, I. L. Goremykin, was unsure what to do in the face of such determined opposition to the state's power. As he noted, the Dukhobors' willingness "patiently to endure sufferings . . . undoubtedly places the battalion administration in an extremely difficult situation, for the exhaustion of all punishment measures requires either to stop future punishments or to take the punishment to a degree of undesirable severity." The continued presence of the Dukhobors in the disciplinary battalions represented "an extreme burden for the military administration," was not achieving its goals of bring the Dukhobors in line, and was having the opposite outcome of disrupting discipline in the military. "In the eyes of others, these sectarians are becoming 'victims' and 'sufferers' for their religious convictions, and with their passive opposition they are providing a basis on which to think that with stubbornness it is possible to stand up against the will of the administration."[111]

In the face of these many challenges, Goremykin proposed a differ-

107. GARF f. 102, 3 d-vo, op. 1895, d. 1053, ch. 1, ll. 546ob, 548–480b, 550–51.
108. Woodsworth, *Russian Roots,* 78.
109. CRCR 1896–02–27g, l. 371.
110. Chertkov and Chertkova, *Dukhobortsy,* 41–43, 55–59.
111. CRCR 1896–02–27g, ll. 370, 371; and Chertkov and Chertkova, *Dukhobortsy,* 53–54.

ent variant to punish those Dukhobors who would actively refuse conscription and military service: banishment to Iakutiia under police surveillance. The minister of war, P. S. Vannovskii, agreed with Goremykin's
estimation and also moved to "free" the military from the Dukhobor conscientious objectors. He worried that the failing measures made the state
look "feeble" and "would give cause to other sectarians to act similarly . . .
and have a harmful influence on the remaining rank-and-file soldiers."
In August 1896, the Emperor agreed to this plan, banishing pacifist
Dukhobors to Iakutiia for a period of eighteen years.[112]

While St. Petersburg officials increasingly came to regard the use of
force toward the Dukhobors as a bankrupt policy, they also realized that
their attempts to block the spread of knowledge about the Dukhobor
movement to the surrounding Transcaucasian population were having
little success. It is not entirely clear to what degree the Dukhobors were
actually involved in proselytism, and it appears that the Caucasian peoples proved generally unreceptive to the Fasters' ideas. Nonetheless, local officials took it as an article of faith that the state's treatment of the
Dukhobors "produced an extremely painful impression on the mass of
neighboring local people."[113] Shervashidze had raised this point in 1895,
and in the years that followed report after report echoed his concerns.
The governor warned: "The exiled sect members are verbally and even
actively promulgating their teachings to which end, apart from persuad-
ing people verbally of the futility and sinfulness of military service and
paying taxes . . . [are] indicating that all people should live in . . . brotherly unity. Such a sermon is very enticing for the dark masses of the peasantry."[114] In parallel, Tolstoyans like Biriukov and Chertkov hoped that
the Dukhobors' use of nonviolent resistance would lead to widespread
support for the pacifist ideas that these intellectuals championed. In line
with the government assessments, they somewhat optimistically noted,
"The hard condition of the Dukhobors, the appalling illegal action carried out on them by the local authorities, and the astonishing meekness
with which the Dukhobors endure all that they are subjected to, arouses
in the Caucasus a general feeling of sympathy to them of all the people—
whatever their religious and political beliefs."[115]

112. Chertkov and Chertkova, *Dukhobortsy*, 53 for quotation; CRCR 1896–02–27g, ll. 371–710b;
GARF f. 102, 5 d-vo, op. 1896, d. 205, ch. 1, 2, 9, 17, and 18; Woodsworth, *Russian Roots*, 82–83,
87; GMIR f. 2, op. 7, d. 489, 1928, ll. 7–8; Biriukov and Chertkov, *Polozhenie*, 21; and Sanborn,
"Non-Violent Protest," 91. On the experience of Dukhobor exile in Iakutiia, see Brock, "Vasya
Pozdnyakov's," 171–76; and Vasia Pozdniakov, "Pravda o dukhoborakh. Zhizn' dukhoborov v Zakavkaz'e i v Sibiri," *EZh*, no. 6 (June 1914): 103–9; and no. 7 (July 1914): 89–101.
113. CRCR 1896–04–23c, l. 3800b.
114. Quoted and translated in Donskov, "On the Doukhobors," 258. Of many examples, see also
Kuropatkin, *Soobrazheniia*, 13; Andrievskii, *Voenno-geografichestkoe*, 60; and Woodsworth, *Russian
Roots*, 102.
115. Biriukov and Chertkov, *Polozhenie*, 11.

Word of the arms burning, the Dukhobors' open defiance of tsarist rule, and the latter's brutal response certainly spread rapidly among South Caucasians. As the Dukhobors were being marched under armed Cossack guard from Akhalkalaki to Gori, they were frequently approached by large crowds of Armenians, Georgians, and Azerbaijanis who were fascinated to find out what had happened, to discover the Dukhobors' beliefs, and to see for themselves the sectarians who had come to take on an almost mythic quality. The government escorts sometimes tried to the keep the locals away with whips and beatings, but preventing all contact was impossible, so the Dukhobors' story spread—of course, the Caucasians were frustrated at the violence they faced for attempting even to talk to the Dukhobors.[116]

Moreover, the Dukhobor movement could not but have had an impact on the neighboring peoples with thousands of sick, starving, religiously devoted Fasters banished to Georgian and Azerbaijani villages. Not only had the earlier collapse of the Dukhobor economy negatively affected the regional one, but now Caucasian villagers were required to live with the Dukhobors, and to offer what assistance they could to mitigate the burdens of exile. It was certainly ironic—one not lost on central officials—that in their efforts to punish the Dukhobors, the local authorities had taken exactly those measures that would most guarantee contact between Fasters and the native peoples. State and Synod agents even reported that the Dukhobor exiles would enter Georgian Church services, criticize the local priesthood and Orthodoxy, and spread their "religious and political propaganda" to their Georgian and Imeretian hosts.[117]

Tsarist efforts to block communication between the Fasters and oppositional intellectuals, such as the Tolstoyans and socialists, met with a similar lack of success. The government fretted that Dukhobor resistance would breathe new life into these larger opposition and revolutionary movements, that the oppositional elites would further radicalize the Dukhobor community, and that the Dukhobors would act as a conduit permitting Tolstoyan views to infiltrate the colonized peoples and further destabilize the area.[118] Golitsyn argued in his report of 1897 that the Tolstoyans were at the root of the Dukhobor opposition, and that further contact needed to be prevented: "The Kars Dukhobors, more radically than others, have adopted the teachings of anarchy and Tolstoyism and are therefore the most convinced and stubborn followers of the criminal

116. Zibarov, O sozhzhenii, 15, 22–23.
117. GARF f. 102, 3 d-vo, op. 1895, d. 1053, ch. 1, ll. 534–340b; Kuropatkin, Soobrazheniia, 15; and RGIA f. 796, op. 442, d. 1612, 1896, ll. 78–790b.
118. Woodsworth, Russian Roots, 102.

anarchist community . . . sometimes literally citing passages from the underground writings of Count L. Tolstoy."[119]

Although state officials frequently overestimated the Tolstoyan influence, the Russian intellectual community (especially the Tolstoyans) did indeed take many important actions to help the Dukhobors. At least initially, Tolstoy saw the Dukhobors as the living fulfillment of his vision of communalist, pacifist peasants: "The realization of what we are striving for, what all our complex activities are leading us to."[120] Tolstoyans viewed the Dukhobor experience as an opportunity to push forward their platform that tsarist subjects "should not have to give up their faith for state demands; should be able to live according to the will of their God in Russia."[121] They worked ceaselessly to document and publicize the Dukhobors' plight and to enlist the support of those who felt that the tsarist state's treatment of the Dukhobors was unacceptable. They lobbied directly with high-level state officials as well as with the commander of the Ekaterinograd disciplinary battalion, asking for leniency toward the Dukhobors. They printed pamphlets in Russia about the Dukhobors in an attempt to circumvent the censorship of Russian periodicals, and in 1897 they broke the wall of internal censorship by convincing a Russian newspaper to publish information about the Dukhobors. Perhaps most important, and certainly most embarrassingly for the tsarist government, Tolstoy published letters in the *London Times* describing the Dukhobors' situation and calling on the international community to come to their aid, which many did, especially Quakers.[122]

ALTERNATIVE RESOLUTIONS AND EMIGRATION

With their policies failing on all fronts, leaders in St. Petersburg urgently considered other options to resolve the confrontation. Beginning in mid-1896, the heads of each of the major ministries and selected regional leaders (Synod, Interior, Justice, Finance, head of civilian affairs in the Caucasus, and chief of Transcaspian region) held a series of meetings in

119. Donskov, "On the Doukhobors," 256. See also GARF f. 102, 3 d-vo, op. 1895, d. 1053, ch. 1, l. 598; Woodsworth, *Russian Roots*, 98–102; and RGIA f. 1405, op. 521, d. 445, 1895–97, l. 3300b.
120. Lidia Gromova-Opul'skaya, Andrew Donskov, and John Woodsworth, eds., *Leo Tolstoy—Peter Verigin Correspondence* (Ottawa, 1995), 2.
121. Biriukov and Chertkov, *Polozhenie*, 16.
122. Tchertkoff, *Christian Martyrdom*, esp. 104–6; J. W. Bienstock, ed. and trans., *Tolstoi et les Doukhobors: faits historiques réunis et traduits du russe* (Paris, 1902); Biriukov and Chertkov, *Polozhenie*, esp. 12–21; GMIR f. 2, op. 7, d. 556, 1896, l. 7; Woodcock and Avakumovic, *Doukhobors*, 109, 112–14, 117; Michael J. de K. Holman, "British Tolstoyans, *The New Order* and The Doukhobors in the late 1890s: Solidarity in Word and Deed," in *Doukhobor Centenary*, 131–48; and Sanborn, "Pacifist Politics," 52–71.

an effort to come to a workable solution. Among numerous ensuing policy proposals in their search for "spiritual missionary ascendancy over the Transcaucasian sectarians," the administrators began to look for other locations where they might settle the "offending" Dukhobors. With the exception of the Synod officials and missionaries, who wanted to keep the Dukhobors isolated in the Transcaucasus, most officials believed that the Veriginites could not be returned to their original homes in Akhalkalaki district for fear that they would once again erupt in antistatism, and because other Dukhobor parties opposed their return. At the same time, they could not be allowed to remain among the Georgian and Imeretian villagers, both because of the Fasters' destitution and the concern that their presence among the colonized peoples would threaten Russian imperial control. Prior to these meetings, Shervashidze argued that the Fasters living in Georgian villages should be banished from Transcaucasia altogether, preferably to Turkey, for which he believed the Dukhobors themselves were lobbying. Barring this, Shervashidze pushed for their relocation to the Transcaspian region, Batumi district, or Abkhazia.[123]

In their early meetings, the ministers did consider the Transcaspian region as a possible new home for the Dukhobors. Despite the years of nonviolent unrest, St. Petersburg was apparently interested in using the Dukhobors as an advance guard of Russian settlement in Central Asia, since such a policy had generally been successful in the South Caucasus. However, the commander in chief of Transcaspia, A. N. Kuropatkin, was reluctant to allow such oppositional Dukhobors into the Turkestan region. He felt that the costs of resettlement and of preparing a new location (particularly irrigation) were prohibitive. At the same time, not surprisingly, there were "political difficulties he foresaw which might arise as a result of relocating sectarian colonists—whose teachings forbid recognition of state authority and who refuse obedience to Government directives—into a newly annexed region among a less than fully acquiescent local population."[124]

A year later, Prince E. E. Ukhtomskii brought forward a not dissimilar proposal to resettle the Dukhobors outside of Russia's borders, into Chinese-held Mongolia. Ukhtomskii again relied on the trope of the sectarians as model colonists that had developed in the middle part of the century: "Motivated by need, these experienced Caucasus toilers would arrive in Mongolia as a sober, meek, Russian force, already accustomed in the Caucasus to dealing with foreigners, and would introduce there our language, our habit of healthy labor, in a word, much of what was ben-

123. Kuropatkin, *Soobrazheniia*, 27–28; Woodsworth, *Russian Roots*, 79; and Donskov, "On the Doukhobors," 258.
124. Woodsworth, *Russian Roots*, 80; and Kuropatkin, *Soobrazheniia*, 40–42, passim.

eficial in the Caucasus." In this case, it was Golitsyn who rejected this project, emphasizing the Dukhobors' "deep hatred of Russian authority and Orthodoxy" and illustrating how much the image of the Dukhobors had shifted in the minds of some state officials. "In view of the Dukhobors' undoubted stubborn and exasperating rejection of the basic principles of our society," he argued, "these people can hardly be regarded as especially useful as colonizers of the adjacent parts of the Chinese empire and they would scarcely be able to facilitate the birth among foreigners of a movement toward Russian norms and to our political structure."[125]

Despite the unacceptability of these particular relocation plans, Golitsyn remained firm in his belief of the necessity to "free Kakheti and Kartli from so harmful and dangerous an element." He made a case to have the internally banished Dukhobors moved within Transcaucasia to Azerbaijani villages in the eastern part of the region where, Golitsyn believed, they would have the most difficulty in spreading their beliefs and opposition. This internal banishment would succeed, he argued—echoing official views of the early nineteenth century—because the Azerbaijani "worldview is not receptive to the propaganda and demoralization of the Dukhobors' false teachings."[126] In 1897 hundreds of Dukhobors were in fact sent out from prisons and Georgian villages to the eastern Transcaucasus. They were settled near the Persian border in Muslim villages either individually or in groups of no more than three. Here, too, they suffered from disease and other health problems, especially fever and hunger.[127] However, even when the tsarist government agreed to send the Dukhobors to eastern Transcaucasia, the internal exile process provoked concern from other Russian elites, splitting the Russian government. No less than Grand Prince Michael sent an angry telegram to the Ministry of Internal Affairs in July 1897, asking, "Is it possible that Dukhobors from Kars territory are being sent to the Mugan steppe?" He was outraged at the prospect of the region's "dangerous climate" killing many of the Dukhobor exiles.[128]

These discussions over where to send the Fasters demonstrate fundamental changes in the way in which state authorities categorized these sectarians. Just as Dukhobor self-definitions shifted over these years, with religious self-conceptions overshadowing any identification as Russian subjects or ethnic Russians, so too did state categorizations change. Un-

125. Quoted and translated in Donskov, "On the Doukhobors," 259–60. On Ukhtomskii, see David Schimmelpenninck van der Oye, *Toward the Rising Sun: Russian Ideologies of Empire and the Path to War with Japan* (DeKalb, 2001), 42–60.

126. GARF f. 102, 3 d-vo, op. 1895, d. 1053, ch. 1, ll. 5550b–600b.

127. GMIR f. 2, op. 7, d. 489, 1928, l. 7; d. 510, n.d., ll. 1–9; ORRGB f. 369, k. 43, d. 1, 1950, ll. 820–24; and Woodsworth, *Russian Roots*, 95.

128. GARF f. 102, 3 d-vo, op. 1895, d. 1053, ch. 1, l. 5810b.

like in the mid-nineteenth century, however, the Dukhobor and state shifts did not move in tandem. Most state officials placed little classificatory weight on their religiosity—despite the spiritual reformation of the New Dukhoborism—seeing them instead as political threats to tsarist power who could no longer be considered loyal subjects or appropriate colonizers. As Golitsyn noted in his discussion of Ukhtomskii's proposal, the Dukhobors were no longer able to transmit Russian norms and values in a colonial situation. The change in identification was not total, however. Officials like Ukhtomskii did continue to see the Dukhobors as excellent colonists, and other officials and educated elites maintained that those sectarians not given to rebellion remained the cream of the colonizing crop.[129]

Significantly, this shift in classification of the Fasters resulted less from their religious difference as an a priori negative characteristic than from their political opposition, challenge to authority, and denial of Russian ethnicity. Thus, unlike the early nineteenth century, when sectarians had been politically and ethnically suspect by virtue of their religious affiliation (and, to a certain degree, by virtue of their actions), by the end of the century the reverse was true: their religious affiliation became suspect because of their antistate resistance. With the exception of the Synod, discussions about the Fasters tended to downplay their sectarianism and highlight their political opposition. Shervashidze claimed that "the Dukhobor sect has been not a religious, but solely a sociopolitical movement with Communist leanings; in their creed religious beliefs and ritual are an additional element necessary for the concealment of their basic social aims." Likewise, Golitsyn called the Veriginites a "criminal anarchist community," Kuropatkin categorized them as "religious anarchists," and even the missionary V. M. Skvortsov found any discussion of the Fasters to hinge on "social-political questions, settled on the soil of a commune and anarchy, under light covering of religious foundations."[130]

The Dukhobors' embrace of their religious identity and their oppositional activities did not affect the state's ethnic categorization of them as Russians, another contrast to the earlier period. The triangular linkage of religious, ethnic, and state identities operated differently in the late nineteenth century. State officials, both Russian and non-Russian, con-

129. Willard Sunderland, "The 'Colonization Question': Visions of Colonization in Late Imperial Russia," *JGO* 48, no. 2 (2000): 223; and Charles Steinwedel, "Resettling People, Unsettling the Empire: Migration, Colonization, and the Challenge of Governance, 1861–1917," in *Peopling the Periphery: Russian Settlement in Eurasia from Muscovite to Soviet Times*, ed. Nicholas B. Breyfogle, Abby Schrader, and Willard Sunderland (forthcoming).
130. For Shervashidze and Golitsyn, see Donskov, "On the Doukhobors," 257 and 256, respectively. For Kuropatkin and Skvortsov, see Kuropatkin, *Soobrazheniia*, 8 and 42.

tinued to see the Faster-Dukhobors as Russians despite the Dukhobors' pacifist resistance, their declarations of a pan-Christian sense of self, and their denial of Russian ethnicity. The Fasters could no longer be relied upon to carry out state duties, but they were Russians nonetheless. Shervashidze, for one, simply could not accept the Dukhobors' denial of Russianness. "While the Dukhobors have renounced their Russian ethnicity [and] do not recognize the Emperor, in the daily routine of life these were mere words; in the depths of their souls they could still not help feeling that they were Russian."[131] Similarly, military officials believed that "on the Asian frontier, every Russian person is a source of strength," whatever their religious affiliation—even if they could no longer be relied upon to defend the Empire in times of war.[132] Well after the Dukhobors emigrated, tsarist officials and educated society continued to claim them as ethnic Russians, lamenting their loss as servants to the Motherland.[133]

The state's efforts to find other places of settlement for the Dukhobors outside of Transcaucasia dovetailed with the Dukhobors' own desire to escape their current predicament by resettling either somewhere within Russia where they "might live and labor in peace" or in a foreign country.[134] Almost immediately after the burning of weapons and internal exile, the Fasters throughout Transcaucasia began to agitate for relocation, "but under the conditions that Fasters from all three provinces will be relocated, and that Verigin and the capital of the Orphan Home would be returned to them."[135] In expectation of imminent resettlement, many stopped sowing their fields and sold off their livestock, clothes, and domestic implements, keeping only what they would be able to carry with them.[136]

In order to achieve these ends, Verigin even wrote to the Empress Alexandra Feodorovna in 1896, attempting to manipulate to the Dukhobors' advantage her presumed gender characteristics (caring, compassionate, maternal) and her well-known role as benefactor of philanthropic causes: "I implore thee, sister in Christ the Lord, Alexandra, pray thy husband Nicholas to spare the [Dukhobors] in the Caucasus from persecution. And there are at this moment more women and children suffering: hundreds of husbands and parents are confined in prisons, and thousands of families are dispersed in the native villages. . . . This falls specially heavily

131. Donskov, "On the Doukhobors," 257–58.
132. Andrievskii, *Voenno-geograficheskoe*, 71; and Kuropatkin, *Soobrazheniia*, 41.
133. RGIA f. 1284, op. 222–1900, d. 98; f. 1291, op. 50, d. 23, 1906; and Woodsworth, *Russian Roots*, Part II.
134. Woodcock and Avakumovic, *Doukhobors*, 116; and GARF f. 102, 3 d-vo, op. 1895, d. 1053, ch. 1, ll. 544, 600–6000b.
135. Kuropatkin, *Soobrazheniia*, 14.
136. GARF f. 102, 3 d-vo, op. 1895, d. 1053, ch. 1, ll. 600–6000b; and Woodsworth, *Russian Roots*, 95.

upon the Christian women!" After laying out the Dukhobors' travails, Verigin suggested a solution to the standoff: either they be allowed to live
together elsewhere in the Empire unmolested by the state or they be
given "the right of emigration into one of the foreign countries. We
would willingly go to England or (which is most convenient) to America,
where we have a great number of brothers in the Lord Jesus Christ."[137]

With the Dukhobor Fasters undesirous of remaining within the Russian Empire and the tsarist government searching desperately for some
solution to the Dukhobor problem, both sides came together to bring
about the emigration of those Dukhobors who wanted to leave. Tsarist officials would have preferred not to lose the manpower and potential contributions of the Dukhobors (despite all that had happened) and only
agreed to their departure when all options for internal resettlement had
been exhausted. Indeed, they placed significant restrictions on those who
might want to leave Russia. "Those of conscription age who have not dis-
charged their military obligations" were forbidden to depart. Those who
did want to proceed with emigration were required to obtain their passports according to standard practice, to pay their own passage, and to sign
a declaration that they would never enter again into Russia, on pain of
exile to outlying regions of the empire.[138] Similarly, not all Dukhobors
wanted to emigrate, and many who initially committed to go later changed
their minds. Not unexpectedly, the internally banished Dukhobors from
Akhalkalaki district were more likely to embrace the emigration project,
while those who had remained in their home villages in Elisavetpol and
Kars were more reluctant.

In the emigration process, Tolstoyans and foreign religious communities (particularly Quakers) played an important role. They raised money
to pay for the Dukhobors' passage, with Tolstoy himself donating the pro-
ceeds from his book *Resurrection*. A number of Tolstoyans accompanied
the Dukhobors on their trip abroad. So great was the involvement that
many tsarist officials erroneously believed that the "Tolstoyan agitators
[were] the initiators of the proposal to send the Dukhobors abroad."[139]
As Golitsyn wrote to Goremykin in August of 1898, "Such actions by the
Tolstoyans, which have paralyzed all our government's efforts to make

137. Translated and quoted in Tchertkoff, *Christian Martyrdom*, 101–3. The original Russian letter is published in Bonch-Bruevich, *Pis'ma*, 89–91. Notably, Verigin was later more ambivalent
about the prospect of emigration. In an 1898 letter to Tolstoy he wrote: "You see, the members
of our community are in need of self-improvement, and so wherever we went we would take our
weaknesses with us; and even though an individual can generally live more freely abroad, I don't
think the difference would be all that great. People are the same everywhere." Translated in Andrew Donskov, ed., *Sergej Tolstoy and the Doukhobors: A Journey to Canada* (Ottawa, 1998), 11–12.
138. Woodsworth, *Russian Roots*, 98–99.
139. Ibid., 98–102; Donskov, "On the Doukhobors," 255–56; idem, *Sergej Tolstoy;* L. A. Sulerzhitsky, *To America with the Doukhobors*, trans. Michael Kalmakoff (Regina, 1982); and Woodcock and
Avakumovic, *Doukhobors*, 107–51.

the Dukhobors they have bewildered listen to reason, are evidently based solely on these agitators' fanatical attempts to make the Dukhobors a prime example of Tolstoy's ideas, to prove, whatever the cost, that their ephemeral socio-political utopia can become a reality."[140]

After an abortive attempt to relocate to Cyprus, approximately 7,500 of the more than 20,000 Dukhobors in Transcaucasia sailed for Canada in 1898 and 1899.[141] The emigration effectively brought an end to the Dukhobor oppositional movement and pacifist insurgency in Russia. Most Small- and Middle-Party Dukhobors stayed in the South Caucasus, along with some Fasters who decided not to make the trip. Other Veriginites remained in exile in Iakutiia until their release after 1905. The majority of Dukhobors, who remained in Russia, began slowly to redevelop symbiotic relations with the tsarist government and to rebuild their social and economic fabric in the wake of more than ten years of conflict and disruption.

This was not the last the world would hear of Dukhobor pacifist opposition, however. For all the calm that emigration brought to the Transcaucasus, the Fasters carried their nonviolent antistatism to Canada, where certain branches of the Dukhobors actively opposed the Canadian government. They became infamous in Canadian society for their refusal to send their children to schools or their men into the army, and for the arson and nudism (as signs of their disavowal of material things) of the Sons of Freedom. Moreover, as Josh Sanborn has recently brought to light, Dukhobors who remained in Russia also later ran afoul of Russian authority: in this case, a Dukhobor resistance movement against Soviet policies in Rostov-on-Don in 1937.[142] For all the traumas that the tsarist state unleashed upon the Dukhobors, the modern world generally held little place for these pacifist peasants who, as Golitsyn remarked, "denie[d] all the principles on which a state is based."[143] The Dukhobors themselves seem to have understood, to a degree, how hopeless their plight was. In one publication, they appealed in anguish to the international community to be moved from Canada to "where there is such a country and such a society, among which they could be tolerated, to settle and feed themselves, and in exchange for this no one would demand for them to give up freedom of conscience or what they consider God's truth."[144]

140. Woodsworth, *Russian Roots*, 102.
141. Donskov, *Sergej Tolstoy;* Sulerzhitsky, *To America;* Woodsworth, *Russian Roots*, 98–191; Woodcock and Avakumovic, *Doukhobors*, 107–51; and GMIR f. 2, op. 7, d. 946, 1924.
142. On the Rostov Dukhobors, see Sanborn, "Non-Violent Protest." On the Canadian Dukhobors, see Koozma J. Tarasoff, *Plakun Trava: The Doukhobors* (Grand Forks, BC, 1982); and Woodcock and Avakumovic, *Doukhobors.*
143. Woodsworth, *Russian Roots*, 102.
144. GARF f. 102, 5 d-vo, op. 1901, d. 509, ll. 44–440b.

FIGURE 18. Dukhobor Axenia Ivanovna Tarasoff with her nephews, Gorelovka, Tiflis province, c. 1916. British Columbia Archives C-01616, published with permission.

PACIFISM AND EMPIRE

The story of the Dukhobor movement is first and foremost about the triumphs and failings of religiously based pacifism in Russia and the difficulties that the modernizing tsarist state had in confronting such opposition. The burning of weapons and refusal of military service remain the most dramatic and among the most important demonstrations of pacifist opposition in Russian history. It certainly grabbed the attention of state leaders and the imagination of pacifists, both in Russia and around the world. Yet, for all the power of the Dukhobors' nonviolent platform, they did not spark a larger pacifist movement, despite their own hopes and those of Tolstoyans and Quakers. Notwithstanding the efforts of Molokans, Tolstoyans, and Mennonites, the Russian soil proved as infertile as elsewhere in Europe for a broad-based pacifist opposition, particularly one based on spiritual foundations. Indeed, the Dukhobors' case demonstrates the long and contingent road to overt pacifist resistance. While nonviolence had for generations been officially part of Dukhobor doctrines—although often honored in the breach rather than the observance—it took an extended period of "compromises" with that violence, an irreparable schism within the religious community, new leadership, and state persecution to bring the Large Party to strict pacifism.

From the state perspective, these pacifists posed a difficult conceptual problem because their nonviolence and civil disobedience could not be beaten out of them. Instead, the state's ineffectual measures of physical repression only made the state look (and feel) like a bully. Given tsarism's turn to universal conscription in 1874 and the military conception of using the army to define the boundaries of the national community, the tsarist state was confronted for the first time with the dilemma of what to do with a large group of people who refused to take up arms and participate in their envisioned national polity. At this time, the notion of granting exceptions—of the possibility of subjects who could be excused from service and yet be considered loyal—was inconceivable (or perhaps unacceptable) for ethnic Russians. Only the Mennonites received a blanket offer of alternative service with the forestry department. To each Dukhobor demand to be allowed to live in peace as Russian subjects and to be excused from duties connected with violence, the state's response was unequivocal: nonservice was not an option. It would be left to the early, heady days of the Soviet period before exclusions from conscription based on religious beliefs would be permitted, and even then only briefly.[145]

The Dukhobors' story is also one about peasant opposition to the

145. On the Mennonites exemption from service, see Peter Brock, *Freedom from Violence: Sectarian Nonresistance from the Middle Ages to the Great War* (Toronto, 1991), 153–63; and Lawrence Klippenstein, "Otkaz ot voennoi sluzhby po motivam sovesti v mennonitskikh obshchinakh tsarskoi Rossii," in *Dolgii put' Rossiiskogo patsifizma*, ed. T. A. Pavlova (Moscow, 1997), 150–71. On questions of conscription policy generally, see Sanborn, *Drafting*. On the exemptions granted to sectarians in the early Soviet period, see Aleksandr Etkind, "Russkie sekty i Sovetskii kommunizm: proekt Vladimira Bonch-Bruevicha," *Minuvshee: istoricheskii al'manakh* 19 (Moscow, 1996): 275–319; A. I. Klibanov, *Religioznoe sektantstvo i sovremennost'* (Moscow, 1969), 188–208; Bruno Coppetiers and Alexei Zverev, "V. D. Bonch-Bruevich and the Doukhobors: on the conscientious-objection policies of the Bolsheviks," *CES* 27, no. 3 (1995): 72–90; and Heather Coleman, "The Most Dangerous Sect: Baptists in Tsarist and Soviet Russia, 1905–1929" (Ph.D. diss., University of Illinois Urbana–Champaign, 1998).

socio-political status quo in Russia. On one level, it highlights the significance of religious factors in generating resistance to tsarist power in the late nineteenth century.[146] On another level, the Dukhobors' nonviolent civil disobedience represents a form of resistance that, while not usually attributed to the "arsenal" of Russian peasants, proved nonetheless a powerful tool in confronting state power.[147]

Moreover, the Dukhobor pacifist movement reflects the myriad complexities of Russian imperialism, colonial settlement, and ethnic politics in the South Caucasus. The increasingly tenuous nature of Russia's presence in Transcaucasia in the 1890s (with the burgeoning national independence movements and regionally based socialist parties) had a clear impact on the way that officials reacted to the Dukhobors' antimilitarism and antistatism, leading them to far more extreme reactions than might otherwise have been the case.[148] Here were the "model Russian colonists" rebelling against the Russian government and refusing to accept the cultural norms that the metropole was imposing. It was an ominous turn of events for state representatives (both Russian and non-Russian) who were compelled to force the Dukhobors back into line, lest sectarian "obstinacy" and resistance spread to the neighboring non-Russians. Moreover, the multi-ethnic situation of the South Caucasus—and the manner in which tsarist officials constructed ethnic difference and manipulated it to govern the Empire—made possible certain policy responses that would not have been options had the Dukhobors lived in the central provinces. The banishment of the Fasters to Georgian and Azerbaijani villages and the installation of Caucasians as *starshiny*, for example, would not have been possible away from the borderlands.

The indigenous population played a variety of roles in the unfolding drama, including both saviors and persecutors of the Dukhobors. The neighboring "natives" could not help but be aware of the Dukhobors' activities and travails. They benefited and were buffeted economically by the Dukhobors' changed relationship to material possessions. In partic-

146. Scholars have noted the religious origins of peasant protest in the seventeenth and eighteenth centuries, especially regarding the Old Believers, but have tended not to address this contributing factor in late Imperial Russia. Georg Michels, *At War with the Church: Religious Dissent in Seventeenth-Century Russia* (Stanford, 1999); and David Moon, *The Russian Peasantry, 1600–1930: The World the Peasants Made* (London, 1999). Recent historians of collectivization have begun to touch on religious aspects of peasant resistance. See Lynne Viola, *Peasant Rebels Under Stalin: Collectivization and the Culture of Peasant Resistance* (New York, 1996); and Sheila Fitzpatrick, *Stalin's Peasants: Resistance and Survival in the Russian Village after Collectivization* (New York, 1994).

147. David Moon highlights four types of peasant protest activity: violence and open rebellion, flight, minor disturbances, or actions that fall under the umbrella of James Scott's "everyday resistance" (such as work slow-downs and dissembling). See his *Russian Peasantry*, 237–81.

148. Ronald Grigor Suny, *Looking Toward Ararat: Armenia in Modern History* (Bloomington, 1993), 52–93; idem, *The Making of the Georgian Nation*, 2nd ed. (Bloomington, 1994), 113–81; and idem, ed., *Transcaucasia, Nationalism, and Social Change: Essays in the History of Armenia, Azerbaijan, and Georgia*, rev. ed. (Ann Arbor, 1996), 109–234.

ular, the complicity of South Caucasians as representatives of the Russian state in quelling the opposition of the Russian settlers sits uneasily and ironically with their own simultaneous nationalist battles against Russification. Yet their activities as state agents reflect the degree to which the Russian Empire provided welcome opportunities for its non-Russian subjects to take on positions of authority within the system. Their willingness to support the Russian state in its efforts to enforce laws, bureaucratic practices, and obedience on the Dukhobor settlers illuminates the degree to which the tsarist empire was not necessarily favorable to colonists who were ethnically Russian.[149]

That said, despite their very significant efforts in "colonizing the colonists," the role of native peoples was also a point of concern for officials in St. Petersburg. The authorities cited the Caucasians' actions in an effort to deflect blame from government policies, arguing that the unrest stemmed from the fact that the Dukhobors had been governed by non-Russians unfamiliar with the sectarians. The lesson of the Dukhobor case, central officials told themselves, was that if the tsarist state was to maintain control of its colonial holdings, these imperial territories would need to be run and controlled by ethnic Russians.

149. See also Jersild, *Orientalism*.

THE END OF AN ERA
AND ITS MEANINGS

MOLOKAN EMIGRATION,
ORTHODOX COLONIZATION

The Dukhobor oppositional movement was a clear sign that the episode of sectarian colonialism in the South Caucasus, which had begun in 1830, was undergoing a fundamental transformation. It was not the only harbinger of change, however. Two other linked processes signaled the end of the dissenters' leading role in tsarist empire-building. First, Molokans in the South Caucasus (and in certain central areas) began to voice their opposition to the demands of the tsarist state in ways that, while less dramatic than the Dukhobors, were equally unsettling to government authority. Eventually, they too called for permission to emigrate, and in the early twentieth century thousands of Molokans (especially Pryguny) left the South Caucasus to begin a new life in the United States and Mexico. Second, in the context of changing religious policies and peasant resettlement practices throughout the Empire, tsarist officials implemented a more aggressive plan for relocating Orthodox Russians to the Transcaucasus. With the sectarians leaving the South Caucasus en masse and Orthodox Russians appearing there in ever greater numbers, the composition of Russian colonists in the region was permanently altered—and along with it the nature of tsarist colonialism. Although more than half of the sectarian population remained, they were increasingly accompanied by large numbers of Orthodox Russians; the use of the South Caucasus as a zone of segregation for these religious nonconformists had come to an end.

Like the Dukhobors, the primary reason for the Molokans' increased dissatisfaction with the tsarist state and their desire to relocate was opposition to military conscription after so many years of freedom from this state obligation. Almost immediately after the imposition of universal male conscription in the South Caucasus in 1887, Molokans of all branches (but especially the Pryguny) began to look for a means of evading such service. They found that the demands of military service countered their religious tenets, particularly, of course, the commandment "Thou shall not kill." Moreover, they complained about a spectrum of problems in army service: about life in the barracks, "where soldiers corrupted their women"; about the prohibitions against practicing their faith in the army; about the army cuisine that required them to eat foods forbidden by their religion; about the obligation to swear an oath of allegiance in violation of their religious beliefs; and about military funerals in which their coreligionists were buried according to Orthodox and not Molokan rites. For many Molokans, the question of military service was the last straw. They were willing to put up with many of the restrictions and obligations placed upon them by the tsarist government, but their insistence that "their children not be taken as soldiers" was not negotiable.[1]

South Caucasian Molokans also felt themselves to be suffering from a range of economic problems that restricted their material lives and threatened their prosperity. Certainly, their communities remained in many respects far better off than other Russian peasants in the central provinces. Nonetheless, they found it harder and harder—both in perception and reality—to maintain the economic levels of preceding decades. In particular, the communities began to experience slowdowns in economic growth because of increasing land shortages. According to one observer, whereas in preceding years Molokan communities in Erevan province held five to seven *desiatiny* per adult male, by the early 1890s that number had dropped to between two and a half and three *desiatiny*. In addition, the average harvest of these villages had decreased by a third. The land shortage was the result of two distinct problems. The first was a rapidly growing population on a generally fixed amount of land. The migration of large numbers of Molokans to Kars territory in the early 1880s briefly relieved these pressures but did not solve the problem. Second, sectarians suffered from land insufficiencies as a result of their economic successes in land-intensive livestock rearing. As Dukhobors and Molokans thrived, the rapid growth of their flocks increasingly taxed their allotments, leading them to rent land from their neighbors.[2] In addition, the

1. GARF f. 102, 5 d-vo, op. 1901, d. 509, ll. 430b, 490b, 50–51; John K. Berokoff, *Molokans in America* (Whittier, CA, 1969), 16–18; Nicholas B. Breyfogle, "Swords into Plowshares: Opposition to Military Service Among Religious Sectarians, 1770s to 1874," in *The Military and Society in Russian History*, ed. Eric Lohr and Marshall Poe (Leiden, 2002), 441–67; A. I. Masalkin, "Iz istorii zakavkazskikh sektantov. Ch. III, Sektanty, kak kolonizatory Zakavkaz'ia," *Kavkaz*, no. 333 (December 16, 1893): 3; GMIR f. 2, op. 8, d. 356, n.d.; RGIA f. 1284, op. 222–1900, d. 69; and *Vsepoddanneishii otchet ober-prokurora sviateishego Sinoda K. Pobedonostseva po vedomstvu pravoslavnogo ispovedaniia za 1896 i 1897 gody* (St. Petersburg, 1899), 150–51.
2. Masalkin, "Kolonizatory," 3. Masalkin also blamed the reduction in output on the Molokans' own land-use practices, which he called "barbaric."

appearance of railways in the South Caucasus in the last quarter of the nineteenth century began to diminish the Molokans' profits from the carting business, depriving them of their lucrative contracts. As a result, Molokans turned increasingly to livestock ranching as a means to fill the void that the railroads had created in their economy, and this shift also exacerbated the problems of land shortage.[3] Faced with these economic challenges, Molokans and Pryguny regularly submitted petitions complaining about the onerous level of tsarist taxation.[4]

Molokans also became increasingly disillusioned with tsarist rule in the South Caucasus because of the restrictions in the practice of their religious faith. Molokans and Pryguny were especially angered by the state's ongoing prohibition against public religious services, the occasional arrests and exile of Molokan preachers and elders, and particularly the government's extensive efforts to forbid the building of designated church buildings for prayer. They voiced frustration at the accelerated construction of state schools in their villages and the government's continued opposition to the Molokans' desire to erect their own schools dedicated to Molokan, rather than Orthodox, Christianity.[5]

Prophecies and expectations of "a journey to eternal refuge" that had long been a component of Molokan and Prygun religious beliefs enhanced their commitment to relocation. The American Molokan author John Berokoff noted decades later that "there was a noticeable undercurrent of a feeling that their settlement in Trans-Caucasia was not permanent. The prophets were frequently moved by the Holy Spirit to remind the people that they should always be prepared to move to a place of Refuge." There were numerous prophecies among the Pryguny about the Journey to Refuge, beginning as early as the 1830s with the prophet David Yesseitch. These prophecies were frequently repeated at prayer meetings so that the idea of eventual movement was firmly entrenched in the minds of the Prygun faithful. Indeed, in what were known as "Spiritual Maneuvers," Berokoff records that "token flights to the refuge would be undertaken by marches of the whole Pryguny congregation

3. I. L. Segal', "Russkie poseliane v Elisavetpol'skoi gubernii (statistichesko-etnograficheskii ocherk)," *Kavkaz*, no. 41 (February 14, 1890): 3. Competition from Caucasian transporters also cut into their business and livelihood. S. Kolosov, "Russkie sektanty v Erivanskoi gubernii," *PKEG na 1902 g.* (Erevan, 1902): otd. IV, 151; N. B., "Ozero Gokcha (iz vospominanii o zakavkazskom krae)," *Kavkaz*, no. 61 (1861): 330; P. Paul', "Iz sel. Elenovki, Erivanskoi gubernii (o vliianii russkikh na korennoe naselenie Novobaiazetskogo uezda," *KSKh*, no. 169 (April 3, 1897): 230; and I. E. Petrov, "Seleniia Novo-Saratovka i Novo-Ivanovka Elisavetpol'skogo uezda," *IKOIRGO* 19, no. 1 (1907–1908): otd. 1, 245.
4. GARF f. 102, 5 d-vo, op. 1901, d. 509, ll. 470b, 50–500b, 51–510b, 540b.
5. Ibid., ll. 430b, 480b–50, 53–540b; GMIR f. 2, op. 8, d. 196, 1913; and Nicholas B. Breyfogle, "Prayer and the Politics of Place: Molokan Church-Building, Tsarist Law, and the Quest for a Public Sphere in Late Imperial Russia," in *Sacred Stories: Religion and Spirituality in Modern Russian Culture*, ed. Heather Coleman and Mark Steinberg (Bloomington, forthcoming).

from one end of the village to the other and back again to the prayer house."[6]

When Molokans first explored the possibility of migration to the Transcaspian region in the 1880s as a means to escape economic problems and military service in the South Caucasus, they called the lands in Turkestan "Tika," endowing the territory with a mythical quality that fit into their prophesies of the Journey to Refuge. Tika was an El Dorado described in one of their venerable songs, and word of Tika was spread by Prygun founder M. G. Rudometkin as well as other prophets. This refuge was to be characterized by "wonderful nature, different fruits and garden, where the trees give fruit twelve times a year."[7]

Another prophet, E. G. Klubnikin, had a vision as a young man in which the Holy Spirit revealed to him that three signs would betoken the appropriate time for the Journey. While he initially kept this prophecy secret, he believed that the three indications took place in the late 1880s and early 1890s. Klubnikin then began to travel around the villages to tell the elders that the time had come for the Journey to Refuge. Augmenting the desire to leave, Klubnikin's prophecies also included predictions that a dire calamity was soon to envelop Russia, before which event the Molokans needed to escape. The Pryguny increasingly became convinced of this and petitioned the tsar for permission to leave the country.[8]

For their part, tsarist officials pointed to the importance of the Dukhobor example for the Molokans in intensifying their opposition to the Russian state and their desire to emigrate.[9] Letters from Dukhobors and their supporters in Canada made their way into the hands of Molokans. Some of this correspondence painted a very tempting picture of the ease and high standard of living in North America, and underscored the freedom of conscience and exemption from military service extended to new arrivals, although it must be said that some of these letters exaggerated the advantages of life in Canada.[10] As in the Dukhobor case, tsarist officials also believed that the Molokans' antistatism resulted from the meddling of anti-tsarist intellectuals (primarily Tolstoyans) who were whipping the

6. Berokoff, *Molokans*, 13.

7. Masalkin, "Kolonizatory," 3.

8. Berokoff, *Molokans*, 15–19; and Pauline Young, *The Pilgrims of Russian-Town: The Community of Spiritual Jumpers in America. The Struggle of a Primitive Religious Society to Maintain Itself in an Urban Environment* (1932; repr. Hacienda Heights, CA, 1998), 12, 58.

9. GARF f. 102, 5 d-vo, op. 1901, d. 509, ll. 430b, 480b–490b, 51–510b. For one Molokan's view of Dukhobor emigration, see GMIR f. 2, op. 8, d. 237, 1910, l. 134.

10. GARF f. 102, 5 d-vo, op. 1901, d. 509, ll. 43, 44–440b, 46–470b, 48, 490b–500b. Not all letters painted a positive picture of the lives of Dukhobors in Canada, and a debate over their fate on the new continent took place not only in private correspondence but also in the pages of the Russian press. That groups of Dukhobors (and Molokans after their emigration) made plans to return to Russia indicates that not all immigrants were happy with their choice. On Dukhobor efforts to return to Russia in the early twentieth century, see Svetlana Inikova, *History of the Doukhobors in V. D. Bonch-Bruevich's Archives (1886–1950s)* (Ottawa, 1999), 83–90.

otherwise peaceable Molokans into a frenzy of opposition. Tsarist officials were especially perturbed because they believed that Molokan emigration would lead to a broader opposition movement among the native
peoples of Kars territory.[11]

The eventual Molokan departure from the South Caucasus took place
in two stages. First, they attempted to find more conducive places to live
within the tsarist empire and lobbied the government for more tolerant
treatment. In the late 1880s, Molokans (along with some Subbotniks) began to request permission to resettle from their homes in Transcaucasia,
especially from Erevan province, to the Transcaspian region.[12] They saw
in Turkestan the opportunity to enhance their economic situation
through better economic conditions, tax relief, and government financial incentives designed to attract Russian settlers to the region, and to
avoid military service, as Russian colonists were given a ten-year reprieve.[13] Settlers to Transcaspia from among the Molokans often returned with positive reports about the abundance of plants and crops
made possible through irrigation, but all complained of the searing heat.
In 1890, almost all of the Pryguny in Erevan province expressed a desire
to migrate eastward to "Tika." In the end, however, only a small number
actually did relocate for good, with the majority returning promptly because of the difficult environment. Additionally, Molokans experimented
with escaping their situation by resettling to other far-flung points in the
Russian Empire, such as into Siberia (especially Orenburg and Tobol'sk
provinces, and Blagoveshchensk on the Amur) or across the Chinese border into Manchuria.[14]

When movement within the Russian Empire proved unsatisfactory or
impossible, Molokans and Pryguny began, in the wake of the Dukhobor
exodus, to agitate for relocation "anywhere abroad." The first Molokan
scouts traveled to the United States to examine the territory in 1900, the
same year that the first of many Molokan petitions for migration to North
America was submitted. According to one petitioner, in 1900 five thousand Pryguny in Kars territory supported their emigration to North
America.[15] Emigration did not take place immediately because the tsarist
government consistently denied the Molokans permission to leave the
Empire. At the same time, the Molokans themselves were unsure whether
North America was the appropriate destination. The reports from the
scouts had been somewhat ambiguous about the quality of life there, and

11. GARF f. 102, 5 d-vo, op. 1901, d. 509, ll. 430b, 45–480b, 490b–50, 510b.
12. A. N. Kuropatkin, *Soobrazheniia nachal'nika Zakaspiiskoi oblasti po voprosu o pereselenii v Zakaspiiskuiu oblast' dukhoborov-postnikov* (n.p., n.d.), appendices 1–5.
13. Masalkin, "Kolonizatory," 3; Kuropatkin, *Soobrazheniia,* appendix 4; and Berokoff, *Molokans,*
17.
14. Masalkin, "Kolonizatory," 3; and GARF f. 102, 5 d-vo, op. 1901, d. 509, l. 540b.
15. GARF f. 102, 5 d-vo, op. 1901, d. 509, ll. 430b–44, 480b–490b, 50–510b.

such migration would be relatively expensive. There was also disagreement over whether America was in fact the place prophesied for their
Refuge, with opponents arguing that Ararat was the actual chosen land.
When the initial forays in the direction of emigration proved unsuccessful, as many as three thousand of the original five thousand potential em-
igrants officially renounced their desire to leave. One reason for the
reduction in interest in emigration was the "administrative measures"
that the officials took to quell the emigration "ferment," particularly by
investigating and exiling some of the leaders of the movement.[16] In the
end, many Pryguny left for the United States and Mexico without state
permission, primarily between 1904 and 1912.[17]

While Molokans and Dukhobors were increasingly unhappy with their
situation and tried to extricate themselves from the South Caucasus, the
tsarist government was simultaneously formulating its own plans to bring
an end to the era of sectarian colonialism. Beginning in the 1880s and
gathering steam throughout the 1890s, Russian officials inaugurated a
series of resettlement policies that introduced larger numbers of Orthodox Russians to Transcaucasia. After 1905, the initial sectarian settlements were swamped by large numbers of Orthodox Russian peasant
migrants, especially to Baku province, although the new Orthodox arrivals do not appear to have been as successful in adapting to their
colonist roles as the sectarians had been.

This shift in tsarist resettlement practice reflected changes in both
central and local policies regarding the borderlands (especially the peasant colonization of frontier lands) and regarding the place of religious
nonconformists in tsarist society. Beginning in the early 1880s and accelerating dramatically over the succeeding decades, St. Petersburg altered the scope and rate of peasant out-migration from central Russian
provinces, especially to Siberia and Central Asia, because of growing concern over the shortage of land for the recently emancipated peasantry.
The full force of this massive resettlement agenda came to the South Caucasus only at the end of the 1890s. Before this time, there were discussions concerning the expansion of ethnic Russian settlement to the
region, but these tended to result in only incremental changes because
the presence of sectarians blocked the way. Russian Orthodox migrants
did arrive in the 1880s and early 1890s, but the great majority came after 1900.[18]

16. Ibid., ll. 490b, 51, 53–540b
17. For the details of Molokan emigration to the United States, see Berokoff, *Molokans,* 12–31;
GARF f. 124, op. 9, d. 481, 1900; f. 102, oo d-vo, op. 1902, d. 622; and f. 102, 5 d-vo, op. 1901,
d. 509.
18. D. I. Ismail-Zade, *Russkoe krest'ianstvo v Zakavkaz'e: 30-e gody XIX–nachalo XX v.* (Moscow, 1982),
esp. 94–283; Firouzeh Mostashari, "Tsarist Colonial Policy, Economic Change, and the Making

As central officials began to encourage ever-increasing waves of Orthodox Russian peasant settlers into the border regions, local officials in Transcaucasia were simultaneously changing their approach to the settlement of ethnic Russians in their territory. South Caucasian authorities began to push for a greater Russian presence in the region, with the dual goals of easing the center economically and reinforcing Russia's control in its frontier regions. G. S. Golitsyn, chief administrator of the Caucasus from 1896 to 1904, was an especially ardent proponent of Russian colonization, pushing the migration project ahead with much greater fervency than his predecessors. He saw Russian appropriation of land as the best means to entrench Russia's imperial presence and to prevent any increase in Armenian landownership. Indeed, Golitsyn was so intent on the colonization project that he ordered his governors to demarcate land for Russian settlement "entirely independent of considerations of the land organization of the natives of Transcaucasia"—a marked departure from the regional leaders before him. Dondukov-Korsakov, for example, had consciously slowed the migration process because there was no way to make land available without dispossessing indigenous peoples.[19] Despite Golitsyn's policy goals, doubts did continue among many local administrators about the appropriateness of settling *any* Russians in the region because of the destructive effects of large-scale colonization on the native inhabitants.

The Orthodox colonization drive took place as certain tsarist authorities—K. P. Pobedonostsev and Synod officials—were assigning renewed importance to Orthodox religious affiliation as an indication of loyalty and commitment to the Empire. On one hand, tsarist officials never left behind their sense of sectarians as disloyal pariahs even as they embraced the idea of the dissenters as model colonists. On the other hand, the Dukhobor movement did little to reinforce any feelings of contentment with the sectarians as Russian representatives in the region. The same was

of the Azerbaijani Nation: 1828–1905" (Ph.D. diss., University of Pennsylvania, 1995), 225–50; Donald Treadgold, *The Great Siberian Migration: Government and Peasant in Resettlement from Emancipation to the First World War* (Princeton, 1957); Willard Sunderland, "The 'Colonization Question': Visions of Colonization in Late Imperial Russia," *JGO* 48, no. 2 (2000): 210–32; idem, "Peasant Pioneering: Russian Peasant Settlers Describe Colonization and the Eastern Frontier, 1880s–1910s," *JSH* 34, no. 4 (Summer 2001): 895–922; and Daniel Brower, "Kyrgyz Nomads and Russian Pioneers: Colonization and Ethnic Conflict in the Turkestan Revolt of 1916," *JGO* 44, no. 1 (1996): 41–53.

19. Golitsyn is quoted in Firouzeh Mostashari, "The Politics of Colonization: Sectarians and Russian Orthodox Peasants in Nineteenth Century Azerbaijan," *Journal of Central Asian Studies* 1, no. 1 (1996): 22. On the anti-Armenian goals of Golitsyn's projects, see Vartan Gregorian, "The Impact of Russia on the Armenians and Armenia," in *Russia and Asia: Essays on the Influence of Russia on the Asian Peoples,* ed. Wayne Vucinich (Stanford, 1972), 184. See also Austin Jersild, *Orientalism and Empire: North Caucasus Mountain Peoples and the Georgian Frontier, 1845–1917* (Montreal and Kingston: 2002), 126–44.

true of the growing Baptist communities in the South Caucasus and of the Prygun movement with their burgeoning demands for relocation. These more local events tied into larger shifts in tsarist religious policy that accompanied Pobedonostsev's tenure as Over-Procurator and the growing unease among Orthodox believers over the expansion of such new sectarian movements as the Shtundists. Beginning in 1899, resettlement laws to the South Caucasus clearly stated that migrants were required to be not only ethnically Russian but also Orthodox. The episode of sectarian colonization was at an end.

THE MEANINGS OF AN ERA

The story of the Molokans, Dukhobors, and Subbotniks who resettled to Transcaucasia between 1830 and 1900 is, on one level, a human narrative about the changing fate of specific communities. Their personal and communal tales are filled with aspirations and disappointments, achievement and tragedy, suffering and joy. Whereas some sectarians were exiled to the southern borderlands for their religious beliefs, many others chose to migrate in the hopes of a better life for themselves. Once there, they encountered new neighbors, new opportunities, and an unfamiliar environment. They experienced high mortality rates as well as economic success, conflict and coexistence with local Transcaucasians, greater freedom in their religious practice and a vibrant devotional life, shifting relations with Russian state power, and changing notions of self-identity. In the process, they altered the world around them even as it transformed them. Characteristic of the spiritual world of tsarist Russia, this story of the sectarians in South Caucasia underscores the integral place of faith and ritual in the daily lives of Russian subjects and in the policy decisions of tsarist officials. It also highlights the evolving nature of religiosity in response to both internal theological developments and the external influences of state authorities, interethnic contact, and the forces of modernization.[20]

On another level, the episode of sectarian colonialism in South Caucasia unveils a Russian Empire that was typically flexible and ad hoc in approach—an Empire that was constructed on a number of often disconnected levels, at times by Russian peasant colonists skeptical of, even

---

20. In this way, this book complements the recent surge of scholarship that is revising our understanding of religion in Russia. See two recent collective volumes that showcase current research: Valerie Kivelson and Robert H. Greene, eds., *Orthodox Russia: Belief and Practice under the Tsars* (University Park, PA, 2003); and Heather Coleman and Mark Steinberg, eds., *Sacred Stories: Religion and Spirituality in Modern Russian Culture* (Bloomington, forthcoming).

unaware of, the larger imperial agenda. Indeed, this study supports the argument of Andreas Kappeler and others that pragmatism and flexibility were central characteristics of tsarist empire-building, resulting in marked administrative and social diversity.[21] In Transcaucasia, as elsewhere across Eurasia, tsarist authorities accommodated their imperial strategies to the human resources available, in this case using pariah "heretics" as colonists. In time, the sectarians played important roles in the imperial process, but these functions were hardly anticipated by the officials who sent them to the southern periphery. Rather, administrators in both St. Petersburg and the South Caucasus came to realize the nonconformists' potential contributions only after resettlement had begun, and improvised new roles and obligations in response.

Such flexibility was both a source of tremendous strength for the Russian Empire and a debilitating weakness. Certainly, if one is to understand how the Russian state managed not only to expand over more than one-seventh of the world's surface but also to maintain that Empire while others crumbled around them, one cannot overestimate the significance of this pragmatic, makeshift approach to imperial management. For a state that was relatively lacking in infrastructure and resources—at least compared with the great imperial powers of Western Europe that were Russia's benchmarks—the decision to use religious dissenters as colonizers maximized the state service that could be obtained from people generally considered socially and politically unreliable. And the tsarist government received much more than they ever expected when the sectarians proved to be extremely competent in their newly allotted imperialist roles. For the dissenters, too, this plasticity was an attractive characteristic of Russian governance, granting them significant freedom and opportunities within the confines of an otherwise autocratic and intolerant state.

This flexibility also proved a significant disadvantage that helped to destabilize Russian power in the South Caucasus. Improvisation and adaptation to local realities ensured that the Russian Empire in the South Caucasus was built in part on the shoulders of sectarian settlers who were at best equivocal imperialists. As a result, while settler and imperial agendas might overlap in many cases, the colonists could not be unreservedly relied upon to support tsarist interests. The Dukhobor movement's challenge to tsarist power, like the burgeoning national opposition movements among many non-Russian communities in the late nineteenth century, reveals the perils of using these peasant dissenters as imperial agents in strategically sensitive borderlands.[22]

21. Andreas Kappeler, *The Russian Empire: A Multiethnic History* (Harlow, UK, 2001), 160–61, passim.
22. E. C. Thaden, ed., *Russification in the Baltic Provinces and Finland* (Princeton, 1981).

Tsarist leaders began to restrict this flexibility in the late nineteenth century, however, with significant consequences for both state and subjects. At that time, Russian imperialism shifted toward greater administrative and cultural standardization, increased prominence of Great Russian nationalism, and expansion of Orthodox borderland colonization.[23] In the South Caucasus, sectarian colonists who had long found the region to be one of relative freedom were confronted with new and unpalatable demands from a standardizing state. Their response was opposition and emigration.

Sectarians as Builders of Empire

While the case of the sectarian colonists in South Caucasia was in some respects unique, the history of sectarian colonization nonetheless demonstrates the pivotal role that peasant settlers played in forging the Russian Empire through the experiences of everyday life in multiethnic contexts. The sectarians functioned as empire builders in at least five ways: by providing administrative, economic, and military support to tsarist officials; as physical agents of "Russification" (*obrusenie*); through relations with the native populations; through interactions with the regional ecology; and as catalysts in the social and cultural formation of a multi-ethnic, multiconfessional Russian realm. These aspects of the peasant colonial experience tell a story about the tsarist empire very different from the narratives of domination/conquest and accommodation/resistance that have colored most histories of Russian geopolitics and imperial governance.

Throughout the nineteenth century, the state's colonizing policy in the South Caucasus was beset by powerful contradictions between the differing religious and imperial goals of sectarian resettlement. As originally envisioned in the 1830 edict, tsarist officials intended to use physical isolation in the southern borderlands to reduce, if not eliminate, the sectarians' communities and to cut off opportunities for contact with Orthodox Russians. Once the "heretics" arrived in Transcaucasia, however, officials also endeavored to use them as agents of imperial governance and control. The tension between these two agendas—one restrictive and intolerant, the other supportive and accommodating—

---

23. Thaden, *Russification;* Jersild, *Orientalism;* Treadgold, *Siberian;* Robert Geraci, *Window on the East: National and Imperial Identities in Late Imperial Russia* (Ithaca, 2001); Eric Lohr, *Nationalizing the Russian Empire: The Campaign against Enemy Aliens during World War I* (Cambridge, MA, 2003); Benjamin Nathans, *Beyond the Pale: The Jewish Encounter with Late Imperial Russia* (Berkeley, 2002); Theodore Weeks, *Nation and State in Late Imperial Russia: Nationalism and Russification on the Western Frontier, 1863–1914* (DeKalb, 1996); and Daniel Brower, *Turkestan and the Fate of the Russian Empire* (London, 2003).

produced complications, compromises, and inconsistencies in tsarist rule, not to mention frequently unfavorable consequences for the colonists themselves. Such contradictory policies were only exacerbated by vacillating official attitudes toward the sectarians that ranged from outright antagonism to grudging praise and acceptance.

The sectarian settlers became a cornerstone of tsarist imperial aspirations in South Caucasia, contributing directly to the achievements of the empire-building enterprise through a variety of economic, government, and especially military functions. Yet for all their many accomplishments the colonists were not simply cogs in the imperialist machinery. Rallying to the cause often reluctantly and on their own terms, they were independent actors who sometimes challenged the Russian state's designs, sometimes supported them, and sometimes were ambivalent. When the sectarians arrived in Transcaucasia, they felt no sense of colonial mission, held little stake in Russian state power, and were indifferent to Russia's geopolitical interests. Even as the sectarians began to develop a sense of shared interests with the tsarist state, they nourished their own priorities and goals, including religious freedom, eternal salvation, and earthly prosperity. When the dissenters supported the Russian military during wartime, they did so in their own way: as noncombatants and for a handsome price. As a result, the sectarian settlers did not acquire the sort of settler mentality that evolved, each in its own way, among the *pieds noirs* in Algeria, the Boers and British in South Africa, and the white settlers in Kenya and Southern Rhodesia.[24]

For their part, tsarist administrators did not consistently consider the sectarian settlers as dedicated agents of empire—there to fulfill central designs—or as equal (or even desirable) partners in the empire-building process. Despite a sincere appreciation of the nonconformists' ample imperial services, the authorities frequently distrusted the sects for their religious nonconformity and only supported settler demands in interactions with the local peoples irregularly. The tsarist practice of settling sectarians as tenant farmers on the lands of non-Russian elites and putting the settlers under the direct authority of Caucasian officials thrust the "colonizers" into a position subordinate to the "colonized." Here, then, the sectarians' religious difference, coupled with their "peasant" social status, created a gap between the colonists and the ruling elites that pre-

24. Alfred J. Rieber, "Struggle over the Borderlands," in *The Legacy of History in Russia and the New States of Eurasia*, vol. 1, ed. S. Frederick Starr (Armonk, NY, 1994), 85; John Comaroff, "Images of Empire, Contests of Conscience: Models of Colonial Domination in South Africa," in *Tensions of Empire: Colonial Cultures in a Bourgeois World*, ed. Ann Laura Stoler and Frederick Cooper (Berkeley, 1997), 178–91; Alan Lester, *Imperial Networks: Creating Identities in Nineteenth-Century South Africa and Britain* (London, 2001); and Dane Kennedy, *Islands of White: Settler Society and Culture in Kenya and Southern Rhodesia, 1890–1939* (Durham, NC, 1987).

vented the development of the cross-class bonds of "whiteness" that existed between imperial authorities and European settlers in British East
Africa, for example.[25]

Sectarian colonists also forged the tsarist empire in Transcaucasia by
acting as an advance guard of biological "Russification." Particularly from
the 1840s on, tsarist officials pictured the settlers as an ethnic anchor—
entrenched in the South Caucasian soil to prevent it from drifting away
from the imperial core. Here too, however, the decision to populate the
South Caucasus with religious sectarians had a contradictory long-term
impact on Russian imperialism. Official fears of sectarian contagion
blocked the settlement of Orthodox Russians in the region until very late
in the nineteenth century. By restricting the overall number of Russian
migrants to Transcaucasia, the original goal of religious segregation
worked against the state's larger vision of integration through colonization. Unlike the North Caucasus or Siberia (or, for that matter, Bashkiria
or the Middle Volga region), which witnessed higher rates of Slavic in-mi-
gration, South Caucasia remained relatively un-Russified. As a result, during the turmoil of both 1917 and 1991 it was easier to uncouple these
regions from the Empire.[26]

The sectarians further acted as empire builders through their relations
with the peoples of the South Caucasus. Indeed, for the Georgians, Armenians, Azerbaijanis, Kurds, and others living in the South Caucasus, the
experience of Russia's imperial presence was shaped in no small way by
their daily contact with the sectarian settlers. These interactions took on
a variety of forms—land disputes, violent clashes, trade, and mutual aid—
and betrayed no permanent division of power between the colonists and
the colonized. The blurring of "dominator" and "dominated" was enhanced by the tsarist practice of subordinating Russian settlers to non-Russian elites, producing a tension within imperial policy between conflicting
ethnic and social power structures. Despite a general belief that Russians
were the most loyal imperial servitors, tsarist imperialism did not have a
strictly ethnic basis that consistently privileged Russians, and local social
status could and often did trump Russian ethnicity. Moreover, whatever
their ethnicity and outlook, tsarist officials were frequently concerned to
ensure that the arrival of the sectarian settlers did not too greatly disrupt
the lives and livelihoods of the indigenous peoples. Certainly, the government did redistribute land, taking from the native peoples and giving

25. Kennedy, *Islands of White*. See also Lester, *Imperial Networks;* and Catherine Hall, *Civilising Subjects: Colony and Metropole in the English Imagination, 1830–1867* (Chicago, 2002).
26. For an insightful comparative discussion of the nexus between colonial settlers, control of territory, and conceptions of empire and state, see Ian S. Lustick, *Unsettled States, Disputed Lands:
Britain and Ireland, France and Algeria, Israel and the West Bank-Gaza* (Ithaca, 1993).

to the Russian settlers or placing the settlers in the supposedly open lands of nomadic pastures. Nevertheless, local officials also strove to protect the interests of the indigenous peoples and were not automatically support-ive of the Russian peasants because of their "Russianness."

The sectarians' relations with their Caucasian neighbors provide im-portant points of comparison with colonial encounters elsewhere. Al-though their experiences had much in common with that of European settlers in North America—aspects of a "frontier exchange economy" and "middle ground," the process of contiguous expansion of the fron-tier, and the role of religious nonconformists in the colonization pro-cess—there were significant differences. The sectarian settlers neither annihilated the indigenous population nor pushed them systematically off their lands. Moreover, unlike European settlers elsewhere in the nine-teenth century, the sectarians did not develop a racially based conception of their Caucasian neighbors, nor did they systematically exploit them economically or sexually.

As scholars of Western European imperialism have shown, imperial expansion often carries with it significant ecological impacts. Unlike other colonized regions both in Russia and elsewhere, however, the nat-ural environment of the South Caucasus was relatively unchanged by the Russian settlers. The overall absence of colonist-induced environmental change was a significant aspect of Russian empire-building, one with far-reaching implications for the peoples of the region.[27]

Finally, the colonists were involved in the building of empire on a so-cial and cultural level. Their communities and daily experiences forged the specific experiential characteristics of nineteenth-century Russia as a multi-ethnic state every bit as much as military conquest or political ad-ministration did. The tsarist empire's multicultural society was a con-stantly evolving organism in which the settlers themselves—in concert with tsarist officials and policies, indigenous peoples, and local environ-ments—created the ever-shifting kaleidoscope of the social and cultural world of the Empire.

Alternative Russias

Just as the colonists played a significant role in the process of empire-building, Russian imperial expansion, with its inclusion of vast territories

---

27. In other arenas, nineteenth-century tsarist empire-building did leave its mark on the climate and environment of South Caucasia, such as in the burgeoning oil industry. However, the largest changes to the environment came in the 1920s and after. Yu. P. Badenkov, A. K. Borunov, A. F. Mandych, A. I. Romashkevich, and V. O. Targulian, "Caucasia," in *The Earth as Transformed by Hu-man Action: Global and Regional Changes in the Biosphere over the Past 300 Years*, ed. B. L. Turner et al. (New York, 1990), 513–31.

and diverse peoples, also transformed the social and cultural worlds of the peasant colonists. By laying open the possibility of resettlement, the very existence of empire gave the migrants the opportunity to refashion themselves in many ways. At the same time, the Empire changed the central provinces by moving out large numbers of people—in this case religious dissenters—that permitted for greater social homogeneity in the interior.

Many significant changes in economic practice developed in the sectarians' communities as a result of their efforts to adapt to the ecology of the Caucasus and, when they could, transform that ecology to serve their own needs. Presented with new opportunities—such as the transportation trade and government contracts—many Russian villagers were able to realize a material existence that contrasted favorably with the suffering of peasants in the central provinces. In this regard, the case of the sectarian colonists mirrors the economic achievements of the Russian peasants who migrated to Siberia at the start of the twentieth century.[28] However, communal enrichment sparked a process of social stratification that was unprecedented—and ultimately unwanted—for these doctrinally egalitarian religious groups.

Still, these alternative Russias of the borderlands often retained much in common with the peasant villages of the Empire's central provinces. While many villagers made dramatic changes in their economic practices, others did not, preferring to stay as close as possible to old ways. Even those who changed did so within the framework of traditional Russian peasant economic practices, characterized by a diversified economy that valued certain crops and forms of cultivation over others.[29] Perhaps more so than in other areas of Slavic migration, the sectarians clung to their customary social and cultural practices, particularly in terms of family life and gender systems. Moreover, as a result of their later emigration, the new worlds generated by sectarian colonists proved much less permanent than those in other parts of the Empire where the settlers put down more lasting roots.[30]

In many respects, the greatest socio-cultural change in this alternative Russia was religious, for the physical journey southward was also a spiritual voyage. The colonists forged new religious identities and theological

28. The source of this economic success was different, however, because the sectarians had distinct religious characteristics and much less access to land, which was highly restricted in Transcaucasia because of extensive preexisting indigenous use. Treadgold, *Siberian.* See also Thomas M. Barrett, *At the Edge of Empire: The Terek Cossacks and the North Caucasus Frontier, 1700–1860* (Boulder, CO, 1999).
29. Regarding peasant economic diversification, see David Moon, *The Russian Peasantry, 1600–1930: The World the Peasants Made* (London, 1999), 118–55.
30. Treadgold, *Siberian.*

systems as they debated which old practices to abandon or fashion anew. The result was a spiritual effervescence that ranks among the most vibrant outpourings of popular religiosity in nineteenth-century Russia. The state's efforts to segregate the sectarians energized their communities by bringing them together for the first time in villages that were purely sectarian. In the relative freedom of the frontier, a spectrum of new and often millenarian religious movements burst into existence. The experiences of life in the South Caucasus during the nineteenth century led directly to the advent of the radical "New Dukhoborism," new Molokan branches such as the Pryguny and Obshchie, and the shift in daily practice from a religiously inspired pacifism to an acceptance of violence in encounters with the Caucasian peoples.

Identity

Understood as both self-description and a state-imposed classification, identity was another locus of significant cultural transformation and flexibility in these new worlds. Categories were of fundamental importance in tsarist Russia, a polity that extensively labeled and divided its population, generating a series of politically and socially significant ascriptive groupings, each endowed with restrictions and privileges. In the eighteenth and early nineteenth centuries, state categorization helped to define the sectarians as discrete groups by fixing them with names—Molokan, Dukhobor, or Subbotnik—that the sectarians themselves later embraced, to varying degrees, as their own. By isolating them on the periphery, the state further consolidated these groups as distinct, self-conscious communities.

Religious identity remained socially and politically valent throughout the nineteenth century, although with significant variances in meaning over time. Prior to resettlement to the Caucasus, the sectarians' religious differences had defined them as outside the fold of both "Russians" (because they were not Orthodox) and "loyal subjects" (because state authorities understood religious pluralism as a political threat and also because obeying secular authority violated the tenets of the sectarians' faith). Once they arrived, however, the state came to identify the non-conformists as model Russian colonists. While the authorities never quite forgot that they were also "heretical pariahs," the application of this new political and ethnic characterization lessened the negative valence that officials had previously attached to their religious distinctiveness. As they showed their political worth to the Empire, lived near non-Russians of contrasting faiths and cultures, and developed their own sense of attachment to, and stake in, state authority, the sectarians' own identity as Russians and imperial subjects also took on new meanings.

Categories such as "Russian," "sectarian," and "loyal subject" often proved unstable, however, because the classificatory borders were developed and maintained through conflicts with state officials over precisely these same labels. Far from being passive, those being classified consciously manipulated the availing categories to take advantage of the benefits and privileges applied to certain labels. Thus, Orthodox peasants wishing to leave their place of residence might take up a sectarian identity to do so, and sectarians wishing to stay in the central provinces underwent the same process in reverse. Once the sectarians arrived in the Caucasus, they naturally tried to manipulate their classification as "Russians" to their benefit.

The Dukhobor movement vividly illustrates the formation, manipulation, and volatile meanings of identity categories in late nineteenth century Russia. Historians have pointed to an increased emphasis on ethnic and linguistic factors as the determinants of nationality in Europe as the nineteenth century progressed, and specialists in Russian history have tended to see a similar, albeit less complete, shift toward ethnic categorizing after the Great Reforms.[31] When viewed from the perspective of the state, the case of the Transcaucasian Dukhobors by and large supports this view. Although the Dukhobors' anti-state activities once again made their religious difference suspect, pushing them out of the fold of loyal tsarist subjects, state officials most frequently classified them not in religious but in ethnic and political terms—as disloyal, untrustworthy Russian subjects. The state's response to the Dukhobor movement suggests that by the turn of the twentieth century tsarist authorities had reduced the importance that they attributed to religious affiliation as a primary mode of social and political classification. This is not to say that religion disappeared as a meaningful marker of state identification. For one, the Synod and Over-Procurator continued to emphasize Orthodox affiliation as essential to political reliability and Russian ethnicity, exerting vigorous influence in ministerial policy debates and in broader societal discussions over the meanings of "Russianness." Moreover, the lesson of the Dukhobor debacle for officials in St. Petersburg was that imperial stability in the South Caucasus required a greater reliance on servitors who were both Russian *and* Orthodox, and less dependence on sectarians and local, non-Russian elites. Nonetheless, a notable shift had taken place in the relative weight that tsarist officials apportioned to religious, ethnic, and political

31. E. J. Hobsbawm, *Nations and Nationalism Since 1780: Programme, Myth, Reality*, 2nd ed. (Cambridge, 1992), 101–30; Charles Steinwedel, "To Make a Difference: the Category of Ethnicity in Late Imperial Russian Politics, 1861–1917," in *Russian Modernity: Politics, Knowledge, Practices*, ed. David Hoffmann and Yanni Kotsonis (Basingstoke, 2000), 67–86; and Paul Werth, *At the Margins of Orthodoxy: Mission, Governance, and Confessional Politics in Russia's Volga-Kama Region, 1827–1905* (Ithaca, 2002), 124–46.

identifications in classifying and controlling the population. If in the early nineteenth century the sectarians' religious dissent had immediately marked them as politically unreliable, by the late nineteenth century the relationship was in many respects reversed: it was their political opposition that branded their religious nonconformity as suspect.

From the sectarians' vantage point, however, religious sense-of-self remained an important identity marker. Veriginite Dukhobors and many Molokans increasingly embraced a Christian identity that fundamentally cut their ties to earthly communities and temporal power. Thus, as the tsarist state strove to order the people of its Empire more consistently through intersecting categories of ethnicity and political loyalty, the nonconformists constructed and coded their self-understanding on a completely different axis, one in which a religious sense of community was paramount. In an increasingly "national" world, however, there was little place for this alternative religious vision.

At the same time, this analysis of identity among the Transcaucasian sectarians underscores that the agents of modernization—railroads, education, and military conscription, for example—did not necessarily act as forces for nation-building, as has been noted in other parts of Europe. Quite the opposite, the appearance of the instruments of "modernity" shattered the connections that had grown up between the sectarians and the Russian polity, and stripped away the pan-imperial identity that had previously tied them to a tsarist, all-Russian Empire. Here, then, religious identity played an important role in blocking the process of state- or nation-building in late Imperial Russia, thereby threatening the long-term survival of the tsarist state.[32]

Center-Periphery Relations and the Meaning of Frontiers in Russian History

The case of the sectarian settlers also speaks to the larger question of center and periphery in Russian history—defined here in spatial terms.[33] Their story undercuts the notion that the South Caucasian "frontier" was simply a geopolitical border between militarily antagonistic bureaucratic empires. It was also the intersection of peoples, one where both cultural

32. Compare to Eugen Weber, *Peasants into Frenchmen: The Modernization of Rural France, 1870–1914* (Stanford, 1976); Caroline Ford, *Creating the Nation in Provincial France: Religion and Political Identity in Brittany* (Princeton, 1993); and Peter Sahlins, *Boundaries: The Making of France and Spain in the Pyrenees* (Berkeley, 1989).

33. On questions of center and periphery, and for insightful discussions of the meanings of "frontier," "borderland," and "border," see Rieber, "Struggle," 61–89; Michael Khodarkovsky, "From Frontier to Empire: The Concept of the Frontier in Russia, Sixteenth–Eighteenth Centuries," *RH* 19, no. 1/4 (1992): 115–28; and Jeremy Adelman and Stephen Aron, "From Borderlands to Borders: Empires, Nation-States, and the Peoples in between in North American History," *AHR* 104, no. 3 (June 1999): 814–41.

creation and imperial conflict could occur. Different societies and polities strove to create a common, mutually shared world in these arenas. Indeed, the Russian periphery proved fertile soil for cultural cross-pollination and the evolution of new social, economic, and political forms. For much of the nineteenth century the borderlands represented a far more vital and diverse area than the geographic and political center—a place of experimentation and innovation with developments of great importance to the nineteenth-century Russian experience.[34]

The South Caucasus remained separate from the center in many ways, but the experiences of the Russian colonists had significant implications for the policies of the center. First, the praise extended to the sectarians for their activities as colonists, their marked economic success, and their support of the tsarist administration at certain junctures had an impact on the treatment of sectarians throughout the Empire. In certain cases, legislation that was extended to the Transcaucasian dissenters in an effort to facilitate their colonizing efforts was later granted to non-Orthodox Russians elsewhere in the Empire. Moreover, the growing sense that the sectarians were unusually good colonists led to their being used in this role—and held up as models—in other regions.[35] Second, Russian intellectual circles became increasingly fascinated by the sectarians and even took action on the sectarians' behalf. Tolstoy's relations with the Dukhobors, his championing of their cause, and the literary and intellectual activities stimulated by his engagement with them are a clear case in point.[36] Third, the inability to apply central policies in the periphery—such as universal military conscription—resonated in efforts to apply such policies throughout the Empire.[37]

As we have seen, the views of tsarist administrators toward the South Caucasian periphery changed over the course of the nineteenth century. Officials initially saw Transcaucasia as a separate part of the Empire: newly acquired, dangerous, and distinct from the center. As a result, they

34. Mark Bassin, "Turner, Solov'ev, and the 'Frontier Hypothesis': The Nationalist Signification of Open Spaces," *JMH* 65 (September 1993): 473–511. For the changeless or slowly changing Russia, see, for instance, Walter G. Moss, *A History of Russia*, vol. 1, *to 1917* (New York, 1997), 372.
35. Willard Sunderland, "Colonization Question," 223; and Charles Steinwedel, "Resettling People, Unsettling the Empire: Migration, Colonization, and the Challenge of Governance, 1861–1917," in *Peopling the Periphery: Russian Settlement in Eurasia from Muscovite to Soviet Times*, ed. Nicholas B. Breyfogle, Abby Schrader, and Willard Sunderland (forthcoming).
36. The same can be said for V. D. Bonch-Bruevich, whose enthrallment with sectarians led to his compulsive collection of documents by and about them. Aleksandr Etkind has extensively explored the meaning of the sectarians for Russian elite culture. See his *Khlyst: Sekty, literatura i revolutsiia* (Moscow, 1998).
37. Joshua A. Sanborn, *Drafting the Russian Nation: Military Conscription, Total War, and Mass Politics, 1905–1925* (DeKalb, 2003), 187. The inability to enforce central directives and policy goals in the Empire's peripheral regions, and the problems that ensued, can also be seen in Weeks, *Nation and State,* 131–92.

used this region as a zone of segregation, a place to jettison unwanted peoples. Their concern was for the central provinces, where they hoped, using a form of utopian social engineering, to create a better, more uniformly Orthodox society. The settlers themselves also attached utopian notions to the center-periphery nexus, but they turned the state's paradigm on its head. For them, the periphery was a place of utopian possibility, whether an earthly land of milk and honey or the heavenly kingdom of the imminent Second Coming.

Later in the nineteenth century, tsarist officials came to see the lands of the South Caucasus as more integral to the imperial whole. The Russian military became increasingly concerned with controlling the periphery and knowing about the kinds of people who lived in the borderland regions. They pushed for mass migrations of non-Russians from and Russians to the frontier zones in order to build loyal border communities that would ensure imperial security.[38] This same period witnessed a rapid increase in the centrifugal forces of nationalism in the Transcaucasus, which forced the state to work even harder to maintain control.[39] This gradual change in the state's view of the periphery was linked to the larger changes in tsarist administration that followed the Great Reforms. As was the case with the Dukhobors, the state began to intervene more directly in the lives of frontier communities. Finally, the industrial drive of the late nineteenth century made the border regions even more essential to the state because of their economic significance.[40] The South Caucasus could no longer serve as a zone for the segregation of the sectarian populations; it would now be settled by Orthodox Russian peasants who would integrate the region more completely with the Empire.

Although the era of sectarian colonialism ended around 1900, the story of Dukhobors, Molokans, and Subbotniks in the South Caucasus has continued. With emigration and the promulgation of new laws on religious toleration in 1905, the remaining nonconformists moved onto a different stage in their history, which included a larger role in late-imperial civil society through publications, associations, economics, and

38. Peter Holquist, "To Count, to Extract, and to Exterminate: Population Statistics and Population Politics in Late Imperial and Soviet Russia," in *A State of Nations: Empire and Nation-Making in the Age of Lenin and Stalin*, ed. Ronald Grigor Suny and Terry Martin (New York, 2001); and Jersild, *Orientalism*, 126–44. On "frontier anxiety," see Rieber, "Struggle," 68.

39. Ronald Grigor Suny, *Looking toward Ararat: Armenia in Modern History* (Bloomington, 1993), 52–93; idem, *The Making of the Georgian Nation*, 2nd ed. (Bloomington, 1994), 113–81; and idem, ed., *Transcaucasia, Nationalism, and Social Change: Essays in the History of Armenia, Azerbaijan, and Georgia*, rev. ed. (Ann Arbor, 1996), 109–234.

40. On the dynamic industrial development of the Empire's peripheries, see Alfred J. Rieber, *Merchants and Entrepreneurs in Imperial Russia* (Chapel Hill, 1982), 219–55, 333–71, passim.

national and local politics.[41] Many moved to the North Caucasus and Southern Russia during the years of war and revolution, but sectarians stayed in Transcaucasia during the Soviet period and continued to play a role as "Russians." In these new times, however, they often lost out under Soviet "indigenization" programs that privileged the native South Caucasian peoples over Russian settlers. They also suffered increasingly from the antireligious legislation of the atheist state.[42] Now that the Soviet Union is no more, the sectarian villages that began to appear in the mid-nineteenth century are finally emptying out. Those few that remain face a host of new challenges from economic downturns to infrastructural collapse and the often unwelcoming ethnic politics of newly independent states. Yet, having seen so many changes and upheavals in their collective lives, their resolve remains strong. "We'll survive," said Luda, a Dukhobor from Gorelovka, in the late 1990s. "We always have."[43]

41. Breyfogle, "Prayer and the Politics of Place."
42. Terry Martin, *The Affirmative Action Empire: Nations and Nationalism in the Soviet Union, 1923–1939* (Ithaca, 2001); Jörg Baberowski, *Der Feind ist überall: Stalinismus im Kaukasus* (Munich, 2003); A. I. Klibanov, *Religioznoe sektantstvo i sovremennost'* (Moscow, 1969), Joshua A. Sanborn, "Non-Violent Protest and the Russian State: the Doukhobors in 1895 and 1937," in *The Doukhobor Centenary in Canada: A Multi-Disciplinary Perspective on their Unity and Diversity*, ed. Andrew Donskov, John Woodsworth, and Chad Gaffield (Ottawa, 2000), 83–102; and S. E. Il'in, *Moia Zakavkazskaia Rossiia* (Moscow, 1998).
43. Quoted in Philip Marsden, *The Spirit-Wrestlers and other Survivors of the Russian Century* (London, 1999), 248.

SELECTED BIBLIOGRAPHY

ARCHIVAL SOURCES

British Columbia Archives (BCA), Victoria
Tarasoff Photo Collection on Doukhobor History

Centre for Research on Canadian-Russian Relations (CRCR), Ottawa
Russian Archival Documents on Canada: The Doukhobors, 1895–1943
Copied Documents from GARF f. 102.

Gosudarstvennyi Arkhiv Rossiiskoi Federatsii (GARF), Moscow
f. 102   Departament politsii ministerstva vnutrennikh del
f. 109   Tret' e otdelenie sobstvennoi ego imperatorskogo velichestva kantseliarii
f. 124   Vremennaia kantselariia po proizvodstvu osobykh ugolovnykh del pri minister-
          stve iustitsii
f. 579   P. N. Miliukov

Gosudarstvennyi Muzei Istorii Religii (GMIR), St. Petersburg
f. 2   V. D. Bonch-Bruevich (op. 7, Dukhobortsy; op. 8, Molokane)
f. 13   I. M. Tregubov
f. 14   Izd. Svobodnoe slovo
f. 17   P. I. Biriukov
f. K1   Sobranie materialov po istorii sektantstva v Rossii.

Manuscript Division, Library of Congress (GKP), Washington
George Kennan Papers

Otdel Rukopisei, Rossiiskaia Gosudarstvennaia Biblioteka (ORRGB), Moscow
f. 369   V. D. Bonch-Bruevich
f. 648   A. I. Klibanov

Peter J. Braun Russian Mennonite Archive (PJBRMA), Toronto
Microfilmed documents from Gosudarstvennyi arkhiv Odesskoi oblasti (f. 89, op. 1)

Rossiiskii Gosudarstvennyi Istoricheskii Arkhiv (RGIA), St. Petersburg
f. 379   Departament gosudarstvennykh imushchestv ministerstva finansov
f. 381   Kantseliariia ministra ministerstva gosudarstvennykh imushchestv
f. 383   Pervyi departament ministerstva gosudarstvennykh imushchestv

f. 384   Vtoroi departament ministerstva gosudarstvennykh imushchestv
f. 391   Pereselencheskoe upravlenie
f. 396   Departament gosudarstvennykh zemel'nykh imushchestv ministerstva gosudarst-
          vennykh imushchestv
f. 398   Departament zemledeliia ministerstva gosudarstvennykh imushchestv
f. 560   Obshchaia kantseliariia ministra finansov
f. 565   Departament gosudarstvennogo kaznacheistva ministerstva finansov
f. 573   Departament okladnykh sborov ministerstva finansov
f. 733   Departament narodnogo prosveshcheniia
f. 796   Kantseliariia Sinoda
f. 797   Kantseliariia ober-prokurora Sinoda
f. 821   Departament dukhovnykh del inostrannykh ispovedanii (MVD)
f. 919   I. I. Vorontsov-Dashkov
f. 932   A. M. Dondukov-Korsakov
f. 1149   Departament zakonov gosudarstvennogo soveta
f. 1152   Departament ekonomii gosudarstvennogo soveta
f. 1263   Komitet ministrov
f. 1268   Kavkazskii komitet
f. 1282   Kantseliariia ministra ministerstva vnutrennikh del
f. 1284   Departament obshchikh del ministerstva vnutrennikh del
f. 1287   Khoziaistvennyi departament ministerstva vnutrennikh del
f. 1291   Zemskii otdel ministerstva vnutrennikh del
f. 1354   Obshchie sobraniia i soedinennye prisutstviia kassatsionnykh departamentov
          senata
f. 1405   Ministerstvo iustitsii
f. 1473   Sekretnyi komitet po delam raskola
f. 1485   Reviziia senatora N. M. Reinke sudebnykh ustanovlenii Tiflisskoi sudebnoi palaty
f. 1574   K. P. Pobedonostsev
f. 1661   K. S. Serbinovich

Sak'art'velos saistorio c'entraluri saxelmcip'o ark'ivi (SSC'SA), Tbilisi

f. 3   Kantseliariia nachal'nika grazhdanskogo upravleniia Zakavkazskim kraem, 1842–
          59
f. 4   Kantseliariia Namestnika Kavkazskogo, 1845–58
f. 5   Kantseliariia nachal'nika glavnogo upravleniia glavnonachal'stvuiushchego grazh-
          danskoi chast'iu na Kavkaze, 1859–83
f. 12   Kantseliariia glavnonachal'stvuiushchego grazhdanskoi chast'iu na Kavkaze, 1882–
          1905
f. 16   Kantseliariia Tiflisskogo voennogo gubernatora upravliaiushchego grazhdanskoi
          chast'iu, 1802–59
f. 17   Kantseliariia Tiflisskogo gubernatora, 1860–1917
f. 26   Tiflisskoe gubernskoe pravlenie, 1802–1919
f. 222   Komissiia po ustroistvu poselenii v Zakavkazskom krae, 1847–52
f. 239   Ekspeditsiia gosudarstvennykh imushchestv pri glavnoi upravlenii Zakavkazskogo
          kraia, 1850–58
f. 240   Departament gosudarstvennykh imushchestv glavnogo upravleniia Namestnika
          Kavkazskogo, 1859–67
f. 244   Tiflisskoe upravlenie gosudarstvennykh imushchestv, 1868–1918
f. 488   Kantseliariia Ekzarkha Gruzii, 1811–1917
f. 1438   Simon S. Esadze and Boris S. Esadze

CONTEMPORARY PERIODICALS

Baku
Dukhovnyi khristianin
Istoricheskii vestnik

Izvestiia Kavkazskogo otdela Imperatorskogo Russkogo geograficheskogo obshchestva
Kars
Kaspii
Kavkaz
Kavkazskie eparkhial'nye vedomosti
Kavkazskii kalendar'
Kavkazskoe sel'skoe khoziaistvo
Molokanin
Molokanskii vestnik
Missionerskoe obozrenie
Novoe obozrenie
Obzor
Otechestvennye zapiski
Pamiatnaia knizhka Erivanskoi gubernii
Pravoslavnoe obozrenie
Pravoslavnyi sobesednik
Russkaia mysl'
Russkaia starina
Russkii arkhiv
Russkii vestnik
Svobodnoe slovo
Sovremennik
Strana
Tiflisskii listok
Tiflisskii vestnik
Tserkovno-obshchestvennyi vestnik
Tserkovnyi vestnik
Tserkovnye vedomosti
Vestnik evropy
Vestnik Gruzinskogo Ekzarkhata
Zapiski Kavkazskogo obshchestva sel'skogo khoziaistva
Zapiski Kavkazskogo otdela imperatorskogo geograficheskogo obshchestva

PUBLISHED PRIMARY SOURCES

Abelov, N. A. "Ekonomicheskii byt gosudarstvennykh krest'ian Geokchaiskogo i Shemakhinskogo uezdov Bakinskoi gubernii." In *MIEB*. Vol. 6, 1–334. Tiflis, 1887.
——. "Ekonomicheskii byt gosudarstvennykh krest'ian Elisavetpol'skogo uezda Elisavetpol'skoi gubernii." In *MIEB*. Vol. 7, 1–140. Tiflis, 1887.
Akty Sobrannye Kavkazskoiu Arkheograficheskoiu Kommissieiu. 12 vols. Edited by A. Berzhe. St. Petersburg, 1886–1904. [Vol. 12 was published twice with different pagination, in 1893 and 1904].
"Alty-Agach (Ot nashego korrespondenta)." *Kaspii* 14, no. 115 (June 1, 1894): 3.
Andreevskii, E. K. "Ot Erzeruma do Tiflisa v. 1878 godu." *IV* 2 (May, 1880): 46–91.
Andrievskii, polkovnik. *Voenno-geograficheskoe i statischeskoe opisanie Kavkazskogo voennogo okruga.* Tiflis, 1908.
Argutinskii, A. M. "Ekonomicheskii byt gosudarstvennykh krest'ian Signakhskogo uezda, Tiflisskoi gubernii." In *MIEB*. Vol. 4:2, 179–385. Tiflis, 1886.
——. [Argutinskii-Dolgorukov, A. M.] "Borchalinskii uezd, Tiflisskoi gubernii v ekonomicheskom i kommercheskom otnosheniiakh." In *RTKE*, 1–323. Tiflis, 1897.
B., N. "Ozero Gokcha (iz vospominanii o zakavkazskom krae)." *Kavkaz*, no. 61 (1861): 328–30.
B., T. "U beregov Kaspiia (iz putevykh zametok i vospominanii) Tri goda nazad." *Kavkaz*, no. 3 (1881): 1; no. 58 (1881): 2–3; no. 75 (1881): 1–2; no. 85 (1881): 2; and no. 91 (1881): 2–3.
Bienstock, J. W., ed. and trans. *Tolstoi et les Doukhobors: faits historiques réunis et traduits du russe.* Paris, 1902.

Biriukov, Pavel Ivanovich, *Dukhoborets Petr Vasil'evich Verigin.* Geneva, 1903.
———. *Dukhobortsy. Sbornik statei, vospominanii, pisem i drugikh dokumentov.* Moscow, 1908.
———. "Kratkii ocherk polozheniia dukhobori za istekshii 1897 god i do nastoiashchogo vremeni." *Svobodnoe Slovo,* no. 1 (1898): 177–218.
Biriukov, P. I. and Vladimir G. Chertkov. *Polozhenie dukhoborov na Kavkaze v 1896 godu i neobkhodimyia sredstva oblegcheniia ikh uchasti.* London, 1897.
Bochkarev, V. P. "Karsskaia oblast'." In *RTKE,* 325–519. Tiflis, 1897.
Bonch-Bruevich, V. D., ed. "Dukhoborcheskaia epopeia." *Obrazovanie,* no. 3 (March 1908): 72–96; no. 6 (June 1908): 117–35.
———, ed. *Pis'ma Dukhoborcheskogo rukovoditelia Petra Vasil'evicha Verigina.* Vol. 1 of *MIIRS.* Christchurch, UK, 1901.
———. *Programma dlia sobranii svedenii po issledovaniiu i izucheniiu russkogo sektantstva i raskola.* St. Petersburg, 1908.
———, ed. *Materialy k istorii i izucheniiu russkogo sektantstva.* 4 vols. Christchurch, UK, 1901–1902.
———, ed. *Materialy k istorii i izucheniiu russkogo sektantstva i raskola.* 6 vols., numbered 1–5, 7. St. Petersburg, 1908–16.
———, ed. *Rasskaz Dukhobortsa Vasi Pozniakova. S prilozheniem dokumentov ob izbienii i iznasilovanii dukhoborcheskikh zhenshchin kozakami.* Vol. 3 of *MIIRS.* Christchurch, UK, 1901.
———, ed. *Raz" iasnenie zhizni khristian i Byl' u nas, khristian, sirotski dom (dve dukhoborcheskiia rukopisi).* Vol. 2 of *MIIRS.* Christchurch, UK, 1901.
———. *Spisok psalmov, pisem, rasskazov i drugikh rukopisei po issledovaniiu ucheniia, zhizni i pereseleniia v Kanadu zakavkazskikh dukhobortsev.* Geneva, 1900.
———, ed. *Zhivotnaia Kniga Dukhobortsev.* St. Peterburg, 1909.
Borozdin, A. K. *Russkoe religioznoe raznomyslie.* St. Petersburg, 1907.
Borozdin, K. A. "Pereselentsy v Zakavkaz'e." *RV,* no. 215 (July 1891): 117–61.
Brock, Peter. "Vasya Pozdnyakov's Dukhobor Narrative." *SEER* 43 (December 1964): 152–76; and 43 (June 1965): 400–414.
Bryce, James. *Transcaucasia and Ararat: being notes of a vacation tour in the autumn of 1876.* London, 1877.
Buniatov, Grigorii. "Byt russkikh krest'ian Loriiskogo uchastka, Borchalinskogo uezda, Tiflisskoi gubernii." In *SMOMPK.* Vol. 31, otd. II, 97–145. Tiflis, 1902.
Buniatov, S. "Khoziaistvennyi byt russkikh poselentsev Borchalinskogo uezda, Tiflisskoi gubernii. I. Sposob pol'zovaniia zemeleiu i zemel'noe dovol'stvo." *KSKh,* no. 121 (May 2, 1896): 2075–76.
Butkevich, T. I. *Obzor russkikh sekt i ikh tolkov.* Petrograd, 1915.
Chertkov, V. G. and A. K Chertkova, eds. *Dukhobortsy v distsiplinarnom batal'one.* Vol. 4 of *MIIRS.* Christchurch, UK, 1902.
Dekonskii, A. G. "Ekonomicheskii byt gosudarstvennykh krest'ian v Shushinskom i Dzhebrail'skom uezdakh, Elisavetpol'skoi gubernii." In *MIEB.* Vol. 4: 1, 221–385. Tiflis, 1886.
Deminskii, F. A. "Nekotoryia svedeniia o Kabristanskom politseiskom uchastke Shemakhinskogo uezda Bakinskoi gubernii." *ZKOIRGO* 22, no. 2 (1901): 1–70.
Devitskii, V. "Kanikuliarnaia poezdka po Erivanskoi gubernii i Karsskoi oblasti." In *SMOMPK.* Vol. 21, otd. I, 79–180. Tiflis, 1896.
Dingel'shtedt, N. D. "Pryguny (Materialy k istoriia obruseniia Zakavkazskogo kraia)." *OZ,* no. 10 (1878): 379–430; and no. 11 (1878): 29–80.
———. *Zakavkazskie sektanty v ikh semeinom i religioznom bytu.* St. Petersburg, 1885.
Donskov, Andrew. "On the Doukhobors: From Imperial Russian Archival Files." *CES* 27, no. 3 (1995): 252–61.
———, ed. *Sergej Tolstoy and the Doukhobors: A Journey to Canada.* Ottawa, 1998.
Dukhobortsy v nachale XIX stoletia. Zapiska 1805 goda. Moscow, 1907.
"Dukhovnye khristiane molokane na Amure." *Molokanin* 1, no. 1 (1910): 35–38.
Dunaev, A. "Sekta prygunov v Zakavkaz'e." In *Russkie sektanty, ikh uchenie, kult i sposoby propagandy,* edited by M. A. Kal'nev, 187–97. Odessa, 1911.
Dzhashi, Illarion. "Obshchestvo Slavianskoe, Elizavetpol'skoi gubernii i uezda." In *SMOMPK.* Vol. 27, otd. 2, 1–41. Tiflis, 1900.
Egorov, Petr. "Zakavkazskaia dorozhnaia zapiski 1851 goda: doroga ot Tiflisa do Shemakhi

i g. Elisavetpolia." *RI*, no. 217 (October 10, 1857): 817; no. 218 (October 11, 1857): 901–3; no. 219 (October 12, 1857): 905–7.

Eliseev, D. Z. "Vnutrennee obozrenie." *Sovremennik*, no. 3 (1865), 57–59.

Eritsov, A. D. "Ekonomicheskii byt gosudarstvennykh krest'ian Borchalinskogo uezda Tiflisskoi gubernii." In *MIEB*. Vol. 7, 367–534. Tiflis, 1887.

——. "Ekonomicheskii byt gosudarstvennykh krest'ian Kazakhskogo uezda, Elisavetpol'skoi gubernii." In *MIEB*. Vol. 2: 3, 1–265. Tiflis, 1886.

"Eshche o Dukhoborakh," *Obzor*, no. 237 (September 6, 1878): 1

Esher, G. M. "Molokany ili khristiane-spiritualisty vostochnoi Rossii." *VE* 14, no. 5 (September–October, 1879): 368–84.

F-v, A. "O raskol'nikakh, poselennykh Tavricheskoi gubernii v Melitopol'skom uezde." *OZ*, ch. 33 (1828): 44–58.

Filibert, Anna. "Predislovie k stat'e 'Neskol'ko slov o molokanakh v Tavricheskoi gubernii.'" *OZ*, no. 6 (June 1870): 292–97.

G., K. "Obshchii vzgliad na vnutrenniuiu zhizn' russkikh sektantov v zakavkazskom krae." *Kavkaz*, no. 141 (1871): 2.

Gorskii, K. "Marazinskaia sel'skaia shkola." *Kavkaz*, no. 130 (1871): 2.

"Gosudarstvennye sberegatel'nye kassy." *Irkutskie gubernskie vedomosti*, no. 8 (February 19, 1897): 8–9.

Grigor'ev, V. "Molokane Ranenburgskogo uezda." *RM*, no. 5 (July 1884): 40–58.

Gromova-Opul'skaya, Lidia, Andrew Donskov, and John Woodsworth, eds. *Leo Tolstoy–Peter Verigin Correspondence*. Ottawa, 1995.

Haxthausen, August von. *Studies on the Interior of Russia*. Edited by S. Frederick Starr. Translated by Eleanore L. M. Schmidt. Chicago, 1972.

Hommaire de Hell, Xavier. *Travels in the Steppes of the Caspian Sea, the Crimea, the Caucasus*. London, 1847.

Ia, E. "Emigratsiia zakavkazskikh molokan." *MO* 10, no. 9 (June 1905): 1417–20.

Iasevich-Borodaevskaia, V. I. *Bor'ba za veru. Istoriko-bytovye ocherki i obzor zakonodatel'stva po staroobriadchestvu i sektantstvu v ego posledovatel'nom razvitii*. St. Petersburg, 1912.

Ikoteli, I. "Iz sela Slavianka, Elisavetpolsk. uezda (urozhai i polevyia myshi)." *KSKh*, no. 139 (September 5, 1896): 2378.

Il'in, S. E. *Moia Zakavkazskaia Rossiia*. Moscow, 1998.

Ispovedanie very Molokan Donskogo tolka Tavricheskoi gubernii. Simferopol', 1875.

Istomin, N. "Dve nedeli v Slavianke." *Kavkaz*, no. 13 (February 13, 1858): 67–68; no. 15 (February 20, 1858): 79–80.

"Istoricheskiia svedeniia o molokanskoi sekte." *PS* 4, no. 9 (September 1858): 42–80; 4, no. 11 (November 1858): 291–327.

Iu. "Dukhovnye khristiane. Ocherk." *VE* 15, no. 6 (November 1880): 1–34.

Iunitskii, A. "Sektantskiia gnezda na Kavkaze (v predelakh Bakinskoi gubernii)." *KhCh*, no. 1 (January–February 1895): 142–64.

——. "Sud i delo nad al'ty-agachskimi skoptsami na Kavkaze." *TV*, no. 20 (May 14, 1892): 318–19.

Iuvachev, I. P. (Miroliubov). "Zakavkazskie sektanty." *IV* 95 (January, 1904): 167–79; (February, 1904): 586–607.

Ivanov, V. V. "Na pomoshch ranenym voinam." *Baptist*, no. 15/16 (1914): 17–18.

Ivanovskii, A. I. "K antropologii zakavkazskikh velikorussov." *Russkii antropologicheskii zhurnal* 6, no. 1/2 (1905): 141–58.

"Iz Signakhskogo uezda (kor. Kavkaza)." *Kavkaz*, no. 15 (February 1, 1877): 3.

"Iz sluzhebnykh vospominanii V. S. Tolstogo." *RA* 22, no. 3 (1884): 55–60.

"K voprosu o zakavkazskikh sektantakh." *Kavkaz*, no. 84 (1881): 1–2.

Kal'nev, M. I., ed. *Russkie sektanty, ikh uchenie, kul't i sposoby propagandy*. Odessa, 1911.

Kalantar, A. "Merinosy v Zakavkaz'e." *KSKh*, no. 206 (December 18, 1987): 839–41; and no. 207 (December 25, 1897): 864–66.

Kalashev, N. "Selenie Ivanovka, Lagichskogo uchastka, Geokchaiskogo uezda, Bakinskoi gubernii." *SMOMPK*. Vol. 13, otd. II, 238–88. Tiflis, 1892.

Karsskii oblastnoi s"ezd dukhovnykh khristian. 1-go, 2-go i 3-go iiunia 1908 g. v sel. Vladikarse, Karsskogo uchastka i okruga. Kars, 1908.

Khakhanov, A. "Sekta Molokan-prygunov v Karrsskoi oblasti." *EO*, no. 3 (1893): 137–49.

——. "Zakavkazskie molokane-pryguny." *EO*, no. 4 (1892): 178–87.
Kharlamov, I. "Dukhobortsy. Istoricheskii ocherk." *RM* 5, no. 11 (November 1884): 138–61; no. 12 (December 1884): 83–115.
"Khronika." *Kavkaz*, no. 212 (September 22, 1883): 1; no. 213 (September 23, 1883): 1; no. 224 (October 7, 1883): 1; no. 234 (October 19, 1883): 1; no. 235 (October 20, 1883): 2; no. 245 (November 1, 1883): 1; no. 247 (November 3, 1883): 1; no. 252 (November 9, 1883): 1.
"Khronika: Iz Lenkorana v Kaspii." *Kavkaz*, no. 208 (September 17, 1883): 1.
Kistenev, D. A. "Ekonomicheskii byt gosudarstvennykh krest'ian Lenkoranskogo uezda, Bakinskoi gubernii." In *MIEB*. Vol. 7, 535–764. Tiflis, 1887.
Kolesnikov, I. F. *Dogmaty i ustav dukhovnykh khristian molokanskogo veroispovedaniia*. Baku, 1910.
Kolonial'naia politika Rossiiskogo tsarizma v Azerbaidzhane v 20–60-x gg. XIX v. 2 vols. Moscow, 1936–37.
Kolosov, S. "Russkie sektanty v Erivanskoi gubernii." *PKEG na 1902 g.* Erevan, 1902. Otd. IV: 143–55.
Kondratenko, E. *Etnograficheskiia karty gubernii i oblastei Zakavkazskogo kraia.* Supplement to *ZKOIRGO* 18 (1896).
"Korrespondentsii Kaspiia: Akhalkalakskii uezd (ot nashego korrespondenta)." *Kaspii* 14, no. 19 (January 25, 1894): 3.
"Korrespondentsii Kaspiia: Sel. Slavianka." *Kaspii* 14, no. 172 (August 11, 1894): 3.
Kostomarov, N. "Vospominaniia o molokanakh." *OZ*, no. 3 (1869): 57–78.
Kratkoe izlozhenie dogmatichesko-religioznogo ucheniia dukhovnykh khristian. Tiflis, 1909.
Kudinov, N. F. *Dukhovye khristiane. Molokane. Kratkii istoricheskii ocherk.* Vladikavkaz, 1913.
—— *Stoletie Molokanstva v Rossii 1805–1905 gg.* Baku, 1905.
Kuropatkin, A. N. *Soobrazheniia nachal'nika Zakaspiiskoi oblasti po voprosu o pereselenii v Zakaspiiskuiu oblast' dukhoborov-postnikov.* N.p., n.d.
Lebedev, Amfian Stepanovich. *Dukhobortsy v Slobodskoi Ukraine.* Kharkov, 1890.
Leont'ev, N. M. "Dukhovnye khristiane sela Ivanovki, Geokchaiskogo u. Bakin. g. (Svedeniia dlia nastol'nogo kalendaria dukhovnykh khristian)." *DKh* 4, no. 1 (January 1909): 18–21.
"Lenkoran," *Kaspii* 1, no. 32 (July 10, 1881): 3.
"Lenkoran," *Kaspii* 1, no. 45 (August 9, 1881): 3.
Lezin, M. P. *Prayerbook of the Spiritual Christian Molokans.* 3rd ed. Los Angeles, 1910.
Liaister, A. F. "'Pryguny' v Erivanskoi gubernii (stranichka iz istorii religioznykh iskanii russkogo cheloveka)." *PKEG na 1912 g.* Erevan, 1912. Literaturnyi otdel, ch. II, 1–20.
Liprandi, A. P. *Kavkaz i Rossiia* (Kharkov, 1912).
Liprandi, I. P. "Kratkoe obozrenie sushchestvuiushchikh v Rossii raskolov, eresei i sekt kak v religioznom tak i v politicheskom ikh znachenii." In *Sbornik pravitel'stvennykh svedenii o raskol'nikakh*. Vol. 2, edited by V. Kel'siev, 91–169. London, 1861.
Litvintsev, Konstantin. "Amurskie sektanty: molokane i dukhobory." *KhCh*, no. 11/12 (November–December 1887): 549–67.
Livanov, Fedor Vasil'evich. *Raskol'niki i ostorozhniki: ocherki i rasskazy.* 4 vols. St. Petersburg, 1872–73.
Lynch, H. F. B. "Queen Lukeria of Gorelovka." *Harper's New Monthly Magazine* 93, no. 553 (1896): 37.
M., G. "Kratkii ocherk istorii i veroucheniia dukhobortsev." *Kavkazskie eparkhial'nye vedomosti*, no. 14 (1882): 482–90; no. 15 (1882): 515–22.
Maksimov, S. V. "Za Kavkazom. (Iz dorozhnykh zametok). I. Subotniki." *OZ*, no. 10 (May 1867): 333–53.
——. "Za Kavkazom. II. Prygunki (otrasl' skoptsov i khlystov)." *OZ*, no. 11 (June 1867): 482–500.
——. "Za Kavkazom. Otryvki iz dorozhnykh zametok. Dukhobortsy i korennye Molokane (Ukleiny)." *OZ*, no. 13 (July 1867): 78–115.
Markov, F. T. "Ekonomicheskii byt gosudarstvennykh krest'ian Erivanskogo uezda." In *MIEB*. Vol. 3: 1, 1–226. Tiflis, 1886.
Masalkin, A. I. "K istorii zakavkazskikh sektantov: I Molokane." *Kavkaz*, no. 306 (November 18, 1893): 2–3.

——. "K istorii zakavkazskikh sektantov: II Subbotniki." *Kavkaz*, no. 307 (November 19, 1893): 2.

——. "Iz istorii zakavkazskikh sektantov. Ch. III. Sektanty, kak kolonizatory Zakavkaz'ia." *Kavkaz*, no. 333 (December 16, 1893): 2–3.

Materialy dlia izucheniia ekonomicheskogo byta gosudarstvennykh krest'ian Zakavkazskogo kraia. 7 vols. Tiflis, 1885–87.

Mekhmandarov, Samed-bek. "V molel'ne u dukhovnykh (prygunov)." *Kaspii* 3, no. 109 (September 25, 1883): 4–5; and 3, no. 110 (September 29, 1883): 2–3.

Mel'gunov, S. P. *Tserkov' i gosudarstvo v Rossii. (K voprosu o svobode sovesti. Sbornik statei).* 2 vols. Moscow, 1907–1909.

Mel'nikov, P. "Zapiski o russkom raskole." In *Sbornik pravitel'stvennykh svedenii o raskol'nikakh.* Vol. 1, edited by V. Kel'siev, 167–98. London, 1861.

Mikhailidis, D. "Iz sela Slavianki, Elisavetpol'skogo uezda." *KSKh*, no. 16 (March 31, 1894): 285–86.

Mikhailovich, Grand Duke Nikolai, *Imperator Aleksandr I: opyt' istoricheskogo issledovaniia.* 2 vols. St. Petersburg, 1912.

"Molokanskii s"ezd v Zakavkaz'e i otmennoe k nemu vnimanie namestnika." *MO* 10, no. 11 (August 1905): 289–91.

N-n, M. "Dukhobory v Dukhobor'e," *Obzor*, no. 159 (June 17, 1878): 3.

"Nekotoroe vliianie dukhobor na mestnye obychai." *KSKh*, no. 198 (October 23, 1897): 678–79.

Nikiforov, N. K. "Ekonomicheskii byt gosudarstvennykh krest'ian zapadnoi chasti Nakhichevanskogo uezda, Erivanskoi gubernii." In *MIEB*. Vol. 1:5, 530–608. Tiflis, 1885.

Nikitin, Zakharii. "Iz sel. Elenovki, Novobaiazet. uezda (Proiskhozhdenie Elenovki i khoziaistvennyi byt naseleniia)." *KSKh*, no. 126 (June 6, 1896): 2169–71.

Nil'skii, Ivan Fedorovich. *K istorii dukhoborchestva i molokanstva.* St. Petersburg, 1886.

Novitskii, Orest. *Dukhobortsy, ikh istoriia i verouchenie.* Kiev, 1882.

——. *O Dukhobortsakh.* Kiev, 1832.

"O pereselentsakh v Karsskoi oblasti." *Kavkaz*, no. 202 (August 1, 1890): 2.

"O poselenii dukhobortsev v Novorossiiskom krae." *RS* 98 (May 1899): 396.

"O russkikh pereselentsakh v Zakavkazskom krae." *Kavkaz*, no. 32 (April 22, 1850): 127–28.

"O sel'skikh zapasnykh khlebnykh magazinakh v Akhaltsiskom uezde." *Tiflisskii vestnik*, no. 31 (1875): 3.

"Obshchestvennye sel'skokhoziaistvennye kapitaly." *Kaspii* 14, no. 17 (January 22, 1894): 2.

Obzor meropriiatii ministerstva vnutrennykh del po raskolu s 1802 po 1881 god. St. Petersburg, 1903.

Ocherk sel'skogo i lesnogo khoziaistva Lenkoranskogo uezda, Bakinskoi gubernii. Baku, 1914.

Ol'khovskii, V. [V. D. Bonch-Bruevich]. "K istorii russkogo dukhoborchestva." *Obrazovanie* 14, no. 9 (1905): 27–56; no. 10 (1905): 145–203; no. 11/12 (1905): 52–80.

Orekhov, I. Ia. "Ocherki iz zhizni zakavkazskikh sektatorov." *Kavkaz*, no. 135 (June 16, 1878): 1–2; no. 136 (June 17, 1878): 1–2; no. 143 (June 25, 1878): 1–2; no. 145 (June 28, 1878): 1.

Otchet dukhovnykh khristian molokan (postoiannykh) po povodu 150-ti letnogo iubileia samostoiatel'nogo ikh religioznogo sushchestvovaniia so dnia opublikovaniia vysochaishogo ukaza gosudaria Rossiiskogo prestola Aleksandra Pavlovicha ot 22-go iiulia, 1805. San Francisco, 1955.

Otchet komiteta po okazaniiu pomoshchi ranenym voinam pri Bakinskoi Obshchin Dukhovnykh khristian (Molokan). S 7-go Sentiabria 1914 g. po 28-oe Fevralia 1915 g. Baku, 1915.

Otchet o Vserossiiskom s"ezde dukhovnykh khristian (Molokan), sostoiavshemsia 22 iiulia 1905 goda. Tiflis, 1907.

Parvitskii, A. V. "Ekonomicheskii byt gosudartsvennykh krest'ian iugo-zapadnoi chasti Novobaiazetskogo uezda, Erivanskoi gubernii." In *MIEB*. Vol. 1:3, 303–81. Tiflis, 1885.

——. "Ekonomicheskii byt gosudarstvennykh krest'ian severo-vostochnoi chasti, Novobaiazetskogo uezda, Erivanskoi gubernii." In *MIEB*. Vol. 4:2, 1–96. Tiflis, 1886.

Paul', P. "Iz sel. Elenovki, Erivanskoi gubernii (o vliianii russkikh na korennoe naselenie Novobaiazetskogo uezda." *KSKh*, no. 169 (April 3, 1897): 230.

———. "Iz sel. Elenovki, Eriv. gub. (material'naia nesostoiatel'nost' russkikh poselentsev)." *KSKh*, no. 123 (May 16, 1896): 2114–15.

Perevalenko, Vasilii. "Pis'mo iz Akhalkalaki (9 Apr. 1852 g.)." *ZV*, April 9, 1852: chast' neofitsial'naia, 79.

Petrov, I. E. "Dukhobory Elizavetpol'skogo uezda." *IKOIRGO* 18, no. 3 (1905–1906): 171–94.

———. "Seleniia Novo-Saratovka i Novo-Ivanovka Elisavetpol'skogo uezda." *IKOIRGO* 19, no. 1 (1907–1908): otd. 1, 226–47.

"Pogrebenie Dukhoborcheskoi prorochitsy—Lukerii Kalmykovoi," *MO* 1, no. 1 (1896): 93.

Pokhilevich, S. I. "Selenie Alty-Agach, Shemakhinskogo uezda Bakinskoi gubernii." *SMOMPK*. Vol. 1, 89–94. Tiflis, 1881.

Polnoe sobranie postanovlenii i rasporiazhenii po vedomstvu pravoslavnogo ispovedaniia Rossiiskoi Imperii. Series 5, vol. 1 (1825–35). St. Petersburg, 1915.

Polnoe sobranie zakonov Rossiiskoi imperii. Series I, II, and III. St. Petersburg, 1830–1915.

"Poselenie dukhobortsev na r. Molochnoi." *RS* 100 (October 1899): 240.

Potapov, Vasilii A. *V plenu u razboinikov: rasskaz*. N.p., 1936.

Pozdniakov, Vasilii. "Pravda o dukhoborakh." *EZh*, no. 6 (1914): 103–9; no. 7 (1914): 89–101; no. 8/9 (1914): 145–54; no. 10 (1914): 71–82.

"Pravda o zhit'e-byt'e i politicheskikh vozzreniiakh zakavkazskikh 'khristian vsemirnogo bratstva,' t. e. dukhobor-postnikov ili anarkhistov." *MO* (June 3, 1898): 833–57.

Prugavin, Aleksandr Stepanovich. "Programma dlia sobraniia svedenii o russkom raskole ili sektantstve." *RM* 2, no. 3 (March 1881): 23–42.

———. "Znachenie sektantstva v russkoi narodnoi zhizni." *RM* 2, no. 1 (January 1881): 301–63.

R.., E. "Russkii raskol i zakonodatel'stvo." *VE* 13, no. 4 (April 1880): 507–52, no. 5 (May 1880): 68–100.

———. "Russkie ratsionalisty. Subbotniki, Dukhobortsy, Molokane, Shtundisty." *VE* 16, no. 2 (February 1881): 650–89; no. 7 (July 1881): 272–323.

Raion Tiflissko-karssko-erivanskoi zheleznoi dorogi v ekonomicheskom i kommercheskom otnosheniiakh. Tiflis, 1897.

"Raskol'niki za Kavkazom. Dukhobortsy." *PS* 5, no. 3 (March 1859): 298–323.

"Raskol'niki za Kavkazom. Dukhovnye. Subbotniki. Obshchie." *PS* 5, no. 4 (April 1859): 432–44.

Rossiiskoe zakonodatel'stvo X–XX vekov. Vol. 6. *Zakonodatel'stvo pervoi poloviny XIX veka*. Moscow, 1988.

Rudometkin, Maksim Gavrilovich. *Kamen' gorlion*. Los Angeles, 1915.

———. *Russian Molokan Book of Prayer and Songs*. Translated by John K. Berokoff. Los Angeles, 1944.

———. *Utrenniaia zvezda*. Los Angeles, 1915.

S-A., K. "Russkie raskol'niki, poselenye v Bakinskoi gubernii." *Kavkaz*, no. 9 (January 21, 1868): 2–3; no. 10 (January 24, 1868): 2–3.

Samarin, I. G., ed. *Dukh i zhizn'—Kniga Solntse*. Los Angeles, 1928.

Sbornik materialov dlia opisaniia mestnostei i plemen Kavkaza. 46 vols. Tiflis, 1881–1929.

Segal', I. L. "Russkie poseliane v Elisavetpol'skoi gubernii (statistichesko-etnograficheskii ocherk)." *Kavkaz*, no. 40 (February 13, 1890): 3; no. 41 (February 14, 1890): 3; no. 42 (February 15, 1890): 3; no. 43 (February 16, 1890): 3.

———. [S-l'., I.] "Religioznoe dvizhenie dukhobortsev." *Kavkaz*, no. 32 (February 4, 1893): 2–3.

Sektanty Kavkaza. Stat'ia. Tiflis, 1890.

"Sel. Slavianka." *Kaspii* 14, no. 243 (November 11, 1894): 3.

"Selenie Semenovka." *Tiflisskii listok* 18, no. 158 (July 13, 1895): 1.

Serebriakov, A. I. "Sel'skoe khoziaistvo v Elisavetpol'skom uezde." *ZKOSKh*, no. 5/6 (1861), 94–190; and no. 1/2 (1862), 1–61.

Sh-v. "Privol'noe," *Kaspii* 2, no. 79 (July 30, 1882): 2–3.

Skvortsov, V. M. *Zapiska o dukhobortsakh na Kavkaze*. N.p., 1896.

"Smert' dukhoborcheskogo kantslera." *MO* 5, no. 1/6 (1900): 481–87.

Sobranie postanovlenii po chasti raskola ostoiavshikhsia po vedomstvu sv. Sinoda. 2 vols. St. Petersburg, 1860.

Sobranie postanovlenii po chasti raskola. St. Petersburg, 1875.

Solov'ev, N. L. *Pol'nyi krug dukhovnykh zakonov.* Moscow, 1907.

Spirit and Life—Book of the Sun. Divine Discourses of the Preceptors and the Martyrs of the Word of God, the Faith of Jesus, and the Holy Spirit, of the Religion of the Spiritual Christian Molokan-Jumpers. Edited by Daniel H. Shubin. Translated by John Volkov. N.p., 1983.

St-v, N. "Obychai i zakon v brachnykh delakh subbotnikov." *Kars,* no. 41 (October 8, 1891): 3.

Stollov, Ananii Ivanov. "Svedenie o molokanakh Tavricheskoi gubernii. (Po povodu stat'i v 'Otech. Zapiskakh' N. Kostomarova: 'O saratovskikh molokanakh')." *OZ,* no. 6 (June 1870): 298–314.

Studzinskii, Sergei. "U nashikh kavkazskikh raskol'nikov." *Slovo* 1 (February 1878): 119–48.

"'Subbotniki' v Erivanskoi gubernii." In *PKEG na 1912 g.* Erevan, 1912. Literaturnyi otdel, ch. III, 1–11.

Sulerzhitsky, L. A. *To America with the Doukhobors.* Translated by Michael Kalmakoff. Regina, 1982.

Suvorov, P. A. *Uchebnik dukhovnykh khristian.* Izd. 1-oe. Baku, 1915.

Svod statisticheskikh dannykh o naselenii zakavkazskogo kraia izvlechennykh iz posemeinnykh spiskov 1886 g. Tiflis, 1893.

Tchertkoff [Chertkov], Vladimir. *Christian Martyrdom in Russia: Persecution of the Spirit-Wrestlers (or Doukhobors) in the Caucasus.* London, 1897.

Tebenkov, M. "Dukhobortsy, ikh uchenie, organizatsiia i nastoiashchee polozhenie." *RS* 27, no. 8 (1896): 256–93; no. 9 (1896): 493–526.

Terletskii, B. N. "Sekta Dukhoborov." In *Russkie sektanty, ikh uchenie, kult, i sposoby propagandy,* edited by M. A. Kal'nev, 8–24. Odessa, 1911.

Tolstoi, V. S. "Velikorossiiskikh bezpopovskikh raskolakh v Zakavkaz'e." *Chteniia v imperatorskom obshchestve istorii i drevnosti rossiiskikh pri Moskovskom Universitete,* no. 4 (October–December 1864): ch. 5, 49–131.

Ustav Bakinskogo Obshchestva Dukhovnykh Khristian (Molokan) goroda Baku i raiona Bakinskogo gradonachal'stva. Baku, 1908.

"V 'Russkom Kur'ere.'" *Kaspii* 2, no. 59 (May 30, 1882): 2.

Varadinov, Nikolai. *Istoriia ministerstva vnutrennikh del.* Vol. 8, Supplementary. *Istoriia raspo-riazhenii po raskolu.* St. Petersburg, 1863.

Vasil'ev, A. "Veroterpimost' v zakonodatel'stve i zhizni v tsarstvovanie imperatora Aleksandra I (1801–1825)." *Nabliudatel'* 6–8 (1896): 35–56, 98–113, 257–96.

Velichko, V. L. *Kavkaz: Russkoe delo i mezhduplemennye voprosy.* 1904. Reprint, Baku, 1990.

Vereshchagin, V. V. *Dukhobortsy i Molokane v Zakavkaz'e, Shiity v Karabakhe, Batchi i Oshumoedy v Srednei Azii, i Ober-Amergau v Gorakh Bavarii.* Moscow, 1900.

Vermishev, Kh. A. "Ekonomicheskii byt gosudarstvennykh krest'ian v Akhaltsikhskom i Akhalkalakskom uezdakh, Tiflisskoi gubernii." In *MIEB.* Vol. 3:2, 1–284. Tiflis, 1886.

"Vliianie malarii na kolonizatsiiu kavkaza." *KK* 54 (1899): otd. II, 35–93.

Vostorgov, Ioann. *Polnoe sobranie sochinenii.* Vol. 4. 1916. Reprint, St. Petersburg, 1995.

Vsepoddanneishii otchet o proizvedennoi v 1905 godu po vysochaishchuiu poveleniiu senatorom Kuzminskim revizii goroda Baku i Bakinskoi gubernii. St. Petersburg, 1906.

Vsepoddanneishii otchet ober-prokurora sviateishego Sinoda po vedomstvu pravoslavnogo ispovedaniia za 1894 i 1895 gody. St. Petersburg, 1898.

Vsepoddanneishii otchet ober-prokurora sviateishego Sinoda po vedomstvu pravoslavnogo ispovedaniia za 1896 i 1897 gody. St. Petersburg, 1899.

Vysotskii, N. G. "Novye materialy iz ranneishei istorii dukhoborcheskoi sekty." *RA* 52, no. 1 (1914): 66–86; no. 2 (1914): 235–61.

Wagner, Moritz. *Der Kaukasus, und das Land der Kosaken.* Quoted and translated in a review in *The Westminister and Foreign Quarterly Review* 50, no. 1 (1849): 261–74.

Woodsworth, John, ed. and trans. *Russian Roots and Canadian Wings: Russian Archival Documents on the Doukhobor Emigration to Canada.* Manotick, Ont., 1999.

Zagurskii, L. P. "Poezdka v Akhaltsikhskii uezd v 1872 godu." *ZKOIRGO,* no. 8 (1873): article 16.

Zaitsev, V. *Iz lichnykh nabliudenii nad zhizn'iu zakavkazskikh sektantov.* St. Petersburg, 1899.

"Zametka o Karsskoi oblasti." *IKOIRGO* 7, no. 1/2 (1882–83): 175–91.

"Zapiski Moskovskogo martinista senatora I. V. Lopukhina." *RA* 52, no. 1 (1884): 85–101.

Zelinskii, S. P. "Ekonomicheskii byt gosudarstvennykh krest'ian v Bambakskom uchastke i v severnoi chasti Shoragial'skogo uchastka, Aleksandrapol'skogo uezda, Erivanskoi gubernii." In *MIEB*. Vol. 3:1, 457–512. Tiflis, 1886.

——. "Ekonomicheskii byt gosudarstvennykh krest'ian v Zangezurskom uezde, Elisavetpol'skoi gubernii." In *MIEB*. Vol. 4:1, 1–220. Tiflis, 1886.

Zhabin, Il'ia. "Selenie Privol'noe, Bakinskoi gub., Lenkoranskogo uezda." In *SMOMPK*. Vol. 27, otd. II, 42–94. Tiflis, 1900.

Zhabin, S. K. *K dukhovnomu svetu. Kratkii kurs Zakona Bozhiia dlia dukhovnykh khristian (postoiannykh molokan).* Tiflis, 1912.

Zibarov, N. S. *O sozhzhenii oruzhiia dukhoborami.* Purleigh, UK, 1899.

SECONDARY SOURCES

Abler, Thomas S. "Scalping, Torture, Cannibalism, and Rape: An Ethnohistorical Analysis of Conflicting Cultural Values in War." *Anthropologica* 34 (1992): 3–20.

Adelman, Jeremy and Stephen Aron. "From Borderlands to Borders: Empires, Nation-States, and the Peoples in Between in North American History." *AHR* 104, no. 3 (1999): 814–41.

Altstadt, Audrey. *The Azerbaijani Turks: Power and Identity under Russian Rule.* Stanford, 1992.

Anderson, Benedict. *Imagined Communities: Reflections on the Origin and Spread of Nationalism.* Rev. ed. New York, 1991.

Argudiaeva, Iu. V. *Krest'ianskaia sem'ia u vostochnykh slavian na iuge Dal'nego Vostoka Rossii (50-e gody XIX v.–nachalo XX v.).* Moscow, 1997.

Arsen'ev, K. K. *Svoboda sovesti i veroterpimosti, Sbornik statei.* St. Petersburg, 1905

Atkin, Muriel. *Russia and Iran, 1780–1828.* Minneapolis, 1980.

Avrich, Paul. *Russian Rebels, 1600–1800.* New York, 1972.

B-v, N. "Molokane." *ES.* Vol. 19:2, 644–46. St. Petersburg, 1896.

Baberowski, Jörg. *Der Feind ist überall: Stalinismus im Kaukasus.* Munich, 2003.

Baddeley, John F. *The Russian Conquest of the Caucasus.* London, 1908.

Badenkov, Yu. P., A. K. Borunov, A. F. Mandych, A. I. Romashkevich, and V. O. Targulian. "Caucasia." In *The Earth as Transformed by Human Action: Global and Regional Changes in the Biosphere over the Past 300 Years,* edited by B. L. Turner et al., 513–31. New York, 1990.

Barrett, Thomas M. *At the Edge of Empire: The Terek Cossacks and the North Caucasus Frontier, 1700–1860.* Boulder, 1999.

——. "Crossing Boundaries: The Trading Frontiers of the Terek Cossacks." In *Russia's Orient: Imperial Borderlands and Peoples, 1700–1917,* edited by Daniel R. Brower and Edward J. Lazzerini, 227–48. Bloomington, 1997.

——. "Lines of Uncertainty: The Frontiers of the North Caucasus." *SR* 54, no. 3 (1995): 578–601.

Barsov, Nikolai. "Dukhobortsy." *ES.* Vol. 11:1, 251–53. St. Petersburg, 1893.

Bartlett, Roger. *Human Capital: The Settlement of Foreigners in Russia, 1762–1804.* Cambridge, 1979.

Bassin, Mark. "Inventing Siberia: Visions of the Russian East in the Early Nineteenth Century." *AHR* 96, no. 3 (1991): 763–94.

——. "Russia between Europe and Asia: The Ideological Construction of Geographical Space." *SR* 50, no. 1 (1991): 1–17.

——. "Turner, Solov'ev, and the 'Frontier Hypothesis': The Nationalist Signification of Open Spaces." *JMH* 65 (September 1993): 473–511.

Becker, Seymour. "The Muslim East in Nineteenth-Century Russian Popular Historiography." *CAS* 5, no. 3/4 (1986): 25–47.

Berokoff, John K. *Molokans in America.* Whittier, CA, 1969.

——. *Selections from the Book of Spirit and Life.* Whittier, CA, 1966.

Billington, James H. *The Icon and the Axe: An Interpretive History of Russian Culture.* New York, 1970.

Blane, Andrew Q. "Protestant Sects in Late Imperial Russia." In *The Religious World of Russian Culture.* Vol. 2, edited by idem, 267–304. The Hague, 1975.

Blum, Jerome. *Lord and Peasant in Russia from the Ninth to the Nineteenth Century.* Princeton, 1961.

Bobrishchev-Pushkin, A. M. *Sud i raskol'niki-sektanty.* St. Petersburg, 1902.

Bonch-Bruevich, V. D. *Izbrannye sochineniia.* Vol. 1. *O religii, religioznom sektantstve i tserkvi.* Moscow, 1959.

———. *Iz mira sektantov. Sbornik statei.* Moscow, 1922.

Bournoutian, George A. "The Ethnic Composition and the Socio-Economic Condition of Eastern Armenia in the First Half of the Nineteenth Century." In *Transcaucasia: Nationalism and Social Change,* edited by Ronald G. Suny, 69–86. Ann Arbor, 1983.

Bowman, R. D. "Messing About with *Bufo Marinus.*" *Origins: Current Events in Historical Perspective* I, no. 2 (1993): 44.

Breyfogle, Nicholas B. "Building Doukhoboriia: Religious Culture, Social Identity and Russian Colonization in Transcaucasia, 1845–1895." *CES* 27, no. 3 (1995): 24–51.

———. "Caught in the Crossfire? Russian Sectarians in the Caucasian Theater of War, 1853–56 and 1877–78." *Kritika* 2, no. 4 (2001): 713–50.

———. "Colonization by Contract: Russian Settlers, South Caucasian Elites, and the Dynamics of Nineteenth-Century Tsarist Imperialism." In *Extending the Borders of Russian History: Essays in Honor of Alfred J. Rieber,* edited by Marsha Siefert, 143–66. Budapest, 2003.

———. "Heretics and Colonizers: Religious Dissent and Russian Colonization of Transcaucasia, 1830–1890." Ph.D. diss., University of Pennsylvania, 1998.

———. "Prayer and the Politics of Place: Molokan Church Building, Tsarist Law, and the Quest for a Public Sphere in Late Imperial Russia." In *Sacred Stories: Religion and Spirituality in Modern Russian Culture,* edited by Heather Coleman and Mark Steinberg (Bloomington, forthcoming).

———. "Rethinking the Origins of the Doukhobor Arms Burning, 1887–1893." In *The Doukhobor Centenary in Canada: A Multi-Disciplinary Perspective on their Unity and Diversity,* edited by Andrew Donskov, John Woodsworth, and Chad Gaffield, 55–82. Ottawa, 2000.

———. "Swords into Plowshares: Opposition to Military Service Among Religious Sectarians, 1770s to 1874." In *The Military and Society in Russian History,* edited by Eric Lohr and Marshall Poe, 441–67. Leiden, 2002.

Breyfogle, Nicholas B., Abby Schrader, and Willard Sunderland, eds. *Peopling the Periphery: Russian Settlement in Eurasia from Muscovite to Soviet Times* (forthcoming).

Brock, Peter. *Freedom from Violence: Sectarian Nonresistance from the Middle Ages to the Great War.* Toronto, 1991.

———. *Freedom from War: Nonsectarian Pacifism, 1814–1914.* Toronto, 1991.

Brock, Peter and John L. H. Keep. *Life in a Penal Battalion of the Imperial Russian Army: The Tolstoyan N. T. Iziumchenko's Story.* York, UK, 2001.

Brower, Daniel. "Kyrgyz Nomads and Russian Pioneers: Colonization and Ethnic Conflict in the Turkestan Revolt of 1916." *JGO* 44, no. 1 (1996): 41–53.

———. *Turkestan and the Fate of the Russian Empire.* London, 2003.

Brower, Daniel R. and Edward J. Lazzerini, eds. *Russia's Orient: Imperial Borderlands and Peoples, 1700–1917.* Bloomington, 1997.

Brubaker, Rogers and Frederick Cooper. "Beyond 'Identity.'" *Theory and Society* 29, no. 1 (2000): 1–47.

Bruess, Gregory L. *Religion, Identity, and Empire: A Greek Archbishop in the Russia of Catherine the Great.* Boulder, 1997.

———. "Religious Toleration in the Reign of Catherine the Great." In *International Perspectives on Church and State,* edited by Menachem Mor, 299–315. Omaha, 1993.

Bullard, Alice. *Exile to Paradise: Savagery and Civilization in Paris and the South Pacific, 1790–1900.* Stanford, 2000.

Burlaka, D. K. and S. L. Firsov, eds. *K. P. Pobedonostsev: Pro et Contra.* St. Petersburg, 1996.

Canadian Museum of Civilization Corporation. The Doukhobors: "Spirit Wrestlers." http://www.civilization.ca/cultur/doukhobors/douo1eng.html.

Cherniavsky, Michael. "The Old Believers and the New Religion." *SR* 25 (1996): 1–39.

Chistov, K. V. *Russkie narodnye sotsial'no-utopicheskie legendy XVII–XIX vv.* Moscow, 1967.

Chulos, Chris. "Peasant Religion in Post-Emancipation Russia: Voronezh Province, 1880–1917." Ph.D. diss., University of Chicago, 1994.

Church, Kenneth W. "From Dynastic Principality to Imperial District: The Incorporation of Guria into the Russian Empire to 1856." Ph.D. diss., University of Michigan, 2001.

Clay, John Eugene. "Orthodox Missionaries and 'Orthodox Heretics' in Russia, 1886–1917." In *Of Religion and Empire: Missions, Conversion, and Tolerance in Tsarist Russia*, edited by Robert P. Geraci and Michael Khodarkovsky, 38–69. Ithaca, 2001.

——. "Russian Peasant Religion and Its Repression: The Christ-Faith [*Khristovshchina*] and the Origins of the 'Flagellant' Myth, 1666–1837." Ph.D. diss., University of Chicago, 1989.

——. "The Theological Origins of the Christ-Faith [*Khristovshchina*]." *RH* 15 (1988): 21–41.

Coates, Timothy J. *Convicts and Orphans: Forced and State-Sponsored Colonizers in the Portuguese Empire, 1550–1755*. Stanford, 2001.

Coleman, Heather. "The Most Dangerous Sect: Baptists in Tsarist and Soviet Russia, 1905–1929." Ph.D. diss., University of Illinois at Urbana-Champaign, 1998.

Comaroff, John. "Images of Empire, Contests of Conscience: Models of Colonial Domination in South Africa." In *Tensions of Empire: Colonial Cultures in a Bourgeois World*, edited by Ann Laura Stoler and Frederick Cooper, 178–91. Berkeley, 1997.

Conovaloff, Andy. The Molokan Home Page. http://gecko.gc.maricopa.edu/clubs/russian/molokan/.

——. Molokan News. http://gecko.gc.maricopa.edu/clubs/russian/molokan/news/.

Conybeare, Frederick Cornwallis. *Russian Dissenters*. 1921. Reprint, New York, 1962.

Coppetiers, Bruno and Alexei Zverev. "V. D. Bonch-Bruevich and the Doukhobors: on the conscientious-objection policies of the Bolsheviks." *CES* 27, no. 3 (1995): 72–90.

Coquin, François-Xavier. "Faim et Migrations Paysannes en Russie au XIXe Siecle." *RHMC* 11 (April–June 1964): 127 44.

——. *La Sibérie: Peuplement et immigration paysanne au XIXe siècle*. Paris, 1969.

Cronon, William. *Changes in the Land: Indians, Colonists, and the Ecology of New England*. New York, 1983.

Cronon, William, George Miles, and Jay Gitlin, eds. "Becoming West: Toward a New Meaning for Western History." In *Under an Open Sky: Rethinking America's Western Past*, 3–27. New York, 1992.

——. *Under an Open Sky: Rethinking America's Western Past*. Edited by William Cronon, George Miles, and Jay Gitlin. New York, 1992.

Crosby, Alfred. *Ecological Imperialism: The Biological Expansion of Europe, 900–1900*. 1986. Reprint, New York, 1996.

Crummey, Robert O. *The Old Believers and the World of Antichrist: The Vyg Community and the Russian State, 1694–1855*. Madison, 1970.

Curtin, Philip D. *Death by Migration: Europe's Encounter with the Tropical World in the Nineteenth Century*. Cambridge, 1989.

Denoon, Donald. *Settler Capitalism: the Dynamics of Dependent Development in the Southern Hemisphere*. New York, 1983.

Diamond, Jared. *Guns, Germs, and Steel: The Fates of Human Societies*. New York, 1999.

Dolzhenko, I. V. "Istoriia pereseleniia i osnovaniia russkikh selenii v Zakavkaz'e." In *Russkie starozhily Zakavkaz'ia: Molokane i Dukhobortsy*, edited by V. I. Kozlov, 22–38. Moscow, 1995.

——. *Khoziaistvennyi i obshchestvennyi byt russkikh krest'ian vostochnoi Armenii (konets XIX–nachalo XX vv.)*. Erevan, 1985.

——. "Pervye russkie pereselentsy v Armenii (30–50-e gody XIX v.)." *VMU, Seriia IX, Istoriia* 29, no. 3 (May–June 1974): 58–66.

——. "Russkie begletsy v Zakavkaz'e (k istorii formirovaniia russkoi diaspory v 1830–1850-e gody)." *EO*, no. 1 (1995): 53–66.

——. "Skotovodcheskoe khoziaistvo russkogo naseleniia Armenii (konets XIX–nachalo XX v.)." *Problemy istorii SSSR*, no. 4 (1974): 145–54.

——. "Struktura i chislennost' semei russkikh krest'ian vostochnoi Armenii (XIX–nachalo XX vv.)." *Istoriko-filologicheskii zhurnal akademii nauk Armianskoi SSR*, no. 3 (1982): 165–73.

"Dukhobor'e." *ES* 11:1, 253. St. Petersburg, 1893.

Dukhovnye khristiane (Molokane). http://www.molokan.narod.ru/.

Dunn, Ethel and Stephen P. Dunn, eds. *The Molokan Heritage Collection*. Berkeley, 1983.

Du Toit, Andre. "No Chosen People: The Myth of the Calvinist Origins of Afrikaner Nationalism and Racial Ideology." *AHR* 88, no. 4 (1983): 920–52.

Eklof, Ben. "Ways of Seeing: Recent Anglo-American Studies of the Russian Peasant (1861–1914)." *JGO* 36 (1988): 57–79.

Elkinton, Joseph. "The Doukhobors, their character and economic principles." *Charities and the Commons (Survey)* 13 (December 3, 1904): 252–56.

Eltis, David, ed. *Coerced and Free Migration: Global Perspectives*. Stanford, 2002.

Engel, Barbara Alpern. *Between Field and City: Women, Work, & Family in Russia, 1861–1914*. New York, 1996.

———. "Engendering Russia's History: Women in Post-Emancipation Russia and the Soviet Union." *SR* 51, no. 2 (1992): 309–21.

Engelstein, Laura. *Castration and the Heavenly Kingdom: A Russian Folktale*. Ithaca, 1999.

———. "From Heresy to Harm: Self-Castrators in the Civic Discourse of Late Tsarist Russia." In *Empire and Society: New Approaches to Russian History*, edited by Teruyuki Hara and Kimitaka Matsuzato, 1–22. Sapporo, Japan, 1997.

———. "Rebels of the Soul: Peasant Self-Fashioning in a Religious Key." *RH* 23, no. 1/4 (1996): 197–213.

Ermolov, A. P. *Biograficheskii ocherk*. St. Petersburg, 1912.

Etkind, Aleksandr. *Khlyst: sekty, literatura i revolutsiia*. Moscow, 1998.

———. "Russkie sekty i Sovetskii kommunizm: proekt Valdimira Bonch-Bruevicha." *Minuvshee: istoricheskii al'manakh* 19 (1996): 275–319.

Faragher, John Mack. "Americans, Mexicans, Métis: A Community Approach to the Comparative Study of North American Frontiers." In *Under an Open Sky: Rethinking America's Western Past*, edited by William Cronon, George Miles and Jay Gitlin, 90–109. New York, 1992.

Fel'dshtein, G. S. *Ssylka. Ocherki eia genezisa, znacheniia, istorii i sovremennogo sostoianiia*. Moscow, 1893.

Field, Daniel. "A Far-off Abode of Work and Pure Pleasures." *RR* 39, no. 3 (1980): 348–58.

———. *Rebels in the Name of the Tsar*. Boston, 1976.

Fisher, Alan W. "Emigration of Muslims from the Russian Empire in the Years after the Crimean War." *JGO* 35 (1987): 356–71.

Fitzpatrick, Sheila. *Stalin's Peasants: Resistance and Survival in the Russian Village after Collectivization*. New York, 1994.

Flanagan, Thomas. *Riel and the Rebellion: 1885 Reconsidered*. 2nd ed. Toronto, 2000.

Ford, Caroline. *Creating the Nation in Provincial France: Religion and Political Identity in Brittany*. Princeton, 1993.

Frank, Stephen. *Crime, Cultural Conflict, and Justice in Rural Russia, 1856–1914*. Berkeley, 1999.

Freeze, Gregory. "The Rechristianization of Russia: The Church and Popular Religion, 1750–1850." *Studia Slavica Finlandensia* 7 (1990): 101–36.

———. "The *Soslovie* (Estate) Paradigm and Russian Social History." *AHR* 91 (1986): 11–36.

Fry, Gary Dean. "The Doukhobors, 1801–1855: The Origins of a Successful Dissident Sect." Ph.D. diss., American University, 1976.

Gammer, Moshe. *Muslim Resistance to the Tsar: Shamil and the Conquest of Chechnia and Daghestan*. London, 1994.

Geertz, Clifford, *The Interpretation of Cultures*. New York, 1973.

Geraci, Robert Paul. *Window on the East: National and Imperial Identities in Late Imperial Russia*. Ithaca, 2001.

Geraci, Robert Paul and Michael Khodarkovsky, eds. *Of Religion and Empire: Missions, Conversion, and Tolerance in Tsarist Russia*. Ithaca, 2001.

Glinka, Sergei. *Opisanie pereseleniia Armian Adderbidzhanskikh v predely Rossii*. 1831. Reprint, Baku, 1990.

Gregorian, Vartan. "The Impact of Russia on the Armenians and Armenia." In *Russia and Asia: Essays on the Influence of Russia on the Asian People*, edited by Wayne Vucinich, 167–218. Stanford, 1972.

Griffiths, Tom and Libby Robin, eds. *Ecology and Empire: Environmental History of Settler Societies.* Seattle, 1997.

Grigulevich, N. I. *Cultural and Ecological Peculiarities of the Traditional Diet of the Russians in Azerbaijan.* Moscow, 1988.

———. *Etnicheskaia ekologiia pitaniia.* Moscow, 1996.

———. "Osnovnye komponenty pitaniia russkikh starozhilov, azerbaidzhantsev i armian." In *Dukhobortsy i Molokane v Zakavkaz'e,* edited by V. I. Kozlov and A. P. Pavlenko, 60–89. Moscow, 1992.

———. "Pitanie kak odin iz osnovnykh pokazatelei adaptatsii pereselentsev." In *Russkie starozhily Zakavkaz'ia: Molokane i Dukhobortsy,* edited by V. I. Kozlov, 183–208. Moscow, 1995.

Grove, Richard. *Green Imperialism: Colonial Expansion, Tropical Island Edens and the Origins of Environmentalism, 1600–1860.* New York, 1995.

Gvozdetskii, N. A. *Kavkaz: Ocherk prirody.* Moscow, 1963.

Hall, Catherine. *Civilising Subjects: Colony and Metropole in the English Imagination, 1830–1867.* Chicago, 2002.

Hechter, M. *Internal Colonialism: the Celtic Fringe in British National Development, 1536–1966.* Routeledge and K. Paul, 1975.

Heffernan, Michael J. "French Colonial Migration." In *The Cambridge Survey of World Migration,* edited by Robin Cohen, 33–38. Cambridge, 1995.

Heffernan, Michael J. and Keith Sutton. "The Landscape of Colonialism: The Impact of French Colonial Rule on the Algerian Rural Settlement Pattern, 1830–1987." In *Colonialism and Development in the Contemporary World,* edited by Chris Dixon and Micheal J. Heffernan, 121–52. London, 1991.

Hewsen, Robert H. *Armenia: A Historical Atlas.* Chicago, 2001.

Hobsbawm, E. J. *Nations and Nationalism Since 1780: Programme, Myth, Reality.* 2nd ed. Cambridge, 1992.

Hokanson, Katya. "Literary Imperialism, Narodnost' and Pushkin's Invention of the Caucasus." *RR* 53, no. 3 (1994): 336–52.

Holman, Michael J. de K. "British Tolstoyans, *The New Order* and the Doukhobors in the late 1890s: Solidarity in Word and Deed." In *The Doukhobor Centenary in Canada: A Multi-Disciplinary Perspective on their Unity and Diversity,* edited by Andrew Donskov, John Woodsworth, and Chad Gaffield, 131–48. Ottawa, 2000.

Holquist, Peter. "To Count, to Extract, and to Exterminate: Population Statistics and Population Politics in Late Imperial and Soviet Russia." In *A State of Nations: Empire and Nation-Making in the Age of Lenin and Stalin,* edited by Ronald Grigor Suny and Terry Martin. New York, 2001.

Horden, Peregrine and Nicholas Purcell. *The Corrupting Sea: A Study of Mediterranean History.* Oxford, 2000.

Hosking, Geoffrey. *Russia: People and Empire, 1552–1917.* Cambridge, MA, 1997.

Hughes, Robert. *The Fatal Shore: The Epic of Australia's Founding.* New York, 1987.

Iamskov, A. N. *Environmental Conditions and Ethnocultural Traditions of Stockbreeding (the Russians in Azerbaijan in the 19th and early 20th Centuries).* Moscow, 1988.

Inikova, S. A., ed. *Doukhobor Incantations through the Centuries.* Translated and edited by Koozma Tarasoff. Ottawa, 1999.

———. *History of the Doukhobors in V. D. Bonch-Bruevich's Archives (1886–1950s),* edited by Koozma Tarasoff. Ottawa, 1999.

———. "Istoriia i simvolika dukhoborcheskogo kostiuma." *Zhivaia starina,* no. 1 (1994): 29–36.

———. "Istoriia patsifistskogo dvizheniia v sekte dukhoborov (XVII–XX vv.)." In *Dolgii put' Rossiiskogo patsifizma,* edited by T. A. Pavlova. Moscow, 1997.

———. "Russkie sekty." In *Russkie,* edited by V. A. Aleksandrov, I. V. Vlasova, and N. S. Polishchuk. Moscow, 1999.

———. "Tambovskie Dukhobortsy v 60-e gody XVIII veka." *Vestnik Tambovskogo universiteta. Ser. Gumanitarnye nauki,* no. 1 (1997): 39–53.

———. "Vzaimnootnosheniia i khoziaistvenno-kul'turnye kontakty kavkazskikh dukhobortsev s mestnym naseleniem." In *Dukhobortsy i Molokane v Zakavkaz'e,* edited by V. I. Kozlov and A. P. Pavlenko, 44–59. Moscow, 1992.

Ismail-Zade, D. I. "Russian Settlements in the Transcaucasus from the 1830s to the 1880s." In *The Molokan Heritage Collection*. Vol. 1, edited by Ethel Dunn and Stephen P. Dunn, section 3: 58–65. Berkeley, 1983.

———. *Russkoe krest'ianstvo v Zakavkaz'e: 30-e gody XIX–nachalo XX v.* Moscow, 1982.

"Iudeistvuiushchie." *ES.* Vol. 13:2, 768–69. St. Petersburg, 1894.

Jersild, Austin. "From Savagery to Citizenship: Caucasian Mountaineers and Muslims in the Russian Empire." In *Russia's Orient: Imperial Borderlands and Peoples, 1700–1917,* edited by Daniel R. Brower and Edward J. Lazzerini, 101–14. Bloomington, 1997.

———. *Orientalism and Empire: North Caucasus Mountain Peoples and the Georgian Frontier, 1845–1917.* Montreal and Kingston, 2002.

Joffe, Muriel. "Autocracy, Capitalism and Empire: The Politics of Irrigation." *RR* 54, no. 3 (1995): 365–88.

Jones, Stephen F. "Russian Imperial Administration and the Georgian Nobility: The Georgian Conspiracy of 1832." *SEER* 65, no. 1 (1987): 53–76.

Journal of World History 4, no. 2 (1993): 267–324.

Kalmakoff, Jonathan Jade. *Doukhobor Genealogy.* http://www.doukhobor.org/index.html.

Kappeler, Andreas. *The Russian Empire: A Multiethnic History.* Harlow, UK, 2001.

Kaufman, A. A. *Pereselenie i kolonizatsiia.* St. Petersburg, 1905.

Kazemzadeh, Firuz. "Russian Penetration of the Caucasus." *Russian Imperialism from Ivan the Great to the Revolution,* edited by Taras Hunczak, 239–63. New Brunswick, 1974.

Kennedy, Dane. *Islands of White: Settler Society and Culture in Kenya and Southern Rhodesia, 1890–1939.* Durham, 1987.

Khachapuridze, G. V. *K istorii Gruzii pervoi polviny XIX veka.* Tbilisi, 1950.

Khodarkovsky, Michael. "From Frontier to Empire: The Concept of the Frontier in Russia, Sixteenth–Eighteenth Centuries." *RH* 19, no. 1/4 (1992): 115–28.

———. *Russia's Steppe Frontier: The Making of a Colonial Empire, 1500–1800.* Bloomington, 2002.

———. *Where Two Worlds Met: The Russian State and the Kalmyk Nomads, 1600–1771.* Ithaca, 1992.

Kingston-Mann, Esther. "Breaking the Silence: An Introduction." In *Peasant Economy, Culture, and Politics of European Russia, 1800–1921,* edited by Esther Kingston-Mann and Timothy Mixter, 3–19. Princeton, 1991.

Kivelson, Valerie. "Patrolling the Boundaries: Witchcraft Accusations and Household Strife in Seventeenth-Century Muscovy." *Harvard Ukrainian Studies* 29 (1995): 302–23.

Kivelson, Valerie and Robert H. Greene, eds. *Orthodox Russia: Belief and Practice under the Tsars.* University Park, PA, 2003.

Kizenko, Nadieszda. *A Prodigal Saint: Father John of Kronstadt and the Russian People.* University Park, PA, 2000.

Klibanov, A. I. "Fifty Years of Scientific Study of Religious Sectarianism." *Soviet Sociology* 8, no. 3/4 (Winter–Spring 1970): 239–78.

———. *Istoriia religioznogo sektantstva v Rossii (60-e gody XIX v.–1917 g.).* Moscow, 1965. [Translated by Ethel Dunn, edited by Stephen Dunn. *History of Religious Sectarianism in Russia (1860s–1917).* New York, 1982.]

———. *Narodnaia sotsial'naia utopiia v Rossii. XIX vek.* Moscow, 1978.

———. "Problems of the Ideology of Peasant Movements." Translated by Stephan P. Dunn and Ethel Dunn. *RH* 11, no. 2/3 (1984): 168–78.

———. *Religioznoe sektantstvo i sovremennost'.* Moscow, 1969.

Klippenstein, Lawrence. "Otkaz ot voennoi sluzhby po motivam sovesti v mennonitskikh obshchinakh tsarskoi Rossii." In *Dolgii put' Rossiiskogo patsifizma,* edited by T. A. Pavlova, 150–71. Moscow, 1997.

Kliuchevskii, V. O. *Sochineniia v deviati tomakh.* Moscow, 1987.

Koval', T. B. *"Tiazhkoe blago": Khristianskaia etika truda.* Moscow, 1994.

Kozlov, V. I., ed. *Russkie starozhily Zakavkaz'ia: Molokane i Dukhobortsy.* Moscow, 1995.

Kozlov, V. I. and A. P. Pavlenko, eds. *Dukhobortsy i Molokane v Zakavkaz'e.* Moscow, 1992.

Kozlov, V. I. and N. A. Dubova, eds. *Russkie starozhily Azerbaidzhana.* 2 vols. Moscow, 1990.

Lang, D. M. "A Century of Russian Impact on Georgia." In *Russia and Asia: Essays on the Influence of Russia on the Asian Peoples,* edited by Wayne Vucinich, 219–47. Stanford, 1972.

———. *The Last Years of the Georgian Monarchy, 1658–1832.* New York, 1957.

Layton, Susan. "Nineteenth-Century Russian Mythologies of Caucasian Savagery." In *Russia's Orient: Imperial Borderlands and Peoples, 1700–1917*, edited by Daniel R. Bower and Edward J. Lazzerini, 80–100. Bloomington, 1997.

———. *Russian Literature and Empire: Conquest of the Caucasus from Pushkin to Tolstoy.* Cambridge, 1994.

Leblanc, Ronald D. "Vegetarianism in Russia: The Tolstoy(an) Legacy." *The Carl Beck Papers,* no. 1507 (May 2001).

Leconte, Daniel. *Les Pieds-Noirs: Histoire et portrait d'une communauté.* Paris, 1980.

Lehning, James R. *Peasant and French: Cultural Contact in Rural France during the Nineteenth Century.* New York, 1995.

Leroy-Beaulieu, Anatole. *The Empire of the Tsars and the Russians.* Vol. 3. *Religion.* New York, 1896.

Lester, Alan. *Imperial Networks: Creating Identities in Nineteenth-Century South Africa and Britain.* London, 2001.

Levin, Eve. *Sex and Society in the World of the Orthodox Slavs, 900–1700.* Ithaca, 1989.

Limerick, Patricia Nelson, Clyde A. Milner II, and Charles E. Rankin, eds. *Trails: Towards a New Western History.* Lawrence, 1991.

Lincoln, W. Bruce. *The Conquest of a Continent: Siberia and the Russians.* New York, 1994.

———. *The Great Reforms: Autocracy, Bureaucracy, and the Politics of Change in Imperial Russia.* DeKalb, 1990.

Lipski, Alexander. "A Russian Mystic Faces the Age of Rationalism and Revolution: Thought and Activity of Ivan Vladimirovich Lopukhin." *Church History* 36, no. 2 (June 1967): 170–89.

Liubavskii, M. K. *Obzor istorii russkoi kolonizatsii s drevneishikh vremen i do XX veka.* Moscow, 1996.

Lohr, Eric. *Nationalizing the Russian Empire: The Campaign against Enemy Aliens during World War I.* Cambridge, MA, 2003.

Lustick, Ian S. *Unsettled States, Disputed Lands: Britain and Ireland, France and Algeria, Israel and the West Bank–Gaza.* Ithaca, 1993.

Mackenzie, John M. "Empire and the Ecological Apocalypse: The Historiography of the Imperial Environment." In *Ecology and Empire: Environmental History of Settler Societies*, edited by Tom Griffiths and Libby Robin. Seattle, 1997.

de Madariaga, Isabel. *Russia in the Age of Catherine the Great.* New Haven, 1981.

Malov, Petr Nikolaevich. *Dukhobortsy, ikh istoriia, zhizn' i bor'ba.* Vol. 1. Thrums, BC, 1948.

Marsden, Philip. *The Spirit-Wrestlers and other Survivors of the Russian Century.* London, 1999.

Marshall, J. P. "British Immigration into India in the Nineteenth Century." In *European Expansion and Migration: Essays on the Intercontinental Migration from Africa, Asia, and Europe,* edited by P. C. Emmer and M. Morner, 179–96. New York, 1992.

Martin, Alexander M. *Romantics, Reformers, Reactionaries: Russian Conservative Thought and Politics in the Reign of Alexander I.* DeKalb, 1997.

Martin, Terry. *The Affirmative Action Empire: Nations and Nationalism in the Soviet Union, 1923–1939.* Ithaca, 2001.

Martin, Virginia. "Barïmta: Nomadic Custom, Imperial Crime." In *Russia's Orient: Imperial Borderlands and Peoples, 1700–1917,* edited by Daniel R. Brower and Edward J. Lazzerini, 249–70. Bloomington, 1997.

———. *Law and Custom in the Steppe: The Kazakhs of the Middle Horde and Russian Colonialism in the Nineteenth Century.* Richmond, UK, 2001.

Maude, Aylmer. *A Peculiar People: the Doukhobors.* 1904. Reprint, New York, 1970.

McConnell, Allen. *Tsar Alexander I: Paternalistic Reformer.* New York, 1970.

McGrew, R. E. *Russia and the Cholera, 1823–1832.* Madison, 1965.

McMillan, David W. and David M. Chavis. "Sense of Community: A Definition and Theory." *Journal of Community Psychology* 14, no. 1 (1986): 8–20.

Meinesz, Alexandre. *Killer Algae.* Translated by Daniel Simberloff. Chicago, 1999.

Michels, Georg. *At War with the Church: Religious Dissent in Seventeenth-Century Russia.* Stanford, 1999.

Miliukov, P. N. *Ocherki po istorii russkoi kul'tury.* Vol. 2, no. 1. *Tserkov', Religiia, Literatura.* 1930. Reprint, Moscow, 1994.

Mochalov, V. D. *Krest'ianskoe khoziaistvo v Zakavkaz'e k knotsu XIX v.* Moscow, 1958.

Moon, David. "Agricultural Settlement and Environmental Change on the Open Steppes of Southeastern European Russia in the Nineteenth Century." In *Peopling the Periphery: Russian Settlement in Eurasia from Muscovite to Soviet Times,* edited by Nicholas Breyfogle, Abby Schrader, and Willard Sunderland (forthcoming).

——. "Peasant Migration and the Settlement of Russia's Frontiers, 1550–1897." *HJ* 40, no. 4 (1997): 859–93.

——. "Peasants into Russian Citizens? A Comparative Perspective." *Revolutionary Russia* 9, no. 1 (1996): 43–81.

——. *The Russian Peasantry, 1600–1930: The World the Peasants Made.* New York, 1999.

——. *Russian Peasants and Tsarist Legislation on the Eve of Reform: Interaction Between Peasants and Officialdom, 1825–1855.* London, 1992.

Moore, Willard Burgess. *Molokan Oral Tradition: Legends and Memorates of an Ethnic Sect.* Berkeley, 1973.

Morgan, Edmund Sears. *American Slavery, American Freedom: The Ordeal of Colonial Virginia.* New York, 1975.

Mostashari, Firouzeh. "The Politics of Colonization: Sectarians and Russian Orthodox Peasants in Nineteenth Century Azerbaijan." *Journal of Central Asian Studies* 1, no. 1 (1996): 16–29.

——. "Tsarist Colonial Policy, Economic Change, and the Making of the Azerbaijani Nation: 1828–1905." Ph.D. diss., University of Pennsylvania, 1995.

Moss, Walter G. *A History of Russia.* Vol. 1. *To 1917.* New York, 1997.

Nathans, Benjamin. *Beyond the Pale: The Jewish Encounter with Late Imperial Russia.* Berkeley, 2002.

Nielsen, Donald. "Sects, Churches and Economic Transformations in Russia and Western Europe." *IJPCS* 2, no. 4 (Summer 1989): 493–522.

Nikol'skii, N. M. *Istoriia russkoi tserkvi.* Moscow, 1930.

Orford, Jim. "Theories of Person-in-Context." In *Community Psychology: Theory and Practice,* 26–29. New York, 1992.

Orudzhev, G. A. "Iz istorii obrazovaniia russkikh poselenii v Azerbaidzhane." *Izvestiia Akademii Nauk AzSSR: Istoriia, Filosofiia, Pravo,* no. 2 (1969): 13–21.

Paert, Irina. *Old Believers, Religious Dissent and Gender in Russia, 1760–1850.* Manchester, 2003.

Pagden, Anthony. *Lords of all the World: Ideologies of Empire in Spain, Britain, and France, c. 1500–c. 1800.* New Haven, 1995.

Pallot, Judith and Denis J. B. Shaw. *Landscape and Settlement in Romanov Russia, 1613–1917.* Oxford, 1990.

Pascal, Pierre. *The Religion of the Russian People.* London, 1976.

Pipes, Richard. "The Russian Military Colonies, 1810–1831." *JMH* 22 (1950): 205–19.

Pivovaroff, Morris Mose. *Moisey: A Russian Christian Molokan.* N.p., 1989.

Polunov, A. Iu. "Gosudarstvo i religioznoe inakomyslie v Rossii (1880–nachalo 1890-kh godov)." In *Rossiia i reformy: Sbornik statei,* vol. 3, edited by M. A. Kolerov, 126–41. Moscow, 1995.

——, ed. "K. P. Pobedonostsev v 1881 godu (Pis'ma k E. F. Tiutchevoi)." In *Reka Vremeni, Kniga pervaia, Gosudar'–Gosudarstvo–Gosluzhba.* Moscow, 1995.

——. *Pod vlast'ia ober-prokurora: Gosudarstvo i tserkov' v epokhu Aleksandra III.* Moscow, 1996.

——. "Politicheskaia individual'nost' K. P. Pobedonostseva." *VMU Seriia 8, Istoriia,* no. 2 (1991): 42–48.

Popoff, Eli Alex. *An Historical Exposition on the Origin and Evolvement of the Basic Tenets of the Doukhobor Life-Conception.* Grand Forks, BC, 1966.

Pyshnova, Iu. T. "Historical-Geographic Aspects of the Development and Settlement of the Black Sea Coast of the Caucasus." *SG* 15, no. 3 (March 1974): 156–63.

Raeff, Marc. "In the Imperial Manner." In *Catherine the Great: A Profile,* edited by idem, 197–246. New York, 1972.

——. "Pugachev's Rebellion." In *Preconditions of Revolution in Early Modern Europe,* edited by Robert Forster and Jack Greene, 161–202. Baltimore, 1970.

——. *Understanding Imperial Russia: State and Society in the Old Regime.* New York, 1984.

Reeds, John. "Hull of a Problem." *Geographical* 71, no. 10 (1999): 26–33.

Reibin, Simeon F. *Trud i mirnaia zhizn'. Istoriia dukhobortsev bez maski.* San Francisco, 1952.

Reisner, M. A. *Gosudarstvo i veruiushchaia lichnost'. Sbornik statei.* St. Petersburg, 1905.

Rhinelander, A. L. H. "The Incorporation of the Caucasus into the Russian Empire: The Case of Georgia, 1801–1854." Ph.D. diss., Columbia University, 1972.

———. *Prince Michael Vorontsov: Viceroy to the Tsar.* Montreal and Kingston, 1990.

———. "Russia's Imperial Policy: The Administration of the Caucasus in the First Half of the Nineteenth Century." *CSP* 17, no. 2/3 (1975): 218–35.

Riasanovsky, Nicholas. *Nicholas I and Official Nationality, 1825–1855.* Berkeley, 1961.

Rieber, Alfred J. "Colonizing Eurasia." In *Peopling the Periphery: Russian Settlement in Eurasia from Muscovite to Soviet Times,* edited by Nicholas Breyfogle, Abby Schrader, and Willard Sunderland (forthcoming).

———. *Merchants and Entrepreneurs in Imperial Russia.* Chapel Hill, 1982.

———. "The Sedimentary Society." In *Between Tsar and People: Educated Society and the Quest for Public Identity in Late Imperial Russia,* edited by Edith W. Clowes, Samuel D. Kassow, and James L. West, 343–71. Princeton, 1991.

———. "Struggle Over the Borderlands." In *The Legacy of History in Russia and the New States of Eurasia,* vol. I., edited by S. Frederick Starr. Armonk, NY, 1994.

Robson, Roy R. *Old Believers in Modern Russia.* DeKalb, 1995.

Rostislavov, Dmitrii Ivanovich. *Provincial Russia in the Age of Enlightenment: The Memoir of a Priest's Son.* Edited and translated by Alexander Martin. DeKalb, 2002.

Rutenburg, V. I. "Kratkii putevoditel' po fondam lichnogo proiskhozhdeniia rukopisnogo otdela Muzeia istorii religii i ateizma." In *Ateizm, religiia, sovremennost'.* Leningrad, 1973.

Sahlins, Marshall. *Islands of History.* Chicago, 1985.

Sahlins, Peter. *Boundaries: The Making of France and Spain in the Pyrenees.* Berkeley, 1989.

———. *Forest Rites: The War of the Demoiselles in Nineteenth-Century France.* Cambridge, MA, 1994.

Sanborn, Joshua A. *Drafting the Russian Nation: Military Conscription, Total War, and Mass Politics, 1905–1925.* DeKalb, 2003.

———. "Non-Violent Protest and the Russian State: the Doukhobors in 1895 and 1937." In *The Doukhobor Centenary in Canada: A Multi-Disciplinary Perspective on their Unity and Diversity,* edited by Andrew Donskov, John Woodsworth, and Chad Gaffield, 83–102. Ottawa, 2000.

———. "Pacifist Politics and Peasant Politics: Tolstoy and the Doukhobors, 1895–99." *CES* 27, no. 3 (1995): 52–71.

Schimmelpenninck van der Oye, David. *Toward the Rising Sun: Russian Ideologies of Empire and the Path to War with Japan.* DeKalb, 2001.

Scheikevitch, Antoine. "Alexandre Ier et l'hérésie Sabbatiste." *RHMC* 3 (1956): 223–35.

Scott, James C. *Weapons of the Weak: Everyday Forms of Peasant Resistance.* New Haven, 1985.

Seed, Patricia. *Ceremonies of Possession in Europe's Conquest of the New World, 1462–1640.* New York, 1995.

Shaw, A. G. L. *Convicts and the Colonies: A Study of Penal Transportation from Great Britain and Ireland to Australia and other parts of the British Empire.* London, 1966.

Shotter, John and Kenneth J. Gergen, eds. *Texts of Identity.* London, 1989.

Slezkine, Yuri. *Arctic Mirrors: Russia and the Small Peoples of the North.* Ithaca, 1994.

Stanislawski, Michael. *Tsar Nicholas I and the Jews: The Transformation of Jewish Society in Russia, 1825–1855.* Philadelphia, 1983.

Staples, John R. *Cross-Cultural Encounters on the Ukrainian Steppe: Settling the Molochna Basin, 1783–1861.* Toronto, 2003.

Starr, S. Frederick. *Decentralization and Self-Government in Russia, 1830–1870.* Princeton, 1972.

Stasiulis, Daiva and Nira Yuval-Davis, eds. *Unsettling Settler Societies: Articulations of Gender, Race, Ethnicity, and Class.* London, 1995.

Steinwedel, Charles. "Resettling People, Unsettling the Empire: Migration, Colonization, and the Challenge of Governance, 1861–1917." In *Peopling the Periphery: Russian Settlement in Eurasia from Muscovite to Soviet Times,* edited by Nicholas B. Breyfogle, Abby Schrader, and Willard Sunderland (forthcoming).

———. "To Make a Difference: The Category of Ethnicity in Late Imperial Russian Politics, 1861–1917." In *Russian Modernity: Politics, Knowledge, Practices,* edited by David Hoffmann and Yanni Kotsonis, 67–86. Basingstoke, 2000.

Stiglmayer, Alexandra, ed. *Mass Rape: The War Against Women in Bosnia-Herzegovina*. Lincoln, 1994.

Stoler, Ann Laura and Frederick Cooper. "Between Metropole and Colony: Rethinking a Research Agenda." In *Tensions of Empire: Colonial Cultures in a Bourgeois World*, edited by idem, 1–56. Berkeley, 1997.

———, eds. *Tensions of Empire: Colonial Cultures in a Bourgeois World*. Berkeley, 1997.

Stone, John. "Internal Colonialism." In *Ethnicity*, edited by John Hutchinson and Anthony D. Smith, 278–81. New York, 1996.

"Subbotniki." *ES*. Vol. 31, 874–75. St. Petersburg, 1901.

Sukhorev, V. A. *Istoriia dukhobortsev*. Winnipeg, 1944.

Sunderland, Willard. "The 'Colonization Question': Visions of Colonization in Late Imperial Russia." *JGO* 48, no. 2 (2000): 210–32.

———. "An Empire of Peasants: Empire Building, Interethnic Interaction, and Ethnic Stereotyping in the Rural World of the Russian Empire, 1800–1850's." In *Imperial Russia: New Histories for the Empire*, edited by Jane Burbank and David L. Ransel. 174–98. Bloomington, 1998.

———. "Making the Empire: Colonists and Colonization in Russia, 1800–1850s." Ph.D. diss., Indiana University, 1997.

———. "Peasant Pioneering: Russian Peasant Settlers Describe Colonization and the Eastern Frontier, 1880's–1910's." *JSH* 34, no. 4 (2001): 895–922.

———. "Peasants on the Move: State Peasant Resettlement in Imperial Russia, 1805–1830s." *RR* 52, no. 4 (October 1993): 472–85.

———. "Russians into Iakuts? 'Going Native' and Problems of Russian National Identity in the Siberian North, 1870s–1914." *SR* 55, no. 4 (Winter 1996): 806–25.

Suny, Ronald Grigor. "Eastern Armenians under Tsarist Rule." In *The Armenian People from Ancient to Modern Times*. Vol. 2. *Foreign Dominion to Statehood: The Fifteenth Century to the Twentieth Century*, edited by Richard G. Hovannisian. New York, 1997.

———. *Looking toward Ararat: Armenia in Modern History*. Bloomington, 1993.

———. *The Making of the Georgian Nation*. 2nd ed. Bloomington, 1994.

———. "'The Peasants Have Always Fed Us': The Georgian Nobility and the Peasant Emancipation, 1856–1871." *RR* 38, no. 1 (1979): 27–51.

———. "Russian Rule and Caucasian Society in the First Half of the Nineteenth Century: The Georgian Nobility and the Armenian Bourgeoisie, 1801–1856." *NP* 7, no. 1 (Spring 1979): 53–78.

———, ed. *Transcaucasia: Nationalism and Social Change*. Ann Arbor, 1983. Rev. ed. Ann Arbor, 1996.

Swietochowski, Tadeusz. *Russian Azerbaijan, 1905–1920: The Shaping of National Identity in a Muslim Community*. Cambridge, 1985.

Tarasoff, Koozma J. *Plakun Trava: The Doukhobors*. Grand Forks, BC, 1982.

Tarasoff, Koozma J. and Robert B. Klymasz. *Spirit Wrestlers: Centennial Papers in Honour of Canada's Doukhobor Heritage*. Hull, 1995.

Thaden, E. C. ed. *Russification in the Baltic Provinces and Finland*. Princeton, 1981.

Tilly, Charles. "Did the Cake of Custom Break?" In *Consciousness and Class Experience in Nineteenth-Century Europe*, edited by John M. Merriman, 17–44. New York, 1979.

Treadgold, Donald. *The Great Siberian Migration: Government and Peasant in Resettlement from Emancipation to the First World War*. Princeton, 1957.

Tumanian, O. E. *Ekonomicheskoe razvitie Armenii*. 2 vols. Erevan, 1954.

Usner, Jr., Daniel H. *Indians, Settlers and Slaves in a Frontier Exchange Economy: The Lower Mississippi Valley Before 1783*. Chapel Hill, 1992.

Velychenko, Stephen. "Identities, Loyalties and Service in Imperial Russia: Who Administered the Borderlands?" *RR* 54, no. 2 (1995): 188–208.

Viola, Lynne. "The Other Archipelago: Kulak Deportations to the North in 1930." *SR* 60, no. 4 (2001): 730–55.

———. *Peasant Rebels under Stalin: Collectivization and the Culture of Peasant Resistance*. New York, 1996.

Vishlenkova, E. A. *Religioznaia politika: ofitsial'nyi kurs i "obshchee mnenie" Rossii Aleksandrovskoi epokhi*. Kazan, 1997.

Volkova, N. G. "Etnicheskie protsessy v Zakakvkaz'e v XIX–XX vv." In *KES*. Vol. 4. Edited by V. K. Gardanov, 3–54. Moscow, 1969.
Waldron, Peter. "Religious Toleration in Late Imperial Russia." In *Civil Rights in Imperial Russia*, edited by Olga Crisp and Linda Edmondson, 103–20. Oxford, 1989.
Walzer, Michael. *On Toleration*. New Haven, 1997.
Wcislo, Francis William. *Reforming Rural Russia: State, Local Society, and National Politics, 1855–1914*. Princeton, 1990.
Weber, Eugen. *Peasants into Frenchmen: The Modernization of Rural France, 1870–1914*. Stanford, 1976.
Weber, Max. *The Protestant Ethic and the Spirit of Capitalism*. Translated by Talcott Parsons. New York, 1992.
———. *The Sociology of Religion*. Translated by Ephraim Fischoff. Boston, 1991.
Weeks, Theodore R. "Defending Our Own: Government and the Russian Minority in the Kingdom of Poland, 1905–1914." *RR* 54, no. 4 (1995): 539–51.
———. *Nation and State in Late Imperial Russia: Nationalism and Russification on the Western Frontier, 1863–1914*. DeKalb, 1996.
Werth, Paul. *At the Margins of Orthodoxy: Mission, Governance, and Confessional Politics in Russia's Volga–Kama Region, 1827–1905*. Ithaca, 2002.
———. "The Limits of Religious Ascription: Baptized Tatars and the Revision of 'Apostasy,' 1840s–1905." *RR* 59, no. 4 (2000), 496–97.
White, Richard. *The Middle Ground: Indians, Empires, and Republics in the Great Lakes Region, 1650–1815*. New York, 1991.
———. *The Roots of Dependency: Subsistance, Environment, and Social Change among Choctaws, Pawnees, and Navajos*. Lincoln, 1983.
Whittock, Michael. "Ermolov: Proconsul of the Caucasus." *RR* 18, no. 1 (1959): 53–60.
Wieczynski, Joseph. "Toward a Frontier Theory of Early Russian History." *RR* 33, no. 3 (1974): 284–95.
Williams, Michael. "Ecology, imperialism, and deforestation." In *Ecology and Empire: Environmental History of Settler Societies*, edited by Tom Griffiths and Libby Robin. Seattle, 1997.
Wirtschafter, Elise Kimmerling. *Social Identity in Imperial Russia*. DeKalb, 1997.
Wolfe, Patrick. "History and Imperialism: A Century of Theory, from Marx to Postcolonialism." *AHR* 102, no. 2 (1997): 388–420.
———. *Settler Colonialism and the Transformation of Anthropology: The Politics and Poetics of an Ethnographic Event*. London, 1999.
Wood, Alan. "Crime and Punishment in the House of the Dead." In *Civil Rights in Imperial Russia*, edited by Olga Crisp and Linda Edmondson. Oxford, 1989.
Woodcock, George and Ivan Avakumic. *The Doukhobors*. Toronto, 1968.
Woodsworth, John, ed. *Russian Archival Documents of Canada. The Doukhobors, 1895–1943: Annotated, Cross-Referenced and Summarized*. 2nd ed. Ottawa, 1997.
Worobec, Christine. *Peasant Russia: Family and Community in the Post-Emancipation Period*. Princeton, 1991.
Wortman, Richard S. *Scenarios of Power: Myth and Ceremony in Russian Monarchy*. Vol. 1. *From Peter The Great to the Death of Nicholas I*. Princeton, 1995.
Wright, James Frederick. *Slava Bohu, the Story of the Dukhobors*. Toronto, 1940.
Yaroshevski, Dov. "Attitudes towards the Nomads of the Russian Empire under Catherine the Great." In *Literature, Lives, and Legality in Catherine's Russia*, edited by A. G. Cross and G. S. Smith. N.p., 1994.
Young, Pauline. *The Pilgrims of Russian-Town: The Community of Spiritual Jumpers in America. The Struggle of a Primitive Religious Society to Maintain Itself in an Urban Environment*. 1932. Reprint, Hacienda Heights, CA, 1998.
"Zhidovstvuiushchie." *ES*. Vol. 11: 2. St. Petersburg, 1894.
Zhitomirskaia, S. V., ed. *Vospominaniia i dnevniki XVIII–XX vv.: Ukazatel' rukopisei*. Moscow, 1976.
Zhitomirskaia, S. V., L. V. Gapochko, and B. A. Shlikhter. "Arkhiv V. D. Bonch-Bruevicha." *Zapiski otdela rukopisei*. No. 25. Moscow, 1962.
Zhuk, Sergei I. "Russia's Lost Reformation: Peasants and Radical Religious Sects in Southern Russia and Ukraine, 1830–1905." Ph.D. diss., Johns Hopkins University, 2002.

INDEX

Page numbers in italics refer to figures.

CPSIA information can be obtained at www.ICGtesting.com
Printed in the USA
238152LV00003B/1/P